The New Republic Reader

The New Republic Reader

EIGHTY YEARS OF OPINION AND DEBATE

Edited by
DOROTHY WICKENDEN

A New Republic Book
BasicBooks
A Division of HarperCollins*Publishers*

Grateful acknowledgment is made for permission to reprint the following:

"Epiphany," copyright © 1977, 1980 by Stanley Kauffmann.
"The Schlepic," copyright © 1988 by Robert Brustein.
"What the Thousand Days Wrought," copyright © 1983 by Arthur Schlesinger, Jr.
"*White House Years* by Henry Kissinger," copyright © 1979 by Ronald Steel.

Published by BasicBooks, A Division of HarperCollins Publishers, Inc.

Designed by Helene Wald Berinsky

LIBRARY OF CONGRESS CATALOGING-IN-PUBLICATION DATA
The New Republic reader : eighty years of opinion and debate / edited by Dorothy Wickenden.
p. cm.
Includes index.
"A New Republic book."
ISBN 0-465-09822-3 (cloth)
ISBN 0-465-09826-6 (paper)
1. United States—Politics and government—20th century. 2. Liberalism—United States—History—20th Century. I. Wickenden, Dorothy. I. New Republic (New York, N.Y.)
E743.N388 1994
320.973—dc20 94-7580
CIP

95 96 97 98 ❖/RRD 9 8 7 6 5 4 3 2 1

Contents

PART III

Race: "The Crisis of Caste"

PART IV

Fights: "What Do the Liberals Hope For?"

Acknowledgments

I am indebted to many colleagues and friends who contributed to the shaping of this anthology. Marty Peretz, who encouraged me to edit the book, made no attempt to determine its outcome. He nevertheless was a critical intellectual influence, as was Leon Wieseltier, who made numerous wise suggestions, both for the contents and for the introductory essay. Andrew Sullivan graciously agreed to give me a three-month leave of absence from the magazine, which made the project possible. I want to thank my editor, Peter Edidin, who worked closely with me in developing the book's themes and in casting the introduction. Thanks also to Michael Mueller for attentively seeing the book through to completion. I relied throughout on the flawless editorial judgment of Ann Hulbert. David Seideman was an invaluable resource, both for his book, *The New Republic: A Voice of Modern Liberalism,* and for his command of early *New Republic* history and lore. John Judis and Rick Hertzberg lent books and excellent counsel, and Mickey Kaus and Mike Kinsley offered astute suggestions of all kinds. Laura Obolensky and Peggy Jarvis Ferrin assisted with archival and other requests. Rafe Sagalyn gave helpful advice as I got started. Eric Konigsberg, Gary Bass, Stephen Rodrick, Jason Zinoman, Lora D. Blum, Hanna Rosin, Gillian Weiss, Dante Ramos, Sue Miller, Nancy Stadtman, and Mary Eng assisted with the tedious tasks of copying, retrieving wayward articles, and checking stray facts. Above all, I am grateful to the countless contributors of eighty years—of whom I was able to include only a tiny and skewed sampling—who turned a laborious exercise into a rediscovery of the energy, eclecticism, and resilience of American liberalism.

INTRODUCTION

Little Insurrections

Twentieth-century liberalism has won. It has inspired democratic revolutions from the Soviet Union to South Africa, and has yet again disabused this country of its prolonged infatuation with conservatism. Yet even now no one is quite sure precisely what liberalism is. Known more for its fractiousness than for its coherence, more for its mutability than for its doctrinal consistency, liberalism is best defined as a state of mind: an attitude toward the possibilities of politics and culture that is both defiantly hopeful and deeply skeptical. As Walter Lippmann wrote in 1919:

> The word, liberalism, was introduced into the jargon of American politics by that group who were Progressives in 1912 and Wilson Democrats from 1916 to 1918. They wished to distinguish their own general aspirations in politics from those of the chronic partisans and the social revolutionists. They had no other bond of unity. They were not a political movement. There was no established body of doctrine. . . . If [American liberalism] has any virtue at all it is that many who call themselves liberals are aware that the temper of tolerant inquiry must be maintained.

Eighty years ago Lippmann helped launch *The New Republic,* a self-proclaimed "journal of opinion" that has defined the liberal project in America. The magazine was conceived to perpetuate the free exchange of ideas in the hope of creating a more civil society. In large part it succeeded, quickly becoming the country's preeminent journal of politics and the arts, respected and reviled, and almost always given a hearing. Herbert Croly, its founder, wrote that his object "was less to inform or entertain its readers than to start little insurrections in the realm of their convictions." This anthology is a record of the magazine's long attempt to incite those insurrections, which are the grounds for all social progress.

In 1909, five years before the birth of *The New Republic,* Herbert Croly, an intensely shy, cerebral architecture critic, published *The Promise of American Life.* His turgid polemic argued that if Americans conscientiously dedicated themselves to the pursuit of freedom and social justice, they could recapture the lofty principles upon which the nation had been built. "The only fruitful promise of which the life of any individual or any nation can be possessed," Croly wrote, "is a promise determined by an ideal. Such a promise is to be fulfilled, not by sanguine anticipations, not by a conservative imitation of past achievements, but by laborious, single-minded, clear-sighted, and fearless work." Croly, then forty years old, had retained his early admiration for Auguste Comte's Positivist faith in science and humanity. But at Harvard he had also absorbed the pragmatic teachings of William James and George Santayana, and he feared that the country's special dispensation was endangered by industrial capitalism, which had created vast disparities between the ruling elite and the mass of exploited workers.

Croly cast aside the tradition of nineteenth-century laissez-faire liberalism favored by most Progressives, with its Jeffersonian emphasis on free competition and natural rights. He replaced it with a vision he described as a "new nationalism," which combined Hamilton's conservative belief in a strong federal government with an argument that the government had to be employed as a progressive social force. Given a forward-looking president and a public-spirited electorate, Croly declared, America not only could reform itself, but also could once again serve as a beacon to peoples around the world who cherished the idea of democracy.

The book made an impression. Its high-minded patriotism was admired by Theodore Roosevelt, who called for a "new nationalism" in his 1912 presidential campaign. It also appealed to Willard Straight, a banker at J. P. Morgan and an imperialistic diplomat who had served in China; and to his idealistic wife, Dorothy, a Whitney and an heir to the Standard Oil fortune. Dorothy urged Croly to start up an independent weekly magazine, and told him that she and her husband would finance it. The Straights bought two brownstones on West Twenty-first Street in New York City's Chelsea district. The editors had spartan offices, but to compensate, they had a wine cellar, a library, a paneled dining room, and a French chef. Croly hired as co-editors two ex-socialists, each of whom had published his own book about American politics: Walter Lippmann (only four years out of Harvard) and Walter Weyl (an economist who had studied at Wharton). Together they began to sketch the contours of their "new republic," a title they reluctantly settled upon only after discarding *One Nation, New Nation, The Republic,* and *FACTS,* which was Straight's own bankerly inspiration.

The times were right for the undertaking. In 1914 the Progressive movement was languishing, World War I had just erupted, and the concentration of capital and industrial power, which had begun with the North's effort to finance the Civil War, was now manifest in an unscrupulous class of businessmen, bankers, and political bosses. It appeared to be just the moment for a moralistic yet reform-minded movement that proposed, as Croly put it, to "do something to keep faith alive in those members of the community who believe in the power of truth to set men free." The editors saw their magazine primarily as a means to achieve sweeping domestic reform in areas such as women's rights, the labor movement, the electoral system, and social welfare. *The New Republic,* choosing as its symbol a ship navigating rough waters, blithely set forth.

From the start, the magazine was unashamedly elitist and calculatedly impudent. "The whole point," Croly said, "is that we are trying to impose views on blind or reluctant people." At the very least, he thought, "we'll throw a few firecrackers under the skirts of the old women on the bench and in other high places." Among those they startled were their own pacifist friends. In the first issue, dated November 7, 1914, the editors–then as now primarily young men from Harvard unhindered by self-doubt–pronounced "The End of American Isolationism." They understood that the "relations between our democratic national ideal and our international obligations" had changed irrevocably—though they were not yet entirely sure just what that meant. By February 1917 they had made up their minds, and boldly came out for interventionism. Lippmann wrote an editorial in which he described German aggression against Britain and France as a war against "the Atlantic community" and "the civilization of which we are a part." In another, he declared, "We are becoming [their] open ally . . . because at the beginning of the war we decided that they were fighting in the main for the kind of world in which we wished to live."

Only three years after its founding, *The New Republic* was shaping the direction of a new liberalism that, the editors believed, realistically addressed America's emerging status and responsibilities as a world power. But not all liberals shared the magazine's confidence that its benign form of nationalism would prevail, and that the Allies could be persuaded to agree to a just peace. Randolph Bourne, the radical social critic and a *New Republic* staff contributor, attacked the editors for their presumptions—an act that made him a hero, John Patrick Diggins notes in *The Rise and Fall of the American Left,* not only to the Greenwich Village intellectuals of his generation but to the New Left of the 1960s as well. Bourne angrily demanded of "the war intellectuals," as he referred to his colleagues: "If the war is too strong for you to prevent, how is it going to be weak enough for you to mold to your liberal purposes?"

Bourne's skepticism was later confirmed at Versailles, in an episode that deeply embarrassed the *New Republic* editors. For years Croly, Weyl, and Lippmann had frequented Teddy Roosevelt's Oyster Bay home and enthusiastically endorsed his politics. But by 1916, at the urging of Lippmann, they had come around to Woodrow Wilson, who had fashioned a more enlightened domestic policy in a bid for liberal support and was heeding the editors' counsel on foreign affairs. Before long Lippmann, a shameless toady, was informally advising the president, dining at the White House, and—along with Croly—paying weekly visits to the New York apartment of Wilson's chief political adviser, Colonel Edward House. In April 1917, when Wilson asked Congress for a declaration of war, Lippmann wrote to Colonel House that it was a "magnificent" address: "We are delighted with it here, down to the last comma." Some months later Lippmann took a leave of absence from the magazine, first to work for the secretary of war, and then to help the president in the secret drafting of the Fourteen Points. As Ronald Steel points out in *Walter Lippmann and the American Century,* the magazine became known in this period, with some accuracy, as a house organ for Wilson. Readers thought it provided an inside glimpse of administration policy, as did stock market speculators, who bribed newsstand operators for advance copies.

However, this proximity to power was problematic for a journal that prided itself on its role as omniscient critic. The closer *The New Republic* came to directly influencing presidential policy, the more it compromised its integrity and institutional intelligence. In the end, Lippmann was appalled at Wilson's unsatisfactory completion of his handiwork, accurately predicting that the punitive peace imposed at Versailles would "balkanize" Central Europe and unleash the destructive forces of nationalism. The magazine turned against the president, and against the idea of the League of Nations, now doomed to inefficacy—a decision, notes Diggins in his seventieth-anniversary essay for *The New Republic,* that caused thousands of readers to decamp to the competing weekly, the pacifist *Nation. The New Republic*'s dalliance with Wilson had taught the editors a Jamesian lesson: in the "great game" of international diplomacy, the pursuit of goodness is not necessarily rewarded. Liberals would carry this lesson forward through World War II, Vietnam, Central America, and numerous smaller entanglements, leading to a foreign policy that was deeply ambivalent about the proper uses of American power.

World War I was only the first shock to Croly's new nationalism, with its assumption that the world, if given a chance, would emulate the spirit and substance of American freedom. The other was provided by the Russian Revolution, which almost from the start simultaneously inspired and depressed the magazine's editors and the liberal mind in general. Although radicals like John Reed and muckrakers like Lincoln Steffens greeted it with ardent approval, the liberals at the magazine were less sure. "The Russian Revolution is magnificent, but it is portentous," the editors wrote amid the upheavals of 1917, and for the next two decades they desperately attempted to make sense of the perils and promise of communism, both in Russia and in China. "I sympathize with those who seek for something good in Soviet Russia. But when we come to the actual thing, what is one to say?" John Maynard Keynes wondered in 1925. "I am not ready for a creed which does not care how much it destroys the liberty and security of daily life, which uses deliberately the weapons of persecution, destruction, and international strife."

Similar fears beset Croly, but there was no denying the rough energy of the Bolshevik Revolution, or the power of Lenin's mesmerizing rhetoric about a "classless society." Capitalism, with its "call of marketplace idolatry," as Harold Laski, the English socialist and *New Republic* regular, put it, had no such intellectual allure, and appeared to be even more stubbornly resistant to change than Croly had anticipated. In a special 1922 supplement in which Croly retooled "The New Republic Idea," he warned that the Great War had imperiled the very foundations of the Western world. The danger arose

> from a science which multiplies machinery much more than it illuminates human nature, from an industry which saves so much human labor and wastes so much human life, from a technology which, while prodigiously productive, is still too sterile to cultivate craftsmanship and creative work, from a nationalism which is opposed to imperialism but which insists itself on being pettily imperialistic, from a liberty which, in spite of so many proofs of its constructive possibilities, remains consciously negative and unedifying. . . . [The American people] feel themselves chained to an economic machine which is grinding their lives smaller, which they cannot control, and which their masters either cannot or will not control. . . . The new gods are headstrong. Their impulses are at once so irresistible and so anarchic that modern society seems incapable of recovering its self-esteem.

Whether or not America felt this way, it was clear that Croly did. Until his death in 1930, he continued to hope that Soviet communism would give way to democracy, and that American capitalism could be redeemed. But he increasingly found solace from the discordant realities of the modern world in a watery form of Christian worship that was expressed in articles for the magazine with titles such as "Christianity as a Way of Life." He even joined the mystical Orage Cult, along with Katherine Mansfield and Hart Crane, whose members, writes David Levy in a biography of Croly, attempted to "liberate the individual by awakening higher consciousness" through diet, breathing exercises, and gymnastics.

By 1920 all the founding editors, in one way or another, had renounced the confident liberalism that had brought them together six years before. While Croly found religion and communed with his consciousness, Walter Weyl turned back to his socialist roots, abandoning *The New Republic,* which he viewed as increasingly conservative, for *The Nation.* "Gone was Weyl's hope," Charles Forcey writes in *The Crossroads of Liberalism,* "that America's 'social surplus' would bring progress without a class struggle. The success of the Soviets completed the disintegration." Meanwhile, Lippmann—with his now undisguised patrician distrust of the mass public—turned right, going to *The New York World* to be a columnist and editor. Before he left the magazine in 1920, Lippmann had refused to print Weyl's essay "Tired Radicals," a barely disguised personal attack on him. The essay, later published posthumously in a collection of Weyl's essays, ridiculed "immature men, grown to clever reactionaries," who, "after shedding all ideas become absorbed in business, practical politics, or pleasure, retaining only an ironical, half regrettable pity for their callow days of radicalism." This early split—rancorous and deeply felt—anticipated the emergence of neoconservatism as an alternative philosophy for disaffected left intellectuals. Then, as later in the century, disagreements over America's role as a world power, and over the best approach to purging the evils of communism and the corruptions of capitalism, appeared to be insurmountable.

Bruce Bliven, who had been the managing editor since 1923, took over as editor upon Croly's death in 1930. More a working journalist than a political philosopher, Bliven took the magazine closer to the tumult of real politics, and for the first time *The New Republic* became unreservedly left-wing. Demoralized by the miscarriage of justice in the 1927 Sacco and Vanzetti trial—which became a nearly obsessive preoccupation for the magazine, as for an entire generation of liberals—Bliven was increasingly pessimistic about America's political order. After visiting the prisoners before their execution in 1927, he wrote, "these two were the haphazard victims of a blind hostility in the community, which was compounded of 'patriotic' fervor, antiforeignism, and of hatred of these men in particular because, as Professor Felix Frankfurter has summed it up, they denied the three things judge and jury held most dear: God, country, and property." The case focused attention on the raw inequities and class prejudices of American life, and helped to account for the magazine's growing doubts about the prospects for true social reform.

The New Deal, which in many ways fulfilled the progressive dreams of the early editors, was initially dismissed by the second generation for not being radical enough. (A now crotchety Lippmann, in his 1937 book, *The Good Society,* attacked FDR from the right for attempting to create a "planned new social order"—precisely what he had called for two decades earlier.) The editors agreed about the failures of industrial capitalism. They simply couldn't come to terms about solutions. George Soule, the magazine's chief advocate for economic planning, was admired by Roosevelt's New Deal administration, which offered him several jobs that he turned down. But as

David Seideman points out in *The New Republic: A Voice of Modern Liberalism,* Soule was regarded with undisguised irritation at the magazine. Felix Frankfurter, a close friend of the founding editors and an adviser to *The New Republic* since its inception, tartly wrote to Bliven of Soule's numbing essays, "I have insisted ad nauseam on more concreteness in NR, instead of repetition of general talk about a planned society." John Dos Passos suggested to Edmund Wilson that *The New Republic* print THIS IS ALL BULLSHIT at the bottom of each page.

Meanwhile, Malcolm Cowley and Edmund Wilson, who took turns as literary editor during the thirties, were calling, if only vaguely, for revolution. Cowley, the preeminent spokesman of the "lost generation," had fled to Europe in the twenties, to find respite from the vapidity of American culture. He and many of his fellow exiles returned with guilty consciences, as Diggins observes, and the Great Depression gave them a new sense of mission. "To the writers and artists of my generation," Edmund Wilson wrote, "who had grown up in the Big Business era and had always resented its barbarism, its crowding-out of everything they cared about, these years were not depressing but stimulating. One couldn't help being exhilarated at the sudden unexpected collapse of that stupid gigantic fraud." Cowley and Wilson were a little scornful of their magazine, with its genteel traditions and old-fashioned decorum. Wilson described it as "a chilly and unfriendly home for anybody but a respectable liberal of at least middle age."

Bliven, Cowley, and Wilson were more ready to forgive the failings of Soviet Russia than those of democratic America. Although Bliven published articles by skeptics such as John Dewey, Max Lerner, Charles Beard, and Vincent Sheean, who warned that Russia was no less dangerous than Germany, he rejected their dour prognostications, accompanying Sheean's critique, "Brumaire: The Soviet Union as a Fascist State" with a dissent called "Common Sense About Russia," in which he attempted to rationalize the Hitler-Stalin Pact of 1939. The previous year he had gone so far as to write an open letter to Stalin, in which he expressed dismay about the purges and show trials, but went on to propose respectfully, among other things, that Stalin consider "withdrawing from the public life" for a time.

The magazine became a proponent of the Popular Front, whose ostensible purpose was the fight against fascism in Europe and reactionary forces in America. In fact, it was an elaborate international deception set up by the Communist Party as a way of recruiting liberals and socialists. Rationalizing this unseemly alliance in 1936, the editors wrote: "It is better to win with the aid of people, some of whom we don't like, than to lose and come under the iron-fisted control of people all of whom we dislike a great deal more." In a famous 1931 essay, "An Appeal to Progressives," Wilson renounced Croly's faith in domestic reform, and advised American radicals and progressives to "take Communism away from the Communists." The American opposition, he rashly declared, "must not be afraid to dynamite the old shibboleths and conceptions and substitute new ones as shocking as possible."

In 1932 Wilson went after Lippmann, Soule, Beard, and Stuart Chase for tinkering around the edges of capitalism with their schemes for liberal planned economies. Even if FDR was elected, Wilson wrote, "it would be the capitalists, not the liberals who would do the planning; and they would plan to save their own skins at the expense of whoever had to bleed." Stuart Chase, a longtime contributor to *The New Republic* (and whose July 1932 series on "A New Deal for America" may have influenced FDR's embrace of the slogan), retorted that Mr. Wilson "has recently been converted to one of the forms of communism, and safe in the arms of Marx can take pot shots at those outside the compound. . . . Well, I'll tell you, Mr. Edmund Wilson. While you were dissecting Proust and other literary gentlemen—and a very pretty job you did—I was dissecting the industrial structure." Wilson conceded his folly in 1937, in "Complaints of the Literary Left," in which he noted the increasing terrorism of Stalin, and in his 1938 book, *To the Finland Station,* excerpted in *The New Republic.* Wilson's apostasy led to a feud with his friend Cowley, who did not fully relinquish his own faith in Soviet communism until after the Hitler-Stalin Pact. This finally brought to an end, at least at the magazine, what W. H. Auden described as "the clever hopes" of "a low dishonest decade."

The New Republic's saving graces in the thirties were its cultural criticism and its social reporting. Cowley's and Wilson's myopia about Soviet communism did not extend to the arts, where they exuberantly explored modernism and its relation to the cultural legacy of the West. In the late twenties and early thirties, Wilson wrote brilliantly about Poe and Hemingway, Dostoyevsky and Joyce, Yeats, and T. S. Eliot. Cowley wrote with equal suppleness about Dada, *Gone with the Wind,* and André Malraux; *Exile's Return,* Cowley's literary memoir, was excerpted in the magazine in 1931. The magazine published William Faulkner, Granville Hicks, the jazz critic Otis Ferguson, Thomas Mann, and Ignazio Silone, among others, and Cowley initiated "Books That Changed Our Minds," an ambitious twelve-part series investigating the intellectual underpinnings of Western thought. "Unlike the Marxist literary left," Diggins writes in his seventieth-anniversary essay, "Cowley and Wilson . . . rejected the 'Progressive' school of American history, in which students were taught to absorb Jefferson, Emerson, and Whitman and to steer clear of Hawthorne, Melville, and Henry James, those 'dark' romantics and realists who cast doubt on progress and reason." The editors' disgust with capitalism even roused them from their editorial armchairs. Cowley, Wilson, and Bliven all ventured out into working-class America, producing riveting accounts of the miseries of class and race, from the mines of Harlan County to the auto industry of Detroit to the racial swamp of Chattanooga. In 1930 and 1931 Wilson published his famous series on social unrest, later collected in *The American Jitters.*

If *The New Republic* couldn't quite bring itself to renounce its battered hopes for communism, it had no such illusions about fascism. In the early thirties, when most of the American public was refusing to acknowledge growing evidence of the Holocaust, the magazine was urgently protesting it, making the European Jews' plight, as Diggins put it, "a new cause of American liberalism." In July 1933 Mary Heaton Vorse, reporting on a bureau set up to help Jews escape Germany, wrote, "here in the hall is the human debris of the cold pogrom which rates Jews as subhuman." However, this new cause of liberalism had little of the optimistic vigor of the old one. Croly had believed that democracy, guided by reason and virtue, would triumph over baser political impulses. Citizens needed only an inspirational leader, and to be "transfigured by a common conviction of the latent regeneracy and brotherhood of mankind." Bliven and his successor in the forties, Michael Straight, were desperately trying to make sense of a world in which fascist dictators derived their power from inciting the unregeneracy of humankind.

Astonishingly, under an editor who had continued the magazine's critiques of American injustice and who recognized the dangers of fascism, *The New Republic* counseled fatalism and restraint in the face of Hitler, Mussolini, and Franco. In September 1939, as the war began with Germany's invasion of Poland, Bruce Bliven and George Soule urged readers to remember the sobering lessons of World War I. In September 1939, in "The Basis of a Lasting Peace," Soule wrote: "Sacrifice and cruelty are necessary, but to what purpose? Last time it was to be for the end of war itself and the creation of a better world. The result is what we see." The treaty writers at Versailles advocated national self-determination. Yet "the new national states which they set up strengthened a hoard of hatreds and grievances." Soule called for "thought and research and public discussion on the problem of the next peace" and, predictably, for "a development of economic planning."

Other contributors were outraged by this hand-wringing. Lewis Mumford flatly charged the editors with moral cowardice. In his April 1940 essay "The Corruption of Liberalism," Mumford denounced the isolationism advocated by most American liberals as "a passive milk-and-water version of the fascist's contemptuous attitude toward the rest of the human race." He was so indignant, notes his biographer, Donald L. Miller, that after he wrote the article, he resigned as a contributing editor. (The magazine's position did indicate a striking reversal. *The New Republic,* which in 1917 had dismissed Randolph Bourne's warnings that the insidious nature of war would defeat liberals' best intentions, now firmly opposed American interventionism for the same reason.) In a mild-mannered rejoinder in the same issue, the editors objected: "Mr. Mumford should be the last to deny that it is possible to feel deeply, and intelligently as well, about the waste and horror of war. . . . It is not a mark of barren isolationism to believe with all one's heart and soul that the best contribution Americans can make to the future of humanity is to fulfill democracy in the United States."

The dispute was put to rest the following year by the new editor, Michael Straight, whose own life charted the tortuous course of liberalism in the thirties and forties. The son of the magazine's benefactors, Michael had joined the student Communist movement while at Cambridge University in 1937, and fell in with the Soviet agents Anthony Blunt and Guy Burgess. Straight returned to the United States the following year, when—according to his 1983 autobiography, *After Long Silence*—he put his Communist past behind him and became a speechwriter for FDR. It was Straight who decided the magazine must stand against the fascist threat, and under his editorship it became a strong proponent of U.S. intervention, calling for a declaration of war four months before the Japanese attack on Pearl Harbor in December 1941.

Mumford too was an interesting case study in liberal angst. Though an implacable opponent of fascism, in the thirties he shared some of the prevailing leftist weakness for communism. Nevertheless, in "The Corruption of Liberalism" he identified a critical vulnerability of American liberalism: its polite, eminently reasonable world view could not comprehend evil. He was one of numerous intellectuals writing for the magazine—including Irving Howe, Lionel Trilling, Alfred Kazin, Reinhold Neibuhr, and Arthur M. Schlesinger, Jr.—who were disturbed by liberalism's paucity of moral imagination and political courage. Throughout the war years, *The New Republic,* like *Partisan Review*, became home to journalists, historians, and theologians who believed that the advent of totalitarianism, the death camps, and the atomic bomb required a tough new kind of historical realism.

One telling example of this view is the wrenching 1944 essay Kazin wrote for *The New Republic,* "In Every Voice, in Every Ban," about an exiled Jewish Pole whose wife and child were killed by the Nazis, and who had recently committed suicide in his London flat.

> Something has been set forth in Europe that is subtle, and suspended, and destructive; and it will break the power-pacts, and the high declarations, and even the armies, since armies are only men. That something is all our silent complicity in the massacre of the Jews (and surely not of them alone; it is merely that their deaths were so peculiarly hopeless). For it means that men are not ashamed of what they have been in this time,

and are therefore not prepared for the future outbreaks of fascism which are so deep in all of us.

Half a century later, as the latest outbreak runs its horrifying course in the former Yugoslavia, his words strike uncomfortably close to home. Once again masses of refugees desperately seek refuge in Europe, while Americans—and *The New Republic,* which has urged measured intervention—debate the country's interests in the matter.

The problem of assessing the interests of any one country, let alone those of humanity at large, grew increasingly complicated after World War II. Walter Lippmann, who occasionally still wrote for the magazine, observed the ominous escalation in the arms race and the ever shifting political configurations across the globe, noting in his 1957 essay "End of the Postwar World": "We have supposed that all the nations would have the same fundamental political ideals which we have, not because they are our ideals but because these ideals are universal." That theory had been disproved at Versailles, and again at Yalta. The world had entered an era, Lippmann wrote, in which no one "can as yet see clearly . . . where we really are and where we ought to go. There are no reliable maps."

American conservatives resolved this difficulty simply by seeing America as locked in a Manichean struggle with the Soviet Union. *The New Republic* attempted a more nuanced approach. Niebuhr, in a 1956 essay called "A Qualified Faith," wrote of the difficulties of exporting democracy to the Third World, correctly arguing that in Asia and Africa, the memory of imperialism and colonialism would, in the short term and despite our best efforts, predispose both those continents toward communism.

Under Straight and subsequent editors, *The New Republic* tried to avoid both the prosecutorial hysteria of the rabid right and the credulous fellow-traveling of the old left. The only exception was Henry A. Wallace, whom Straight hired in 1946—a decision he quickly regretted. Wallace routinely emblazoned on the cover his calls for one-worldism and for "jobs, peace, and freedom," in a bloviated prose style that Dwight Macdonald unforgettably described as "Wallese." In 1948 the Progressive Party was formed, led by Wallace, which was found to have ties to American Communists. This was anathema to the ex-Communist Straight, who immediately asked Wallace to step down, which he did. Straight saw, as he put it in a 1975 article on his "Days with Henry Wallace," that "the gap between the liberal line and the Communist line is going to go on widening." (Straight's own loyalties, however, remained a little murky, as he revealed in his autobiography. In March 1951, Burgess ran into Straight in Washington, D.C., and admitted that he had passed along to Moscow the U.S. plans to advance into North Korea. Straight warned his old friend that he would turn him in. He did approach a British official, but changed his mind when he was told that many others had come forward with information on Burgess. "I told myself," he wrote, "that Guy was gone forever, and that Anthony had been rendered harmless.")

In 1950 *The New Republic* had moved to Washington, the center of political affairs in postwar America. The following year, amid the omnipresent paranoia of McCarthyism, the editors implored the Senate to expel the junior senator from Wisconsin, and continued to defend unequivocally the civil liberties of teachers, intellectuals, and members of the Communist Party. Nevertheless, they did not hesitate to point out that, abhorrent as the government's tactics were, not everyone who was convicted of spying for the Soviet Union was innocent. The most explosive case of the decade was that of the convicted atomic spies Julius and Ethel Rosenberg. As the couple's clemency plea was about to be considered by President Eisenhower in January 1953, the editors declared that "the Rosenbergs are guilty," but argued that their death sentence should be commuted to life imprisonment: "One of our chief weapons against Russia is the accusation of excessively harsh sentences, and the execution of the Rosenbergs will greatly weaken our future use of this line of attack. We will benefit far more by not competing with the Communists in this field." Twenty-two years later, under Martin Peretz, the magazine revisited the case in an essay by Sol Stern and Ronald Radosh that evolved into an important book, *The Rosenberg File,* by Radosh and Joyce Milton. These authors too believed that the death sentence was profoundly unjust, but found that Julius (not Ethel) had been at the center of a Soviet espionage network after the war. Predictably, a contingent of readers, who still marched to the causes of the 1930s left, registered their outrage in letters to the editor.

The magazine's search for a firm stand against both Soviet communism and the American right wing later became further complicated by the ethical and political chaos of Vietnam and Watergate. Under Gilbert Harrison, the owner and editor from 1953 to 1974, *The New Republic* denounced the escalation of the war in Indochina under Kennedy, Johnson, and Nixon, while resisting the New Left's romanticization of the Communist National Liberation Front. Christopher Jencks, reporting in October 1967 for *The New Republic* on a meeting in Czechoslovakia between a group of Americans and two delegations of Vietnamese revolutionaries, wrote: "The common bond between the New Left and the NLF is not . . . a common dream or a common experience but a common enemy: the U.S. Government, the system, the Establishment. The young radicals' admiration for the NLF stems from the feeling that the NLF is resisting The Enemy successfully, whereas they are not."

The American values of patriotism and freedom, which had seemed so patently honorable to the founding editors, were being wrenched grotesquely out of shape. George Orwell had demonstrated, in his famous

1946 essay on "Politics and the English Language," how to spot the corruption of political belief in the debasement of language. "In our time, political speech and writing are largely the defense of the indefensible," he wrote, consisting "of euphemism, question-begging and sheer cloudy vagueness. Defenseless villages are bombarded from the air, the inhabitants driven out into the countryside, the cattle machine-gunned, the huts set on fire with incendiary bullets: this is called *pacification*." This essay, with its notion of destroying villages in order to save them, predicted with uncanny precision the kind of rhetoric the U.S. government began to use to justify the prosecution of a war that could be neither won nor morally justified. Meanwhile, the Vietcong were mouthing American rhetoric about independence and "just wars," and New Leftists were ridiculing their own country as "Amerika." It was somehow appropriate that the nation's preeminent foreign policy maker at the time, Henry Kissinger, was, as Ronald Steel points out in his *New Republic* review of Kissinger's memoirs, *White House Years,* incanting "such phrases as 'equilibrium,' 'balance of power,' and 'national interest,'" which floated "errantly in an undefined void."

Trying somehow to fill this void, *The New Republic* in the 1960s and early 1970s became a forum for a liberalism fiercely at odds with itself and the country. On the domestic front, the magazine contained articles by "new conservatives" like Peter Viereck, who in 1964 attacked members of his own movement as "rootless, counter-revolutionary doctrinaires"; and by New Leftists like James Ridgeway, who covered the farcical New Politics convention of 1967 in an article called "Freak-Out in Chicago," which described the strange stew of participants: white radicals, black militants, Communists, Quakers, and various addled hippies. ("Represent yourself. You are free. Dig? It's like we got a choice, man.") It also published unreconstructed social democrats like Michael Harrington, who defied the "militant negativism" of conservatives and some liberals by arguing in 1970 that the New Deal, the Fair Deal, and the Great Society had not gone far enough. Meanwhile, each week the magazine monitored the mounting scandals of Watergate through indignant editorials and its cantankerous, painstaking White House correspondent, John Osborne. His weekly "Nixon Watch" columns, which were written with a mixture of revulsion and pity, were avidly read as the presidency began to self-destruct. On August 24, 1974, he concluded his final column on Nixon: "Thank God, he's gone. I'll miss him and I wish him the mercy that he doesn't deserve and probably won't get."

The New Republic conducted a liberal wake in its sixtieth anniversary issue in 1974—the year Martin Peretz bought the magazine from Harrison—with a supplement called "This Fractured Democracy." The consensus among the contributors (Irving Howe, Hans J. Morgenthau, C. Vann Woodward, Marcus G. Raskin, James Chace, and Abe Fortas) was that liberals had lost their moral courage and political bearings, retreating into a shell of baffled defeatism. Morgenthau was the gloomiest of the lot, writing: "The charisma of democracy, with its faith in the rationality and virtue of the masses, has no more survived the historic experience of mass irrationality and the excesses of fascism and of the impotence and corruption of democratic government, than the charisma of Marxism-Leninsm has survived the revelations of the true nature of Communist government." He warned that "no new political faith has replaced the ones lost," and that "no civilized government that is not founded on such a faith and rational expectation can endure in the long run." Morgenthau underestimated American democracy's miraculous appeal to oppressed peoples around the world, but he was right that the impotence and corruption of democratic government remained intransigent problems for liberals.

Peretz, a sixties leftist active on a number of fronts, had grown personally dismayed and ideologically disillusioned by the time he took over as editor-in-chief in 1975. He hoped that *The New Republic* could help restore liberalism's sense of direction and its backbone. He made it clear that the views of the New Left were not welcome in the magazine, demanding that readers face up to the unpleasant lessons of history. Under his editorship, the magazine became more widely read than it had ever been (growing from 86,000 subscribers in 1975 to 104,000 in 1993), but it attracted critics commensurate with its status. In 1976 Peretz hired Michael Kinsley as managing editor, a twenty-five-year-old Harvard graduate and law school student who infused the magazine with an iconoclastic, sardonic approach to the follies of domestic politics. Peretz directed the magazine's position on foreign policy, giving it a neoconservative cast. Along with senior editors Charles Krauthammer and Morton Kondracke and the literary editor, Leon Wieseltier, he articulated a hard-line view of Soviet adventurism and unstinting support for Israel.

In 1957 Reinhold Niebuhr had written of the Arab nations' vow to "throttle Israel in its cradle" and of the pathos "in the fact that the Jews should have exchanged the insecurity of Europe for the collective insecurity of the Middle East." Peretz shared Neibuhr's fear about Israel's security, particularly after the 1967 Six-Day War. While the New Left championed the cause of Palestinian nationalism, *The New Republic* urgently described the threats posed to the solitary democracy in the region. (In 1967 Peretz and Michael Walzer wrote an essay in *Ramparts* magazine called "Israel Is Not Vietnam.") The anarchic world of the Middle East, as Walzer wrote in 1975, had come to represent the breakdown of a political code. "The New Terrorism," perpetrated by the Palestinian Liberation Organization and a bewildering array of other fanatical groups, was "a total war against nations, ethnic groups, religions."

Throughout the 1980s many liberals charged that *The New Republic,* like *Commentary,* had become reflexively right-wing about foreign policy in general and about Israel in particular. The magazine was accused by countless readers of being an abject apologist for Israel, and of harboring contempt for the rights, needs, and interests of other groups in the Middle East. Yet the picture is more complicated. Zionism had always been a defining feature of *The New Republic,* embraced by the early editors along with friends like Louis D. Brandeis and Felix Frankfurter. And under Peretz *The New Republic* periodically spoke out in behalf of oppressed groups that didn't much interest the mass media, like the Bahai in Iran and the Kurds in Iraq and Turkey.

Moreover, the magazine has insisted that the Israelis, like the Palestinians, must make politically unpalatable compromises on the occupied territories. Writing on the twentieth anniversary of the Six-Day War, the editors noted that "power also brings responsibilities, and among the responsibilities of power acquired by Israel in the '67 war was the Palestinian problem. . . . For reasons of security—and for reasons of justice—Israel must use its new power wisely. Unfortunately, it does not always do so." In 1988 Leon Wieseltier warned Israel not to relinquish its own democratic ideals in its struggle with the Palestinians. "The Palestinians are not a nation of terrorists," he wrote. "And Israel, too, has blood on its hands. To say that Israel cannot deal with Palestinians who call themselves 'PLO' is to say that there can be no deal. It is to transform an argument against terrorism into an argument against politicians. That is, into another excuse."

However, the decade's defining battle between left and right, and within the left, took place over Central America. Those who supported aid to the Nicaraguan *contras* claimed American support was the surest guarantee against the spread of communism in the region. Others responded that the *contras* couldn't win, that they were unworthy American surrogates, that the United States should avoid further entanglements in a region where it had such an unsavory past. Still others believed that the Sandinistas were the saviors of the Nicaraguan people.

Although *The New Republic* pitilessly attacked Ronald Reagan's domestic policies under both Michael Kinsley (the editor from 1976–81 and 1985–89) and Hendrik Hertzberg (who twice took over from Kinsley), and though its editors disagreed among themselves about the dispute, a majority agreed to a policy of aid to the contras. They supported The Reagan Doctrine (a term popularized by Charles Krauthammer in a 1985 essay for *Time*), which granted U.S. support for insurgencies battling Soviet-supported regimes. "We believe that preventing the establishment of a Leninist dictatorship in Nicaragua is a goal worthy of American support," the editors declared in March 1986, "and that those willing to fight for this cause are deserving of American assistance." This position led many frustrated readers to charge the editors with "schizophrenia," and caused a revolt among intellectuals affiliated with the magazine. Soon afterward, thirteen contributing editors wrote an aggrieved rebuttal, insisting that their disagreement was not "rooted in isolationism, defeatism, willful blindness, or a double standard of 'scrupulousness' about the sovereignty of 'states rule by pro-Soviet Leninists,'" but stemmed rather "from a judgment that the means the administration proposes—themselves morally dubious—cannot accomplish the ends it envisions."

The dissident editors claimed vindication the following year, when it was discovered that the Reagan administration, in a particularly imaginative perversion of presidential power, had sold arms to its sworn enemy Iran (as part of a scheme to secure the release of American hostages held in Lebanon), and used the proceeds to fund an illegal *contra* war. The magazine continued to insist that the goals, at least, of the administration were laudable, and that it was the persistent application of American pressure that eventually forced the Sandinistas to agree to democratic elections.

"Iranamok," as the magazine facetiously dubbed the whole mess, seemed to prove Hans Morgenthau's point about the vanishing charisma of liberal democracy. Presidents who lie to Congress and the electorate and betray the Constitution, Morgenthau claimed, take on the attributes of the authoritarian and totalitarian regimes they deplore. The public rewards them with cynicism and mindless cheerleading. In 1974, with Watergate and Vietnam in mind, Morgenthau wrote that "shame, the public acknowledgment of a moral or political failing, is virtually extinct . . . a disgraced President moves easily into the position of an elder statesman receiving confidential information and giving advice on affairs of state." In 1988 Reagan was politely escorted out of the White House, and Oliver North became, for some, an American hero.

The founding editors of *The New Republic* would have been appalled by Watergate and Iranamok. They expected that an energetic, inventive federal government would solve America's political ills, not catalyze them. Of course, they had counted on the triumph of progressive government and an engaged electorate. Painfully aware of the corruption of domestic politics and of the country's social and economic inequities, the editors simply believed the problems must be addressed and corrected. If children and workers were being exploited by industry, new labor laws must be enacted and unions strengthened. Blacks and immigrants must be shielded from bigotry and assisted in their efforts to join the American mainstream. Women must be enabled to work outside the home, and be given access to birth control and the right to abortion. The economy must be regulated and government programs like unemployment insurance and Social Security introduced to protect the poor and the vulnerable from the punishing fluctuations of capitalism. Many of these causes were in due course enacted, most dramatically in the New Deal, and the liberals' most divisive disagreements resolved.

Race, however, the most visceral issue of American politics, has defied the liberals' predilection for social engineering, defeating all of their favored remedies. As the editors said in a 1927 editorial, "Realistic Liberalism," foreshadowing the magazine's neoliberalism in the 1980s, liberals had made "a well-intentioned but inconsiderate attempt to redeem human nature without asking human beings to participate in their own redemption, except by devising social programs, winning elections, passing laws, inventing more machines, and increasing individual and social capital." Croly recognized this weakness and, citing Santayana, concluded *The Promise of American Life* by asking the common citizen to be "something of a saint and something of a hero, not by growing to heroic proportions in his own person, but by the sincere and enthusiastic imitation of saints and heroes." Croly had in mind a leader like Abraham Lincoln, about whom he wrote in his 1920 essay "The Paradox of Lincoln": "He embraced them all, rich and poor, black and white, rebel and loyalist, as human beings."

Unfortunately, Lincoln had long since been transported to the realm of myth. Far more paradigmatic of twentieth-century race relations was the 1932 trial of the "Scottsboro boys," nine black youths accused and convicted of raping two white girls. The editors saw the case, like that of Sacco and Vanzetti, as an ominous failing of the courts to protect defendants' constitutional rights. This time the abrogation of justice took place along the lines of race, not class. As Edmund Wilson described it in "The Freight-Car Case," a fair trial was out of the question, given the inordinate interest the case had aroused and the court's refusal of a change of venue. To complicate matters, the defendants were quickly swept up in another political battle, as the Communists' International Labor Defense and the National Association for the Advancement of Colored People (NAACP) fought over who would represent them. The case was appealed numerous times and reversed twice by the Supreme Court, until twenty years later, as William Manchester writes in *The Glory and the Dream,* the last of the prisoners died of cancer: "The Communist Party made 'the Scottsboro Boys' known around the world, and their persecution provided incalculable fuel for black despair and, later, militancy." The case was also an instructive lesson for future racist demagogues, from George Wallace to Louis Farrakhan, who saw the politics of race as an opportunity to be exploited rather than as an evil to be overcome.

As the courts began to devise legal solutions to segregation in the 1950s, the underlying tensions of race relations became more fraught than ever. The editors wrote in 1960, "The fight against segregation in the South is advancing to a new stage—from the courts and the Congress into the market place, where emotions can be as taut as in the school yard." Most white politicians misread this development. Even John F. Kennedy, whom the magazine rapturously welcomed, in part because of his sensitivity to the issues of race and poverty, "underestimated the moral passion" behind the civil rights movement, as Arthur F. Schlesinger, Jr., conceded in his 1983 retrospective for *The New Republic.* If there was a figure in this era who rose to saint/hero status in the eyes of America, it was not JFK, who moved cautiously on racial issues, or even his brother Bobby, but Martin Luther King, Jr., possibly the country's most remarkable public figure since Lincoln.

Yet even before King's assassination, his all-encompassing vision of American society was being supplanted by the sectarianism of Malcolm X and the Black Panthers, and by the increasing radicalism and truculence of Students for a Democratic Society and the New Left. The original liberal goal had been to erase the boundaries of race, class, and gender. But by the late sixties, the New Left, as Diggins points out, had come to see these as "social categories that one must embrace to discover the self. Somehow the categories that once were used to discriminate and keep people oppressed came to be seen as forces for change and freedom." It was an early expression of the multiculturalism that swept American universities in the 1980s. Andrew Kopkind, writing ten months after the 1965 Watts riots, noted the pervasive Malcolm X sweatshirts, the use of "black" for "all that is good or true," the black schools "teaching soul" and nationalist doctrine, and the gangs, reconstituted as self-help organizations. In January 1966 Stokely Carmichael, then field secretary of the Student Nonviolent Coordinating Committee, contributed to a series in the magazine called "Thoughts of the Young Radicals," in which he called Johnson's concept of the Great Society "preposterous" and denied that "the goal is for Negroes and other excluded persons to be allowed to join the middle-class mainstream of American society as we see it today."

The New Republic was willing to give the "young radicals" a chance to explain themselves. It even, at one point, endorsed the black militants' own assesssment of American racism. The magazine, commenting on Johnson's Commission on Civil Disorders report in 1968, interpreted it as saying, "in effect, don't blame conspirators, outside agitators, Rap Brown, Stokely Carmichael, Communists, sexual irregularity, drugs, neglect in childhood, handguns or slaves, sloth, dirt, rats. Blame Whitey. It's a harsh judgment, and true." Nevertheless, there were many signs of the magazine's emerging conservatism on racial issues. Perhaps inevitably, given the skeptical strain of *New Republic* liberalism, the editors came to reject both the black militants' critique of American racism and the hopes of moderate liberals that the answer to the crisis—as to many baffling social dilemmas—lay in legal remedies and in generous government entitlements.

Gunnar Myrdal expressed the magazine's evolving position in his 1964 essay "The War on Poverty," in which he declared that "the goals of social justice and economic progress . . . are compatible," but warned that even after legal equality had been achieved, "Negroes will still suffer the lasting effects of poverty, slum existence, previous exclusion from easy access to education and housing" and that a vast number of those in the poverty pockets were not only unemployed but also unemployable. The same year Christopher Jencks questioned the viability of Johnson's poverty programs, which relied on education, training, and character building to change ghetto culture. "Can such a plan succeed? Not this year or next, certainly. Not, probably, in a decade or a generation. . . . [H]ave we the means to abolish the attributes of the poor? Ignorance? Incompetence? Short-sightedness? Apathy? Despair? Illness? Not for $1 billion a year, and probably not for $10 billion either."

This early, pessimistic line of argument was taken up by Peretz, who made the underclass one of the magazine's primary domestic themes. The editors frequently warned that despite the rapid advances made by the black middle class since the 1954 *Brown* v. *Board of Education* decision, in some respects American society was becoming more segregated than ever. Teenage boys in inner cities sought escape through drugs and power through guns; and girls, as Ann Hulbert explained in a 1984 article on teenage pregnancy, hoped to find some affirmation of their status by having babies. In 1989, in "The Crisis of Caste," C. Vann Woodward said bluntly, "there seems to be no reasonable hope in the foreseeable future for color-blind assimilation."

In the 1970s, under the guidance of the legal scholar Alexander Bickel, a longtime *New Republic* contributing editor, the magazine had also begun to argue against the well-meaning social activism of the Warren Court. Bickel wrote the magazine's first editorial on *Roe* v. *Wade* in 1973, saying that the decision was "derived from fashionable and humane notions of progress," not from the text of the Constitution—a position the magazine has stubbornly stuck to ever since. He also wrote several signed articles in which he frankly discussed the unintended consequences of busing and school desegregation. To the alarm of numerous liberals, he declared that "to dismantle the official structure of desegregation is not to create integrated schools. Actual integration is enormously difficult, if possible at all." This set off a flurry of rebuttals by Marian Wright Edelman and other civil rights advocates, who said that Bickel—like the Nixon administration—was "conceding that the constitutional rights of blacks are those that the white majority is willing to permit and nothing more." Today, however, blacks themselves often choose not to mingle with whites at integrated schools and universities, and many have come to argue against integrating black universities. Some white liberals, meanwhile, are reluctantly coming around to Bickel's conclusion that "federal help for coherent local efforts to improve primary and secondary education" was the most promising role for the government to play. He even proposed school choice as one alternative, an idea that some liberals reluctantly began to reconsider two decades later, when the Bush administration began stealing education from the Democrats as a popular political issue.

Throughout the late seventies and eighties, the magazine staked out a defiant position on affirmative action. Unlike the Democratic Party, which remained faithful to the coalition politics first forged by FDR and which stressed group demands, *The New Republic* emphatically placed the highest value on the rights of the individual. As the editors said in 1983: affirmative action in hiring and schooling is "an unexceptionable notion when it means vigorously recruiting qualified black applicants, a controversial (and, to us, unacceptable) one when it means, as it often does, quotas." In its 1978 editorial on the Court's tortured *Bakke* decision, through which a white student won admission to the University of California at Davis on the grounds that the school's rigid quota system had unfairly excluded him, the editors pointed out the ironies of court-mandated remedies to social problems:

> The trouble with many affirmative action programs, certainly with quota systems such as the one at Davis, is that they substitute simplistic group identifications for evaluations of individual worth. There are two problems with such programs. One is that they demean and insult both those who are admitted and those who are excluded as a result. The other is that they encourage group hostility and suspicion in society at large.

The dangers of "groupthink," as the editors called it, borrowing Orwell's phrase, had been apparent ever since George McGovern's crushing defeat to Richard Nixon in 1972, a turning point for *The New Republic* and for many others who had clung to the vestiges of New Left politics. The magazine had endorsed McGovern, despite his inability to articulate a credible political position. As Tom Geoghegan wrote in "Miami and the Seeds of Port Huron," the McGovernites "are caught between [Tom] Hayden's world, where politics is expected to deal with the whole man and his sense of helplessness, and the Great Society, where a faceless bureaucracy indemnifies anyone or any group big enough to make trouble for it." It was a mistake the editors would not make again. In an election postmortem, the magazine struck a note it repeated with every subsequent Democratic defeat: the party was substituting interest-group politics for ideological integrity, becoming nothing more than a mix of "independent and heterogeneous principalities with interests so divided it can't even be called a coalition."

In the 1980s Peretz continued to impress this point upon *New Republic* readers, reminding them of a conservative truth that the Democrats had forgotten: to affect policy, you need to get elected; and to get elected, you need to know what your voters believe. The Democrats were ignoring, at their own peril, the demands of the middle class, an enormous voting bloc that was worried about crime and taxes and abysmal public schools. In 1983 Henry Fairlie, one of a number of Britons to assign himself the role of America's conscience in the magazine, wrote a widely discussed cover story on why the Democrats deserved to lose the election. As much as he despised the Reaganites, he feared "the Democratic Party will return to the White House before it is ready to govern from there, and that, squandering its opportunity yet again, it will forfeit . . . the chance to reverse the narrow-minded, dry-hearted, pinch-souled conservative mood that now prevails in America." Not unlike Croly, Weyl, and Lippmann, the editors in the eighties—disgusted with traditional party politics and with the mindless greed and upbeat untruths of the reigning conservatives—proposed a "neoliberal" program, which combined fiscal prudence, a strong defense, and enlightened government social policies. In 1992, after twelve years of Republican rule, a Democrat was finally reelected President by adopting a similar platform.

In the "post-ideological" era, the problems—let alone the solutions—are even less clear than they were in 1914. This anthology arrives at a time when once again history has suddenly accelerated, destroying the certitudes of all political groups. Not surprisingly, given the ragged course of liberalism over the century, *The New Republic* retains little of the righteous indignation and reformist zeal that propelled its early contributors. The founding editors' calls for a more aggressive foreign policy have been complicated by global technology, the end of the cold war, the rise of Japan as an economic world power, and the ruinous national and ethnic animosities of countless aggrieved peoples.

The magazine occasionally hazards an ambitious new social agenda, such as the one laid out in Mickey Kaus's 1992 essay "The End of Equality." Kaus proposed the heretical notion that liberals stop attempting to redistribute wealth and begin building a new public sphere—through universal health care, a draft, and welfare reform—that would create true "social equality" in the face of capitalism's inevitable material inequality. The "front of the book" also continues to publish historians, philosophers, and critics such as C. Vann Woodward, Michael Walzer, Nathan Glazer, and, until his death in 1993, Irving Howe, who snub conventional political and scholarly trends and ask the reader to reflect upon the broader cultural and historical context of political events. But in general *The New Republic,* while retaining its irreverence, has dropped much of its early solemnity, offering more brisk news analysis than earnest soul-searching about the future of liberalism. This can be seen in its popular weekly columns, Michael Kinsley's "TRB from Washington" and Fred Barnes's "White House Watch"; and in its more clipped editorials fashioned by the current editor, Andrew Sullivan, another undoctrinaire British conservative. Meanwhile, "the back of the book," under the stewardship of Leon Wieseltier and Ann Hulbert, continues its more distanced assessment of the fractious worlds of politics and culture.

In a 1939 essay for *The New Republic* Charles Beard wrote, "Herein lies a test of the perspicacity of TNR's editors in formulating their program. They did with remarkable insight divine the future. . . . Their labors were far from vain, for history, that merciless judge of all man's proposals, has thus far, in large measure, vindicated their projections of 1914." Beard, a faithful friend of the magazine, was being generous. The triumph of liberalism is not that it divined the future, but that it helped remake the future by adhering to a few core beliefs about independence, equality, and justice. As the editors declared in the seventy-fifth anniversary issue, "We still believe in the possibility of change, in the moral and historical grandeur of individual and social action—and in the importance of ideas as the seeds of change and the springs of action." If nothing else, the essays in the following pages testify to the importance of intellectual honesty in the face of mass uncertainty and of recapturing Herbert Croly's belief in the power of truth to set people free.

DOROTHY WICKENDEN

PART I

The New World Order: "After the Revolution"

The End of American Isolation

EDITORIAL

NOVEMBER 7, 1914

The self-complacent isolation of a great people has never received a ruder shock than that which was dealt to the American nation by the outbreak of the European war. We have long been congratulating ourselves on something more than an official independence of Europe. We considered ourselves free in a finer and a deeper sense—free from the poison of inherited national antipathies, free from costly and distracting international entanglements, free from a more than incidental reliance on foreign markets for the sale of our products, free to make mistakes with impunity and to gather fruits by merely shaking the tree. We were more nearly self-contained, more completely the master of our own destiny, than any other nation of history. Yet this consummate example of political independence has been subjected to a visitation of fate almost as disconcerting as those which beset wandering Indian tribes. There broke over the country a European war which the American people individually and collectively were powerless to prevent or to mitigate, yet which may have consequences upon the future and policy of the country as profound and far-reaching as our self-made Civil War. Independence in the sense of isolation has proved to be a delusion. It was born of the same conditions and the same misunderstandings as our traditional optimistic fatalism; and it must be thrown into the same accumulating scrapheap of patriotic misconceptions.

The American nation was wholly unprepared to cope with such a serious political and economic emergency. It possessed no organization and no equipment with which to protect its citizens against the loss and the suffering caused by the war. It was equally unprepared to take advantage of the opportunities for an increase in foreign trade which the sudden belligerency of the European powers thrust into its hands. No disposition was shown to sit down patiently under the affliction. The industries and interests whose prosperity was affected jumped swiftly to the conclusion that a loss which was the result of an international crisis, and which was serious enough to threaten their own subsequent economic efficiency, should not fall upon themselves alone, but should be redistributed. They all promptly appealed to the government for assistance either in carrying the burden or in taking advantage of the unexpected opportunities. The railroads demanded an increase in rates as compensation for diminution in business. The cotton-growers tried to draw an additional five cents a pound for their cotton out of the United States Treasury. Congress was asked to provide the ships which were needed to transport American products to foreign countries; and it actually consented to place upon the nation the extraordinary risks of marine insurance. In every direction the need of more flexible and responsible national business organization was apparent, yet everywhere the country was obliged to put up with unsatisfactory makeshifts. There was no adequate political and business machinery for dealing with an essentially collective business emergency. Winter will soon set in without the making of a proper provision for the relief of the greatest sufferers from the war, who are not railroads or cotton-growers or brokers, but the increasing body of unemployed wage-earners. The national economic system has been wholly unable to meet the obligations, which in the opinion of the great majority of American citizens the war had imposed upon it.

The American people were as ill-prepared to meet the spiritual challenge of the war as they were to protect themselves against its distressing economic effects. Their sense of international isolation has bred in them a combination of crude colonialism with crude nationalism. In the beginning they constituted themselves into a supreme court, whose affair it was to sit in judgment on the sins of Europe. They passed the day in objurgating the war, in abusing Europe for bringing it to pass, and in crying for peace at a moment when there could and should be no peace. But their protests against the war did not prevent them from taking sides violently for or against the Allies, and from giving expression to latently bellicose sympathies and antipathies. They traveled so far along this road that President Wilson felt obliged to read them a lecture on the expediency and the moral grandeur of being neutral.

The instinctive colonialism of American public opinion was balanced by a similarly inconsiderate expression of national self-assertion. The United States was going to penalize Europe for engaging in the war by snatching away many of its existing superiorities. American manufacturers proposed to capture European trade in South America and the Orient. The profits of financing international commerce were to be transferred from London to New York. Fashions for women would be designed on Fifth Avenue rather than the Rue de la Paix. A great national revival in the fine arts would follow a cessation of the importation of painting, sculpture and music. The United States would be thrown back upon its own resources, and then it would show to Europe a full measure of national accomplishment.

When Americans indulge in these expectations they are merely being pursued by the evil spirit of their traditional national delusion—the delusion of isolated newer worldliness. The European war has done nothing except in certain fugitive respects to make them independent of Europe, or to give them an advantage over Europe. Less than ever before will their geographical isolation result in genuine independence. No matter who is victorious, the United States will be indirectly compromised by the treaty of peace. If the treaty is one which makes for international stability and justice, this country will have an interest in maintaining it. If the treaty is one which makes militarism even more ominously threatening, this country will have an interest in seeking a better substitute. Neither will our merchants derive permanent advantages in their own or foreign markets as a result of the war. When it is over, European nations will immediately become both more efficient and more insistent competitors for foreign trade than they were before it began. They will be obliged as a matter of popular subsistence to reconquer and extend their markets, and they will therefore be better organized and equipped for the work. Thus the war has brought with it increasingly numerous and increasingly onerous American national and international obligations.

In its deepest aspect, then, the European war is a challenge to the United States to justify its independence. The nation can not be independent in the sense of being isolated. It can be independent in the sense of being still more completely the master of its own destiny. The control of its own destiny will not mean, as it has done in the past, merely the renunciation of European entanglements, because entanglements will inevitably ensue from the adoption of the positive and necessary policy of making American influence in Europe count in favor of international peace. Neither will the control of its own destiny by the American nation mean, as it has done in the past, its own control by a triumphant prophecy of prosperity. What it will mean is a clearer understanding of the relation between our democratic national ideal and our international obligations, and such an understanding should bring with it a political and economic organization better able to redeem its obligations both to its own citizens and to a regenerate European system.

The Duty of Harsh Criticism

REBECCA WEST

NOVEMBER 7, 1914

Today in England we think as little of art as though we had been caught up from earth and set in some windy side street of the universe among the stars. Disgust at the daily deathbed which is Europe has made us hunger and thirst for the kindly ways of righteousness, and we want to save our souls. And the immediate result of this desire will probably be a devastating reaction towards conservatism of thought and intellectual stagnation. Not unnaturally we shall scuttle for safety towards militarism and orthodoxy. Life will be lived as it might be in some white village among English elms; while the boys are drilling on the green we shall look up at the church spire and take it as proven that it is pointing to God with final accuracy.

And so we might go on very placidly, just as we were doing three months ago, until the undrained marshes of human thought stirred again and emitted some other monstrous beast, ugly with primal slime and belligerent with obscene greeds. Decidedly we shall not be safe if we forget the things of the mind. Indeed, if we want to save our souls, the mind must lead a more athletic life than it has ever done before, and must more passionately than ever practise and rejoice in art. For only through art can we cultivate annoyance with inessentials, powerful and exasperated reactions against ugliness, a ravenous appetite for beauty; and these are the true guardians of the soul.

So it is the duty of writers to deliberate in this hour of enforced silence how they can make art a more effective and obviously unnecessary thing than it has been of late years. A little grave reflection shows us that our first duty is to establish a new and abusive school of criticism. There is now no criticism in England. There is merely a chorus of weak cheers, a piping note of appreciation that is not stilled unless a book is suppressed by the police, a mild kindliness that neither heats to enthusiasm nor reverses to anger. We reviewers combine the gentleness of early Christians with a promiscuous polytheism; we reject not even the most barbarous or most fatuous gods. So great is our amiability that it might proceed from the weakness of malnutrition, were it not that it is almost impossible not to make a living as a journalist. Nor is it due to compulsion from above, for it is not worth an editor's while to veil the bright rage of an entertaining writer for the sake of publishers' advertisements. No economic force compels this vice of amiability. It springs from a faintness of the spirit, from a convention of pleasantness, which, when attacked for the monstrous things it permits to enter the mind of the world, excuses itself by protesting that it is a pity to waste fierceness on things that do not matter.

But they do matter. The mind can think of a hundred twisted traditions and ignorances that lie across the path of letters like a barbed wire entanglement and bar the mind from an important advance. For instance, there is the tradition of unreadability which the governing classes have imposed on the more learned departments of literature, such as biography and history. We must rebel against the formidable army of Englishmen who have achieved the difficult task of becoming men of letters without having written anything. They throw up platitudinous inaugural addresses like wormcasts, they edit the letters of the unprotected dead, and chew once more the more masticated portions of history; and every line they write perpetuates the pompous tradition of eighteenth century "book English" and dissociates more thoroughly the ideas of history and originality of thought. We must dispel this unlawful assembly of peers and privy councillors round the well-head of scholarship with kindly but abusive, and, in cases of extreme academic refinement, coarse criticism.

That is one duty which lies before us. Others will be plain to any active mind; for instance, the settlement of our uncertainty as to what it is permissible to write about. One hoped, when all the literary world of London gave a dinner to M. Anatole France last year, that some writer would rise to his feet and say: "Ladies and gentlemen, we are here in honor of an author who has delighted us with a series of works which, had he been an Englishman, would have landed him in gaol for the term of his natural life." That would have shown that the fetters of the English artist are not light and may weigh down the gestures of genius. It is not liberty to describe love that he needs, for he has as much of that as any reasonable person could want, so much as the liberty to describe this and any other passion with laughter and irony.

This enfranchisement must be won partly by criticism. We must ridicule those writers who supply the wadding of the mattress of solemnity on which the British governing classes take their repose. We must overcome our natural reverence for Mrs. Humphry Ward, that grave lady who would have made so excellent a helpmate for Marcus Aurelius, and mock at her succession of rectory Cleopatras of unblemished character, womanly women who, without education and without the discipline of participation in public affairs, are yet capable of influencing politicians with wisdom. When Mr. A. C. Benson presents the world with the unprovoked exudations of his temperament, we may rejoice over the Hindu-like series of acquiescences which take the place of religion in donnish circles. The whole of modern England is busily unveiling itself to the satirist and giving him an opportunity to dispute the reverences and reticence it has ordained.

But there is a more serious duty than these before us, the duty of listening to our geniuses in a disrespectful manner. Criticism matters as it never did in the past, because of the present pride of great writers. They take all life as their province to-day. Formerly they sat in their studies, and thinking only of the emotional life of mankind—thinking therefore with comparative ease, of the color of life and not of its form—devised a score or so of stories before death came. Now, their pride telling them that if time would but stand still they could explain all life, they start on a breakneck journey across the world. They are tormented by the thought of time; they halt by no event, but look down upon it as they pass, cry out their impressions, and gallop on. Often it happens that because of their haste they receive a blurred impression or transmit it to their readers roughly and without precision. And just as it was the duty of the students of Kelvin the mathematician to correct his errors in arithmetic, so it is the duty of critics to rebuke these hastinesses of great writers, lest the blurred impressions weaken the surrounding mental fabric and their rough transmissions frustrate the mission of genius on earth.

There are two great writers of to-day who greatly need correction. Both are misleading in external things. When Mr. Shaw advances, rattling his long lance to wit, and Mr. Wells follows, plump and oiled with the fun of things, they seem Don Quixote and Sancho Panza. Not till one has read much does one discover that Mr. Shaw loves the world as tenderly as Sancho Panza loved his ass, and that Mr. Wells wants to drive false knights from the earth and cut the stupidity and injustice out of the spiritual stuff of mankind. And both have to struggle with their temperaments. Mr. Shaw believes too blindly in his own mental activity; he imagines that if he continues to secrete thought he must be getting on. Mr. Wells dreams into the extravagant ecstasies of the fanatic, and broods over old hated things or the future peace and wisdom of the world, while his story falls in ruins about his ears.

Yet no effective criticism has come to help them. Although in the pages of Mr. Shaw enthusiasm glows like sunsets and the heart of man is seen flowering in a hundred generous and lovely passions, no one has ever insisted that he was a poet. We have even killed his poetry with silence. A year ago he lightened the English stage, which has been permanently fogged by Mr. Pinero's gloomy anecdotes about stockbrokers' wives and their passions, with "Androcles and the Lion," which was a miracle play and an exposition of the Christian mysteries. It taught that the simple man is the son of God, and that if men love the world it will be kind to them. Because this message was delivered with laughter, as became its optimism, English criticism accused Mr. Shaw of pertness and irreverence, and never permitted the nation to know that a spiritual teacher had addressed it. Instead, it advised Mr. Shaw to return to the discussion of social and philosophical problems, in which his talent could perhaps hope to be funny without being vulgar.

Mr. Wells' mind works more steadily than Mr. Shaw's, but it suffers from an unawareness of the reader; an unawareness, too, of his material; an unawareness of everything except the problem on which it happens to be brooding. His stories become more and more absent-minded. From *The Passionate Friends* we deduced that Mr. Wells lived on the branch line of a not too well organized railway system and wrote his books while waiting for trains at the main line junction. The novel appeared to be a year book of Indian affairs; but there were also some interesting hints on the publishing business, and once or twice one came on sections of a sympathetic study of moral imbecility in the person of a lady called Mary, who married for money and impudently deceived her owner. And what was even more amazing than its inchoateness was Mr. Wells' announcement on the last page that the book had been a discussion of jealousy. That was tragic, for it is possible that he had something to say on the subject, and what it was no one will ever know. Yet this boat of wisdom which had sprung so disastrous a leak received not one word of abuse from English criticism. No one lamented over the waste of the mind, the spilling of the idea.

That is what we must prevent. Now, when every day the souls of men go up from France like smoke, we feel that humanity is the flimsiest thing, easily divided into nothingness and rotting flesh. We must lash down humanity to the world with thongs of wisdom. We must give her an unsurprisable mind. And that will never be done while affairs of art and learning are decided without passion, and individual dulnesses allowed to dim the brightness of the collective mind. We must weepingly leave the library if we are stupid, just as in the Middle Ages we left the home if we were lepers. If we can offer the mind of the world nothing else we can offer it our silence.

Soviet Russia

J. M. KEYNES

OCTOBER 28, 1925

It is extraordinarily difficult to be fair-minded about Russia. And even with fair-mindedness, how is a true impression to be conveyed of a thing so unfamiliar, contradictory, and shifting, about which almost no one in England has a background of knowledge or of comparable experience? No English newspaper has a regular correspondent resident in Russia. We rightly attach small credence to what the Soviet authorities say about themselves. Most of our news is from prejudiced and deceived Labor deputations or from prejudiced and untruthful émigrés. Thus a belt of fog separates us from what goes on in the other world where the Union of Socialist Soviet Republics rules and experiments and evolves a kind of order. Russia is suffering the penalty of years of "propaganda," which by taking away credence from words, almost destroys, in the end, the means of communication at a distance.

Leninism is a combination of two things which Europeans have kept for some centuries in different compartments of the soul—religion and business. We are shocked because the religion is new, and contemptuous because the business, being subordinated to the religion instead of the other way round, is highly inefficient.

Like other new religions, Leninism derives its power not from the multitude but from a small minority of enthusiastic converts, whose faith and zeal and intolerance make each one the equal in strength of a hundred indifferentists. Like other new religions, it is led by those who can combine the new spirit, perhaps sincerely, with seeing a good deal more than their followers, politicians with at least an average dose of political cynicism, who can smile as well as frown, volatile experimentalists, released by religion from truth and mercy but not blinded to facts and expediency, and open therefore to the charge (superficial and useless though it is, where politicians, lay or ecclesiastical, are concerned) of hypocrisy. Like other new religions, it seems to take the color and gaiety and freedom out of everyday life and to offer but a drab substitute in the square wooden faces of its devotees. Like other new religions, it persecutes without justice or pity those who actively resist it. Like other new religions, it is unscrupulous. Like other new religions, it is filled with missionary ardor and oecumenical ambitions. To say that Leninism is the faith of a persecuting and propagating minority of fanatics led by hypocrites, is, after all, to say no more nor less than that it *is* a religion and not merely a party, and Lenin a Mahomet, not a Bismarck. If we want to frighten ourselves in our capitalist easy chairs, we can picture the Communists of Russia as though the early Christians led by Attila were using the equipment of the Holy Inquisition and the Jesuit Missions to enforce the literal economics of the New Testament; but when we want to comfort ourselves in the same chairs, can we hopefully repeat that these economics are fortunately so contrary to human nature that they cannot finance either missionaries or armies and will surely end in defeat?

There are three questions which need an answer. Is the new religion partly true, or sympathetic to the souls of modern men? Is it on the material side so inefficient as to render it incapable to survive? Will it, in the course of time, with sufficient dilution and added impurity, catch the multitude?

As for the first question, those who are completely satisfied by Christian capitalism or by egotistic capitalism untempered by subterfuge, will not hesitate how to answer it; for they either have a religion or need none. But many, in this age without religion, are bound to feel a strong emotional curiosity towards any religion, which is really new and not merely a recrudescence of old ones and has proved its motive force; and all the more when the new thing comes out of Russia, the beautiful and foolish youngest son of the European family, with hair on his head, nearer both to the earth and to heaven than his bald brothers in the West—who, having been born two centuries later, has been able to pick up the middle-aged disillusionment of the rest of the family before he has lost the genius of youth or become addicted to comfort and to habits. I sympathize with those who seek for something good in Soviet Russia.

But when we come to the actual thing, what is one to say? For me, brought up in a free air undarkened by the horrors of religion with nothing to be afraid of, Red Russia holds too much which is detestable. Comfort and habits let us be ready to forgo, but I am not ready for a creed which does not care how much it destroys the liberty and security of daily life, which uses deliberately the weapons of persecution, destruction, and international strife. How can I admire a policy which finds a characteristic expression in spending millions to suborn spies in every family and group at home, and to stir up trouble abroad? Perhaps this is no worse and has more purpose than the greedy, warlike and imperialist propensities of other governments; but it must be far better than these to shift me out of my rut. How can I accept a doctrine which sets up as its bible, above and beyond criticism, an obsolete economic textbook which I know to be not only scientifically erroneous but without interest or application for the modern world? How can I adopt a creed which, preferring the mud to the fish, exalts the boorish proletariat above the bourgeois and the intelligentsia who, with whatever faults, are the quality in life and surely carry the seeds of all human advancement? Even if we need a religion, how can we find it in the turbid rubbish of the red bookshops? It is hard for an educated, decent, intelligent son of Western Europe to find his ideals here, unless he has first suffered some strange and horrid process of conversion which has changed all his values.

Yet we shall miss the essence of the new religion if we stop at this point. The Communist may justly reply that all these things belong not to his true religion but to the tactics of revolution. For he believes in two things—the introduction of a New Order upon earth and the *method* of the Revolution as the *only* means thereto. The New Order must not be judged either by the horrors of the Revolution or by the privations of the transitionary period. The Revolution is to be a supreme example of the end justifying the means. The soldier of the Revolution must crucify his own human nature, becoming unscrupulous and ruthless and suffering himself a life without security or joy—but as the means to his purpose and not its end.

What, then, is the essence of the new religion as a New Order upon earth? Looking from outside, I do not clearly know. Sometimes its mouthpieces speak as though it was purely materialistic and technical in just the same sense that modern capitalism is—as though, that is to say, communism merely claimed to be in the long run a superior technical instrument for obtaining the same materialistic economic benefits as capitalism offers—that in time it will cause the fields to yield more and the forces of nature to be more straitly harnessed. In this case there is no religion after all, nothing but a bluff to facilitate a change to what may or may not be a better economic technique. But I suspect that, in fact, such talk is largely a reaction against the charges of economic inefficiency which we on our side launch, and that at the heart of Russian Communism there is something else of more concern to mankind.

In one respect communism but follows other famous religions. It exalts the common man and makes him everything. Here there is nothing new. But there is another factor in it which also is not new but which may, nevertheless, in a changed form and a new setting contribute something to the true religion of the future, if there be any true religion. *Leninism is absolutely, defiantly non-supernatural, and its emotional and ethical essence centres about the individual's and the community's attitude towards the Love of Money.*

I do not mean that Russian Communism alters, or even seeks to alter, human nature—that it makes misers less avaricious or spendthrifts less extravagant than they were before. I do not merely mean that it sets up a new ideal. I mean that it tries to construct a framework of society in which pecuniary motives as influencing action shall have a changed relative importance, in which social approbations shall be differently distributed, and where behavior, which previously was normal and respectable, ceases to be either the one or the other.

In England today a talented and virtuous youth, about to enter the world, will balance the advantages of entering the Civil Service and of seeking a fortune in business; and public opinion will esteem him not less if he prefers the second. Money-making, as such, on as large a scale as possible, is not less respectable socially, perhaps more so, than a life devoted to the service of the State or of Religion, Education, Learning, and Art. But in the Russia of the future it is intended that the career of money-making as such will simply not occur to a respectable young man as a possible opening, any more than the career of a gentleman burglar or acquiring skill in forgery and embezzlement. Even the most admirable aspects of the love of money in our existing society, such as thrift and saving, and the attainment of financial security and independence for one's self and one's family, whilst not deemed morally wrong, will be rendered so difficult and impracticable as to be not worth while. Everyone should work for the community—the new creed runs—and, if he does his duty, the community will uphold him.

This system does not mean a complete leveling down of incomes—at least at the present stage. A clever and successful person in Soviet Russia has a bigger income and a better time than other people. The Commissar with $25 a week (*plus* sundry free services, a motor-car, a flat, a box at the ballet, etc., etc.) lives well enough, but not *in the least* like a rich man in London. The successful Professor or Civil Servant with $30 or $35 a week (*minus* sundry impositions) has, perhaps, a real income three times that of the proletarian worker, and six times those of the poorer peasants. Some peasants are three or four times as rich as others. A man who is out of work receives half pay, not full pay. But no one can afford on these incomes, with high Russian prices and stiff progressive taxes, to save anything worth saving; it is hard enough to live day by day. The progressive taxation and the mode of assessing rents and other charges are such that it is actually disadvantageous to have an acknowledged income exceeding $40 to $50 a week. Nor is there any possibility of large gains except by taking the same sort of risks as attach to bribery and embezzlement elsewhere—not that bribery and embezzlement have disappeared in Russia or are even rare, but anyone whose extravagance or whose instincts drive him to such courses runs serious risk of detection and penalties which include death.

Nor, at the present stage, does the system involve the actual prohibition of buying and selling at a profit. The policy is not to forbid these professions, but to render them precarious and disgraceful. The private trader is a sort of permitted outlaw, without privileges or protection, like the Jew in the Middle Ages—an outlet for those who have overwhelming instincts in this direction, but not a natural or agreeable job for the normal man.

The effect of these social changes has been, I think, to make a real change in the predominant attitude towards money, and will probably make a far greater change when a new generation has grown up which has known nothing else. A small, characteristic example of the way in which the true Communist endeavors to influence public opinion towards money is given by the campaign which is going on about the waiters in communal restaurants accepting tips. There is a strong propaganda to the effect that to give or to receive tips is disgusting; and, as a result, it is becoming impolite to offer a tip in a public way, and a not unknown thing for a tip to be refused!

Now, all this may prove utopian, or destructive of true welfare, though, perhaps, not so utopian, pursued in an intense religious spirit, as it would be if it were pursued in a matter-of-fact way. But is it appropriate to assume, as almost the whole of the English and American press do assume, and the public also, that it is insincere or that it is abominably wicked?

The Movies and Reality

VIRGINIA WOOLF

AUGUST 4, 1926

People say that the savage no longer exists in me, that we are at the fag-end of civilization, that every thing has been said already, and that it is too late to be ambitious. But these philosophers have presumably forgotten the movies. They have never seen the savages of the twentieth century watching the pictures. They have never sat themselves in front of the screen and thought how, for all the clothes on their backs and the carpets at their feet, no great distance separates them from those bright-eyed, naked men who knocked two bars of iron together and heard in that clangor a foretaste of the music of Mozart.

The bars in this case, of course, are so highly wrought and so covered over with accretions of alien matter that it is extremely difficult to hear anything distinctly. All is hubble-bubble, swarm and chaos. We are peering over the edge of a cauldron in which fragments of all shapes and savors seem to simmer; now and again some vast form heaves itself up, and seems about to haul itself out of chaos. Yet, at first sight, the art of the cinema seems simple, even stupid. There is the King shaking hands with a football team; there is Sir Thomas Lipton's yacht; there is Jack Horner winning the Grand National. The eye licks it all up instantaneously, and the brain, agreeably titillated, settles down to watch things happening without bestirring itself to think. For the ordinary eye, the English unæsthetic eye, is a simple mechanism, which takes care that the body does not fall down coal-holes, provides the brain with toys and sweetmeats to keep it quiet, and can be trusted to go on behaving like a competent nursemaid until the brain comes to the conclusion that it is time to wake up. What is its surprise, then, to be roused suddenly in the midst of its agreeable somnolence and asked for help? The eye is in difficulties. The eye wants help. The eye says to the brain, "Something is happening which I do not in the least understand. You are needed." Together they look at the King, the boat, the horse, and the brain sees at once that they have taken on a quality which does not belong to the simple photograph of real life. They have become not more beautiful, in the sense in which pictures are beautiful, but shall we call it (our vocabulary is miserably insufficient) more real, or real with a different reality from that which we perceive in daily life? We behold them as they are when we are not there. We see life as it is when we have no part in it. As we gaze we seem to be removed from the pettiness of actual existence. The horse will not knock us down. The King will not grasp our hands. The wave will not wet our feet. From this point of vantage, as we watch the antics of our kind, we have time to feel pity and amusement, to generalize, to endow one man with the attributes of the race. Watching the boat sail and the wave break, we have time to open our minds wide to beauty and register on top of it the queer sensation—this beauty will continue, and this beauty will flourish whether we behold it or not. Further, all this happened ten years ago, we are told. We are beholding a world which has gone beneath the waves. Brides are emerging from the Abbey—they are now mothers; ushers are ardent—they are now silent; mothers are tearful; guests are joyful; this has been won and that has been lost, and it is over and done with. The War sprung its chasm at the feet of all this innocence and ignorance, but it was thus that we danced and pirouetted, toiled and desired, thus that the sun shone and the clouds scudded up to the very end.

But the picture-makers seem dissatisfied with such obvious sources of interest as the passage of time and the suggestiveness of reality. They despise the flight of gulls, ships on the Thames, the Prince of Wales, the Mile End Road, Piccadilly Circus. They want to be improving, altering, making an art of their own—naturally, for so much seems to be within their scope. So many arts seemed to stand by ready to offer their help. For example, there was literature. All the famous novels of the world, with their well known characters, and their famous scenes, only asked, it seemed, to be put on the films. What could be easier and simpler? The cinema fell upon its prey with immense rapacity, and to this moment largely subsists upon the body of its unfortunate victim. But the results are disastrous to both. The alliance is unnatural. Eye and brain are torn asunder ruthlessly as they try vainly to work in couples. The eye says: "Here is Anna Karenina." A voluptuous lady in black velvet wearing pearls comes before us. But the brain says: "That is no more Anna Karenina than it is Queen Victoria." For the brain knows Anna almost entirely by the inside of her mind—her charm, her passion, her despair. All the emphasis is laid by the cinema upon her teeth, her pearls, and her velvet. Then "Anna falls in love with Vronsky"—that is to say, the lady in black velvet falls into the arms of a gentleman in uniform, and they kiss with enormous succulence, great deliberation, and infinite gesticulation on a sofa in an extremely well appointed library, while a gardener incidentally mows the lawn. So we lurch and lumber through the most famous novels of the world. So we spell them out in words of one syllable written, too, in the scrawl of an illiterate schoolboy. A kiss is love. A broken cup is jealousy. A grin is happiness. Death is a hearse. None of these things has the least connection with the novel that Tolstoy wrote, and it is only when we give up trying to connect the pictures with the book that we guess from some accidental scene—like the gardener mowing the lawn—what the cinema might do if it were left to its own devices.

But what, then, are its devices? If it ceased to be a parasite, how would it walk erect? At present it is only from hints that one can frame any conjecture. For instance, at a performance of *Doctor Caligari* the other day, a shadow shaped like a tadpole suddenly appeared at one corner of the screen. It swelled to an immense size, quivered, bulged, and sank back again into nonentity. For a moment it seemed to embody some monstrous, diseased imagination of the lunatic's brain. For a moment it seemed as if thought could be conveyed by shape more effectively than by words. The monstrous, quivering tadpole seemed to be fear itself, and not the statement, "I am afraid." In fact, the shadow was accidental, and the effect unintentional. But if a shadow at a certain moment can suggest so much more than the actual gestures and words of men and women in a state of fear, it seems plain that the cinema has within its grasp innumerable symbols for emotions that have so far failed to find expression. Terror has, besides its ordinary forms, the shape of a tadpole; it burgeons, bulges, quivers, disappears. Anger is not merely rant and rhetoric, red faces and clenched fists. It is perhaps a black line wriggling upon a white sheet. Anna and Vronsky need no longer scowl and grimace. They have at their command—but what? Is there, we ask, some secret language which we feel and see, but never speak, and, if so, could this be made visible to the eye? Is there any characteristic which thought possesses that can be rendered visible without the help of words? It has speed and slowness; dartlike directness and vaporous circumlocution. But it has also, especially in moments of emotion, the picture-making power, the need to lift its burden to another bearer; to let an image run side by side along with it. The likeness of the thought is, for some reason, more beautiful, more comprehensible, more available than the thought itself. As everybody knows, in Shakespeare the most complex ideas form chains of images through which we mount, changing and turning, until we reach the light of day. But, obviously, the images of a poet are not to be cast in bronze, or traced by pencil. They are compact of a thousand suggestions of which the visual is only the most obvious or the uppermost. Even the simplest image: "My love's like a red, red rose, that's newly sprung in June," presents us with impressions of moisture and warmth and the glow of crimson and the softness of petals inextricably mixed and strung upon the lilt of a rhythm which is itself the voice of the passion and hesitation of the lover. All this, which is accessible to words, and to words alone, the cinema must avoid.

Yet if so much of our thinking and feeling is connected with seeing, some residue of visual emotion which is of no use either to painter or to poet may still await the cinema. That such symbols will be quite unlike the real objects which we see before us seems highly probable. Something abstract, something which moves with controlled and conscious art, something which calls for the very slightest help from words or music to make itself intelligible, yet justly uses them subserviently—of such movements and abstractions the films may, in time to come, be composed. Then, indeed, when some new symbol for expressing thought is found, the film-maker has enormous riches at his command. The exactitude of reality and its surprising power of suggestion are to be had for the asking. Annas and Vronskys—there they are in the flesh. If into this reality he could breathe emotion, could animate the perfect form with thought, then his booty could be hauled in hand over hand. Then, as smoke pours from Vesuvius, we should be able to see thought in its wildness, in its beauty, in its oddity, pouring from men with their elbows on a table; from women with their little handbags slipping to the floor. We should see these emotions mingling together and affecting each other.

We should see violent changes of emotion produced by their collision. The most fantastic contrasts could be flashed before us with a speed which the writer can only toil after in vain; the dream architecture of arches and battlements, of cascades falling and fountains rising, which sometimes visits us in sleep or shapes itself in half-darkened rooms, could be realized before our waking eyes. No fantasy could be too far-fetched or insubstantial. The past could be unrolled, distances annihilated, and the gulfs which dislocate novels (when, for instance, Tolstoy has to pass from Levin to Anna, and in so doing jars his story and wrenches and arrests our sympathies) could, by the sameness of the background, by the repetition of some scene, be smoothed away.

How all this is to be attempted, much less achieved, no one at the moment can tell us. We get intimations only in the chaos of the streets, perhaps, when some momentary assembly of color, sound, movement suggests that here is a scene waiting a new art to be transfixed. And sometimes at the cinema in the midst of its immense dexterity and enormous technical proficiency, the curtain parts and we behold, far off, some unknown and unexpected beauty. But it is for a moment only. For a strange thing has happened—while all the other arts were born naked, this, the youngest, has been born fully clothed. It can say everything before it has anything to say. It is as if the savage tribe, instead of finding two bars of iron to play with, had found, scattering the seashore, fiddles, flutes, saxophones, trumpets, grand pianos by Erard and Bechstein, and had begun with incredible energy, but without knowing a note of music, to hammer and thump upon them all at the same time.

Heil, Hitler!

H. V. KALTENBORN

FEBRUARY 14, 1933

It is extremely difficult for American correspondents to see Hitler. He has a deep-rooted suspicion of them all. It was only after I had been passed upon by the press department of the National Socialist party that I was permitted to visit the new Chancellor at his summer "Town House" a hundred or so miles from Munich. Here he was living with his secretaries and his bodyguards, seeing the many callers who flocked to his house daily.

His greeting, when I was introduced to him, was perfunctory, suggesting latent hostility, and my first question brought this forth into full flame. I had asked him whether his anti-Semitism concerned Jews everywhere or whether he had something specific against German-Jews as such.

"In America you exclude any would-be immigrants you do not care to admit," he said emphatically. "You regulate their number. Not content with that, you prescribe their physical condition. Not content with that, you insist on the conformity of their political opinions. We demand the same right in Germany. We have no concern with the Jews of other lands, but we are very much concerned about the anti-German elements within our country. We demand the right to deal with these elements as we see fit. Jews have been the intellectual proponents of subversive anti-German movements, and as such they must be dealt with."

On foreign affairs Hitler proved uncompromising. In spite of the concessions which Germany had recently received at Lausanne, he considered France to be playing the bully, holding down a helpless opponent and choking him to death.

"How can we have friendly relations with France while this attitude continues?" he asked. He referred to separatist movements in Germany which he evidently feels are receiving aid from French sources. He summed up his comment with this sentence: "The existence of our sixty-five million people is a fact with which France must reckon; they want to live!"

Germany's relations with Russia are always important and I asked him what a National Socialist government would do about that country.

"It is possible, of course, to differentiate between a government and its policies," he said. "The Fascist government of Italy has dealings with Soviet Russia and at the same time carries on vigorous prosecution of Communists in Italy. But it is impossible for any country to have really good relations with Russia if it has a large number of Communists within its own borders."

Some National Socialists visualize a bloc of fascist states extending from the Mediterranean to the Baltic. Such a grouping might include Albania, Italy, Hungary, Austria, Germany, Finland, Esthonia and Latvia. Hitler's reaction to the suggestion of this possibility was interesting. "There will be no fascist bloc of states," he said. "But remember that Europe is accustomed to being governed by systems which extend over many countries. Many times in the past, governmental systems and ideas have crossed frontiers, acquired local color and flourished. Mussolini once said that fascism was not an article of export. I would say the same thing of our National Socialism.

"Europe," he continued, "cannot maintain itself, riding the uncertain currents of democracy. Europe must have authoritarian government. In the past this authoritarian leadership was provided by the monarch or by the Catholic Church. The form which the authority takes may differ. But parliamentarism is not native to us and does not belong to our traditions. Yet because the parliamentary system has not functioned we cannot substitute brute force. Bayonets alone will not sustain any government for any length of time. To be viable a government must have the support of the masses. A dictatorship cannot be established in a vacuum. Any government that does not derive its strength from the people will fail the moment it confronts a crisis. The soldier and the policeman do not constitute the substance of a state. Yet dictatorship is justified if the people declare their confidence in one man and ask him to lead."

Hitler's mind is resourceful, but not flexible. Its operations are not under complete control. For some minutes his statements may be logical, then suddenly he runs off on a tangent and gets away from the matter in hand. He speaks with such force and torrential speed that it is difficult for an interviewer to interject questions.

Sometimes his logic is hard to follow. He insisted that with little more than one-third of the German vote he had the right to complete control. Here is his argument: "Under the rules of democracy, a majority of 51 percent has the right to control the country. I now have 37 percent of all the votes. That is 75 percent of the necessary power. I am entitled to three-fourths of the power and my opponents to one-fourth. In the run-off election for President I stood alone and won thirteen million votes. That is my hardearned capital. I slaved for it and risked my life for it. Without my party, no one can govern Germany today. Let us consider the German government as though it were a business. I am bringing into this business 75 percent of the total investment. Whoever furnishes the rest, whether it is the President or the political parties, is only contributing 25 percent of the total capital. Moreover, every unit of the 75-percent investment which I make is worth twice as much of that of the others. I have the bravest, the most energetic, yes, and the best disciplined Germans in my ranks. That is why I don't have to march on Berlin—I am already there. The only question is, who will have to march out of Berlin? My fifteen million voters are actually worth thirty million. That is no mean capital investment. It can be put to work in the business of governing Germany forthwith without any majority votes, without commissions or committees. It can be put to work on the say-so of one man—myself."

This last sentence allowed me to put this question: "Which is more important to the success of a movement, the personality of its leader or the policies of his party?" to which he replied, "There is no fundamental sense in which you can separate the leader from his party. They are identical. It is only after the period of organization has passed, after party ideas have been translated into governmental action and after this action has been tested by experience, that you can dispense with the leader, or remove him if he should be guilty of transgressions.

"No idea can be launched without a leader. You cannot separate fascism from the personality of Mussolini. Had Frederick the Great died prematurely, there would have been no state of Prussia. If Bismarck had died in 1869, there would have been no German Empire. Ten years later he might have been dispensed with. Only after a movement has been under way for a long time can it develop the historic background, and the traditions that would enable it to carry on without a strong leader."

The National Socialist party platform has had much to say about the iniquities of Big Business. Department stores were to be socialized, interest was to be reduced or abolished, land was to be confiscated for social purposes and income without labor was to be abolished. The only part of the program specifically mentioned in Hitler's radio appeal to the German electorate is compulsory labor service. Nor was there much radicalism—Hitler's answer to my question as to why he opposed Big Business. "I do not oppose Big Business in all cases," he replied. "I am well aware that you cannot build an ocean liner or a locomotive without business organization. But we believe in the wide distribution of wealth. We live next door to a country that has abolished private property. We do not wish to do that, but we must see to it that the average man has a chance to acquire property. In your country everyone still carries the marshal's baton in his knapsack. Not so in Germany. Yet I cannot tell sixty-five million Germans that they should be satisfied with nothing because fifty thousand Germans happen to have a great deal. The more millions of our people own property, the better it will be for our whole nation and the less temptation there will be for our people to follow the Russian experiment. The collectivist idea cannot mean real progress. There must be competition. But the competition must promote individual welfare."

Hitler reveals a much sounder social and economic philosophy in private conversation than when he speaks in public. He has the orator's instinct for exaggeration and popularization, and is utterly conscienceless about speaking for effect. He knows the mob mind, and has gone out to win it. In speaking with me, he indicated that he would never take the chancellorship unless and until he had the power to enforce his party program. But he has now accepted power with crippling handicaps. Von Hindenburg, von Papen, Hugenberg, Defense Minister von Blomberg, Foreign Minister von Neurath are every one opposed to many of his policies and principles. Yet they are his associates in the government of Germany. He is sworn to obey the Constitution and is likely to do so. The time for a Fascist coup d' état is past. Hitler himself had definitely lost prestige and power before he won the chancellorship. Whatever the result of the March fifth election, it will not give Adolf Hitler the opportunity to establish his long heralded *Drittes Reich*.

Man's Solitude

MALCOLM COWLEY

JULY 4, 1934

Man's Fate is a novel about the Chinese revolution written by a soldier of fortune who risked his life in the revolutionary cause, and yet it is not in essence a revolutionary or even a political novel. Brutal, tender, illuminating, it ends by casting more light on our own bourgeois society than on the Chinese Communists who died to change it.

This doesn't mean that it shows political events in false perspective. Malraux is writing about two days that helped to decide the history of China. On March 21, 1927, the Communists of Shanghai declared a general strike and, acting in alliance with Chiang Kai-shek, seized control of the largest city on the Asiatic mainland. Many people then believed that all China would go communist quickly and without much bloodshed. Chiang Kai-shek had Russian officers training his troops and Russian political advisers; the great formless mass of peasants and coolies was leavened with communist ideas. But three weeks later, on April 11, Chiang betrayed his Communist allies, dissolved their labor unions, captured their local posts and executed all his prisoners after torturing most of them; the Communist leaders were boiled in vats of oil or thrust living into the fireboxes of locomotives. The streets of the big cities ran with blood, but the revolution continued to live in the countryside, where the peasants were beginning to organize their own soviets. Malraux not only participated in these events: he has since reflected on their political meaning and has learned to estimate the part that was played in them by personal ambitions, by foreign money, by class antagonisms. Everything he says about the Chinese revolution seems keen and convincing.

But the revolution, instead of being his principal theme, is the setting and the pretext for a novel that is, in reality, a drama of individual lives. It is true that these lives are bound together by a single emotion, but this emotion is not the desire to revolt or to achieve justice. Malraux's real theme is a feeling that most men nurse, secretly, their sense of absolute loneliness and uniqueness, their acknowledgment to themselves of inadequacy in the face of life and helplessness against death—that is what he means by *la condition humaine;* this is man's lot, his destiny, his servitude. And he has chosen to depict this emotion during a revolutionary period because it is then carried, like everything else that is human, to its pitch of highest intensity.

All of his characters, though drawn from different nations and ranks of society, are obsessed by this feeling of personal solitude. All of them try to escape from it, either through dissipation or else through establishing a bond with others at the cost of no matter what sacrifice. Thus, little Ch'en, the former student in a missionary college, escapes from his loneliness by adopting terrorism as a career; he wants to found a religion of political murder and self-immolation—finally, clutching a bomb in his hand, he hurls himself under the automobile in which he thinks Chiang Kai-shek is riding. Ferral, the banker and exploiter, tries to escape from his own sterility by dominating others, and ends by despising them only a little more than he despises himself. Clappique tries to evade his personality by playing imaginary roles; he keeps repeating that "the Baron de Clappique does not exist." May finds her escape in love, and Katov finds his in an absolute devotion to the revolutionary cause. Old Gisors, the French philosopher who used to teach at the University of Peking, has two means of avoiding himself: opium and his love for Kyo, his son by a Japanese wife; after Kyo's death, he has only opium.

As for Kyo Gisors, the hero of the novel, "his life had a meaning, and he knew what it was: to give to each of these men whom famine, at this very moment, was killing like a slow plague, the sense of his own dignity." It was through his love for human dignity that Kyo became a Communist, and through dignity, too, that he met his death. On April 11, the one man who might have saved his life was König, the German commander of Chiang Kai-shek's secret police—and König, having forfeited all respect for himself during the civil war in Russia, had learned to hate every man who was not self-seeking and a coward. When Kyo refused to betray his comrades, König ordered him to be taken to Section A, the part of the prison reserved for those who were to be burned to death.

Man's Fate is a novel packed tight with contradictions: one feels in it the dilemma of people ill prepared by a peaceful childhood to face one of the most brutal and cataclysmic periods in human history. It is a philosophical novel in which the philosophy is expressed in terms of violent actions. It is a novel about the East that expresses the soul rather of the West. It is a novel written sympathetically about communists by a man whose own mentality has strong traces of fascism (perhaps this explains why it has been so popular in Italy) and a novel about proletarian heroes in which the technique is that developed by the Symbolists of the Ivory Tower. It is a good novel too, extraordinarily rich in characters and perceptions, and yet it becomes difficult to read—the emotions are so taut that one feels the need of laying down the book, lighting a cigarette, turning on the radio, doing anything to break the intolerable tension.

But if one persists, one comes at last to a scene as tragically stirring as anything in modern literature. It is a scene that might be compared with the terrible chapter in *The Possessed* in which Kirillov is ordered to commit suicide and finally obeys, except that Malraux is describing several suicides and around them two hundred prisoners waiting for the firing squad—the whole thing is magnified to the point of intolerable melodrama, and yet is rendered true and humanly bearable by the feeling of brotherhood existing among the prisoners. . . . Katov, the old revolutionist, is lying wounded in the famous Section A, which is nothing but a half-empty space along the wall of a crowded prison yard. Beside him in the darkness lies the dead body of Kyo, who has taken the cyanide that all members of the Communist Central Committee kept hidden in their square belt buckles as a final means of escaping their tortures. Katov, too, has his cyanide and is waiting to use it. Two new prisoners, young Chinese, are brought into Section A; they have no poison and know that for them there is no possible escape from being thrown into the firebox of the locomotive whistling outside the prison (all this, I might add, is a faithful picture of what happened that night in Shanghai; Malraux doesn't exaggerate). The two young men are weeping and Katov gives them his cyanide to divide between them; it is his supreme sacrifice.

But the scene doesn't end there; if it did, one might conceivably forget it instead of lying awake to brood over it. One of the young men has been wounded in the hand; he drops both the little packages of poison; and the three of them grope in the darkness among the pebbles and bits of broken plaster that litter the prison yard, looking for death as if they were looking for diamonds. This is the picture that sticks in one's mind—this and the sense of pitiful fraternity among the three searchers, expressed in a few words whispered by one of the young Chinese when he suddenly took Katov's hand, pressed it and held it. "Even if we don't find it . . . " he said. A moment later the two boys clutched the poison and gulped it down.

Malraux is saying that here in the prison yard, the effort to escape from man's solitude and the search for a purpose by which life is dignified both found their goal. The individual dramas and the great revolutionary drama merged into each other. Here in the darkness, Katov poured himself out in "that absolute friendship, without reticence, which death alone gives"; and here among his comrades condemned to be burned alive, Kyo felt that "he was dying, like each of these men, because he had given a meaning to his life. What would have been the value of a life for which he would not have been willing to die? It is easy to die when one does not die alone."

The Future of Democracy

BERTRAND RUSSELL

MAY 5, 1937

I do not believe that "political democracy is on the wane." There is nothing new about the present anti-democratic movements; there were similar movements after the French Revolution, and after the revolutions of 1848, not to mention the age of Louis XIV. The two Napoleons were closely analogous to modern dictators; they owed their success to French inexperience in working democratic government. My grandfather, Lord John Russell, in a letter written from France in 1871, expressed the general opinion when he said: "I fear that a Republic like that of America is not practicable in France. They would prefer a military hero, or a civil despot, to any quiet wise man who can bear liberty in others." So people now speak of Germany—let us hope with equal lack of truth. Italy and Germany had only a brief period of democracy; Russia had none. America, Great Britain and the self-governing dominions show no tendency to abandon political democracy; in France, since 1870, all movements toward dictatorship have been defeated. It cannot be maintained that the regime is secure in either Germany or Italy; certainly it is not likely to survive defeat in war. There are good reasons for supposing that Russia will gradually develop a democratic system. We are in a period of reaction, analogous to that of the Holy Alliance after the previous Great War; but I see no ground for supposing that the reaction will be permanent, or will destroy democracy in the United States, France or Britain.

"Is authoritarian government superior to democracy?" One must ask: superior for what? Perhaps, for purposes of war, there is a short-term superiority to be obtained by establishing a popular authoritarian government in a country that had previously been democratic. But (a) most authoritarian governments soon cease to be popular, (b) the absence of free criticism soon produces bureaucratic conservatism which is fatal to success in war. Ever since the beginning of the eighteenth century, victory in every important war has gone to the side that had the most nearly democratic institutions. Apart from war, it may be argued that authoritarian government is better than democracy in that it allows more consistent planning. I think it must be admitted that, if any important economic change is to be successfully carried out, a government will need some years of free initiative. This, however, is not incompatible with democracy, which consists in the occasional exercise of popular control, but does not demand the constant hampering of the executive. The ultimate power of the majority is very important to minimize the harshness inevitably involved in great changes, and to prevent a rapidity of transformation which causes a revulsion of feeling. I do not believe, therefore, that an authoritarian government is better than a democracy, though I believe that, in times of crisis, a strong and temporarily unhampered executive is necessary.

"Are security and freedom for the individual compatible?" As to this, it should be said, first, that freedom and democracy have only an accidental and external connection with each other. In time of war, a democracy may exact a very rigid control over the individual; in China, while the Emperor was nominally omnipotent, the individual had a degree of freedom which is now unknown in the Western world. Economic security for the average citizen is incompatible with economic freedom for the capitalist; economic freedom is necessarily limited to a small minority, and as industry becomes concentrated into fewer organizations, the minority becomes smaller. Economic freedom, as conceived by the friends of peasant proprietorship and small businesses, belongs to a stage of industrial development which is past. Economic power, nowadays, must be centralized, and the only question is whether it shall belong to an oligarchy or to a democratic State. The latter gives some chance of general security; the former, none.

The kinds of individual freedom that are important are cultural: freedom of religion, of opinion, of art and science. It is difficult to reconcile these with modern large-scale economic organization. At present, in nominally democratic countries, artists and men of science depend for their success upon the rich; in dictatorships, they depend upon the governments. The problem of obtaining for them some degree of liberty is difficult, and has never yet been solved; Homer had to flatter chiefs, and so did Virgil, Shakespeare and Walt Whitman. The problem has its importance, but it is a very much smaller importance than that of the problem of economic and political power. To cause *both* these to be evenly distributed is the chief task of our age; it is necessary to solve it not only for happiness, but for stability. So long as there are either rich and poor, or rulers and ruled, there will be danger of wars—both civil wars and wars of conquest. And so long as the danger of war continues, our scientific civilization may at any moment destroy itself.

A Letter to Stalin

BRUCE BLIVEN

MARCH 30, 1938

Josef Stalin
The Kremlin, Moscow, U.S.S.R.

Dear Josef Stalin:

The government of which you are the head has now proposed a conference of nearly all the world powers, except the three chief fascist nations, for the purpose of considering ways of checking the menace of those three. On the assumption that there is still time, and that a major world conflict has not begun while this issue of *The New Republic* is on the press, I, like millions of others, hope with all my heart that this meeting can be held and will prove effective. The fact, however, that your government is issuing such a call makes appropriate a few remarks about the attitude of the outside world toward the USSR and your responsibility in regard to it.

The latest of the famous Moscow trials has ended. Eighteen of the defendants, after pleading guilty with abject self-abasement, have been executed. Three others have received prison sentences averaging twenty years each. Since they are elderly men, it seems unlikely that they will survive their imprisonment, unless its terms are mitigated.

At the same time, the cables from Moscow tell us that fresh purges and additional trials are contemplated. I take it for granted that your heart sinks at this prospect, as do those of millions of other persons throughout the world. No one outside Russia and very likely no one within its borders knows exactly how many individuals have been exiled, imprisoned or executed since that unhappy day when Kirov was slain. Estimates of the total, based upon accounts in Soviet newspapers, range upward from 1,200. The list of well known persons is a staggering one, embracing a former premier, top-ranking commissars, presidents and other high officials of individual Soviet republics, foreign ambassadors and editors of chief newspapers. It must now be true that at least 90 percent of the best known men who made the revolution have lost their places or both places and lives. You yourself have commented on the strain and tension produced within the Soviet Union by the purges of recent months, by the excesses of mistaken zeal. Testimony from many sources indicates that executives hesitate to take responsibility, people are reluctant to be promoted into the limelight and that this is doing the economic program of the USSR grave harm.

It would be natural for you to say that this is nobody's business but Soviet Russia's; such an attitude has been held by many great rulers throughout history. But you are too wise, I am sure, to hold this view. The Soviets are not only a country but an idea, and it is certainly your ultimate hope that it will spread throughout the entire world. You yourself in your recent letter to a youthful comrade accused of Trotskyism called upon the proletariat of the world to stand by Soviet Russia in case of an attack from the league of fascist powers. You have, moreover, in recent years, sought energetically to make alliances with other countries, whatever their form of government, that might stand with you against the threatened attack. That the public opinion of these other countries is important you have recognized by agreements to refrain from propaganda among their nationals. The proposal a few days ago for a worldwide anti-fascist conference is only the latest of a long series of developments recognizing the fact that the Soviet Union cannot exist in a sealed vacuum any more than can any other power.

You are no doubt already aware that the series of trials of traitors, spies and saboteurs has had a bad effect upon world public opinion. I question, however, whether you realize just how bad this effect has been. It is in one sense a real tragedy for the world that you, with your remarkable abilities and intelligence, should never have traveled outside the borders of the USSR, and should not be conversant with languages other than your own. If like Lenin you had remained long abroad, in several lands, you might appreciate more keenly the fact that people do live, even in the capitalist countries, by ideas as well as by bread.

In briefest summary, the series of trials in the Soviet Union has had unhappy repercussions in many parts of the world. They have made Germany, Japan and Italy more aggressive. It is not at all impossible that they may, through Japan's grossly overestimating the internal difficulties of the USSR, have helped create the decision for Japan to attack China in 1937 rather than at a later time. They did great harm to the People's Front in France, which for this and other reasons was momentarily impotent at a major turning point in European history, when Hitler went into Austria. They have helped to alienate important and hitherto friendly sections of opinion in the United States, including the President. Perhaps most serious of all, they upheld the hands of the anti-Soviet faction in the British government. In all human probability, they strongly influenced Chamberlain in his move toward rapprochement with Germany and Italy which in turn gave Hitler his chance to seize Austria, gave Hitler and Mussolini their chance to make a last desperate assault on the Loyalist government of Spain. At a critical moment in the history of modern Europe, it was said throughout the world and believed by many that Soviet Russia had turned to a bloody-handed dictatorship, that a great part of her population was in a state of potential revolt, that Russia no longer counted and that a new orientation of the powers must be found from which she should be excluded. These statements may all have been false, but a false statement on which people act may be as disastrous as a true one.

What I now urge upon you is a revision of your policy to take account of world opinion. Much has already been lost, but not everything. There may still be time to convince the world not only that Soviet Russia is strong, but that her strength can be counted with the democracies against the tyrannies.

I suggest, first, that in future treason trials, a procedure should be followed more compatible with that of the countries under the Anglo-Saxon or the Roman law tradition. Soviet court procedure in most types of trials is admirable; it is only in these treason cases that the actual trial takes place in the form of long preliminary hearings at which confessions are made under conditions never revealed to the public. It may be unjust of the Americans, for example, to suspect that torture is used in these cases; but in the United States there is a nationwide and long continued tradition of police brutality, of extorting confessions by torture in every sort of case from petty larceny to murder. It is inevitable that this country should look with suspicion upon confessions obtained in secret hearings, however plausible these confessions may be on their face.

My second point is one that will be particularly hard for you to understand, yet it is of high importance. I suggest that in the future you shall not merely present to the world testimony which many people in all countries find incredible, without some attempt to make its credibility apparent. I do not mean by this that it is enough for such testimony to be accepted by your own zealous followers, but that it shall be reasonable and plausible to the great mass of the people who constitute the foundation of that curious phenomenon called public opinion. Repeated experience has proved that, for the reasons given above, it is not enough simply to publish the verbatim text of the open court proceedings: so much of the most important aspect of every trial has been that part conducted in preliminary secret investigation. I suggest that on matters regarding which almost the whole world is skeptical, you should publish every scrap of documentary evidence that is available, including transcripts of all preliminary interrogations. After all, we must not forget that the chief purpose of the public trials is to convince the citizens of the Soviet Union and of other countries that the decisions already made were just and deserved. If these proceedings are not convincing, there is no point in holding them.

My third suggestion arises partly from personal prejudice, partly from recognition that many other persons share my view. It is that you shall abolish the death sentence for these and all other crimes. Your own experience amply proves that it is not a deterrent. It is not needed for the safety of the state: Soviet Russia's prisons and concentration camps are safe enough. The recurring line in news dispatches from Moscow, "The prisoners were all shot," has done inestimable harm to the reputation of the USSR. They shoot people freely in Germany and Italy, too. For you to abolish the death penalty would do more than any other single thing you could do to prove that the dictatorship of the proletariat is not on all fours with the dictatorships of the fascists.

My fourth and final suggestion will be still harder for you to accept. I propose that in view of the great emergency that now exists you should make an important change in the internal organization of the USSR. My recommendation is that you offer an amnesty to all opponents who have not yet been guilty of any crime under the normal civil code, on a pledge on their part of future good behavior. I suggest further that these elements be organized into a formal and legal Opposition. It is important to remember that most of these opponents, in so far as they can be judged by their own statements, disagree with you only about means, and not ends. While they have repudiated some present policies, very few of them have repudiated Marx and Lenin. By creating a legal Opposition, which would be permitted to participate in parliamentary debate, you would canalize all that disagreement which now finds expression in traitorous acts and comes to an end, in many cases, before the firing squad. I need not underline the difference that would be made in foreign opinion. I need not underline, either, the fact no loyal friend of the Soviet Union could believe that such a development would do harm to the future of the USSR.

There is one other thing you might do. I will not add it formally to the list above, because I realize there is probably no chance of its being accepted, and I do not propose to make my suggestions mere breath in the wind. Many men throughout the world say there is incongruity in your appeal against the dictators because you are yourself a dictator. You could answer them once and finally by withdrawing from the public life of your country for a stipulated length of time, perhaps a year or eighteen months. You would, naturally, first obtain guarantees from your colleagues that during this period no one of them would seek an abnormal degree of influence at the expense of the others. Upon your return I assume you would resume your present degree of importance in Soviet affairs. I am profoundly convinced that nothing you could do for the USSR by remaining in office for that length of time could be as great a service as the demonstration that among 190 million comrades no one is indispensable, that those foreign critics who lump together "Hitler, Stalin and Mussolini" have been and are altogether wrong.

"In Every Voice, in Every Ban"

ALFRED KAZIN

JANUARY 10, 1944

On May 12 of this year, a man named Shmuel Ziegelboim, who was a Socialist, a Jew and a Pole, was found dead by his own hand in a London flat. His wife and child had been killed by the Nazis in Poland; and no doubt he had had his fill of Polish politics—even (or especially) in London. I had never heard of Shmuel Ziegelboim before I read of his death; and so many Socialists, Jews and Poles have died in these last few years that it is possible—conscience and memory being what they are even for one's own—that I would never again have thought of him had he not left a letter that was published in a negligible corner of *The New York Times*.

His letter was addressed in Polish to the President of Poland and to Sikorski, who was then Premier. What he wrote was this:

> I take the liberty of addressing to you my last words, and through you to the Polish government and the Polish people, to the governments and peoples of the Allied states—to the conscience of the world.
>
> From the latest information received from Poland, it is evident that the Germans, with the most ruthless cruelty, are now murdering the few remaining Jews in Poland. Behind the ghetto's walls the last act of a tragedy unprecedented in history is being performed. The responsibility for this crime of murdering the entire Jewish population of Poland falls in the first instance on the perpetrators, but indirectly it is also a burden on the whole of humanity, the people and the governments of the Allied states which thus far have made no effort toward concrete action for the purpose of curtailing this crime.
>
> By the passive observation of the murder of defenseless millions, and of the maltreatment of children, women and old men, these countries have become the criminals' accomplices. I must also state that although the Polish government has in a high degree contributed to the enlistment of world opinion, it has yet done so insufficiently. It has not done anything that could correspond to the magnitude of the drama being enacted now in Poland. From some 3,500,000 Polish Jews and about 700,000

other Jews deported to Poland from other countries—according to official statistics provided by the underground Bund organization—there remained in April of this year only about 300,000, and this remaining murder still goes on.

I cannot be silent—I cannot live—while remnants of the Jewish people of Poland, of whom I am a representative, are perishing. My comrades in the Warsaw ghetto took weapons in their hands on that last heroic impulse. It was not my destiny to die there together with them, but I belong to them, and in their mass graves. By my death I wish to express my strongest protest against the inactivity with which the world is looking on and permitting the extermination of my people.

I know how little human life is worth today; but, as I was unable to do anything during my life, perhaps by my death I shall contribute to breaking down that indifference of those who may now—at the last moment—rescue the few Polish Jews still alive from certain annihilation. My life belongs to the Jewish people of Poland and I therefore give it to them. I wish that this remaining handful of the original several millions of Polish Jews could live to see the liberation of a new world of freedom, and the justice of true socialism. I believe that such a Poland will arise and that such a world will come.

I trust that the President and the Prime Minister will direct my words to all those for whom they are destined, and that the Polish government will immediately take appropriate action in the fields of diplomacy. I bid my farewell herewith to everybody and everything dear to me and loved by me.

S. ZIEGELBOIM

After the text, the newspaper report added: "That was the letter. It suggests that possibly Shmuel Ziegelboim will have accomplished as much in dying as he did in living."

I bring the matter up now because I have been thinking about the meaning of that letter ever since I clipped it out of *The Times,* and because I hope I can now write thoughtfully about it, since I no longer feel any hatred for the newspaper writer who added with such mechanical emotion that possibly "Shmuel Ziegelboim will have accomplished as much. . . ." Of course the newspaper writer did not believe that he had accomplished anything; nor did the Polish National Council, which released it to the world; nor do I. Shmuel Ziegelboim died because some men can find their ultimate grace only in the fulfilment of their will—even if their will, in 1943, is toward a death that has so desperate a symbolism. He died because the burden of carrying our contemporary self-disgust became too much even for a man who believed that a new world of freedom would come, "and the justice of true socialism." And he died because his wife and child were dead, and the millions in the great Jewish worlds of Poland, and the thousands and thousands of his comrades in the Jewish Labor Bund—the disenchanted and dispossessed Jews who lived on air and were called *Luftmenschen*, but helped to defend Warsaw when the colonels fled.

I think I know how great and indirect a wish for immortality can go into any suicide. I shall believe that men want to die only when I hear of men living (or writing) in complete anonymity. I know something of the ultimate and forgivable egotism of any human spirit, and that the one thing we can never afford to lose is the promise of our identity. Shmuel Ziegelboim wrote at the end with the instinctive rhetorical optimism of those who feel that they are dying without too much division in themselves, and for something greater than their own ambitions. But I have wanted to believe, and now do believe, that Shmuel Ziegelboim died because he was finally unable to withstand the real despair of our time—which arises not out of the burning and the killing and the endless political betrayals, but out of a humiliation which some of us can still feel before so terrible a break in human solidarity. I think he died, as so many greater men have already died morally, because he was unable to believe in a future built on so unrecognized and unreported a human isolation and barbarism as we know today. Shmuel Ziegelboim came from a ghetto-driven, self-driven, but spiritually generous culture; and I honestly believe that he was thinking not only of his own people at the end, but of the hollowness of a world in which such a massacre could have so little meaning. In any event I should like to think that I am more "fortunate"—that is, relatively untouched and able to think about what freedom is. And that is why I bring the matter up now, as a token of what Shmuel Ziegelboim died for, and in an effort to say some very elementary things which liberals especially have not always cared to face.

I do not speak here of the massacre of the Jews, for there is nothing to say about it that has not already been said. I can add nothing, nor would I wish to add anything, to the private imprecations and the public appeals. I do not say that they are useless, for I do not dare to believe that anything here will be useless. It is merely that something has already been done—and not by the Nazis—which can never be undone, except as we seek to understand it and to grow human again (or expectant, or merely wise) through it. For the tragedy is in our minds, in the basic quality of our personal culture; and that is why it will be the tragedy of the peace. The tragedy lies in the quality of our belief—not in the lack of it, but in the unconsciousness or dishonesty of it; and above all in the merely political thinking, the desperate and unreal optimism, with which we try to cover up the void in ourselves. Yet I speak pragmatically: I am thinking of concrete situations. For Hitler will leave anti-Semitism as his last political trick, as it was his first; and the people who have been most indifferent to the historic meaning of the massacre of the Jews will be just those who will wonder why all the pacts and all the armies and all the formal justice will have done so little to give them their pre-fascist "security" again. If liberal optimism is false now, it will seem cruel later, when in even a post-Hitler Europe men will see again (many of them know it now, but for other, for purely political, reasons) that fascism remains, even though fascists, too, can die.

The treatment of the Jews, historically, has always been a touchstone of the degree of imagination, of Christian confidence, really, which formally Christian countries have been able to feel in themselves. Historically, no massacre was ever unexpected, no act of cruelty ever so great that it violated the professions of a civilization—every civilization being what it was, even when the cathedrals rose highest. But surely there was never so much self-deception about our essential goodness or our dream of "social security," so little philosophic (or moral) searching of the lies our hopes build on our lack of community, as there is today. The real materialism of our time has nothing to do with our intellectual naturalism, which is indispensable to those who do not believe in magic; or to our complete technological reliance upon ourselves, which is what it is. The real materialism, the real heresy, is the blindness of those who, declining to believe that there is a prime cause in the heavens, believe bitterly that society is always the prime cause of what we are. It is the materialism that comes with passing the buck so persistently to everyone but yourself that you never know whom to blame, even when you are Koestler's Rubashov in Lubyanka. It is the materialism of those who believe, as radicals, that you can begin by lying and making your victim lie (especially in public; a public life has a public apotheosis)—and that *then* you can build a brave new world based on the ultimate good sense of coöperativeness and the higher self-interest. It is the materialism of those who believe, as reactionaries, that you can build a tolerable society by appealing to an inner contempt among men for their "romantic"—and quite indestructible—hopes. It is the materialism of those who believe, as liberals, that you so fascinate men in a legality of good intentions, or even philanthropy, that you will

> *By faith, and faith alone, embrace,*
> *Believing where we cannot prove . . .*

But it is above all the materialism of all those—not liberals, not radicals, certainly not reactionaries—who want only to live and let live, to have the good life back—and who think that you can dump three million helpless Jews into your furnace, and sigh in the genuine impotence of your undeniable regret, and then build Europe back again.

That is the central point—not a "moral" point which any true unbeliever need be afraid of for its own sake, but the coarsely shrewd point based on the knowledge that life is also a process of memory, and that where so great a murder has been allowed, no one is safe. I do not believe in ghosts; if I did, I could be falsely heroic and satisfyingly sentimental, and say that the blood of the Jews over Europe is like that Christ's blood which Marlowe's Faustus saw streaming in the firmament. For I know that the indifference—the historic contemporary indifference, with everything it suggests about our governments as well as ourselves: I do not forget the rulers in describing the ruled—is far more terrible than physical terror and far more "tangible" than conscience. And what I am saying is not that the peoples will be remorseful (did we do it?), but that they will be betrayed by the human practices encouraged by the massacre of the Jews. Something has been set forth in Europe that is subtle, and suspended, and destructive; and it will break the power-pacts, and the high declarations, and even the armies, since armies are only men. That something is all our silent complicity in the massacre of the Jews (and surely not of them alone; it is merely that their deaths were so peculiarly hopeless). For it means that men are not ashamed of what they have been in this time, and are therefore not prepared for the further outbreaks of fascism which are so deep in all of us. It means that we still do not realize why

In every Infant's cry of fear,
In every cry of every Man,
In every voice, in every ban,
The mind-forg'd manacles I hear.

Blake knew it, as we can still know it: the manacles are always forged by the mind. Can the mind still break them free? Can it?

On Roosevelt

WINSTON CHURCHILL

APRIL 15, 1946

NBQ223 INTL=N LONDON VIA WUCABLES 189/185 28 528P

PRESS MANAGING EDITOR NEWREPUBLIC=

DURING THE YEARS OF CLOSE CONTACT AND COOPERATION BETWEEN THE ENGLISH SPEAKING WORLD THE LATE PRESIDENT ROOSEVELT BECAME TO ME NOT ONLY A DEAR AND VALUED FRIEND BUT ALSO THE PERSONIFICATION OF THE FIRM AND BRAVE SPIRIT WHICH CHARACTERIZES THE AMERICAN PEOPLES STOP I RECALL HOW AT THE HEIGHT OF OUR PERIL IN THE DARK HOURS OF DUNKIRK HIS VOICE CAME TO US WITH MESSAGES OF CHEER AND HOPE FROM THE MORE FORTUNATE BUT NONE THE LESS ENDANGERED LAND ACROSS THE OCEAN STOP AND AS THE YEARS OF OUR LIFE-STRUGGLE PROGRESSED HE INSPIRED US ALL WITH WORDS AND DEEDS OF POWER AND UNDERSTANDING STOP HIS VISION AND HIS JUDGEMENT OF INTERNATIONAL AFFAIRS HIS COMPREHENSION AND SYMPATHY FOR THE PROBLEMS OF THE ORDINARY MAN AND THE WARMTH AND HUMANITY OF HIS PERSONALITY ENDEARED HIM TO HIS OWN COUNTRYMEN AND TO ALL FELLOW-FIGHTERS IN THE GLORIOUS YEARS THROUGH WHICH WE HAVE TRAVELLED TO VICTORY STOP WE DO WELL TO HONOUR HIS NAME AND BE PROUD THAT WE HAVE LIVED IN HIS TIME=

WINSTON CHURCHILL.

Politics and the English Language

GEORGE ORWELL

JUNE 24, 1946

In our time it is broadly true that political writing is bad writing. Where it is not true, it will generally be found that the writer is some kind of rebel, expressing his private opinions and not a "party line." Orthodoxy, of whatever color, seems to demand a lifeless, imitative style. The political dialects to be found in pamphlets, leading articles, manifestos, White Papers and the speeches of undersecretaries do, of course, vary from party to party, but they are all alike in that one almost never finds in them a fresh, vivid, home-made turn of speech. When one watches some tired hack on the platform mechanically repeating the familiar phrases—*bestial atrocities, iron heel, bloodstained tyranny, free peoples of the world, stand shoulder to shoulder*—one often has a curious feeling that one is not watching a live human being but some kind of dummy: a feeling which suddenly becomes stronger at moments when the light catches the speaker's spectacles and turns them into black discs which seem to have no eyes behind them. And this is not altogether fanciful. A speaker who uses that kind of phraseology has gone some distance toward turning himself into a machine. The appropriate noises are coming out of his larynx, but his brain is not involved as it would be if he were choosing his words for himself. And this reduced state of consciousness, if not indispensable, is at any rate favorable to political conformity.

In our time, political speech and writing are largely the defense of the indefensible. Things like the continuance of British rule in India, the Russian purges and deportations, the dropping of the atom bombs on Japan, can indeed be defended, but only by arguments which are too brutal for most people to face, and which do not square with the professed aims of political parties. Thus political language has to consist largely of euphemism, question-begging and sheer cloudy vagueness. Defenseless villages are bombarded from the air, the inhabitants driven out into the countryside, the cattle machine-gunned, the huts set on fire with incendiary bullets: this is called pacification. Millions of peasants are robbed of their farms and sent trudging along the roads with no more than they can carry: this is called *transfer of population* or *rectification of frontiers*. People are imprisoned for years without trial, or shot in the back of the neck or sent to die of scurvy in Arctic lumber camps: this is called *elimination of unreliable elements.* Such phraseology is needed if one wants to name things without calling up mental pictures of them. Consider for instance some comfortable English professor defending Russian totalitarianism. He cannot say outright, "I believe in killing off your opponents when you can get good results by doing so." Probably, therefore, he will say something like this:

> While freely conceding that the Soviet regime exhibits certain features which the humanitarian may be inclined to deplore, we must, I think, agree that a certain curtailment of the right to political opposition is an unavoidable concomitant of transitional periods, and that the rigors which the Russian people have been called upon to undergo have been amply justified in the sphere of concrete achievement.

The great enemy of clear language is insincerity. When there is a gap between one's real and one's declared aims, one turns as it were instinctively to long words and exhausted idioms, like a cuttlefish squirting out ink. In our age there is no such thing as "keeping out of politics." All issues are political issues, and politics itself is a mass of lies, evasions, folly, hatred and schizophrenia. When the general atmosphere is bad, language must suffer.

But if thought corrupts language, language can also corrupt thought. A bad usage can spread by tradition and imitation, even among people who should and do know better. The debased language that I have been discussing is in some ways very convenient. Phrases like *leaves much to be desired, would serve no good purpose, a consideration which we should do well to bear in mind,* are a continuous temptation, a packet of aspirins always at one's elbow. Look back through this essay, and for certain you will find that I have committed the very faults I am protesting against.

I said earlier that the decadence of our language is probably curable. Those who deny this would argue, if they produced an argument at all, that language merely reflects existing social conditions, and that we cannot influence its development by any direct tinkering with words and constructions. So far as the general tone or spirit of a language goes, this may be true, but it is not true in detail. Silly words and expressions have often disappeared, not through any evolutionary process, but owing to the conscious action of a minority. Two recent examples were *explore every avenue* and *leave no stone unturned,* which were killed by the jeers of a few journalists. There is a long list of flyblown metaphors which could similarly be got rid of, if enough people would interest themselves in the job; and it should also be possible to laugh the *not un-* formation out of existence,* to reduce the amount of Latin and Greek in the average sentence, to drive out foreign phrases and strayed scientific words and, in general, to make pretentiousness unfashionable. But all these are minor points. The defense of the English language implies more than this, and perhaps it is best to start by saying what it does *not* imply.

To begin with, it has nothing to do with archaism, with the salvaging of obsolete words and turns of speech, or with the setting-up of a "standard English" which must never be departed from. On the contrary, it is especially concerned with the scrapping of every word or idiom which has outworn its usefulness. It has nothing to do with correct grammar and syntax, which are of no importance so long as one makes one's meaning clear, or with the avoidance of Americanisms, or with having what is called a "good prose style." On the other hand, it is not concerned with fake simplicity and the attempt to make written English colloquial. Nor does it even imply in every case preferring the Saxon word to the Latin one, though it does imply using the fewest and shortest words that will cover one's meaning. What is above all needed is to let the meaning choose the word, and not the other way about. In prose, the worst thing one can do with words is to surrender to them. When you think of a concrete object, you think wordlessly, and then, if you want to describe the thing you have been visualizing, you probably hunt about till you find the exact words that seem to fit it. When you think of something abstract you are more inclined to use words from the start, and unless you make a conscious effort to prevent it, the existing dialect will come rushing in and do the job for you, at the expense of blurring or even changing your meaning. Probably it is better to put off using words as long as possible and get one's meaning as clear as one can through pictures or sensations. Afterwards one can choose—not simply *accept*—the phrases that will best cover the meaning, and then switch round and decide what impression one's words are likely to make on another person. This last effort of the mind cuts out all stale or mixed images, all prefabricated phrases, needless repetitions and humbug and vagueness generally. But one can often be in doubt about the effect of a word or a phrase, and one needs rules that one can rely on when instinct fails. I think the following rules will cover most cases:

1) Never use a metaphor, simile or other figure of speech which you are used to seeing in print.
2) Never use a long word where a short one will do.
3) If it is possible to cut a word out, always cut it out.
4) Never use the passive where you can use the active.

*One can cure oneself of the *not un-* formation by memorizing this sentence: *A not unblack dog was chasing a not unsmall rabbit across a not ungreen field.*

5) Never use a foreign phrase, a scientific word or a jargon word if you can think of an everyday English equivalent.

6) Break any of these rules sooner than say anything outright barbarous.

These rules sound elementary, and so they are, but they demand a deep change of attitude in anyone who has grown used to writing in the style now fashionable. One could keep all of them and still write bad English, but one could not write the kind of stuff that I quoted in the first part of this article.

I have not here been considering the literary use of language, but merely language as an instrument for expressing and not for concealing or preventing thought. Stuart Chase and others have come near to claiming that all abstract words are meaningless, and have used this as a pretext for advocating a kind of political quietism. Since you don't know what fascism is, how can you struggle against fascism? One need not swallow such absurdities as this, but one ought to recognize that the present political chaos is connected with the decay of language, and that one can probably bring about some improvement by starting at the verbal end. If you simplify your English, you are freed from the worst follies of orthodoxy. You cannot speak any of the necessary dialects, and when you make a stupid remark its stupidity will be obvious, even to yourself. Political language—and with variations this is true of all political parties, from Conservatives to Anarchists—is designed to make lies sound truthful and murder respectable, and to give an appearance of solidity to pure wind. One cannot change this all in a moment, but one can at least change one's own habits, and from time to time one can even, if one jeers loudly enough, send some worn-out and useless phrase—some *jackboot, Achilles' heel, hotbed, melting pot, acid test, veritable inferno* or other lump of verbal refuse—into the dustbin where it belongs.

EDITOR'S NOTE: This was the second of a two-part essay. The first part appeared in the June 17, 1946, issue

Sigmund Freud

W. H. AUDEN

OCTOBER 6, 1952

Today, thanks to Freud, the man-in-the-street knows (to quote by an inaccurate memory from *Punch*) that, when he thinks a thing, the thing he thinks is not the thing he thinks he thinks, but only the thing he thinks he thinks he thinks. Fifty years ago, a girl who sprained her ankle on the eve of a long-looked-forward-to ball, or a man who suffered from a shrewish wife, could be certain of the neighbors' sympathy; today the latter will probably decide that misfortune is their real pleasure. The letter of apology to the hostess whose dinner invitation you have forgotten is much more difficult to write than it used to be. If an Isolde worries all day lest her absent Tristan should be run over by a bus, the dumbest Brangaene could warn her that her love includes a hope that he will never return. As for parents, not only the few who have read up on the Oedipus Complex and Erogenous Zones, but also the newspaper-reading mass, the poor things are today scared out of their wits that they will make some terrible mistake; the Victorian, even the Edwardian, paterfamilias who knew what was right is almost extinct, which is, perhaps, a pity. (However, if the bearded thunder god has turned into a clean-shaven pal, there is still the iron-toothed witch.)

It always comes as a shock to me to remember that, when Freud was born, *The Origin of Species* had not yet appeared, and that he was in his fortieth year before he published his first "freudian" papers. Freud's formative years, that is, were a time when the great intellectual battle was between Science and the sort of bourgeois idealist manicheeism of which, in 1875, Mrs. Eddy became Popess. The feeling that matter and the body are low or unreal and that the good and the real are spiritual or mental is always likely to become popular in a society where wealth and social prestige go to those who work with their heads; as long as the aristocracy thinks of itself as the warrior class, it is protected from this heresy because, while it may depise manual labor, athletic fitness is a badge of class: further, as long as their work is really manual, the market value of physical strength and manual skill prevents the working classes from underestimating the body, but with the coming of the machine which can be minded perfectly well by an unskilled child, white-collar manicheeism infects them as well. The great dramatic interest of the second half of the nineteenth century lies in the fact that, at the very time when the scientific advances which were being made in the natural sciences like chemistry and biology seemed to suggest that all reality might ultimately be explicable in terms of quantity and necessity, the development of society was making the notion of any relation of the good and the beautiful to matter peculiarly repugnant. One cannot read either the scientists or the naturalistic novelists of the period without feeling, in the very passion with which they assert that man is *only* an animal, their selection for portrayal of the ugliest "nature" they can find, the same horror as was exhibited by their episcopal opponents; they see themselves as preaching the truth, but none of them thinks that the truth is good news. Freud is no exception; the very man who has done most to free us from a manicheean horror of sex quotes more than once, with an unmistakable shudder of distaste, the Church Father who pointed out that we are born *inter urinas et faeces*. Some wag once summed up the message of psychoanalysis as saying: "We are born mad; we grow sane and unhappy; then we die." There are photographs of Freud in which he almost looks as if he would agree.

In this battle between those who asserted that the egg is only a dream of the hen and those who asserted that the hen is only a dream of the egg, Freud certainly thought of himself as a dyed-in-the-wool egg-fancier. He observes all the egg-fancier tabus; Beatrice, for instance, becomes the Love Object and the four-letter words always appear veiled in the decent obscurity of the Latin language. (The child-like faith of even the most anti-clerical members of the medical profession in the magical properties of that tongue is extremely comic and warrants psychoanalytic investigation.)

But Freud is a clear and beautiful example of a revolutionary thinker—it probably holds good for them all—who is much more revolutionary and in quite another way than he himself realizes.

Had one asked a doctor in the 80's and 90's to forecast the future of psychology, he would almost certainly have replied somewhat as follows:

It seems probable that we shall soon be able to describe all mental events in terms of physical events in the brain, but even if we cannot, we may safely assume:

1) Like the human body, the human mind has a constant nature, typical for the species; individual variations are either pathological or insignificant.

2) The behavior of this mind can be explained in terms of stimulus

and response. Similar stimuli will necessarily produce similar responses. Both are quantitatively measurable in terms of intensity and duration.

3) Mental development is like physical growth, i.e., the mind passes from a younger or earlier phase into an older or later one. This process can be arrested or become morbid, but two phases cannot exist simultaneously any more than an oak can be an acorn at the same time.

4) The neuroses and psychoses must be typical diagnostic entities, identical in every patient. To discover a cure for one means to discover the procedure which is effective independently of the individual doctor or the individual patient.

One has only to read a few lines of Freud to realize that one is moving in a very different world, one in which there are decisive battles, defeats, victories, decisions, doubts, where things happen that need not have happened and even things which ought not to have happened, a world where novelties exist side by side with ancient monuments, a world of guilt and responsibility, a world, heaven help us, that has to be described with analogical *metaphors.* The Master may sometimes write as if he thought that saying a three-year-old child wishes to commit incest with his mother were the same kind of statement as saying he wishes to go to the bathroom, but we are not deceived. Whatever we may think of that famous trio Ego, Super-Ego and Id, we can see that they are like Prince Tamino, Zorastro and The Queen of The Night and not like mathematical equations. We may find the account of the Fall in *Totem and Taboo* more or less plausible than the account in Genesis (the Bible version which makes the psychological sin, and therefore the sense of guilt, prior to the moral crime seems to me the more "freudian"), but we shall not dream of applying the standards of "scientific" evidence employed in Chemistry or Biology to either.

In fact, if every one of his theories should turn out to be false, Freud would still tower up as the genius who perceived that psychological events are not natural events but historical and that, therefore, psychology as distinct from neurology, must be based on the pre-suppositions and methodology, not of the biologist but of the historian. As a child of his age who was consciously in a polemic with the "idealists," he may officially subscribe to the "realist" dogma that human nature and animal nature are the same, but the moment he gets down to work, every thing he says denies it. In his theories of infantile sexuality, repression, etc., he pushes back the beginnings of free will and responsibility earlier than even most theologians had previously dared; his therapeutic technique of making the patient re-live his past and discover the truth for himself with a minimum of prompting and interference from the analyst (meanwhile, one might add, doing penance by paying till it hurts), the importance of Transference to the outcome of the therapy, imply that every patient is a unique historical person and not a typical case.

Freud is not always aware of what he is doing and some of the difficulties he gets into arise from his trying to retain biological notions of development when he is actually thinking historically. For example, he sometimes talks as if civilization were a morbid growth caused by sexual inhibition; at other times he attacks conventional morality on the grounds that the conformists exhaust in repression the energies which should be available for cultural tasks: similarly, he sometimes speaks of dream symbolism as if it were pure allegory, whereas the actual descriptions he gives of the dreaming mind at work demonstrate that, in addition to its need to disguise truth, it has an even greater need to create truth, to make historical sense of its experience by discovering analogies, an activity in which it shows the most extraordinary skill and humor. In a biological organism, everything was once something else which it now no longer is, and change is cyclical, soma-germ-soma; a normal condition is one that regularly re-occurs in the cycle, a morbid one is an exception. But history is the realm of unique and novel events and of monuments—the historical past is present in the present and the norm of health or pathology cannot be based on regularity.

Freud certainly expected opposition and obloquy from the conventional moralists and the man-in-the street for his theories about human sexuality; in actual fact, the general public took him to their bosoms rather less critically, perhaps, than they should have done, while the real opposition came and still comes from the behaviorists, the neurologists and all the schools of psychiatry that regard their subject as a natural science and are therefore outraged by the whole approach of the psychoanalysts, irrespective of any particular theory they may hold.

The opposition can certainly find plenty of ammunition in psychoanalytic literature; for, while it is possible to do important work (though not, I believe, the greatest) in the natural sciences without being a wise and great man, the most routine exercises in a field that involves the personal and historical demand wisdom, and a psychoanalyst who lacks it cannot write a five-minute paper without giving himself away as a vulgar nincompoop.

The same holds for the reader; a man may fail to understand a text-book of physics but he knows he has not understood it and that is the end of the matter; but he may read a psychoanalytical treatise and come out more of a damned fool at the end than he was before he began it. Or more of a crook—every defense lawyer in a seemingly hopeless criminal case knows how to instruct his client in his unloved childhood to embarrass Bench and Jury.

In the long run, however, the welcome given to psychoanalysis by the public is based on a sound intuition that it stands for treating every one as a unique and morally responsible person, not as a keyboard—it speaks of the narcissism of the Ego, but it believes in the existence of that Ego and its capacity to recognize its own limitations—and that in these days is a great deal. The behaviorists are certainly right in one thing; the human mind does have a nature which can be tampered with: with a few drugs and a little regular torture every human mind can be reduced to a condition in which it is no longer a subject for psychology.

Psychoanalysts and their patients may sometimes seem funny little people, but the fact that they exist is evidence that society is still partly human.

A Qualified Faith

REINHOLD NIEBUHR

FEBRUARY 13, 1956

The Asian junket of Bulganin and Khrushchev coming just after the Summit conference is instructive. The two Communist bosses were saying in effect: "We have eliminated the possibility of atomic warfare; now we have the chance to carry on political warfare against the democratic world with a minimum of risk; we will center upon those parts of the world where our creed will seem most plausible and relevant." They thereupon hurled insults at the "imperialists" and "colonialists," assured the Burmese that they were civilized long before their former masters, the British, were. They posed as representatives of Asia, even though they could not possibly make themselves "colored." The technical aid they offered was symbolic of the fact that Russia had negotiated the hazardous road to technical modernity without achieving or appreciating "a democratic" society.

The plausibility of the Communist creed to the two colored continents is enhanced by the fact that the Marxist interpretation of the class struggle and its analysis of the class structure, though always too simple to fit the facts, is much more relevant to the social facts in a decaying feudal structure than in an advanced capitalistic one. It is not surprising that Marxism succeeded only in the agrarian and feudal economies of semi-Asiatic Russia and in China; nor surprising that it still appears to be relevant to the recently emancipated nations of Africa and Asia, who have suffered or still suffer from foreign domination; and whose suffering has not ended with their throwing off of the foreign yoke.

American idealists are inclined to neglect all the political complexities of Asia and Africa and to imagine that "free elections" represent a meaningful goal to the people who live there. They think democracy is a matter of accepting a democratic constitution and they are oblivious to the tortuous history by which justice was established in a free society through an equilibrium of political and economic forces. If they are more realistic, our idealists propose a technical assistance program for the non-technical nations, but only few recognize that technical advance breaks the molds of organic communities. Political chaos may go hand in hand with a rise in living standards. A free society is not as simple an alternative to the old feudal society as is the collectivism of communism which promises technical competence; promises but does not grant, economic justice; and does *not* promise the individual freedom which the peoples of Asia and Africa have never enjoyed and which seems in any case to be beyond their reach.

But whatever mistakes our idealists make in presenting an open society as a simple alternative to past injustices, they are trumped by the mistakes of our "realists" who insist on regarding our contest with communism primarily a problem of military strategy.

The right-wing "realists" of the Republican Party still insist, for example, that China might have been saved from communism if the nationalists had been given adequate military support. They close their eyes to obvious political and moral weaknesses of the nationalist cause and to our loss of prestige in the whole of Asia throughout our persistent military championship of that cause long after it had proved its inability to win and hold the loyalty of the Chinese masses.

Secretary Dulles manages to combine the mistakes of the idealists *and* the realists. He has a purely "idealistic" approach to the problems of Asia and Africa when he defines the issues between ourselves and the Communists as a contest between those who believe in the "moral law" and those who do not. He is a military "realist" when he contrives military defense pacts which enrage our neutralists "allies" by driving a wedge between India and Pakistan, and another in the Middle East between the various members of the Arab League. These defense pacts are modeled after the European NATO model; but Mr. Dulles does not seem to appreciate that the analogy he uses to justify them is faulty. For the European community is solid, or nearly solid, in its devotion to the standards of democratic civilization and can be conquered only by military force. In non-European nations on the other hand, subversion and political conspiracy are the Communists' chief weapons.

In addition to these mistakes Secretary Dulles has managed to perpetuate an error which was originated before his administration: letting Asian politics be governed by our relations to our European allies, some of which, particularly France, are still deeply involved in "colonialism." Thus he allowed himself to issue a joint statement with the Portuguese Ambassador on the subject of the disputed Portuguese "province" of Goa, off the coast of India, a statement prompted by our desire to renew a lease with Portugal for a military base in the Azores. The consequences to our prestige in India were catastrophic: particularly as the statement coincided with the India visit of the two Soviet leaders.

Dulles' mistake was not, of course, the first of its kind. Long ago we committed ourselves to Bao Dai, the French puppet Emperor of Viet-Nam, in order to shore up a precarious French Government. Subsequent French Governments have continued to be precarious, and we gained nothing from our adventure in "realpolitik" but increasing the plausibility of the caricature of ourselves as an "imperialist" nation.

The essential problem which democracy faces in Asia and Africa can be briefly stated: Democracy is at once a more tainted and a more impossible ideal than we have realized. It has been tainted for the Asian and African nations because the democratic nations are also the technically most powerful nations, whose initial impact on the continents was imperialistic. Democracy seems an impossible ideal because it seems to lack the essential conditions for attaining justice and stability, within the framework of a free society. Asians and Africans also usually lack the religio-cultural foundation for individual freedom; their religions either lose the individual in the social whole, the family or the tribe (as in Confucianism and in the more primitive religions of Africa), or are mystical religions which seek for the annullment of individuality.

But even if these peoples should manage to gain an appreciation of the value of the individual, more like our own, they must still prove that individual liberty, so much prized by the West, can be made compatible with *both* justice and stability. Freedom is not an absolute value. We think so because we take the values of justice and stability for granted. But these values have been made compatible with freedom by very slow processes of history in the West. If freedom could not be made compatible with justice, the Communist case against a free society would be proved. If free societies could not achieve stability, the Communists would finally profit from the resulting chaos.

Justice requires an equilibrium of political and economic power. The equilibrium of political power was broadly achieved by universal suffrage. But a tolerable justice was not achieved in Western civilization until the industrial workers achieved both political *and* economic power through political and trade union organizations.

Further, the stability of a free society requires not only justice but a measure of moral and political wisdom which sets limits to party conflict and the competition of conflicting interests within the community. The wisdom expressed in the "limited warfare" of parliamentary government is not the simple fruit of literacy or even of intelligence. It is also an historical product, usually the fruit of generations of living together in freedom. The justice and stability which we take for granted have not been achieved in most Latin American nations, though they may have ideal Constitutions.

Such an analysis would seem to make our democratic alternative to communism impossible for nations of Asia and Africa. But while the difficulties must be appreciated, the alternative is not impossible. The possibility rests upon the ability of men to transfer political skills and wisdom from one culture in which they matured into another culture in which they are not indigenous. This ability requires rare co-operation between the tutor nation and the apprentice; and resentments against the imperial tutor frequently make this co-operation extremely difficult. But the experience of Britain in India and our experience in the Philippines, and, less impressively, the Dutch experience in Indonesia, prove that it is possible to transfer historically acquired skills. The British have proved in the Gold Coast of Africa that it can be done, even if the apprentice is a budding nation with a primitive culture.

Yet the difficulties of the task make it evident that we have a long-range program before us, requiring not only ingenuity but patience. Naturally it is necessary to resist communism whenever it presents itself in terms of military aggression, as in Korea, and to prevent the Communist movement from gaining supremacy in weapons, nuclear and otherwise, with which modern warfare is bound to be conducted. Military force is always the *ultima ratio* in the contest between nations. But this ultimate form of logic in the international relations cannot obviate the significance of competition on all other levels—moral, political and economic.

The long ardors of competitive co-existence to which we will be subjected perhaps for a century cannot be understood at all or borne with patience, if we do not realize that the contest between a free society and a tyranny is one in which the tyranny has all the immediate advantages in the colored continents, while we have all the ultimate ones. That is why time is on our side, however much the battle may run against us for decades.

End of the Postwar World

WALTER LIPPMANN

APRIL 15, 1957

Within recent weeks, our government has announced that a cessation of nuclear bomb tests is not feasible, that atomic warheads will be made available to our NATO allies in the event of an emergency, that long-range guided missiles will be delivered by us to the British. The British in turn have revolutionized their defense program, relying on hydrogen bombs and ballistic rockets. The Russians have reacted sharply by promising to "strengthen most decisively the Warsaw Pact," by charging that our weapons agreement with Britain has increased . . . the threat of a new war," by broadcasting warnings of devastating retaliation against the Netherlands, Britain and West Germany, by informing Denmark that it would be suicidal to permit use of her bases for atomic strikes against the USSR, by threatening Norway with a destructive blow, and by telling France and Israel that any attempt to defend the right of free passage through the Gulf of Aqaba by force would create an immediate risk of "broad military conflict." Against this background of threats and counter-threats, the search for some area of possible East-West agreement continues. In the opinion of Walter Lippmann, "the issue of war and peace will be decided primarily in Europe." Thus, he suggests, there must be a new diplomatic approach to an all-European settlement.

No one, I think, not even at the top of affairs and therefore on the inside of all of the available information, can as yet see clearly, can as yet see as a whole, where we really are and where we ought to go.

Everyone knows, of course, that we are in a time of rapid, radical and complicated change. Now, in itself, change is far from being a new experience for the generation to which I belong. We have lived amidst great events for which we were unprepared. We have become involved in wars which we expected to stay out of. We have hoped great things from victory and we have never seen a good peace. But now, if I may put it that way, the world is changed for Americans, not only in the degree of our involvement with the outer world, but in the very kind of our involvement with the rest of the world.

Throughout the 19th Century, and during the two world wars of this century, we have thought that we were living in one world. We have thought that this world had its political center in the Western society, the society which consists of Europe and the Americas, the society to which we belong.

Even the most anti-imperialistic among us has assumed this. We have supposed that all the nations—the old ones who were breaking with the past, the new ones who were emerging from colonial status—that all the nations would have the same fundamental political ideals which we have, not because they are our ideals but because these ideals are universal.

The greatest and most fundamental change of our time is that this picture of ourselves and of our place in the world and of our role in the history of mankind is no longer valid. The culture, the ideology of the Western society is no longer recognized as universal. It is challenged as it has not been challenged since Christendom was challenged by the expansion of Islam.

The one world which we always have taken for granted in our thinking has been succeeded by many worlds. We now live amidst these many worlds. They compete with one another, they coexist with one another. They trade with one another and, in varying degrees, they co-operate with one another. This change from one world to several worlds is a deep change. It is a change not only in what we think about our foreign policy but in the very way that we have to think about it.

In our political thinking, that is to say in the thinking of the Western world, it is a change comparable with the change from the Ptolemaic to the Copernican astronomy, from the view that this earth is the center of the universe to the view that this earth is only a planet, a big planet no doubt, but still a planet in a much larger solar system. It is this new situation which we are trying to understand. It is in this new situation that we are trying to get our bearings and to feel our way forward.

But in order to do this, we must first look back and see how United States foreign policy was, until very recently, controlled by the underlying conception of the 19th Century—the conception of one world whose political center was in the North Atlantic region of the globe.

In the First World War we were drawn in when Britain and her ally, France, were threatened with defeat. We were no longer able to remain isolated from Europe and unentangled with the wars of Europe, as we had been during the 19th Century. But how were we drawn in the First World

War? We were drawn in to reinforce Great Britain. We were the auxiliaries and the reserves. We called ourselves an associated power, and our troops fought in Europe under a supreme commander who was a French general and our Navy was under the overall command of the British admiralty.

When the war ended in 1918, we hoped and believed that we had won a victory for the idea that the principles and ideals of the Western society are universal. Woodrow Wilson proclaimed a world order. But it was a world order based on our Western principles and ideals. Moreover, it was to be an order in which the nations of the North Atlantic region would continue to be the political leaders of mankind.

On the surface, there was in 1918 much to justify this optimistic view. The North Atlantic community had won a smashing military victory, and the United States emerged as a new and powerful member of the Western society. Russia was still a primitive country in the throes of a deep social revolution. China was a feeble and backward country, divided up among foreign powers. India was still under British rule. North Africa, the Middle East, and Southeast Asia were under British or French imperial dominion. On the surface, in Woodrow Wilson's time it looked as if Britain and France, reinforced by the United States and Canada, could prolong indefinitely the world order that had existed in the 19th Century.

We now know that this was a brilliant illusion. Both France and Britain were profoundly weakened by their fearful losses in the First World War. As representatives of the Western philosophy, they were challenged as imperialists over all Asia and Africa. We did not know this in 1918. We took it for granted that with American military and financial help the worldwide predominance of the Atlantic community would continue.

In the Second World War, the role played by the United States was no longer that of an associated power bringing up the reinforcements and the reserves. But before Pearl Harbor, and before we actually entered the Second World War, we still thought of ourselves in terms of World War I. We used to talk, you may remember, about aiding the Allies to defend America. In fact, however, it was soon plain that we must take up the whole burden of the war in the Pacific, including the defense of Australia and of New Zealand. In Europe, the French Army had been defeated and Great Britain was under violent assault and strained to the limit. We had not only to supply the weapons and other economic necessities, but we had to raise a great army ourselves.

The difference between the two world wars is marked by the fact that in the second, as distinguished from the first, the supreme commanders on sea and on land were Americans. Nevertheless, until World War II ended, we could still believe—perhaps I should say that we tried still to believe—that when Britain and France and western Europe recovered from the damages of the war, the North Atlantic community would still be the political center of the world.

I venture to believe that in the last analysis this was the underlying assumption in the minds of both Churchill and Roosevelt at the close of the war. They believed that with Britain and America acting as partners, they could handle Russia and have the deciding voice in the postwar settlement. They were mistaken.

The fact of the matter is that Churchill himself was so big that he made British power look bigger than it was. It soon appeared that Britain, though it was a great power by the old standards, was not like the United States and the USSR, a superpower. It was soon evident that in the postwar world the Atlantic community, with the British-American partnership at its core, was no longer the paramount power in the world.

We achieved our independence amidst the rivalry of the North Atlantic powers. We developed this continent in security behind the supremacy of the British powers. We fought the First World War as the auxiliary of the Atlantic powers. We fought the Second World War as the leading power of the Atlantic community. Now this is fundamentally altered.

The greatest powers with which we have to concern ourselves are no longer in the North Atlantic region. They are in eastern Europe and in Asia. While the welfare of the Atlantic community is a close and vital interest of the United States, the Atlantic community is no longer the political center of the world. We are living amidst the decline of Britain as one of the leading powers of the world, and we find ourselves without a powerful ally in the face of the new powers of eastern Europe and of Asia and of Africa.

To dramatize the rapid changes in the past 100 years, we might say that through most of the 19th Century the world capital was London. After the First World War, the world capitals were London and Washington. After the Second World War, the world capitals were Washington, Moscow, and London. Now the world capitals are Washington, Moscow, London, Peiping, Delhi, and, who knows, perhaps eventually, also Cairo.

We are in a wholly new situation. It is not a clearly visible situation with all its landmarks and features well defined. There are no reliable maps. This is, in part, because so much of the world is hidden by censorship and obscured by propaganda.

But another reason, and perhaps a more compelling reason, why there are no reliable maps is that so much of the world is in the midst of revolutionary changes of which we cannot foresee the outcome.

Nevertheless, we must try to find our bearings, to find out where we are and what is around us. And one way to do this is to look back and to remind ourselves where we came from and how we got where we are.

We must, I think, go back about twelve years to the winter of 1945 when

Roosevelt and Churchill were on their way to Yalta in the Russian Crimea. The end of the world war was in sight. They were on their way to Yalta in order to negotiate with Stalin about the armistices which would end the fighting.

As we all know, they did not reach an agreement on what should be the terms of the peace treaties with the two powerful enemies they expected soon to defeat. But they did agree on the general terms of the armistices they expected to make with Germany and Japan.

I hope I can say what I have to say here about Yalta without entering into and stirring up again the furious controversy which has raged about it ever since. The point about which there cannot be serious dispute is that Yalta was followed in May by the German armistice and in August by the Japanese armistice.

Now, an armistice is essentially an agreement, first to stop shooting, and then it is an agreement as to where the armed forces are to stand still. In substance, the armistices of 1945 reflected and registered the military situation as the Big Three at Yalta expected it would be when the fighting ended. The lines of the armistices of the Second World War are what we have since come to know as the line of the Iron Curtain. The Iron Curtain is where the Red Army settled down when the fighting stopped. This line still divides Germany. It still divides Europe. And in Asia the line which now divides the Communist from the non-Communist powers is essentially the line of the American occupation at the time of the ceasefire.

This, then, was the situation of the postwar world as it took shape from the armistice lines. Today we are living amidst the breakup and the disintegration of the postwar world. The question I should now like to discuss is how this disintegration started, and what caused this breakup.

As a result of the Yalta conference the world was divided into two great spheres of influence. In the one sphere, where the Soviet Union was supreme, Stalin tried to create a new Russian Empire. This empire was founded primarily on the power of the Red Army. In fact, the empire was the territory occupied by the Red Army. Stalin's purpose was to make the people of eastern Europe docile satellites or colonies of the new Russian Empire.

The other sphere comprised the rest of the world. It was an unorganized collection of old and new states. It consisted not only of western Europe, Latin America, and the United States, but also of the old European empires, which then extended across North Africa, Egypt, and the Middle East through India and Southeast Asia to the Dutch Empire in Indonesia. In this sphere, the United States took the initiative in trying to make sure that the Soviet Union did not extend its empire.

As the principal military arm of the Communist sphere was the Red Army, so the principal military arm of the non-Communist sphere was the United States Strategic Air Force equipped with atomic bombs.

This situation lasted until about 1950, as long as only the Soviets had an effective army and only the United States had the atomic bomb. In this uneasy balance of power, the Red Army was supreme on the ground in all of Europe and Asia; the United States Strategic Air Force was supreme in the air over Europe and Asia. Each acted as a deterrent on the other. As against an invasion by the Red Army, western Europe was wholly defenseless. Yet the Red Army did not and could not overrun western Europe. It was contained because the Kremlin knew what the United States Air Force could do to Russian cities.

On the other hand, one might say vice versa, the United States was held in check by the Red Army. Let me say a word about how we were held in check. The very highest American military authorities knew that if we struck at the Russian cities, the Red Army, which was already in eastern Europe, would overrun western Europe. It would occupy the countries of western Europe against which we could not use the atomic bomb, countries such as western Germany, the Netherlands, Belgium and France. When the Red Army did that it would destroy the existing governments. It would liquidate the existing leaders in all classes and, before it could be forced to retire, it would probably destroy the big cities and the industrial plants of western Europe.

This was the postwar stalemate, the Red Army as against the atomic bomb.

The breakup of the postwar world was fairly foreseeable as soon as this original postwar stalemate was broken. In September 1949, the Soviet Union set off an atomic bomb of its own. This event announced to the world that the American monopoly was over and that a situation, which was radically different from that of the postwar years, would now develop.

The breaking of the American monopoly meant the beginning of a race in nuclear armaments. This was a terrifying prospect. It set in motion a strong tendency towards disintegration inside both the Stalinist empire and inside the Western coalition.

Once it was evident that there were going to be two rival superpowers, each armed with nuclear weapons, the nations which had no nuclear weapons began to feel desperately insecure. They were in danger of being destroyed in a war that would be fought with weapons they themselves did not possess. They could not defend themselves against those weapons. They could not strike back. They were bound, therefore, to make it their central national purpose to stay out of a big war if, because of acts of criminal folly, a big war could not be prevented. It was under these conditions that what we call neutralism was born and soon began rapidly to spread.

If we say that at Yalta the postwar world was divided into two great spheres of influence, then I would say that when the race of nuclear armaments got underway—beginning in 1949 but rising to a climax with the hydrogen bomb—the two great spheres of influence began to disintegrate. No doubt there were other reasons. But the trigger which set the forces of disintegration in rapid motion in both spheres was the race of nuclear armaments. On both sides of the Iron Curtain the pent-up forces of nationalism were released. On our side of the Iron Curtain these forces invoked the slogan of anti-colonialism and anti-imperialism. On the other side of the Iron Curtain, they have been invoking the slogan of anti-Stalinism.

These upheavals have, of course, a long history. The liquidation of the western empires is one of the great historical phenomena of the 20th Century, and the national opposition by Hungarians and Poles to Russian domination began long ago in the past. But when the atomic race began in 1949, nationalism and neutralism became urgent and passionate because they offered a means of self-defense, and indeed a means of survival.

The terrifying destructiveness of the hydrogen bomb was demonstrated between November 1952, when we exploded ours, and August 1953, when the Soviets exploded theirs. Politically and psychologically, these gigantic explosions have jarred loose, they have dislocated and pulled apart, much of the political structure of the postwar world. The disintegration of the old European empires in Asia and Africa has been accelerated. The disintegration of the new Russian empire in Europe has been started. The structure of alliances on both sides of the Iron Curtain has begun to crumble.

It was when he realized this that President Eisenhower made his historic declaration that there is now no alternative to peace. The Russians had also realized what the revolution in military weapons meant. This common realization in Moscow and Washington led to the famous meeting at the summit, which took place in Geneva a year and a half ago, in July of 1955. At that meeting, Russia and the United States acknowledged publicly to each other and before the world that with the advent of the new weapons they could not, they would not, they dared not contemplate war.

At the time of the Geneva meeting, we were all aware that, beyond these mutual declarations against war, there were no serious agreements reached, or even brought any nearer, on any of the great practical issues of the time—on, for example, the reunification of the two Germanies, on the problem of the status of the satellites in eastern Europe, on the future of the Middle East.

There is no way of telling whether or not the opportunity existed to go on from Geneva to settlements of some of these problems. If the opportunity existed, it was missed. On our side, the President fell ill and was unable for some time to take the initiative in foreign affairs. On the other side, the Russians stood pat and were unyielding. We do not know what might have been. But what has actually happened is that while we have come no nearer to settlements in Europe, in the Middle East and in the Far East, there has been a rapid disintegration of empires and of alliances.

We can see what has happened to the French in North Africa and the British in the Middle East. We know from what has happened in Poland and in Hungary that the Soviet empire in eastern Europe is undermined, and that the Soviet military system, which is known as the Warsaw Pact, is profoundly affected. We know that if NATO is going to survive, it is going to have a very different future from what we expected.

A few months ago, at the end of October, the course of events, which I have been describing, burst into violence. It is a remarkable fact, which historians will long be studying and trying to explain, that the explosion in Hungary and the explosion in Egypt took place at approximately the same time. The fact that the two explosions came so very close together may not have been a mere accident. It may well be that the Israeli government decided to strike when it saw that the Soviet Union was deeply entangled by the rebellion in Hungary. But the two explosions would not have happened if both in eastern Europe and in the Middle East the situation had not become explosive. These two explosions marked the disintegration of the postwar world.

You will want me to say before I conclude what I see emerging from all this. This is not so easy, and no doubt I am foolish to try. But here at least are some of the things I see coming out of it.

There will remain the fundamental stalemate between the Soviet Union and the United States, the stalemate which was recognized by the President and the Soviet leaders at Geneva in 1955.

In all probability, neither of the superpowers will decide deliberately to make war against the other. On the other hand, both in Europe and in the Middle East, there are very grave issues which, if they cannot be settled by negotiation, may burst into violence. They may become uncontrollable, and they could involve Russia and America in a war they are both trying to avoid.

In Europe the question is whether the Soviet empire can be liquidated in a peaceable and orderly way. If it is not, we must be prepared to see the kind of thing that has happened in Hungary spread to eastern Germany. If there is armed rebellion in eastern Germany and the Red Army is used to suppress it, there is little likelihood that the West Germans will sit quietly on the sidelines. They will almost certainly join in, perhaps not officially at first, but as volunteers, and this will put the American and the British Armies in western Germany in a very dangerous predicament. For one could hardly expect the Russians to leave West Germany alone if it becomes the base of a rebellion in eastern Germany. All of this could readily enough lead to a world war.

The supreme question is whether we can, by a great effort of statesmanship, negotiate a settlement which averts these dangers. I am not saying that we can. But at least one can imagine such a settlement. It will have to be a settlement negotiated by the Western powers with the Soviet Union and ratified by the two Germanies. It will have to provide for the reunification of the two Germanies. It will have to provide for the gradual but nevertheless definite evacuation of the European Continent up to the Soviet frontier by the Red Army in the east, and by the British and American armies in the west. Only in this way can Poland, Hungary, and the other satellites be liberated.

But that will not be enough. The withdrawal of the armies, the unification of Germany, the liberation of the satellites will be possible, will be conceivable—only if we can construct by negotiation an all-European security system which is underwritten by the Soviet Union and the United States. It will have to be a system which guarantees the European nations among themselves, and particularly against a revived and reunited Germany. It will have to be a system which guarantees all of Europe against Russia, and it will have to be one which guarantees Russia against Europe. Within such a European system there ought to develop an all-European economy, and beyond that—on the far horizons of hope—the prospect of a European political confederation.

In my view the issue of war and peace will be decided primarily in Europe, and, so to speak, along the line of Iron Curtain. The greatest question in the world is whether Europe can cease to be divided and can become united by negotiation and peaceable means.

I would go so far as to say that if we could engage the Russians in a serious negotiation which looked to a general European settlement, the problem of the Middle East would become—I won't say soluble—but manageable. I say this because Russia is not vitally interested in the Middle East. She does not need the oil, and she cannot be invaded from the Middle East. Russia is, however, vitally interested in Europe, particularly in Germany and in Poland, and it is there in Europe that we must make a settlement or live in continual danger of a gigantic war.

When I look into the future I think of this country as having two great missions to perform. The one is to bring about the European settlement I have just been describing. On this, as I have just said, depends the issue of peace or war. From such a settlement would come a new Europe, a Europe which had lost its empires overseas but had found a new strength, security, and prosperity in its own unity. Our other mission is, I firmly believe, to work out a new relationship between the Western nations and the newly emancipated peoples of Africa and Asia. The imperial and colonial age is over. The age which is to follow is only in its dim beginnings, and it is our mission to play a leading part in working out the terms on which the peoples of the East and the peoples of the West can live side by side in confidence, in security and in mutual respect.

When Castro Heard the News

JEAN DANIEL

DECEMBER 7, 1963

Havana

It was around 1:30 in the afternoon, Cuban time. We were having lunch in the living room of the modest summer residence which Fidel Castro owns on magnificent Varadero Beach, 120 kilometers from Havana. For at least the tenth time, I was questioning the Cuban leader on details of the negotiations with Russia before the missile installations last year. The telephone rang, a secretary in guerrilla garb announced that Mr. Dorticós, President of the Cuban Republic, had an urgent communication for the Prime Minister. Fidel picked up the phone and I heard him say: *"Como? Un atentado?"* ("What's that? An attempted assassination?") He then turned to us to say that Kennedy had just been struck down in Dallas. Then he went back to the telephone and exclaimed in a loud voice, *"Herido? Muy gravemente?"* ("Wounded? Very seriously?")

He came back, sat down, and repeated three times the words: *"Es una mala noticia."* ("This is bad news.") He remained silent for a moment, awaiting another call with further news. He remarked while we waited that there was an alarmingly sizable lunatic fringe in American society and that this deed could equally well have been the work of a madman or of a terrorist. Perhaps a Vietnamese? Or a member of the Ku Klux Klan? The second call came through: it was hoped they would be able to announce that the United States President was still alive, that there was hope of saving him. Fidel Castro's immediate reaction was: "If they can, he is already re-elected." He pronounced these words with satisfaction.

This sentence was a sequel to a conversation we had held on a previous evening and which had turned into an all-night session. To be precise, it lasted from 10 in the evening until 4 in the morning. A good part of the talk revolved about the impressions I recounted to him of an interview which President Kennedy granted me this last October 24, and about Fidel

Castro's reactions to these impressions. During this nocturnal discussion, Castro had delivered himself of a relentless indictment of U.S. policy, adding that in the recent past Washington had had ample opportunity to normalize its relations with Cuba, but that instead it had tolerated a CIA program of training, equipping and organizing a counter-revolution. He had told me that he wasn't in the least fearful of his life, since danger was his natural milieu, and if he were to become a victim of the United States this would simply enhance his radius of influence in Latin America as well as throughout the socialist world. He was speaking, he said, from the viewpoint of the interests of peace in both the American continents. To achieve this goal, a leader would have to arise in the United States capable of understanding the explosive realities of Latin America and of meeting them halfway. Then, suddenly, he had taken a less hostile tack: "Kennedy could still be this man. He still has the possibility of becoming, in the eyes of history, the greatest President of the United States, the leader who may at last understand that there can be coexistence between capitalists and socialists, even in the Americas. He would then be an even greater President than Lincoln. I know, for example, that for Khrushchev, Kennedy is a man you can talk with. I have gotten this impression from all my conversations with Khrushchev. Other leaders have assured me that to attain this goal, we must first await his re-election. Personally, I consider him responsible for everything, but I will say this: he has come to understand many things over the past few months; and then too, in the last analysis, I'm convinced that anyone else would be worse." Then Fidel had added with a broad and boyish grin: "If you see him again, you can tell him that I'm willing to declare Goldwater my friend if that will guarantee Kennedy's re-election!"

This conversation was held on November 19.

Now it was nearly 2 o'clock and we got up from the table and settled ourselves in front of a radio. Commandant Vallero, his physician, aide-de-camp, and intimate friend, was easily able to get the broadcasts from the NBC network in Miami. As the news came in, Vallero would translate it for Fidel: Kennedy wounded in the head; pursuit of the assassin; murder of a policeman; finally the fatal announcement: President Kennedy is dead. Then Fidel stood up and said to me: "Everything is changed. Everything is going to change. The United States occupies such a position in world affairs that the death of a President of that country affects millions of people in every corner of the globe. The cold war, relations with Russia, Latin America, Cuba, the Negro question . . . all will have to be rethought. I'll tell you one thing: at least Kennedy was an enemy to whom we had become accustomed. This is a serious matter. An extremely serious matter."

After the quarter-hour of silence observed by all the American radio stations, we once more tuned in on Miami; the silence had only been broken by a rebroadcasting of the American national anthem. Strange indeed was the impression made, on hearing this hymn ring out in the house of Fidel Castro, in the midst of a circle of worried faces. "Now," Fidel said, "they will have to find the assassin quickly, but very quickly, otherwise, you watch and see, I know them, they will try to put the blame on us for this thing. But tell me, how many Presidents have been assassinated? Four? This is most disturbing! In Cuba, only one has been assassinated. You know, when we were hiding out in the Sierra there were some (not in my group, in another) who wanted to kill Batista. They thought they could do away with a regime by decapitating it. I have always been violently opposed to such methods. First of all from the viewpoint of political self-interest, because so far as Cuba is concerned, if Batista had been killed he would have been replaced by some military figure who would have tried to make the revolutionists pay for the martyrdom of the dictator. But I was also opposed to it on personal grounds; assassination is repellent to me."

The broadcasts were now resumed. One reporter felt he should mention the difficulty Mrs. Kennedy was having in getting rid of her bloodstained stockings. Fidel exploded: "What sort of a mind is this!" He repeated the remark several times: "What sort of a mind is this? There is a difference in our civilizations after all. Are you like this in Europe? For us Latin Americans, death is a sacred matter; not only does it mark the close of hostilities, but it also imposes decency, dignity, respect. There are even street urchins who behave like kings in the face of death. Incidentally, this reminds me of something else: if you write all those things I told you yesterday against Kennedy's policy, don't use his name now; speak instead of the policy of the United States government."

Toward 5 o'clock, Fidel Castro declared that since there was nothing we could do to alter the tragedy, we must try to put our time to good use in spite of it. He wanted to accompany me in person on a visit to a *granja de pueblo* (state farm), where he had been engaging in some experiments. His present obsession is agriculture. He reads nothing but agronomical studies and reports. He dwells lyrically on the soil, fertilizers, and the possibilities which will give Cuba enough sugar cane by 1970 to achieve economic independence.

We went by car, with the radio on. The Dallas police were now hot on the trail of the assassin. He is a Russian spy, says the news commentator. Five minutes later, correction: he is a spy married to a Russian. Fidel said: "There, didn't I tell you; it'll be my turn next." But not yet. The next word was: the assassin is a Marxist deserter. Then the word came through, in effect, that the assassin was a young man who was a member of the "Fair Play for Cuba Committee," that he was an admirer of Fidel Castro. Fidel declared: "If they had had proof, they would have said he was an agent, an accomplice, a hired killer. In saying simply that he is an admirer, this is just to try and make an association in people's minds between the name of Castro and the emotion awakened by the assassination. This is a publicity method, a propaganda device. It's terrible. But you know, I'm sure this will all soon blow over. There are too many competing policies in the United States for any single one to be able to impose itself universally for very long."

We arrived at the *granja de pueblo,* where the farmers welcomed Fidel. At that very moment, a speaker announced over the radio that it was now known that the assassin is a "pro-Castro Marxist." One commentator followed another; the remarks became increasingly emotional, increasingly aggressive. Fidel then excused himself: "We shall have to give up the visit to the farm." We went on toward Matanzas from where he could telephone President Dorticós. On the way he had questions: "Who is Lyndon Johnson? What is his reputation? What were his relations with Kennedy? With Khrushchev? What was his position at the time of the attempted invasion of Cuba?" Finally and most important of all: "What authority does he exercise over the CIA?" Then abruptly he looked at his watch, saw that it would be half an hour before we reached Matanzas and, practically on the spot, he dropped off to sleep.

After Matanzas, where he must have decreed a state of alert, we returned to Varadero for dinner. Quoting the words spoken to him by a woman shortly before, he said to me that it was an irony of history for the Cubans, in the situation to which they had been reduced by the blockade, to have to mourn the death of a President of the United States. "After all," he added, "there are perhaps some people in the world to whom this news is cause for rejoicing. The South Vietnamese guerrillas, for example, and also, I would imagine, Madame Nhu!"

I thought of the people of Cuba, accustomed to the sight of posters like the one depicting the Red Army with maquis superimposed in front, and the screaming captions "HALT, MR. KENNEDY! CUBA IS NOT ALONE. . . . " I thought of all those who had been led to associate their deprivations with the policies of President John F. Kennedy.

At dinner I was able to take up all my questions. What had motivated Castro to endanger the peace of the world with the missiles in Cuba? How dependent was Cuba on the Soviet Union? Is it not possible to envisage relations between Cuba and the United States along the same lines as those between Finland and the Russians? How was the transition made from the humanism of Sierra Maestra to the Marxism-Leninism of 1961? Fidel Castro, once more in top form, had an explanation for everything. Then he questioned me once more on Kennedy, and each time I eulogized the intellectual qualities of the assassinated President, I awakened the keenest interest in him.

The Cubans have lived with the United States in that cruel intimacy so familiar to me of the colonized with their colonizers. Nevertheless, it was an intimacy. In that very seductive city of Havana to which we returned in the evening, where the luminous signboards with Marxist slogans have replaced the Coca Cola and toothpaste billboards, in the midst of Soviet exhibits and Czechoslovakian trucks, a certain American emotion vibrated in the atmosphere, compounded of resentment, of concern, of anxiety, yet also, in spite of everything, of a mysterious, almost imperceptible, rapprochement. After all, this American President was able to reach accord with our Russian friends during his lifetime, said a young Cuban intellectual to me as I was taking my leave. It was almost as though he were apologizing for not rejoicing at the assassination.

"Unrepentant, Unyielding": An Interview with Viet Cong Prisoners

BERNARD B. FALL

FEBRUARY 4, 1967

Lai-Khé, South Vietnam

Two years ago, Lai-Khé was a tranquil place hardly an hour's ride from Saigon, and the home of the *Institut de Recherches du Caoutchouc du Vietnam,* a research institute jointly financed by the French rubber plantations in Vietnam. There was some rubber production as such, but the low, yellow-stuccoed laboratory building with its neat rows of glittering instruments and vats full of creamy latex, the clean native village of the rubber tappers, and the spacious villas for the French scientists and administrators, gave the whole place the air of a well-funded American agricultural college. The war changed all that, for Lai-Khé is at the edge of a forest complex situated between two rivers which eventually merge about 20 miles from Saigon, thus forming a triangle pointing at South Vietnam's capital. In a series of swift attacks on the Vietnamese Army posts at the edge of the forest in late 1964, the Viet Cong had completely dismantled the whole government civilian and military apparatus in the area and taken over the town of Ben-Suc, a pleasant little place inside a meander of the Saigon River, big enough to appear on most maps of Vietnam.

Repeated attempts by the Vietnamese to retake the area failed (the stripped hulls of three American M-113 armored personnel carriers lost to accurate Viet Cong fire still lie near the road to Ben-Suc), and even a push by the U.S. 173rd Airborne Brigade in 1965 yielded no tangible results. Progressively, the 210 square miles of forest between Ben-Suc and Ben-Cat acquired its sinister reputation as the "Iron Triangle," said to contain not only crack VC elements, but also the command structure of MR-4, the Liberation Front's 4th Military Region covering the Saigon area. It was from the Iron Triangle that the repeated successful VC penetrations of Saigon's huge Tan Son Nhut airbase had come. As long as the Iron Triangle existed, Saigon itself would be exposed to the threat of attack. The decision was therefore made late in 1966 to destroy the Iron Triangle in the largest concentrated attack by

U.S. Forces since the Vietnam war began. The operation, begun on January 8, opened with the 1st Infantry in position on the Iron Triangle's northern base, with the 25th Infantry Division 196th Light Brigade blocking all escapes on the left flank across the Saigon River, while the ARVN's 5th Division and parts of the 173rd Airborne Brigade held the right flank. Other units, including the ARVN 8th Infantry which, the year before, had broken at Ben-Suc, further reinforced the assault units. In all, 28 combat battalions—over 30,000 men with their logistical support—and 35 artillery batteries (140 field guns) had converged on the Triangle. But the key actors, on the American side, were not the men, but the unleashed machines.

For days before the actual attack, the windows of Saigon had been rattling from concentrated B-52 raids on the Triangle, at least 13 of them in eight days, unloading hundreds of tons of heavy explosives on every raid, plowing under the Viet Cong's incredibly extensive network of underground tunnels and depots. Thanks also to American technology, the Air Force cartographers are capable of providing the military with fantastically detailed photo maps in color within a few hours after the strikes. On these maps, the trails of the bomb carpets in the jungle look like the tracks of tiger claws on an animal's skin—claw marks that are three miles long and over 100 feet wide. Whenever the strategic bombers were not over the Triangle, artillery barrages and the hammering of the light fighter-bombers saw to it that no Viet Cong would try to break out from the hell that the Triangle had become.

But the newest weapon of them all and, in its own way, the most incredibly impressive for all its civilian normality, was an assemblage of perhaps 80 bulldozers, in many cases airlifted into the midst of the jungle by huge "Skycrane" helicopters or the somewhat smaller "Chinooks." Their job was simple: eliminate the jungle once and for all. By the third day of the battle, huge yellow scars had begun to be clearly visible in the deep jungle green as the bulldozers began to plow down the jungle as if some insane developer were suddenly hell-bent on covering Vietnam with Levittowns or parking lots. Such Viet Cong hideouts or tunnels as there were, either were crushed or their exits bulldozed shut, for in many cases the adversary (as well as civilians) hiding in the tunnels disappeared in their deepest recesses rather than surrender. "Tunnel rats," American soldiers specially picked for their small size and equipped with gas projectors and what looked like flamethrowers, sometimes penetrated for hundreds of meters into the burrows, looking for what was said to be a veritable "subway" crossing the whole Triangle. It was never found and perhaps never existed.

Inexorably, the bulldozers bit into the countryside, cutting huge swaths of cleared land right across the Triangle. They were followed by flame-thrower tanks and teams on foot, destroying the felled trees with fire. And not only the trees: every human inhabitation within the beaten zone, be it an isolated hut which may have been used by the Viet Cong, or a whole little hamlet inhabited for years by charcoal kilners—non-white Saigon cooks with charcoal almost exclusively—went up in flames. There was one day toward the end of the week in which the air was totally still and the sky as transparently fresh and pure as on a spring day in America. Yet as I joined a new unit within the Triangle by helicopter, the whole sky, literally in a 360° circle, was framed in by perfectly straight black columns: the earth was being scorched on the whole perimeter of the Iron Triangle. And the town of Ben-Suc was among them.

Ben-Suc had been occupied in less than two minutes by two battalions of the 28th Infantry, followed by Vietnamese troops, while overhead loud-speaker helicopters instructed the population to stay put, for "anyone seen running away will be considered a Viet Cong." The 3,500 women, children and old men (there was not one able-bodied man in the lot) stayed put as Vietnamese Navy landing craft beached in front of the village and began to take aboard the population for a 10-mile ride downstream to a temporary refugee camp at Phu-Cuong. They went without offering resistance, believing that they would merely be taken away temporarily until the operation was over. But Operation "Cedar Falls" (the code name for the whole undertaking) was, in the words of a briefing officer, an "operation with a real difference"—there would be no coming back, because Ben-Suc would be put to the torch and then razed with bulldozers, just like the forest and part of the rubber plantation. A clamor arose as the women begged to be allowed to return long enough to dig up their meager treasures, for as in Europe during the Thirty Years War, the peasants of Vietnam have long resorted to burying their money and jewelry in earthenware jars to keep them from being pilfered by government troops or taxed away by the Viet Cong. The respite was granted and the American troops even made arrangements to evacuate the most precious movable belongings of the villagers, their buffaloes and wagons.

"Make damn' sure the buffaloes stay with the refugees and don't end up in the market place," I overheard the earnest young major in charge of the evacuation say to one of his subordinates escorting the landing craft.

As the burning houses began to collapse and the bulldozers methodically bit into the remaining standing walls, a new town seemed to emerge altogether from the debris. Ben-Suc was honeycombed with tunnels, trenches and stone-lined bunkers, and every house was built atop huge rice caches carefully lined with wicker mats. There were hundreds of tons there (the total "take" in the Triangle was 3,170 tons), far in excess of what Ben-Suc could have produced, let alone saved from previous crops.

"You see," said the young major, "Ben-Suc was a major transit point of supplies both for War Zone 'C' and probably the VC's central headquarters. The stuff would come up here by motor sampan and the population then transfers it on its buffalo carts and off it goes into the deep jungle in escorted convoys."

"Look at the rice," he said, picking up a handful which he carried in the breastpocket of his combat jacket, "there are at least 20 different brands here from all over South Vietnam and probably from the U.S., too. I've sent a batch down to Intelligence. They'll find out where it came from."

He looked back on smoking Ben-Suc with real affection as he held its rice in his hand.

"Would you believe that we offered the women that they could take the rice with them as their own if they told us where the rice caches were? *Not one* of them spoke up. Now *that's* loyalty."

As he spoke, he opened his hand to let the golden rice grains fall on the ground, stopped in mid-gesture, and put the rice back into his pocket. I scooped up a handful from the smoldering heap to my right and put it in one of my pockets. That much of Ben-Suc would stay alive. Later, what was left of Ben-Suc would be obliterated by Air Force bombers in order to destroy whatever underground caches and depots had been missed by the bulldozers.

In the evening at the mess tent, the day's doings were toted up as officers from nearby units came in for briefing and for a hasty bite to eat. There were over 400 dead by "body count," 62 prisoners, 18 machine-guns (including three brand-new American M-60's), more than 200 individual weapons (there would be close to 400 by the end of the operation, along with 508 enemy dead and 6,000 displaced civilians), and miles and miles of destroyed tunnels.

A whole jungle hospital, with two levels below ground and one above ground, had been captured.

"You should have seen the equipment," said the G-2. "Some of the stuff was good enough to be used in our hospital. West German surgical scissors at $45 apiece by the trunkful; French antibiotics."

Now, according to an order issued by General Westmoreland, on September 20, 1966, in compliance with Article 33 of the 1949 Geneva Convention, "captured or abandoned medical supplies or facilities will not be destroyed intentionally." I was told, however, how the field hospital had been disposed of.

"Well," said an eyewitness, "we removed all the medical equipment, and then all there was left was just another empty bunker and tunnel system. So we destroyed it like everything else." The same also happened to a smaller VC aid station.

An NBC television crew with a neighboring outfit witnessed and photographed the mutilation of a dead enemy soldier, but the NBC hierarchy in New York, mindful of the uproar created more than a year ago when an enterprising CBS cameraman filmed the burning of a village with cigarette lighters, "killed" the sequence. Conversely, a reporter for a Texas newspaper was wounded that day by a VC sniper while he was flying about in a medevac helicopter clearly marked with large red crosses. It is this kind of mutual barbarization, the needless cruelties inflicted far beyond military necessity, which will make the Vietnam war stand out in modern history.

"You should see 'em," said the burly prison camp commander. "Unrepentant, unyielding. The only thing they're sorry for is that they got taken alive."

He was referring to Professor Vinh Long and Middle-Level Teacher Tran Van Tan, captured in the Iron Triangle, and probably the highest-ranking Liberation Front cadres thus far to fall into American hands. Both were native Southerners, Vinh Long being born in Danang, and Tan in the province of the Iron Triangle. Both had gone to North Vietnam in 1954 when the country was partitioned, and both had gone on to higher studies. Long got his AB in physics and mathematics in 1963, Tan an AB in education in 1962. Both were "finds" in their own right, since they were involved in running the general education department of MR-4. *[For security reasons, we have substituted fictitious names for the real names of the prisoners interviewed by Mr. Fall.*—THE EDITORS]

The prisoner-of-war enclosure of the 1st Division was a small clearing in the rubber tree forest, surrounded by concertina barbed wire in which two squad tents had been erected. Within the enclosure was an even smaller enclosure, housing three captive women, one of them a pretty 19-year-old Eurasian girl with long red hair and freckles, but almond-shaped eyes. "She was a cook in the outfit," explained an escort.

Vietnam can be bitingly cold in January, and we were shivering in our jungle combat uniforms, particularly after a night spent rolled in a poncho liner. The prisoners were lying on normal Army cots and had been issued three woolen blankets each, and each of them seemed to have his share of C-rations. Courteously sitting up on their cots as we approached, they looked, wrapped in their blankets, like green-clad desert Arabs. Intelligent, ascetic faces with deep-burning eyes, showing no fear—just curiosity as to what next. I first sat down with Vinh Long, flanked by a Vietnamese sergeant acting as an interpreter, and an American captain. The captain was showing signs of a very bad cold, sneezing and fumbling through his pockets for an absent handkerchief. The Vietnamese prisoner picked up the C-ration box, searched around in it and came up with the tiny roll of toilet paper it contains, which he handed to the captain.

Long said that he spoke no French, but he spoke Russian. I explained to him in Russian that I was a college professor myself, not a soldier, and that I was not interested in military information. I also apologized for my bad Vietnamese and for the fact that I'd have to use an interpreter. That's all right he said, now clearly relaxed. Who had ordered him to return South?

"The party. But I would have gone in any case because I wanted to. I was happy. I visited Hanoi before I left."

He had left the North in December 1963 for the Duong Minh Chau area—the headquarters area of the Liberation Front. Before his departure from the North, where he has been stationed with the 338th Division at Xuan-Mai (he offered no information on units except those already known from papers captured with him), he had been briefed on the war here.

"We were given an accurate picture of what was going on in the South and told that victory would be easy. Of course, with the Americans here, it's not so easy." He picked up a cigarette in the C-ration carton, offered the others around, and then looked straight at me.

"But we'll win, anyway. Every country in the world helps us. Look at the American, Morrison, who committed suicide because he disagreed with American policies."

True, I said. But how about the other 200 million Americans who don't kill themselves?

"The Liberation Front forces will win in any case, because all the Vietnamese people help us. This war can only be settled among the Vietnamese themselves. The Americans and their allies must go."

But he had seen the Americans, now. Realistically, could they be made to go?

"Lots of American soldiers do get killed in battles. Look at Chulai, Pleiku, Tayninh. We can do it."

To the Viet Cong, those battles, which we either claim as having won ourselves (Chulai), or as having suffered only minor losses (Pleiku), represent major victories. I said that I feared he was confusing the Americans with the French. The French weren't one-tenth as powerful as the Americans.

"Oh, I know the French were weaker than the U.S. is, but we'll still win because our cause is right. Do Americans think they can stay with this kind of war for 30, 40 years? Because that is what this is going to take."

The members of the Front are known to practice self-criticism. If he were to criticize himself for his activities over the past year, would he do something differently? There was a momentary lowering of the head, and a great deal of pride in the short answer: "I wouldn't change a thing."

And what would he do after all this was over?

"When I get out of this a free man, I will again work for the Liberation Front."

There was a poem, in wartime France, about a resistance member who had given exactly that answer to a German military court:

Et si c'était à refaire
Je referais ce chemin . . .

Yes, but that was 23 years ago, and the Nazis were the bad guys, and here the Free World is fighting the good fight with billions of dollars' worth of firepower against bad guys like Long and the freckle-faced cook.

"I told you," said the captain. "Unrepentant. Unyielding."

Tan was less tense than Vinh Long; perhaps because we had switched from a Vietnamese interpreter to an American GI (one of the few real side-benefits of the whole mess is that the U.S. Armed Forces are going to have more Vietnamese linguists than all the universities of the whole world taken together; and that is not a figure of speech). Tan, in addition to education, had minored in anatomy and physiology and had been the inspector of the VC's educational system for the military zone. Though having fought in the Viet Minh against the French since 1950, he only joined the Communist Party here in South Vietnam in 1966, and like Vinh Long, he was sure that his side was winning.

"It's only natural that we should receive help from North Vietnam. After all, we're all Vietnamese, aren't we? Just as the Saigon government gets American help, the Front gets help from the socialist countries." There was a pause, and Tan said with great emphasis. "And it will never stop. *Never.* Even if their help does not rise above the present level, we'll win."

How did he feel he was being considered in the movement, being an intellectual, I asked. Wasn't he treated with a certain amount of suspicion?

"Oh, there is a certain amount of suspicion against intellectuals, but that is understandable. After all being intellectuals, they are divorced from the masses and the working class, in particular.

"We Southern cadres are not discriminated against by the Northerners, although it did happen that some of the 'regroupees' [Southerners who went to the North in 1954 and then were reinfiltrated. B.F.] would desert from homesickness once they came South again. It doesn't affect our status at all."

But as a man trained in dialectical materialism, how could he dismiss

American power so lightly in his estimates of the outcome of the war? That, to him, was no problem at all:

"After all, the Front is fighting a just war, as a true representative of the South Vietnamese people. This being a just war, we shall win."

But other "just wars" were lost in other places . . .

"Indonesia?" he interjected helpfully.

No, I said, but Greece, Malaya and the Philippines for example. As an intellectual, he could not dismiss these defeats lightly, unless he felt that these wars weren't "just wars."

"Not at all. They were just wars, to be sure, and the people were defeated, but only temporarily. The will to fight on remained in their hearts and they surely will rise again. But here, there won't be even such a temporary setback. The party has been active in South Vietnam for 36 years and thus defeat of its organization is impossible now."

"Here, the guerrillas will become stronger and stronger with the help of the socialist countries."

Yes, but did not the Sino-Soviet split introduce a weakening factor in this aid effort? Now he was on the defensive for the first time.

"Those struggles for greater socialist unity no more affect the socialist camp's effort in Vietnam than the French-American dispute affects power relationships in the West."

Come now, I said, if you read *Pravda* and the *Peking Review* and the incredibly severe mutual accusations between Peking and Moscow, you wouldn't describe this as a "struggle for greater unity."

"Let's not get into this. We'll win in any case."

Even if South Vietnam is totally destroyed in the process by American artillery and bombers? He had seen what happened here. It's happening all over the country. There was a hurt look in his eyes as the implication sunk in: "If South Vietnam is lost, we have got nothing left to live for. We would rather be dead than live as slaves. Have *you* ever seen anybody who wants to live as a slave?"

No, I had never seen anybody who wanted to, but I'd seen plenty of cases where people *had* to because they were given no choice. And I cited, on his side of the fence, the Budapest uprisings, and on our side, the Dominican Republic operation.

"These are small things," was his reply. And what did he think of how this whole war got started, I asked.

"Ah, the Americans are sly and clever," said Tan, whereupon the Americans present broke out in uncontrolled laughter. The interpreter explained to Tan that the Americans themselves never thought of themselves as either sly or clever. He nodded pensively, as if this were an important revelation.

"You know, they never smile," said the captain to me. I told him that considering their position and what was in store for them—transfer to the far-from-tender South Vietnamese—I wouldn't smile, either.

"The Americans," Tan went on, "took over military planning for the Saigon government. Their economic experts forced the South Vietnamese to work for them and Diem persecuted everybody. He would have killed us all, and that is why we revolted."

Tan, who had been silent for a moment, looked up and asked the interpreter if he, too, could ask me a few questions since I was a professor. Of course, he could.

"Do you know whether we will be treated as prisoners according to the Geneva Convention?"

Obviously, word must have gotten around among the Viet Cong about how badly most of the prisoners are still treated on this side, all promises of improvement notwithstanding, with the Americans reluctant to intervene once the prisoners have been transferred. All that I could say lamely was that he was being treated according to the Convention right now.

"Do American families approve of their soldiers here killing innocent people?"

Most of them weren't aware of innocent people being killed here, I said. As for the soldiers themselves, they were carrying out orders just as he was.

"Yes, but I'm here as a Vietnamese, in my own country. Why are the Americans all over the place, in Greece, in Laos?"

Well, they were helping their own allies, just as he expected the socialist camp to help him. But the socialist camp's aid was "political," he retorted. To which I answered that the Chinese weapons we had captured yesterday did not look "political" to me. A quick fleeting smile conceded the point to me.

"You may be right on that, but after all, it is the Americans who are the aggressors."

Why were the North Vietnamese so difficult about negotiations? I asked. On this, he was probably to the left (or was it right?) of official Front and North Vietnamese policy. Like Ambassador Henry Cabot Lodge here, who feels that negotiations are pointless if "victory by fade-out" can be achieved—a point which he has repeatedly made ever since September 1965—Tan felt that there was little to negotiate since his side was winning and since Vietnam was "one country."

Contrary to the Front's and Hanoi's avowed programs, he felt that reunification would come rapidly if the Americans were to leave. In fact, he did not believe that a divided Vietnam would "work." I told him that, for the sake of world peace, both Germany and Korea had accepted more or less permanent division.

"That's all right for them. But we rose up and fought for our own independence. We don't want to stay divided."

Yet, when asked what he would have done differently, Tan said that he would have negotiated last year, before the massive input of American troops, and he came through with a small truth which confirmed what intelligence specialists here had been wondering about for quite a while:

"You know, this is no longer the 'Special War' General Taylor talked about, but a new type of war [here the interpreter was faced with one of those party neologisms for which there was no acceptable single word] where outside forces became primary.

"The decision that the character of the war had changed was made late last year here in the South, either by the People's Revolutionary [*i.e.*, South Vietnamese Communist] Party, or by the Central Committee of the Liberation Front. But when I was captured I did not yet know what this decision entailed."

As far as is known, the decision entails the maintenance of large units in reserve at more or less secure bases, while small forward units inflict heavy losses on the allied forces. How well this tactic works was shown this week, when the U.S. suffered the highest casualties of the war (1,200 in one week)—all as a result of dozens of pinprick attacks.

But Tan knew that he was on the right path. As I was getting up to leave, he said earnestly: "We are not fighting here to have a cease-fire and prolonged division. It is the Americans who sent their troops here. They will have to make the decision to leave. Nobody can make it for them."

As I walked out, after he had ceremoniously shaken hands with the captain, the interpreter and me, Tan said something very rapidly.

"He's asking you to thank the American people and Lord Russell for what they are doing."

Back at Division, reports were still filtering in. Ben-Suc was now totally evacuated. A herd of 61 reluctant buffaloes which proved intractable to adult Americans—it seems to be true that buffaloes find the white man's smell offensive—had required the re-airlifting in of 10 Vietnamese buffalo-boys aged six to 10 who rounded up the two-ton beasts without much difficulty. The town was now bulldozed flat and awaited its final airstrike.

Standing in his map tent, the brigade commander was going through the details of the pull-out, for after all the blood and the firepower spent here, the Iron Triangle would not be held.

"We just haven't got the troops to stay here, and the Arvins [for ARVN, the South Vietnamese Army] simply won't."

"In other words," I said, "the VC will move right back in again."

"Sure," said the general. "But they'll find their dugouts smashed, huge open lanes in the forest, and at least we'll have helicopter LZ's [landing zones] all over the place. Next time's going to be easier to get back in."

As I walked out of the command post, a short, whitewashed obelisk caught my eye, standing at the entrance to Lai-Khé. It was a monument to the dead of the 2nd Moroccan Spahi Regiment, the 2nd Cambodian Mobile Battalion, the 3rd and 25th Algerian Rifle Battalions, and 3rd Battalion, 4th Tunisian Rifles, who had died for the Iron Triangle between 1946 and 1954.

Chinese Checkers

JOHN OSBORNE

MARCH 11, 1972

This account of the Nixon trip to China, written in Washington after the President's return, begins with a remembered scene in the banquet hall of the Hang-chou Hotel in the resort city of Hang-chou, the capital of Chekiang Province, where Generalissimo Chiang Kai-shek was born 85 years ago. Premier Chou En-lai is seated at the President's right, Mrs. Nixon at her husband's left. Through an interpreter, also a woman, Pat Nixon and the wife of a Chinese official are talking with a show of great animation. Premier Chou and the President have fallen silent. They have the look of men who for the moment have had more than enough of each other, and no wonder. It is the last night but one of the President's seven days in China, the days that he is soon to say made up "the week that changed the world." He and Chou have been nearly 40 hours together at public dinners and entertainments and in private converse. They have just spent a cold and windy afternoon in a tour of West Lake, the glory of China and of Hang-chou, and its lovely islets set at the foot of misty mountains, smiling into cameras and feeding goldfish and acting out for the world their portrayal of old enemies learning and trying to be friends. Premier Chou, a grey little man of 72, gazes straight ahead . . . for minutes on end. Mr. Nixon cups his chin in his right hand and stares upward at the high ceiling. He and his host for the evening, Chairman Nan Pinh of the Chekiang Revolutionary Committee, have delivered their respective toasts, mercifully brief for once. The several hundred Chinese in the huge room have applauded the President's quotation of the saying that "heaven is above and beneath are Hang-chou and Soochow" and have then received in stony and puzzled quiet his added observation that "the proud citizens of this province would say that Peking is the head of China, but Hang-chou is the heart of China." They would say, an embarrassed Chinese official explains to a table of reporters, that Peking is the head and heart of China. Suddenly, the President's third public dinner of the week and his fourth in Chou's company is over. Nixon and Chou rise and, with the others of the official party, walk slowly up a long aisle from the head table to the exit. American reporters are standing along the aisle and the President introduces some of them to Chou. Near the door, during one such pause, the President remarks that he and the Premier have been hard at work all week and still have work to do that night. Chou smiles dimly and with his right hand gives the President a gentle shove toward the door, as if to say that's right and let's get on with it. Mr. Nixon halts once more, in a cluster of reporters, and Chou again touches his shoulder and urges him toward and finally through the door. Walking behind them, an American official clutches his stomach in mock dismay and murmurs his thanks to God that only one more Chinese banquet lies between the Nixon party and the journey home.

This observer wouldn't know how Mr. Nixon came over on this and other public occasions to the home and worldwide television audience, the audience that the President twice declared with evident pleasure to be the largest that had ever witnessed an event. To a reporter tagging along with him in China, the President seemed to be strikingly and consciously diffident throughout the visit. He kept his hands, those famous twitching hands, under rigid control. This was easier than usual to do, because at no point from the arrival in Peking to the departure from Shanghai did the Chinese authorities allow crowds to assemble in his honor and invite the familiar Nixon salute. The interpreters and other functionaries who accompanied the press invariably said that the few hundreds of Chinese noted along the streets traveled by the Nixon party would have been there anyhow. Even when they were seen to be watching the motorcades, any special interest in their improbable visitor was explicitly denied.

One could guess that the President had been forewarned and had determined not to obtrude himself upon his Chinese hosts and the Chinese scene any more than his presence demanded. The result, in any case, was that an occasion that might have been expected to elicit some new and enlightening aspects of the Nixon personality was curiously barren in this respect. His talent for the utterance of banalities was unimpaired, as he demonstrated when he remarked at the Great Wall that "you have to conclude that this is really a great wall" and called upon Secretary of State William P. Rogers and nearby reporters to agree that it was. Mrs. Nixon, industriously providing the television crews with something to do when the President was immured in private conferences, emitted a daily stream of bright inanities. In the kitchens of the Peking Hotel, where favored guests who don't rate the handsome government guest houses are lodged in funereal grandeur, she stated that the boggling piles and varieties of Chinese food laid out for her inspection looked good enough to eat. When her host at the moment, the chairman of the hotel revolutionary committee, invited her to stay for lunch and sample the food, the consternation that sated Western guests in the Far East are bound to feel from time to time was evident as she begged off and promised to return for that pleasure at some later date. In the freezing cold at the Great Wall and the Ming Tombs, in the light snow that fell over the Forbidden City and its fantastic succession of ancient palaces and museums when the President visited them, Nixon appeared as usual without a hat and was dutifully trailed by the Secretary of State and ranking aides in a condition of hatless and obvious discomfort that their master chose to ignore. When he invited the American press party to pose with him for a group picture at the guest house assigned to him in Hang-chou, he turned up in the open and chilly patio where the photograph was taken with neither hat nor topcoat and for 12 petrifying minutes assured the journalists that he understood their need for hard news from his closed and secret conferences with Chinese officials and was sorry that he couldn't do much about it until a joint communique was issued in Shanghai. These incidentals intrigued the reporters and, the Hang-chou picture episode excepted, amused them. But there was something about the China adventure that made all this seem irrelevant and inconsequential. It was as if the event and the results that could follow it dwarfed the Nixons and their less impressive characteristics and invested the President with a stature that he could not attain by and for himself alone.

The secrecy that cloaked the President's and Henry Kissinger's meetings with Premier Chou En-lai and Chairman Mao Tse-tung, and Secretary Rogers' huddles with lesser officials, was soon to affect and distort the reporting and interpretation of the announced results. The few details that could be extracted from the President's press spokesman and other American officials in China and after the return to Washington did throw some light upon the proceedings, however. It turned out to be true, as had been supposed and reported, that the President and Kissinger were as surprised as everybody else was when the rarely seen or accessible Chairman Mao received them on the Monday of their arrival. At 78, often reported in recent years to be either dead or incapacitated, Mao appeared to Nixon and Kissinger during their hour with him to be in excellent health, alert, and in total command of the People's Republic. With necessary breaks for translation allowed, the half hour or so of substantive talk that the President and Kissinger had with Mao could hardly have encompassed the range of issues that the Americans wanted the press to believe it did. Nothing whatever about the substance of the talk with Mao was divulged. The only fact that emerged, other than the Chairman's appearance of bouncy health, was that Premier Chou, who on other occasions seemed to the Americans to be the paramount and controlling figure on the China scene, played the part of a humble follower and subordinate when he was in Mao's presence with them. Chou's demeanor presumably contributed to the impression, reported by Kissinger, that the Premier checked with Mao at every important stage of the secret discussions. Nixon and Kissinger had never been told when and where they would meet Mao, and they didn't know for sure until they were about to leave China that they wouldn't have a second meeting with him.

It was intimated to Kissinger during his preparatory visits in July and October that the Chinese authorities would be offended if the President traveled within China in American rather than People's Republic aircraft. Mr. Nixon's *Air Force One* (properly and pompously the *Spirit of '76*) and a second Boeing 707 jet delivered him and his supporting party to the Peking airport. After that, on the short flights from Peking to Hang-chou and from Hang-chou to Shanghai, the President and his assistants traveled in two Ilyushin 18s. The same planes transported the press party ahead of the President, then were flown back to Peking and Hang-chou to pick up the Nixon group. Because other Ilyushins were to be seen at the Peking and Shanghai airports, always grounded while the President was anywhere near, the reporters assumed that only these particular planes and their crews had been checked out for safety and competence, to the satisfaction of solicitous Chinese officials. By comparison with the spacious Boeings of the presidential fleet, the Ilyushins are cramped and noisy jet-prop craft. They could not have carried even the minimal communications equipment that a U.S. President requires. Presumably without offense to the sensitive Chinese, the President's Boeing followed the Ilyushins by 15 minutes and was parked as inconspicuously as possible at the Hang-chou and Shanghai airports. At the Hang-chou airport, a rather touching symbol of Chinese pride and anxiety to measure up to the logistical demands of the Nixon visit was observed. It was a large and attractive terminal building, beside a smaller and shabby old one, the larger erected within 40 days by some 10,000 laborers and artisans last September and October after it was certain that the President would be coming to Hang-chou.

In deference to Chinese sensibilities, the President and his companions relied entirely upon interpreters provided by the People's Republic. The same young women who served in this capacity at the public and televised appearances translated for the President and Kissinger at the closed conferences. The confidence thus reposed in Chinese officialdom was not completely unalloyed, however. John Holdridge, a Kissinger assistant who speaks and understands Mandarin Chinese, sat in at all of the President's and Kissinger's meetings with Chou. Two State Department language specialists accompanied Rogers at his sessions. Holdridge and his State Department colleagues, Alfred Jenkins and Roger Freeman, kept quiet (and generally unneeded) check upon the Chinese translation and prepared voluminous records of the proceedings for White House and State Department files.

One may be sure that these records are far more complete and revealing than the "complete and adequate report" provided by the President and his spokesmen in Shanghai and Washington proved to be. The report so described by the President's press secretary, Ronald Ziegler, consisted of the joint American and Chinese communique issued in Shanghai the evening before the President left China, Henry Kissinger's cautious elaboration of the communique at a press conference in Shanghai, and the speech that Mr. Nixon delivered when he landed at Andrews Air Force Base. The comment that follows is written with the assumption that readers of this journal have had a surfeit of quotation from the communique, the Kissinger press conference, and the Nixon address. My purpose in the remainder of this report is to summarize the understandings of what did and didn't transpire in China that the administration wants to convey and my estimate of the Nixon account.

I find it believable that the President and his Chinese conferees reached no "written or unwritten agreements." The few concrete accomplishments that are claimed—moves toward expanded trade, cultural exchanges, regular diplomatic communication short of formal recognition—justify the rather exalted Nixon estimate of their importance only in the sense that they signify the beginnings of accommodation between two powers that have been isolated from each other and in a state of declared hostility to each other since the People's Republic was founded in 1949. I doubt that the opportunity given Nixon on the American side and Chou and Mao on the Chinese side to explore and test out each other's perceptions of the world and its problems, as a somewhat enchanted American adviser to the President put it after the return to Washington, is as important and as promising for the future as Mr. Nixon is said to think it is. Since Kissinger visited Peking last July, the same informants have been telling Washington reporters how fully and admirably steeped in American lore and attitudes Premier Chou En-lai is. If Mr. Nixon had to go to Peking, as he said he did, to learn in person from the Chinese leaders of "their total belief, their total dedication to their system of government," then he and his countrymen are in a sad plight. It was not anything that Nixon could have learned anew about his Chinese hosts and their purposes, that gives the Nixon visit to China substantial significance. What makes it meaningful is the fact that it occurred; that the Chinese Communists were willing to receive him and that he was willing to go to them, in defiance of ingrained and powerful prejudices and preconceptions in both countries. The enchanted American adviser whom I have just quoted, rather disparagingly, was closer to reality when he said after his return to Washington that Chou and Mao are likely to have at least as much trouble with the extremist factions in their society, in the Nixon aftermath, as the President is already having with some of his disillusioned conservatives.

The conservatives are principally alarmed by what they take to be the evidence in the Shanghai communique that Nixon has agreed to sell out Chiang Kai-shek and his Republic of China on Taiwan in return for a Chinese Communist undertaking to further a negotiated settlement of the Vietnam and Indochina war. There can be no doubt that the U.S. interest in Taiwan has taken second place to the U.S. interest in achieving a full accommodation with Communist China. But the interest in Taiwan and the commitment to defend it against mainland military aggression were in decline before Mr. Nixon went to Peking. The suspicion that the President persuaded the Peking leadership to push the Hanoi Communists toward a settlement of the war, at the Taiwan government's expense, rests only upon the semantics and omissions of the Shanghai communique. My hunch, based upon no better evidence, is that if there was a failure in Peking it was the President's failure to make any progress toward a negotiated end of the Indochina war.

On the Disaster

EDITORIAL

MAY 3, 1975

The collapse of the American adventure in Indochina came just as we were embarking on the Bicentennial observances. A pall would in any case have been cast over the festivities: how could it have been otherwise as long as the United States continued to fuel a fratricidal war and impede a negotiated peace? But the events unfolding so quickly in Vietnam and Cambodia seemed almost to turn our days of national celebration into judgment days. Two hundred years have passed since the farmers of Lexington and Concord fired the first shots of the revolution; and for 25 of those years our might has been deployed to frustrate an indigenous political and social revolution in Vietnam. Finally it was clear that American power had failed in its squalid mission.

No just cause is served by idealizing the Vietnamese revolution or minimizing its proclivity to cruelty. The late Paul Mus, perhaps the wisest student of Vietnamese culture, saw "great violence and extreme coercion" as inevitable features of change in Vietnam—even if the French and the Americans had not intruded into its history. The victory of Hanoi is not, then, an intrinsically joyful event. But the excruciating agony suffered by Vietnam and Cambodia is largely of our making. No reparations we could pay will balance the evil we did there.

The Vietnam debacle should occasion a reassessment of both the purposes and limits of our power; if the Bicentennial helps us focus on the contrast between our idealism and our crimes, so much the better. Those who have moved among the mighty will urge that the reassessment be general, almost abstract. They will call this restraint "avoiding recriminations," an unexceptionable aim. But we should not be excessively generous. A genuine reappraisal, moreover, should not fix only on the present incumbents and their policies, for the enormity before us was crafted as well by some of the most eminent latter-day doves. Nor would it be wholly out of place for the peace movement to review its role in allowing the government to sustain the war. For an end to the killing always entailed—as it does now—a coalition in Saigon willing to negotiate a political settlement with the NLF. Rather than discuss the complexities of a coalition, most popular antiwar politicians opted for facile sloganeering over withdrawal deadlines which, while hastening the return of the American troops, did little to stop the war.

Much of this may seem like ungrateful quibbling; but our stakes in self-scrutiny are great.

The New Terrorists

MICHAEL WALZER

AUGUST 30, 1975

Conceived as a form of political warfare against the established order, terrorism is now about 100 years old. The terrorism of governments, of course, is much older and, except in histories of the French Revolution, is rarely given its proper name. But the terrorism of dissident groups has its origins in the 1860s. It has been a feature of far left and ultra-nationalist politics ever since, though its legitimacy has been much debated and many leading leftists and nationalists have condemned it. Throughout these debates it's been assumed that a single phenomenon was at issue: killing for a cause, strategic murder. In fact two very different activities are hidden here behind a single name, and in the years since World War II, terrorism has undergone a radical transformation.

Until about the middle of the 20th century, terrorism was most often a modernist version of the older politics of assassination—the killing of particular people thought to be guilty of particular acts. Since that time terrorism has most often taken the form of random murder, its victims unknown in advance and, even from the standpoint of the terrorists, innocent of any crime. The change is of deep moral and political significance, though it has hardly been discussed. It represents the breakdown of a *political code*, worked out in the late 19th century and roughly analogous to the laws of war, developed at the same time.

I can best describe this code by giving some examples of "terrorists" who acted or tried to act in accordance with its norms. I have chose three historical cases, from different parts of the world. The first will be readily recognizable, for Albert Camus made it the basis of his play *The Just Assassins*.

• In the 1870s, a group of Russian revolutionaries decided to kill a Czarist official, the head of a police agency, a man personally involved in the repression of radical activity. They planned to blow him up in his carriage, and on the appointed day one of their number was in place along his usual route. As the carriage drew near, the young revolutionary, a bomb hidden under his coat, noticed that the official was not alone; on his lap he held two small children. The revolutionary looked, hesitated, decided not to throw his bomb; he would wait for another occasion. Camus has one of his comrades say, accepting this decision: "Even in destruction, there's a right way and a wrong way—and there are limits."

• During the years 1938–39, the Irish Republican Army waged a bombing campaign in Britain. In the course of this campaign, a republican militant was ordered to carry a pre-set time bomb to a London power station. He traveled by bicycle, the bomb in his basket, took a wrong turn, and got lost in the maze of London streets. As the time for the explosion drew near, he panicked, dropped his bike, and ran off. The bomb exploded, killing five passers-by. No one in the IRA (as it was then) thought this a victory for the cause; the men immediately involved were horrified. The campaign had been carefully planned, according to a recent historian of the IRA, so as to avoid the killing of innocent bystanders.

• In November, 1944, Lord Moyne, British Minister of State in the Middle East, was assassinated in Cairo by two members of the Stern Gang, a right wing Zionist group. The two assassins were caught minutes later by an Egyptian policeman. One of them described the capture at his trial: "We were being followed by the constable on his motorcycle. My comrade was behind me. I saw the constable approach him . . . I would have been able to kill the constable easily, but I contented myself with . . . shooting several times into the air. I saw my comrade fall off his bicycle. The constable was upon him. Again I could have eliminated the constable with a single bullet, but I did not. Then I was caught."

What is common to these three cases is a moral distinction, a line drawn between people who can and people who cannot be killed—the political equivalent of the line between combatants and noncombatants. The obliteration of this line is the critical feature of contemporary terrorism. In former times children, passers-by and sometimes even policemen were thought to be uninvolved in the political struggle, innocent people whom the terrorist had no right to kill. He did not even claim a right to terrorize them; in fact his activity was misnamed—a minor triumph for the forces of order. But today's terrorists earn their title. They have emptied out the category of innocent people; they claim a right to kill anyone; they seek to terrorize whole populations. The seizure of hostages (barred now in wartime) symbolizes a general devaluation of human life, which is most clearly expressed when the terrorist's victims are not held for ransom but simply killed. A bomb planted on a streetcorner, hidden in a bus station, thrown into a cafe or pub: this is a new way of taking aim, and it turns groups of people, without distinction, into targets.

I don't want to recommend assassination. It is a vile politics; its agents are usually gangsters (and sometimes madmen) in political dress. But we do judge assassins to some degree by their victims, and when the victims are Hitler-like in character, agents of oppression and cruelty, we may even praise the assassin's work. It is at least conceivable, though difficult, to be a "just assassin," while just terrorism is a contradiction in terms. For the assassin fights a limited war: he aims at known individuals and seeks specific political and social changes.

The new terrorism, on the other hand, is a total war against nations, ethnic groups, religions. Its strategic goals are the repression, exile or destruction of entire peoples. Thus the victory of the FLN in Algeria forced the emigration of the French *colons*, while the victory of the OAS would have brought savage repression for Algerian Arabs. If the Provisional IRA were ever to triumph in Northern Ireland, the majority of Protestants would have to leave. The PLO would destroy the Israeli state and force most of its citizens into exile, if it were able. Such goals cannot be kept secret; they are the unmistakable message of random murder—whatever the official program of the terrorist group. The line that marks off political agents from uninvolved men and women, officials from ordinary citizens, is critically important. Once it has been crossed, there is no further line to draw, no stopping place beyond which people can feel safe. Terrorism is the ultimate lawlessness, infinitely threatening to its potential victims, who believe (rightly, it seems to me) that no compromise is possible with their would-be murderers.

And yet terrorists operate today in what has to be called a permissive atmosphere. Statesmen rush about to make bargains with them; journalists construct elaborate *apologias* on their behalf. How is this indefensible activity defended? It is said that contemporary terrorists are not doing anything new; they are acting as revolutionaries and nationalists have always acted, which is demonstrably false. It is said that terrorism is the inevitable product of hardship and oppression, which is also false. Both these statements suggest a loss of the historical past, a kind of ignorance or forgetfulness that erases all moral distinctions along with the men and women who painfully worked them out. Finally it is said that random murder is an effective political strategy; the terrorist will win the day—which, if true, is the most frightening assertion of all, less a defense of the terrorist, than an indictment of the rest of us.

"The revolution," says one of Camus' characters, "has its code of honor." At least it once had. Political militants struggling against forms of oppression as cruel as anything in the contemporary world taught one another that there are limits on political action: everything is not permitted. These were not necessarily gentle, or even good, people. Many of them were all too ready to kill officials, collaborators, traitors to the cause. In discussing means and ends, they were often ruthless and, once in power, they were often tyrannical. But except for a few deranged individuals, seizing hostages and killing children lay beyond their ken, outside the range of their strategic considerations. They did not want the revolution to be "loathed by the whole human race."

Today, in many parts of the world, radical politics has been taken over by thugs and fanatics. One of the reasons they are as strong as they are is that the rest of us have lost the courage of our loathing. To deal with terrorists, police work is necessary; so is intelligence work, and all the security devices of an advanced technology. But none of these will be enough unless we can also restore a collective sense of the moral ugliness of terrorism. For the moment we are only confused: frightened, defensive, weakly indignant. The American consul in Kuala Lampur, released in Libya by the "Red Army" a few weeks ago, earnestly told reporters that his captors had been "perfect gentlemen." I suppose he was grateful not to have been beaten or shot, but the description could not have been more inaccurate. Prepared to kill some 50 hostages, already responsible for acts of murder in Japan, Western Europe and Israel, these were revolutionaries entirely without honor. Nothing is more important than to recall the code that they have consciously rejected. It is, to be sure, little more than the minimal standard of political decency. But reasserting minimal standards would right now be a great advance for civilization.

Jimmy Parts the Red Sea

TRB FROM WASHINGTON

SEPTEMBER 30, 1978

They were just sitting there, Sunday afternoon, having coffee in the Legion Hall press headquarters when ABC's Sam Donaldson burst up the stairs. The Summit was over—the Summit they had blown up and down in hope and gloom for 13 days. There would be a briefing in Washington at 9 PM, Carter at 10:30, with the others. *Others*? they roared. What others? Begin, Sadat, everybody! All hell broke loose. There was a two-way rush to telephones and cars.

Eight miles away at Camp David, Hamilton Jordan caught the President's eye through a window. Carter gave a big, jubilant thumbs up. Just then came the damndest crack of thunder ever heard. Maybe it's legend—I don't know; already it's part-myth. But it was no myth what happened at the parking lot outside the Legion Hall: 100 crazy cars trying to nose out simultaneously through a narrow channel; pelting, pouring rain; gutters wouldn't hold it; everybody soaked to the bone; Dave Garcia of ABC using a fruit box as an umbrella.

So that's when I picked it up. Why was it like Pearl Harbor, December 7, 1941? That was on a Sunday, too. This time the *NBC News* interrupted with a flash—the Summit's over, Carter on at 10:30. Telephone rings . . . White House calling . . . briefing at 9. Yes, I'll be there.

The floor of the briefing room slopes slightly like a theater, seats 150; it fills up with reporters—exhilarated, excited, electrified. Ice-cold Brzezinski doesn't chew gum; his jaws seem to be reacting as he keeps his cool; he presents the intricate timetable to reporters struggling between cynicism and euphoria. He is clear, precise, incomprehensible. Modalities . . . what are modalities? Jody Powell, only man in the room wearing a vest (let alone coat), says if we leave immediately we can see them arrive by helicopter on the South Lawn.

The lovely White House glows luminously. Grass is thick, springy. Harry Truman's balcony looks down, and the porch where I saw FDR give his fourth inaugural, in January, 1945. (They lifted him around like a potato sack. The bare boughs had snow on them.) Now it is mild, muggy; a moth darts in the lights, the fountain plays at the far end; over behind looms the great flood-lit Monument, ethereal as a dream. Distant planes at the airport sound like subway cars. I try to make notes in the dark. This setting, those stage-scenery trees—it isn't real; anything can happen; is happening. The moon peek-a-boos down. (There was a moon, too, at Pearl Harbor; a crescent, and it saw grim senators go in to FDR and come out still grimmer.)

The pop-popping of a helicopter; the huge hulk lands delicately on the lawn, giant blades rotate with another little egg-beater on the tail. "United States of America," it says. The door opens: there they are—Carter, Begin, Sadat; incredible; everything's incredible. A little applause. Moon comes out full. We dash for the press room.

This is prime time, Sunday night, three networks; ABC showing something called "Battlestar Galactica" with ray guns; poof, you're killed. Suddenly they are giving an instant replay of the South Lawn landing we have just witnessed. A miracle, that is, too! Carter starts; always the potential Sunday school teacher, he says "prayers have been answered beyond any expectations." Swarthy Sadat gives testimony next ("let us join in prayer to God Almighty"); tough little Begin follows, ex-terrorist, dedicated, looking more and more like Felix Frankfurter. He praises God; Jewish teachings; "habemus pacem"; the "Jimmy Carter Conference"; Shalom, Shalom. He is in high fettle. They all praise Jimmy. They are all born again. What an unlikely trio for a revival: Arab, Jew, Christian. The first two are so happy they ham it up—look (cheers) they are hugging each other!

Outside on the front lawn as I come away I pause to hear Senators Jackson and Percy giving a floodlit interview after just leaving the East Room. They are nonplussed, prompting, corroborating, babbling. A crowd clings to the iron rails on Pennsylvania Avenue looking in. (A crowd always gathers at the rails at great moments; they were here at Pearl Harbor too—tried to sing "America, the Beautiful." Only that time it was war; this is peace, maybe.)

Next day, 11:30 AM, Monday, September 18—Vance gives the briefing. Sadat's foreign minister, Kamel, has resigned. Again there is irrefutable testimony how Carter worked at Camp David, hour by hour, night and day, urging, cajoling, persuading. Punch-drunk reporters begin to get a sense of the thing. Yes, it is real. The Red Sea has parted, Jimmy Carter is leading them through, with a wave of "ifs" on either side. Vance goes 50 minutes. More modalities.

So here I am, finally, in the press gallery for Carter's talk to the joint session of Congress, where this thing must stop. Again the atmosphere is crucial. I have watched many times; this is noisier, more high-spirited—like a birthday party. In the President's gallery, flaxen-haired Amy rotates rapidly to shake out her ringlets. Sadat and Begin enter, with girlish-looking Mrs. Carter between them. The applause rises, and rises; crests in an ovation. The clerk shouts: "Mister Speaker, the President of the United States!" Sixty seconds of applause. He hails Sadat, Begin, more applause, standing; the frame of no other government could create a scene like this. Men's summer suits are tan, beige, light blue; the carpet is figured red and green; an occasional woman's dress . . . the big chamber vibrates; even Carter's anointed delivery can't dull it. He ad libs a bit; uses a teleprompter, addresses four vital audiences simultaneously—Congress, the nation, Sadat and Begin, and the people of the Middle East. He tries to wall in Begin and Sadat with flattery till they can't escape. He is folksy—"the three of us together." He hails Vance (huge applause). And he ends movingly: "Blessed are the peacemakers, for they shall be [called] the children of God." A great moment.

Begin and Sadat love it; they do their act again, they embrace, they hug. . . . I have seen everything.

So now, what do we say about Jimmy Carter? He is the despised kid at school who stepped up to bat and clouted one over the fence, bases loaded. He is so easy to underestimate. Enemies didn't hate him; they patronized him. He is soft-spoken, a poor speaker, almost unctuous; America has never had a president quite like him, perhaps. He will have more ups and downs. He is facing an inflation-recession now and doesn't know the answer, I think. (Nor does anybody else.) The post-Summit agreement may collapse. Those polls may sink again. But how hard he is trying.

White House Years
by Henry Kissinger

RONALD STEEL

DECEMBER 15, 1979

Of few other books could it more appropriately be said that there is less here than meets the eye. Or the hand. For this massive volume, impossible to carry on the bus or even to read in bed, tells us far more than we need to know about the author's first four years as Richard Nixon's foreign policy adviser. This book harbors many gems, to be sure, but they are deeply encased in padding, like a set of old dishes packed in styrofoam. Henry Kissinger, or "Doctor," as he prefers to be addressed in the academic title he quaintly brought along with him into the corridors of power, has not resisted the attempt to tell nearly everything he knows. And a good deal more besides.

He cannot resist the temptation to pontificate, a habit no doubt induced by years of lecturing to captive students, or of demonstrating his erudition. Thus, before each major foreign trip, the reader is treated to a slide-show capsule history. "Bordered on the south by the Indian Ocean, on the north by the Himalayas, and on the west by the Hindu Kush mountains that merge with the heavens as if determined to seal off the teeming masses, and petering out in the east in the marshes of Bengal, the Indian subcontinent has existed through millennia as a world apart," we are told in preparation for his celebrated "tilt" toward Pakistan in the 1971 war. This lecture, which goes on and on for paragraphs, reveals the good doctor's talent for travelogues, but also why his text runs to 1,476 pages.

Unfortunately the exigencies of a huge publisher's advance, said to amount to some five million dollars, and the 1980 presidential elections, in which, as an unemployed statesman, he has a professional interest, did not permit him to write the reflective volume of which he is no doubt capable. This one is more in the nature of what might be called a campaign autobiography: the campaign for his return as secretary of state in some future Republican administration.

Nonetheless, buried deep in these multitudinous pages is a book worthy of his scholarly, as well as of his worldly, ambitions. One gets glimpses of it from time to time, particularly in the canny vignettes of the great and the not so great. Here Kissinger's unexpected talents as a biographer, and his well-known expertise at vindictiveness and flattery, are put to good use.

In a few striking paragraphs the author draws portraits of some of the foreign leaders he encountered in his years at the top—Mao, Chou, Brezhnev, De Gaulle, Wilson, Heath—and twists his rapier in the back of those who, like McGeorge Bundy, have given him less than he believes to be his due. The capsule biography form also offers him the opportunity to lay flowery wreaths at the bier of past benefactors, such as Nelson Rockefeller, to whom he has most appropriately dedicated the volume, and at the feet of such possible future ones as John Connally. Any future employer, however, would do well to watch his step. Kissinger's comments on his former boss, Richard Nixon, are sly, vicious, and dripping with innuendo. Doctor Kissinger proves himself to be, on a very high level indeed, accomplished both as a flatterer and a character assassin.

But Kissinger is not Keynes, and one does not read his little essays in biography for revelation. One is merely surprised that they are written so deftly. Nor does one read Kissinger to find out what the guiding principles of American foreign policy ought to be. For what is most striking about this book is that the celebrated diplomatist does not seem to know. He does, to be sure, incant such phrases as "equilibrium," "balance of power," and "national interest," but they tend to float errantly in an undefined void.

For him the purpose of foreign policy is simply the aggrandizement of the power of the state. The uses to which such power may be put are purely incidental. There are, to be sure, a few ritualistic curtsies to "morality." No foreign policy text would be completed without them. But the author uses the word in a very special sense. For him it does not mean equity, justice, self-determination, or dedication to principles higher than the law of nations. Rather, as he makes clear in relating his part in the devastation of Cambodia, the plotting against Allende's Chile, the unqualified support of the shah of Iran, and the encouragement of Pakistani genocide, morality is whatever seems most advantageous to the power of the state he happens to serve.

Kissinger does not offer a view of foreign policy so much as a set of negotiating tactics. He tells us how to pin an opponent to the ground, or even how to cripple him for life, but not the reasons why he should be considered an opponent. For Henry Kissinger such questions do not even seem to arise. Life is a struggle for supremacy. Victory goes to the strongest. Anything that stands in the way—the Congress, the press, a recalcitrant public—should be cajoled, lied to, intimidated, "contained."

But we live in a country that expects its foreign policy to have at least some relation to moral values. And so Kissinger tells us, in recounting the resignation of three of his key aides over the invasion of Cambodia, that "morality can best be demonstrated not by a grand gesture but by the willingness to persevere through imperfect stages for a better world." But the decision to devastate "poor Cambodia" was most definitely, he assures us, "not a moral issue." It was all part of what he calls, in a frequent incantation, a "Greek tragedy." Presumably by that phrase he does not mean what the Greeks meant—the moment of searing revelation that comes in the aftermath of blind and violent passion. If so, there is no indication of such self-knowledge here, only self-justification.

No, this is not a book about morality in foreign policy, and Kissinger is ill-advised even to raise an issue that can only cast doubt on his motives, if not his decency. Any man who can calmly recount how he plotted to overthrow the democratically elected government of another country—in this case Chile—does not have a serious claim to our attention on moral grounds.

The case of Chile is instructive and, together with the chapter on the India-Pakistan war over Bangladesh, perhaps the most significant in the book. Not because it deals with events that captured the attention of many Americans—the long sections on the Indochina war have understandably aroused greater controversy—but because it reveals the assumptions that govern Kissinger's view of foreign policy. Salvador Allende was expendable on three counts. First, having won only a 36 percent plurality, he was not "really" elected. (By this logic Woodrow Wilson, who in 1912 garnered but 41 percent of the vote in a three-way race, should have been replaced by William Howard Taft in a British-engineered coup.) Second, he might not observe "democratic guarantees" (although Kissinger fails to note that Allende did hold a democratic election three years later and increased his plurality in parliament). Third, and obviously most important, he had "avowed his dedication to totalitarian Marxism-Leninism."

We can forget about the problem of democratic guarantees, which seemed not to concern Kissinger at all with regard to the shah of Iran, whom he describes as a "gentle, even sentimental man" whose authoritarian methods were "in keeping with the traditions" of his society. No, Allende's sin was that he was an "admirer of the Cuban dictatorship and a resolute opponent of 'American imperialism.'" That being the case, it was clearly "neither morally nor politically unjustified for the United States to support those internal political forces seeking to maintain a democratic counterweight to radical dominance." In other words, it was "moral" to funnel money into opposition parties and, after Allende won the election, to foment civil unrest, encourage a military coup d'état, and finance terrorist groups that, in a botched kidnapping attempt, murdered the head of the Chilean armed forces when he refused to go along with a coup. "I cannot accept the proposition that the United States is debarred from acting in the gray area between diplomacy and military intervention," Kissinger blandly observes. This is, to be sure, a logical policy, given his premises. But to pretend it has anything to do with morality is unworthy of such an avowed exponent of realpolitik. Kissinger should, like Dean Acheson, whom he professedly admires, have the courage not to pay lip service to sentiments he so clearly despises.

What are his convictions? That we live in a Hobbesian world where power is the only arbiter and the only morality. That international life is an incessant struggle for dominance. That the weak are meant to be victims and that the strong can avoid that fate only by being merciless. What he refers to as the "national interest" must be based upon such principles. Anything else, to use one of his favorite derogatory terms, is purely sentimental. Thus those State Department officials who wondered whether it was right for the United States to try to prevent Chileans from electing a president of their choice are contemptuously dismissed for "confusing social reform with geopolitics." Secretary of State William Rogers, Kissinger's hated bureaucratic rival, is described as having "no grasp of geopolitical stakes." And what are those stakes? "By geopolitical," he explains, "I mean an approach that pays attention to the requirements of equilibrium." And what is equilibrium? Essentially the balance of power, which is to say, the status quo.

One could, of course, argue over the morality of a policy dedicated to counterrevolution and the perpetuation of the status quo. Such an argument might be interesting, but not to Kissinger. Even on his grounds, however, one could ask whether such a policy is realistic. Is it really in America's "national interest" to go to war in defense of the status quo? Is it reasonable to interpret any political change anywhere as a threat to the balance of power? Is every third world palace coup equally crucial to America's vital interests? (The trouble with Kissinger's definition is that it is devoid of any sense of proportion or priority—the failing that led him to pursue "honor" for four futile years in Vietnam and to attempt an intervention in Angola.) He still has not learned the difference between a vital interest and a peripheral one. For him it is all "linkage."

It is this curious concept of linkage that led him to prolong the war in Vietnam and to devastate Cambodia. Obsessed with the Soviets and indifferent to the moral claims of others less powerful, he sees the world as a vast chessboard with two kings, a few rooks, and a field of pawns. Thus the revolt of the Bengalis in 1971 against the murderous Yahya Kahn regime in West Pakistan is seen only in terms of Kissinger's own diplomatic preoccupations. "There was no doubt about the strong-arm tactics of the Pakistani military," he admits of the slaughter in Bangladesh. "But Pakistan was our sole channel to China." Too bad for the Bengalis, who got in the way when Kissinger needed a postman to deliver his *billet-doux* to Chou En-Lai. To have failed to back the Khan regime "would have undone our China initiative." That the Bengalis might have had priorities that, to their minds, were more important than ensuring that Henry Kissinger had pressed duck in Peking is apparently not worthy of a serious statesman's consideration.

But it may be worthy of ours. Particularly since Kissinger reveals that he was urging Nixon to threaten the Soviet Union with war if it put pressure on China. The logic goes something like this. The Indians, with Russian weapons and encouragement, were backing the Bengali secessionists and making vague threatening noises at West Pakistan. The Pakistanis had linked up with India's old nemesis, China. If Pakistan were humiliated by a friend of Moscow, that is, India, then the Chinese would not take Uncle Sam "seriously." Thus the puzzling "tilt" toward Pakistan. "The major problem now is that the Russians retain their respect for us," Kissinger explained to Nixon in their coded language of geopolitics. "We have to prevent India from attacking West Pakistan." If the Indians did attack—and it is questionable that they ever intended to—then the United States would "have no choice" but to aid China. And if the Soviets should then threaten Peking, Washington "would not stand idly by."

So, folks, while the fighting in Vietnam was still going on, we almost got embroiled in a war with Russia in order to save face for China—a nation which at that time we did not even officially recognize. Such is realpolitik as played by the masters: the same kind that plunged Europe into war over the assassination of the Archduke Ferdinand by Serbian nationalists in 1914. Thus does Nixon, in Kissinger's words, deserve our everlasting thanks for having the courage to "preserve the world balance of power for the ultimate safety of all free peoples."

Kissinger's obsession with the Russians leads him down other curious byways. Allende, for example, had to be overthrown not only because he was a "Marxist-Leninist," but because halfway around the world the Syrians, presumably with a wink from Moscow, had made forays into Jordan. And to wrap it all up, Washington was at the time putting pressure on the Russians to dismantle their nuclear submarine refueling base in Cuba. This, in Kissinger's language, was an example of "linkage." There is a kind of logic in all this; there is also a kind of madness. Not madness of the certifiable sort, to be sure, for it takes a great deal more to certify a statesman than it does an ordinary citizen, but madness nonetheless. Linkage may have its uses, but only if the connection between events remains somewhere this side of paranoia. One gets the impression that around the White House it was not only Nixon who had to be humored lest he go off the deep end, but the good doctor himself.

Diplomacy as conducted by Kissinger, for all its Byzantine intricacy, was hobbled by an intellectual straightjacket. Kissinger's tendency to see every nationalistic contretemps everywhere in the world as linked to the Russo-American cold war suggests not only intellectual blinders, but intellectual narcissism as well. That is, an incapacity to see the world except in reference to an abused and insufficiently appreciated self. His celebrated megalomania, which he often uses as the object of gentle jokes designed to charm his admirers and disarm his critics, is merely the other side of an ill-concealed insecurity. Fame and power seem to have made Kissinger more at ease with the insecurity, but have made him no less intolerant of those with other views on how the world operates.

All of this would be of no public consequence—certainly we are all entitled to our own neuroses—did it not deeply affect his perception of international relations and his conduct of American diplomacy. An inability to perceive the validity of others is matched by an incapacity to view their struggles as anything more than an extension of one's own. Thus the Cambodians, Bengalis, Chileans, and Vietnamese, for example, are not only treated as pawns in the great battle of the superpowers, but viewed as entities of a lesser order of reality. A diplomacy that sees the world in terms of pawns may or may not be immoral. But it is certainly self-deceiving and prone to dangerous obsessions. Were Kissinger still directing American foreign policy we would, no doubt, long ago have sent the Marines into Nicaragua to defend Somoza—"a friend of our country and a pillar of stability in a turbulent and vital region," to use Kissinger's description of another free world friend, the shah of Iran. We would be aiding the Moroccans in the Sahara war and the South Africans against Angola. And it would all be done in the name of the higher logic of "equilibrium" and the balance of power.

Kissinger is in no sense an ideologue. He is a game player, as bored by matters of ideology, not to mention morality, as are the Soviets themselves. The game is all, and what makes it worth playing is a competitor worthy of one's own guile. Were the French, for example, as powerful as the Russians, he would be absorbed in containing them. He is a counterrevolutionary, to be sure, but because he lives in a satiated status quo country. Were he an Iranian or a Cuban he would be calling for a "new international order." Kissinger gets on with the Soviets because he shares their view of the world as a jungle in which every beast is out for his own advantage. He could serve their government, or any other, with equal distinction because he is concerned only with the mechanics of foreign policy, not its political content or moral weight. Indeed, one can almost see him in Andrei Gromyko's shoes, or Brezhnev's, for that matter, cynically manipulating other countries for the greater glory of his own, piously defining the exercise of his nation's power as coterminous with the interests of mankind, brutally squashing rebellious satellites, bankrolling congenial dictators, and defending it all as a "historical responsibility for preserving the balance of power."

Henry Kissinger's world is one where power is exercised for its own sake, power devoid of moral restraint, of responsibility for its consequences, even at times of rational objective. There is something compelling about such a cynical use of power, particularly when it is rationalized with such intellectual verve. Kissinger not only appeals to the "Sockless Joe" in all of us, the redneck who wants to give some pesky little runt a sock in the jaw, but provides a certified Ph.D. reason for doing so. Thus the continuing fascination Kissinger holds over the public mind, not to mention itchy politicians and moonstruck journalists.

Doctor Henry Kissinger has constructed a diplomacy for a Hobbesian world. When he exercised that diplomacy he helped create the kind of world that would justify it. This book tells how he did it. And it also reveals what might happen were he to regain the power for which he so palpably yearns.

The League of Frightened Men

SHIRLEY HAZZARD

JANUARY 19, 1980

To act with doubleness towards a man whose own conduct was double, was so near an approach to virtue that it deserved to be called by no meaner name than diplomacy.

Something like this view of George Eliot's may have influenced Iranian leaders in their contemptuous dismissal of Kurt Waldheim last week in Tehran. There was no reason for any of the prevailing factions in Iran to negotiate with an official who had ignored the atrocities of the previous regime, and had made himself an eager instrument of the shah's policy of buying respectability through donations to overseas institutions. Year after year, as Amnesty International presented documented reports of gross violations of human rights in Iran, the United Nations secretariat—supposed custodian of rights—courted funds from the shah and, in return, helped him to furbish his image.

Returning from Tehran, an unnerved Waldheim appeared on ABC's "Issues and Answers." He indignantly denied that the United Nations had done nothing about the abuses of the shah and SAVAK. "I received hundreds and thousands of complaints, and we always dealt with them. We sent them to the—and I even spoke to the Iranians. When I was in Iran two years ago, I did raise the question, but the there authorities said that they wouldn't discuss the matter with me." This tragic charade—referring reports of atrocities back to the offending government for consideration—is indeed standard United Nations procedure. It is augmented by the UN Commission on Human Rights, a discredited body presided over for a time by Princess Ashraf, the sister of the shah.

Princess Ashraf recently placed a full-page ad in some American newspapers to remind Waldheim about his past appreciation of her brother's favors. Her tactless *aide-memoire* included a photograph of a jubilant Waldheim clutching the princess with one hand and a large Pahlavi check with the other. It quoted rhapsodic tributes to the humanitarian ideals of the Pahlavis from Waldheim and his assistant, Mrs. Helvi Sipila. Princess Ashraf chaired a variety of UN rights bodies in the 1970s, and was given a leading role in the chaotic International Women's Conference held at Mexico City in 1975 and made possible by Iranian munificence. Until events overtook them, there were plans for a United Nations training institute for women in Iran, with a proposed Iranian budget of one million dollars. Despite this seeming preoccupation with women's rights, Kurt Waldheim demonstrates massive discrimination against women within his own staff. He showed no support for the Iranian women who bravely marched in thousands last year in Tehran to protest repression by the ayatollah.

During the shah's ascendancy, Waldheim administered an annual award of $50,000, known as the Pahlavi Prize, paid for by guess-who and conferred for environmental services. The first recipient was Waldheim's own colleague, Maurice Strong, who was leaving the United Nations Environment Program after a short and turbulent career.

When Kurt Waldheim set foot in Iran on New Year's Day, his first utterance was characteristically negative: "You cannot expect from such a first visit to solve immediately all problems. That is not being realistic." Much more unrealistic was his supposition that the world observed the capers of United Nations officials with any residual optimism. Last October, the *Guardian* of London discussed Waldheim's role (non-existent) in ending the Cambodia tragedy: "As so often when anything important is taking place in the world, the UN itself is silent. It is aided, abetted and guided in that silence by the inactivity of the Secretary-General himself. . . . Why does not Kurt Waldheim make a strenuous effort to overcome the deadly punctilio in which his office has taken refuge?"

In fact, the deadly punctilio is organic. The method for selecting secretariat leaders is the only UN official process that can be described as finely honed. United Nations senior officers are systematically chosen for their very lack of moral courage and independent mind. The office of secretary general is the pinnacle on which this negative capability culminates. In Waldheim, the position has found its consummate expression.

Kurt Waldheim was born in Austria in 1918. He came to manhood, as it were, with the Anschluss, dutifully following the normal path by taking part in the Nazi youth movement and serving in Hitler's army in various campaigns including the Eastern Front. To do otherwise would have been to exhibit a rare heroism—and, incidentally, to disqualify himself, had he survived, for the future position of United Nations secretary general. Unflawed by any such aberration Waldheim moved on through the Austrian diplomatic service and foreign ministry into the political life of his country apparently intent on gaining high office. In 1971, shortly before his installation as UN secretary general, he was an unsuccessful candidate for the Austrian presidency. His UN appointment was sought, and possibly attained, through intensive lobbying.

When Waldheim's predecessor, the Burmese U Thant, retired as secretary general, it was—as was remarked of Asquith's fall from power—as if a pin had dropped. Waldheim inherited from Thant a position steeped in self-righteous timidity and administrative incapacity. The first UN secretary general, Trygve Lie—whose background as a labor lawyer and member of Norway's wartime government-in-exile might have promised better—had demolished any germ of a true international civil service by conspiring to violate the charter before its ink was dry. In the UN's infancy, Lie contracted a secret agreement with the United States government whereby Washington was given control over United Nations administrative procedures. The U.S. used this control to dominate the secretariat for 20 years, with incalculable adverse effect on United Nations potential, and in the end with particularly negative results for the United States.

The most powerful member of the United Nations secretariat in the organization's formative years was not Trygve Lie, but the administrative chief, Byron Price, an American of destructive tendencies who was in effect Washington's chief covert agent at UN headquarters. During the McCarthy years, the secretariat administration expelled, repelled, persecuted, intimidated, or alienated virtually every free-thinking employee in its senior and intermediate grades. This left a dross from which the present administrative edifice was formed. (The danger to be avoided, in the view of member governments, was the possibility that a truly international civil service might be created, in accordance with the provisions of the United Nations Charter, to represent the moral principles that governments were likely to ignore.) The organization was convulsed over this issue for six years. Lie's legal officer, an American, committed suicide; and Lie himself, along with Byron Price, eventually resigned—but not before they had installed a branch of the United States Federal Bureau of Investigation at UN headquarters, on international territory, for the purpose of "screening" the staff. The FBI office was retained by Dag Hammarskjöld until it had completed its "task." No senior UN official was heard to object.

Despite its systematic exclusion of persons of character from the secretariat, and its rejection of candidates with even a mild show of unorthodoxy in their backgrounds, the United Nations administration has knowingly recruited, and retained in prolonged employment at senior grades, agents of the KGB and CIA—and, presumably, of every other national secret police on earth. That is entirely consistent with a UN precept that the only unforgivable offense a senior official can commit is to lose the endorsement of the relevant member government—not necessarily his own. When the double agent Shevchenko defected to the United States last year from his high UN post, it was announced that even though he had violated every contractual obligation, his UN pension would be paid. The former head of the United Nations mission in Cyprus, Prince Alfred zur Lippe-Weissenfeld, who resigned last September after repeated complaints from the government of Cyprus about his massive thefts of Cypriot antiquities, also will receive his UN annuity.

Waldheim's own past presented no obstacle to his United Nations appointment. When the United Nations was founded, former members of fascist organizations in the belligerent states were declared ineligible for UN service. But this prohibition was rescinded quietly in 1952, at the very time when rigorous provisions were introduced against infusions of nonconformity. To have embraced a status quo, fascist or otherwise, apparently connoted the desired team mentality. What the United Nations abhorred was individual distinction. This view follows the precedent set in the 1930s by the League of Nations, whose officials declined to recognize the plight of German and Austrian Jews.

The field of human rights is where the United Nations secretariat had, and cast away, its supreme opportunity. In the intensifying violence of the last three decades, United Nations bodies of human rights and the leaders of the UN secretariat have remained virtually silent: about American ravages in Asia, and about Pol Pot; about genocide in Biafra and Indonesia, starvation in Ethiopia, torture in Greece, Chile, Argentina, Guatemala, the Philippines, and Uganda; about punitive mutilation in Saudi Arabia, and about the vast prison network of the Soviet Union.

Into the vacuum created by United Nations inaction on human rights has come an active humanitarianism by individuals and private agencies that has gradually formed itself into a moral force—a force of the kind that a different United Nations might have inspired and led. This is the most hopeful development of the past decade. Organizations like Amnesty International operate with voluntary contributions: they offer their workers no exorbitant salaries or inane revels, and no delusions of self-importance. Nevertheless, they mobilize inestimable resources of human fellowship and proper indignation, and have assumed the task that the United Nations, with its colossal funds and massive bureaucracy, would not attempt. Only since the human rights movement burgeoned into a force not to be ignored has the United Nations made any effort to overcome its own paralysis in this area. Even so, Amnesty International has received no action on any of the thousands of documented cases it has submitted to the United Nations over many years.

In his Nobel address, Aleksandr Solzhenitsyn denounced the United Nations as a place where individuals have no voice or right of appeal:

> It is not a United Nations organization but a United Governments organization . . . which has cravenly set itself against investigating private grievances—the groans, cries and entreaties of single, simple individuals . . . and abandoned ordinary persons to the mercy of regimes not of their choosing.

Solzhenitsyn cannot address the United Nations. Terrorists bearing arms can address UN assemblies, but not the moral heroes and martyrs of our violent age. The only notable recognition of his existence that Solzhenitsyn has received from the United Nations was a clandestine attempt by Waldheim and his associates, at the Soviets' behest, to suppress his works in commercial bookshops on United Nations territory. Meanwhile in Moscow, in September 1977, Waldheim presented Leonid Brezhnev with the United Nations peace medal, "in recognition of his considerable and fruitful activities in favor of universal peace and people's security."

Each December a handful of Soviet citizens demonstrate to commemorate the promulgation of the United Nations Universal Declaration of Human Rights. They are inevitably and invariably arrested by the Soviet police within moments of their appearance. No UN medals have been conferred on them, nor has a United Nations official ever publicly raised a voice on their behalf.

The UN secretariat is a disordered and hypertrophic institution whose continuance, as a United Nations official recently remarked, "defies the laws of logic and gravity." This is reflected in the quality of all United Nations services, most tragically in the conception and execution of relief programs and technological aid. A systematic public inquiry into the competence of UN management and its cost effectiveness is overdue. It would be interesting to compare the true proportion of the budget spent on administrative costs in UN projects to that in private relief agencies. The United States Senate Committee on Government Operations found in 1977 that United Nations salaries and material benefits ran 50 percent to 650 percent higher than the corresponding rewards to United States civil servants.

Any effort to shed light on this pleonexia is characterized by the United Nations as a blow to world peace. Generally it arouses the only show of moral outrage at which UN circles excel. In the past year, realistic reporting on the United Nations by Morton Mintz of the *Washington Post* and a series in the same paper by Ronald Kessler about UN finances brought hysterical denunciation from both the United Nations and the U.S. State Department. Charles Maynes, assistant secretary of state for international organizations, confirmed that Kessler's statistics were accurate, but told the *Post* that "an article on the overall financial situation of the UN system would be used unfairly by political critics of the United Nations." Maynes said that a story on the subject "will do tremendous damage to the United Nations. . . . The damage will be incredible. It will be devastating." And so on.

United Nations officials were not called upon to testify at the cursory congressional inquiry that followed the *Post* story because, as a congressional aide explained, "the United Nations prohibits its employees from testifying before a member country's legislative committees." As it happens, dozens of American United Nations employees did appear many years ago before the McCarran Internal Security Subcommittee, which made political sport of them and ruined their careers. Not only did the UN administration make no objection to this procedure, but it made clear that any employee who refused the summons would be dismissed.

It is hard to see how significant reform of the present United Nations system could ever be effected. In any case, a juster system, based on merit as decreed by the UN Charter, could not be introduced without scuttling the corrupt political basis of the present bureaucracy. It is among the intermediate and junior staff of the United Nations that decency has lingered, like a trace of archaic culture in a totalitarian state. The extirpations of early years silenced resistance for a generation; and the staff in general remains an extremely conditioned and intimidated group. Nevertheless, with the entry of younger people into the lower and middle grades, where appointments are not yet exclusively dictated by governments, some courage has filtered back.

The labor mediator Theodore Kheel recently has undertaken, for a nominal fee, to represent the UN staff in its struggle with the administration. Kheel says that he has never encountered anything approaching the UN administration's authoritarian attitude in 40 years of labor mediation, and compares the UN leadership to "the court of Henry VIII." Kheel says, "Waldheim would be a better international mediator if he'd eschew the role of ayatollah toward his own staff."

When Pliable, in *The Pilgrim's Progress*, turned back at the Slough of Despond and found his way home, he was at first "held greatly in derision among all sorts of people." But soon he recovered confidence. In Waldheim's case, too, with his recent excursion to Iran, the hollowness of his office has been only briefly exposed. But the question of Waldheim's reelection is imminent, and the Iranian debacle—which has yet to run its course—may put an end to his United Nations career. This could provide an opportunity for the public, for the first time, to observe and criticize the appointment of his successor.

Throughout the modern world, fear has created a heightened consciousness of human rights. The rise of active human rights agencies outside the United Nations suggests the form that a future world body might take. Whether public apprehension can be engaged toward the creation of rational international instruments depends, to a large extent, on serious treatment of this theme in the world's press, where it has as yet been little explored. Having almost no realistic information on the United Nations, the public cannot frame hard questions, and takes the organization at the UN's own trivial valuation, as an innocuous captive of incompatible national demands.

Lebanon Eyewitness

MARTIN PERETZ

AUGUST 2, 1982

Much of what you have read in the newspapers and newsmagazines about the war in Lebanon—and even more of what you have seen and heard on television—is simply not true. At best, the routine reportorial fare, to say nothing of editorial or columnists' commentary, has been wrenched out of context, detached from history, exaggerated, distorted. Then there are the deliberate and systematic falsifications: remarkably little of what has been alleged in various published protest statements against the Israeli action in Lebanon is fact. I know; I was there.

Few of us are immune to the impact of the thirty-second TV news update, the headline that tells all but what's important, the human-interest particular that misrepresents by universalizing, the analogy that warps rather than illumines. (The most obscene of this last is the comparison of Beirut, where six thousand PLO gunmen hold a civilian population hostage to their last-ditch battle with Israel, with the Warsaw ghetto, all of whose inhabitants were marked by ascription for death by the Nazis. This likening of the Jews to the Nazis and of the PLO to the Jews is sometimes made less directly by characterizing the Israeli invasion as "genocidal" and Israeli war aims as "the final solution to the Palestinian problem." Mass culture makes much of our politics derivative of such superficialities: the media, fast-paced for multiple deadlines—early edition, late edition, morning news, 7 o'clock news, 11 o'clock news—are always after new, vivid images of conflict, violent if possible, even if they beg, unrequited, for explanation. Why would anyone be interested in buildings that have remained standing or in bodies that have remained whole?

But those who take their opinions from photographs or verbal evocations of war victims are not pacifists; few of the condemnations of Israel are based on pacifist principles or even on vaguely pacifistic sentiment. And few of those who condemn Israel today condemn others when their actions make for similar photographs, or worse ones. In any case, pacifism is not politics. All wars hurt, but some wars are conducted differently from others—yes, more humanely, and to more humane purpose. This I argue—this I saw with my own eyes—is Israel's war in Lebanon. It's a war too complicated to tell about quickly, too taxing by way of historical understanding for correspondents armed with a peculiarly American mixture of ignorance, cynicism, and brashness, who jet from crisis to crisis—looking for Vietnam, and, if possible, for Watergate, too.

About ten days into the war, *The New Republic* noted editorially that there had been "terrible civilian casualties . . . terrible Israeli callousness." With the specificity that the computer age requires, two numbers had by then been bruited about in the media. One widely cited report numbered the dead at 10,122; another, at 9,583. The figure that took hold in the public's imagination was a neat 10,000 fatalities, to which were added anywhere from 16,000 to 40,000 wounded, and no fewer than 600,000 refugees. TNR had been skeptical of the statistics from the first, but, deep down, I feared that perhaps the Israelis had actually been "unforgettably bloody," as the *Post* would later put it, causing "widespread slaughter of civilians." I too had seen on television the bombed-out buildings of Sidon.

There is no way to be pleasantly surprised as one travels north from sleepy Nahariya, on Israel's Mediterranean coast, into Lebanese territory. Waterside roads have been strafed, trees uprooted, cars damaged, roofs of the occasional shoreline houses blown out; PLO artillery pieces, carcasses of a self-defeating illusion, litter the landscape. The UNIFIL outposts—those preposterous redoubts of French, Nepalese, Fijian, and Dutch witnesses to the inability of international authority to keep the promise made to Israel after 1978 that Palestinian terrorists would not again assault its settlements—are untouched. The fighting here was fast, and, as army types aseptically put it, "light." No one says that south of Tyre many civilians, or any, were caught in harm's way.

Tyre is where the controversy about civilian casualties starts and Sidon is where it ends. The casualties of West Beirut, whose destiny the PLO holds in its hands, were never counted in the early estimates that first provoked indignation. Tyre and Sidon fell to the Israelis after forty-eight hours of heavy fighting. The cities were bombed from the air, shelled from the sea, set upon over the land. These were not, said a saddened Israeli colonel, "manicured attacks." But neither were they indiscriminate or wholesale; this was no war against a civilian population, Lebanese or Palestinian. Whomever I talked to on the streets—and there are many eager to talk, Christian and Moslem, in French or English or Arabic—pointed out that what the Israelis had targeted were invariably military targets. A friend in the States later remonstrated that this observation implicitly faults the PLO for resisting the invasion. It's not that, not that at all—but rather that the PLO resisted, as it had previously aggressed, from the midst of civilian life, and of Lebanese as well as of Palestinian civilian life. With excruciating consistency, the PLO's commanders seemed to favor for their antiaircraft batteries the courtyards of schools, for their tanks and artillery the environs of hospitals, apartment buildings, and—easiest for them and most devastating for their families—the labyrinthine alleys of the refugee camps, Rashidiye at Tyre and in Ain el-Hilwe at Sidon. The PLO was not alone in turning noncombatant areas into war zones: Jonathan Randal in the *Post* gingerly admits from Aazzouniye that "there were also confused reports of Syrian soldiers being in the area of the sanitarium during the fighting." In Jezzin, more beautiful than Aspen, the reports were not confused. Dr. Naji Kannan told me that he had evacuated patients to his own home from his hospital because the Syrians had installed themselves in its confines and wouldn't leave.

On whom, according to the Geneva Convention's laws of war aiming to set inhibitions on the killing of innocents, falls the onus for civilian casualties incurred in populated areas? Had the Israelis, I asked, shelled areas from which there was no fire? No one suggested they had. The entrance to Sidon and the city center were devastated—and, I was told by locals, that's exactly where PLO arms and fighters were most densely concentrated. The bombed-out, skeletal evidence of a military infrastructure proved it. In this primarily Moslem locale, PLO headquarters stood directly between the Shabb hospital and Al Fatah's own infirmary. All the same, it was apparent that Israeli forces took pains not to damage such buildings, likely to hold civilians. Even in heavily hit areas, many mosques and other public institutions seemed miraculously to survive unscathed.

You've seen the destroyed areas on television; you've probably not seen the vast areas adjacent to them or those five or ten minutes away. In the hills beyond Sidon and Tyre, toward the interior, the countryside has been wholly undisturbed. Here and there are shell marks; natives date them vaguely to five or six years ago. The press has systematically ignored the fact that much of the destruction, in the cities and in other locales like Damour, that it describes and portrays on television is a result of seven years of bitter fighting.

In both major coastal cities, hours before the Israeli attack, leaflets had been dropped, calling on the inhabitants to flee to the beaches, which would be guaranteed by the Israelis as open or war-free zones. That's what the cities could have been had the PLO entrenched themselves in the hills and not in the cities. In Sidon, I was told by a local merchant, the PLO fire-bombed a street of shops to emphasize its intent that people not leave. . . . Dr. Pinhas Harris, Israel's Scottish-born deputy surgeon-general, who returned from leave at Walter Reed Hospital in Washington, D.C., to direct the medical relief effort in the south, estimated that more than 100,000 people, perhaps 150,000, took refuge on the beaches north and south of Sidon. Two weeks after the fighting, I could see that there had been a vast encampment. Israelis told me that food had run out quickly. "It is not a happy circumstance to escape to the beaches," Dr. Harris conceded, "but had more civilians heeded our warnings, listened to our importunings, the number of dead would have been infinitesimal."

What were the numbers? "Please don't tell us," Mary McGrory wrote Menachem Begin in an open letter in *The Washington Post* "that the figures given by the Lebanese of 9,000 civilian dead are exaggerated." But was it not the numbers which flared tempers? Was it not the numbers which in Richard Cohen's meticulous calculus (the *Post*) of just how little Israel had suffered from recent terrorist attacks—and not what it had prevented in the past and prevented for the future—that made its response "totally out of proportion"? People who talk about proportionality need to be scrupulous about numbers.

Numbers have always been a problem in Lebanon: there has been no census for more than a generation, lest fresh figures disrupt the political formula for denominational representation which alone allows Lebanon to be imagined as one country. The PLO will not allow UNRWA to do a count of the refugees in the camps lest allocations be reduced. As on Chicago's voting rolls, old people don't really die in the camps; their food rations go on forever. The population of Lebanon is said to be about three million; this makes the figure of 600,000 new refugees in the south transparent nonsense, since that is roughly the total number of inhabitants of the war zone, from the Mediterranean in the west to the Syrian front in the east. Even the scaled-down number of 300,000 refugees defies logic and one's eyes. A number that never seemed to change is of those in West Beirut. Although for weeks correspondents have described—and I saw—long lines of cars laden with people and belongings leaving the PLO-held sector, there always were 500,000 people left; the Israelis' guess is between 200,000 and 250,000. So what's one or two hundred thousand among journalists? If no one quibbles about these big numbers, no one should quibble about a mere few thousand in the death count.

Given the impossibility of accurately judging the number of the living, it is not surprising that sloppiness and propaganda determine the number of the dead. In the beginning the high toll seemed to carry the cachet of international relief agencies. Maybe that's why Senator Charles Percy, not ordinarily inclined to see the best in the Israelis anyway, accepted the 10,000 figure as close to the truth. But the source was never actually the International

Red Cross or any UN agency, though they have been widely cited. The numbers came originally from the Palestinian Red Crescent, of which Yasir Arafat's brother is president. Some early Lebanese estimates were close to his. But the numbers from Beirut about the deaths in the south also defy logic and experience. This past winter there were airplane crashes in Washington and Boston; it took more than a week to know exactly how many were dead. But last month in Lebanon, we received and accepted precise daily figures—and not even from authorities on the spot but from Israel's enemies in besieged Beirut—and elsewhere. Chancellor Bruno Kreisky of Austria, joining the litany for the 10,000 dead, said his source was unicef. But in Geneva a spokeswoman for unicef declared, "We have not reported any casualty figures at all."

This leaves the International Red Cross, which seems absolutely beside itself to deny responsibility for the casualty numbers. David Ottaway reported in the *Post* that Franceso Noseda, head of the Red Cross mission in Lebanon, claimed that "we did not mention here any figure approaching 10,000." He did say that the only numbers the Red Cross had provided were the counts of 47 dead and 247 wounded in Tyre—and these figures, interestingly, are lower than those put out by Israeli authorities. In Tyre, Dr. El Khalil estimated that between 57 and 63 persons had been killed, including civilians from the refugee camps. Dr. Harris told me that Israel "doesn't estimate the dead. We count them. This is why we couldn't give numbers as readily as the people in Beirut. We had no real numbers until the fallen-in buildings were dug out. Maybe there are a few more we won't find." The Israelis didn't hazard an official number until June 22. They admit to some 250 dead in Sidon. In Nabatiye, the PLO's main base in the center, where the resistance was spotty because Palestinian regulars had run, no one really challenges the Israeli number of ten civilian dead. In a Nabatiye hospital with 60 patients, Dr. Kanon told me there was only one war-wounded, from Sidon.

The refugee estimates have also been brought into perspective. Many of the refugees, in fact, are those *returning* to their homes in the south, abandoned after the PLO usurpations since 1976. The fact is that the invasion has solved or redressed a refugee problem even as it has created or perpetuated one.

Representatives of Oxfam and other agencies are now all over Lebanon, trying to find a way to spend the money they've raised and are still raising. Some of them have gotten into squabbles with the Israelis over bureaucratic obstacles put in the way of distributing supplies. But the truth is that there is no emergency in basic human needs: food is plentiful and cheap. An uproar in Israel and abroad quickly rectified the tendency of both Israelis and Lebanese to ignore the Palestinians' suffering; in the few areas where electricity was still out, there was a shortage of flashlights; many people said there was not enough gasoline or kerosene; one farmer told me that insecticide was scarce. The hospitals are, as one medical director put it, "not especially worse off than before"; *Medicins Sans Frontières* is operating freely but without as much to do as it had expected. "The one real need is for construction supplies to help people rebuild," the supervisor of the Joint Distribution Committee's operation in Lebanon told me. "But the need is not insurmountable and it is being addressed." There is already functioning a joint task force from the Israeli Army and the frail Lebanese government to do what's needed in the warm months ahead. Most people said to have been displaced were displaced for only a few days. One indication: David Ottaway, in the *Post,* reported that Jezzin "is said to have become a major refugee center with 200,000 now camping in and around it." When I spent a day in Jezzin a week later they were not there. I don't think Ottaway would vouch for his numbers.

What is clear is that Israel's attack was measured and careful. I was also in Lebanon after "Operation Litani" in 1978, another Israeli action that was, in my view, neither measured nor careful. A slap-dash improvisation, it did not go as far north as this recent campaign and did not embroil big cities. But many villages and towns I saw then were hit, bombed mostly, as nothing—not even the armed Palestinian center, Damour, once and for centuries a Christian town—was hit this time. The inhabitants I saw then were enraged at the indiscriminate harshness of Israel's attack. . . . This time, Lebanese of all persuasions and origins have expressed—I heard it myself dozens of times—gratification at their liberation from the PLO.

It is by now certain that the casualties reported out of southern Lebanon were false. "Arabs exaggerate," said an Arab friend to me coyly in Jerusalem. But we need no instruction in national character to know about Palestinian hyperbole. The front page of *The Washington Post* on June 12 should have been an object lesson. "Minutes before a ceasefire went into effect," Richard Homan reported, "Israeli bombers destroyed a Beirut apartment building housing the PLO's military command center. A PLO communiqué said more than 100 persons had been killed." Homan went on to report what is probably closer to the truth: "Beirut radio put the toll at five dead." It's not hard to understand why the PLO, which attacks civilians as a strategy and as a chosen alternative to engaging armed units, is profligate with estimates of the dead caused by Israel: it's one way to try to establish a parity of immorality. On June 25, 1981, the Palestine Information Office published an advertisement in *The Christian Science Monitor* charging that "over 500 people in Palestinian refugee camps and Lebanese villages had been killed in the previous month by the Israeli military air raids and attacks." On July 7 the

Monitor published a most unusual correction of a paid advertisement. It stated that 100, not 500, had been killed from May 25 to June 25, and "of these about 90 resulted from Syrian shelling, about 10 from Israeli attacks." The correction went on to note that, according to Lebanese sources, the total number killed since April 1 had been about 700. "The great majority of the losses resulted from shelling by Syrian forces. About 40 to 50 were the result of Israeli attacks." It is just possible, it may even be likely, that more civilians were killed in Lebanon by the Syrians alone—leaving aside the routine homicidal rampages of the various Palestinian factions and the Lebanese militias—in that virtually unnoticed fighting last spring than in this entire Israeli war, which has riveted so many influential Americans to their seats of judgment.

The relentless trolling of the PLO and its partisans about civilian casualties is directed at two audiences. With elite opinion in the West, it seems for the moment to have won a round. The other target is Israeli opinion, and, more particularly, the fighting spirit of Israel's citizen army.

Many Israeli soldiers with whom I spoke were desolated by the consequences of what they saw as their acts of necessity. They did not need the inflated casualty figures of "many thousands" to feel grief for what they had wrought. "We must be able to weep also for victims of just wars," said Yuval, a nineteen-year-old paratrooper in the elect Golani Brigade. But Yuval went on to insist that army training establishes fastidious rules about avoiding harm to civilians in warfare. "I do not believe that we Israelis are wholly alone in the world in being so fixed on this issue. But I have no evidence that our neighbors care about it at all, and certainly not the PLO."

In English, the phrase is clumsily rendered as either the "purity of arms" or the "morality of arms." In Hebrew, the doctrine is called *tohar haneshek*; its origins go back to the 1930s, when, as a companion piece to *havlagah* or restraint, it established clear and self-denying rules of what was militarily permissible. Zionism then was an intensely ideological movement, measuring its successes against scrupulous moral standards. The semi-official Jewish self-defense force, the Haganah, insisted on so many prohibitions on exposing unarmed Arabs to risk that, as one old veteran told me, "we took on the most terrible risks ourselves." The Haganah also got itself into an ongoing dispute with the far less meticulous and more indurated Revisionist wing of Zionism, Menachem Begin's precursors in British Mandate Palestine. In the post-independence Israel Defense Forces, the partisans of *tohar haneshek* went unchallenged. "Has the sway of the doctrine atrophied," I asked Shlomo Avineri, "with the ascendancy of the Revisionists?" Avineri is one of the world's leading political theorists, a specialist on Marx who teaches at the Hebrew University, and director-general of the Foreign Ministry in the last Labor government. He is not a friend of the incumbents or their theories. His answer was clear. "If anything, the restraints of the doctrine of *tohar haneshek* are more compelling now than before," he said. "The army's professionalism, which protects it, is sure. The lapses of Operation Litani have been corrected, strenuously. Moreover, precisely because the Likud is in power and the Labor opposition waiting to pounce on deviations from the army canons, there was much greater sensitivity to the fate of civilians during wartime."

Most of the soldiers I know, like most of the Israelis I know, are people of the left, all of them critics of this government, some of them critics of this war. Udi is one of them. He is a reservist in field intelligence in the armored corps—made up of those infernal tanks which, once hit by heat-seeking weapons, don't give anyone half a chance to survive. In civilian life, he is a young therapist in training. He takes *tohar haneshek* seriously. "The most awful moment of the war was when, searching through my binoculars for the source of RPGs [rocket-propelled grenades] being hurled at our tanks, I found the faces of twelve- or thirteen-year-olds. What was I to do?" After the fighting was over, he suggested that just possibly they were somewhat older. Probably they weren't older; captured PLO recruitment documents say clearly, "those under 12 years of age will not be accepted." So were these children civilian casualties? One of Udi's friends fought hand-to-hand in a refugee camp. Fire seemed to come from everywhere and could come from anywhere. Even in pursuit of terrorists, however, he wouldn't throw grenades into rooms where they might be hiding. He wouldn't understand a phrase like "generate no prisoners." Why, after all, does Israel now hold between 5,000 to 6,000 PLO prisoners from this Lebanon operation? There were six days of close combat in one of the camps. How many Israelis died there? Wouldn't fewer have died if the Israelis relied more on bombing?

Soldiers, like other Israelis, have political opinions and political differences. In contrast to most other armies, these are aired in routinely arranged seminars or bull sessions, even on the front. Such exchanges are part of army life. Professor Avineri, for example, was in Lebanon last week on a reserve assignment with the army education unit, and conducted "fully free and open" discussions with officers and ordinary soldiers on various vexing topics, including whether it would be right or wrong for Israel to move against West Beirut.

The only big demonstration anywhere in the Middle East against the war in Lebanon was in Tel Aviv, organized by an army officer-initiated movement called Peace Now. But, as the very dovish Israeli novelist Amos Oz reminds us in the July 11 *New York Times Magazine*, "Not a single member of Peace

Now disobeyed the mobilization orders. . . . Some of them died in the fighting." The first night I was in Israel I met a young Peace Now reservist who had volunteered to fight even though he hadn't been called up. "My unit goes, I go."

The dissent was mostly political or strategic, not moral. It was registered in advance of the war, and also during it. No one really disagreed with the goal of removing the PLO threat in the north; but some thought the costs too high or the goal impossible to achieve. It is a strange army, needing no home-front jingoism to support it; as a lieutenant I know said, "Except for some blatherings from the Prime Minister, we heard no jingoistic slogans. It's better that way." A study done at Bar-Ilan University, released while I was in Israel, shows that, proportionally, more ex-members of the most left-wing of Israel's youth movements, the Hashomer Hatza'ir, join combat units in the army than from any other Zionist flank.

Israel did not go to war against the PLO in Lebanon on behalf of the Lebanese people. Had it done so, its purpose might have been thought illegitimate. So if some alien rump had set up a state-within-a-state, as the PLO had done in southern Lebanon and Beirut since 1976, yet had not at all threatened Israel, there might have been laments in Jerusalem but little or no action from there.

And, of course, there are Israelis who didn't want action from Jerusalem, even if taken solely in Israel's interests. "I was one of them," said Clinton Bailey. "I was dead-set against this war." Bailey, 46, is a native of Buffalo, New York; he is now an Israeli. He is senior lecturer in Middle Eastern history at Tel Aviv University and now finds himself in Sidon, after a stint in Nabatiye, as adviser on Arab affairs to the Israeli military in southern Lebanon. He comes by this post because he is a prominent Arabist; he teaches courses on Palestinian nationalism and Bedouin culture. He's been a burr under the saddle of successive Israeli governments, having become a tribune for the nomadic Bedouins displaced by modernization in general and, specifically, by the air bases now being completed in the Negev to replace those evacuated in the Sinai. He knows the Arabs and likes them, and not in a patronizing way. A Lebanese municipal official in Nabatiye told me that Bailey was particularly sensitive to questions of Arab dignity, "which is why he made sure that the administration of the city was quickly given over to the Lebanese. We had not really had it for six years."

That's the story I was told by Lebanese all over southern Lebanon, in the big cities and the smaller towns, by Christians and Moslems, by people of all classes and educational levels. "I had thought that the PLO had fought for a foothold in Lebanon," Bailey told me. "Not till I came here and spoke to the Lebanese themselves did I realize what the PLO had done here, that they had established a stranglehold."

That is the great untold story of the last six years. It unfolds in every encounter with a Lebanese, even from those few still sympathetic to the plight of the Palestinians. Everyone has his own grievance, his own memories. The simplest, perhaps the most existential, is that the PLO endangered everyone's lives by making southern Lebanon a target of the Israeli military. But it rarely stops with that. The PLO, it turns out, was not a guerrilla army in a friendly sea.

Khalil, a 25-year-old Moslem who had just left West Beirut, told me that his brother had been killed by a sniper shooting from a Palestinian stronghold. Jabber, slightly younger, said that his family's car had been confiscated by a PLO faction. Hussein said that his sister was constantly being accused of being an Israeli spy: "Not true; she resisted some Palestinian's advances." Ahmet said, "They got their way always by showing the pistolet; if not the pistolet, the Kalashnikov." Toufek—his brother called him Tommy—said, "This was our land and they ran it as if it were theirs."

Moustafa Mouein was the representative of the Lebanese Ministry of the Interior in the Nabatiye district, including 42 surrounding villages. Nabatiye, I was told, was deserted over the years by much of its populace. "I walked on mines," Mouein said. "I could not hang the Lebanese flag in my office or the picture of the president." This civil servant described the disintegration of the courts. "An injured Lebanese could get no justice from a Palestinian. The courts were courts of force." He groped for words. A more articulate, more cagey official, Ednan Ibrahim, the town's deputy mayor, arrived. "There was no normal society in the south," he said, in elegant French. "Civil society was paralyzed. There were no functioning judges, no lawyers really. If a judge pronounced a fair decree, who would execute it? The police were the Palestinian militias." It was a tale of kangaroo courts, and of vengeance. This had a wider meaning he wanted to share. "There had not been a civil war between Moslem and Christian in Lebanon. There was a war on the land of Lebanon by two exterior forces to destroy the government and make the country their own. I mean the PLO and the Syrians. The PLO wanted to solve its problems on our territory."

I asked them whether Western journalists had asked them about life with the PLO during the previous six years. Both said no. One went further: "You couldn't talk to journalists without permission." Later, in the hallway, a minor functionary volunteered, "We were glad the journalists didn't come with their questions. We would have been afraid to tell the truth."

That the journalists didn't come with their questions is clear. On four successive days in March 1981, *The Washington Post* ran articles, running to almost six pages, on "South Lebanon: The Forgotten War." The series, by William Claiborne and Jonathan Randal, is very tough on Major Haddad, the leader of an uneasy coalition between Shiites and Christians just north of the Israeli border, and tougher still on Israel. There is, for example, the suggestion that people left Nabatiye because of the Israelis rather than because of the PLO. "The Palestinians and their leftist allies exercise a kind of wild and woolly control," Claiborne and Randal wrote, "but they are hemmed in by the Syrian Army, which came to Lebanon as a peacekeeping force in 1976." How fortunate for the Lebanese that the PLO was hemmed in; but was the PLO really just wild and woolly? No, not exactly. In Shiite villages, "the Palestinians misbehaved, ruined orchards and crops, and the Israelis simply raised the pain threshold." Even today *Post* correspondents describe the PLO occupation in benign terms. Tyre "had been run by a local PLO commander in cooperation with local residents until the Israeli invasion." Some Lebanese, of course, did cooperate with the PLO, like the Jumblatt clan. (In Lebanon, extended families are political movements.) But is "cooperation" the word the residents of Tyre used? "Sidon had been a PLO protectorate. . . ." Perhaps a broad meaning of protection is intended here. Alas, it was not the war in southern Lebanon that was forgotten, but the people. That's what Deputy Mayor Ibrahim thinks: "Lebanon wasn't considered during the last six years." And then, with his dignity suddenly turning plaintive, "There is a Lebanese people."

But it was from Beirut that the narrative of the Palestinian grievance was being written. From Beirut last week, Randal cavalierly reduced a complex historical dispute to a phrase: ". . . the Palestinians were expelled from Israel." Simple. It's also in Beirut where the PLO's dreams for redress are formulated and its heroes anointed. In the *Post* on July 7 Ed Cory eulogized PLO Colonel Azmeh Seghaiyer, apparently killed by the Israelis in Sidon. Azmeh "had participated in training and preparations for a number of operations against Israel including the coastal road assault of 1978 in which more than 30 Israelis were killed. . . . I always thought of him as an honorable military officer. . . . You can admire a man even when he is part of deeds you cannot admire—the coastal raid, for example."

The PLO's behavior in the south does not quite fit the neat image its propagandists convey to the press. Confiscations, harassments, young people forced into the militias, schools closed, rapes, molestations, commandeering of licenses, passports, services, offices: this was the stuff of everyday life in the web of the PLO's "state-within-a-state." A doctor in the former PLO "protectorate" of Sidon reported that the PLO regularly sacked hospitals and doctors' offices for medical supplies. "We couldn't keep our ambulances. The local population suffered." So much so that whole villages and towns were evacuated, sometimes leaving only the aged and the infirm—the Shiite village of Arnon, for example, in the far south, near Beaufort, or Rihane farther north.

I spent some time in others. Aichiye is one. It was a Maronite village of maybe 3,000 people, emptied save for 30, maybe 40, since shortly after a PLO massacre that took 75 lives. I have before me the names of comparable towns with comparable recent histories: Brih, Kaa, Jdaidet Baalbeck, Kaddam. You've probably never heard of them. I hadn't till last month. There is a similar list of Lebanese towns shot up by the Syrians. No one pretends that the massacres were one-sided—Maronites shed the blood of Moslems, too, rivers of blood. Even Père Boulos Oneid, Aichiye's mayor-priest, admits that. But he still seemed stunned by the world's indifference, and even the Pope's, to the PLO's "rape of my native village. I am happy to be back. Ten or fifteen families return every day. Maybe with the grim lessons of the past behind us we will be able to live better with our neighbors."

It won't be easy. When—and if—the foreigners leave, the local militias, manned by lithe young toughs, smiling and polite and probably trigger-happy, will still be around, armed with the hate-filled memories of old men. The Lebanese hatred of the Palestinian is something awful. The Hebrew paper *Ma'ariv* reported on July 9 that the motto of one xenophobic Maronite militia commands, "It is the duty of every Lebanese to kill one Palestinian." A blood-curdling *Times* interview on July 10 with two Christian poets left the Israeli colonel who'd accompanied correspondent Henry Kamm "so sick" that he "wanted to leave." Bailey told me, "You can't casually ask a Lebanese doctor to treat a Palestinian patient." It is a human tragedy.

But you can't begin to be able to deal with that tragedy until you look at the sources of the hatred—and the sources of the relief at the coming of the Israelis. Randal has found at least one Lebanese made happy by the war: "Dr. Labib Abu-Zahr . . . could scarcely conceal his joy. 'I'm a son of a millionaire orange grove owner. . . . Now we want to build Lebanon again with marble floors,' he said, flourishing a cigar." But is it only Lebanon's vulgar rich who are relieved by the developments in their country? I met no one rich in Lebanon, and everyone I did meet was relieved that the Israelis had lifted from them the burden of the PLO. And not all that far from Damour, where wretchedness has been the fate sequentially of Christians and Palestinians, stands the glaringly plush little community of Doha. It must have been to the nicer parts of Beirut what Bel Air is to Beverly Hills, Hobe Sound to Palm Beach. Doha showed no scars of war; its elegant homes and gardens are islands of corrupt indifference. Huge crates of granite and marble wait to be put into an unfinished house. War had intruded in Doha only when an Israeli general was killed by a PLO gunman in hiding. How had Doha, so close to ravaged Damour and other scenes of heavy fighting these last six years, remained unscathed? "The residents paid high taxes to the PLO and they provided a patrol," I was told by a less protected neighbor who lived nearby. So the PLO, a revolutionary movement of the downtrodden, not only confiscated from those with little but also cosseted those with much. Rowland Evans and Robert Novak, long-time critics of Israel, wrote from Sidon in their syndicated column that for the Lebanese "surviving the PLO was another kind of hell." The PLO was "itself an occupying power." The character of PLO rule may just have been an augury of what was planned for the "secular democratic state in Palestine." Maybe that's why those who look forward to that state weren't eager to examine the model already taking form in Lebanon.

Doubtless if the Israelis don't extricate themselves from Lebanon, they will be seen as an occupying power, as they have become in the West Bank. For now, though, the contrast between the Israelis and the PLO in southern Lebanon is vivid and welcome, a manifestation also of *tohar haneshek.* "Civilized soldiers," a schoolteacher called them. Do the Israelis loot, I asked? Toufek's sister—we were not introduced—answered from outside the circle of men, "Not a cigarette." But even well-behaved foreign soldiers, around too long, will be seen as intruders. The West Bank is historically disputed territory. Southern Lebanon is not; there is no Palestinian claim to it whatever. So try to figure out why you've heard and seen and read so much about the Israeli occupation of the West Bank and so little about the Palestinian (and Syrian) occupations of southern Lebanon, two chunks of land roughly comparable in size and population, one on everyone's tongue, the other till last month the home of the forgotten Lebanese. Not eyeless in Gaza, but eyeless in Lebanon.

I write from the safety of the seashore. The radio reports heavy casualties in Beirut, today in both parts of the city. Again, the death of innocents. Enough have been killed; no one needs the pornography of inflated numbers. West Beirut is the biggest hijacked plane in history, its population hostage of a vanquished army that has not even been asked to surrender but only to leave foreign territory with flag and song and small arms, for elsewhere, perhaps to those countries which have paid them all these years to operate out of poor Lebanon.

The radio also reports harsh repressive measures by Israel in the West Bank. These make a mockery of the victory in Lebanon which, with the PLO militarily defeated, makes it possible for Israel to take steps, however tentative and groping, toward a more generous peace. Israel is now itself hostage to Begin's ideological hubris, and to his will to be brutal. *Tohar Haneshek* has run its course in the West Bank, and because of Israel's ruling politicians, not its army. The struggle in Israel, I console myself, is not over Lebanon, but over the West Bank, which is what the struggle should be about, the struggle to disgorge, the struggle to find Arab partners in a territorial compromise.

The Palestinians have always been hostage to the recalcitrance of their leaders. For sixty years a compromise was possible between the two peoples whose pasts and futures are inextricably tied to the one land of historic Palestine. But no compromise satisfied the Arab leadership—not even the tiny little statelets proposed for the Jews by the British in the 1930s, not even the partition plan of 1947. The PLO was formed, it is urgent to remember, in 1964, when the West Bank and Gaza and East Jerusalem were all still in Arab hands. Always the Palestinians were hostage to the dream of a map without Israel. That's why the leadership never really permitted the mass resettlement of refugees anywhere. Their homelessness was to fester and explode; the camps were to be the launching pad for the "the return." UNRWA, initially a humanely motivated operation, became hostage to the refusal of the Arabs to find a compromise. It is shocking, but not illogical, that an UNRWA school in Siblin should have served as a training base for PLO terrorists. When Camp David was ratified, committing the parties to negotiations for full autonomy and free elections that might eventually have developed, despite Begin's designs, into an Arab sovereignty, no West Bankers or Gazans came forward to press their case at the conference table. Some of their well-wishers never quite grasped why the Palestinian Arabs did not seize the opportunity provided by Camp David. But the Israelis understood, and rightly, that to the PLO and to those who feared it, any compromise was too compromising. And those who hinted they might want to come forward met with death at the hands of the PLO.

The Arabs of Palestine suborned their rights to the exiles in Lebanon, and the exiles chose armed struggle. The truly enormous caches of arms I saw, heavy arms, from the Soviet Union and North Korea and France and the U.S., far too many for those who would fight, held the Palestinians in thrall to the idea of some decisive defeat of the Israelis. It was the PLO which, having chosen armed struggle, inevitably provoked it, and was decisively defeated in it. Surrounded and isolated in Beirut, its fighters are hostage now to the idea of dying for Palestine. As in Sidon and Tyre, cities held hostage for six years, they don't care who dies with them, and their partisans don't really seem to care either.

Lebanon's freedom to struggle through to its own complicated destiny depends on the removal of the PLO from Lebanese soil. So, too, only the removal of the PLO from Lebanon will free the Palestinians, there and in the West Bank, from their captivity to the intoxicating and death-dealing notion of no compromise. Those are the stakes in Beirut. What happens in the next days in Beirut will determine whether the Palestinians will be allowed at long last to face reality. The Israelis have won their military victory; this surely is a precondition for peace. But it is not the only precondition; there are others, political ones. Whether the present Israeli government can move to create these remains to be seen. It, too, must face reality.

Isolationism, Left and Right

CHARLES KRAUTHAMMER

MARCH 4, 1985

It is a wonder that for a continental nation protected by two oceans and bordered by two weak and friendly neighbors isolationism should be an epithet. Yet Pearl Harbor made it so, and ever since it has been mandatory for any serious political actor to deny being isolationist. Consequently, even those advocating the most radical retrenchment of American commitments overseas protest that they do not call for isolating the United States from the world, economically or even diplomatically. This attempt to retire the word is not very convincing. Isolationism has never meant total withdrawal from the world. It has always meant *selective* disengagement from *certain* relationships (alliance, military) in *certain* parts of the world. Classical 19th-century isolationism avoided European entanglements only. As the historian Seilig Adler wrote, "Our isolationist barricade had only one wall. We shut only our eastern door." Nor did classical isolationism mean passivity and neutrality. During its pre–World War I isolationist heyday, American foreign policy was selectively active and expansionist, extending American hegemony southward under the Monroe Doctrine and westward all the way to the Philippines and to China through the Open Door.

After World War II the United States became the dominant power in the world and internationalism became the guiding ideology of its foreign policy. Internationalism reached its rhetorical high-water mark with John Kennedy's "bear any burden" inaugural pledge. That was soon put into practice in Vietnam. Since then there has been a gradual but marked retreat. From the cutoff of aid to Saigon and the Clark amendment (banning U.S. intervention in Angola) to the retreat from Beirut and the Boland amendment (restricting aid to the Nicaraguan *contras*) the United States has selectively, though hardly systematically, sought to reduce its international commitments.

It is debatable whether the decline in America's relative dominance was inevitable. It is not debatable that there have been strong and articulate

American voices arguing that such a contraction of America's reach and responsibilities is desirable. Although as explicit an isolationist vision as George McGovern's "Come Home America" is still a rarity, a new isolationism has clearly emerged, picking up the strands of a tradition 200 years old.

We tend to think of that tradition as a property of the right, since at its apogee on the eve of Pearl Harbor, isolationism had become almost totally identified with anti-New Deal, far right America Firsters. We tend to forget the pre-war tradition of left isolationism. It included Socialists (such as Norman Thomas), Progressives (such as William Borah and Robert LaFollette), and periodically, i.e., when Moscow so instructed, Communists. (Thomas, for example, argued that the cost of foreign commitments would prevent economic reconstruction at home, a familiar argument today on Capitol Hill.) With World War II, both left and right isolationism went into eclipse, not to reemerge until Vietnam.

Today isolationism has regained its voice. It is no longer a philosophy of political eccentrics, as it was from World War II until the mid-sixties. Nor is it, as conservatives now like to charge, the exclusive property of the left. It has reconstituted itself in both parties, finding, as in the pre-war era, two distinct forms of expression.

The first of these, left isolationism, has become the ideology of the Democratic Party, not of its ("McGovernite") fringes but of its mainstream. Modern left isolationism is defined by a paradox: its ends remain truly internationalist, but its approved means have turned radically anti-interventionist. There is no retreat from the grand Wilsonian commitment to the spread of American values. These tend now to be called human rights rather than democracy, but the commitment to their success has lost none of its Wilsonian universalism or moral urgency. "The cause of freedom is indivisible," declared Walter Mondale in a major foreign policy address in November 1983. He followed with a *tour d'horizon* of the world's top human rights violators from South Korea to Poland to South Africa. Mondale's detailed interest in what human rights violators rightly call their "internal affairs" is not an isolated burst of Wilsonianism. Universal human rights has become *the* foreign policy cause of the post-Carter Democratic Party, and for that matter, of post-Vietnam liberalism. This cause is as grandly internationalist in its reach as any since Wilson, FDR, and Truman. Only in its means is it novel.

"American restraint on intervention, military action, and covert operations does not mean American indifference," said Gary Hart. "We care about human rights and democratic values and economic development; and we can show our concern in our diplomacy, our aid programs. . . ." Diplomacy. Aid. Something is missing. "You don't bring in democracy at the point of a bayonet," said Daniel Moynihan about Grenada. That idea will come as a surprise to Germans and Japanese (and now Grenadans, too), the beneficiaries of an earlier Democratic internationalism that defined itself (vs. pre-war isolationism) precisely by its insistence on the relationship between democracy and bayonets.

Left isolationism is the isolationism of means. And the modern Democratic Party is its home. In the 1984 Democratic campaign the principal disagreement over Central America was whether the United States should station 20 advisers in Honduras (Walter Mondale's position) or zero (Gary Hart's). On Angola, El Salvador, Grenada, Lebanon, and Nicaragua, the Democratic position has involved some variety of disengagement: talks, aid, sanctions, diplomacy—first. In practice this invariably means—only. Force is ruled out, effectively if not explicitly.

Why? Like their pre-war socialist and progressive forebears, today's left isolationists consider the international status quo unjust and do not want American power used to preserve it. Walter Lippmann and *The New Republic,* for example, came out against the League of Nations because it meant the United States would have to defend Versailles and the territorial ambitions of the victorious European powers that Versailles sanctioned. Today liberals find the United States the status quo power. And for those on the wrong side of history, as the left likes to say, force is not only wrong, it is futile. "The gravest political and security dangers in the developing world," explains the 1984 Democratic platform, "flow from . . . poverty, repression, and despair. Against adversaries such as these, military force is of limited value." What is of value, then? "Such weapons as economic assistance, economic and political reform, and support for democratic values by, among other steps, funding scholarships to study at U.S. colleges and universities." These must be "the primary instruments of American influence in the developing countries."

What does it mean in practice to rely on cultural, economic, and diplomatic tools? No one seriously believes that cultural exchange will secure American interests anywhere. Its effects are at best diffuse and very long-term. What to use in the meantime? Say, in this century?

Economic aid is always cheap to advocate in the abstract. Giving it is another matter. Congressional Democrats, so emphatic that Central America's root problems are economic and social, gagged on the Kissinger Commission's recommendation of eight billion dollars in aid.

But the problem with economic weapons is not just the sincerity of its advocates. The fact is that poverty in most of the world is endemic and totally unresponsive to any imaginable American economic intervention. To identify poverty as the principal cause of instability—and thus the principal threat to American interests—is to admit that instability is intractable and our interest not defendable.

It is not just giving economic aid that is so limited an instrument—so is invoking economic sanctions. Experience with South Africa, Russia, Poland, and Iran has shown that embargoes fail. Democracies hate to interrupt free trade or to expend taxpayers' money to promote non-economic ends. The boycotter invariably loses heart and caves in. Jimmy Carter's courageous grain embargo was attacked by everybody, from his presidential opponent to, four years later, his own former running mate. Last week, in criticizing the idea of sanctions against New Zealand for barring U.S. warships, *The New York Times* argued that it would "punish American consumers of lamb at least as much as New Zealand's producers." ANZUS bows before the lamb-eater lobby.

That leaves diplomatic tools. At its most unserious level, this means talk—anywhere, anytime, with anyone. There were even complaints that the Reagan administration had not tried to negotiate with Grenada's Bernard Coard, a little tyrant with whom even Maurice Bishop, considerably more attuned to Coard's thinking, had some difficulty communicating.

There is, however, a serious core to the contemporary Democratic notion of diplomacy as the preeminent foreign policy tool. It is the idea of multilateralism: collective action by peace-loving countries against international malefactors. Multilateralism is the great Democratic defense against the charge of isolationism. "The Republicans have always been unilateralists—go-it-aloners," said Arthur Schlesinger in an interview with Morton Kondracke. "The Democrats are traditional internationalists who believe we can't run the world ourselves." Jimmy Carter's deputy chief of the National Security Council, David Aaron, argued that the isolationist charge "misses the entire thrust of Democratic policy from Truman to John Kennedy to Walter Mondale. What all of them have tried to do is create some sort of stable world order that respects international law and allows for economic development and the spread of prosperity. The Republicans . . . are still unilateralist."

True. For 50 years multilateralism has been central to the internationalist idea. It was to be the principal instrument of world order. In its service were fashioned a host of institutions. Some were global, like the League of Nations, the UN, and the World Court. Some were regional, like NATO, ANZUS, and the OAS. (Remember SEATO? CENTO?) Collective security, which we had failed to implement in the interwar period, was to be the guarantor of peace and stability.

Aren't today's multilateralists the real heirs to FDR and Truman, as Schlesinger claims? Only in form. Multilateralism means something very different today than it did in the immediate postwar period. Then, when the

United States was by far the overwhelming power in the world, multilateralism was indeed the preferred means for American action—*and was no real restraint on it.* In 1950 the United States could push through a "Uniting for Peace" resolution in the General Assembly, and in effect, act unilaterally in Korea under multilateral auspices. Kennedy and Johnson could justify intervention in Vietnam by appeal to SEATO obligations and by the presence of "allied" troops from South Korea and Australia. Johnson intervened in the Dominican Republic under cover of the OAS. "For the very strong," says Robert Tucker, "multilateralism . . . does not materially restrict behavior." It is, in fact, "an advantage in that it gives their actions a legitimacy that they might otherwise not possess."

For the strong, multilateralism is a cover for unilateralism. For the rest, it is a cover for inaction. Today the United States is part of the rest. The global multilateral institutions, like the UN, have been captured by a hostile Third World-Communist majority. The regional institutions are paralyzed by reluctant allies. (The OAS, for example, would never have approved Grenada. That is why we went not to it but to the Association of Eastern Caribbean States, an alliance of dubious existence, to provide the 82nd Airborne with a flag of convenience.) Multilateralism, now a true hindrance to American action, is a synonym—an excuse—for paralysis. It has become what Lippmann once called "the internationalism of the isolationist."

The irony is that classical isolationism opposed multilateral entanglement for fear it would draw America into foreign conflicts. Modern isolationism embraces multilateralism because it keeps America out of foreign conflicts. The reason for the change is a simple reversal in the power relations. In the 19th and early 20th centuries, the United States was a junior partner to the aggressive, imperial powers of Europe. Today the United States is the preeminent, dynamic power. Its allies want nothing more than to tend their vineyards undisturbed. Exquisite concern for their wishes is a guarantee of inaction.

It is also at the heart of Democratic foreign policy. The 1984 platform contains, by my count, no fewer than ten references to multilateralism. Significantly, six are in a single section—the section on the Western Hemisphere, the one area where one might expect the United States, because of tradition, interest, and a preponderance of power, to claim a unilateral right to action (what used to be called the Monroe Doctrine).

Listen to Gary Hart's critique of the Reagan administration in his major foreign policy speech of the campaign (Chicago, March 1984): "[It] made no effort to send peace-keeping forces from the UN or from neutral nations to Lebanon; to invoke OAS sanctions for Grenada; to back the *Contadora* governments' efforts for a peaceful resolution in El Salvador and Nicaragua. . . .

The Reagan administration has turned its back on . . . *North-South dialogue* between rich and poor nations; turned its back on the *World Bank's* efforts to offer some opportunity and hope to the world's neediest people; turned its back on *United Nations* efforts to curb racist rule in South Africa. . . ." (My italics.)

Or Walter Mondale. Immediately after the Grenada invasion, he criticized the President because he failed to "adequately consult with our allies." He noted that Margaret Thatcher opposed the invasion and her advice should have been "fully weighed" because Grenada is a Commonwealth nation. "I understand the French were not consulted at all and have opposed the invasion." The French? "At a time when we are relying on their cooperation and assistance in Lebanon, we should be making every effort to keep their confidence." Oh. Later he charged that "Mr. Reagan ignored the nonintervention provisions of our treaty obligations, as well as opportunities for multilateral action under the OAS charter."

One measure of how far this line of reasoning has penetrated Democratic thinking is a recent speech given by Senator Moynihan. Moynihan takes internationalism very seriously. So much so that he argued that "had the Democratic Party not failed in its foreign policy mission in 1919–20 [to support the League] the world likely could have escaped the Nazis" and World War II. We had a second chance with the UN, he argued, and we made it work. "Something, however, had changed in the world from the time of Wilson." That was "the rise of totalitarianism." As a result, "the world order Wilson and Roosevelt had envisioned was not really a practical arrangement and perforce we fell back on military alliances, vast rearmament, and eventually a succession of limited wars."

So Moynihan acknowledges that while multilateralism may once have been, it no longer is adequate to meet the new threat to world order. What to do? Continue the forms of American unilateralism (including "limited wars") that we have had to fall back on in the recent past? His answer: "The age of the totalitarian state is waning. . . . The Soviet Union is a declining power." So? "Our grand strategy must be to wait out the Soviets." In other words: between now and then, when the totalitarian threat will wane and permit a Wilsonian internationalism to prevail, there is nothing to be done! While the rest of the party spells out a program of multilateral paralysis, its most serious foreign policy thinker presents waiting-it-out as a bold new foreign policy idea. Such is the state of left isolationism.

Left isolationism has received much attention because it has captured the majority party, the party that invented internationalism. However, there is a second species of contemporary isolationist thought, less developed, less noticed, but crucial. These isolationists are weary of, indeed largely indifferent to, the world and any dream of reforming it. They call for retreat from Wilsonian goals. They accept Irving Kristol's distinction between foreign policy (the defense of interests) and diplomacy (the maintenance of [the fiction of] an international order). They have little use for the latter.

They have even less use for multilateralism. Schlesinger is right. They are go-it-aloners. They are the classic isolationists of the right: their ends are nationalist, not internationalist; their means uni-, not multilateralist.

Right isolationism has yet to capture a party, but its proponents, still in opposition, are growing in strength and confidence. Kristol, for example, in his essay "Does NATO Exist?" (his answer is no), makes the most radical case for the United States to get out of Europe. Henry Kissinger probes the idea more tentatively with a proposal (last year in *Time*) for cutting U.S. forces in Europe by "perhaps up to half." Owen Harries follows with a proposal to turn from an Atlantic to a "Pacific Community." (There is an echo here. "General MacArthur," wrote Lippman, "argu[ed] that our interests in Europe are at best an expensive form of philanthropy and that our true destiny is to go it alone in the Pacific and in East Asia.") In Congress, the leader of the effort to cut U.S. troops in Europe is a conservative Democrat, Sam Nunn. Even within an administration that promised a return to a robust internationalism, there is a dissenting column: Caspar Weinberger and the joint chiefs opposed intervention in Lebanon, only reluctantly went along with Grenada, and are now most wary about involvement in Central America. And the Europeans rightly perceive behind much of the conservative enthusiasm for strategic (Star Wars) defense, the promise of an America that relies exclusively on itself for its own defense—the traditional nationalist-unilateralism of the right.

This is the isolationism of selective disengagement. It is a direct descendant of pre-war conservative isolationism: it wants to redraw the American security perimeter, both to reduce the dangers caused by the current imbalance between ends and means, and to restore American freedom of action that is now so constrained by paralyzing alliances.

Administration officials, charged with the day-to-day management of vast overseas commitments, are not as free as conservative intellectuals (or out-of-power Democrats) to indulge their isolationist instincts in public. Which is what makes Weinberger's November 28, 1984, speech, "The Uses of Military Power," despite concurrent and subsequent qualifications, such a remarkable right isolationist text.

It is remarkable because of its insistence on the hallmarks of right isolationism: nationalism and unilateralism. Weinberger first gives ritual nods to "the fulfillment of our responsibilities as a world power." He does not want to frighten half the world to death. He even makes a point of attacking "people [who] are in fact advocating a return to post–World War I isolationism." But interspersed with internationalist boilerplate are references to a much narrower definition of American interests: "We should only engage *our* troops if we must do so as a matter of our *own* vital national interest. We cannot assume for other sovereign nations the responsibility to defend *their* territory—without their strong invitation—when our own freedom is not threatened." (Emphasis Weinberger's.) It is hard to imagine *any* foreign event that can threaten the freedom of a continental power protected by two oceans and possessing 10,000 nuclear warheads. And invitations, no matter how strong, are easily ignored. When Egypt closed the Straits of Tiran in May 1967, Israel asked Britain, France, and the United States to honor written guarantees to maintain free passage through the Straits. No one moved a ship.

Weinberger then proceeds to elaborate six conditions for American intervention abroad. Point four is devoted to national interest. "We must continuously keep as a beacon applied before us the basic questions, *'Is this conflict in our national interest?'* 'Does our national interest require us to fight, to use force of arms?'" (His emphasis.) Not a single mention of international law, multilateral action, or consulting with allies passes Weinberger's lips. The idea that intervention must be "internationally defensible" and "open to independent scrutiny" (two of Mondale's six conditions in his 1983 speech) is totally alien to right isolationism.

But what is being rejected is not just multilateralism as a means of action. Weinberger is obviously uncomfortable with internationalism as a guide to action. The references to national interest, as opposed to alliance obligations, are reinforced by point five: no intervention without advance assurance of domestic support. This clearly is a policy of prudence (and perhaps a backhanded slap at Secretary of State George Shultz for Lebanon). But it is more than that.

This particular requirement establishes profound limitations on any possible intervention. Domestic opinion, in advance of any intervention, is likely to define national interests very narrowly. "No unpopular war" is almost a prescription for "no wars," certainly for none at the margins of the free world. Domestic support can be counted on (apart from three-day mismatches like Grenada) only for answering direct attacks on the United States: Pearl Harbor and nothing less. This is the *pre*-war standard. Indeed, in January 1938 congressional isolationists went exactly the suggested Weinberger route: they brought to a vote a constitutional amendment to make war, except in response to invasion, subject to a national referendum. It took an extraordinary appeal from President Roosevelt to keep the House from passing what all knew would amount to (again: save direct attack) a guarantee of isolation. To insist on prior domestic support is to reinforce the narrowest nationalist basis for intervention.

Where does nationalist-unilateralism lead? What commitments are to be given up? Right isolationists draw different lines. Weinberger's criteria necessarily exclude from America's defensive perimeter much of the Third World. Some of the old right, like Barry Goldwater, are Monroe doctrinaires. They want to draw a line around this hemisphere. ("Restore the Monroe Doctrine" graces the letterhead of the Conservative Caucus.) About Europe there is great ambivalence. When Owen Harries suggests a turn from an Atlantic to a Pacific Community, he is suggesting more than a tactical ploy to force Europe to defend herself and to permit one form of American disengagement. He is echoing the classic isolationist policy of shutting the eastern door and pursuing American destiny to the west, where American actions have traditionally been less encumbered. Even the logical extreme of the right isolationist view—Fortress America—has its proponents (the most articulate of which was Robert Tucker in his 1972 book, *A New Isolationism*).

Although right isolationists draw different lines, the sentiment animating their efforts is the same: a sense that America has let itself be drawn into commitments that serve not its interests but that of others. From Washington's farewell address on, that sentiment has always animated classical isolationism, particularly pre-war right isolationism. It was never abandoned, not even during the interlude of Vandenbergian internationalism that immediately followed World War II. Even then, the right never fully renounced its nationalist-unilateralist ideology. It did reconsider tactics. Chastened by the interwar failure of the European system, it came to accept the view that American interests could best be served through American-dominated internationalist vehicles. That domination now ended, many conservatives want out. They want to redraw the lines of the American sphere, and withdraw to its unencumbered defense.

The political monopoly enjoyed by postwar internationalism is at an end. It is now faced with a continuing, two-front isolationist challenge. Does internationalism have an adequate defense?

In my view the left isolationist challenge is more easily met. That is because it fails on its own terms. Jesse Jackson's Third World school of American foreign policy, which is not isolationist, is at least coherent. It supports "progressive" (i.e., anti-American) forces abroad and welcomes an encumbering multilateralism and the renunciation of (American) force as the way to further that cause. On the other hand, mainstream Democratic foreign policy, from Hart to Moynihan, professes different goals—the success of the Western idea in the world—but resolutely abjures the means of securing them.

That leads to two results, one dangerous, one merely peculiar. The danger comes from the commitments retained, like the nuclear guarantee for Europe. The enthusiasm on the left for curtailing the military might behind this commitment—the freeze, no-first-use, a moratorium on Pershings, cutting the military budget (which is devoted overwhelmingly to conventional defense)—increases the risk of such commitments. It ensures that were they ever to be challenged and we foolish enough to honor them, the consequences would be catastrophic.

The peculiarity comes from the means renounced. To renounce unpleasant kinds of pressure—those requiring force—is, in effect, to decide for only one kind of intervention: against friends only. The reason is simple. To influence enemies requires the application of means, while to influence friends, simply their withdrawal. Hence the obsessive Democratic focus on the Philippines, El Salvador, Korea, Taiwan, and so on, regimes that do, in fact, violate Wilsonian ideals—not *because* they are friends of the United States, but because, being friends, they are susceptible to the most passive of foreign policy instruments, the only ones left isolationists are prepared to use. To find the origin of this selectivity in a blame-America-first reflex, as does Jeane Kirkpatrick, is to miss the mark. The charge does fit Jesse Jackson but not, for example, Mondale—the choice of San Francisco Democrats—or Hart or Moynihan or Nunn or any other representatives of the party's mainstream. The selectivity of the fervor for reforming the world comes not from anti-Americanism; it is the natural consequence of an incoherent policy that is internationalist in ends but isolationist in means.

Right isolationism is more difficult to refute, not because, in my view, it is any less misguided, but because the argument hinges on a question of values, not logic.

Right isolationist logic is powerful. Arthur Vandenberg is said to have turned internationalist when he saw London fall under German V-rocket attack in 1944. "How can there be any immunity or isolation when men can devise weapons like that?" he said. The opposite lesson, elaborated by Robert Tucker among others, is more compelling: it is precisely the new weaponry, specifically, strategic nuclear weaponry, that permits a return to isolation. It restores the conditions that once made such a policy possible: the unilateral possession of a preponderance of deterrent power. In the interwar period the United States did not have that, and suffered the consequences (World War II) of pretending it did not need it. America needed European allies to create a preponderance of power to deter the enemy (the

Axis). No longer. Strategic weaponry has given the United States unilateral possession of that deterrent power. In fact, alliances are a threat to U.S. security. They make the United States risk its own national existence for interests (like Europe) on which its physical security does not depend.

Are American troops in Korea and Berlin there to defend American security? It is not so easy a case to make. South Vietnam fell, and with it all of Indochina. Has that jeopardized the physical security of the United States? Even if all the dominoes fell right up to Rio Grande, no adversary in his right mind would dare cross it. In terms of a simple calculation of physical danger, to risk our existence on guarantees to weak and exposed allies is the riskiest of all strategies. We are always listening for the sounds of exploding "powder kegs." An isolated America would not have so cocked an ear.

In the nuclear age, alliances are much harder to justify as physical buffers. The counter to the right isolationist argument, therefore, must begin with the question: What is worth fighting for? If America stands only for its defense, if its mission is physical security—if, in other words, its nationalism is like all other nationalisms—then, indeed, why not as narrow a definition of American interests, as tight a circle around our borders as possible? A Finlandized Europe will trade with the United States. Finland does. And so does the rest of world, which, from Angola to the Soviet Union, is eager for American commerce.

The ultimate response, therefore, to right isolationism must be the assertion that an alliance of free nations, as the locus and trustee of Western values, is a value in itself. In other words, the answer to right isolationism must be Wilsonian.

Not that freedom is indivisible. That woolly Wilsonian claim is both empirically false and dangerous. It is false because freedom has been lost in half of Europe and Indochina—it can be lost in, say, Afghanistan—without it being lost everywhere, certainly not in the United States. It is dangerous because the belief that freedom is indivisible involved us, among other things, in imprudent defenses of freedom in places like Vietnam.

A new Wilsonianism must argue not that freedom is indivisible, but that it is valuable. A sustained internationalism rests on a large vision of America, an America that stands for an idea. Liberty and democracy are intrinsic to American nationhood as they are not, say, to France or Britain, where the state predates the democratic idea. As Tucker admits, "The price of a new isolationism is that America would have to abandon its aspirations to an order that has become synonymous with the nation's vision of its role in the world." He adds, "Isolationism is opposed, among other reasons, because it is equated with indifference to the fate of others. . . . It undoubtedly is and no useful purpose is served by evasiveness on this point."

And it is exactly on this point that the nationalist and the internationalist part ways. The internationalist may decide not to intervene in particular areas for prudential reasons, but not out of indifference. A wise internationalism and right isolationism differ not on prudence but purpose. It is one thing to admit that we will bear not *any* burden, but only *some* burdens—those within our (relatively) reduced means—for the success of freedom. It is another to say that we will bear burdens only for national interest.

A century ago a foreign policy of such narrow nationalism could be consistent with American's idea of itself. America was weak and could indeed best serve the idea of freedom by preserving itself and through the power of example. Today, as a superpower, that is not enough. Action, sometimes unilateral action, is necessary. It is American power that guarantees the survival of freedom. In Europe, the burden of whose defense has grown too heavy for some, the borders of freedom are defined by a thin line of American soldiers, not by the reach of American example. Czechoslovakians know of the American example.

To disengage in the service of a narrow nationalism is a fine foreign policy for a minor regional power, which the United States once was and which, say, Canada or Sweden are now. For America today it is a betrayal of its idea of itself. Most of all, it seems a curious application of American conservatism, which usually holds liberty to be the highest of political values. Does that idea now stop at the nation's shores?

After the Revolution

ADAM MICHNIK

JULY 2, 1990

Politics is the art of achieving political goals—of achieving what is possible in a given situation, that is, in a situation that has its conditions and its limits. In this respect, the ethical point of view, the consideration of what is good and what is bad, what is fair and what is unfair, what is honest and what is dishonest, is external to politics. An ethical action, like an unethical action, is usually analyzed by politicians purely in pragmatic terms. Does it lead toward the goal or does it lead away from it? Montaigne observed, in his famous polemic against Machiavelli, that if a politician rejects ethical norms it can make him untrustworthy, and sometimes deprive his political actions of effectiveness.

Politics and ethics belong to different worlds. Yet we, the men and the women of the anti-totalitarian opposition movements, have a different view of politics, and of our participation in it. The politics of those totalitarian regimes was, after all, an open attack on ourselves, on our freedom, on our dignity, on truth. The elementary reflex of defending those elementary values entangled us in politics, transformed people of culture into people of politics. Thus there was born the phenomenon of an artist or a humanist occupying the center of the political stage in our part of Europe. Thus there was created the political idea of building civil societies outside the totalitarian state (for example, the Workers Defense Committee, or KOR), what George Konrad has called anti-political politics, what Vaclav Havel has described as politics based on the power of the powerless.

Now we are leaving totalitarianism behind. Our nations are shedding the fetters of dictatorship, spitting the gag of censorship. We are engaged in a great experiment of confrontation between the idea of politics based on the power of the powerless and a social reality that was shaped when politics was based on the power of the powerful. We have always announced that our politics will be carried out without violence, without hatred, without revenge. True to the Christian message of our culture, we have always distinguished between the sin and the sinners. We have always tried to behave according to this difference, and we are trying to behave like this now.

But we are encountering the resistance of the social fabric. We see acts of violence, we hear shouts of hatred, we come upon calls for revenge. Sometimes we feel like the sorcerer's apprentice, who released forces that he could not control. These aroused ambitions, these displays of belated courage, these intrigues and personal conflicts, these slanders, these accusations of embezzlements against any adversary, or of being secret agents or crypto-communists—where do they come from? We look around and ask, Where does this taste for kicking those who are down come from, this ever-growing area of intolerance, this urge to imprison people of the ancien régime, this dream of vengeance, this chauvinism, this xenophobia, this egalitarian demagoguery proper to populism that conceals simple envy? Where does this return to the idea of a nationalist state come from? This explosion of hatred for everyone—for gypsies, for AIDS patients, for all who are different?

What is the mechanism behind this revival of hatred for adversaries in public life? we wonder with concern. And we wonder, after all, whether we are not all children of totalitarian communism, whether we do not all carry inside ourselves the habits, the customs, and the flaws of that system. The death of the communist system does not mean the end of totalitarian habits. The carefully bred slave of communism did not die with the end of the Communist Party's reign. Even the enemy of communism was often formed in the likeness of the system he was fighting.

We must reflect on what these new developments mean. The hateful chauvinism is a degenerate reaction to the human need for national identity and national sovereignty, a need that was beaten down by communism. The envious populism is a degenerate reaction to the human longing for a just social order. Into the place left empty by communist ideology, these two fiends steal. Like a cancer attacking the fragile human organism, they attack the tender emerging organism of our pluralist European democracy and our normal market economy.

Let us recall that historically, in our region, nationalism mixed with populism produced fascism. The central contest of this period of transition from totalitarianism to democracy is not mainly a contest of parties or political programs, but a contest of two cultures. It is best symbolized by the names of two outstanding Russian activists of the anti-communist opposition, Andrei Sakharov and Igor Shafarevich. Sakharov was an exponent of the European tendency within Russian culture; he rejected communism because it trampled on human freedom and human dignity, because it was the dictatorship of the minority *nomenklatura* over the majority of society, and at the same time it persecuted all minorities in the Soviet Union. Shafarevich rejected communism because it was a system foreign to Russia, because he perceived it as a European creation brought to the Russian land by foreigners, and because it preached a godless ideology. So we are returned again to the fundamental dilemma that was formulated by Leszek Kolakowski many years ago. Is communism evil because it is atheist or because it is totalitarian? Do the Communists sin by not adhering to a doctrine or did they stifle the very essence of human and national freedom?

The present period of transition from dictatorship to democracy must consist of a compromise among the main political forces. There must be a pact for democracy. The breaking of this pact makes public life brutal, and introduces anarchy, and eventually chaos. And chaos cannot be reformed. Chaos leads inevitably to dictatorship.

Every revolution, bloody or not, has two phases. The first phase is defined by the struggle for freedom, the second by the struggle for power and revenge on the votaries of the ancien régime. The struggle for freedom is beautiful. Anyone who has taken part in this struggle has felt, almost physically, how everything that is best and most precious within him was awakened. Revenge has a different psychology. Its logic is implacable. First there is a purge of yesterday's adversaries, the partisans of the old regime. Then comes the purge of yesterday's fellow oppositionists, who now oppose the idea of revenge. Finally there is a purge of those who defend them. A psychology of vengeance and hatred develops. The mechanics of retaliation become unappeasable: witness the Jacobin terror and the Iranian revolution.

We inherited from the totalitarian era, like a birthmark, the conviction that wisdom is the same as permanent suspicion. Jozef Tischner is right in saying that this is one of the most serious threats to democratic order in Poland. And yet contemporary Europe provides examples of countries that were able to stop after the first phase of the anti-dictatorial revolution, and thanks to that, they may now enjoy democratic order and wealth. Take Spain. Its transition from dictatorship to democracy demonstrates that a state can be built in which yesterday's political adversaries, the prisoners and their guards, do not lose their political identity, but can, and wish to, live next to each other in a common state, in a state in which they are able to respect the rules of pluralism, tolerance, and honest political struggle.

But we know, if only from looking into the mirror, or deep into our own hearts, how perverted we are by totalitarian communism. We lack democratic culture and democratic institutions. We lack the tradition of democratic coexistence in the framework of a democratic order. In Central and Eastern Europe, each of our countries has its distinct biography, its own secret knowledge about threats to democratic order.

I think of Poland. The Polish experience is well symbolized by Józef

Pilsudski. Pilsudski was, in my view, the incarnation of the best Polish traditions of struggle for freedom and for independence. He was, after 1918, the first chief of the independent state, the guarantor of the first free parliamentary elections, and of the passage of the most democratic constitution in Europe. He was also the guarantor of the first democratic election of the president of Poland, Gabriel Narutowicz. *And* he was witness to the moment when Poles suddenly lacked the sense of compromise, the moment when this first democratically elected president was murdered following a brutal campaign of hatred in the press and in the streets. Pilsudski retreated to Sulejówek, and the Polish Parliament proved incapable of creating a stable government. Three years later, in 1926, he returned to power at the point of a bayonet. The long and painful agony of Polish parliamentary democracy began.

In sum, the man who fought and won freedom for Poland, the father of Polish independence, also laid the foundation for dictatorship in Poland. He hurled abuses at parliamentarians and at Parliament; he offended political adversaries and was responsible for the shameful Brzesc trials, in which some of his parliamentary opponents, on the left and the right, were imprisoned. The dramatic story of Pilsudski holds a dramatic warning for us. We must always bear in mind this fragment of our heritage of independence, this time when, without Communists and without Soviet advisers, we squandered our opportunity to build a democratic and lawful state.

An intellectual is pretty helpless in the face of these dangers: as a political man he must be efficient, as a man faithful to the ethical origin of his commitment he knows that he must abide by the truth. That is how we are, divided in two. We know how fragile are the bases of democratic order in Poland, and we know that to denounce continuously the slippages in our democracy will make it even more fragile. We face, in these circumstances, a peculiar conflict of loyalties. What is more important, we ask ourselves, the fragile democratic order or the defenseless truth? None of us has a ready answer to the question of which of these two loyalties should prevail. We are doomed to inconsistency. We are doomed to live in a state of tension, uncertainty, permanent risk.

Still, it is not true that we know nothing. We are children of a certain tradition. And we know that this tradition does not permit us to renounce the truth with impunity. We are the children of our Judeo-Christian culture, and we know that this culture, which recommends loyalty toward the state, commands us to bend our knees only before God. We know, therefore, that we should put faithfulness to truth above participation in power. We know, by reaching for our roots, that the truth of politics resides, in the end, in the politics of truth; that every political order is polluted by the original sin of imperfection. We reject the belief in political utopia. We know that our future is an imperfect society, a society of ordinary people and ordinary conflicts—but, precisely for this reason, a society that must not renounce its ethical norms in the name of political illusions.

Yes, it is true that we are helpless before the many ethical traps of contemporary politics. It is then that we reach out for the truth of our own roots, for the ethics of the power of the powerless, or simply for the Ten Commandments. The rest is lies, and has the bitter taste of hypocrisy.

Highway to Hell

MICHAEL KELLY

APRIL 1, 1991

Captain Douglas Morrison, 31, of Westmoreland, New York, headquarters troop commander of 1st Squadron, 4th Cavalry, 1st Division, is the ideal face of the new American Army. He is handsome, tall and fit, and trim of line from his Kevlar helmet to his LPCS (leather personnel carriers, or combat boots). He is the voice of the new American Army too, a crisp, assured mix of casual toughness, techno-idolatrous jargon, and nonsensical euphemisms—the voice of delivery systems and collateral damage and kicking ass. It is Tom Clancy's voice, and the voice of the military briefers in Riyadh and Washington. Because the Pentagon has been very, very good in controlling the flow of information disseminated in Operation Desert Shield/Storm, it is also the dominant voice of a war that will serve, in the military equivalent of stare decisis, as the precedent for the next war. In the 100-hour rout, Captain Morrison's advance reconnaissance squadron of troops, tanks, and armored personnel carriers destroyed seventy Iraqi soldiers and took many more prisoner. In its last combat action, the company joined three other American and British units to cut in four places the road from Kuwait City to the Iraqi border town of Safwan. This action, following heavy bombing by U.S. warplanes on the road, finished the job of trapping thousands of Saddam Hussein's retreating troops, along with large quantities of tanks, trucks, howitzers, and armored personnel carriers. Standing in the mud next to his humvee, Morrison talked about the battle.

"Our initial mission was to conduct a flank screen," he said, as he pointed to his company's February 26 position on a map overlaid with a plastic sheet marked with the felt-tip patterns of moving forces. "We moved with two ground troops [companies] in front, with tanks and Bradleys. We also had two air troops, with six 0-H50 scouts and four Cobra attack helicopters. It is the air troops' mission to pick up and ID enemy locations, and target handoff to the ground troops, who then try to gain and maintain contact with the enemy and develop a situation."

The situation that developed was notably one-sided. "We moved into the cut at 1630 hours on Wednesday [February 27, the day before the cease-fire]," Morrison said. "From 1630 to 0630, we took prisoners. . . . They didn't expect to see us. They didn't have much chance to react. There was some return fire, not much. . . . We destroyed at least ten T-55S and T-62S. . . . On our side, we took zero casualties."

There hadn't been much serious ground fighting on the two roads to Iraq because, as Morrison put it, "the Air Force had previously attrited the enemy and softened target area resistance considerably," or, as he also put it, "the Air Force just blew the shit out of both roads." In particular, the coastal road, running north from the Kuwaiti city of Jahra to the Iraqi border city of Umm Quasr, was "nothing but shit strewn everywhere, five to seven miles of just solid bombed-out vehicles." The U.S. Air Force, he said, "had been given the word to work over that entire area, to find anything that was moving and take it out."

The next day I drove up the road that Morrison had described. It was just as he had said it would be, but also different: the language of war made concrete. In a desperate retreat that amounted to armed flight, most of the Iraqi troops took the main four-lane highway to Basra, and were stopped and destroyed. Most were done in on the approach to Al-Mutlaa ridge, a road that crosses the highway twenty miles or so northwest of Kuwait City. There, Marines of the Second Armored Division, Tiger Brigade, attacked from the high ground and cut to shreds vehicles and soldiers trapped in a two-mile nightmare traffic jam. That scene of horror was cleaned up a bit in the first week after the war, most of the thousands of bombed and burned vehicles pushed to one side, all of the corpses buried. But this skinny two-lane blacktop, which runs through desert sand and scrub from one secondary city to another, was somehow forgotten. Ten days after what George Bush termed a cessation of hostilities, this road presented a perfectly clear picture of the nature of those hostilities. It was untouched except by scavengers. Bedouins had siphoned the gas tanks, and American soldiers were still touring through the carnage in search of souvenirs. A pack of lean and sharp-fanged wild dogs, white and yellow curs, swarmed and snarled around the corpse of one soldier. They had eaten most of his flesh. The ribs gleamed bare and white. Because, I suppose, the skin had gotten so tough and leathery from ten days in the sun, the dogs had eaten the legs from the inside out, and the epidermis lay in collapsed and hairy folds, like leg-shaped blankets, with feet attached. The beasts skirted the stomach, which lay to one side of the ribs, a black and yellow balloon. A few miles up the road, a small flock of great raptors wheeled over another body. The dogs had been there first, and little remained except the head. The birds were working on the more vulnerable parts of that. The dead man's face was darkly yellow-green, except where his eyeballs had been; there, the sockets glistened red and wet.

For a fifty- or sixty-mile stretch from just north of Jahra to the Iraqi border, the road was littered with exploded and roasted vehicles, charred and blown-up bodies. It is important to say that the thirty-seven dead men I saw were all soldiers and that they had been trying to make their escape heavily laden with weapons and ammunition. The road was thick with the wreckage of tanks, armored personnel carriers, 155-man howitzers, and supply trucks filled with shells, missiles, rocket-propelled grenades, and machine-gun rounds in crates and belts. I saw no bodies that had not belonged to men in uniform. It was not always easy to ascertain this because the force of the explosions and the heat of the fires had blown most of the clothing off the soldiers, and often too had cooked their remains into wizened, mummified charcoal-men. But even in the worst cases, there was enough evidence—a scrap of green uniform on a leg here, an intact combat boot on a remaining foot there, an AK-47 propped next to a black claw over yonder—to see that this had been indeed what Captain Morrison might call a legitimate target of opportunity. The American warplanes had come in low, fast, and hard on the night of February 26 and the morning of the 27th, in the last hours before the cease-fire, and had surprised the Iraqis. They had saturated the road with cluster bombs, big white pods that open in the air and spray those below with hundreds of bomblets that spew at great velocity thousands of razor-edged little fragments of metal. The explosions had torn tanks and trucks apart—the jagged and already rusting pieces of one self-propelled howitzer were scattered over a fifty-yard area—and ripped up the men inside into pieces as well.

The heat of the blasts had inspired secondary explosions in the ammunition. The fires had been fierce enough in some cases to melt windshield glass into globs of silicone that dripped and hardened on the black metal skeletons of the dashboards. What the bomb bursts and fires had started, machine-gun fire finished. The planes had strafed with skill. One truck had just two neat holes in its front windshield, right in front of the driver.

Most of the destruction had been visited on clusters of ten to fifteen vehicles. But those who had driven alone, or even off the road and into the desert, had been hunted down too. Of the several hundred wrecks I saw, not one had crashed in panic; all bore the marks of having been bombed or shot. The bodies bore the marks too.

Even in a mass attack, there is individuality. Quite a few of the dead had never made it out of their machines. Those were the worst, because they were both exploded and incinerated. One man had tried to escape to Iraq in a Kawasaki front-end loader. His remaining half-body lay hanging upside down and out of his exposed scat, the left side and bottom blown away to tatters, with the charred leg fully fifteen feet away. Nine men in a slat-sided supply truck were killed and flash-burned so swiftly that they remained, naked, skinned, and black wrecks, in the vulnerable positions of the moment of first impact. One body lay face down with his rear high in the air, as if he had been trying to burrow through the truck bed. His legs ended in fluttery charcoaled remnants at mid thigh. He had a young, pretty face, slightly cherubic, with a pointed little chin; you could still see that even though it was mummified. Another man had been butterflied by the bomb; the cavity of his body was cut wide open and his intestines and such were still coiled in their proper places, but cooked to ebony.

As I stood looking at him, a couple of U.S. Army intelligence specialists came up beside me. It was their duty to pick and wade through the awfulness in search of documents of value. Major Bob Nugent and Chief Warrant Officer Jim Smith were trying to approach the job with dispassionate professionalism. "Say, this is interesting right here," said one. "Look how this guy ended up against the cab." Sure enough, a soldier had been flung by the explosion into the foot-wide crevice between the back of the truck and the driver's compartment. He wasn't very big. The heat had shrunk all the bodies into twisted, skin-stretched things. It was pretty clear some of the bodies hadn't been very big in life either. "Some of these guys weren't but 13, 14 years old," said Smith, in a voice fittingly small.

We walked around to look in the shattered cab. There were two carbonized husks of men in there. The one in the passenger seat had the bottom of his face ripped off, which gave him the effect of grinning with only his upper teeth. We walked back to look at the scene on the truckbed. The more you looked at it, the more you could imagine you were seeing the soldiers at the moment they were fire frozen in their twisted shapes, mangled and shapeless. Smith pulled out a pocket camera and got ready to take a picture. He looked through the viewfinder. "Oh, I'm not gonna do this," he said, and put the camera away.

Small mementos of life were all around, part of the garbage stew of the road. Among the ammunition, grenades, ripped metal, and unexploded cluster bomblets lay the paltry possessions of the departed, at least some of which were stolen: a Donald Duck doll, a case of White Flake laundry soap, a can of Soft and Gentle hair spray, squashed tubes of toothpaste, dozens of well-used shaving brushes, a Russian-made slide rule to calculate artillery-fire distances, crayons, a tricycle, two crates of pecans, a souvenir calendar from London, with the House of Lords on one side and the Tower on the other, the dog tags of Abas Mshal Dman, a non-commissioned officer, who was Islamic and who had, in the days when he had blood, type O positive.

Some of the American and British soldiers wandering the graveyard joked a bit. "Crispy critters," said one, looking at a group of the incinerated. "Just wasn't them boys' day, was it?" said another. But for the most part, the scene commanded among the visitors a certain sobriety. I walked along for a while with Nugent, who is 43 and a major in the Army's special operations branch, and who served in Vietnam and has seen more of this sort of thing than he cares for. I liked him instantly, in part because he was searching hard to find an acceptance of what he was seeing. He said he felt very sad for the horrors around him, and had to remind himself that they were once men who had done terrible things. Perhaps, he said, considering the great casualties on the Iraqi side and the extremely few Allied deaths, divine intervention had been at work—"some sort of good against evil thing." He pointed out that there had not been much alternative; given the Allied forces' ability to strike in safety from the air, no commander could have risked the lives of his own men by pitching a more even-sided battle on the ground. In the end, I liked him best because he settled on not a rationalization or a defense, but on the awful heart of the thing, which is that this is just the way it is. "No one ever said war was pretty," he said. "Chivalry died a long time ago."

Live Souls

VASSILY AKSYONOV

SEPTEMBER 16 & 23, 1991

The Red plotters in Moscow preyed upon, and planned to exploit, two basic biological feelings: fear and hunger. For the former they had tanks; for the latter, sausages. Cynical imbeciles, that is to say, typical products of "materialistic philosophy," they regarded the people as Pavlovian dogs. (The prime minister in the Committee of Eight was named Pavlov.) They had no doubt that Muscovites frightened by tanks could be appeased by the immediate delivery of unheard-of stocks of food to the stores, and thus harmony between the people and their new rulers could be immediately established.

For it's logical, isn't it, that anyone confronted with the choice between mortal danger and a good chew would choose the latter? These plotters, in short, appear to have had no idea of the higher reaches of human nature. It never occurred to them that their attempt to restore communism would broach other alternatives to the people of Moscow: between dignity and servility, between humiliation and freedom. Least of all did they suspect that inside the tanks rode human beings, with their own notions of the alternatives.

What a triumph, what a sense of joy, of revelation, of pride, of gratitude! People of my own generation cannot but remember Prague 1968. Why did the bastards again choose the third week in August—to help us experience the historical parallel more perfectly? If so, they certainly succeeded. Twenty-three years ago we were filled, in that third week in August, with hatred and despair; we did not even dare to dream that the Czech liberals would resist or that the Soviet tankmen would not open fire. This time, in this third week of August, the wildest, most metaphorical dreams of our generation came true. The miracle took place. The spiritual revolution envisaged by Tolstoy came to pass.

One analyst wrote of the coup that it was Dostoyevsky at the beginning, the Marx Brothers at the end, that the twilight struggle turned into farce. Not quite. For me it was more a musical development: nameless and faceless dodecaphony at the beginning, then Beethoven, Mozart, Rossini, and at the end a real Rite of Spring.

In a way, Russians should be grateful to the bastards for helping them to attain the sense of a new national identity. These three August days and nights resolutely repudiated the cynical idea that Russians want nothing but order, that lousy old euphemism for brutal pseudo-patriotic rule. The Russians proved, without any reservations, that they seek a new, civilized relationship with each other, that they wish to be a part of the civilized world.

It is amazing how wrong the Slavophile chauvinist writers and intellectuals have turned out to be. There is no doubt that they were paving the way for the putsch. One thousand percent Russian, they knew best what Russians really want. Some of them even took part in the final preparations. Three weeks before Gorbachev's arrest and the deployment of the tanks in Moscow, the right-wing newspaper *Sovetskaya Rossiya* published an "Appeal to the Russian People," and among the list of signatories, along with some of the top military brass, could be found some of the most active Nazi-Bolshevik writers, such as Yuri Bondarev, Valentin Rasputin, and Aleksandr Prokhanov.

The wording of this appeal looks like a draft for the junta's communiqué. It was surely written not by people in uniform, but by those "engineers of human souls" in the service of the great fatherland. And in precisely the same spirit the junta deplored, among other things, "the hydra of pornography." The spread of this hydra over the holy land since the beginning of perestroika was one of the major reasons for the arrest of the president and the ordering of troops into the streets of Moscow.

The hysterical screams of the ultra-patriots among the writers have been heard for quite some time, but nobody took them very seriously. The liberal writers had no time to waste on such matters, and so nobody was alarmed, even though there was evidence of close ties between the Slavophiles and the KGB, the Party apparatus and the military establishment. Strangely enough, the only serious reply to the "Appeal" came from their fellow Slavophile, the writer Viktor Astafiev. "Don't trust them," the old novelist warned the television audience, "they want to return you to Communist slavery. They are the bandits of the Black Hundreds!"

In the first week in August I drove by the Gorbachevs' resort near Sevastopol, in the southern Crimea, and noticed the two navy vessels anchored in the coastal waters to guard the president. They turned out to be bad at their job. That same night I saw Colonel Viktor Alksnis, the curly-haired leader of Soyuz, the reactionary group in the Soviet Parliament, on television. I remember being struck by the thought that he sounded like nothing but the spokesman for a draconian regime that is just around the corner. I'm sure that I was not the only viewer to be alarmed by Alksnis's statements; but again they were not taken seriously, because such statements had all been heard before.

In those early days in August the Russian air was filled with ambiguity, with hopes and fears, with lust and fatigue. Young balladeers in the streets sang songs about the White Army's "irreproachable knights." And towering over them were the same old heavy statues of Lenin, with the same old slogans: "Lenin's ideas are immortal because they are eternal." And finally the ghosts of the past materialized, in the forms of a dozen high-ranking bastards and a thousand tanks.

What happened next might be called, without exaggeration, the greatest and most glorious page in the history of Russia. Challenging what the plotters thought was "common sense," a tall, broad-shouldered man, a former apparatchik himself, repeated almost step by step the famous move made by the Communists' idol seventy-four years ago. With one rather substantial difference: Lenin climbed onto the armored car to announce that communism's time had come. Yeltsin did so to announce that communism's time had gone.

It appears that miracles have been taking place in the souls of millions. "Enough!" shouted everyone. "Never again!" Old women and street punks, Afghan vets and factory workers, militiamen and teenage rockers (the bikers were especially useful as messengers for the resistance), journalists and musicians, intellectuals and bricklayers—all stood arm in arm in their own Tiananmen Square, which the Moscow street, thank God, never became.

I imagine that the intoxication of solidarity can make a man fearless. Happily that same intoxication overwhelmed the tankmen, too, and all the troops that had been readied for a massacre. The disobedience of the soldiers provided the final chords in the great symphony of Russia's spiritual revolution. God's spark was lit in all the hearts in the crowd, including the hearts in uniform. And there was still another call to the nation: of the three young heroes who lost their lives in the confrontation with the coup, two were Russians and one was a Jew. What do you think of *that*, Comrade Rasputin?

These were the happiest days in the life of our generation. Whatever fate has in store for us, now we can say that everything we lived, beginning with the very first steps of resistance decades ago, was worth living. If there is a sense of bitterness in my soul, it is only because I left Moscow for Paris on the quiet Sunday morning of August 18, just one day before the event. While my son stood on the barricades, and my wife joined the crowd that surrounded the White House in the expectation of an assault, I sat with a stack of newspapers in Montparnasse. Paris, with all its glitter, looked dull to me.

After Memory

LEON WIESELTIER

MAY 3, 1993

> ***Dear God, let us exchange our memories—***
> ***I will recall the beginning, you will remember the end.***
>
> —A. SUTZKEVER

I.

Once upon a time the past was the danger. It stifled, with all its dictates and demands, all its presumptions upon the present; and so it came to be identified as a "burden" that had to be resisted. We are still living in the culture of that resistance. The instruments of resistance to the "burden" were many. There were fantasies of the past's destruction, which became plans, which became revolutions. (Which became the past, which inspired fantasies of the past's destruction, which became plans, which became revolutions.) Perhaps the unlikeliest method of beating back the past, however, was the study of history. The critical scrutiny of sacred texts that began in earnest in the seventeenth century and flourished in the nineteenth century taught a powerful lesson: that knowledge is a form of mastery. Objectivity, the principled dissociation from one's circumstances that history took from the sciences, seemed to give the knower power over the known; or at least it stole from the past some of the mystery to which it owed its authority. The detachment that originated as an ideal of science was swiftly promoted into an ideal of life. And so for a while the terror went out of the past.

But almost immediately the costs of detachment were plain. The shiny, secular, unhaunted contemporaneity that was to have remained in the wake of "the burden of the past" turned out not to inspire or to incite in quite the strenuous old way. And the deposing of the sacred in the name of history ended in the sacralization of history. History became God, the nineteenth and twentieth century's paltry contribution to the ranks of the divine; but this was a God that did not address, that could not be addressed, that was trapped in time, that never intervened except as "development," that seemed to justify any conceivable human outcome. Historical awareness became merely a modern kind of dogma; and the scholarly study of history came to seem like a desiccating activity, a means for depleting the primal energies of individuals and peoples. History seemed to lack the vitality of memory. Historiography seemed unable to nourish to transmit the traditions that it studied to the generations that awaited them. Suddenly the past was not the danger, the past was itself in danger. And the "burden of the past" was not the problem; the real problem was the burden of the burden of the past: the dourness and the dutifulness of the historical attitude the sense that all that remains for the heirs of the past is to recover and to record, to be grateful and custodial.

And so there arose, in reaction to the transports of historical consciousness, the modern romance of memory. Memory would battle history, for the prize of a living past. Of course, this was ironic, insofar as historiography had developed precisely as a response to the inadequacies of annals and chronicles based substantially on memory, or as a response to the fear that memories were being lost. The modern discovery of memory as a superior avenue of access to the past was made first in philosophy and literature and psychology, in Bergson and Proust and Freud, and came later to professional historians; but in recent decades it has thrown the historians, too, into a condition of crisis. Pierre Nora has nicely described the contradiction between memory and history:

> Memory is life, borne by living societies founded in its name. It remains in permanent evolution, open to the dialectic of remembering and forgetting, unconscious of its successive deformations, vulnerable to manipulation and appropriation, susceptible to being long dormant and periodically revived. History, on the other hand, is the reconstruction, always problematic and incomplete, of what is no longer. Memory is a perpetually actual phenomenon, a bond tying us to the eternal present; history is a representation of the past. Memory, insofar as it is affective and magical, only accommodates those facts that suit it. . . . History calls for analysis and criticism. . . . Memory takes root in the concrete, in spaces, gestures, images and objects; history binds itself strictly to temporal continuities, to progressions and relations between things. Memory is absolute, while history can only conceive the relative. At the heart of history is a critical discourse that is antithetical to spontaneous memory. History is perpetually suspicious of memory, and its true mission is to suppress and destroy it.

Nora is a historian who takes the side of memory. It is, as I say, a romantic view, even an elegiac one, which longs for organic communities with seamless traditions that retain their meanings in practices and settings that sufficiently approximate the original practices and the original settings to make genuine continuity possible. There is a mystical quality to such a view of memory. About collective memory, certainly, there will always be a mystical quality, since it consists in the unaccountable capacity to remember—not to know, but to remember—things that happened to others. The Jews in particular pioneered these refreshing abolitions of time and space: it may be said that memory, in its ritual and legal and liturgical expressions, protected the Jews from history. (And from historiography, too: it was not until the spectacular dislocations of the sixteenth century that the Jewish obsession with the past issued in a methodologically strict and secularizing study of it.) A generation ago the Jew was the alienated one. Now the Jew is the one who remembers. Thus Nora, in a typical simplification: "In [the Jewish] tradition, which has no other history than its own memory, to be Jewish is to remember that one is such." Of course, there is something brackish and circular (and historically incorrect) about such a characterization of Jewish identity; but the contemporary prestige of memory appears to carry all before it. In the view of many historians and critics, it was the interference with memory, by means of the critical study of history and the reform of the ritual and liturgical carriers of memory, that left modern Judaism with a rupture that has not yet healed.

The contest between memory and history becomes acute, even excruciating, when the subject of the backward look is catastrophe. One of the many ways in which the Nazi war against the Jews was unprecedented was that it occurred in the age of historical consciousness. The savage assaults on the Jewish communities in Ashkenaz, or the Rhineland, during the Crusades of 1096 and 1146 were the first significant attempt (there was a similar attempt at extermination in Visigothic Spain, about which little is known) to wipe out an entire Jewry physically; yet the Ashkenazic literature in the wake of the atrocities is stunning for its reticence about the events. Liturgical lamentations were written, and chronicles of the events were produced that were probably also intended for liturgical use; but otherwise Jewish literature in the aftermath of the trauma is remarkable for the absence from it of any extended expression of a documentary impulse.

The atrocities of 1933–45, by contrast, were perpetrated in a culture that was drenched in historicity. Indeed, the killers themselves, animated by a philosophy of history, had a pathologically documentary mentality; they left a great deal of paper and film. (The killers' films of the killings, some of which may be seen at the United States Holocaust Memorial Museum in Washington, are a rape of the eye.) And lying in wait for the historical consciousness of the killers was the historical consciousness of the survivors and the scholars. They proceeded swiftly to produce a body of evidence of the genocide that is staggering in its size and its sophistication. The historiography of the Holocaust was an act of intellectual heroism, not least because it was the intention of the Nazis to make precisely such a historiography impossible. They weirdly believed that they could cover the traces of their crime, that the evidence of the death of the Jews would die with the Jews. "Among ourselves it should be mentioned quite frankly," Himmler told a group of SS officials in Poznan in 1943,

> and yet we will never speak of it publicly. . . . Most of you must know what it means when a hundred corpses are lying side by side or five hundred or a thousand. To have stuck it out and at the same time—apart from exceptions caused by human weakness—to have remained decent men, that is what has made us hard. This is a page of glory in our history, which has never been written and is never to be written.

But some of Himmler's victims were, in their way, also hard. The historiographical labor was begun by the victims themselves, in the Warsaw Ghetto and elsewhere. The page was written, though not quite as Himmler would have written it. In the war between History and history, history won.

In assembling the record of the Nazi war against the Jews, moreover, history and memory worked together. The survivors brought precise pain and the scholars brought painful precision. Without betraying its own methods, history approached memory's proximity to its subject. It was, in Nora's admiring term, "concrete." To be sure, the rise of "Holocaust Studies" and its professionalization has had a certain anesthetizing effect; the chat of these experts can chill your bones. (In the historian of evil, however, intellectual poise is a spiritual accomplishment.) Yet soon the survivors will be gone, and only the scholars will remain. It is no longer true, as the ancient Indian saying has it, that an event lives only as long as the last person who remembers it; the historians have stalled oblivion. Still, it will not be long before we find ourselves in a more customary, more distant, more mediated, more indirect relationship to the Holocaust.

Will we mourn the loss of memory? Will the loss of memory mean the loss of the past? "We speak so much of memory," Nora writes ruefully, "because there is so little of it." Well, yes; the elders die. The slippage of immediacy is inevitable. (For the survivors of the catastrophe, of course, this slippage is an easing, a passing into peace.) Not least for this reason, we had better be careful about the idealization of memory, and the disparagement of the historical attitude.

But there are other reasons, too. Remembering is the twin of forgetting. Memory is not retention, it is selection. (Memory is precisely what a computer does *not* have.) The memory of an event is an interpretation of an event; and the interpretation may be beautiful, or moving, or necessary for a certain end, but it leaves the mind with work to be done. The traffic between memory and history is a traffic between magic and doubt. Without magic, there is no continuity; without doubt, there is no contemporaneity. Traditions decay or disappear if they are not remembered, but they do not flourish in the hands of those who live in the past. And memory, too, may cloud or clog one's view of one's time. Even when it is true, memory is demagogic. It compels; but the world is not suffering from too little compulsion. And so the brake of history is not a bad thing.

And sometimes memory alienates more powerfully than history; or rather, it is too inalienable to be of any use. Memory is not always, or only, an instrument of knowledge; it is also a confinement, an irreversible sentence of individuation. Listen to a survivor, say, at a kitchen table in Brooklyn recall her experiences of Poland, 1943. If you grasp the meaning, you will grasp the distance. You are being addressed across a gulf, through a thick wall of glass, from the farthest corner of a banished heart. You listen carefully, but an approximation of her experience is the best you can hope for. And the love that you feel for this woman makes the sense of impassability even harder to bear. You begin to understand that there are situations in which memory is not a privilege, in which history is preferable to memory: if history is your only source of knowledge about the darkness, then you were one of the lucky ones. You look at this woman in the work of recollection and you no longer remark on the beauty of memory, or on its utility for the perpetuation of the knowledge of the disaster, you wish only that memory would falter and die, and you bless the moments of forgetfulness and all the divagations of ordinary life after the end of the world.

Memory, in sum, is not only authentic, and radiant, and poetic. It is also hurtful, and fragile ("who, after all," asked Hitler, "speaks today of the annihilation of the Armenians?"), and, in a strict sense, untransmittable. Therefore it needs the fortifyings of history: the corrections, the comparisons, the conclusions. (Memory is color, history is line.) The first of the many accomplishments of the United States Holocaust Memorial Museum, which opens this week on the Mall in Washington, is the paradox of its name: a memorial museum, a house of memory *and* history. Here the vividness of recollection joins the sturdiness of research. The stinging subjectivity of the testimonies of the survivors is met in these galleries by the tart objectivity of photographs, films, maps, statistics and objects.

In the creation of a memorial, moreover, there is another reason that memory must be accompanied by history, and feeling must be annotated by fact; and that is the fickleness of memorials themselves. These things shed their meanings with almost cynical alacrity. The public spaces of modern cities are littered with figures and markers that are more or less illegible. Their opacity is itself a kind of release from the particulars of the past.

Instead of history, they give a warm sensation of historicity. They say only: once there was someone who wanted something remembered here. Before these figures and markers nobody any longer stops, or thinks, or shudders. They are bulwarks against thought, devices for the prevention of any intrusion of the past into the present. "There is nothing in this world as invisible as a monument," wrote Robert Musil: "They are no doubt erected to be seen—indeed, to attract attention. But at the same time they are impregnated with something that repels attention, causing the glance to roll right off, like water droplets off an oilcloth, without even pausing for a moment. . . . This can no doubt be explained. Anything that endures over time sacrifices its ability to make an impression. Anything that constitutes the walls of our life, the backdrop of our consciousness, so to speak, forfeits its capacity to play a role in that consciousness."

The proliferation of Holocaust memorials in the United States poses the problem starkly. The banality of the memory of evil, you might call it. According to James E. Young, in an interesting survey of Holocaust memorials called *The Texture of Memory*, just published by Yale University Press, "Today, nearly every major American city is home to at least one, and often several, memorials commemorating aspects of the Holocaust." This is affecting, and this is revolting. It certainly makes the fear that the Holocaust will be forgotten seem faintly ridiculous. And worse, it ensures that if the Holocaust is forgotten, or if it is pushed to the peripheries of consciousness and culture, then it will be partly owing to the memorials themselves, which will have made the horror familiar and thereby robbed it of its power to shock and to disrupt. Of the memorial in Tucson, Young writes that "the monument now functions as the architectural entryway visitors pass through on their way into a stunning complex of auditoriums, cavernous gymnasiums, weight rooms, swimming pools and tennis courts. Built as it is into the wall and the plaza, the memorial houses and thus lends a certain cast to all the activities that take place in the center." The Raoul Wallenberg Tennis Classic?

Remembering saves; but it also salves. Too little memory dishonors the catastrophe; but so does too much memory. In the contemplation of the death camps, we must be strangers; and if we are not strangers, if the names of the killers and the places of the killing and the numbers of the killed fall easily from our tongues, then we are not remembering to remember, but remembering to forget. Of course, the banalization of the memory serves many purposes. It suits the poverty of American Jewishness. "It's a sad fact," said the principal philanthropist of the grotesque Simon Wiesenthal Center in Los Angeles, "that Israel and Jewish education and all the other familiar buzzwords no longer seem to rally Jews behind the community. The Holocaust, though, works every time." His candor was refreshing, even if it was obscene. On the subject of the extermination of the Jews of Europe, the

Jews of America are altogether too noisy. They need the subject too much. Those Jews of the Rhineland in the twelfth and thirteenth centuries who omitted their experience of atrocity from so many of their liturgical verses and legal rulings and pietistic sermons and mystical speculations had not forgotten it. Indeed, they were, in their commemorations of their martyrs, the inventors of Jewish morbidity in the Diaspora. But their Jewishness was too great for their morbidity to overwhelm.

Between 14th Street and 15th Street in Washington, the memorial will be saved from the fate of memorials by the museum, and the museum will be saved from the fate of museums by the memorial. The designers of this institution have made a provision for shock. One of the achievements of the Holocaust Memorial Museum is that it leads its visitors directly from history to silence. Its exhibition ends in a Hall of Rememberance, a six-sided, classically proportioned chamber of limestone, a chaste vacancy, seventy feet high, unencumbered by iconography, washed in a kind of halting light, in a light that seems anxious about its own appropriateness. There are steps all around the cold marble floor that will most likely serve as seats. The least that you can do, after seeing what you have just seen, is sit down and be still.

The Hall of Remembrance is a temple of ineffability. This, then, is the plot, the historical and spiritual sequence got right, of the infernal display on the Mall: memory, stiffened by history, then struck dumb.

II.

The museum is a pedagogical masterpiece. It begins at the beginning and it ends at the end. It illustrates the sufferings of all who suffered. It resists the rhetoric about *Shoah v'Gvurah*, Holocaust and Heroism, as if there was as much heroism as there was holocaust. It does not prettify or protect the visitor from the worst. (Nazi footage of killings in the pits, and of medical experiments in the camps, is shown on monitors behind walls that are too high for children to see over. Adults may wish that the walls were higher still.) And it does not conclude its narrative in triumph. There was no triumph, at least for the Jews. There was a narrow escape, that is all. The Nazis did not win their war against the Jews. But they did not lose it, either.

The building itself teaches. It seems to have been distilled, but not abstracted, from its subject. Its principal materials are brick and steel and brick bolted with steel. The exhibits are located in eight towers, each topped by a kind of sentry box, which surround a huge atrium, into which you enter. The impression is elegant and oppressive. The industrial atmosphere is ominous. This is an atrium without air; it holds the opposite of air, the end of air. A staircase that looks like a railroad track rises into a wall of black marble, into which a doorway has been cut and set in brick in the shape of the entrance to Birkenau, which was the killing center at Auschwitz. The skylight, too, puts you in mind of a train station, until you begin to notice that this gigantic frame of steel is warped, twisted, a derangement of rational design. Above the skylight, from one of the glass bridges that connect the towers, the deformity is truly terrifying. The building seems to be held together by what is tearing it apart. Like survivors; like Jews.

A large part of the instruction that this museum imparts is tactile. Alongside the maps and the charts and the films and the photographs, there are the objects, the stuff, the things of the persecutions and the murders. The museum is a kind of reliquary. The relics are sacred and profane; and while there are things in the world more sacred, there surely are none more profane. Here is the blackened metal chassis on which corpses were burned at Mauthausen when the ovens were too full to receive them, and here are the canisters and the crystals of Zyklon-B gas. Here is a pile of umbrellas and tea strainers and can openers and toothbrushes that Jews brought to Auschwitz. Here is the wooden frame of the ark that held the Torah scrolls in the synagogue at Essen, stabbed and scratched and scarred across the words that warned the worshiper to remember before Whom he stood, provoking now an almost Christian desire to touch the wound. Here is a madly detailed model of the Lodz Ghetto sculpted out of a suitcase by a Jew in hiding. Here is what remains of a Mauser rifle and a Steyn pistol used by Jewish fighters in the Warsaw Ghetto. Here is a Danish fishing boat that carried hundreds of Jews to safety. (Here you smile. It is the only spot in the building where you do.)

Perhaps the most startling passage in Claude Lanzmann's *Shoah* was its reconstruction of the trajectory of a killing van in Chelmno, because it was filmed in real time: nothing was abridged or abbreviated, the van was filmed along the local roads for exactly as long as it would have taken for the gas in the van to kill the people inside it. In the Holocaust Memorial Museum, there is real space. Here is a railway car, of the Karlsruhe kind, number 31599-G, and in this railway car Jews were carried to the death camps. The freight car weighs fifteen tons; its ceiling is mean and low, with four small slatted windows and iron bolts on its doors. It carried about a hundred Jews every time it traveled. Now, in the semidarkness of an exhibition hall in America, you stand inside it, and are defeated. Its wooden walls are thoroughly scratched and splintered, and to every scratch and splinter you ascribe a panicked hand. Though it is empty, it feels crowded and cramped. You wish that you could smell a human smell, but there is only the smell of old wood, and a general stench of technocratic efficiency. It occurs to you that you are standing in a coffin. It also occurs to you that there are survivors visiting this museum who may find themselves in this coffin for the second time.

And here are barracks from Auschwitz. More real space. More old wood. The living quarters of the dying. The prisoners slept, whatever that means, six in a row, on three levels. You realize, looking at these structures, that they may have given respite, but they never gave rest. The wood is hard, and unexpectedly smooth to the touch; it appears to have been polished by all the flesh that passed over it. There is no room to sit up or to stretch out. Here men, or what was left of men, were merely stored in rows for the night. You try to imagine the desolation of returning in the evening to these planks. And you keep running your hands over them, because their materiality wakens you. It reminds you that all this dying was lived.

But lived by whom? The conventional answer is: by Jews, Gypsies, homosexuals, Communists, Jehovah's Witnesses and so on. But those appellations describe groups, not individuals; and when, in the remembrance of the catastrophe, the victims are seen as individuals, it is usually in the period between the completion of their life and the completion of their death, in the purgatory between the ramp and the oven, as starved, naked, shaved, numbered, emaciated men and women whose physical extremity, and its fearful inscription in their faces, makes you stop before the photographs and consider them one by one. By that time, however, these people were already gone; they were just not yet dead. The victims of the Holocaust are known too much by the manner of their death.

In the museum on the Mall, however, there is a tower of photographs, three stories high. They are photographs of the Jews of Ejszyszki, a town in Lithuania. Jews lived in Ejszyszki for 900 years, until 1941, when the Jewish community of Ejszyszki was shot to death in two days. (There were more than 4,950 cities, towns, villages, and hamlets in which the Nazis and their Polish, Ukrainian, Latvian, Lithuanian, Estonian, Slovakian, Hungarian, and Croatian accomplices destroyed the Jewish population.) In the years before the war, four local photographers set out to produce a pictorial record of the Jews of Ejszyszki; and now their pictures rise high into the tranquil brick tower, rows and rows of them, all around you, in black and white and sepia, and finally you see *who died*.

There are gymnasts and teachers and merchants and rabbis and nannies and writers and carpenters. There are preening male bathers by the sea; humorless Zionist activists of the right and the left; families in gloomy, paneled interiors, gathered around tables heavy with cutlery and cakes; cantors, looking silly in the cantorial way, assembled for their graduation; a girl and a boy lazing on a hammock in the woods; a rabbi in wrinkled gabardine strolling up a hill, his hands behind his back and his text in his head; a man in a Mickey Mouse suit on bended knee before a slightly startled girl in a park; a group of young women smartly turned out to ski; a father propping his son up on his shiny new car.

One picture crushed me. A girl sits, her legs crossed, on a sofa. She wears a woolen cap and a plaid shirt and a long skirt pulled tightly over her thighs and (in Ejszyszki!) cowboy boots. She is in her teens. In her hand is a cigarette. On the wall above her hangs a picture of a dashing, medieval-looking cavalier. And close to her, very close to her, sits a young man in a rocking chair. He looks nothing like the cavalier. He seems a little bookish, in glasses and jacket and tie. She bends toward him confidently and confidently he lights her cigarette. They do not look like they are lovers, though they might be lovers. They do not look like they are going to die, though they are going to die.

That is what is missing from so many accounts of the end of Jewish life in Europe: the eros of Jewish life in Europe before the end. These slaughtered Jews loved the world. They were at home in it, exile or no exile. The melancholy in the tradition that they inherited seems not to have sapped them. Their piety and their impiety were equally robust. Around the thousands of people in these hundreds of photographs there is not a trace of the angel of death. Only the contemporary viewer sees it hovering, impatiently, in every frame. And for that reason there is no room in this great and grisly building that you visit more bitterly. In the other rooms, the ones that show death, you learn the lesson of finality. In this room, the one that shows life, you learn the lesson of perishability. I am not sure which lesson is the harder one. How do you choose between sorrow and fear?

III.

In the weeks leading up to the opening of the Holocaust Memorial Museum in Washington, Germany was nervous. According to Marc Fisher in *The Washington Post*, the German government offered the museum "millions of dollars" to include an exhibit on postwar Germany and its decades of democracy. The government's press spokesman immediately denied that such an offer was made, but he added that "the federal government would have welcomed it if the museum had included information on German resistance to National Socialism [it does] as well as on the successful construction of a state based on the rule of law and of a liberal democracy in postwar Germany." A historian in Munich who acts as an informal adviser to Helmut Kohl observed that "it would have been good for educational reasons to show that Germany has changed since 1945. It was a mistake for the museum not to include other cases of genocide." A writer in the *Frankfurter Allgemeine Zeitung* observed that the museum's emphasis on gas chambers and death camps "has less to do with the German past than with the American present"; and the paper's Washington correspondent wondered whether "half a century after war's end it is advisable to lead millions of visitors through a museum that ends in 1945 and thereby may leave the lasting impression [that] these are the Germans and this is Germany."

There is something comic about the Germans asking the Jews to help them with the image of what the Germans did to the Jews. Finally, though, the comedy is thin. This complaint, that a true depiction of the German war against the Jews is an expression of hostility to Germany, has been heard before. When *Shoah* appeared, it was attacked for its uncomplicated attitude toward the killers, for its unembarrassed hatred of the Germans it filmed. Now, in the dark halls of the museum on the Mall, as you file by these pictures of German doctors in their laboratory coats posing over their fascinating corpses, and German soldiers politely escorting women into the woods, and German officers smiling as they put a bullet into the head of a Jew perched at the edge of a pit, the problem of hatred will be posed again. And so I would like to say a few things in defense of hatred.

First, that hatred is not always the enemy of, or the obstacle to, understanding. Sometimes, and certainly in the instance of radical evil, hatred may be evidence that a state of affairs has been properly understood. I will give, as an example, the report of an atrocity that broached this problem for me many years ago. When I was a boy, I was told of a Nazi satrap in Galicia, in Poland, in the early 1940s, who picked up a Jewish baby by its legs and tore it apart. My sense of the world has not yet recovered from that anecdote. I remember vividly my response. It was hatred: hatred of the man, hatred of the deed, hatred of the circumstances in which the deed could have been committed.

I was, as I say, a boy; but when I reflect now upon that man, and that deed, and those circumstances, I do not conclude that my hatred was something that I must overcome, for the purpose of a more accurate or a more humane analysis. Quite the contrary. Were I not to hate that man, and that deed, and those circumstances, or were I left in confusion about whether or not I should hate them, there would be reason to wonder whether I had understood what I had been told, I mean the plain meaning of the story, or worse, whether I had understood what we mean by understanding, that is, the axioms by which our civilization orders and evaluates human experience. There would have been reason to wonder, in short, whether I was what we call a moral idiot.

That epithet quite properly links judgment to intelligence. Not to recognize moral idiocy, however, is itself a form of moral idiocy. If, by hatred, we mean an attitude of condemnation accompanied by an intensity of feeling, then the absence of hatred in the face of radical evil would constitute not merely an ethical failure, but also an intellectual one. If I had not hated the Nazis, I would not have understood them. The relations between knowing and judging are complicated; the empirical and the moral cannot be easily disentangled. It is not always true that *tout comprendre c'est tout pardonner.*

Comprehension does not always lead to forgiveness. In certain cases, indeed, forgiveness may signify the absence of comprehension. The hatred of the Jew for the Nazi was not just a feeling, it was the emotional expression of a correct analysis of the position of the Jew in the Nazi world.

Nor is all hatred like all other hatred. There is, I suppose, a similarity of the surface—a man who hates is more like a man who hates than a man who loves—just as there is a similarity of the surface between the Nazi who killed a Jew and the Jew who killed a Nazi. They were, both of them, killers. But distinctions must be made. There was a difference between the hatred of the Nazi for the Jew and the hatred of the Jew for the Nazi. The Nazi hated the Jew because he believed that the Jew was not human. The Jew hated the Nazi because he believed that the Nazi was human, but had betrayed his humanity. The Jewish hatred, Lanzmann's hatred, the hatred that you feel in this museum before, say, the German film of the massacre at Libau in Lithuania, is premised finally on the assumption of a commonality between the oppressed and the oppressor, and it amounts to a defense of that commonality against those who would deny it.

There were also decent and brave Germans who tried to resist the Nazis and to assist the Jews. The failure to acknowledge and to honor those Germans amounts to a notion of collective guilt, which is a very Nazi notion. Contrary to its German critics, the Holocaust Memorial Museum acknowledges the German heroes and honors them. In this respect, moreover, Lanzmann's critics were right: it *was* disgraceful that none of the dissenters and the rescuers appeared in his film. But, I hasten to add, it was only a little disgraceful. There is the matter of proportions. The few, however admirable, were not the equal, or the exoneration, of the many. The historical truth is brutal. It may be simplistic, but it is not false, to describe these events in Europe between 1933 and 1945 as an attempt by a people called the Germans to destroy a people called the Jews. The assault on the Jews was, actively and passively, a collective assault. It is a distortion of the past to deny the dissenters and the rescuers a place in the history of the catastrophe; but it is also a distortion to give them a pride of place.

There is more. Just as hatred is not necessarily an intellectual failure, it is not necessarily a moral failure. In the debate about *Shoah*, it was suggested that Lanzmann's hatred of the evildoers made him resemble them. He, too, it was said, was making absolute distinctions between human beings. As one of the critics wrote, "If one sees no resemblance between self and other, and believes all evil to be in the other and none in oneself, one is (tragically) condemned to imitating one's enemy. If, on the other hand, one discovers one's resemblance to the enemy, and recognizes the evil in oneself as well as the good in the other, then one is truly different from the enemy." There is nobility in these words, and perversity: the executed had about as much in common with the executioners as the dead had in common with the living.

It is odd, this worry about the virtue of the victims. ("It would have been more fair and more open," wrote the historian from Munich about the museum in Washington, "to show that Jews care about other acts of genocide.") I wonder how many of those who preach this loftiness about the evil in all of us have considered the extent to which it would damage the capacity for resistance to evil. What, exactly, does the evil of another time or another place have to do with the evil of this time and this place, except to inhibit the fight against it? Can devils be opposed only by saints? The conclusion of such reasoning is *fiat justitia pereant Judeii*: let justice be done and the Jews perish. In 1943 such reasoning led Simone Weil to the outrageous insistence that France's colonies robbed it of the moral authority to fight Germany. Surely the difference between the man who points the gun and the man at whom the gun is pointed is greater, at least at the moment of their encounter, than the similarity between them. It is trivial at any moment, and it is grotesque at that moment, to point out that one day the relation may be reversed because there is evil in all of us. Of course there is evil in all of us; but not all of us act on our evil.

On April 13, 1943, in the Warsaw Ghetto, Emanuel Ringelblum entered these words in his diary:

> Spent the two Passover nights at Schachna's. There was an interesting discussion about vengeance. Mr. Isaac, who had been interned in a prison camp in Pomerania, demonstrated that vengeance would never solve anything. The vanquished would in turn plan their own vengeance, and so it would go on forever. There was talk that raising the moral level of humanity was the only solution.

Mr. Isaac's idealism is heartbreaking. But Ringelblum was skeptical. His gloss on the discussion at the seder introduces a different moral voice. "The Jewish revenge [is] that the Jews are very forgiving. The Germans are only people after all"—and then he adds, "except for the Gestapo!" Do those final four words diminish Ringelblum ethically? Do they catch him in a resemblance to his enemy? I do not think so. For the Gestapo were not "only people." His exclusion of them from his sense of humanity indicated only that he had understood them properly.

It also allowed him to act against them. If knowing did not run into judging, if critical thought did not make way for moral action, then the triumph of the Nazis over the Jews would have been total. But Ringelblum became one of the organizers of the revolt in the Warsaw Ghetto, which took place ten days later. And on March 7, 1944, he was executed, with his wife and his son, in the ruins of the ghetto. The Holocaust Memorial Museum opened in Washington on the fiftieth anniversary of the Warsaw Ghetto revolt, and the milk can that hid Ringelblum's archive of the ghetto may be found on the second floor. For its faithfulness, its color of rust has turned a color of gold.

IV.

But why this museum, and this memorial, on the Mall?

The question is not a new one. In 1946, A. R. Lerner, a Viennese journalist who fled the Nazis and came to New York, where he tirelessly spread the news of what the Nazis had done to the Jews, proposed that a monument to the "Heroes of the Warsaw Ghetto and the Six Million Jews Slain by the Nazis" be established in New York. Mayor O'Dwyer and Parks Commissioner Moses agreed, and the sculptor Jo Davidson chose a spot in Riverside Park. (I take this tale from Young's book.) On October 10, 1947, thousands of people came to Riverside Park to dedicate the site. *The New York Times* wrote the following day that "it is fitting that a memorial to 6 million victims of the most tragic mass crime in history, the Nazi genocide of Jews, should rise in this land of liberty." But the monument was never raised, not least because the opinion of the *Times* was not shared by everyone. In 1964, when a design for the monument was submitted to the city's Arts Commission, one of the commissioners, the sculptor Eleanor Platt, declared that it would "set a highly regrettable precedent. How would we answer other special groups who want to be similarly represented on public land?" And Newbold Morris, the city's parks commissioner, further objected that "monuments in the parks should be limited to events of American history."

The proposal to create a museum and a memorial to the Holocaust on the Mall in Washington, on the hallowed ground of the American republic, was similarly controversial. In 1987 the architecture critic of *The Washington Post*, in a churlish column called "In Search of a Delicate Balance," repeated Morris's objection, and worried about "the symbolic implications of the memorial's placement—that the Nazi extermination of 6 million Jews [could be considered] an integral part of the American story." Of course, nobody ever suggested that the Holocaust was an event in American history. What the delicate balancer seems to have forgotten, however, is that this is a country of immigrants. The past of America is elsewhere. (Here the past *is* a foreign country.) The collective memory of this country will always include names and dates foreign and far away. Pluralism makes demands on the imagination.

And yet the objection is not hard to understand. This is a tolerant country, but it is not an innocent country. It is permanently stained with the fate of the Native Americans and the African Americans; and neither the memories nor the histories of those wretched Americans may be met on the Mall.

And there are still other genocides that haunt still other Americans—the Armenians, for example—that are unacknowledged. (A home to all the peoples of the world is a home to all the scars of the world.) For a time there was talk of a separate wing in the Holocaust Memorial Museum that would document and commemorate all the catastrophes, but the wing was never built.

It is now clear that a Hall of Genocide would have been a ghastly mistake, a macabre multiculturalist insult to the memories of all. For the most lasting impression that the Holocaust Memorial Museum leaves is of human foulness. This building interferes not only with your opinion of Germany, or Europe, or Western civilization; it interferes with your opinion of the human world. A Jew who wanders through these galleries feels pity for his people turn into pity for his race. There occurs a general darkening of outlook. For there is a sickening sense in which a corpse is a human being that has been returned to its sheerest humanity; there is something truly universal about a corpse. Anybody who looks at these images of corpses and sees only images of Jews has a grave moral problem.

It is true, as Jewish historians and theologians have argued, that the Holocaust was in some way "unique"; but it was in no way so "unique" that it does not press upon the souls of all who learn of it. The story of the life and the death of the Jews in Europe is one of the great human stories (which, by the way, is also one of the reasons that Jews should study it). I am not sure that the memory of that story, or the history of it, will suffice to stay the hand of the malicious and the murderous, or that a museum and a memorial will stand much in the way of prejudice and its appetite for power. The world fifty years later does not seem especially restrained by the world fifty years before. Still, it is not just Jews who will be warned by what they see in this building on the Mall. All are warned. Here is the precedent. Just because it was the worst does not mean that it will be the last.

And so it is right that the first thing you notice, when you leave the Hall of Remembrance, is the figure of Thomas Jefferson. Across the calming waters of the Tidal Basin he presides perdurably over his own memorial, an architect of the only political system in the history of the world that made men free without thinking too highly of them. You think, in the light of what you have just seen, that it was no small achievement to found a democracy upon a pessimistic view of human nature. And you think, in the light of what you have just seen, that it was just as well.

PART II

Scenes from America

In a Schoolroom

RANDOLPH S. BOURNE

NOVEMBER 17, 1914

The other day I amused myself by slipping into a recitation at the suburban high school where I had once studied as a boy. The teacher let me sit, like one of the pupils, at an empty desk in the back of the room, and for an hour I had before my eyes the interesting drama of the American school as it unfolds itself day after day in how many thousands of classrooms throughout the land. I had gone primarily to study the teacher, but I soon found that the pupils, after they had forgotten my presence, demanded most of my attention.

Their attitude towards the teacher, a young man just out of college and amazingly conscientious and persevering, was that good-humored tolerance which has to take the place of enthusiastic interest in our American school. They seemed to like the teacher and recognize fully his good intentions, but their attitude was a delightful one of all making the best of a bad bargain, and co-operating loyally with him in slowly putting the hour out of its agony. This good-natured acceptance of the inevitable, this perfunctory going through by its devotees of the ritual of education, was my first striking impression, and the key to the reflections that I began to weave.

As I sank down to my seat I felt all that queer sense of depression, still familiar after ten years, that sensation, in coming into the schoolroom, of suddenly passing into a helpless, impersonal world, where expression could be achieved and curiosity asserted only in the most formal and difficult way. And the class began immediately to divide itself for me, as I looked around it, into the artificially depressed like myself, commonly called the "good" children, and the artificially stimulated, commonly known as the "bad," and the envy and despair of every "good" child. For to these "bad" children, who are, of course, simply those with more self-assertion and initiative than the rest, all the careful network of discipline and order is simply a direct and irresistible challenge. I remembered the fearful awe with which I used to watch the exhaustless ingenuity of the "bad" boys of my class to disrupt the peacefully dragging recitation; and behold, I found myself watching intently, along with all the children in my immediate neighborhood, the patient activity of a boy who spent his entire hour in so completely sharpening a lead-pencil that there was nothing left at the end but the lead. Now what normal boy would do so silly a thing or who would look at him in real life? But here, in this artificial atmosphere, his action had a sort of symbolic quality; it was assertion against a stupid authority, a sort of blind resistance against the attempt of the schoolroom to impersonalize him. The most trivial incident assumed importance; the chiming of the town-clock, the passing automobile, a slip of the tongue, a passing footstep in the hall, would polarize the wandering attention of the entire class like an electric shock. Indeed, a large part of the teacher's business seemed to be to demagnetize, by some little ingenious touch, his little flock into their original inert and static elements.

For the whole machinery of the classroom was dependent evidently upon this segregation. Here were these thirty children, all more or less acquainted, and so congenial and sympathetic that the slightest touch threw them all together into a solid mass of attention and feeling. Yet they were forced, in accordance with some principle of order, to sit at these stiff little desks, equidistantly apart, and prevented under penalty from communicating with each other. All the lines between them were supposed to be broken. Each existed for the teacher alone. In this incorrigibly social atmosphere, with all the personal influences playing around, they were supposed to be, not a network or a group, but a collection of things, in relation only with the teacher.

These children were spending the sunniest hours of their whole lives, five days a week, in preparing themselves, I assume by the acquisition of knowledge, to take their places in a modern world of industry, ideas and business. What institution, I asked myself, in this grown-up world bore resemblance to this so carefully segregated classroom? I smiled, indeed, when it occurred to me that the only possible thing I could think of was a State Legislature. Was not the teacher a sort of Speaker putting through the business of the session, enforcing a sublimated parliamentary order, forcing his members to address only the chair and avoid any but a formal recognition of their colleagues? How amused, I thought, would Socrates have been to come upon these thousands of little training-schools for incipient legislators! He might have recognized what admirably experienced and docile Congressmen such a discipline as this would make, if there were the least chance of any of these pupils ever reaching the House, but he might have wondered what earthly connection it had with the atmosphere and business of workshop and factory and office and store and home into which all these children would so obviously be going. He might almost have convinced himself that the business of adult American life was actually run according to the rules of parliamentary order, instead of on the plane of personal intercourse, of quick interchange of ideas, the understanding and the grasping of concrete social situations.

It is the merest platitude, of course, that those people succeed who can best manipulate personal intercourse, who can best express themselves, whose minds are most flexible and most responsive to others, and that those people would deserve to succeed in any form of society. But has there ever been devised a more ingenious enemy of personal intercourse than the modern classroom, catching, as it does, the child in his most impressionable years? The two great enemies of intercourse are bumptiousness and diffidence, and the classroom is perhaps the most successful instrument yet devised for cultivating both of them.

As I sat and watched these interesting children struggling with these enemies, I reflected that even with the best of people, thinking cannot be done without talking. For thinking is primarily a social faculty; it requires the stimulus of other minds to excite curiosity, to arouse some emotion. Even private thinking is only a conversation with one's self. Yet in the classroom the child is evidently expected to think without being able to talk. In such a rigid and silent atmosphere, how could any thinking be done, where there is no stimulus, no personal expression?

While these reflections were running through my head, the hour dragged to its close. As the bell rang for dismissal, a sort of thrill of rejuvenation ran through the building. The "good" children straightened up, threw off their depression and took back their self-respect, the "bad" sobered up, threw off their swollen egotism, and prepared to leave behind them their mischievousness in the room that had created it. Everything suddenly became human again. The brakes were off, and life, with all its fascinations of intrigue and amusement, was flowing once more. The school streamed away in personal and intensely interested little groups. The real world of business and stimulations and rebounds was thick again here.

If I had been a teacher and watched my children going away, arms around each other, all aglow with talk, I should have been very wistful for the injection of a little of that animation into the dull and halting lessons of the classroom. Was I a horrible "intellectual," to feel sorry that all this animation and verve of life should be perpetually poured out upon the ephemeral, while thinking is made as difficult as possible, and the expressive and intellectual child made to seem a sort of monstrous pariah?

Now I know all about the logic of the classroom, the economies of time, money, and management that have to be met. I recognize that in the cities the masses that come to the schools require some sort of rigid machinery for their governance. Hand-educated children have had to go the way of handmade buttons. Children have had to be massed together into a schoolroom, just as cotton looms have had to be massed together into a factory. The difficulty is that, unlike cotton looms, massed children make a social group, and that the mind and personality can only be developed by the freely inter-stimulating play of minds in a group. Is it not very curious that we spend so much time on the practice and methods of teaching, and never criticise the very framework itself? Call this thing that goes on in the modern schoolroom schooling, if you like. Only don't call it education.

The Matter with Congress

W. L. STODDART

FEBRUARY 20, 1915

One great thing the matter with Congress is Congressmen. There are other things the matter with it, but the chief trouble is the men who make it up. Back of these men, and converting them seemingly into mere manifestations of it, is the terribly ancient system of doing Congressional business which pertains in the Capitol at Washington. In a sense the system is the matter with Congress, not Congressmen; but if ever liberation is to come it will be had at human hands, and the hands will be those of the slaves of the system who alone can strike off their shackles. And the chief thing the matter with Congressmen is that they have not the time to think; the system won't let them, and they won't change the system.

Theoretically Washington is a city set apart for statesmanship. It is a non-commercial city; a city planned wisely and fairly well, with wide streets and fair avenues, with parks and playgrounds and many monuments to the earnest bad taste of the creators of it; a city located on an historic stream, with not a thing to do but to buy and sell real estate, food, clothes and knicknacks, and to legislate. The Washington correspondents always make much of the idea that "national opinion" is formed in Washington, and the average reader of the newspapers, when he reads under a Washington date line that "it is believed here that the Administration" will do so and so, invariably feels that "they" in Washington are holding wise council and are really deliberating with common purpose about real things. In the mind's eye the principal occupation of Congressmen is considering the welfare of the nation. How else can they be amusing themselves, freed as they are from the rush and hurry of farm or city life, freed from the cares of struggling along in Podunk Corners on a salary of less than seventy-five hundred, without carfare at twenty cents a mile, than by studying and pondering, statesmanlike, the needs of the country? Few can imagine how else they can be spending the long and weary sessions between campaigns.

In the average Congressman's working day of somewhat less than ten hours, the periods for thought and study are few and the spaces between them are wide. The morning mail of a man who represents 220,000 people is likely to be large, and if the man is a candidate for the continuing favor of the voting fraction of the 220,000, the task of answering it must be handled with skill and a certain degree of personal attention. This takes time. It takes time to call up by telephone or physically journey to three or four government offices for the purpose of adjusting important district business. It takes time to sit as a member of one or two committees. It takes time to sit in the daily sessions of the House, where time more than energy is consumed in the interest of the public weal. It takes time to tow about Washington the inevitable brides and grooms, the equally inevitable delegations of suffragists, prohibitionists and protestants in one cause or another. It takes time to prepare the few perfunctory speeches which even the average Congressman must prepare during a season—or have someone prepare for him, and this may eventually take more time. And it takes endless, awful periods to talk and discuss and lobby and intrigue for the smallest favors from the machine that controls Congress and thus governs Congressmen. The few Congressmen who accomplish the ordinary routine things and manage in addition to do something noteworthy outside of the rut are strong men.

For example: Mr. Oscar Underwood, the Democratic leader of the House, estimates that during the last Congress a total of fifty-five legislative days, or two legislative months, was consumed in the mere vocal calling of the roll, a tedious process dating from primitive parliamentary era. Converted into money, represented by economies in salaries and running expenses, this means a yearly cost to the country of $50,000—enough money to run a couple of government bureaus, to pay the wages of half a dozen Congressmen, or to provide three-quarters of the salary of the President of the United States. Far more wasteful in the time that could be utilized for taking thought, however, is the obsolescent *viva voce* roll-call. Yet we discover a Representative from the state of Georgia, Mr. Frank Parks, fearing that the installation of a system of electrical voting would "flood this country with legislation, and the people can never get out from under it. The faster you vote," he added, "the more legislation you pass."

Most of the machinery of the Capitol at Washington is like the slow old roll-call, calculated to consume time and to prohibit study. The ventilating system, for example, is bad, though thousands of dollars have been sunk on it. This means that lungs breathe poor air, that blood is sent through the brain unpurified, and the processes of the mind impaired. Ancient habits such as the reading of a journal to which none listens are still retained. Useless and doddering political henchmen clog the doorways. Of expert clerical assistance there is little, and that little is tributary to a system of private contracting firms from whom can be bought copies of documents belonging to the public. Distribution of publications is chaotic and wasteful.

Records of committees are kept or not, lost or not, published or not, as suits individual whims. Two days ahead—a day ahead, even—no one knows what may be the order of business; there is no program of the physical acts of Congress and of Congressmen, no arrangement, no care. The National Voters' League is attempting to run down the various forms of petty graft which exist, it claims, in the House of Representatives. "The public knows nothing about the opportunities which numerous members have of diverting into their own pockets the money value of perquisites intended to aid them in their work."

Grown astray from the paths of what a legislature should be is our national body at Washington. The throwing of the average Representative into the maelstrom of Washington—a converging point for hundreds of streams of thought and a focal center of many rays of national consciousness—is a dangerous act. It is comparable to throwing a boy of twenty into a university and, instead of giving him time and an opportunity to study, ordering him to run both the university and the outside world. No boy could do it, and no sensible person would expect him to. Similarly, hardly a Congressman ever reaches his head above the strong tide of custom which grabs him almost the moment he steps into his job. The things he has to do in order merely to tread water and stay alive are too many for him. He cannot construct because he cannot meditate, dream or digest ideas even if—which also is a rare case—he is capable of receiving dreams or ideas.

A year ago there was smuggled into an appropriation bill an item establishing a bureau or division of legislative reference in the Library of Congress. The item had to be smuggled in because every attempt to secure the frank and open passage of a bill providing for a legislative reference and bill-drafting division had failed. These attempts had failed because of the opposition of Congressmen who thought that they, being the statesmen and legislators, should not delegate any of their work to subordinate officers. Among objectors on these grounds was a highly distinguished and educated Representative from the north shore of Massachusetts. Luckily in spite of him the division, shorn of its bill-drafting feature, was created. It is at work, and it is being used by some of the few thoughtful Congressmen. The majority, however, are enjoying that immunity from mental action, that separation from intellectual effort, and that absence of brain-filling which make life, after all, just about what it is, in Congress as well as out.

A Middle-Class Wife

ALICE AUSTIN WHITE

JANUARY 20, 1917

I have two babies; I hope they may never know how warmly at this moment I hate them. I have a husband; we were married because we were very much in love—and him I hate too. I have a large stock of relatives, and them I hate with the heart and should hate with the hand if I had not the misfortune to be well brought up. This emotion of mine, especially in connection with my spouse and offspring, is, up to the present, local and temporary; indeed I think it will not grow into a permanent hatred, but will gradually assume two peculiar forms: toward my children a passionate and slavish devotion, which will make me resent my daughters-in-law; and toward my husband regards, reasonably kind, which will be reciprocated. My feeling toward my relatives, on the other hand, is becoming quite, quite fixed.

It is all the fault of the children. I wanted children very much; I am fond of children, mentally and physically; and the sheer normality of having them I rejoice in. Furthermore, having been an only child myself, I wanted my children close together so that they might enjoy one another all the way up. I seemed to think I could have babies as easily as a geranium has red blossoms. But I find they commonly come rather hard and that I am not the only woman who for months after a baby is born has an aching body and a dull mind and a defective sense of humor. During this period one's husband is very fatherly toward one, and one begins to feel the small asp of hate nipping one's heart.

The semi-invalidated stage that I have gone through with each of my babies is well past. I am normally sturdy—I have to be. I shall not tell over the tale of the things there are to do, cooking and mending and washing and baby-tending. It happens that I relate my daily household misadventures in a way diverting to my relatives, and they think I dote on housework. A really *model* wife and mother, say my kin; so unexpected, they say, considering her *education*, and all. And when I crawl to bed at half past eight, no thought save detail of housework and child-rearing has found place in my mind all day; I have done no reading save snips from a book propped against the sink faucets while I washed dishes; and I have simply heard, not shared even mentally, such stimulating conversation as my husband brings home to dinner.

I know house and children ought not to take all my day and all my strength. If I had had special training in domestic science and child-psychology and nursing I should doubtless be able to do my work in less time and with far less effort. But in college and university I flew straight in the face of providence, which is a war-name of advising relatives, and worked at mathematics, while in the spare time which I might have devoted to stray courses in home economics as a sop to the gods, I took 'cello. Furthermore, I am glad of it. If I were to have a vacation tomorrow and a financial windfall, I should take two courses in mathematics at the university, and a 'cello lesson a week, and bask in it as my sister-in-law does in chiffon underwear.

You *ought* to have help, say my relatives, and I add a verse to my hymn of hate for them. Among the qualities for which I love my husband are generosity, sensitiveness, modesty and conscientiousness, and I take it each of these characteristics has lower money-making value than the others. Some day when we have got middle-aged, we shall have the salary we need now; and just about that time our relatives will die and leave us money we could get on without. If I happened to be male instead of female, which God forfend, I could double the family income by teaching at the university, but the university does not yet see its way to employing women on its teaching staff, and I therefore scrub the square of my kitchen floor instead.

The truth is, however, that it is not a floor-scrubber and dishwasher that I desire. I could get along with that work or leave it happily undone. It is the care of two children under three that concerns me. It is unremitting and nerve-tearing, and the day in and day out of it is undermining mercilessly my ability to be lovable and to love. Furthermore, I have not the qualifications that would justify entrusting me with sole responsibility for the growth of human beings. Maternal instinct I have in normal amount; I could be trusted to rescue my infants from a burning building, but that is a very different matter from knowing what to do with twenty-four hours' worth of bodily and mental development every day. I do not want a nursemaid; I have no training for my job, but I have an occasional vagrant idea, and it does not appeal to me to exchange my services to my offspring for those of a handmaiden with neither training nor ideas. The helper for me should be a trained psychologist, a child-lover, to be sure, but a child-lover with expert knowledge of the needs of growing minds. She should have also training in the treatment of the smaller physical ailments of children. She ought to cost me two thousand dollars a year, but in the present state of women's wages I have no doubt I could get her for a thousand. And I want her only half the day—five hundred dollars. Our income is sixteen hundred.

Such a woman as I have in mind, however, could take charge of a very appreciable number of children along with my important two. For five or six hours a day she could take care of a nursery-full, and still have time for life and love; while the sigh of relief that a mother breathes when she ties her son's Windsor under his chin and posts him off to school would be breathed five years earlier. Indeed she might enjoy her children, and the sigh be dispensed with. Four hours a day of freedom for us educated, reasonably intelligent, good-stock, middle-class mothers—! The possibilities are limitless. We might even have more children.

The Paradox of Lincoln

HERBERT CROLY

FEBRUARY 18, 1920

In listening to John Drinkwater's legendary drama of Abraham Lincoln, I found obtruding upon my mind an irrelevant and disconcerting observation. I was watching the performance of a play about the life of the man whom the American people have canonized as half hero and half saint. He had earned their gratitude by helping them to steer a true course into and out of a civil war, which, had they gone astray, would have shattered the moral and political continuity of American national life. A new generation of his fellow-countrymen had just emerged as one of the victors in another war—one of the most bloody and costly which history has to record. Yet this play contained passages in which their national hero rebuked an attitude of mind toward the war of his day which no actor could have repeated with safety on the stage in any large American city during the war of our day. He said to Mrs. Blow, "You come to me talking of revenge and destruction and malice and enduring hate. These gentle people [the pacifists] are mistaken, but they are mistaken cleanly and in a great name. It is you that dishonor the cause for which we stand." No actor would have dared, we repeat, to speak these words on an American stage during the war. The prevailing opinion in America had yielded utterly to the obsession of fear, destruction and hatred which Lincoln rebuked in the person of Mrs. Blow. It treated the pacifists whom Lincoln defended as morally contemptible criminals.

The contrast illustrates a characteristic of Lincoln's which his biographers have never sufficiently emphasized. His mind was capable of harboring and reconciling purposes, convictions and emotions so different from one another that to the majority of his fellow-countrymen they would in anybody else have seemed incompatible. He could hesitate patiently without allowing hesitation to become infirmity of will. He could insist without allowing insistence to become an excuse for thoughtless obstinacy. He could fight without quarrelling. He could believe intensely in a war and in the necessity of seeing it through without falling a victim to its fanaticism and without permitting violence and hatred to usurp the place which faith in human nature and love of truth ordinarily occupied in his mind. When, for instance, the crisis came, and the South treated his election as a sufficient excuse for secession, he did not flinch as did Seward and other Republican leaders. He would not bribe the South to abandon secession by compromising the results of Republican victory. Neither would he, if she seceded, agree to treat secession as anything but rebellion. But although he insisted, if necessary, on fighting, he was far more considerate of the convictions and the permanent interests of the South than were the Republican leaders, who for the sake of peace were ready to yield to her demands. In the same spirit he insisted during the war on continuing the fight until the South was ready to return to the Union without conditions and to free the slaves. But his determination to fight until the Northern army had overcome the obstacles to the vindication of the political objects of war did not interfere in his mind, as it did in the minds of so many bitter-enders, with "the hope of love and charity on earth and the spirit of just and merciful dealing."

It is not only, however, that he harbored purposes, convictions and feelings which were incompatible one with another in the minds of other people. He expressed and acted on these usually incompatible motives and ideas with such rare propriety and amenity that their union in his behavior and spirit passes not only without criticism but almost without comment. His fellow-countrymen, who like to consider him a magnified version of the ordinary American and to disguise flattery of themselves under the form of reverence for him, appear not to suspect how different he is from them. He seems to them a simple man whose feelings, motives and words are composed of familiar and homely material and whose values they can sum up in a few simple formulas. He *is* a simple man in the sense that power, responsibility and intensity of personal experience never divided him from his own people who had none of these things. More than any other statesman in history he is entitled to their trust and veneration. But he was not a simple man as simplicity is ordinarily understood. He was an extremely complicated and sophisticated product of a kind of moral and mental discipline which sharply distinguishes him from his fellow citizens both of his own day and today. His simplicity was not a gift. It was the expression of an integrity of feeling, mind and character which he himself elaborately achieved, and which he naturalized so completely that it wears the appearance of being simple and inevitable.

The ordinary characterization of Lincoln as "a man of the people," who rose by his own efforts from the humblest to the most eminent position in American life interprets him as a consummate type of the kind of success which all Americans crave and many achieve. The superficial facts of

Lincoln's life verify this interpretation, but it is none the less profoundly untrue. He did, of course, rise from the occupation of a rail-splitter to that of President of the American Republic. He could not have won the confidence of his fellow-countrymen unless he had appropriated all that was wholesome and fruitful in their life and behavior. He shared their kindliness and good nature, their tenacity of purpose, their good faith and, above all, their innocence. His services to his country and the achieved integrity of his personal life depended on his being good natured, resolute, faithful and innocent. But these comparatively common traits were supplemented in his case by others of a very different complexion. By some miraculous flight of the will he had formed himself into an intellectually candid, concentrated and disinterested man and into a morally humane, humble and magnanimous man. These qualities, which were the very flower of his personal life, neither the average nor the exceptional American of his day or our day can claim to possess. Not only does the American fail to possess these qualities but he either ignores, misunderstands or disparages them. . . .

While Americans do not understand how complicated, many-sided and distinctively individual Lincoln is, his influence on them is the child as much of his many-sidedness as it is of his deceptive simplicity. They find in his words or in his actions, just as they do in the words and actions of Jesus, persuasive precedents for very different kinds of behavior. During the war, for instance, those who wished to fight on to the finish, those who considered it essential to keep political discussion alive and subordinate military action to political purposes, and those in whom war did not extinguish the spirit of fair play and good will—people who represented all these divergent points of view found consolation and support in Lincoln's deeds and phrases. In our own day he serves almost equally well as the prophet both of conservatism and radicalism. The National Industrial Conference Board has issued a leaflet, intended obviously for circulation among wage earners, in which Lincoln figures chiefly as the spiritual forerunner of Calvin Coolidge. They quote him as the advocate of hard work, thrift, the indefeasible right of private property and law and order, and the quotations are, of course, unimpeachably authentic. But the Labor Party of New York carries on its letterhead an emphatic affirmation by Lincoln of the prior claim of labor as compared to capital on the product of industry; and the *New York World* reproduces a passage from the First Inaugural about the right of revolution.

The interests, the sects and the parties all labor to exploit for the benefit of their own propaganda the name of Lincoln, but although they can usually find sentences and acts which they construe for their own benefit, the man himself as a spiritual force always breaks out of the breastworks of any particular cause. He never purveyed one particular political, moral or social specialty. His generation was particularly given to spiritual sectarianism and social crotchets. He himself was extremely accessible to generous emotions and humane ideas. But he was too complete a man to allow his mind to pass into the possession of any cause. And just as he freed himself from the obsessions of the reformer, so he was also too much of a man to yield to the weakness of a tolerant and balanced intelligence and take refuge in intellectual eclecticism. He was first of all himself. With the tact of moral genius he appropriated all that he needed from his surroundings and dismissed apparently without hesitation or struggle all that was superfluous and distracting. Whatever he appropriated he completely domesticated in his own life. The memory of Bismarck belongs chiefly to the German national imperialists; the memory of Gladstone belongs chiefly to *laissez-faire* liberalism; even the memory of Washington belongs more than anything else to the successors of the Federalists. But the memory of Lincoln belongs to all his fellow-countrymen who can guess what magnanimity is. Alone among modern statesmen he is master of every cause and every controversy which entered into his life. He did not flourish principles which he had not assimilated. He never relaxed his grip upon a truth which he had once thoroughly achieved. The action of his mind was always formative. Instead of being enervated and cheapened by its own exercise, as it was in the case of so many of his contemporaries and successors, it waxed steadily in flexibility, in concentration, in imaginative insight and in patient self-possession.

Hence it is that Lincoln is at once the most individual and the most universal of statesmen. In externals he fairly reeks of Middle Western life during the pioneer period. No man could reflect more vividly the manners and the habits of his day and generation. He is inconceivable in any other surroundings. But with all his essentially and intensely Middle Western aspect, he achieved for himself a personality which speaks to human beings irrespective of time and country. He had attained the ultimate object of personal culture. He had married a firm will to a luminous intelligence. His judgments were charged with momentum and his actions were instinct with sympathy and understanding. And because he had charged himself high for his own life he qualified himself to place a high value on the life of other people. He envisaged them all, rich and poor, black and white, rebel and loyalist as human beings, whose chance of being something better than they were depended chiefly on his own personal willingness and ability to help them in taking advantage of it.

Finally Lincoln obtained the mastery of his own life not merely or chiefly as the result of tenacity of purpose and strength of will. When the Divine Comedy of the modern world comes to be written, we shall find all the houses in one of the suburbs of Purgatory occupied by people who were esteemed during life chiefly for strength of character. It was his intelligence and insight which humanized his will. Not only were his peculiar services to his fellow-countrymen before and during the Civil War born of his ability to see more clearly and think harder than the other political leaders, but the structure of his personal life and the poignancy of his personal influence depends most of all on the quality of his mind. It was his insight which enabled him to keep alive during the Civil War the spirit of just and merciful dealing and the hope of love and charity on earth. He knew that without just and merciful dealing human nature could not be redeemed in this or in any other world, and because he knew this, the goblins of war could not lead him astray. Both the integrity and the magnanimity of his life were born of this humane knowledge. Others willed when he did not and much good their willing did. But he *knew* when others did not know and he knew the value of knowledge. In a neglected passage of one of his last speeches he recommends to his fellow-countrymen the study of "the incidents" of the Civil War "as philosophy to learn wisdom from and none of them as wrongs to be revenged." That sentence furnishes the key to the interpretation of Abraham Lincoln. He studied the incidents of his own life, of the lives of other people and the life of his country not as an excuse for revenge or for any kind of moral pugnacity or compensation, but as a philosophy to learn wisdom from.

The Front Porch in Marion

CHARLES MERZ

OCTOBER 6, 1920

Another week or two, and no more pilgrims. In Marion the dusk is falling. Delegations come and go; when Marion's day is done it will be said that Senator Harding has managed to align himself with the best of them. Out of the variety of his early experience and the capacity of his memory he has attained that personal touch which makes each stranger feel at home. For the band, he recalls days when he himself once blew upon a horn. He tells the railway workers of boyhood longings to become an engineer and of a day he helped "wood up" on the old Atlantic and Great Western. The schoolteachers he reminds that once upon a time he taught a country school. For baseball players from Chicago, he recalls his own experiences at first base. For veterans of the Spanish War he can recall "emotions in my breast the day the boys from Marion marched away. . . . I remember also when the *Maine* was sunk." For delegates from certain native Indian tribes, he has this message: "I wish I could take you about here and introduce you to the musical names in this section that all come from the Indian days. . . . I was raised along the banks of the old Olentangy." And for visitors from Richland County, he can recall a Richland County grandmother on her way to market pursued by wolves—"I feel myself almost a part of Richland County."

The Senator is the ideal host.

You feel that, when you arrive in front of the green house in Mount Vernon Avenue with the wide porch that runs around the corner. There is a policeman on duty near the hedge. He does not warn you off the gravel lawn. He does not bid you keep your distance. To those visitors gathering on the walk before the house he points out marks of interest. "Yes, that flagpole came from Canton. Yes, it used to stand on President McKinley's lawn. That's all right, lady. You can go right up and take the little fellow's picture on the steps. Senator Harding doesn't mind a bit. What's that? No, that's not the Senator. I reckon it's one of the newspaper writers. On the porch? That lady? Let's see. Yes, the lady's Mrs. Harding." Mrs. Harding, eh? Two visitors especially are interested. They reveal themselves to the policeman. Between them, he is informed, they constitute the Court of Pettis County, Missouri—Republican now, thank God, and likely to stay Republican forever. They happen to be out looking at courthouses. Their own, not long ago, burned down. If that is really Mrs. Harding . . . ? Sure, says the policeman; go right up and introduce yourselves.

He is only the symbol, this Chesterfield in uniform, of Republican principle in 1920. For a party that may fly apart, whenever it attempts to reach agreement upon a definite issue, self-preservation advises postponement of the possible catastrophe. . . . There is more of a crowd now, and it surges respectfully across the lawn as the Senator appears with the newspapermen who have followed him from his office. He is still answering questions. The crowd holds back. The Senator disengages himself from the newspapermen and comes to greet his callers. He takes the nearest hand. "And what portion of the state do you come from?" he asks. "Ashland," replies his happy guest, and adds: "Motored in this morning." "Roads good?" asks the Senator. "Fine." The Senator turns to an elderly woman. She has been teaching school for forty years, she says, and she wants the Senator's interest in a teachers' pension bill. The Senator assures her that while he recognizes in America no special classes, and while he conceives the Presidency as at best co-equal with the legislative and judicial powers, nevertheless he is ready to promise that the teachers' pension bill will have his close attention. More handshaking follows. But the Senator sights his campaign manager, Mr. Daugherty, and wants a game of quoits. Bolder portions of the crowd adjourn with the contestants to the Harding alley. The Senator removes his coat. The crowd whispers its recognition of a democrat when it sees one, and the moving-picture men start grinding. The Senator pitches six horseshoes. Mr. Daugherty pitches six. It cannot truthfully be said that any of the twelve arrive. But the Senator is declared a winner. The crowd accompanies him around to the front of the house again. And the moving-picture men remain. They push their cameras nearer to the little stake and start taking close-ups. The finished picture must show at least one bull's-eye. So they grind away while an understudy stands just outside of camera range and drops horseshoes accurately upon the hitherto neglected stake. A knockout, the moving-picture men agree.

The Senator now has disappeared. There are delegations coming, delegations from six Ohio counties, and an official porch reception is to follow. Crowds are gathering along Mount Vernon Avenue, awaiting the parade. There are people sitting on the curbstones, sandwich boxes open on their knees. Come upon a crowd waiting like this anywhere else in America and you would guess that Barnum and Bailey themselves were the attraction. But all Barnum's horses and all Bailey's men could not tempt these people from their present posts.

Down the street at the head of a procession comes the first band on its way to the front porch in Mount Vernon Avenue. The Harding-and-Coolidge Club of East Liberty, Ohio, wheels in sight. The Logan County Women's Club for Harding follows. "Save the Constitution," its banners read. "League of Nations? No, We Know Our Business." Other delegations follow, from Ottawa County and from Tuscarawas. They march four or five abreast. They have come to greet the next President of the country. The Champaign County delegates appear with white-and-green-striped parasols. The crowd sends up a cheer. A moment later there is is a second burst of cheering. Knox County has arrived with a bandmaster who can throw his great baton above his head and catch it, spinning, with an arm behind his back.

The long line of pilgrims has been marshaled into position for a battery of cameramen, told to take its standards down, told to close its ranks up, told to take its hats off. Various minor celebrities have appeared upon the porch. The crowd has guessed at their identity. There is a moment of suspense. The Senator appears upon the porch. The crowd cheers. There is an ovation which lasts four seconds by the watch. Without difficulty the crowd is silenced by the unidentified celebrity who acts as master of ceremonies. "Ladies and Gentlemen," he announces, "we will first hear from the Tuscarawas County Quartet." The quartet follows with a lively song. There is another cheer. Various chairmen of county delegations are introduced. They tell the Senator he will win overwhelmingly in November. He is, they wish to assure him, the greatest statesman of his party. He will restore the country from the decay of Democratic rule, bring down prices, harmonize capital and labor, safeguard American honor and fan the sacred fire of the Fathers. He is the greatest statesman since Lincoln. To each generous tribute the Senator bows, not in false modesty, but as a man conscious of his worth and humbled by it. Between compliments he stands erect, eyes raised above the heads of those who watch him. On his face is stamped an almost tragic resignation. The times have summoned him: very well, he will obey the call. An octet of Negro singers leaps up the steps and bursts into ragtime. Here is a real sensation. The octet sings an encore. The crowd shouts its joy again. And then, suddenly, and with no more preparation, the Senator himself. . . .

"Fellow citizens of the Republic—America uncovers today in observance of the 133rd anniversary of the birthday of the nation. I do not say the birthday of American freedom which we celebrate variously though always patriotically on July Fourth in reverence for the Declaration of Independence, but this is the anniversary of the literal birthday of our American nation. . . . In that first convention were men of every type of mind. . . . It was difficult timber out of which to erect the enduring temple of the Republic which I think it worth our while to recall to lead us to greater appreciation. . . ."

Heads bared to the summer sun, they hear him out. They do not cheer especially, except when he has finished. It is his turn now, and he shall have it. He has been the perfect host. It has been a splendid day. They have come chiefly for the purpose of saying that they have been, and with this philosophy nothing can take the edge off their satisfaction. They pack banners, balloons and tired children into trains and motorcars and start back home again. Only a few more pilgrims will stand upon that gravel lawn. In Marion the dusk is falling. Not alone the merchants and innkeepers of Marion, but all those—everywhere—who cherish the performance of a perfect act will mourn the passing of the day.

The Graveyard of Youth

ONE OF THEM

AUGUST 9, 1922

They are all government clerks. Some are called specialists, and some are called stenographers, and some are called editors. But they are all government clerks.

The majority are very old. They have been in the service twenty, thirty, forty years. Over half of them are white-haired. The men have heavy figures. They are bent, and their faces are either a dead white or a splotchy red. To these old people who have been in the same place for so many years, their desks are their sanctums; to move them is sacrilege. These desks of theirs are like attics—full of queer odds and ends of things, all jumbled together—old papers yellow with age which are always about to be filed; new reports which they read as they rest them on top of a jumble of papers, for there is never any cleared space on their desks; an eraser which some one has had for ten years; a green shade for the eyes; an inkwell which has not been cleaned for months; a piece of string; pencils that are never sharpened; a tumbler; and everywhere, reports, always reports, spread open, bottom up, at a certain page, and buried under more reports. These desks are never cleared up. And the minds of these old men are never cleared up. They grow mouldier year by year.

The women's figures are heavy, too. Like square-rigged brigantines, they bear down upon you in the hall, all sails set, heavily under way. They are incased in corsets over which their white shirtwaists are drawn tightly without a wrinkle. Or else they are of the angular type whose shirtwaists hang upon them, *all* wrinkles. Their mouths are grim; their chins are settled into their collars; their eyes are always passing judgment, with the petty, narrow judgments of the small town. They are not workers. They are defeated bourgeoisie. And they have not forgiven the world their defeat.

There is just one group that is young, and that is the stenographers. And they are the most pathetic of all, for they are no younger in spirit. Their flesh is smooth and velvety, their ankles are slender and shapely, their figures are slight, and they sway as they walk. They make a brave showing in clothes. All their tiny wages must go into clothes in the attempt to capture before their youth goes what is to them the great adventure—man and marriage. Their youth is such a precarious thing. It is in their ankles, in their hair, in their slim figures. But it is not in their eyes or their mouths. There is no life there, no sparking curiosity, no promise of growth. Their pathetically young profiles are as old as the old women's in their lack of alertness, in the deadness of their expression. Their eyes do not light up except on two topics—man and dress. And the years are fleeting. And soon *they* will be heavy-footed, and their figures will "settle," and they will begin wearing stiff, starched shirt-waists instead of fluffy, transparent bits of chiffon. And so they appear each week in some new dress, and they fill their desk drawers with the latest thing in cosmetics, and they look always with hostility upon these old people moving so inexorably among them—reminding them, reminding them.

They flutter in terror and futile hate—futile for they cannot escape since they have no youth in their hearts. Youth is growth, and what chance have they to grow, doing day after day tasks that mean nothing to them, with no incentive or opportunity to express themselves in their work, hemmed in by petty restrictions, cast-iron hours, and copying, forever copying, long-winded, stodgy, meaningless reports?

And so their youth dies before it has a chance. And their bodies shrivel and harden into unlovely shapes, and their mouths become straight and tight, and their eyes hard and lifeless, because there is no fountain of inextinguishable youth within them, no eager intellectual curiosity, no insatiable desire to find out about life and this amazing, ever-changing world in which we live.

A few days ago, a woman came into the wash room where everyone was getting washed up preparatory to going home. She had evidently been weeping, her face was distorted with pain, her eyes were miserable and imploring as she cried out to us, "Has anyone seen my silver spoon, my silver fruit spoon? I have had that spoon twenty-five years, just as long as I have been in the service. It would break my heart if I lost that spoon."

All the old women in the room, with their white aprons and black aprons on and their hair screwed up in all the queer shapes of the hair-dressing of fifty years ago, gathered fussily about her, condoling with her. The stenographers stood for a moment with their lip-sticks poised in mid-air as they turned their young, intolerant, disdainful faces on the woman who had lost her spoon—and then they suddenly turned back to the mirrors and applied the lip-sticks to their young lips, almost with fury.

Washington Notes

TRB FROM WASHINGTON

MARCH 9, 1927

What a wonderful lot of laughs the average American misses by being a dolt about politics! What a shame it is that the ordinary citizen, allegedly educated and supposedly intelligent, is not sufficiently acute and informed in his comprehension of public men and matters to assimilate more than the material prepared for him in the daily press! How much gayer life could be if it were possible for him really to see the unconsciously funny side of the avowedly solemn show put on by these little men who now strut the national political stage. Always, in both parties and at all periods, it has undoubtedly had its humorous side; but in the Republican party, at this particular time, things are funnier than in the memory of anyone now in Washington—always provided, of course, that you view the show from the right angle. Otherwise it isn't funny in the least.

The mere fact that Calvin Coolidge is President of the United States is in itself as droll a thing of its kind as can well be imagined. Coolidge as President, Coolidge dealing with great questions of international relations, Coolidge kowtowed to by the great men of finance and business, inviting to dinner and placidly patronizing the eager and flattered publishers of the daily and weekly press with the largest mass circulation—in all this, to the few who have known Mr. Coolidge best and who are at once too clear-eyed to be blinded by the glamor of the great office he holds, and too well informed not to know what is really back of the journalistic and financial support by which he has up to now been buttressed and held up—there is irresistible humor.

Certainly, too, no one not obviously unfitted to express an opinion on anything will deny that it is a wonderful joke to have John Garibaldi Sargent, one of the leading lawyers of Ludlow, Attorney General of the United States. If you know the whole story, John Garibaldi as Attorney General is just a little funnier to contemplate than Mr. Coolidge as President.

The amusing features of having Frank B. Kellogg, who, since the Nicaragua-Mexican mess, has done more to justify his Senate sobriquet of "Nervous Nellie" than before, are too patent to need pointing out, and make it possible to pass more quickly to the suggestion that the case of that august personage, Andrew W. Mellon, Secretary of the Treasury, is not altogether without its humorous aspects. I know that this will be considered treason of a terrible sort by presidents of national banks and trust companies, by newspaper publishers who have dined at the White House, sailed on the Mayflower, or who are in the higher-bracket class as income-tax payers, and by most successful business and professional men who take seriously the eloquent eulogies of this administration by the *Saturday Evening Post* publicists—who were at one time such frequent White House guests that it was hard to go in or out without bumping into one.

Perhaps Mr. Mellon is not funny personally, but is there not, just the same, something essentially comic in having him, the third richest man in the country, interested in more income-paying corporations than any other individual, the owner of great banks and trust companies that are in constant contact with the department he directs, the controller of more companies that do business with the Internal Revenue Bureau than any other single person, personally the head of the department where these business interests of his have to come to have their taxes adjusted and their claims adjudicated? Also, is there not some slight humor when the punishing power of this department of which Mr. Mellon is the head is used in an attempt to collect a claim of many millions of back taxes from his personal enemy in the Senate, who charged on the floor of that body, and still does, that the effort is an act of reprisal, due entirely to his leadership in the Senate investigation of Mr. Mellon's department?

I must confess that this situation is not without its humorous appeal to me. To my mind, when it is fully grasped, it also makes ridiculous the question asked me so often by apparently earnest and intelligent men—some of them, strange as it may seem, members of the Senate—why neither Mr. Coolidge nor Mr. Mellon, both concededly men of personal honesty and unblemished character, seemed unable to see the argument against putting men on boards or commissions where they have regulatory power over corporations and concerns in which they previously had long and intimate financial interest. It even seems funny to me that those stern Republican Senators who opposed Mr. Cyrus Woods's appointment to the Interstate Commerce Commission, because of "the principle of the thing," do not appear to see that if they hold fast to that principle it logically compels them to assume the attitude that Mr. Mellon himself ought not to be Secretary of the Treasury.

However, enough about Mr. Mellon and Mr. Coolidge and Mr. Sargent and Mr. Kellogg. If they are jokes, as they often seem to the irreverent, they are by this time pretty old jokes, and I did not really start out this week to write about them at all. What got me off on this tack about the humorous side of the administration was not a sudden realization of it, so far as Mr. Coolidge in the White House is concerned. That has always appealed to my sense of the ridiculous. I appreciate that under some conditions it would not be a thing to laugh about. In a time of such unprecedented national prosperity and well-being, however, and in the absence of any public crisis requiring a strong hand, it seems to me much better to laugh at it, and the people who permit it, than to get irritated by it, as, I regret to say, some of my most orthodox Republican friends show a deplorable tendency to do.

What I really started to write about today were the two or three recent developments that ought to give the American people a good laugh, if only they knew enough to see the point of such things, which apparently they don't. One of these was the comment of Republican leaders in New York, printed in all the New York newspapers, in which they strongly disapproved Nicholas Murray Butler's opinion that the third-term tradition would be fatal to a Coolidge reelection, and that the wet and dry issue ought to be faced by the Republican party instead of being dodged. They were quoted as declaring Dr. Butler's words to be "indelicate and uncalled for" and "calculated to make trouble." They feared he might "raise an issue over which there would be room for wide differences of opinion." There may be in me an ineradicable tendency to scoff at serious things, but try as I will, I cannot help thinking this funny.

Likewise, there was some fun to be got out of Secretary of the Navy Wilbur's speech in New York, in which he pulled out the old Bolshevist bogey again and seriously warned us against the "Red Menace." So far as I am concerned, the amusing part of this speech was not so much in what the good Curtis said on this occasion as that it seemed it must surely recall, to those with memories longer than a minute, his performance during the 1924 campaign, when he dug up the old Bloody Shirt out in Denver and wildly waved it until he was yanked off the stump by wire, rushed back to Washington by aeroplane, and, it was publicly believed, made aware of the intense pain in the stomach he had caused the austere Calvin. So far as I can recall, this is one of the few speeches Mr. Wilbur has made since the 1924 incident. And here he is seeing red again. Of course he is much safer this time. For one thing, there is no campaign on. For another, the State Department has recently and more publicly seen more redly than he. Still, I don't care what anyone says—it is funny.

One other funny thing I should like to mention before I close—and that is the Borah-Butler debate on the prohibition issue in Boston before the Roosevelt Club in April. I admit it is necessary to use the imagination to see the fun in this, because the debate itself is not funny at all. It ought to be interesting and worth hearing. The funny phase comes when you stop to consider the feelings of Calvin Coolidge while it is going on. Here are Borah and Butler, two notable members of his own party, both of whom he has often entertained at the White House, who say they are his "personal friends," one of whom publicly proclaims that he cannot be reelected and the other of whom certainly thinks he ought not to be, agreeing to debate on an issue that is likely to cause him more political embarrassment in the long run than farm relief. And in Boston. And at a Roosevelt Club. There is not a doubt in the world that the President finds himself in full accord with those New York Republican leaders who deplore the whole business as "indelicate and uncalled for."

There is a lot of fun in life—even political life—if you know how to recognize it.

In Dedham Jail: A Visit to Sacco and Vanzetti

BRUCE BLIVEN

JUNE 22, 1927

The automobile slides through a pleasant green New England landscape: parks and ponds and big houses set far back from the road, among Louisa Alcott's own lilacs. A sharp turn through the elms, a hundred feet down a side road, and here we are.

It does not look like a prison, this nondescript, rambling structure, painted white and gray, and, like the houses, set back in a lawn, with a curving driveway and wooden stables at one side. It looks like a private school—or do all private schools look like prisons?. . . The stables have been converted to garages, but even so, there is such an air of 1880 about them that involuntarily you lift your eyes to the gable for the galloping horse, silhouetted in iron, which should be there as weather-vane. Up a flight of steps, through a door, and now we know where we are. Before us is another door, made of big vertical steel bars. A guard lets us in—an elderly, silver-haired New Englander, like a lobsterman come ashore. We are in a huge rectangular space, flooded with sunshine on this lovely June day. It is hardly a room. So much wall space has been removed and so many iron bars substituted, that it is like a cage; and here come those it encloses. No ball-and-chain, no lockstep; but men in single file, heads bent, arms folded on their breasts. They look young and healthy, on the whole; there are some fine faces and well modeled heads, and others which are less pleasing. These men wear trousers of gray stuff, uncouthly cylindrical—since they never have been pressed and never will be—and gray-and-white-striped shirts, cheap and coarse. They mount the stairs and pass along the balcony before the cell block, falling out of line one by one. The air resounds with the clash of metal, ringing harshly in our ears, as they lock themselves in. Every few minutes during the next half-hour, another such file passes through, silhouetted against the bars and the lush green of grass and trees, climbs the stairs and breaks up as it enters the cells.

From the cell block they appear, these two most famous prisoners in all the world, walking briskly, side by side. No bars are interposed between them and their visitors; we are introduced, shake hands, sit down on a bench and some chairs, like so many delegates to a convention, meeting for the first time in a hotel lobby. They are in prison garb like the others; they look well, seem in good spirits. Both are of average height, both black-haired, both somewhat bald in front, a baldness which somehow gives them a mild domestic air. Vanzetti wears a big, bristling Italian moustache; Sacco is clean shaven and his hair is clipped rather close on his round Southern skull. Vanzetti is expansive, a glowing friendly temperament, with bright eyes, an expressive face; Sacco is intelligent, too, but less emotional. He listens acutely, interjects a shrewd word or two at times. He judges men's specific acts, pessimistically, in the light of general principles, and usually for the purpose of deflating Vanzetti's too-generous view of human nature. What he says sounds true; and sometimes profound as well. He is not sullen. Neither of them reveals to the casual visitor any trace of that warping of the faculties which the experts say has been produced in them.

Today is an anniversary of a sort, for these two. One month from today, or within the six days thereafter, they are to die. Unless the Governor of Massachusetts acts to stay the process of the law, these strong and healthy men, eager and full of life, will sit in the electric chair, their heads tonsured, their trouser legs split, for the electrodes, and say farewell to life. Thus the state will take its Old Testament revenge for a murder which someone committed seven years ago.

Well, perhaps Sacco and Vanzetti were members of the band which did that deed, though I know what I am talking about when I say that the chances against it are a thousand to one. But that they did not have a fair trial, there is no doubt whatever. No intelligent man has ever read the record of what happened in the courtroom, coming to the case with an open mind, without being convinced that these two were the haphazard victims of a blind hostility in the community, which was compounded of "patriotic" fervor, anti-foreignism, and hatred of these men in particular because, as Professor Felix Frankfurter has summed it up, they denied the three things judge and jury held most dear: God, country and property.

We try, sitting now on these hard chairs in Dedham jail, to speak of their plight, to offer the words of cheer which decency seems to dictate. They listen gravely, and we read in their eyes the disbelief which they are too courteous to put into words. When you have been under the shadow of death for seven years, you do not any longer clutch at straws of hope. "We'll be glad if you are right," says Vanzetti politely; but it is as though one said to a baby, "It will be nice, if you can reach the moon." They have long expected that their martyrdom, which has already been so incredibly cruel, will be completed, and that they will die in the chair.

They are willing to spend but a moment on their own case, however.

Vanzetti's mind is full of something else, and now, impatiently, he pours it out. He is troubled about Tom Mooney, who is dying of a broken heart in a bleak gray California prison by the Golden Gate. He looks at us appealingly, his words tumble out. God in Heaven! This man, who is to die in four weeks, is thinking only of another man 3,000 miles away, victim of an injustice like his own. Could we do something, Vanzetti asks, for poor Tom Mooney? He himself has been doing all he can—writing, writing, letters to many people, especially to some Austrian friends, urging them to keep up the fight. "I may not be able to help much longer," says Vanzetti, with a twisted little smile. "And he needs help, Tom Mooney. He's a sick man. If they don't look after him, he'll die."

Vanzetti's English, if not always idiomatically correct, is fluent and, on the whole, accurate. Sacco, perhaps, does not do quite so well; but it is fair to remember that most of the time they try to say things that are not too easy, even in one's mother tongue. You must not be deceived by an accent, or by the workingman's easy way they have of sitting on a hard bench as though they were used to it. These are book men. Their political faith is philosophic anarchism, and they know its literature from Kropotkin down. In this year's graduating class at Harvard, there will not be twenty men who, on their own initiative, have read as many difficult, abstruse works as these gray-clad prisoners.

Since today's visitors are in no mood for abstract controversy, the hosts, ever courteous, follow their lead. The homes of these two men in Italy are mentioned. Have we ever been there? We never have, but we have been not far away. Florence, we all agree, is charming. The polite Americans call it Firenze, the polite Italians give it the Anglicized form. And Naples! Ah, yes, lovely, is it not? And we go on to speak of a famous Italian wine; and one says, "When you are free, you will perhaps go back to Italy and drink again the *lacrimae Christi*?"

"When we are free . . . " says Vanzetti thoughtfully. Does he see against the bars a great clock which is ticking away his life and that of his companion?—"*Tick, tock*! thirty-one days to live! *Tick, tock*! thirty days to live!"

One does not know. He says nothing for a few minutes, and then speaks quietly of exercise. Lately they have been given an Italian lawn-bowling set, which they use during the hour and a half they are permitted to be out-of-doors. "It is good," says Sacco, and Vanzetti corroborates: "It makes you sweat." Besides this, every morning in his cell, Vanzetti takes setting-up exercises; he flexes his biceps to show you, lest his English may not have conveyed the idea. The prison food, he goes on, is not well selected, too much starch. Before they had the set of lawn-bowls, Vanzetti had terrible indigestion much of the time. Now things are better. In their earlier years in prison, these men were treated with abominable cruelty. As their plight has become better known around the world, things have been made easier for them. Indeed, they have little to complain of, if you overlook their deadly peril of being victims of a foul judicial murder.

One of their visitors loses the thread of the conversation, thinking about that murder. One can understand a good hot-blooded killing; some day I shall commit one myself, if the organ grinder keeps on playing under my window. But to murder in blood that is seven years cold!—to assassinate men in order to bolster the prestige of an unbalanced judge. . . . And now to find majority opinion in a great American community supporting that murder!. . .

He comes back from this by-path with a start, to hear Vanzetti speaking of his other trial, the one at Plymouth, which was even more brazen in its denial of common justice and common decency than the joint ordeal with Sacco. He remembers, Vanzetti does, with mild reproach, that some of the little fund which his friends—poor people, like himself—had raised to defend him was squandered. A man took money to get an automobile and interview possible defense witnesses. (Judge Thayer subsequently failed to take these witnesses seriously, on ground that they were Italians and that their testimony, therefore, could not be important.) But this man who was given funds to get an automobile, instead of seeing witnesses, went joy riding instead. Was that fair? Vanzetti asks.

He has a hatred of injustice, one sees that in him perhaps most clearly of all. With his philosophical and political ideas this writer does not happen to agree; and yet one must recognize that no other sect in the modern world comes as close to primitive Christianity as his. He is opposed equally to Mussolinism in Italy and Sovietism in Russia, and for the same reason—he is against any rule supported by force. They do not believe in force, these two men who (according to the state's official theory) after a lifetime of sober industry, on a given day suddenly turned murderers to get money "for the cause," when the cause didn't need it; planned a crime which bore every earmark of the expert professional, didn't get any of the money when it was over, and made no effort to hide or escape afterward.

And now they are to die in four weeks.

Four weeks! Our conversation has halted for a little; we all have things to think about. We learn now—by accident—that we are keeping our hosts from their dinner; if they are delayed much longer it will be cold, or they will get none. And so we stand up and shake hands and say good-bye. "Good-bye." "Good-bye." "You see my friend Mr. A—in New York? You tell him I thank him so much. Perhaps you do something to help Tom Mooney?"

And they walk away toward the cell-block, these three—Sacco and Vanzetti and the unseen gray-robed figure which is ever at their side; and we go out into the glorious June evening, to the car and the chauffeur and the road home.

Justice Holmes and the Liberal Mind

JOHN DEWEY

JANUARY 11, 1928

When men have realized that time has upset many fighting beliefs, they may come to believe even more than they believe the very foundations of their own conduct that the ultimate good desired is better reached by free trade in ideas—that the best test of truth is the power of truth to get itself accepted in the market, and that truth is the only ground upon which their wishes can be carried out. That, at any rate, is the theory of our Constitution. It is an experiment, as all life is an experiment.

Were I to select a single brief passage in which is summed up the intellectual temper of the most distinguished of the legal thinkers of our country, I think I should choose this one. It contains, in spite of its brevity, three outstanding ideas: belief in the conclusions of intelligence as the finally directive force in life; in freedom of thought and expression as a condition needed in order to realize this power of direction by thought, and in the experimental character of life and thought. These three ideas state the essence of one type, and, to my mind, the only enduring type, of liberal faith. This article proposes, then, to consider the identity of the liberal and the experimental mind as exemplified in the work of Justice Holmes.

If it were asserted that Justice Holmes has no social philosophy, the remark would lend itself to misconstruction, and, in one sense, would not be true. But in another sense, and that in which the idea of a social philosophy is perhaps most often taken, it would be, I think, profoundly true. He has no social panacea to dole out, no fixed social program, no code of fixed ends to be realized. His social and legal philosophy derives from a philosophy of life and of thought as a part of life, and can be understood only in this larger connection. As a social philosophy, "liberalism" runs the gamut of which a vague temper of mind—often called forward-looking—is one extreme, and a definite creed as to the purposes and methods of social action is the other. The first is too vague to afford any steady guide in conduct; the second is so specific and fixed as to result in dogma, and thus to end in an illiberal mind. Liberalism as a method of intelligence, prior to being a method of action, as a method of experimentation based on insight into both social desires and actual conditions, escapes the dilemma. It signifies the adoption of the scientific habit of mind in application to social affairs.

The fact that Justice Holmes has made the application, and done so knowingly and deliberately as a judge, and in restriction to legal issues, does not affect the value of his work as a pattern of the liberal mind in operation. In his own words, "A man may live greatly in the law as well as elsewhere; there as well as elsewhere his thought may find its unity in an infinite perspective; there as well as elsewhere he may wreak himself upon life, may drink the bitter cup of heroism, may wear his heart out after the unattainable. All that life offers any man from which to start his thinking or his striving is a fact. And if this universe is one universe, if it is so far thinkable that you can pass in reason from one part of it to another, it does not matter very much what that fact is. Your business as thinkers is to make plainer the way from something to the whole of things; to show the rational connection between your fact and the frame of the universe." Justice Holmes has shown fondness for the lines of George Herbert:

Who sweeps a room as for Thy laws,
Makes that and th' action fine.

But he takes it as having "an intellectual as well as a moral meaning. If the world is a subject for rational thought it is all of one piece; the same laws are found everywhere, and everything is connected with everything else; and if this is so, there is nothing mean, and nothing in which may not be seen the universal law." The field which Justice Holmes has tilled is a limited one, but since he has "lived greatly in it," his legal and social philosophy is great, not limited. It is an expression of the processes and issues of law seen in an infinite perspective; that of a universe in which all action is so experimental that it must needs be directed by a thought which is free, growing, ever learning, never giving up the battle for truth, or coming to rest in alleged certainties, or reposing on a form in a slumber that means death.

"The Constitution is an experiment, as all life is an experiment." According to the framework of our social life, the community, the "people," through legislative action, the seat of social experiment stations. If Justice Holmes has favored giving legislative acts a broader and freer leeway than has, in repeated instances, commended itself to fellow judges, it has not been because he has always thought the specific measures enacted to be wise; it is not hard to see that in many cases he would not have voted in favor of them if he had been one of the legislators. Nor is his attitude due to a belief that the voice of the people is the voice of God, or to any idealization of popular judgment. It is because he believes that, within the limits set by the structure of social life (and *every* form of social life has a limiting structure), the organized community has a right to try experiments. And in his ken, this legal and political right is itself based upon the fact that experimentation is, in the long run, the only sure way to discover what is wisdom and in whom it resides. Intellectual conceit causes one to believe that his wisdom is the touchstone of that of social action. The intellectual humility of the scientific spirit recognizes that the test can only be found in consequences in the production of which large numbers engage. Time has upset so many instances of fighting private wisdom that, even when one's own wisdom is so mature and assured that for one's own self it is the very foundation of one's own conduct, one defers to the beliefs of others to the extent of permitting them a free competition in the open market of social life. Judicial decisions amply prove that it demands courage as well as a generosity beyond the scope of lesser souls to hold that "my agreement or disagreement has nothing to do with the rights of a majority to embody their opinions in law," and to declare that "constitutional law like other contrivances has to take some chances."

The faith that, within certain large limits, our social system is one of experimentation, subject to the ordeal of experienced consequences, is seen in Justice Holmes' impatience with the attempt to settle matters of social policy by dialectic reasoning from fixed concepts, by pressing "words to a drily logical extreme." "There is nothing I more deprecate than the use of the Fourteenth Amendment beyond the absolute compulsion of its words to prevent the making of social experiments that an important part of the community desires." "It is important for this court to avoid extracting from the very general language of the Fourteenth Amendment a system of delusive exactness." It is impossible to state in any short space the full practical implications of Justice Holmes' repeated warnings against "delusive exactness," where exactness consists only in fixing a concept by assigning a single definite meaning, which is then developed by formal logic, and where the delusion consists in supposing that the flux of life can be confined within logical forms. "The language of judicial decision is mainly the language of logic. And the logical method and form flatter that longing for certainty and repose which is in every human mind. But certainty generally is illusion, and repose is not the destiny of man. Behind the logical form lies a judgment as to the relative worth and importance of competing legislative grounds. . . . You can give *any* conclusion a logical form." "To rest upon a formula is a slumber, that prolonged, means death."

Yet nothing could be further from truth than to infer that Justice Holmes is indifferent to the claims of exact, explicit and consistent reasoning. In reality, it is not logic to which he takes exception, but the false logic involved in applying the classic system of fictitious fixed concepts, and demonstratively exact subsumptions under them, to the decision of social issues which arise out of a living conflict of desires. What he wants is a logic of probabilities. Such a logic involves distinctions of degree, consideration of the limitation placed upon an idea which represents the value of one type of desire by the presence of ideas which express neighboring, but competing interests. These requirements can be met only by employing the method borrowed, as far as possible from science, of comparison by means of measuring and weighing. He objects to domination of law by classic logic in the interest of a logic in which precision is material or quantitative, not just formal. To rely on deduction from a formal concept of, say, liberty as applied to contract relations is but a way of hindering judges from making conscious, explicit, their reasons of social policy for favoring the execution of one kind of desire rather than another. Thus the formal logic becomes a cover, a disguise. The judgment, the choice, which lies behind the logical form is left "inarticulate and unconscious . . . and yet it is very root and nerve of the whole proceeding." "I think the judges themselves have failed adequately to recognize their duty of weighing considerations of social advantage. The duty is inevitable, and the result of the often proclaimed aversion to deal with such considerations is simply to leave the very ground and foundation of judgments inarticulate and unconscious." Formal logic has become a mask for concealing unavowed economic beliefs concerning the causes and impact of social advantage which judges happen to hold. It is hard to imagine anything more *illogical* than leaving the real premises for a conclusion inarticulate, unstated, unless it be the practice of assigning reasons which are not those which actually govern the conclusion.

Upon the positive side, Justice Holmes has left us in no doubt as to the logical method he desires to have followed. "The growth of education is an increase in the knowledge of measure. . . . It is a substitution of quantitative for qualitative judgments. . . . In the law we only occasionally can reach an absolutely final and quantitative determination, because the worth of the competing social ends which respectively solicit a judgment for the plaintiff or the defendant cannot be reduced to number and accurately fixed. . . . But it is of the essence of improvement that we should be as accurate as we can." In deprecating the undue share which study of history of the law has come to play, he says that he looks "forward to a time when the part played by history in the explanation of a dogma shall be very small, and instead of ingenious research we shall spend our energy on the study of ends to be attained and the reasons for desiring them." More important than either a formal logical systematization of rules of law or a historical study of them is "the establishment of its postulates, from within, upon *accurately measured* social desires instead of tradition." And so he says in another address: "For the rational study of the law the black-letter man may be the man of the present, but the man of the future is the man of statistics and the master of economics." Summing it all up: "I have had in mind an ultimate dependence of law [upon science] because it is ultimately for science to determine, as far as it can, the relative worth of our different social ends. . . . Very likely it may be with all the help that statistics and every modern appliance can bring us there will never be a commonwealth in which science is everywhere supreme. But it is an ideal, and without ideals what is life worth?"

There is a definitely realistic strain in the thinking of Justice Holmes, as there must be in any working liberalism, any liberalism which is other than a vague and windy hope. It is expressed in his warning against the delusive certainty of formal logic, against taking words and formulas for facts, and in his caution to weigh costs in the ways of goods foregone and disadvantages incurred in projecting any scheme of "social reform." It is found in his belief that intelligent morals consist in making clear to ourselves what we want and what we must pay to get it; in his conception of truth as that which we cannot help believing, or the system of our intellectual limitations. It is seen in his idea of a rule of law as a prediction where social force will eventually impinge in the case of any adopted course of conduct. At times, his realism seems almost to amount to a belief that whatever wins out in fair combat, in the struggle for existence, is therefore the fit, the good and the true.

But all such remarks have to be understood in the light of his abiding faith that, when all is said and done, intelligence and ideas are the supreme force in the settlement of social issues. Speaking in commemoration of the work of Justice Marshall, he remarked: "We live by symbols. . . . This day marks the fact that all thought is social, is on its way to action; that, to borrow the expression of a French writer, every idea tends to become first a catechism and then a code; and that according to its worth an unhelped meditation may one day mount a throne, and . . . may shoot across the world the electric despotism of an unresisted power." Again and again he says that the world is today governed more by Descartes or Kant than by Napoleon. "Even for practical purposes theory generally turns out the most important thing in the end." Just because facts are mighty, *knowledge* of facts, of what they point to and may be made to realize, is mightier still.

We live in a time of what is called disillusionment as to the power of ideas and ideals. The seeming eclipse of liberalism is part of this distrust. To believe in mind as power even in the midst of a world which has been made what it is by thought devoted to physical matters, is said to evince an incredible naïveté. To those whose faith is failing, the work of Justice Holmes is a tonic. His ideas have usually been at least a generation ahead of the day in which they were uttered; many of his most impressive statements have been set forth in dissenting opinions. But patience as well as courage—if there be any difference between them—is a necessary mark of the liberal mind. I do not doubt that the day will come when the principles set forth by Justice Holmes, even in minority dissent, will be accepted commonplaces, and when the result of his own teachings will afford an illustration of the justice of his faith in the power of ideas. When that day comes, the spirit of Justice Holmes will be the first to remind us that life is still going on, is still an experiment, and that then, as now, to repose on any formula is to invite death.

The American Scene

HAROLD J. LASKI

JANUARY 18, 1928

The English traveler who sees post-war America after long absence is impressed immediately by three things. Coming from a continent of poverty and depression, American prosperity is, at first, overwhelming. The confidence of the people, their clothes, their cars, seem to convey an air of solid and widespread well-being that has something of novelty in the history of civilization. He is struck, secondly, by the apartness of politics from the rest of the national life. There is little interest in, or awareness of, the issues (prohibition apart) which settle the acts of Congress. The politicians do not make, and sometimes hardly seem to influence, the temper of social thought. They live in a world into which the ordinary man does not choose to enter, and he does not seem to think either of them or of their doings as implicated in the essentials of his existence. And, more subtle than either of these, more difficult, therefore, to convey, he cannot help but note a certain complacency or condescension. It is as though the typical American had taken his achievement of material comfort as the mark of a final social well-being; or, if he has a further ambition, it is to achieve a greater material comfort than he already has. A bigger house, a bigger car, a more expensive radio set, a new fur coat, these (on the installment plan) seem to the observer to be regarded as ideals. He cannot help a sense of doubt whether this satisfaction is not an index to a dangerous spiritual poverty. He recognizes the pace of American life, the urgency of American effort; he is not convinced that there is purpose or direction, chosen consciously for what they are morally worth, in the swift movement that he sees about him.

That America has achieved material prosperity for the average citizen upon a scale previously unknown in history, it is not, I think, possible to deny; nor that it is a prosperity which, broadly speaking, reaches far wider among the mass of men than in the past. Yet it is possible to be skeptical about its value. Virtuous materialism makes the mind cling to little objects; and while this may not corrupt, it does, in general, seem to enervate.

America, to the outsider, seems in its present temper to make for an unprecedented number of men with small ambitions, but a disproportionately small number with ambitions of a noble kind. Nor is that all. The average American one meets is curiously egocentric; he attends to his own business, he speaks of his own concern, as if he were alone in the world, or as if, when he recognizes a neighbor, the latter is primarily the consumer of some commodity he has to sell. And because he is self-centered, he makes the present too much his concern. He ceases to have a sense of responsibility for the future. Let him extend his material possessions, and he has attained social good in the process of extension. There is no ultimate and spiritual bond between one man and another, no sense of sharing in a great common fellowship. Each man is exploiting an avenue that may lead to his enrichment, without thinking of the consequence to his neighbors of success in that exploitation.

I am not seeking to suggest that material prosperity is a mistake; but I am concerned to wonder, as I have observed America, whether material prosperity pursued as a deliberate end does necessarily enhance the quality of civilization. Even more, I am concerned to doubt the American affirmation (which I found in many for whom I have high respect) that when material prosperity has been achieved a spiritual increase is added unto us. The temper of American life is set by the successful business man. His standards, of ethics, of art, of intellectual insight, do not strike me as attractive. He seems to believe that the ethics of success means the success of ethics. He lacks the ability to doubt. He has no real sense of impalpable values. He equates bigness with grandeur. He believes that to teach men to want more is to increase civilization without regard to the problem of what is wanted. He confuses the announcement of right with the achievement of right. He has nothing of that communion with things unseen, that eternal self-questioning, that fellowship with the great spirits of the past, which have made the lives of poor and humble men happy and full in a sense unknown to him. He contents himself with material well-being; and so to do is, at least possibly, to lose the art of securing well-being itself. The very instability of his material desires is surely an index not only to the lack of an inner harmony in himself, but also to that over-zeal for the immediate which makes him angry with the long view. The result is his passion for the obvious; and great things are seldom obvious. He has, it may be granted, firm hold of the fact that the world is made for the energetic man to conquer. But he rarely inquires, he would probably think it sacrilegious to inquire, into what channels his energy should be directed.

This attitude pervades every class and area in America. The art of salesmanship is its chief contribution to the technique of living; and its addition to happiness is the prospect it offers of buying the material commodities you want before you have the means to pay for them. The universities even are influenced by this atmosphere; and students to whom Dante might have sung are taught that art of retail selling which consists in persuading your customer to buy something he need not want. Even science has been captured by the ghoul of publicity; and one reads in the press of pronouncements that serve only to betray both its ideals and personalities. It invades the world of letters; and one big (often adventitious) success not only produces an immediate crop of imitators without direct vision, but drives the creative artist himself to premature and over-abundant production lest he lose his public. For salesmanship means advertisement; and advertisement means keeping hold of the attention you have so hardly won. It is easier, I believe, to gain the attention, and also easier to lose it, of Americans than of any other people. That means a feverish haste in life that is fatal to the art of thought about difficult or ultimate things. The creative artist can hardly arise or mature in an atmosphere where the significance of leisure is thus lost.

I believe myself that the consequences of American prosperity are seen nowhere so vividly as in the political sphere. No one can observe the legislature or the executive without the sense that their composition represents the apotheosis of mediocrity. The best elements of American life regard them either with scorn or with indignation. The average element asks only of its government the maintenance of order; I am not certain that this is not a step on the road to slavery. No man expects the statesman to set great objects above himself. No one—as the scandals of the Harding administration testify—is indignant when corruption is revealed. No one is alert for new theories of government, or interested in schemes of social innovation; too often they are merely regarded as irksome and dangerous. The despotism of parties that have ceased even to know what they stand for is accepted without question; they have learned the art of being able to degrade, without tormenting, their constituents. They give to the latter security, prosperity, pleasure, upon the saving condition that their minds do not play about matters of ultimate social constitution. The combination of a spasmodic popular sovereignty with a continuous administrative despotism produces an inert people; and, in the end, no inert people knows how to choose its governors. The political system having ceased either to debate great matters, or to devote itself to great purposes, ceases to be capable of educating those who are influenced by its results. To a considerable extent, indeed, this is the consequence of the form of American government; but it is also the result of a prosperity which offers great rewards to those willing to be absorbed by a purely private life. Politics, to the mass of men, seems not so much unimportant as irrelevant. It does not enter into the fabric of their daily lives. It does not absorb any substantial part of their thought. Even the simple function of voting arouses less and less of their interest.

Explanations, of course, have been offered for this phenomenon. Americans, it is said by some, do for themselves what, in Europe, is done for the people by their governments; and this is a proof of the superior initiative and independence of the new world. Yet I should argue that the contrast with certain European phenomena, the control of hours of labor, social insurance on a national scale, the defective quality of the American civil service are all of them representative of a weakness in the American concept of the state. They represent a failure of the average man to conceive of himself as a citizen. He does not see that what is done at the center of affairs is done in his name; and it is a moral weakness on his part to regard himself as disinterested. For the result is written in things like the recent happenings at Passaic, in the tragedies of Ludlow and Lawrence and half a score of similar events. The inattention of Americans to the growth of their imperialism is only a different phase of a similar negligence. No state can ultimately prosper in which the vast majority inertly surrenders its responsibility for sovereign acts.

Others believe that it is the outcome of the real inability of democracy to cope with its own problems. They are, it is said, too big and too complex for the average man to follow the nature of the solution. But this is, I believe, to confound the details of a solution with its underlying principles. There are few political questions, especially where ideas are related to men, on which the judgment of an interested average man is not helpful. The expert who controls ultimately betrays simply because he will not know what the average man wants; and only as the latter explains his desires and announces the degree to which they have been satisfied are the habits of a democratic community really fostered. The fault here of the new America is surely that it has mistaken that fluidity of classes which constitutes social equality there for political equality. In fact they are completely different.

For political equality is impossible without liberty; and liberty implies an active interest by the many in affairs of state. The social equality which Americans enjoy offers small comforts of a material kind to many; and it is possible that the flavor of liberty is so subtle as to be obscured by them. But political equality means that the engines of state work for the general interest; and those who direct them have to be watched a little grimly if this is to be achieved. The refusal of the average man to regard the work of Congress and the state legislatures as emphatically his business makes him unfree because it makes him significant only in his private context. It means that on the vital subjects there is no American opinion. It means that the framework of the national life, the mold through which it has to flow, is being shaped by men who do not need to consult those who will, at least in the long run, be profoundly affected by the result. That does not, perhaps, matter greatly in an era of prosperity; but, in a sudden crisis, it means that the instruments which control the national destiny, and ought to be responsive to the national will, can in fact be careless of these because they have passed outside their control. Inertia in politics on the part of the people always pays a heavy penalty in the end. That is why the real groundwork of democratic security is a system which makes political power the highest prize of ambition in a community. It is, I think, a tragedy that in America men of high distinction should regard the honor to be won in the arena of politics either as ignoble or futile. For the field is then left to be cultivated by others whose purpose is unworthy of the end to be achieved.

I should myself argue that the circumstance under which the presidency of the United States fell to Mr. Coolidge is itself of high significance in this regard. That the position of greatest political importance in modern civilization should be the reward of chance is surely either tragedy or an offering on the altar of ironic genius. But it is, I think, more useful to note the expression of this temper in the quality of American political speculation during the last half-century. Much work of a valuably laborious kind has doubtless been achieved; but in really creative thought, in that inventiveness which is typified in England by the name of Bentham, there has been no name of real eminence since Abraham Lincoln. A great crisis enabled President Wilson to voice great aspirations greatly; but it is not unimportant in this context that he could not secure from his own people concerted effort for their fulfillment. American political thought impresses most European observers as at once timid and conservative. It is either occupied with description or obsessed by machinery. It has forgotten the great truth that political thought of a seminal kind is born only when the character of the people has been elevated to great purposes by great leadership. That was the secret of Washington and Hamilton, of Jefferson and of Lincoln. The banker, the manufacturer, the stockbroker, the organizer of a vast department-store, do not function on the plane where their actions raise the moral stature of their generation. Yet they are regarded by most Americans as their leaders. The men who in England or France or Germany set the temper of discussion are in America of comparatively little importance. The Cabinet officer, the Senator, the Congressman, are not the tried leaders of the people; and those who have replaced them are not so related to the national life as to educate by the counsel they are either able or willing to offer.

Were I an American, considerations such as these would give me a sense of profound disturbance about the future of my country. I should not feel that the bond between man and man was a union of spiritual purposes. I should feel that the equality was of a character too purely social to be related to the forces of permanent well-being. I should consider the present prosperity an opportunity to organize for high and conscious ends, a period for self-examination, rather than an occasion for complacency. It does not profit a people to be rich unless it has also won the right to moral self-respect. And that right is gained only upon the plane of the spirit.

Generalizations about any people are always too wide to be quantitatively true, and any examination which approached an indictment would only reveal its own inadequacy. There are elements in American life which weigh heavily and significantly against the considerations I have here urged. American literature, for example, reveals a spirit of restless self-criticism which is at once arresting and important. It suggests that the spirit of skepticism, the desire for a conscious and direct purpose for which I have been pleading, are already in the throes of birth. The discontent of American youth, even if on a small scale, is notorious and suggestive; for, as Disraeli said, the youth of a nation are the trustees of posterity. Certain American judges reveal a temper in their decisions which is worthy of the great names of legal history. It is possible, moreover, that the law schools of America will, by the sheer quality and independence of their work, rescue American lawyers from their present and painful dependence on the business man; will, also, in the next generation, do the work in political philosophy which its technicians should perform. One can think, also, of isolated scholars in a number of universities, who, deaf to the call of marketplace idolatry, give themselves to their various sciences with a devotion of heart and a quality of mind which makes a European envy America their possession.

Above all, there is the emphatic sense, borne in upon every traveler to America, that, while it is complacent, it is not happy. It has somewhere buried, beneath its surface, the realization that the heart must lie where the treasure is, and that the heart of America does not lie there. Why does America yearn so eagerly for the creative genius in art, in poetry, in philosophy, unless it is uneasy about their absence from itself? The very generosity of its wealthy men is not merely a form of insurance, but also a pathetic striving to attain a self-respect that mere possessions do not confer. The presence, in every great center of population, of groups of younger men who, sometimes a little willfully, reject the standards of their environment, is important and arresting. It may well be that, unobviously to the stranger, the period of critical doubt has already begun in America. Certainly, if it comes, the very energy of the American character should make it a period of great importance in world history. For if America is able to save herself by her energy, it is at least possible that she may help to save Europe by her example.

The Birth-Control Raid

MARGARET SANGER

MAY 1, 1929

"This is *my* party!" shouted Policewoman Mary Sullivan, in the midst of her personally conducted raid on the Birth Control Clinical Research Bureau in New York City, last week. Subsequent developments have demonstrated that this boast was as premature as it was untruthful. For Policewoman Sullivan's little raiding party, carried out with a vigor that swept aside as unnecessary such things as common courtesy and ordinary good manners, has proved to be of vital interest to every thinking member of this community. And the end is not yet in sight. As I write these indignant words, the announcement comes that Chief Magistrate William McAdoo now admits that the police, in seizing the case histories of our patients, had exceeded the scope of the search warrant he had issued authorizing this raid—an act on their part which constitutes a misdemeanor.

After you have spent some fifteen years, slowly and with infinite pains and patience working for the right to test the value of contraceptive practice in a scientific and hygienic—and lawful—manner, without interfering with the habits or the morals of those who disagree with you, it is indeed difficult to submit with equanimity to such brutal indignities as were gratuitously thrust upon us at the clinic a week ago. Compensations there have been, of course—mainly in the enlightened attitude of such dailies as *The New York Herald Tribune* and others, and the generous offers of aid from distinguished physicians. But even these can scarcely counterbalance the evidence of the sinister and secret power of our enemies.

As in the breaking up of the birth-control meeting in the Town Hall, in 1921, the raid on the Birth Control Research Bureau gives us a glimpse of the animus which may direct the action of the police. In their futile efforts to annihilate a social agency which had already been given a clean bill of health by the health department of the municipality, by the state board of charities and by the Academy of Medicine, our hypocritical antagonists have not the courage to fight us squarely, in the open, but adopt the cowardly subterfuge of utilizing minor and crassly ignorant members of the police force. Our research bureau has been functioning since 1923, operating within the law, and cooperating with recognized charitable institutions.

From whatever point of view it is analyzed, Policewoman Sullivan's "party" was a deplorable failure. A failure, first of all, because it has exposed a complete lack of intelligence in those who conducted it, and a woeful lack of coordination in the police department itself. It is not enough for Grover Whalen or District Attorney Banton to disclaim all foreknowledge of the raid. Modest as may be the headquarters of the research bureau, it is highly significant and important. Therefore, to permit minor members of the police force, or hostile assistants in the office of the District Attorney, to pass judgment upon its fate, denotes either a lack of coordination of powers, or a bland carelessness in directing them. Certainly no official of the city government, cognizant of awakened public opinion concerning the social value of contraception, and aware, moreover, of the searching criticism to which the police department of New York City is now subjected, would ever have chosen the present moment as one psychologically suited to inaugurate a brutal raid upon a modest unadvertised clinic which was functioning quietly and successfully in an obscure side street, minding its own business and hoping that its powerful ecclesiastical neighbors would mind theirs. At a time when the criminal elements of the city—racketeers, gangsters, gunmen and hijackers—are so active and successful, it would seem to a bystander that all the intelligence, skill, and brawn of the force should be mobilized and focused upon "crime control."

Even the thrill of satisfaction we have had in the offers of distinguished doctors to testify in our behalf, in the letters to the press, and the courageous outspoken editorials, cannot obliterate the memory of Policewoman Sullivan standing in the clinic and shouting vigorously and victoriously "This is my party!" I would rather forget that here was a woman fighting against other women who were devoting their lives to succor and to save their fellow women. By trickery and hypocrisy she had obtained her "evidence," and now she triumphantly commanded the doctors and nurses into the waiting patrol wagons.

Whatever the outcome of this raiding party, I hereby call upon the citizens of New York to find out for themselves how and where it originated, and why it was carried out. I ask them to recall the breaking up by the police of the birth-control meeting in Town Hall, with the subsequent revelation that this illegal action was instigated by Roman Catholic ecclesiastical authorities. We are paying, and paying heavily, for the support of a great police force. It is our right and duty to insist that it shall function in an efficient, legal, and socially effective manner. Policewoman Sullivan's "party" exposes it as operating in a manner which suggests the gratification of private prejudices and unreasoning emotion, rather than the even-handed administration of justice and the law.

Out of the Red with Roosevelt

JOHN DOS PASSOS

JULY 13, 1932

They came out of the Stadium with a stale taste in their mouths. Down West Madison Street, walking between lanes of cops and a scattering of bums, the crowds from the galleries found the proud suave voice of the National Broadcasting Company still filling their jaded ears from every loud-speaker, enumerating the technical agencies that had worked together to obtain the superb hook-up through which they broadcast the proceedings of the Democratic Convention of 1932. Well, they did their part: the two big white disks above the speakers' platform (the ears of the radio audience) delicately caught every intonation of the oratory, the dragged-out "gre-eats" when the "great Senator from the great state of . . . " was introduced, the deep "stalwart" always prefixed to "Democrat" when a candidate was being nominated, the indignant rumble in the voice when the present administration was "branded" as having induced "an orgy of crime and a saturnalia of corruption"; the page with the portable microphone in his buttonhole had invariably been on hand when a delegate was recognized from the floor; the managers for NBC had been there all the time, stage-managing, moving quietly and deftly around the platform, with the expression and gestures of old-fashioned photographers; coaxing the speakers into poses from which they could be heard; telegrams had been read giving the minute-to-minute position of the nominee's plane speeding west, the radio voice of Wally Butterworth had whooped things up describing the adverse flying conditions, the plane's arrival at the airport, the cheering throngs, the jolly ride from Buffalo, the Governor's nice smile; but when Franklin D. Roosevelt (in person) walked to the front of the rostrum on his son's arm while the organ played the "Star Spangled Banner" and an irrepressible young lady from Texas waved a bouquet of red, white and blue flowers over his head, to greet with a plain sensible and unassuming speech the crowd that had yelled itself hoarse for an hour for Al Smith three days before, that had gone delirious over the Wet plank and applauded every phrase in the party platform, and sat with eager patience through the week-long vaudeville show—nothing happened. Courteous applause, but no feeling. The crowd in the huge hall sat blank, blinking in the glare of the lights. Neither delegates nor the public seemed to be able to keep their minds on what the candidate, whom they had nominated after such long sessions and such frantic trading and bickering downtown in their hotel rooms, had to say. As he talked the faces in the galleries and boxes melted away, leaving red blocks of seats, even the delegates on the floor slunk out in twos and threes.

Starting on Monday with the "Star Spangled Banner" and an inaugural address of Thomas Jefferson's read by a stout gentleman with a white gardenia in his buttonhole; through the Senator from Kentucky's keynote speech, during which he so dexterously caught his glasses every time they fell from his nose when he jerked his head to one side and up to emphasize a point; through Wednesday's all-star variety show that offered Clarence Darrow, Will Rogers, Amos 'n' Andy, and Father Coughlin "the radio priest" (who, by the way, advised the convention to put Jesus Christ in the White House), all on one bill; through the joyful reading of the platform with its promise of beer now and a quietus by and by on prohibition snoopers and bootleggers; through the all-night cabaret on Thursday, with its smoke and sweaty shirts and fatigue and watered Coca Cola and putty sandwiches and the cockeyed idiocy of the demonstrations: Governor Byrd's band in plumes and rabbit's fur (which he kindly loaned to Ritchie and to Alfalfa Bill when their turn came) and the pigeons and the young women who kept climbing up on the platform and bathing in the klieg lights like people under a warm shower, and the sleepy little Oklahoma girls in their kilties; and the grim balloting while the sky outside the windows went blue and then pink until at last the sun rose and sent long frightening bright horizontal shafts through the cigar smoke and the spotlights and the huddled groups of worn-out politicians; through the nominating speeches, and the seconding speeches and the reseconding speeches, and the old-time tunes, "The Old Gray Mare," "A Hot Time in the Old Town Tonight," "I've Been Working on the Railroad". . . through all the convention week and flicker of flashlight bulbs and the roar of voices there had been built up a myth, as incongruous to this age as the myth of the keen-eyed pilot at the helm of the ship of state that the Republicans tried to revitalize three weeks ago; the myth of the young American working his way by honesty and brawn, from Log Cabin to President. This stalwart Democrat was to rise in his might, wrench the government out of the hands of the old bogey Republicans, Wall Street, Privilege, Graft and Corruption, return it to the people and thus in some mystic way give a job to the jobless, relieve the farmers of their mortgages, save the money the little fellow had deposited in the tottering banks, restore business to the small storekeeper and producer and thereby bring the would-be Democratic office holders massed on the floor back to the fleshpots of power. A powerful myth and an old myth. But when, largely through the backstage efforts of Mr. McAdoo, the myth took flesh in the crippled body and unassuming speech of the actual Governor of New York, the illusion crashed. Too late.

You come out of the Stadium and walk down the street. It's West Madison Street, the home address of migratory workers and hoboes and jobless men all over the Middle West. Gradually the din of speeches fades out of your ears, you forget the taste of the cigar you were smoking, the cracks and gossip of the press gallery. Nobody on the street knows about the convention that's deciding who shall run their government, or cares. The convention is the sirens of police motorcycles, a new set of scare headlines, a new sensation over the radio. There are six-day bicycle races and battles of the century and eucharistic congresses and big-league games and political conventions; and a man has got a job, or else he hasn't got a job, he's got jack in his pocket, or else he's broke, he's got a business, or else he's a bum. Way off some place headline events happen. Even if they're right on West Madison Street, they're way off. Roosevelt or Hoover? It'll be the same cops.

You walk on down, across the great train yards and the river to the Loop, out onto Michigan Avenue where Chicago is raising every year a more imposing front of skyscrapers, into the clean wind off the lake. Shiny store-fronts, doormen, smartly dressed girls, taxis, buses taking shoppers, clerks, business men home to the South Side and North Side. In Grant Park more jobless men lying under the bushes, beyond them sails in the harbor, a white steamboat putting out into the lake. Overhead pursuit planes fly in formation advertising the military show at Soldiers' Field. To get their ominous buzz out of your ears, you go down a flight of steps, into the darkness feebly lit by ranks of dusty red electric lights of the roadway under Michigan Avenue. The fine smart marble and plate-glass front of the city peels off as you walk down the steps. Down here the air, drenched with the exhaust from the grinding motors of trucks, is full of dust and grit and the roar of the heavy traffic that hauls the city's freight. When your eyes get used to the darkness, you discover that, like the world upstairs of store-fronts and hotel lobbies and battles of the century and political conventions, this world too has its leisure class. They lie in rows along the ledges above the roadway, huddled in grimed newspapers, gray sag-faced men in worn-out clothes, discards, men who have nothing left but their stiff hungry grimy bodies, men who have lost the power to want. Try to tell one of them that the *gre-eat* Franklin D. Roosevelt, Governor of the *gre-eat* state of New York, has been nominated by the *gre-eat* Democratic party as its candidate for President, and you'll get what the galleries at the convention gave Mr. McAdoo when they discovered that he had the votes of Texas and California in his pocket and was about to shovel them into the Roosevelt band wagon, a prolonged and enthusiastic *Boooo*. Hoover or Roosevelt, it'll be the same cops.

FDR Gives Marching Orders

EDITORIAL

JANUARY 19, 1942

President Roosevelt's annual message to Congress on the state of the nation will rank as one of the great utterances of a leader whose state papers are already the most impressive in the history of the presidency. Speaking to the American Congress the President was actually speaking to the American nation and to the democratic peoples of the world. His message was in essence the marching orders for the war effort in 1942.

The marching orders are good ones. They show that the President has in at least one phase—that of boldness of imagination and grasp—the qualities of a great war leader. He does not underestimate the enemy's strength, preparation and ruthlessness. He sees what the aim of the Japanese attack was—to deliver so stunning a blow that we would divert our whole strength to a single theater of the war; and seeing the enemy's trap, he is determined not to fall into it.

He understands not only the power politics and military strategy of total war, but also the vast moral gulf that today separates the two causes and the two conceptions of world order; and he has the ability to state this insight in terms the common man will understand. "The militarists of Berlin and Tokyo started this war, but the massed, angered forces of common humanity will finish it. . . . The world is too small to provide adequate living room for Hitler and God." He has the capacity to speak of the enemy in terms of intensity that steel our will against them, without indulging in the hysterical violence and hate-mongering of Hitler's speeches.

He has the daring to speak realistically of the long and arduous war road ahead of us, and to set correspondingly high directives for the production effort of America. "We must raise our sights," he tells us, "all along the production line." This is a good form of political warfare. "I rather hope," the President improvised after he had stated our 1942 goals for planes, tanks, anti-aircraft and shipping production, "that all these figures . . . will become common knowledge in Germany and Japan." For here, in the great prestige of the American industrial potential all over the world, lies part of the role

America can play in psychological war. Finally, the President understands the importance of underlining the collaboration toward a grand strategy already achieved by the United Nations, the need for promising a shift from a defensive to an offensive war, and the value of opening the broad perspectives of an equally determined effort for peace and security after the war.

These are brave words, bold words, heartening words. But how about carrying them out? Our enemies profess to believe that we don't have what it takes to do so. We had better search our minds and wills and hearts to make certain that we are equal to what we are undertaking. Let us start with the President himself. He has always been rather better in the statement of directives than in the sheer economic and administrative problems of follow-through. It is not that he lacks principle or purpose or strength. It is rather that his political training and his great gifts of amiability have made him use all too generously the methods of compromise and concession, the methods of yielding to an embittered opposition rather than fighting it out. This is not so damaging in a peacetime program of social reform, where the crucial thing is the steady forward movement and everything does not hang in the balance of months. But in wartime it is not enough to say that time is of the essence ("our task is unprecedented and the time is short"). It is necessary to blast like dynamite through the tangles and obstructions of vested interests and old ways of thought and action. Is he ready to tell his lieutenants frankly that in the crucial phases of the economic effort—tooling-up, plant expansion, raw-material piles, putting-out of orders to the small business unit, procurement and supply, conversion from civilian to war production—they have botched their jobs? If so, let him start with William Knudsen and Jesse Jones, with men in his own Cabinet, with the dollar-a-year men in the OPM. That would be giving us the marching orders of the deed and not only of the word.

And what applies to the President applies to an even greater degree to Congress, to the business men, to the men in the administrative services. They are the means for transmuting plans agreed on by our leaders into tasks clear enough, specific enough, manageable enough to be undertaken by the people themselves. Whether the American people as a people have the stamina and realism and sheer fighting heart to see through to the end a war effort of the magnitude projected by the President, only history will determine. Our own conviction is that we have these qualities. But we cannot exercise them while Congress starts to consider a price-control measure and ends by passing a farm-relief measure, when business men are more interested in fighting a plan for war production because of its labor source than in testing it in actual practice, when we place administrative power in the hands of men trained not to the tasks of collective leadership but to the multiplying of profits and the restriction of production.

As we look back at how the Western world came to its present impasse we must lay the blame on three types of failure in the ruling economic and political groups. One was a failure of knowledge. They simply did not understand the forces loose in our world, how revolutionary those forces were, how archaic they made the Old Order of an unplanned and anarchic capitalism. The second was a failure of will. In the face of the Nazi threat they were like a hen hypnotized by a snake. The third was the failure to replace private incentive by public dedication. They went in pursuit of blind class interest when it should have been clear that the strength of a nation lay in its capacity to marshal its forces for public purposes.

Those are the lessons our spokesmen and technicians, our business men and workers, our thinkers and our plain people must learn if they are to carry out the high marching orders of the President. Mr. Roosevelt mentioned the "almost superhuman will and courage" of the Russian people. He mentioned the Chinese, who "have withstood bombs and starvation and have whipped the invaders time and again." These are good allies to have fighting on our side. But if we are to be worthy of such allies, we must replace our smugness by knowledge, our inertia by organized will, our habitual seeking for private profit and security by a dedication to the common good. And this involves not only inspiration and heart-searching, but hard and basic changes in the structure of economic and political decision.

Arthur Miller's Conscience

RICHARD H. ROVERE

JUNE 17, 1957

"I will protect my sense of myself," Arthur Miller told the House Committee on Un-American Activities when he refused to identify some writers who had once been Communists. "I could not use the name of another person and bring trouble on him." The refusal brought Miller a conviction for contempt of Congress from a judge who found his motives "commendable" but his action legally indefensible.

A writer's sense of himself is to be projected as well as protected. It becomes, through publication and production, a rather public affair. For this and other reasons, it is fitting that what Miller saw as the testing of his integrity—the challenge to his sense of himself—was a question involving not himself but others. Of himself, he had talked freely, not to say garrulously. He chatted, almost gaily, about his views in the Thirties, his views in the Forties, his views in the Fifties, about Ezra Pound and Elia Kazan and other notables, about the Smith Act and Congressional investigations and all manner of things. When he was asked why he wrote "so morbidly, so sadly," he responded patiently and courteously, rather as if it were the "question period" following a paid lecture to a ladies club. His self-esteem was offended only when he was asked to identify others.

Thus, one might say, it was really a social or political ethic that he was defending, while of his sense of himself he gave freely. In legal terms, this might be a quibble, for there is no reason why a man should not have a right to his own definition of self-respect. In a literary sense, it is not a quibble, for Miller is a writer of a particular sort, and it was in character for him to see things this way. He is, basically, a political, or "socially conscious" writer. He is a distinguished survivor of the Thirties, and his values derive mostly from that decade. He is not much of a hand at exploring or exploiting his own consciousness. He is not inward. He writes at times with what may be a matchless power in the American theater today, but not with a style of his own, and those who see his plays can leave them with little or no sense of the author as a character. He is not, in fact, much concerned with individuality of any sort. This is not an adverse judgment; it is a distinction, or an attempt at one. What interests Miller and what he can often convey with force is the crushing impact of society upon its members. His human beings are always on the anvil, awaiting the hammer, and the act that landed him in his present trouble was an attempt to shield two or three of them from the blow. (It was, of course, a symbolic act, a gesture, for Miller knew very well that the committee knew all about the men he was asked to identify. He could not really shield; he could only assert the shielding principle.) What he was protecting was, in any case, a self-esteem that rested upon a social rule or principle or ethic.

One could almost say that Miller's sense of himself *is* the principle that holds "informing" to be the ultimate in human wickedness. It is certainly a recurrent theme in his writing. In *The Crucible*, his play about the Salem witchcraft trials, his own case is so strikingly paralleled as to lend color—though doubtless not truth—to the view that his performance in Washington was a case of life paying art the sincere flattery of imitation. To save his life, John Proctor, the hero, makes a compromise with the truth. He confesses, falsely, to having trafficked with Satan. "Did you see the Devil?" the prosecutor asks him. "I did," Proctor says. He recognizes the character of his act, but this affects him little. "Good, then—it is evil, and I do it," he says to his wife, who is shocked. He has reasoned that a few more years on earth are worth this betrayal of his sense of himself. (It is not to be concluded that Proctor's concession to the mad conformity of the time parallels Miller's testimony, for Proctor had never in fact seen the devil, whereas Miller had in fact seen Communists.) The prosecutor will not let him off with mere self-incrimination. He wants names; the names of those Proctor has seen with the Devil. Proctor refuses; does not balk at a self-serving lie, but a self-serving lie that involves others will not cross his lips. "I speak my own sins," he says, either metaphorically or hypocritically, since the sins in question are a fiction. "I cannot judge another. I have no tongue for it." He is hanged, a martyr.

In his latest play, *A View from the Bridge*, Miller returns to the theme, this time with immense wrath. He holds that conscience—indeed humanity itself—is put to the final test when a man is asked to "inform." Eddie, a longshoreman in the grip of a terrible passion for his teen-age niece, receives generous amounts of love and sympathy from those around him until his monstrous desire goads him into tipping off the Immigration officers to the illegal presence in his home of a pair of aliens. His lust for the child has had dreadful consequences for the girl herself, for the youth she wishes to marry, and for Eddie's wife. It has destroyed Eddie's sense of himself and made a brute of him. Yet up to the moment he "informs" he gets the therapy of affection and understanding from those he has hurt the most. But once he turns in the aliens, he is lost; he crosses the last threshold of iniquity. "In the garbage can he belongs," his wife says. "Nobody is gonna talk to him again if he lives to a hundred."

A View from the Bridge is not a very lucid play, and it may be that in it Miller, for all of his wrath, takes a somewhat less simple view of the problem of the informer than he does in *The Crucible*. There is a closing scene in which he appears to be saying that even this terrible transgression may be understood and dealt with in terms other than those employed by Murder, Incorporated. I think, though, that the basic principle for which Miller speaks is far commoner in Eddie's and our world than it could have been in John Proctor's. The morality that supports it is post-Darwinian. It is more available to those not bound by the Christian view of the soul's infinite preciousness or of the body as a temple than it could have been to pre-Darwinian society. Today, in most Western countries, ethics derive mainly from society and almost all values are social. What we do to and with ourselves is thought to be our own affair and thus not, in most circumstances, a matter that involves morality at all. People will be found to say that suicide, for a man or woman with few obligations to others, should not be judged harshly, while the old sanctions on murder remain. Masochism is in one moral category, sadism in another. Masturbation receives a tolerance that fornication does not quite receive. A man's person and his "sense of himself" are disposable assets, provided he chooses to see them that way; sin is only possible when we involve others. Thus, Arthur Miller's John Proctor was a modern man when, after lying about his relations with the Devil, he said, "God in heaven, what is John Proctor, what is John Proctor? I think it is honest, I think so. I am no saint." It is doubtful if anyone in the 17th Century could have spoken that way. The real John Proctor surely thought he had an immortal soul, and if he had used the word "honest" at all, it would not have been in the sophisticated way in which Miller had him use it. He might have weakened sufficiently to lie about himself and the Devil, but he would surely not have said it was "honest" to do so or reasoned that it didn't really matter because he was only a speck of dust. He was speaking for the social ethic which is Arthur Miller's—and he resisted just where Miller did, at "informing."

It is, I think, useful to look rather closely at Miller's social ethic and at what he has been saying about the problems of conscience, for circumstances have conspired to make him the leading symbol of the militant, risk-taking conscience in this period. I do not wish to quarrel with the whole of his morality, for much of it I share—as do, I suppose, most people who have not found it possible to accept any of the revealed religions. Moreover, I believe, as Judge McLaughlin did, that the action Miller took before the committee was a courageous one. Nevertheless, I think that behind the action and behind Miller's defense of it there is a certain amount of moral and political confusion. If I am right, then we ought to set about examining it, lest conscience and political morality come to be seen entirely in terms of "naming names"—a simplification which the House Un-American Activities Committee seems eager to foist upon us and which Miller, too, evidently accepts.

A healthy conscience, Miller seems to be saying, can stand anything but "informing." On the one hand, this seems a meager view of conscience. On the other, it makes little political sense and not a great deal of moral sense. Not all "informing" is bad, and not all of it is despised by the people who invariably speak of it as despicable. The question of guilt is relevant. My wife and I, for example, instruct our children not to tattle on one another. I am fairly certain, though, that if either of us saw a hit-and-run driver knock over a child or even a dog, we would, if we could, take down the man's license number and turn him in to the police. Even in the case of children, we have found it necessary to modify the rule so that we may be quickly advised if anyone is in serious danger of hurting himself or another. (The *social* principle again.) Proctor, I think, was not stating a fact when he said, "I cannot judge another"—nor was Miller when he said substantially the same thing. For the decision *not* to inform involves judging others. "They think to go like saints," Proctor said of those he claimed he could not judge, and Miller must have had something of the sort in mind about the writers he refused to discuss. He reasoned, no doubt, that their impulses were noble and that they had sought to do good in the world. We refuse to inform, I believe, either when we decide that those whose names we are asked to reveal are guilty of no wrong or when we perceive that what they have done is no worse than what we ourselves have often done. Wherever their offenses are clearly worse—as in the case of a hit-and-run driver or a spy or a thief—we drop the ban.

If the position taken by Miller were in all cases right, then it would seem wise to supplement the Fifth Amendment with one holding that no man could be required to incriminate another. If this were done, the whole machinery of law enforcement would collapse; it would be simply impossible to determine the facts about a crime. Of course, Congressional committees are not courts, and it might be held that such a rule would be useful in their proceedings. It would be useful only if we wished to destroy the investigative power. For we live, after all, in a community, in the midst of other people, and all of our problems—certainly all of those with which Congress has a legitimate concern—involve others. It is rarely possible to conduct a serious inquiry of any sort without talking about other people and without running the risk of saying something that would hurt them. We can honor the conscience that says "I speak my own sins. I cannot judge another," but those of us who accept any principle of social organization and certainly those of us who believe that our present social order, whatever changes it may stand in need of, is worth preserving cannot make a universal principle of refusing to inform. If any agency of the community is authorized to undertake a serious investigation of any of our common problems, then the identities of others—*names*—are of great importance. What would be the point of investigating, say, industrial espionage if the labor spies subpoenaed refused to identify their employers? What would be the point of investigating the Dixon-Yates contract if it were impossible to learn the identity of the businessmen and government officials involved?

The joker, the source of much present confusion, lies in the matter of *seriousness.* Miller and his attorneys have argued that the names of the writers Miller had known were not relevant to the legislation on passports the Committee was supposed to be studying. This would certainly seem to be the case, and one may regret that Judge McLaughlin did not accept this argument and acquit Miller on the strength of it. Nevertheless, the argument really fudges the central issue, which is that the Committee wasn't really investigating passport abuses at all when it called Miller before it. It was only pretending to do so. The rambling talk of its members with Miller was basically frivolous, and the Un-American Activities Committee has almost always lacked seriousness. In this case, as Mary McCarthy has pointed out, the most that it wanted from Miller was to have him agree to its procedure of testing the good faith of witnesses by their willingness to produce names. It was on this that Miller was morally justified in his refusal.

Still, Miller's principle, the social ethic he was defending, cannot be made a universal rule or a political right. For it is one thing to say in *The New Republic* that a committee is frivolous or mischievous and another to assert before the law that such a judgment gives a witness the right to stand mute without being held in contempt. As matters stand today, Miller was plainly in contempt. At one point in *The Crucible*, John Proctor is called upon to justify his failure to attend the church of the Reverend Mr. Parris and to have his children baptized by that divine. He replies that he disapproves of the clergyman. "I see no light of God in that man," he says. "That is not for you to decide," he is told. "The man is ordained, therefore the light of God is in him." And this, of course, is the way the world is. In a free society, any one of us may arrive at and freely express a judgment about the competence of duly constituted authority. But in an orderly society, no one of us can expect the protection of the law whenever we decide that a particular authority is unworthy of our cooperation. We may stand by the decision, and we may seek the law's protection, but we cannot expect it as a matter of right. There are many courses of action that may have a sanction in morality and none whatever in law.

Yet the law is intended to be, among other things, a codification of morality, and we cannot be pleased with the thought that a man should be penalized for an act of conscience—even when his conscience may seem not as fully informed by reason as it ought to be. In a much more serious matter, war, we excuse from participation those who say their consciences will permit them no part in it. One of the reasons the order of American society seems worth preserving is that it allows, on the whole, a free play to the individual's moral judgments. In recent years, Congressional committees have posed the largest single threat to this freedom. The issues have often been confused by the bad faith of witnesses on the one hand and committee members on the other. Still and all, the problem is a real one, as the Miller case shows. If there is not sufficient latitude for conscience in the law, then there ought to be. It would be unrealistic, I think, simply to permit anyone who chooses to withhold whatever information he chooses. The Fifth Amendment seems to go as far as is generally justified in this direction. Changes in committee procedures have often been urged, but it is doubtful if much clarification of a problem such as this can be written into rules and by-laws. The problem is essentially one of discretion and measurement; it is, in other words, the most difficult sort of problem and one of the kind that has, customarily, been dealt with by the establishment of broad and morally informed judicial doctrines. It is surely to be hoped that in the several cases, including Arthur Miller's, now in one stage or another of review, the courts will find a way of setting forth a realistic and workable charter for the modern conscience.

These New Men

EDITORIAL

JULY 25, 1960

Some of the shrewdest political observers have been struck, if not bowled over, by the drama of the "new men" taking command of the Democratic Party. It is not simply that the youthful Mr. Kennedy has won the Presidential nomination; it is that he has done it largely on his terms, through his own efforts and the efforts of men of his own generation; he is not the candidate because of his religion, or because of labor or ADA, or because of the old pros, or because of a single region. "1960," Walter Lippmann believes, "marks the passing of the old political generation and the appearance of the new." "A new kind of party is coming into being," Marquis Childs writes, "under the sponsorship of new men." Ralph McGill says that "an old political order is passing. . . . The Old Guard of the Democratic Party is finished." James Reston reports that there has been a "shift in power from men born in the 19th Century to the new generation born in the 20th, and from a very few all-powerful political bosses to a much larger group of younger and more intelligent political figures, many of them comparative amateurs." And *The Economist* of London, in a lead editorial of July 9 entitled "The New Men," suggests that "it should not necessarily be a cause for anxiety among America's allies if the [nation's] choice should in fact fall on a young man. . . . Many of his most important dealings, from the very beginning of his term, will be with leaders of new states whose inexperience may be apparent but whose youthful enthusiasms have to be grasped and understood. . . . The need is for a President who will allow new ideas to reach the top and circulate effectively among the policy-makers." The transition was inevitable, if not in 1960 then four years hence, but what does it signify? What kind of a new Democratic Party may emerge, to whom is it appealing, and what is its principal . . . business? The New Guard speaks to the voter who has come of political age since World War II. Theirs is the party of coffee-hours in living rooms, of television, of the kind of precinct organization that can be staffed by housewives—a party most of whose members are literate, high-school and college graduates, sophisticated and reasonably well-off. For them, windbag oratory or the spectacle of the torchlight parade have charm only as curiosities. For them, the social services of the old-time party organization are and should be provided out of taxes. Instead of a basket of groceries, they expect from their politicians action on unemployment, depressed areas, transportation, social security and medical care.

The leaders of this new party are not all devotees of Senator Kennedy's nomination—Eugene McCarthy is a shining example of that—but they are of his age, few of them are creatures of long-established political machines, they see eye to eye on the role of 20th-century government, they accept without regret involvement of this country in what happens on every continent. It is nonsense, of course, to say that Mr. Kennedy lacks "experience." He is one of the most experienced politicians of the day, not only in the tactics of battle but in his understanding of what the battle is all about. And as for the world, he is closer in touch with realities overseas than either Mr. Truman or General Eisenhower dreamed of being when they stepped into the White House. Senator Kennedy and those who are his closest allies take it for granted that the distinction between "foreign" and "domestic" issues has lost meaning; they perceive the connections between what is done here and events abroad. They sense too that this century will not, as some thought 20 years ago, be an "American Century," and that the world will not be shaped in the image of our democratic capitalism. Implicit in the platform these men wrote in Los Angeles and in the speeches of Senator Kennedy is an awareness that we can no longer assume the indefinite continuance of the bipolar conflict in the form in which it has been familiar during the past 15 years—or its end in "victory" for one side or the other.

But these new men, so eager to take over, have some mountains to climb and some rapids to swim before they can reach their destination—effective control of the party, especially in the Congress. "It is not only what we have inherited from our fathers that exists again in us," Ibsen remarks, "but all sorts of old dead ideas and all kinds of old dead beliefs and things of that kind. They are not actually alive in us; but there they are dormant all the same, and we can never be rid of them. Whenever I take up a newspaper and read it, I fancy I see ghosts creeping between the lines." If only they were ghosts! The progressive newer leaders will be haunted by flesh-and-blood committee chairmen in the Congress, notably in the House Rules Committee.

Can these "more intelligent political figures," as Mr. Reston calls them, win effective control of Democratic politics? Senator Johnson has been kicked upstairs, and if the ticket wins in November there will be a new Majority Leader in the Senate—one, presumably, with whom the President is compatible. Mr. Rayburn's retirement cannot be far off, which could mean the selection of a Kennedy-stripe Congressman, such as Richard Bolling, for the Speakership. This, of course, is conjecture. It is far too early to say who will come to the top, or when. But the responsibilities of the newer generation are identifiable. Nuclear energy, missiles, earth-circling satellites, for example, have made rubbish of many orthodox doctrines of defense and call in question both the utility of many of our overseas bases and the character of our alliances. Henceforth no diplomatic or military policy will have force unless it rests not merely on the consent of the governed here, but on the full consent and confidence of public opinion in a very large and growing number of non-Communist nations. How much we trade, with whom, how much of what we give of our productive skills or resources, to whom and under what conditions—cannot henceforth be settled solely by Congressional committees. Improved living standards and political stability in Asia, Africa and Latin America will mean more, not less, collective effort; more, not less, international cooperation.

The "new men" aren't starting from scratch. America for years has been burgeoning, not only with challenges to our capacities and our compassion, but with blueprints on how to progress more rapidly. What has been missing is will, imagination, an experimental spirit at the top. Our 179.3 million population of today will, within five years, have gone up by another 15 to 20 million. A Rockefeller Report foresees a doubling of the costs of public elementary and secondary school education in the sixties—and that bill must be paid for by higher taxes, or a larger Gross National Product, or a different allocation of resources—or all three. The nation must have soon not only more and better schools and teachers, but more hospitals and clinics, nursing homes, medical schools, research facilities.

In particular, there must be made available through social security services by which the growing population of older people can be assured of adequate health care, remembering that about three-fifths of the aged who are not in institutions still have cash incomes of under $1,000 a year and that we must anticipate, by 1975, 21 million Americans over 65. We need not only more lower- and middle-income housing, but a more sensible and attractive planning of the communities where they are built. It will take years to rid our cities of slums, the tangle of traffic, the foul air urban residents now breathe. The retirement of more and more families from farming must be anticipated as more food and fiber is produced on less and less land.

And why not a Taste Cultivation Program? TV's unadventurous "adventures," its nerveless dramas, its constricted wails in echo chambers that pass for popular folk music; the endless hokum of advertising, the selling short of the best in this creative country pitching all appeals to the largest number of potential consumers—all this is as inappropriate to the 1960's as is Eisenhower's notion that business is the most reliable custodian of our national well-being.

Above all, if the "new men" are to offer something more than new faces, they must have a commitment to the widest possibilities of life. The dry rot that eats away at morale is the uncertainty in the minds of so many now coming to maturity whether there is a socially useful role for them. "The chief moral failing of Americans in the Fifties," William Lee Miller wrote in a recent issue of *Christianity and Crisis*, "was not that in a complicated new organizational world some of us could not be individually honest, but rather that more of us could not be socially responsible." Security and the obscurity of a slot in a corporation's table of organization is not the dream of the best young Americans.

We share the sense of great-things-in-the-making. We are impressed by the idealism of such men as Eugene McCarthy, Orville Freeman, Gaylord Nelson, Leroy Collins, Mennen Williams, Gale McGee, George McGovern, Lee Metcalf, Frank Coffin, Steward Udall, Richard Bolling, Chester Bowles, John Brademas, Sidney Yates, Frank Thompson, Hubert Humphrey, and scores of others. It is not an idealism that expends itself in moral pronouncements. These men are not romantics; they find no satisfaction in defeat. Politics to them is more a business than a game. They are untouched by the sentimentalities of the thirties about the character of communism, but also less inhibited than the Old Guard by the Cold War rules drafted in the Stalinist forties and early fifties. They all have a controlled impatience; they want action, but they calculate the odds. They will use the power of government to expand and strengthen the economy, provide more social services, reconcile our defense policies with the new technological and political realities, and invest as we have never invested before both money and hope in nations born since 1945.

These new men know the score. And a large number of them know too that, in John Buchan's words, "in the greater matters of life, the mind must fling itself forward beyond its data," and that the possession of this instinct is what constitutes "the difference between the great and the less great among mankind."

There is a "new frontier," as Senator Kennedy said in his acceptance speech, unlimited by national frontiers unenclosed by the space above us, unapproachable by narrow paths of the past—but there for discovery and mastery by those who have the requisite intelligence, courage and imagination.

Nothing But Ads

PAUL GOODMAN

FEBRUARY 9, 1963

In an average stretch of TV time, only the ads make a strong aesthetic appeal, sensual and passionate. She caresses her arms after using Thrill (liquid) detergent and touches her fingertips to the nap of a Turkish towel laundered in Tide, and hangs up the wash, done with Ivory, on a softly blowy line. Warmly erotic, she presses her cheek close to his because she has used Ban that stops odor for 24 hours. In a surprisingly poetic action he blows on shiny chromium and sees his breath, but he doesn't know how his breath smells until he uses a Mouth Wash whose name I don't remember. Her face expresses the passionate suffering of a headache (she has controlled herself) until, like an addict, she takes an aspirin. (She's in control again.) And with studied persuasiveness, a mobile brow, a knowing eye, and a little smile, he tells you about the Spin filter on Old Golds. The ads almost always exploit the formal possibilities of the TV medium: montage; combinations of photography, graphics, speech, noise, and music; variety and novelty of expression. They are tight in structure and concise in statement.

In the nature of the case, the ads must be aesthetically superior to the programs because only they want and are designed to have an effect on the watcher, to come home to him, to activate him. The programs—whether dramas, games, panel-discussions, or routine newscasts—are tactical operations to hold passive attention, while the ads are the strategic action on the audience and speech to the audience. The ads have real content, commodities, and an authentic contact with social reality—sales. From the ads something is supposed to happen; from the programs nothing.

There are also, let us keep in mind, the more prestigious and aesthetically duller institutional ads of giant corporations, where the program itself is selected to enhance the Image (this point was repeatedly insisted on by the companies in one of Mr. Minow's hearings). One has the impression, in these cases, that it is not a matter of vulgar marketing but of using up a swollen budget for Advertising and Public Relations.

Of course the formula—commercial action as the real business of life for which sex, education, community, politics, etc. are just the setting—is generic in our society and applies to other mass arts. But in television, for historical and technical reasons, it poses peculiar difficulties and has peculiarly displeasing effects. There is a clash, except in the institutional ads, of the real content and the programs; and it is frustrating and rather disgusting that the merely attention-holding programs claim so much time and foreground.

In the economics of magazines like *Esquire, Mademoiselle, The New Yorker*, and so forth, we must distinguish, just as in TV, the "sustaining part," the ads, from the "non-sustaining" part, the stories, articles, and cartoons. The readers do not support the magazines; circulation is kept up and expanded for the ads. These magazines exist, however, in a tradition of publishing, back to Sam Johnson and Fleet Street, in which the audience did directly support authors and booksellers without patronage; and in a literary tradition, back to antiquity, in which artists gave real rather than token entertainment and instruction to their audiences. Further, every such magazine is established to reach a segment of the public that likes its particular format and attitude and for which its staff has hopefully an affinity. The ads are selective, both in their products and their style, for this special public. In *Mademoiselle*, for instance, one can hardly distinguish the chief editorial content (the fashions) from the ads, and the residual content (the articles and stories) can be astoundingly anything at all—sometimes even good. In *Esquire* or *The New Yorker*, the attitudé of the staff, the writing, and the ads more nicely merge. This gives the artists a relative freedom: if they meet the prejudices of the staff and are willing to be rewritten in the right format, they can breathe and prosper within the fairly wide limits of not flatly insulting the advertisers or seriously subverting the social system altogether. And the audiences can pick and choose among many magazines. Very important, finally, is the technical fact that, concentrating on an article or story from beginning to end (even though continued on page 78), a reader needs hardly notice the ads unless he is interested. From all this it follows that parts of these magazines can live together and the non-sustaining parts might sometimes touch some reality, though not so much reality as the ads.

Historically, radio and TV programs have drawn on no free tradition at all. What is their tradition? Hollywood movies, official newspapers, and regimented universities. Even vaudeville, the best part of the tradition, was moribund when radio began and dead when TV began. From the very beginning the programs were patronized; they never breathed a free marketplace nor were a forum for unadministered authors. Fine authors accept censorship, pretaping, and being pushed around by format on TV that they would indignantly reject from a publisher or editor. Further, the broadcasters have tried from the beginning to corral "mass" audiences, without specific group or individual needs, and the networks have hugely succeeded.

(This is what betrays the fine authors, for they cannot resist the lure of a million watchers.) Broadcasting has followed the common-denominator line—bland *cum* sensational—of the general-public press, like *Life* or some of the tabloids. All this has put the non-sustaining programs in a weak position.

Finally, technically, on TV and radio the non-sustaining programs exist in the same continuous experience of broadcasting time as the real content, the ads, that are the economically sustaining part. The effect of this is peculiarly unfortunate. Sometimes the aesthetically interesting ads are interrupted by the bland programs; other times the programs, desperately trying to hold or lull the audience, are interrupted by the agitating ads. Since the seconds are sold, everything is hurried. If there happens to be an important communication that is programmed for its general interest, like a crisis in the UN, it is devastatingly interrupted by a beer-jingle, a soothing soap ad, with heaven knows what effect on the citizens. Where the program depends on its sensational appeal, *e.g.*, a bloody Doctor show, there is a fierce clash with its luscious food ad. Where the program by exception presents something that has an intrinsic value, *e.g.*, an interview with a genuine and interesting man, it is trivialized by the ads; the man is insulted. (The interviewer is sometimes apologetic, usually just rude.) And of course the sale of the time-stretch to the advertiser necessarily favors him: either the program is interrupted by the ads irrelevantly to its own structure, or it is irrelevantly structured to be interrupted by the ads.

I am told that there are studies—I have not seen them—that demonstrate that the more authentically interesting a program is, the more stimulating beyond routine sensationalism, superficial excitement, or mere prestige, the *less* the memory of the commercial. This figures. However exciting the ads may be aesthetically, their contents are only ordinary familiar commodities that cannot compete for attention against novel reality unless one happens to be terribly hungry or needy. And certainly interrupting anything really interesting must lead to resentment, and blotting-out of the interrupter. If indeed there is a competition of this kind, between program interest and ad retention, the programs must become blander or even more superficially sensational. Only the most prestigious name-corporations, DuPont, Ford, U.S. Steel, Standard Oil, etc., could dare to sponsor interesting programs without fear of vanishing from memory, resting secure in being the pillars of society that can allow even the interesting to occur—if it endangers the image.

What is the solution? In my opinion, the watchers ought to pay for free communication and demand what they need. Free broadcasters, including cooperatives of technicians and artists, ought to run the stations and control the ads as they see fit. The FCC ought to give TV back to us.

None of this is realistic. Given the temper of the Americans and the realities of our society, perhaps the most humane and popular realistic solution would be rather to drop the programs and expand the commercials into more leisurely and extensive information and entertainment to replace them. There is no doubt that, at present, most of the best talent, peculiarly anonymous, is devoted to producing the ads anyway; it would be reasonable to give it its head. The incursion of the ads into the programs is now not uncommon—*e.g.,* Jack Paar, coyly—but this has the tendency to reduce the person in the program to the stature of a man who would say such words, a disastrous result when the person is supposed to have some authority, like Dr. Joyce Brothers. (Gene Shepherd, of course, tried to avoid the reduction by speaking the ad sardonically or sarcastically.) It is better to go the whole way toward commercial carnival. Certainly the most characteristic invention of TV, the Giveaway shows (*The Price Is Right* or the Quizzes), giving away commodities and climactically Money itself, have worked in this direction, with the most pleasant bridging of format and ads, the liveliest excitement of the participants, the most authentic content, namely goods and competitiveness, and immense audience popularity.

The attitude of Newton Minow is apparently just the opposite: to "contain" the ads, to diminish their time and muffle their decibels! and at the same time to "improve" the programs, but under the same network auspices and commercial patronage. In my opinion, such a policy must result in making the TV even more official, controlled, and phony than it is. The basic commercial reality, the need for the expanding mass-audience, remains. The basic political reality, to affirm the status quo, remains. The higher-level programming would be entirely factitious and pompous: Establishment art, news, and information. My guess is that with more pretentious programming the big corporations would be even more in evidence. This is no doubt exactly what Establishment people, like the Administration, think is dandy. I don't.

The world of TV is a peculiarly pure product of our public policy of an expanding economy with artificial demand (plus annual increases in the arms budget), to maintain both high profits and adequate employment. It has the aesthetics and human values that fit that policy.

The War on Poverty

GUNNAR MYRDAL

FEBRUARY 8, 1964

Having to live with large pockets of poverty-stricken people in their midst is not a new experience in the American nation. Right from slavery the masses of Negroes formed such pockets, both in the rural South and in the cities South and North. Such pockets were also formed by other colored people who immigrated to work as laborers from Asia, Mexico and Puerto Rico. Most American Indians in their reservations were also poor and isolated as they are today. There were also, as there are still, pockets of "poor whites," ordinarily of old American stock, who lived by themselves in abject poverty and cultural isolation.

I believe it is important to have in our minds this broad picture of the historical reality of American poverty as a background to the discussion of the problems facing us today. The regular, prosperous Americans have become accustomed to living with unassimilated groups of people in their midst, about whom they know in a distant and general way that they are very poor. The fact that in earlier times they themselves lived under the risk of being thrown out of work and losing their livelihood, if only temporarily, made it easier for them to feel unconcerned about the people who more permanently were enclosed in the pockets of poverty. Otherwise, the existence of all this poverty in the midst of progressive America stood out in blunt contradiction to the inherited and cherished American ideals of liberty and equal opportunity, as these ideals increasingly had been interpreted, particularly since Franklin D. Roosevelt and the New Deal.

Automation and other changes are all the time decreasing the demand for unskilled and uneducated labor. Standards are rising fast even in household and other menial work. Something like a caste line is drawn between the people in the urban and rural slums, and the majority of Americans who live in a virtual full-employment economy, even while the unemployment rate is rising and the growth rate of the economy is low. Except for a lower fringe, they experience a hitherto unknown security, for it is a tacit understanding in America, as in the rest of the Western world, that a recession will never again be permitted to develop into anything like the Great Depression. But there is an underclass of people in the poverty pockets who live an ever more precarious life and are increasingly excluded from any jobs worth having, or who do not find any jobs at all.

I want to stress one important political fact. This underclass has been, and is largely still, what I have been accustomed to call the world's least revolutionary proletariat. They do not organize themselves to press for their interests. The trade union movement comprises only about one-fourth of the workers, mostly its upper strata who in the main belong to the prosperous majority. To a relatively higher extent than normally they do not register and vote at elections—even apart from the large masses of Negroes in the South who are prevented from doing so.

In very recent times we have seen one important break of this empirical rule of the political apathy of the poor in America. I am, of course, referring to the rebellion of the Negroes in Southern and Northern cities. Without any doubt, this is a true mass movement—so much so that the Negro leaders in the upper and middle class have had to run very fast to remain in the lead, as have, on the other side of the fence, the Administration and other whites responsible for American policy.

I am not at this time going into the question of how this movement, so exceptional to what has been the pattern of passivity on the part of the poor in America, has come about. But I should mention two things about which I am pretty sure. One is my belief that the outbreak of this rebellion just now is not unconnected with the high and, as a trend, rising rate of unemployment, which as always runs much higher—about double—for Negro workers than for whites. Another thing of which I am convinced is that this movement will not abate unless very substantial reforms are rapidly undertaken to improve the status in American society of its Negro citizens. I am optimistic enough to forecast that in the next 10 years the Negroes will get legal rights equal to the white majority, and that these will be enforced. What will still be needed are, in particular, social sanctions to defend the Negroes' equal opportunities to employment, against the resistance of trade unions more than employers and the business world, particularly big business. And even when all this is accomplished, the Negro masses will nevertheless continue to suffer all the lasting effects of the disabilities and disadvantages of their poverty, their slum existence and their previous exclusion from easy access to education and training for good jobs.

Indeed, it is easy to understand why some of the Negro leaders, and some white liberals, are now raising the demand for a new Marshall Plan to make good the effects of the maltreatment in America of the Negroes from slavery and up till this day. Nevertheless, I am convinced that this demand for a discrimination in reverse, *i.e.*, to the advantage of the Negroes, is misdirected. Nothing would with more certainty create hatred for Negroes among other poor groups in America, who have mostly been their bitterest enemies as they have been the only ones who have felt them as competitors. Moreover, special welfare policies for Negroes are not very practical. Negro housing cannot very well be improved except as part of a plan to improve the housing situation for poor people in general. The same is true of education. Special welfare policies in favor of the Negroes would strengthen their exclusion from the main stream of American life, while what the Negroes want is to have equal opportunities.

What America needs is a Marshall Plan to eradicate poverty in the nation. This is a moral imperative. The unemployed, the underemployed and the now unemployables are also America's biggest wastage of economic resources. The poor represent a suppressed demand which needs to be released to support a steady rapid growth of American production. The goals of social justice and economic progress thus are compatible. A rapid steady economic growth is impossible without mobilizing the productive power of the poor and clothing their unfilled needs with effective demand. The existence of mass poverty in the midst of plenty is a heavy drag on the entire economy.

The statistics on unemployment in America do not tell the whole story. Besides the four million unemployed there are the workers who are only part-time employed, those who have given up seeking work, and all the underemployed. It is an ominous fact that even the prolonged upturn in production from 1961 and onward has not implied a substantial decrease in the rate of unemployment. Nobody seems to expect that the continuation of the present boom will bring down unemployment to a level that could be considered even to approach full employment. And nobody assumes that there will not be a new recession, if not this year then the next. It is reasonable to expect that the unemployment rate will then reach a new high point. There are definite signs that the trend is rising.

For this there are explanations. I believe it is important to stress that none of the specific explanations put forward makes a rising trend of unemployment inevitable, or could by itself prevent the attainment of full employment. Only in conjunction with each other do these influences have the present disastrous result. If in the Sixties exceptionally many young workers enter the labor market, this should not necessarily mean more unemployment. Production could expand rapidly enough to absorb them, and all the new workers could have been properly educated and trained so that they fitted the demand for labor as it has been changing. Long ago, Professor Alvin Hansen and other economists, including myself, used to think that in rich countries, where capital is plentiful, a rapid population increase would rather act as a spur to expansion. It would stimulate the demand for new housing and all the goods and services accessory to housing, and for new schools, teachers, and productive capacity.

Likewise, automation should not by itself lead to unemployment if output expanded enough and the labor force were adjusted to fit the change in demand, caused by automation itself among other things. There are countries with full employment that have an equally rapid pace of automation. There, automation is viewed as driven forward by the scarcity of labor and as resulting in higher productivity of labor, higher earnings and a rising consumers' demand for products and services: in America, as a cause of unemployment.

What type of society are we moving toward in the modern rich countries? A continually smaller part of our total labor force will be needed in agriculture, manufacturing industry, heavy transport, distribution of commodities, banking and insurance. If we could countervail Parkinson's law, which for various reasons is working with particular force in America, even many sectors of public service would demand less labor.

It is the serious lag in adjusting the education and training of our labor force to the needs of this new society which is the general cause of the situation where we have serious overemployment in some sectors of our economy, at the same time as there is an uncomfortably large and growing residue of structural unemployment and underemployment that cannot be eradicated by an expansion of our production that is feasible.

Against this background it is easy to establish the broad lines of the policies that we will have to apply in order to cure our economic ailments. Huge efforts will have to go into education and vocational training, not only on the higher levels but on the level of grade schools and high schools. Particularly will we have to lift the level of elementary education for the poor people in the urban and rural slums, who are not now getting an education that fits them to the labor market. We must at the same time undertake the retraining of the older workers who are continuously thrown out of jobs without having the abilities to find new ones in our changing society.

I see it as almost a fortunate thing that America has such vast slums in the big cities and smaller ones in the small cities; so many dwellings for poor people that are substandard; so many streets that need to be kept cleaner; such crying needs for improved transport. To train unskilled workers to do such jobs should be easier than to make them teachers or nurses.

It should be stressed, however, that a primary condition for success is rapid and steady economic expansion of the national income. Without an increased demand for labor, no efforts for training and retraining workers on a mass scale can succeed. This is the important argument for the view that expanding the economy is the essential thing. Expansion is, in a sense, the necessary condition for any effort to readjust the supply of different types of labor to demand.

A common characteristic of all the reforms directed at raising the quality of the labor force and eradicating poverty in the midst of plenty is that the increased expenditure will be public expenditure. Even when poverty is gone, when there is little or no unemployment or underemployment, a relatively much larger part of the nation's needs will have to be met by collective means. In the future society toward which we are moving, where our productive efforts will increasingly have to be devoted to the care of human beings, health, education, research and culture, and to making our local communities more effective instruments for living and working, public spending will be an ever larger part of total spending. This is because it is not very practical and economical, and in most cases not even possible, to rely on private enterprise for filling these types of demands.

This brings up the problem of balancing or not balancing the federal budget. Large sections of the public and Congress hold, on this question, an opinion that has no support in economic theory and is not commonly held in other advanced countries: that, in principle, expenditures of the federal budget should be balanced by taxation.

A recent experience from my own country Sweden must seem curiously up-side-down to Americans. In a situation of threatening overfull employment and inflationary pressure, the Swedish social democratic government, which has been in power almost a third of a century, felt that it needed to put on brakes, and decided to raise taxation to a level where, for a while, we actually had a balanced budget in the American sense. The political parties to the *right* of the party in power criticized the government fiercely for overtaxing the citizens, and insinuated that this was a design to move our economy in a socialistic direction, by robbing the citizens and private business of the funds they needed. So differently can the problem of balancing the budget appear in two otherwise very similar countries. In fact, you have examples nearer at hand. When the railroads were built in America, the federal government favored the railroad companies in various ways, which occasionally broke the rule of balancing the budget.

The analogy that a nation must handle its purse strings with the same prudence as an individual is false. An individual is not in the position to borrow from himself. Moreover, if the implication is that the government should not borrow even for productive purposes, it is a rule which no private householder follows, or should follow, if he is wise and prudent. And we know that there has been a huge increase, both absolutely and relatively, of private borrowing by business as well as by consumers.

This does not mean that Congress should not carefully weigh each dollar that is spent and each dollar that is taken in by taxation or other means. But the weighing should be in terms of progress and welfare for the nation. I can see no virtue in America having decreased its national debt in postwar years to half its size compared with the national income, while abstaining from undertaking a great number of public expenditures that would have been highly productive from a national point of view. America has been satisfied for a whole decade with a rate of growth of only a little more than one percent per head, and with unemployment rising to the present high level. In the interest of public enlightenment I would wish my American colleagues to spend a little more of their time disseminating some simple truths about budget balancing and related issues. America cannot afford to remain the rich country that has the highest rate of unemployment, and the worst and biggest slums, and which is least generous in giving economic security to its old people, its children, its sick people and its invalids.

LBJ Isn't JFK

TRB FROM WASHINGTON

MARCH 28, 1964

Lovely spring is turning Washington yellow with forsythia and the time has come at last to quit disparaging Lyndon Johnson because he isn't John F. Kennedy. He isn't, and that's that. He is a powerful figure in his own right who has already got Congress to pass the biggest tax cut in history; he is giving all-out support to the most far-reaching civil rights bill in 100 years; he has proposed a "war on poverty" which—even with superlatives drained off—remains a splendid bundle of beginnings; he will try to enact Medicare, and he will do his best with foreign aid in the face of a broadly hostile Congress and a generally indifferent public.

Mr. Johnson is operating in a world where the Opposition almost seems not to want to win. We have always suspected that of Goldwater: he told the Press Club here not long ago that he had thought seriously of withdrawing after JFK's death and continued only from loyalty to his friends; something of a defeatist admission, we thought.

Republicans are no nearer picking a leader than three months ago; the NH primary was a debacle for the two leading contenders. One begins to wonder if it matters much who ultimately gets the nod; the problem is to salvage the party. Goldwater extremists have just captured the Republican Assembly in California; Governor Rockefeller has mounting troubles in his own GOP legislature. Democratic hopes look up in the two largest states.

This is too bad in a way. The country needs a strong two-party system. There is plenty about the Administration to criticize, but nobody to do it effectively, not, at any rate, until the Republicans have straightened themselves out.

President Johnson is popular, but not too popular. His position is illustrated by the story of the thank-you note written by the little girl to her grandmother for the gift of a thimble. "Thank you, Granny," she wrote, "I like your present, but not very much." The approval of Mr. Johnson is widespread, but nobody can say how deep it is; it seems to lack both the passionate support and dislike that most leaders create in time.

As a matter of fact, this mood of muted approval may express something important within the country; Mr. Johnson elicited it in his hour-long TV interview, in which he did not make any slips, but evoked instead a feeling that was cozy, relaxed, comfortable and bored. Maybe the country wants to be bored a bit. Mr. Johnson implied that he loves everybody; that he wants to be a "prudent progressive"; favors a "better deal" and just adores free enterprise. The viewer could snap off the set and turn to more interesting things, satisfied that Mr. Johnson was probably safe and sound, precisely the feeling the President probably sought to elicit.

Is Mr. Johnson then nothing more than an intelligent Eisenhower? He is a lot more, we think. He said about the civil rights bill, for example, "I believe they [the Senate] can pass it and I believe they will pass it and I believe it is their duty to pass it, and I am going to do everything I can to get it passed."

Ike never made an affirmation like that in eight years, save perhaps about the dangers of galloping inflation.

Take 20 historians and ask them to write down adjectives that describe the typical American; then let half a dozen Johnson friends write down his predominant characteristics as they see it. There will be a close resemblance, we guess, between the lists. He is proud, sensitive, impulsive, flamboyant, sentimental, compassionate; he is a doer not a thinker, and he won't alarm people (as JFK did) with startling new notions. He is optimistic, a worrier, quick-tempered, impatient, tough, hard-driving and boastful; he is earthy as Truman, and tends to leave culture and art to his wife (who is a great asset, by the way). He is an exponent of moderation, compromise and manipulation, and on big issues, he is careful and cautious. He works 18 hours a day.

All the time he does corny things that embarrass ivory-tower intellectuals, like going around and turning the White House lights off; but how many votes do the intellectuals have? The man in the street understands the symbolism, and the businessman thinks that LBJ is somehow safer than JFK because "he isn't a spender." Well, we'll see.

Miami and the Seeds of Port Huron

TOM GEOGHEGAN

SEPTEMBER 2, 1972

> ***Beneath the reassuring tones of the politicians . . . is the pervading feeling that there simply are no alternatives, that our times have witnessed the exhaustion not only of utopias, but of any new departures as well.***
>
> —THE PORT HURON STATEMENT, 1962

> ***And is it any wonder that the people are skeptical and cynical of the whole political process?***
>
> —THE DEMOCRATIC PLATFORM, 1972

You can't fool the GOP with any phony populism or New Politics. Their platform exposes the once-great Democratic Party bent on surrender abroad and "convulsive leftward lurches" at home, duped by a radical clique which would "scorn our nation's past and would blight its future." The only past that Republicans scorn, apparently, is "the nightmarish time" of the sixties, those bad old days of riots and Vietnam and radical social programs. Oddly enough, it seems Senator McGovern will mention very few such programs in his campaign this year. He preaches a sober bookkeeper's radicalism, an almost passive reordering of priorities—one that takes away defense funds and supplements incomes.

But the Republicans are right to sense that their old rivals are groping for new targets, though they aren't quite sure what these might be. The Democrats as a party have given them few clues. With a morbid eye on Archie Bunker's vote, they are more concerned than ever to sound folksy, like all those farmers-cabbies-housewives they kept splicing into the dead air of their telethon last month in Miami. Even the platform—this year, for once, an important document—was a showpiece of populist zip. "For the People" rambles on for nine chapters, and though it does little more than repackage the Great Society grocery list, it tries in its new folk wisdom to sound restless with the nostrums of liberal reform. It hankers after the homegrown, radical rhetoric of the 19th-century Populists and 20th-century Bull Moosers, but without finding much there it can use. Except for a swipe at the railroads (an anachronistic plank in the age of Amtrak), the main thrust of the 1892 platform of the People's Party was to encourage the people to keep their spare change. When the Populists pronounced that "wealth belongs to him who creates it," they could have been spouting either a Marxist theory of value or small-fry capitalist homiletics. The Populist obsession with liquidity extended even to their own pygmy governments: "All state and national revenues shall be limited to the necessary expenses of government, economically and honestly administered." We do not demean the radicalism of Tom Watson or Sockless Jerry Simpson by suggesting their limited value to the phrasemakers of the New Politics of the '70s.

Nor were the Progressives of 1912, the party of Herbert Croly and Herbert Hoover, a ready source of inspiration or direction for the Democrats in Miami Beach this year. Progressive broadsides against "invisible government" of special interests catch moods the Democrats wish to capture, but the Bull Moosers didn't have the feisty proletarianism of the New Politics. Apostles of referenda and primaries, the Progressives had a fairly elitist faith in "a new instrument of government" more likely to co-opt than destroy the big trusts. They were angry, aroused, and yet quaintly confident that sound business methods could put the country aright.

The true ancestor of the Miami platform is still hidden in the closet—the SDS charter first drafted 10 years ago in Port Huron by Tom Hayden. With SDS today in disrepute, blasted even by the *new* New Left for being out of touch with "the people," this kind of victory is hollow but always logical, with the radical left always running out of steam and the moderate left always running out of ideas.

In *A Populist Manifesto*, Jack Newfield and Jeff Greenfield jeer at SDS for slighting the "concrete economic interests" of working people (forgetting the Progressive Labor faction, which made a fetish of them) and for indulging their middle-class malaise. But Populism, narrowly defined as an attack on economic privilege, is what the Miami Beach Democratic platform rejects: the problems of the people are deeper than their concrete economic interests. "The people" of the 1972 platform are straight out of Port Huron—not the John Q. Publics or the aggrieved farmers reaching for their pitchforks but the alienated, the bored, the apathetic. There's no biblical wrath here, the platform just delivers some old New Left rabbit punches: "the people are *skeptical*" of all platitudes; "the people are *cynical*" about promises. And the Democrats of 1972 will "speak to those doubts." "No government can by itself restore the lost faith," the platform modestly admits, for the people must struggle with a vast bureaucracy that is demoralizing. Impersonal, not authentic government, Port Huron called it. The party half-articulates the Port Huron challenge of turning federal government into participatory democracy. No more cheap talk in Hayden's platform about throwing the rascals out: the people are isolated from one another, they must be brought together into a community as a means of finding meaning in personal life," one that is "personally authentic."

In its bolder passages, the Miami Beach platform takes a few small steps into the Rousseauistic future:

"What do the people want?"

"They want three things:

- They want a personal life that makes us all feel that life is worth living;
- They want a social environment whose institutions promote the good of all; and
- They want a physical environment whose resources are used for the good of all."

It may be the first campaign commitment of a major national party to soul-satisfying "authenticity." At this point, the platform breaks for an interlude of new Populism, rejecting the dole and demanding law-and-order, but it then returns to this inchoate "right to full participation in government and the political process." And how is this right to be exercised? Mainly through more quotas and primaries around election year, as if through some sort of McGovern-Fraser guidelines there could be popular takeover of a remote federal machine. Port Huron called for "public groupings," not groupings of representatives, which would help people make direct, primary decisions about even their personal lives. The Port Huron statement, however, did not resolve the tension this would create between a new radical individualism and a new popular sovereignty. The Democrats also ignore that dilemma, a platform being no place for dialectics.

But parties are at least expected to have programs to match their rhetoric. The Democrats just furrow their brows and say, "It is time now to rethink and reorder the institutions of this country so that everyone . . . can participate in the decision-making process inherent in the democratic heritage to which we aspire." This is at best an ethic and at worst bombast.

Ironically, only the George Wallace Democrats made serious use of the old SDS rhetoric to criticize American institutions. Their minority report has a ruthless democratic thrust. It asks tough questions about judges who ignore Congress to make laws, Presidents who ignore Congress to make wars and bureaucrats who ignore Congress to "pursue abstract and artificial social theories." It suggests Americans will have to sit down and write the social contract all over again. In contrast, the McGovern Democrats have no intention of letting participatory democracy undermine the constitutional status quo. For all the talk about personal fulfillment, their platform trails off into interest group liberalism—a few more welfare programs, a little more bargaining and dealing with tenant organizations, welfare rights groups, veterans, elderly, American Indians, consumers—but without any institutional reforms. In brief, the Democrats promise more old-left new deals in the language of the New Left, a tactic almost calculated to escalate apathy.

The danger of the Democratic platform (and its so-called "populist" rhetoric) is that by its explicit promise of social reintegration, it exploits the political potential of the "new anxieties" of private identity. It wants ordinary people to take more responsibility for complex social crises—without having any more power than they did before. Even if more politics were the cure for the distresses in our lives, the Democrats don't seem to have the stomach to give real power to the people. The logic of participatory democracy, as the Wallace Democrats know, requires, for instance, a reshuffling of the judiciary to give the majority of people control over the root-and-branch issue in American politics—race—which David Broder has called the single issue with enough emotional punch to realign the parties.

But the courts are only one stumbling block to participatory democracy. The huge federal leviathan, which survived unscathed at Miami, is sure to compromise any new populist attack on economic privilege and corporate conspiracy. In our economy, the people's government is not another policeman on the block but the air which all big business must breathe. After a century of progressive effort, Washington is regulating and subsidizing and even drawing up the entire demand curve of many large firms. "Consumers, citizens and taxpayers constitute too diffuse and amorphous a group to compete in this league," Richard Posner wrote last fall in *Public Interest.* "The larger the role of government in the economy . . . the worse the problem of public powers employed for private ends will become." Though calling for tougher antitrust laws against big-business establishment, the Democratic platform accepts a federal establishment already too mammoth to work properly.

Thus, the New Democrats are caught between Hayden's world, where politics is expected to deal with the whole man and his sense of helplessness, and the Great Society, where a faceless bureaucracy indemnifies anyone or any group big enough to make trouble for it. The Democrats can't promise, like Wallace, to throw briefcases into the Potomac, nor will they tear down the *ancien régime* in the name of Port Huron. In place of genuine participation, then, the Democrats are left only with cant about truth-in-government, inspired by the Pentagon papers, and a cult of "sin-cere-ness" inspired by Ellsberg and McGovern himself. More than the war itself, the Pentagon papers have deflected radical Democrats into conspiracy theories and image politics. A bread-and-butter issue like tax reform now figures in their rhetoric as just a particularly good example of hypocrisy in high places.

Larry O'Brien told the Miami Beach convention that the Democrats would level with the people. But before you level, you must have something to level about. It may be fine to open up FBI files and close down army spy rings, but it is ludicrous to expect thousands of honchos at HEW and HUD to start "leveling" with the people when the Democrats return to power. The platform hails a new era of participatory democracy, but the politicians simply promise a new era of good feelings between the people and government.

It may be that, bankrupt as it is of better ideas for fuller participation, the Democratic Party can do no more than incant the name of the people. I'd like to suggest, however, that there is still time to go through an almost discredited exercise in 18th-century political science: to think through the republican principles on which Americans founded their constitutional government, see how far we have strayed from them and whether and how we might return to them. The Miami platform rightly addresses popular distrust of those in public authority. But it ignores the first halting steps of Congress to reclaim its position as the central institution in federal government—so far the most dramatic response to the so-called "crisis of confidence." For the lessons of this crisis, whether its particular form be Vietnam or housing, are laid out not in the Pentagon papers but in *The Federalist Papers.*

The *Federalist* authors saw the United States as a republic, with government in the hands of delegates necessarily removed from the general citizenry. But they had a peculiarly modern concern for protecting the citizen from government tyranny and faction through a system of checks and balances. The genius of the document is that it was written to fend off monsters like "a standing army," not to mention a standing army bankrolled at $80 billion per annum.

The *Federalist* authors assumed Congress would be a more popular representative institution than the presidency, if only because it had more people to represent *the* people. Today Congress may be the last institutional alternative to the civic ennui that the Miami platform indicts. Liberals have sneered at Congress, particularly the "popular" branch—the House—because they confuse legitimate institutions, which Congress is, with progressive institutions, which Congress often is not. To strengthen the legitimate representative character of the government we may have to sacrifice a little of its progressive character. For however frustrating, Congress is not impersonal or "inauthentic." It helps foster independent publics, voluntary and legitimate face-to-face relationships with agencies and bureaucrats. Institutional reform at this level would throw any issue into new relief. Poorly staffed and financed, Congress defers to the "experts." In every area of government, it has delegated too much decision-making to trade associations, private groups and public corporations that even the President cannot control. Though it is foolish to expect warm, meaningful relationships between the people and their federal agencies, it is not too much to expect these agencies to have precise standards to follow—and the setting of those is a legislative responsibility.

Should Congress begin again to hoard its authority, the Democrats might have to accept greater limits on presidential government. That would not be bad. They have put too much faith in the power of the FDRs and JFKs to pull the people into the political process. Presidential elections can educate and entertain, but they are not the vehicles by which the people debate and decide issues.

The Miami platform is faithful to the spirit of centralized government, content with the post-parliamentary stage which most Western liberal democracies have entered. Its New Left rhetoric of participation may evoke nostalgia for the old sense of group responsibility that Tocqueville saw in American life. It may be a half-conscious itch for a government by public discussion at the national level, for congressional leadership. But in place of such leadership, the platform talks plebiscites and presidential democracy. What the party did in Miami was turn the Port Huron statement on its head, thundering at the beast and then promising to feed it. The Wallace Democrats had a populist last word: "What this platform says is 'Government has failed—give us more government.'"

Abortion

EDITORIAL

FEBRUARY 10, 1973

The Constitution, said Justice Holmes in a famous dissent in 1905, "is made for people of fundamentally differing views." Very seldom, therefore, do the Constitution's text and its history return a single comprehensive answer to questions of social and economic policy. When he wrote those words, the justices were grinding out annual answers to social and economic questions on the basis of their own convictions of what was wise—derived, as it happens, from the laissez-faire philosophy of Herbert Spencer. That would not do, Holmes told them, and it did not, although it took 30 years for a majority of the justices to see it and Holmes was gone by then.

Nobody has since reread Herbert Spencer into the Constitution, but in the 1960s, a majority of the justices, under Earl Warren, again began dictating answers to social and sometimes economic problems. The problems now were not regulation of economic enterprise, not labor relations, but the structure of politics, educational policy, the morals and mores of the society. And the answers were differently derived, not from the *Social Statics* of Herbert Spencer, but from more fashionable and perhaps humane notions of progress. Again, it seems, it may take some time before the realization comes that this will not do. On January 22, the Supreme Court, paying formal tribute to Holmes' 1905 dissent, but violating its spirit, undertook to settle the abortion issue. Most states have abortion statutes. They are not uniform in their provisions. Some are old and some are new. All are currently in controversy and in flux. In their place, the Supreme Court has now prescribed a virtually uniform statute of its own, allowing very little variation. During the first three months of pregnancy, the Court decreed, a woman and her physician may decide on an abortion quite free of any interference from the state, except as the physician may be required himself to be licensed by the state. During the second three months, the state may impose some health regulations, but it may not forbid abortion. During the last three months, the state may if it chooses forbid as well as regulate.

That may be a wise model statute, although there is considerable question why the Court foreclosed state regulation of the places where the abortion is to be performed. The state regulates and licenses restaurants and pool halls and Turkish baths, and God knows what else in order to protect the public, and it is difficult to see why it may not similarly regulate and license abortion clinics, or doctors' offices, if abortions are to be performed in them. In any case, with this and perhaps one or another exception, the Court's model statute is an intelligent one. But what is the justification for its imposition on the country by the Court? If this statute, why not one on proper grounds for divorce, or on adoption of children or on anything you please?

There is a body of medical evidence now in existence, the Court tells us, showing that abortions during the first three months of pregnancy present no great risk. Well and good. It is also clear that the fetus is not a life in being at the early stages of pregnancy, and is not entitled to constitutional protection. The Constitution cannot be construed to forbid abortion. Well and good. But the fetus is a potential life, and the Court acknowledges that society has a legitimate interest in it as such. And so does the individual—the woman and perhaps also the father—and the individual interest may be characterized as a claim to personal privacy, which in some contexts, all of them markedly different, the Constitution has been found to protect. The individual interest, the Court holds, completely overrides the interest of society in the first three months of pregnancy, and subject only to health regulations, also in the second. In the third trimester, society is in charge again.

Why? The Court never says. It simply asserts the result it has reached. That is all the Court can do because there is no answer that moral philosophy, logic, reason or other materials of law can give to this question. If medical considerations were the only ones involved, perhaps a satisfactory rational answer could be arrived at. But as the Court acknowledges, they are not. That is why the question is not for courts, but should have been left to the political process, which in state after state can achieve not one but many accommodations and adjust them from time to time as attitudes change.

There were, astonishingly enough, only two dissenters—Justices White and Rehnquist. The Court's decision is an "extravagant exercise" of judicial power, said Justice White; it is a legislative rather than judicial action, suggested Justice Rehnquist. So it is, and if the Court's guess concerning the probable and desirable direction of progress is wrong, it will nevertheless have been imposed on all 50 states, and imposed permanently, unless the Court itself should in future change its mind. Normal legislation, enacted by legislatures rather than judges, is happily not so rigid, and not so presumptuous in its claims to universality and permanence.

Unpardonable Offense

EDITORIAL

SEPTEMBER 21, 1974

We are instructed to do justly and to love mercy, but we do not know what it means to do justly except by reference to laws and customs. They are the foundation of our liberty and order. Without them we are in Hobbes' state of nature: "No arts, no letters, no society and, which is worst of all, continual fear and danger of violent death, and the life of men solitary, poor, nasty, brutish and short." So the Constitution of the United States commands that the President "shall take care that the laws be faithfully executed." Is that what Mr. Ford has done by pardoning Mr. Nixon? Now President Ford has not said that anyone is above the law. Rather he has perceived, and at the start only in the case of Mr. Nixon, that there is an obligation to be merciful, which is above the law. That is a civilized perception, given formal recognition by the Constitution in Article 2, Section 2: "The President . . . shall have Power to grant Reprieves and Pardons for Offenses against the United States, except in cases of Impeachment." Our objection to the pardon is that the power has been used too hastily, too indiscriminately, and that in consequence confidence in the applicability of equal justice and in the President's judgment have been further weakened. When the force of law is laid only on the backs of errand boys—and perhaps not even on their backs—justice is discredited, all considerations of compassion notwithstanding.

Abuse of a presidential power, deception of aides and the public—characteristics of the disgraced previous administration—likewise marked the process that led up to pardoning Mr. Nixon for "all offenses against the United States which he . . . has committed or may have committed or taken part in" from January 20, 1969 through August 9, 1974. Suddenly that openness and candor that Mr. Ford had led us to think would be the hallmarks of his presidency had vanished. Ten days earlier he had assured his press conference that immunity from prosecution would be "unwise and untimely" before any "legal process has been undertaken." That was a sensible comment; it still is. Moreover, while the pardon was under study, Mr. Ford's press secretary and through him newsmen and the public were being advised by top Ford aides that no such move was being explored.

The blunder was not in the deceptiveness that accompanied it or the inconsistency. What was wrong was to pardon a man for offenses that were not specified (to use a favorite word of Mr. Nixon's early defenders on the House Judiciary Committee), or proven or confessed to by the pardoned "offender." Mr. Ford was reduced to unpardonable vagueness; "certain acts or omissions occurring before his [Nixon's] resignation. . . ." The failure to itemize the misdeeds surely lends support to Mr. Nixon's blithe view of the scandals as nothing more than "a complex and confusing maze of events, decisions, pressures and personalities." The record—and it is incomplete—allows no such easy escape into ambiguity. For example there's the June 23, 1972 tape, which shows that six days after the Watergate break-in Mr. Nixon approved a plan for the CIA to block the FBI investigation, disproving Mr. Nixon's assertion that he erred only "in not acting more decisively and more forthrightly in dealing with Watergate particularly when it reached the stage of judicial proceedings . . . [in January 1973]." It was the unanimous finding of the House Judiciary Committee that almost immediately after the burglars were caught in June 1972, the former President personally and through subordinates "made it his plan and did direct" the subsequent criminal obstruction of justice. If Mr. Nixon was to be pardoned, was it not incumbent on Mr. Ford to state such facts as these, so we might know what the pardon was for? And is it not legitimate to ask whether this pardon for unknown crimes is to be followed by a pardon to unknown persons, whose names and deeds may surface after further revelations? For instance there are more than five dozen Watergate-related White House tapes whose contents are known today only by Mr. Jaworski and Judge Sirica—and Mr. Nixon.

The indictment of the former President and a trial or a negotiated plea—none of which is now possible—would have put on record the accusatory evidence, requiring Mr. Nixon to rebut specific allegations or at least rationalize them. For the first time, he would have been held accountable by due process on particular charges for particular acts, a situation he initially avoided by publicly lying about his conduct, then resigning in advance of an inevitable Senate impeachment trial. How will a future public understand what was behind the impeachment drive or the true cause for Richard Nixon's resignation? By reading the incomplete report of the Judiciary Committee? By reading Mr. Nixon's interpretation? Already one hears it said he was "driven from office," as if by partisan furies.

Who is there who does not want the wounds of Watergate to be healed? But they won't be healed by concealing the infection, its nature and cause; it will only fester. That's why full disclosure and legal certification of responsibility and remedial action are necessary. Many of the abuses of power referred to in the House committee's second article of impeachment need further congressional scrutiny. To take one aspect of the case, Mr. Nixon's departure and the presidential pardon have not foreclosed future White House misuse of the Internal Revenue Service, the Central Intelligence Agency or FBI wiretaps. Information on these matters developed by the special prosecutor, had it been laid out and examined during a trial of Mr. Nixon would have spurred Congress to revise preventive administrative or legislative remedies. Unless this information now comes out in some other way, Congress is going to have to dig out the facts on its own.

Mr. Ford could limit some of the damage caused by his ill-timed and ill-considered act. Under Justice Department regulations, Special Prosecutor Jaworski has authority to issue reports. That regulation was to have permitted the first prosecutor, Archibald Cox, to explain publicly at the conclusion of his work why prosecutions were being brought. Cox also expected to file a general report on Watergate. A similar report by the Jaworski staff, completed only after a full Nixon investigation has been concluded, can still be written. The 11 areas of the Nixon inquiry under way at the time of the pardon encompass a range, from the Watergate cover-up to the handling of campaign funds by Mr. Nixon's friend Charles Rebozo. Where criminal violations implicating others than Mr. Nixon are discovered, prosecutions are still in order. And in those instances where Mr. Nixon was a party to illegalities, his role could be described in the Jaworski report. That may not be full justice, but at least the opportunities for historical falsification or partisan mischief would be minimized.

President Ford could review and then release such a document, thereby putting his prestige behind its findings. This becomes important in light of the fact that prior to release of the June 23, 1972, tape, then-Vice President Ford was a steady defender of Mr. Nixon's innocence, going so far as saying that no impeachable offense had been committed and calling the Judiciary Committee's passage of impeachment article one a partisan vote. Since assuming the presidency Mr. Ford has spoken only of Mr. Nixon's desire for peace and the suffering he and his family have borne. Both are true but not the whole truth. Never has President Ford assigned any blame to Mr. Nixon for what Ford describes as the "years of bitter controversy and divisive national debate."

Perhaps President Ford still believes his predecessor did no wrong. If so he has made it more difficult to prove the contrary. Perhaps Mr. Ford looks upon Watergate as a political caper, blown up by the anti-Nixon press in concert with the Democrats. If that is so, his description of Mr. Nixon's actions as "bad dreams that continue to open a chapter that is closed" rings honest. But it is a mistaken judgment. Justice has not been done, and mercy has been shown for behavior that has not been identified or admitted. We can't go back to cover-ups. If the book on Mr. Nixon's misuse of his authority as the President is to be firmly shut and sealed as Mr. Ford wants, Congress and Mr. Jaworski must follow through, going ahead wherever the evidence leads them.

Decline of Democratic Government

HANS J. MORGENTHAU

NOVEMBER 9, 1974

If democratic government is defined as the choice by the people at large, according to preestablished rational procedures, of the personnel and, through it, of the policies of the government, then the decline of democratic government throughout the world is an observable fact. Most of the nations that still comply with the procedure of periodic elections are one-party states, where elections do not provide the electorate with a choice among different persons, and hence, policies. Rather they are in the nature of plebiscites through which the electorate, as a matter of course, confirms the rulers in their power and gives them a mandate for whatever policies they wish to pursue.

Many of the nations that used to offer the people a genuine democratic choice or at least paid their respects to democratic legitimacy through plebiscitarian elections are governed by military dictatorships. Of the new African states only one, Gambia, can still be said to have a multiparty system offering the people a genuine choice of men and policies; close to half of them are governed by military dictatorships. In Latin America the number of military dictatorships has steadily increased at the expense of genuine democracies; more particularly the few attempts at return to democratic rule have met with seemingly insuperable difficulties. Even in countries such as France, Italy, Great Britain and the United States, where democratic procedures appear to be unimpaired, the substance of democratic rule has been diminished. France and Italy for a quarter of a century have, as a matter of principle, deprived one-quarter and close to one-third of the electorate, respectively, of any direct influence upon the personnel and the policies of the government by excluding the Communist Party from it. In Great Britain a general political malaise has begun to crystallize in calls for non-democratic solutions to problems parliamentary democracy appears to be unable to solve.

Finally and most importantly, the United States has experienced two presidencies in succession whose arbitrary, illegal and unconstitutional rule tended to reduce democratic choice to exercises in futility. Those who voted in 1964 for one candidate because they preferred the policies for which he campaigned, found him, when he was elected, to pursue the policies of his defeated opponent with a ruthlessness and deception the latter might not have been capable of. Lyndon B. Johnson, whom I called in March 1966 "The Julius Caesar of the American Republic," was followed by Richard M. Nixon, who bids fair to become its Caligula. Nixon, as pointed out in this journal on August 11, 1973, introduced into the American system of government four practices of a distinctly fascist character: the deprivation of the minority of an equal chance to compete with the majority in the next elections; the establishment of the "dual state" in which the official statutory agencies of the government, subject to legal restraints, are duplicated by agencies performing parallel functions, which are organized by the ruling party and responsive only to the will of the leader; the invocation of "national security" as justification for any government action, however arbitrary, unconstitutional or illegal; and, finally, a nihilistic destructiveness, only thinly disguised by the invocation of conservative principles and patriotic and religious slogans.

Aside from the intangible damage these two presidencies have done to the practices of the American government and to the relations between that government and the people, they have given us the first President who owes his position not to a popular election but primarily to the choice by his predecessor (congressional approval having been a foregone conclusion), who had to leave office in order to escape impeachment for "high crimes and misdemeanors." They are likely to give us a Vice President, next in line to succeed to the presidency during the present incumbent's term of office, who owes his office primarily to the present incumbent's choice (congressional approval being in the nature of ratification rather than of genuine choice). Thus at the very least with regard to the incumbent President and Vice President the democratic processes of choosing among a number of candidates have been attenuated to the point of virtual disappearance. If one wants to give free rein to one's morbid imagination one can visualize the incumbent Vice President ascending to the presidency, who then will appoint a new Vice President, and so forth. But it requires nothing more than some knowledge of ancient history to be reminded of the Roman emperors appointing their successors with the approval of the Senate, given either as a matter of course or under the threat of physical violence.

In order to understand the reasons for the decline of the democratic order throughout the world and, more particularly, in the United States, it is necessary to consider the fundamentals of government, regardless of the type, and its relations with the people over whom it rules. We leave out of consideration only the theocratic type of government, which derives its justification from divine origin or grace.

Men expect their governments to perform for them three basic functions: to protect them from themselves and from their fellow men, that is, to protect them from violent death; to give them the opportunity to put their abilities to the test of performance, that is, to protect a sphere of freedom, however defined; to satisfy at least some of their basic aspirations, that is, to fulfill the requirements of substantive justice, however defined. It is to these expectations that the Declaration of Independence referred as "Life, Liberty and the pursuit of Happiness." Not all men will expect at all times their governments to live up in the same measure to all these requirements. Yet it can be said that a government that consistently falls short of one or the other of these requirements loses its legitimacy in the eyes of its citizens: its rule will be suffered since it cannot be changed, let alone gotten rid of, but it will not be spontaneously supported.

Applying these standards to contemporary governments, one realizes that the crisis of democratic governments is but a special case of the crisis of government as such. That is to say, contemporary governments—regardless of their type, composition, program, ideology—are unable to govern in accord with the three requirements of legitimate government. They are no longer able to protect the lives, to guarantee the liberty, and to facilitate the pursuit of happiness of their citizens. Governments are thus incapacitated because their operations are hopelessly at odds with the requirements or potentialities of modern technology and the organization it permits and requires.

It has become trivial to say—because it is so obvious and has been said so often—that the modern technologies of transportation, communication and warfare have made the nation-state, as principle of political organization, as obsolete as the first industrial revolution of the steam engine did feudalism. While the official governments of the nation-states go through the constitutional motions of governing, most of the decisions that affect the vital concerns of the citizens are rendered by those who control these technologies, their production, their distribution, their operation, their price. The official governments can at best marginally influence these controls, but by and large they are compelled to accommodate themselves to them. They are helpless in the face of steel companies raising the price of steel or a union's striking for and receiving higher wages. Thus governments, regardless of their individual peculiarities, are helpless in the face of inflation; for the relevant substantive decisions are not made by them but by private governments whom the official governments are unwilling or unable to control. Thus we live, as was pointed out long ago, under the rule of a "new feudalism" whose private governments reduce the official ones to a largely marginal and ceremonial existence.

The global corporation (misnamed "multinational") is the most striking manifestation of this supercession of national governments not only in their functional but also territorial manifestations. For while the territorial limits of the private governments of the "new feudalism," as first perceived about two decades ago, still in great measure coincided with those of the nation-state, it is a distinctive characteristic of the global corporation that its very operations reduce those territorial limits to a functional irrelevancy.

The governments of the modern states are not only, in good measure, unable to govern, but where they still appear to govern (and appearances can be deceptive) they are perceived as a threat to the welfare and very existence of their citizens. National governments, once hailed as the expression of the common will, the mainstays of national existence, and the promoters of the common good, are now widely perceived as the enemy of the people, a threat to the citizen's freedom and welfare and to his survival. That is to say, the fear that governments have always inspired as a potential threat to the concerns of the citizens (*vide:* the philosophy of the *Federalist Papers*) has now become not only a reality of everyday life, but a reality that the citizen can neither counter nor escape. For it is the great political paradox of our time that a government, too weak to control the concentrations of private power that have usurped much of the substance of its power, has grown so powerful as to reduce the citizens to impotence.

That reduction, by an unchallengeable government, of the citizen to an impotent atom is, of course, most strikingly evident in authoritarian and totalitarian societies; Mandelstam and Solzhenitsyn bear eloquent testimony to the individual's helpless plight in such societies. Yet in liberal democracies, too, the capacity to maintain oneself and find redress against the government is markedly reduced. How many of the innocent public officials who were ruined socially and professionally by the government during the McCarthy era were able to restore their good name and recover their livelihood? What effective redress does a citizen have whose income tax returns are audited year after year for suspected but unprovable political reasons and with results both drastic and absurd?

Most importantly that drastic shift of power from the citizen to the government has rendered obsolete the ultimate remedy for the government's abuses—popular revolution. It is not by accident that the last popular revolutions occurred in Russia and China, then technologically backward nations, and that this is the age of the coup d'état, especially its military variety, that is, the takeover of the government by an elite enjoying a monopoly of the modern technologies of transportation, communication and warfare. But a modern government that can count on the loyalty of the technological elites is immune to displacement by the wrath of the people. It is so not only for technological but also moral and intellectual reasons. The political consequences of Watergate are a case-in-point.

Although we have a new President, we are still governed by the same people who governed us before Nixon's downfall. Although the power of the Nixon administration was not sufficient to conceal all its misdeeds—thwarted by its own incompetence, scrutinized by a free press, and subject to the rule of independent courts—the individual citizen cannot help but wonder how many secrets will remain hidden forever; he cannot but marvel at the generosity of some of the judgments and sentences (a former Attorney General who appears to have committed perjury going for all practical purposes scot-free); and he cannot but be amazed at the chumminess between the disgraced former President and his successor. In ancient Athens politicians dangerous to the state were ostracized without any charge being brought against them. In America an administration whose prominent members are accused or convicted of common crimes and guilty of subverting the public order, blends easily into its honorable successor without a drastic change in personnel.

Shame, the public acknowledgement of a moral or political failing, is virtually extinct. The members of the intellectual and political elite whose judgments on Vietnam proved to be consistently wrong and whose policies were a disaster for the country remain members of the elite in good standing; a disgraced President moves easily into the position of an elder statesman receiving confidential information and giving advice on affairs of state. Thus the line of demarcation between right and wrong, both morally and intellectually, is blurred. It becomes a distinction without lasting moral or political consequences. To be wrong morally or politically is rather like a minor accident, temporarily embarrassing and better forgotten. That vice of moral and intellectual indifference is presented and accepted as the virtue of mercy, which, however, as forgiveness and dispensation with the usual reaction to vice, supposes a clear awareness of the difference between vice and virtue.

The people are not only deprived of the traditional effective means of stopping the abuses of government, but they are also helpless in the face of the ultimate abuse, their own destruction. A government armed with the modern weapons of warfare, even of a nonnuclear kind, holds the life of the citizens in its hands. The weapons acquired for the purpose of defense or deterrence also serve as a provocation to a prospective enemy similarly armed, and that dialectic of defense-deterrence, threat and counterthreat seeks and assures the destruction of all concerned. The universal destructiveness of that dialectic is of course pushed to its ultimate effectiveness in the nuclear field where effectiveness is the equivalent of total destruction, obliterating the conventional distinction between defense and offense, victory and defeat.

The individual faces this prospect in complete helplessness. He cannot forestall it; he cannot hide from it; he cannot escape from it. He can only wait for the ultimate disaster. Looking, as is his wont, to the government for protection, he realizes that he continues to be alive only because his government and a hostile government threaten each other with total destruction and have thus far found the threats plausible. Thus his life is for all practical purposes the function of the will of two unprecedentedly mighty governments who have the power and proclaim to have the will to destroy utterly their respective populations.

Man throughout the world has reacted to his attrition as the center of political concern—according to Aristotle, individual happiness is the purpose of politics—by political apathy, political violence and the search for new communities outside the official political structure.

Apathy can be a comprehensive reaction all by itself. It then manifests itself simply as a retreat from politics, nonparticipation in political activities and a contemptuous unconcern with traditional political procedures. Since the individual has no influence upon the policies of the government and his vote appears to be meaningless, providing normally only a choice between Tweedledee and Tweedledum, since more particularly political corruption appears to be endemic, regardless of the individuals and the parties in power and of the policies they embrace, the individual turns his back upon politics altogether and tends his own garden, trying to get as much advantage as possible for himself at the expense of his fellows and his government.

Although this apathy as a self-contained attitude is widespread throughout the world, as expressed by popular political attitudes and, more particularly, large-scale abstention from voting, it can also form a backdrop for political activism, seeking by violence the destruction of the existing political order or the substitution of a new and radically different one for the existing one. The violence that we witness in the form of hijacking, kidnapping, torture, indiscriminate killing, differs from traditional violence in the form of political assassinations and the destruction of political institutions in that it is in general politically aimless. Rather than being a rational means to a rational end, it is an end in itself, as such devoid of political rationality.

One could argue that though this kind of violence, as isolated and sporadic acts, is indeed devoid of political rationality, it becomes endowed with that quality when it is part of a concerted action seeking a clearly defined political change. Yet it is a common characteristic of individual violence throughout the world—Argentina, France, Germany, Great Britain, Italy, Japan, the United States—that it does not serve a rationally defined political aim, but finds its fulfillment in the act of destruction itself. It is an act born not of political concern but of political frustration and despair. Unable to change the political order from within through the procedures made available by that political order, unable likewise to overthrow that political order through concerted acts of violence, that is revolution, the political activist finds in indiscriminate destruction a substitute for the meaningful political act. He substitutes for the revolution, which aims at changing the world, the revolutionary tantrum, which for a fleeting moment satisfies him psychologically and frightens the supporters of the status quo without having any lasting effect upon the character and the distribution of power within society.

The individual, frustrated by his own loss of power and threatened by the unchallengeable power of the state, has still another avenue of escape. He can turn his back upon the existing social order and its institutions and search for and build a new society that makes him at home by giving meaning to his life and a chance for his abilities to prove themselves. Throughout long periods of history otherworldly religions have offered this alternative, and the monastery became the refuge of frustrated political man. In our period of history man thus frustrated must build his own monastery in the form of communes for living, political cooperation, esthetic pursuits and manual labor, searching for a "counterculture" of some kind that in time shall fill the void left by the disintegration of the old one.

It is against this background of general political decay and disintegration, affecting democratic and nondemocratic societies alike, but in different ways, that one must consider the decline of democratic government. Democracy suffers from what ails all governments, but it does so in a specific way. Democratic government is sustained by two forces: consensus upon the political fundamentals of society, and government with the consent of the governed through the people's ability to choose from among several policies by choosing among different men. These two forces must be sharply distinguished both for diagnostic and therapeutic purposes.

All democratic societies take for granted that the fundamental issues bearing upon the nature and distribution of power in society have been settled once and for all. Such settlements are typically the result of revolutions and civil or international wars. They are generally codified in written constitutions and, as such, they are not subject to public debate, let alone change by majority rule. They are the stable foundation upon which democratic institutions are erected, and the framework within which democratic processes operate. In other words men, if they can help themselves, will not allow the issues that are most important to them to be subjected to the vagaries of parliamentary or popular vote. They willingly submit to the vote of the majority only those issues that are not vital to them, that is, with regard to which they can afford to be outvoted. The really vital issues, which are, as it were, issues of political or economic life and death, are not susceptible to democratic settlement. Rather the viability of the democratic processes is predicated upon their settlement by the free interplay of military, economic and political forces.

It is the common character of the great issues, which have either wrecked or paralyzed democratic governments, that by their nature they are not susceptible to democratic settlement. They concern basically the distribution of economic and, through it, political power within the state. Thus it is that democratic elections appear not to settle anything of vital importance; for what needs to be settled cannot be settled by democratic procedures. In consequence democratic elections tend to resemble more and more charades, which at best result in adjustments within the status quo without even raising the fundamental issues of the distribution of economic and political power. Democratic challenges to the economic and political status quo are staved off by the manipulation of the electoral and parliamentary procedures, as in France and Italy or, where that manipulation appears to be insufficient, by military force, as in Argentina, Brazil or Chile. Considering the attempts at changing the basic distribution of economic and political power in the United States from populism to the Great Society, one cannot but marvel at the staying power of the status quo, which has not only maintained itself against attempts at radical reform but also has co-opted its main enemies by transforming the main body of the labor movement into its defenders.

Insofar as the popular challenge to the status quo is feeble, the democratic procedures are irrelevant to the fundamental issues that agitate society. Insofar as that challenge is perceived as a genuine threat by the ruling elite, the democratic procedures will be shunted aside if it appears to be necessary for the defense of the status quo. Thus the lack of consensus on the fundamentals of power in society renders government with the consent of the governed, that is democracy, either irrelevant or obsolete. The opposition turns its back on democracy because democracy withholds the chance to get what it wants. The powers that be dispense with democratic procedures because they fear to lose what they have. Thus frustration causes political apathy in all its forms, and fear reduces democratic procedures to means to be used or discarded on pragmatic grounds.

However, as concerns the weakness of democracy, frustration and fear are not distinct social phenomena. But they are organically connected, one stimulating the other and both cooperating in weakening democracy. Each manifestation of alienation in the form of violence and competitive social structures of counter-culture increases the fear for the viability of the status quo. That fear, in turn, translates itself into measures of defense which are chosen primarily in view of their service to the status quo and without regard for the requirements of democracy. Thus democratic government, by dint of its political dynamics, comes to resemble more and more the plebiscitarian type of pseudo-democracy. The people have still the legal opportunity of registering their dissent, and the government still observes the more conspicuous restrictions of its power; but neither has a genuine choice. For the relevant decisions are made neither by the people at large nor by the official government, but by the private governments where effective power rests, and they are made not in deference to democratic procedures but in order to save the economic and social status quo.

The decline of official government, both in general and in its democratic form, has still another consequence, transcending the confines of politics. In a secular age men all over the world have expected and worked for salvation through the democratic republic or the classless society of socialism rather than through the kingdom of God. Their expectations have been disappointed. The charisma of democracy, with its faith in the rationality and virtue of the masses, has no more survived the historic experience of mass irrationality and the excesses of fascism and of the impotence and corruption of democratic government, than the charisma of Marxism-Leninism has survived the revelations of the true nature of Communist government and the falsity of its eschatological expectations. No new political faith has replaced the ones lost. There exists then a broad and deep vacuum where there was once a firm belief and expectation, presumably derived from rational analysis.

No civilized government that is not founded on such a faith and rational expectation can endure in the long run. This vacuum will either be filled by a new faith carried by new social forces that will create new political institutions and procedures commensurate with the new tasks; or the forces of the status quo threatened with disintegration will use their vast material powers to try to reintegrate society through totalitarian manipulation of the citizens' minds and the terror of physical compulsion. The former alternative permits us at least the hope of preservation and renewal of the spirit of democracy. Neither alternative promises us the renewal of the kind of democratic institutions and procedures whose 200th anniversary we are about to celebrate.

Epiphany

STANLEY KAUFFMANN

DECEMBER 10, 1977

> ***. . . to Adams the dynamo became the symbol of infinity. . . . Before the end, one began to pray to it; inherited instinct taught the natural expression of man before silent and infinite force. Among the thousand symbols of ultimate energy, the dynamo was not so human as some, but it was the most expressive.***
>
> —*The Education of Henry Adams*

Close Encounters of the Third Kind (Columbia) is not so much a film as an event in the history of faith. Seventy years ago Henry Adams saw it coming, in its quintessence, just as J. M. W. Turner's paintings of steel furnaces 160 years ago foresaw the electronic-nuclear age. More and more, the motions of science have been utilized by fiction, more assiduously in fiction than in pure science itself, to represent a "silent and infinite force," to fill the growing theological vacancies in the Western world. Heaven with a capital H is being replaced by the heavens, and the fiction of the field is a chief pulse in the change.

Science fiction is ancient—the usually given starting date is the second century A.D. with the work of Lucian of Samosata. Then the line is traced exiguously through the centuries until the intensification in the periods of Verne and Wells. The graph leaps up around 1940: there were five SF magazines in the U.S. in 1938, 13 in 1939, and 22 in 1941. (See Kingsley Amis's *New Maps of Hell.*) It hardly seems strained to connect that surge with political events of the time, with some increase in terrestrial despair.

Ten years later, in the early 1950s, I was editor-in-chief of a firm that, among other kinds of books, published an SF book every month, so I had first-hand evidence of the strong, steady, increasingly discriminating appetite for science fiction. By then it was a commonplace that SF was the field where unfettered speculation could precede factual scientific accomplishment: we heard stories of the FBI's shock in the war years when an SF magazine published fiction that uncannily predicted the Manhattan Project.

There was a belief that SF was the best place for contemporary satire by extrapolation (a favorite word) into the future: e.g., the way that advertising agencies rule the universe in *The Space Merchants* by Frederik Pohl and C. M. Kornbluth. And there was the religious-theological aspect of SF, which was the most interesting to me, that had long been present in the field, and was brought to a new height by Arthur C. Clarke's novel *Childhood's End* in 1953. In that story the Overlords, creatures from outer space who are much more intelligent than humans, finally decide that humans have progressed to the point where it's worthwhile to visit the earth and take over. (The last line of Clarke's prologue: "The human race was no longer alone." The advertising slogan for *Close Encounters:* "We are not alone.")

In the film world the passion for SF began at just about the moment that the first camera-crank turned. From the work of Georges Méliès before the turn of the century until today, the technical comforts of the film medium have made the marriage with SF fated and happy. Every kind of SF, from stories built on data to the wildest fantasy, has been plentifully filmed. My personal grievance is that, though SF is so well fitted to the medium, not many of these films have meant much to me.

That's precisely relevant to the effect of *Close Encounters*. I'm not an SF-film fan. The two big SF hits of the last 10 years, *2001* and *Star Wars*, were differently boring, I thought. The first was technically ingenious but so infatuated with its ingenuity that it lapsed into stupor. The second was a consciously juvenile work, with a repellent, cooked-up, kids-again, moral freshness. So I was not aching to see *Close Encounters*, especially since I had disliked the previous work of its director, Steven Spielberg. His first feature, *The Sugarland Express*, had seemed facile, fake-honest naturalism. His second, *Jaws*, was made for one purpose, to scare, and flopped with me because it was so clumsily done. I was utterly unprepared for this third kind of close encounter with Spielberg. I was particularly unprepared for the last 40 minutes of this 135-minute film, in which two things happen. First, and less important, the SF film reaches its pinnacle to date. Second, the movement of SF as vicarious religion and the movement of (what I've called) the Film Generation meet, unify, and blaze.

The script, written by Spielberg, is not much. It's like a 19th-century opera libretto: it serves as an armature, with some passable and some feeble devices, on which to string a progressive series of splendors that are part of, yet, distinct from, the story. The plot functions to make two people aware of and affected by UFOs: Richard Dreyfuss, an Indiana power-company employee, and Melinda Dillon, a neighbor (widow? divorcée?) with a small son. Dreyfuss forgets wife and children in his obedience to psychic clues about the place of a forthcoming major UFO landing. Dillon's little boy has been snatched up in a whirlwind created by a UFO visit, so she has a strong interest in getting to that major landing place.

They and some other people are psychically haunted by two phenomena: a five-note tune and the shape of a mountain. The U.S. government, publicly disclaiming the seriousness of all this, has nevertheless taken the tune as a signal of greeting and the shape as a sign of where the meeting will take place—a huge wind-carved butte in Wyoming. After the government sets up a false panic to clear inhabitants out of hundreds of square miles, they secretly build a special airfield below the butte. To that guarded rendezvous point, Dreyfuss and Dillon fight and sneak their way. There, after a heralding crescendo of small space ships, the gigantic flagship of the outer-space fleet lands. That landing and the exchanges that follow occupy the last 40 minutes, and—blue-white under the night sky, immense, beautiful—they form one of the most overpowering, sheerly cinematic experiences I can remember.

François Truffaut, who figures prominently throughout the film, has the key moment in that sequence. He is a French scientist who believed that some day contact would be made and who tracked down evidence all over the globe. (One of Spielberg's best-directed sequences is Truffaut's visit to India, to question a mass of people who are chanting that outer-space tune—a sequence that courses excitingly with its huge cast and moves to a climactic gesture.) The fact that most of Truffaut's dialogue has to be translated or subtitled, in an English-language film, provides an advance node of the greater difficulties of extraterrestrial exchange; and Truffaut himself, with his sensitive face and warm personality, helps to certify the humane base of the enterprise.

It seems right that he should be the one to make the first personal contact with the visitors. I don't want to describe too much: although there'll be some pleasure in seeing this film a second or third time, the first time needs its quota of discovery. I'll say only that I thought Spielberg had made his first serious mistake when he let the outer-space creatures actually emerge from their ship, but that I was proved wrong by Truffaut's brief exchange with one of them.

From the very opening sequence, in which some old U.S. military planes that had mysteriously disappeared 30 years earlier are discovered intact in the middle of a Mexican desert sandstorm, the sound-track establishes that it's going to be a major part of the film's presence—in a wide stereophonic range. Frank Warner was in charge of the sound, John Williams provided a score that magnifies pop strophes into magnificence. (It's crucial that you see this film in a stereophonically equipped theater with a true Panavision screen.) Some of those who have panted like puppies about Robert Altman's use of overlapping sounds have complained that Spielberg's track is sometimes jumbled. Altman's sound complexities often seem to me attempts to create complexity where none really exists. The *Close Encounters* track provides *in its very method* an analogue of the emotional states caused by the

UFOs. It's always subtly shaded, from the large to the intimate, to convey the right planes of space, and the frequent overlays always convey something clear in their seeming frenzy. I was not only never confused by the soundtrack, I was happily engulfed by it.

Visually—and visually it's nearly perfect—*Close Encounters* is the work of many hands and eyes. Spielberg himself is credited with the original visual concepts; they were executed, and then some, by Douglas Trumbull, most celebrated for his work on *2001.* The director of photography was Vilmos Zsigmond, but additional photography was done by William Fraker, Douglas Slocombe, John Alonzo, and Laszlo Kovacs. This is amazing. Each of these men is a recognized cinematographer in his own right. I know of no such previous ensemble of cinematographic stars; yet the film is seen with visual consistency throughout. The list of all other associates—camera, effects, design, sound and so forth—is about nine times as long as the list of featured actors. This proportion seems quite right for the film: the non-actors are the central performers. And, with no rudeness to Spielberg, they help to explain the difference in quality between his earlier pictures and this one. (I saw *Close Encounters* at its first public screening in New York, and most of the audience stayed on and on to watch the credits crawl lengthily at the end. For one thing, under the credits the giant spaceship was returning to the stars. For another, they just didn't want to *leave* this picture. For still another, they seemed to understand the importance of those many names to what they had just seen.)

What happened here? Basic, I think, to some understanding is the fact that, at this moment, there is not one smallest scrap of hard *proof* that any life of any kind exists out there. There are logical inferences and statistical assumptions, there are plentiful rumors and reports, there is hope. Hope, obviously, implies need. That need runs, as it does in all matters of faith, far ahead of proof.

The long, last, thrilling scene overpowers us because, given any reasonable chance to be overpowered by it, we *want* to be overpowered by it. The film does everything in idea and execution to make it possible. Outer-space creatures, if they ever come, may in fact prove to be malevolent, or stupider than we are. Those possibilities are not part of the faith. We need them to be benevolent and brighter, and that's what *Close Encounters* gives us.

Inevitably the film was made by a young man—Spielberg is just 30. He is right in the heart of an American generation that grew up with revised attitudes toward film and electronic media, with those media as refuge, as structures of self and fantasy before they even *got* to the function of communication. If Spielberg is what's called a post-literate, he has the strengths as well as the defects of post-literacy. The modern self that he represents may be straitened, even narcotized, as against the historical self of Western tradition, but that self, forlorn religiously, distraught politically, finds its consoling expression in the size and shaking powers of the finale of this film. That finale doesn't bring us salvation—there is no hint of what will come out of the encounter—it brings us companionship. We are not alone. That belief seems potent in itself, if not all that one could possibly want, and the film makes the belief believable. The way to faith seems to be through the transubstantiation of the 12-track Panavision film.

So we come back to Henry Adams, to what he envisioned in the dynamo. One of the chief attractions of the film form for the Film Generation is, I think, that an art dependent on technology seems the most fitting means of expression for an age dominated by technology. The finale of *Close Encounters* is a dazzling epiphany of that idea. The technology of the film makes the faith tenable, but the technology itself becomes indistinguishable from what it is conveying. Prayers are being answered by the act of answering. It's not a case of the medium being the message; the medium is a function of the recipient, the audience, through its delegates, Spielberg and company. We made the technology that is making the answer, as we made the dynamo in which Adams foresaw the new divinity. If there is no god in heaven, we have created something that can create something to bring us at least a little peace.

To be in that huge theater at the first public showing, to hear the exclamations and applause all during the film, was to see the audience's self-ordained god dispensing miracles of reassurance. Even though nobody really knows whether there's any life out in space, during those 40 minutes our technology made us masters of unimaginable cosmic mystery. A black man, walking out ahead of me after the picture, said to his companion, "I feel *good*, man, I feel *good*." So, certainly, did I. It has worn off to a great extent, but I know that I can go back to that film again and get the feeling again, through technology. The materialism that so severely circumscribed the spiritual in that last few centuries has moved out of the material into magic.

Spare the Rod, Spoil the Party

HENRY FAIRLIE

APRIL 25, 1983

As things stand now, I can see no reason why any Democrat, apart from the candidates themselves, should wish his party to win the Presidential election in 1984.

Let me begin by making clear what I am not saying. I am not saying that things cannot or will not change. I am not saying how I think anyone should vote next year. I am not saying that I would like to see President Reagan or any other Republican win the election. I am not saying that it would be desirable to support a third party or independent candidate, as *The New Republic* supported John Anderson in 1980. I am not saying that some special circumstance (such as the prospect of a large number of openings on the Supreme Court) may not make it imperative to support any Democrat, however undistinguished. Perhaps I should emphasize above all that, in looking beyond the next election to 1988, I am not saying that the Democrats should wait for Edward Kennedy.

I am merely saying that the Democratic Party today is in such a state that for the good of its soul and the sake of its future, it would be better if a Democrat did not recapture the White House next year. If I were in charge of the fortunes of the Democratic Party at the moment, I would concentrate on winning back the Senate, on increasing the party's majority in the House of Representatives, and on strengthening its hold on the governorships and state legislatures, before being much interested in whether it wins the Presidential election nineteen months from now.

I am arguing from what I believe to be the interests of the Democratic Party. But what of the interests of the country, it may be asked, and of the alliance of which America is the leader? My answer is that I despise the present Administration more than I fear it. As long as the Democrats are powerful somewhere else in the political system—and the American voters are skillful at producing that corrective and that balance when they think it is needed—I see no particular reason to fear a second Republican term in the

White House. I fear much more that the Democratic Party will return to the White House before it is ready to govern from there, and that, squandering its opportunity yet again, it will forfeit, perhaps for the rest of this century, the chance to reverse the narrow-minded, dry-hearted, pinch-souled conservative mood that now prevails in America.

It is because I believe that the only hope for America lies with a restored Democratic Party that I ask whether it has been in the wilderness long enough. We can survive the next five years or so, even with the alarms of Star Wars. What makes me anxious is the more distant future.

In 1984 it will be thirty-two years since Eisenhower won the White House, and for twenty of those years the Republicans will have held the Presidency. The Democrats have broken into this dominance only twice—with Kennedy's victory in 1960, reinforced by Johnson's in 1964, and with Carter's in 1976—and it cannot be said that they have acquitted themselves well. In fact the Democrats themselves have done more than the Republicans, more even than the conservatives, to make many ordinary people impatient with them. The condition of the Democratic Party today does not suggest that it would do any better if it occupied the White House between 1985 and 1989. For who can doubt that such a Presidency would last only one term; that at the end of it no one would know any better than at the beginning what the Democrats stand for; and that the right wing would then be poised, after four years of regathering itself in opposition, to sweep to an even larger, even more conservative, victory than in 1980?

Although the candidates themselves do not seem to me the most important factor, they are naturally where all thoughts of the 1984 election begin. No Democratic candidate who has entered the lists so far, or is expected to enter them, can excite anyone's rational interest for long, quite apart from exciting any impulsive enthusiasm or even much genuine hope that he will govern persuasively. It is hard to believe that even those whose duty it will be to place their names in nomination at the Democratic Convention will acclaim any one of them as a wise and indomitable leader of the nation.

The renovation of Walter Mondale, though not taking quite as long as the renovation of the South Bronx, has been going on for some time. In fact, we ought perhaps to use for him the word we reserve for a particular kind of renovation in our cities: gentrification. It is true that he cares about the unfortunate and the downtrodden, and that he has found a new rhetoric—by Edward Kennedy out of the Democratic-Farmer-Labor Party—to give more vibrant expression to his undoubtedly sincere concerns. In this mood today, before captive audiences of Democrats or union members, Mondale is a walking, talking Statue of Liberty. "Give me your tired, your poor,/Your huddled masses, yearning to breathe free." This rhetoric may stir his self-selected audiences, and might even win him the nomination; it will not win him the election, any more than the similar rhetoric of Edward Kennedy would have done in 1980, and no one knows that better than Mondale. Hence the gentrification.

We all know what is meant by gentrification. Take a rundown terrace house that would have sold for $30,000 in 1968, knock down a wall or two inside, replace the old window frames, paint the front door a pastel mauve or olive, put a wooden tub of geraniums on either side, and sell it to somebody "upscale" for $210,000 in 1984. That is exactly all the renovation of Walter Mondale that we will be able to observe if he should ever have the opportunity to turn from winning the nomination to winning the election in the suburbs even of the Northeast and Middle West, where, however soured the voters are by Mr. Reagan's performance, they show very little inclination to be persuaded by a gentrified liberal and party hack. It is an unfortunate fact that he makes good causes seem a bore and himself an irrelevance.

So a second claim is made for Mondale: at least he knows the ropes of government. The metaphor always seems to me unfortunate, since the boxer who best knows the ropes is the one who is being battered into submission against them, as Reagan would surely batter Mondale. Attorney General of Minnesota for four years, a forgotten thirteen years as a United States Senator in the shadow of Hubert Humphrey, and Vice President for four years, during which, we are now sedulously being told, he made something of that office (a claim that was equally made for Spiro Agnew, until it was found that what he was making out of it was a bundle); this is not a political record that, in the absence of more convincing reasons for voting for Mondale, is likely to persuade many voters of the virtue of knowing the Washington ropes.

John Glenn is the media candidate, in the most ominous sense of the word. The media and no one else of any weight is trying to project him. In a classic insider's column in *The Washington Post* on March 30, David Broder wrote of the political importance of the Gridiron Dinner, a juvenile occasion at which Washington journalists and politicians preen themselves in each other's company. "Personal relations of the kind that are fostered on such light-hearted evenings," wrote Broder, "really are essential to making government function." In the middle of this cockeyed nonsense, and true to its character, Broder then observed: "Senator John Glenn of Ohio, the Democratic speaker of the evening, laughed his reputation as a tedious orator away—maybe for good—by turning the President and Vice President—to say nothing of a distinguished political columnist of *The New York Times*—into helpless straightmen for a monologue that can fairly be called a triumph." Observe that "maybe for good," as if one trivial performance before the elect of Washington, on their most self-congratulatory evening, can turn a Buckeye sow's ear into a Presidential silk purse.

But David Broder's ecstasy over "the special ambience" of the Gridiron Dinner, at which "politicians and reporters . . . manage to rise above themselves," is only the most flagrant example, so far, of the media's attempt to get Glenn to the launching pad for takeoff. No one will deny that Lt. Col. John Glenn, D.F.C. (eight times), Air Medal (eighteen clusters), is a legitimate hero of the Space Age. But putting him into orbit as a Presidential candidate will be rather like the Russians putting the dog Laika into space, and should call forth the same protests from those who believe that we do not have the right to abuse harmless and trusting household animals.

The media is manufacturing Glenn as a Presidential candidate out of the very political weightlessness that should disqualify him. He is one of those politicians who in a different set of circumstances from those existing in his own state might just as well have become a candidate for the other party. What is certain is that if the media succeeds in nominating and then electing him, it will not be because he's a Democrat. His appeal and his policies will neither clarify nor strengthen what the Democratic Party stands for or ought to stand for now. He will have been elected solely because of the appeal implicit in the headline on a recent cover of *New York* magazine—JOHN GLENN: THE RIGHT STUFF?—and we may as well prepare for the day when the saving question mark is dropped.

The opportunism of Gary Hart makes one recall what one English politician once said of political ambition: that it should, like the cuffs of a gentleman's shirt, show a little below the sleeves of his jacket, but not too much. Hart's opportunism shoots out three inches or so below his jacket's sleeves. Smart and agile and facile, he is in many ways tailored (the word springs naturally to mind) for a contemporary political campaign: the campaign of the media consultant and the pollster and the direct mail wizard, and above all the campaign guided by computerized calculations of how not to upset anybody. In place of a vision is a fast-thinking grasp at fad and trend. The neoconservatives have won a great deal of publicity for themselves; what a felicitous thought, then, to invent oneself as a neoliberal. Technology is a neutral and apolitical answer to the problems of industry and the economy; how ingenious, then, to be known as an Atari Democrat, until someone suggested that the Atari Democrats should ponder the fact that Atari is decamping to Asia with 1,700 jobs, which rather spoils the image of technology as a deus ex (video) machina. Hart runs so hard to appear up to date that, when he catches up with it, he is as out of date as last year's *Time* covers. One can put the question bluntly: what would the Democratic Party discover of itself—and it desperately needs to discover its contemporary identity—by assisting Gary Hart to the White House?

These are the three men most persistently mentioned as contenders.

One might comb through the rest of the names, most of them worthy men in the offices they now hold, asking why they presume to be President. Two other Senators are putting themselves forward: Alan Cranston, who is experienced and thoughtful, and Ernest Hollings, who is civilized and charming. (Dale Bumpers recently withdrew from the race.) Each is the kind of man who would raise the quality and competence of any legislative body. But Cranston is a one-issue (arms control) candidate in a multi-issue time, and Hollings is a total stranger to the national scene. The Presidential ambitions of the remaining candidate, Reubin Askew, were ignited by one successful keynote speech at a Democratic convention; that fire having been lit, no doubt it will not die. But it would be a very daring observer who predicted for him a career in national politics very different from that of Harold Stassen in the Republican Party: the perennial, never seriously considered, candidate. Askew and Hollings are both former Southern governors. One has the sneaking suspicion that they were emboldened to join the race more by the anomalous success in 1976 of another former Southern governor than by any large qualifications of their own; and one suspects as well that they would mistake the White House for a statehouse. Given the unconvincing appearances of even the dark horses, one is left wondering why the Democratic Party does not run a ticket of Eugene McCarthy and Mo Udall, who might at least persuade the nation that the business of America is jokes.

If we turn from the candidates to policy, we find lists instead of visions. I do not believe that an opposition party needs a program, a catalog of what it will do in every conceivable field, given in meaningless detail. The voters are intelligent enough to know that the position papers of a candidate describe the very positions he will perforce abandon in office. Hugh Gaitskell elaborated his position on so many issues when he was leader of the opposition in the British general election of 1959, that Harold Macmillan, who easily trounced him, said afterward that Gaitskell's trouble had been that he behaved as if he were prime minister even before he had been elected. He thus incurred all the disadvantages of being in office while enjoying none of its advantages; and it is indeed a little ridiculous when a Presidential candidate defines his policy in such detail—McGovern? Carter?—that he almost seems to be running more on his "record" than the President in office.

Far more important and urgent than drawing up a program is the need for the Democratic Party and its Presidential candidate to have some clear idea of the people whom it is seeking to represent. Let us look for illustration at the elections of 1928 and 1932.

By 1928 there had been a long succession of Republican Presidents that had been unimpressively interrupted now and then by the Democrats, and then quite impressively interrupted by Woodrow Wilson, to the extent that it could be said in 1928 (as it might be said now) that the Republicans were the Presidential party. After filling in time with two dud candidates in

1920 and 1924, the Democrats then made the brave choice of Al Smith—Catholic, wet, Tammany—a choice that ensured that they would lose the 1928 election, but that prepared the ground for twenty years of continuous and commanding Democratic rule after 1932. One can only be grateful in retrospect that the Democratic victory was delayed in 1928, and this can tell us something about the present weakness of the Democrats.

There are two points to be made. The Democratic Party was not ready to assume office, and it was not ready in a special and critical sense. The mass of immigrant (and children of immigrant) voters in the cities were by then only beginning to feel their power, and to arrange themselves behind the Democratic Party in order in turn to make that power felt. The many studies of voting behavior in Chicago in those years, for example, show with what complexity during the 1920s the multiple ethnic groups shifted about, trying to find the ground from which they could exert their new political weight in a sustained manner, until at last they formed themselves behind the brilliant Anton Cermak. But in 1928 that realignment was incomplete, and so would have been a Democratic victory.

Too much is made of the New Deal "coalition" that F.D.R. put together after 1932, which was still strong enough to give Truman his victory sixteen years later. Parties draw their basic strength from below, rather from their leaders or establishments, a fact that much misguided American political science has managed to obscure. As a New York governor who could scarcely ignore Tammany, F.D.R. understood what was happening in the cities in the 1920s, and when he at last reached the White House, his political genius enabled him to weld the famous coalition that the Republicans and conservatives are still trying to dismantle today. But his initial opportunity was given to him less by his own political skill and intuition, less by the Democratic Party and its machines, than by a profound social and political movement of voters who felt themselves disenfranchised.

Those Democrats who are seriously interested in the future of their party should be ready to consider the fact, however unwelcome, that it is the Republicans who in recent years have been appealing to masses of voters who have considered themselves disenfranchised. It is the Republicans who have been appealing to "the silent majority," even to the extent of echoing F.D.R.'s appeal to "the forgotten man." The long pull of the Republicans back to power in the past twenty years has been based on this reach to the "middle Americans" who felt themselves left out by the Democrats' neglect.

Today there is no mass of voters who are shifting their ground to place themselves behind the Democratic Party. The result is what we see: a number of Democratic candidates who, with various degrees of emphasis, are trying to attract the support of various interest groups, which they hope to bind together into a fanciful "coalition." It is wholly to the point that these interest groups are usually identified and identify themselves as *minorities*, and it is precisely there that the analogy with the New Deal "coalition" can be seen today to be misleading and unprofitable. Beyond the appeasement of various minorities, the New Deal was addressed, first and foremost, to the *majority* in terms of their common citizenship. The genius of the New Deal was not the "coalition," but the appeal to the *majority sense* of the nation.

The second point helps us to judge more clearly the inadequacy of the Democratic candidates today. Whatever else may be said of the political contribution of F.D.R., the most important point to make in this context is that he had an astonishing sense of the nation. However shrewdly he moved to meet the needs of the farmers or the unemployed or the unions, of the Middle West or the South or any other region, of the Poles, the Lithuanians, the Slovaks, the Bulgars, and even of the artists and writers in the W.P.A., it was not in terms of a coalition of minorities that his impact was so dramatic and far-reaching. What he communicated was a sense of the nation, not divided against itself but united by a common citizenship to which his Administration's policies, as well as his own words, gave a meaning that ordinary people felt almost personally.

There can be many explanations of his personal sense of the nation, including that generous, aristocratic embrace which seemed to include everyone. But above all it was political, as it must be in America, perhaps more than elsewhere. America has no Throne; it has no Church. Where then does the nation exist, except in its politics and its government? In its national politics, above all, and its national government. *E pluribus unum.* Where is the *unum* outside the activity of the federal government? It is not in the states. (One thought that question had been settled long ago.) But it is also not in Wall Street, in the "private sector." There is no *unum*, by definition, in the market. Neither does the nation exist in those intermediary associations that are so fashionably touted these days. People may need those intermediary associations for much of their daily lives, and no one can sensibly question that the healthier they are, the better those lives will be. But it is not in them that the nation is to be found. Even more to the point, the New Deal understood one thing: that in a modern society the intermediary associations need the active support and constant intervention of the national government.

The one thing common to all the Democratic candidates today—renovated liberals, neoliberals, and "moderates" alike—is that they all talk of the national government as if it needs to be justified. What should be the role of government? one hears them ask. But government is not the sum of its roles. One would think from the way in which the candidates now talk of adding one or two more roles to government that it is a kind of table to which they would pull up one or two more chairs than the Republicans do. Government does, they say, a little more than what the Republicans think it should do; whereas to a Democrat (and to a democrat) the whole point should be, as F.D.R. knew, that government is. Government is, and so the nation is. Until the Democrats shift their whole rhetoric about government back to that simple proposition, they will only be confused in office and do not deserve it.

For all President Reagan's promise to restore the vigor of American foreign policy, and for all his poking about the world to find places of no very clear significance where he can give an impression of vigor, the fact is that the foreign policy of America can no more be called a national policy than it could under his predecessor; he has failed just as lamentably to create a national commitment to a policy that the people understand. This was predictable. If you dismantle the nation at home, there is no nation to act abroad. The Democratic candidates today whom I have heard under questioning are all pathetically weak on foreign policy, and there can be little doubt that, apart from the issue of the nuclear freeze (on which the ground could so easily be cut from under them), they would prefer to ignore foreign policy. Again, this is not surprising. Patching together "coalitions" of minorities that have a grievance against the present Administration—grievances that may not necessarily be carried to the ballot box at the election—they have no way of creating that majority sense of the nation that might support a coherent policy. The Republicans are dismantling the nation, the Democrats are proposing to patch it. In between, America is lost.

Returning to Walter Mondale, since at the moment he is leading the pack, it is worth recalling his mentor. Why do so many people today miss Hubert Humphrey? One reason is surely that no one can imagine a renovated Hubert Humphrey. No one can imagine Humphrey changing his style or his rhetoric to suit what the polls seem to demand of a candidate or what is said to be the mood of the country. But there is another reason. Humphrey had as all-embracing and generous a sense of the nation as did Roosevelt. He would not be guarding his words. When did Humphrey ever guard his words? He would not be out talking to the unemployed as unemployed, to the blacks as blacks, to the suburbs as Atari players, to the teachers as teachers, but to Americans as Americans, all of them. He would be talking to Americans as citizens, talking of their common concerns and the possibilities of common endeavor. He would not be talking of the "role" of government. "Your government," he would say, believing it, as F.D.R. believed it. Until the Democrats find another like Hubert, how can they have the heart to wish for office?

Away with a Manger

TRB FROM WASHINGTON

OCTOBER 31, 1983

It's getting to be that time of year again, and Christmas just wouldn't be Christmas without the American Civil Liberties Union's annual campaign to rid the nation of religious displays on government property. (Mary McGrory once accused the ACLU of "pursuing the spirit of Christmas across the land like a thief.") Washington got a foretaste of this beloved seasonal rite, like a snowstorm in October, when the Supreme Court, on day two of its new term, heard oral arguments about a nativity scene in Pawtucket, Rhode Island.

According to the ACLU brief, the offending tableau is ten by fourteen feet and "includes a stable approximately four and one-half (4½) feet high, together with thirteen to fifteen figures ranging in height from one (1) foot"—guess who?—"to five (5) feet. The figures include a baby lying in a manger, arms outstretched, two angels, several animals, and several figures kneeling in a posture of worship." This threat to our freedom was purchased in 1973 for $1,365.

The ACLU may be right that government-sponsored nativity scenes violate the First Amendment's injunction against the "establishment of religion." Past Supreme Court rulings about the establishment clause have been a bit confusing. When I was studying for the bar exam, we were taught that the best way to guess which pro-religion government activities pass muster was the mnemonic device of the letter "t": *t*extbook subsidies for parochial schools, charitable *tax* deductions, and so on. Parochial school lunches ("*t*una fish") are okay, too. On the other hand, the court ruled in 1980 that posting the *T*en Commandments in public schools is unconstitutional, so my education is clearly out of date. Recreating a central moment of Christianity in the center of town does seem to imply some sort of endorsement, despite comic claims by the Justice Department (which supports Pawtucket) that it merely recognizes the religious element in a secular folk tradition.

Nevertheless, it wearies me to see the ACLU expending its limited resources of money and good will playing the Grinch like this. Obviously the mere fact that its position is unpopular is no reason for the ACLU to shy away. Unpopular causes are the only ones that need civil liberties protection. The ACLU's greatest glory of recent years was defending the rights of Nazis to march in Skokie, Illinois.

But that was a defense of free expression—the ACLU's central mission—and a rejection of intolerance. The anti-crèche campaign has nothing to do with free expression (of religion or speech), and in a funny way it reflects a spirit of intolerance. What, after all, is wrong with a publicly sponsored crèche? It's obviously not the money, which is trivial compared to other ways government supports religion (tax deductions, for example). The problem is that the appearance of official sanction, which is taken as an affront.

"On a practical level," the ACLU writes, "a child whose family does not believe in the Divinity of Christ must view the public crèche as a symbolic representation of his or her status as an outsider. The child will question . . . his identification with the American culture."

I think that's right. But I also think this child had better learn early on to question his identification with the American culture, because it's a tough question that will follow him all his life no matter how successful the ACLU is in banning nativity scenes. There *is* a majority culture in this country. It is Christian, white, middle-class. Jews and nonbelievers (I am both) *are* outsiders to some extent in that culture. So are blacks, homosexuals, Orientals, and so on. This is so even though we are a society that is constantly remaking itself, and a society committed to protecting the civil rights and economic opportunities of minorities. The battle for minority rights goes on, of course, but does final victory require eradication of the majority culture? And is every manifestation of that culture an insult to those who aren't fully a part of it?

People who want to go through life with nothing to remind them of their minority status ask too much. They will not get it, and full civil equality does not require it. Furthermore, in the name of ethnic or religious or racial or sexual awareness, they would impose a vast unawareness on national life in which, for official purposes, most Americans are of no particular race or religion (or equally divided among all).

In theory, there is a difference between the society and the polity. In practice, the difference is impossible to police. The majority culture needs some degree of government sanction, and attempts to prevent the government from recognizing this are futile. December 25 has to be a national holiday. If we are going to get any work done at all we can't add Hanukkah and Ramadan.

Anyone who is truly affronted by the sight of a publicly sponsored crèche is (to repeat Joel Sayre's famous crack about John O'Hara) "a master of the fancied slight." This official recognition of the majority culture totally lacks the unnerving gratuitousness of, say, the late Interior Secretary James Watt's terminal asininity about women, blacks, Jews, and cripples. What was so chilling about this remark? The labels themselves, except for "cripple," were not insulting. What shocked, I think, was the unwitting revelation of how aware a man like Watt is of the "otherness" of people around him, and the implicit contrast to himself as a whole, white, male, Christian American. It reminded me of an eerie occasion in high school when I went to a friend's house and his mother told me, apropos of nothing, that she didn't know how to make chicken soup.

Far from being a handicap, a sense of "outsiderness" can be a great asset in a society that does, in the end, try to protect the rights of cultural outsiders. It energizes, promotes skepticism, gives perspective. I would not want my child to grow up completely comfortable in his surroundings, never forced to "question . . . his identification with the American culture." The enormous literary contribution of homosexuals, the prominence of Jews in courageous social causes of all sorts, the creation of jazz by blacks all derive in part from the discomfort of being outside the majority culture. I am happy to be a bit of an outsider in my own country. I am no less an American for it, and may even hope to be a better one as a result.

What the Thousand Days Wrought

ARTHUR M. SCHLESINGER, JR.

NOVEMBER 21, 1983

He glittered when he lived, and the whole world grieved when he died. In the twenty years since, his memory has undergone vicissitude. Grief nourishes myth. The slain hero, robbed of fulfillment by tragic fate, is the stuff of legend. But legend has a short run in modern times. "Every hero," as Emerson said, "becomes a bore at last." So in retrospect John F. Kennedy, the slain hero, the bonny prince, the king at the Round Table, the incarnation of youth and glamour and magic, is the object of disillusion and the target of attack.

The whole idea of Camelot excites derision. In fact, I am sure Kennedy would have derided it himself. No one at the time ever thought of his Washington as Camelot. It was a stricken Jacqueline Kennedy who first so portrayed it to Teddy White a week after Dallas. The Camelot idea was the initiation of the legend. It was not J.F.K.'s sort of thing. He was no romantic, but a realist and ironist.

All right, forget Camelot. How in his own terms does John Kennedy stack up as President? His reputation, revisionist scholars assure us, rests on style, not on substance. No doubt he had wit, charm, grace, and eloquence. But his soaring rhetoric roused expectations that politics could never realize; and, in any event, he cared less about passing legislation than about projecting his "image." In domestic policy, revisionists continue, history will remember him as a minor President of inconsequential achievement. Basically a conservative, he feared to risk popularity in the cause of reform. His liberalism was expedient and contrived, designed to seduce, not to succeed. His New Frontier was feeble and inauthentic next to the Great Society of his volcanic successor: Kennedy promised, Johnson delivered. Even his leadership in the civil rights struggle was forced upon him by events.

If revisionism finds Kennedy hopelessly cautious in domestic policy, it finds him (or the predominant school does) hopelessly bellicose in the world. He was, we are told, a rigid and embattled cold warrior, the reckless high priest of a cult of toughness. Where his predecessor, General Eisenhower, was a man committed to peace, Kennedy was a man addicted to crisis. He was a mindless activist, a war lover, who found macho relish in danger and felt driven to prove manhood by confrontation. Loving crisis, he provoked the crises he loved without regard to the perils for humanity. He brought the world needlessly to the brink of nuclear holocaust over the Soviet missiles in Cuba, entangled us in the Vietnam morass, ordered the assassination of Castro and probably Diem too, and was, in the words of the British historian Eric Hobsbawm, the "most dangerous and megalomaniac" of Presidents.

Thus the predominant school. A minority school, however, sees Kennedy as incorrigibly weak and vacillating in foreign affairs. The Bay of Pigs, snorted the peace-loving Eisenhower himself, should be called a "Profile in Timidity and Indecision." As for the Cuban missile crisis, Kennedy, in Richard Nixon's judgment, "enabled the United States to pull defeat out of the jaws of victory." Instead of eliminating Castro, we guaranteed his safety against invasion and even left a Soviet brigade behind in Cuba, to be rediscovered by Jimmy Carter in 1979. "So long as we had the thumbscrew on Khrushchev," said Dean Acheson, "we should have given it another turn every day. We were too eager to make an agreement with the Russians."

Then there is the question of Kennedy's private life. We live in an age obsessed with sex. It titillates us to know that Jefferson, F.D.R., Eisenhower, Johnson, and Martin Luther King had (or may have had) mistresses. This obsession has bred the *National Enquirer* school of biographers, which includes people like Garry Wills and Ralph Martin, who collect unsubstantiated and unattributed rumors, treat them as if they were indisputable facts, and use them as the basis for a highly speculative character analysis. Every claim by anyone to have slept with John Kennedy is taken as gospel, though if half the claims were true he would have had time for little else. (One scholar has suggested that I write a sequel to *A Thousand Days* and title it *A Thousand Nights*.) As one who worked at the White House throughout the Kennedy years, I can testify that, if anything untoward happened at all, it did not interfere with Kennedy's conduct of the Presidency.

Still, the allegations have unquestionably contributed to the demolition of the Camelot myth—not that Camelot was a place known for marital fidelity. And the cumulative effect of these varieties of revisionism on some has been disappointment edging into bitterness, resentment bordering on rage. Remembering their days of naive faith and ingenuous hope, they now feel that they were manipulated, seduced, betrayed, and abandoned. Did he fool us? Did we fool ourselves? In meditating on this question, I must, as one who worked in Kennedy's White House, declare an interest. Still, let us consider dispassionately what Kennedy was up to as President.

Kennedy's campaign appeal in 1960 was to get the country moving again. He meant this in a large sense, hoping to lead an intellectual breakaway from the complacency and stagnation of the Eisenhower years. He meant it too in a more immediate economic sense; for the Eisenhower years had seen limping growth and three recessions, the last of which had bequeathed the Kennedy Administration 7 percent unemployment. Kennedy responded with a set of expansionist policies: the investment tax credit, the liberalization of tax depreciation guidelines, the containment of long-term interest rates through the "monetary twist," the promotion of worker training programs, and finally the proposal of general tax reduction, enacted in 1964. During the Kennedy years, economic growth averaged 5.6 percent, unemployment was brought down to 5 percent, and inflation was held at 1.3 percent.

Not a bad record; and the last item deserves particular notice. Inflation was not the issue in the early 1960s that it became later. Nonetheless it was a problem much on Kennedy's mind. He understood the vital relationship between inflation and productivity: increased productivity was the only way to absorb higher wages without driving up prices. The problem therefore was to keep wage increases within the limits of advances in productivity. To do this, Kennedy introduced his "wage-price guideposts" in 1962. It was United States Steel's cavalier rejection of the guideposts that led to the great steel battle late that year. When U.S. Steel raised its prices after the Administration had persuaded the union to accept a noninflationary wage contract, Kennedy exploded in cold anger—"My father always told me that all businessmen were sons-of-bitches, but I never believed it till now"—and forced the company to retract its action.

Kennedy's wage-price guideposts constituted a form of what we today call incomes policy. A basic dilemma of modern capitalism is the conundrum, thus far unanswered, of achieving full employment without inflation. Our recent Presidents—Ford, Carter, Reagan—have been able to figure out no way to slow inflation except by inducing mass unemployment, and no way thereafter to restimulate the economy without rekindling inflation. The Reagan Administration brought down inflation at the cost of nearly 11 percent unemployment. Recovery, given the present structure of the economy, will infallibly produce new inflation. So in recent times we have been on a dismal roller coaster: resorting to recession to combat inflation, and then resorting to inflation to combat recession. This is a hell of a way to run a railroad. The only way to combine high employment and stable prices is through incomes policy—through devising an institutional means of relating wages, prices, and profits to productivity. Kennedy perceived this twenty years ago. We will have to recapture that perception if we are ever to get off the roller coaster and bring stability into our economic life.

Kennedy thus sought, with skill and success, to ensure his expansionist policies against inflationary aftereffects. At the same time, he recognized that general fiscal stimulus, while it would increase aggregate output and employment, would not reach into pockets of localized and "structural" poverty. Income tax reduction, for example, was of limited help for people too poor to pay income taxes. The plight of the demoralized and inarticulate poor greatly concerned him. He had seen them in the black valleys of West Virginia when he campaigned for the Democratic nomination in 1960. He began to attack the "culture of poverty" with the Area Redevelopment Act of 1961 and the Appalachia program; and in 1963 he decided that, if these forgotten Americans were to be helped, tax reduction required a counterpart in the form of a comprehensive assault on poverty. "First we'll get your tax cut," he told the chairman of the Council of Economic Advisers before his death, "and then we'll get my expenditure programs." Lyndon Johnson's war against poverty was the fulfillment of Kennedy's purpose.

In economic management, Kennedy was a most effective President. But his ambition for larger social programs—Medicare, federal aid to education and to the cities, civil rights—was frustrated by his parliamentary situation. For he had been elected President in 1960 with a slim margin of 120,000 in the popular vote. Though his Congress in 1961 was nominally Democratic, he lacked a working majority in the House of Representatives. Like every Democratic President since Roosevelt after 1938, he faced a House controlled by a conservative coalition made up of Republicans and Southern Democrats. With much of his legislative program thus blocked, he devoted himself to laying the groundwork for future action by education and persuasion.

The issue of equal opportunity for nonwhite Americans posed particular problems. If anyone had asked Kennedy in 1960 how he really felt about civil rights, he might have answered something like this: "Yes, of course, we must achieve racial justice in this country, and we will; but it is an explosive question, so let us go about it prudently." Like most white politicians, he underestimated the moral passion behind the movement. The protests of the Freedom Riders on the eve of his departure for his 1961 meeting with Khrushchev irritated him. He stalled on fulfilling his campaign promise to issue an executive order ending discrimination in housing financed by federal loans and guarantees; this was in part because he wanted Congress to create a new department of urban affairs, to which he planned to appoint Robert C. Weaver, a black economist, as secretary. (The House Rules Committee, fearing the idea of the first black cabinet member in history, killed the proposal anyway—which indicates why Kennedy despaired of getting comprehensive civil rights legislation.) He appointed Southern judges who turned out in some cases to be bitter-end segregationists; this was in part because he wanted the Senate Judiciary Committee, then headed by Jim

Eastland of Mississippi, to clear the appointment of Thurgood Marshall to the federal circuit court. It was a time when advance seemed possible only by small trade-offs.

But in the country a flame had been lit. Led by Martin Luther King, Jr., civil rights workers, white and black, were bravely challenging the white supremacists. James Meredith applied for admission to the University of Mississippi, and the courts decreed he must be admitted. Governor Ross Barnett responded that Mississippi would "not surrender to the evil and illegal forces of tyranny." Kennedy, hoping to avoid violence, tried to work things out with Barnett. Negotiation was unavailing. An angry mob tried to prevent Meredith's enrollment. Kennedy sent in the Army to gain the black man his constitutional rights. It was the beginning of the mighty change, in Alabama and in the nation. Twenty-one years later Barnett attended a memorial service in Mississippi for Medgar Evers, who as state director of the National Association for the Advancement of Colored People had encouraged Meredith's action and who was himself murdered a year later.

The change received new impetus in 1963 when Bull Connor, the police commissioner of Birmingham, Alabama, loosed police dogs against a nonviolent march led by Martin Luther King. "You shouldn't all be totally harsh on Bull Connor," Kennedy later told the black leaders. They were stunned until he added: "After all, he has done more for civil rights than almost anybody else." The shocking photographs of Bull Connor's dogs, teeth bared, lunging viciously at the marchers, transformed the national mood. Legislation now was not only necessary: it was possible. "I shall ask the Congress," Kennedy said, ". . . to make a commitment it has not fully made in this century to the proposition that race has no place in American life or law." It was, he said, "a moral issue"—an issue "as old as the scriptures" and "as clear as the American Constitution." No President had ever spoken such words.

Kennedy was now fully committed. The political risks were acute; the fight drove him down in the polls from an overwhelming 76 to 13 approval in January 1963 to 59 to 28 in November (still not bad by latter-day standards). Opponents said that the civil rights movement was a Communist conspiracy, that Martin Luther King was under Communist control. Both John Kennedy and his brother, Attorney General Robert Kennedy, publicly went to bail for King. Privately they acceded to J. Edgar Hoover's demand that King be wiretapped, confident that this would disprove the allegations. Kennedy took King for a walk in the Rose Garden to warn him that he was under F.B.I. surveillance. (King, noting the fact that Kennedy had first taken him into the garden, reflected, "I guess Hoover must be bugging him too.")

King did not hold the wiretaps against Kennedy, and, despite a general policy of not endorsing political candidates, planned to endorse him for reelection in 1964.

The civil rights bill was moving toward enactment when Kennedy was killed; so was the tax reduction bill. Grief speeded enactment; but, as Mike Mansfield, the Senate Democratic leader, later said, "The assassination made no real difference. Adoption of the tax bill and the civil rights bill might have taken a little longer, but they would have been adopted." What soon made a real difference was the 1964 Presidential election, which gave the Democrats an extra thirty-seven seats in the House, nearly all from the North, and thereby made Lyndon Johnson the first Democratic President since F.D.R. to have a working progressive majority in Congress.

Johnson was a man of formidable skills in dealing with Congress, and he used these skills brilliantly in the sessions of 1965–66. Still, what was decisive was the congressional arithmetic. In 1965 and 1966 Johnson won passage of more progressive legislation than any President since F.D.R.; but when he lost his working majority in the 1966 election, his Great Society petered out. Had Johnson been elected in 1960 with Kennedy as his Vice President, and had Johnson offered the 87th Congress the program actually offered by Kennedy, he would have had no more success than Kennedy—perhaps less, because he appealed less effectively to national opinion. If Johnson had died in 1963 and Kennedy had beaten Goldwater in 1964, then Kennedy would have had those lovely extra votes in the House; and political pundits would no doubt have contrasted his cool and efficient management of Congress with the ham-handed efforts of his predecessor. Too much has been attributed to parliamentary sorcery that is really due to the political mathematics.

One other point might be noted, in view of the White House feuds and the money scandals that have disgraced so many recent Presidencies. Kennedy's White House was small, generally harmonious, and honest. So was his Administration. Someone asked the columnist Jack Anderson, the Mormon Savonarola, which of the many Presidencies he had covered stands out as the cleanest. Anderson replied, "The John Kennedy Administration."

Looking back in the fall of 1963, Kennedy was unhappy that he had been able to devote so little time to domestic policy; that would be his priority in the second term. But foreign affairs had been exigent: "each day was a new crisis." Two weeks before his inauguration, Khrushchev had given a notably truculent speech in Moscow, promising Communist victory in the third world through wars of national liberation, while at the same time arguing the impossibility of nuclear war between the superpowers. We can see now that Khrushchev had a double purpose: he was trying to tell the

Chinese Communists, then in a fiercely militant mood, that he favored world revolution and the Americans that he favored peaceful coexistence. Inevitably, Beijing and Washington each believed the part of the message intended for the other. Kennedy's inaugural response, with its extravagant rhetoric about paying any price, bearing any burden, meeting any hardship, supporting any friend, opposing any foe in order to assure the success of liberty, resounded at the time, but in retrospect it was an overreaction. The distinctive note of the inaugural expressed a different concern. "Let us never negotiate out of fear," Kennedy said, "but let us never fear to negotiate."

Still, during his first months in office, each day did seem to bring a new crisis: Laos, where Eisenhower told him that the United States should, if necessary, fight "unilaterally"; the exile invasion of Cuba, which Eisenhower recommended should "be continued and accelerated"; the Congo; the Soviet astronaut in space; the assassination of Trujillo; the ardent Soviet support of "national-liberation wars" in Algeria, Cuba, and Vietnam; the Vienna meeting with Khrushchev and the Soviet effort to drive the allies out of West Berlin; the Soviet resumption of nuclear testing. It was a grim year.

Contrary to revisionist myth, Kennedy did not relish confrontation. "Prudence" was one of his favorite words. He well understood the limits of American power. When Barry Goldwater was crying "Why not victory?," Kennedy, in a speech nine months after the inaugural, reminded his countrymen ". . . that the United States is neither omniscient nor omnipotent, that we are only 6 percent of the world's population, that we cannot impose our will upon the other 94 percent of mankind, that we cannot right every wrong or reverse each adversity, and that therefore there cannot be an American solution to every world problem."

But there could not be a Soviet solution either. Lines had to be drawn, and positions held. When Khrushchev refused a global standstill agreement at Vienna and threatened to disturb the international equilibrium by negotiating a separate treaty with East Germany, Kennedy forced him to retreat. And, if national-liberation wars were to be the great new Soviet weapon, ways had to be found to check such wars. This led Kennedy for a season into the fantasy of counterinsurgency—a mode of warfare for which Americans were ill-adapted, which nourished an American belief in the capacity and right to intervene in foreign lands and which was both corrupting in method and futile in effect.

Cuba became a particular target for covert action—the Bay of Pigs and thereafter infiltration, arms drops, sabotage. All this gave special power to the C.I.A., which carried its dark deeds further, judging by available evidence, than Kennedy knew. The project to assassinate Fidel Castro originated in the Eisenhower Administration (which recruited gangsters to do the dirty work). It continued through the Kennedy Administration and two years into the Johnson Administration. The argument is made that, because Kennedy was President, he *must* have known what the C.I.A. was doing. The argument applies equally to Eisenhower and to Johnson. There is no evidence that any of the three Presidents authorized or knew about (except as something over and done with) the C.I.A.'s assassination policy.

In the Kennedy years, the C.I.A. officers directing the assassination project did not even inform John McCone, whom Kennedy had appointed to succeed Allen Dulles as C.I.A. director. If they ever told Kennedy, they would have had to add, "By the way, don't mention this to McCone; he doesn't know about it"—an implausible bureaucratic situation. In the autumn of 1963 Kennedy altered his Cuban policy and explored through emissaries a possible normalization of relations with Castro. Ambassador William Attwood was set to make a secret visit to Cuba. But the C.I.A. kept determinedly and secretly on the assassination track. On November 22, 1963, a C.I.A. officer provided a Cuban defector with murder weapons for use against Castro. Kennedy was in Dallas.

Vietnam presented the most troubling case of national-liberation war. Kennedy accepted the line drawn by the previous Administration, and on occasion even endorsed Eisenhower's "domino" theory. He increased the number of American military advisers to more than sixteen thousand, of whom seventy-three were killed in combat. But he steadily opposed Pentagon recommendations for the despatch of American military units, and steadily pressed the authoritarian Ngo Dinh Diem to broaden his base through political and economic reform. Diem disdained such advice, and his brutal repressions led his generals to plot his overthrow. A message from Washington, later characterized by Kennedy as a "major mistake," informed the generals that the United States would recognize a successor regime. Nine weeks later the generals deposed and—despite American plans to fly him out of the country—murdered Diem.

Kennedy expressed his basic view in September 1963 when he said of the people of South Vietnam, "It is their war. They are the ones to win it or lose it." He had watched the French Army flounder in Vietnam a dozen years before and was sure that large-scale American military intervention would only rally the forces of nationalism against the invader. Among the revelations of the Pentagon Papers was Kennedy's plan for the complete withdrawal of American advisers from Vietnam by 1965—a plan canceled by Johnson a few months after Dallas. Kennedy confided to Mike Mansfield that his goal was total withdrawal; "but I can't do it until 1965—after I'm reelected." Otherwise the Republicans might beat him in 1964 over the "loss" of Indochina as they had beaten the Democrats in 1952 over the "loss" of China. Yet he never disclosed his intention lest the prospect undermine the Saigon regime. Though he privately thought the United States "overcommitted" in Southeast Asia, he permitted the commitment to grow. It was the fatal error of his Presidency.

The search for military remedies in the third world was a wretched chapter in the history of American foreign policy. Nor have we yet shaken off the delusion. Instead we are repeating the folly in El Salvador, Nicaragua, and Grenada. Though he had his counterinsurgency binge, Kennedy's long-term approach to the third world was not to repress symptoms but to cure maladies. "Those who make peaceful revolution impossible," he told the Latin American ambassadors in 1962, "will make violent revolution inevitable." His Alliance for Progress was designed precisely to encourage peaceful change. Even Castro called it "a good idea . . . a politically wise concept put forth to hold back the time of revolution." After Kennedy's death, his policy of supporting reform governments in Latin America was abandoned. Yet his Alliance is still a good idea, and we will have to return to something like it if we are ever to have a democratic hemisphere.

Kennedy saw nationalism as the most powerful political emotion of the time. His abiding purpose was to adjust American policy to what he called the "revolution of national independence" he saw going on around the world. His vision was of a "world of diversity"—a world of nations varied in institutions and ideologies "where, within a framework of international cooperation, every country can solve its own problems according to its own traditions and ideals." He summed up his policy in a deliberate revision of Wilson's famous line about making the world safe for democracy. "If we cannot now end our differences," he said, "at least we can help make the world safe for diversity."

In the nuclear age, he saw no alternative to a policy of prudence. "Mankind must put an end to war," he told the United Nations in 1961, "or war will put an end to mankind." General and complete disarmament was "a practical matter of life and death." When Khrushchev sneaked nuclear missiles into Cuba in 1962, Kennedy had no doubt that they would have to be removed. Revisionist critics call it a needless crisis and condemn Kennedy for not negotiating the missiles out by trading them for the American missiles in Turkey. It is clear now that this is exactly what he did. Had the missiles stayed, the '60s would have been the most dangerous of decades. And if the Kennedys had really been consumed by a mania to eliminate Castro, the missiles would have supplied the perfect pretext. Instead, Robert Kennedy led the fight against the surprise air attack, and John Kennedy made the decision against it.

Once the missiles were out, Kennedy forgot recrimination, forbade gloating, and moved purposefully toward a reduction of international acrimony. He worried, as he told me the morning after the crisis ended, that people would draw all the wrong conclusions; that they would suppose that in dealing with the Russians you had only to be tough and they would collapse. The missile crisis, he went on, had three distinctive features: we enjoyed local superiority; Soviet national security was not directly threatened; and the Russians lacked a case they could justify before the world. Things would be different, he said, when the Russians felt they were in the right and when their vital interests were involved.

His great concern, now more anguished than ever, was nuclear war. "I am haunted," he told a press conference in 1963, "by the feeling that by 1970 . . . there may be ten nuclear powers instead of four, and by 1975, fifteen or twenty." He got his timing wrong, but his point haunts us still. In his speech at American University in June he called on Americans as well as Russians to rethink the cold war. Both sides, he said, were "caught up in a vicious and dangerous cycle in which suspicion on one side breeds suspicion on the other, and new weapons beget counterweapons." Khrushchev called it "the greatest speech by any American President since Roosevelt." Twenty years after, alas, we are caught up in the same vicious cycle again.

Kennedy's first step in breaking out of the cycle was the limited Test Ban Treaty. To get this treaty ratified, he had to persuade, or at least silence, the congressional hawks and the military. He did this partly by minor concessions and partly by a speaking tour across the country. "One of the ironic things," he mused that year, ". . . is that Mr. Khrushchev and I occupy approximately the same political positions inside our governments. He would like to prevent a nuclear war but is under severe pressure from his hard-line crowd, which interprets every move in that direction as appeasement. I've got similar problems. . . . The hard-liners in the Soviet Union and the United States feed on each other." He was a peacemaker. "I had no cause for regret once Kennedy became President," Khrushchev wrote in his memoirs. "It quickly became clear that he understood better than Eisenhower that an improvement in relations was the only rational course."

Far from being a confrontationist, Kennedy was by temperament a conciliator. His greatest disappointment, he told Bobby in the fall of 1963, was that he had not been able to make more progress toward disarmament. He had proved his manhood on the PT boat in the Solomon Islands and felt no need to prove it vicariously by sending young men to kill and to die. He had the capacity to refuse escalation—as he did in the Bay of Pigs, in Laos, in the Berlin crisis of 1961, in the Cuban missile crisis, and as he surely would have done in Vietnam. He was always hopeful that differences could be rationally worked out, whether with Khrushchev or with Ross Barnett; force was the last resort, and only to be used with restraint and circumspection. He liked to quote a maxim of the British military strategist Liddell Hart: "Never corner an opponent, and always assist him to save his face. Put yourself in his shoes—so as to see things through his eyes. Avoid self-righteousness like the devil—nothing is so self-blinding."

His brief days in the White House were days of steady growth—growth in confidence, in understanding, and in purpose. He made mistakes but candidly acknowledged them and always learned from them. He knew the world was changing, and he had the courage and flexibility to adapt to change. It is impossible to predict what Presidents who died might have done had they lived; it is hard enough, heaven knows, to predict what living Presidents will do. Still, one can reasonably suppose that Kennedy, had he lived, would have reached his New Frontier in his second term with a strengthened mandate and a more cooperative Congress. If he had followed his own plan, he would have withdrawn American troops from Vietnam in 1965, instead of Americanizing the war that year as Johnson did. And had Kennedy lived, Khrushchev might well have stayed in power longer (Castro later told an American reporter that he thought Kennedy refrained from tightening the thumbscrew during the missile crisis "to save Khrushchev"); and the two men, who had stared down the nuclear abyss together in that tense October, might have taken the world a good deal farther along the road to disarmament and peace.

He never had the chance. But he had his impact. Did he fool us? I think not. The public man was no different from the private man. He had humor, incisive intelligence, courage—not just the courage of war but the quieter courage that enabled him to endure illness and agony without complaint; "at least one-half of the days he spent on this earth," his brother Robert once recalled, "were days of intense physical pain." He had confidence in human reason and hope for human nature. His commitment was to a sane, rational, and civilized world, and he believed such a world attainable. His contagious optimism gave his country the sense that, with sufficient ingenuity, steadfastness, and goodwill, we could meet our responsibilities. He was sure that there was a great reservoir of idealism, especially among the young, a selfless desire to help the poor and the powerless. He proposed to tap that idealism through undertakings like the Peace Corps abroad and a domestic peace corps (later realized in VISTA) at home. His directness and openness of mind, his faith in reasoned discussion, his ironic, often self-mocking wit, and his generous vision of American possibility broke the crust that had settled over the country in the 1950s. His irreverence toward conventional ideas and institutions provoked a discharge of critical energy throughout American society. He came to be loved in the black community and was the first President since F.D.R. with anything to say to the young. In other lands he was seen as a carrier of American idealism and a friend of humanity. For a moment he made politics seem in truth (in the phrase he cherished from John Buchan's *Pilgrim's Way*) "the greatest and most honorable adventure."

Why then the reaction against him? Fluctuations in the reputations of Presidents are entirely predictable. A low point generally comes in the period fifteen to twenty-five years after a President's death. When I was in college in the '30s, Theodore Roosevelt (d. 1919) was regarded as a blustering jingo and Woodrow Wilson (d. 1924) as a deluded fanatic. Roosevelt and Wilson stocks have long since recovered on the historical exchange. F.D.R. and Harry Truman had their periods of eclipse a short while back; now their stocks have recovered too. It is as if we swim for a moment in the hollow of the historical wave. Not until we reach the crest of the next wave can we look back and see with clarity what went before. If every hero becomes a bore at last, history eventually strikes a balance.

Our politics too flows in cycles. We have tides of action, passion, idealism, and reform that continue until the country is worn out. Then the tide goes out, and we enter into seasons of drift, quiescence, hedonism, and cynicism until our problems accumulate, our batteries recharge, and we are ready for a new surge ahead. We live today in a time of public apathy. We hate being reminded of nobler and more demanding days. We hate being nagged to think about the poor and the powerless. We hate the idea that we should not ask what our country can do for us but ask what we can do for our country. Because we cannot bear the challenge that John Kennedy embodied, we seek refuge in cynicism and sniggering gossip, dwelling on his failings in order to excuse our own failure.

But periods of irresponsibility do not go on forever. In this century it has been roughly a thirty-year cycle from one time of idealism to another: Theodore Roosevelt in 1901, Franklin Roosevelt in 1933, John Kennedy in 1961, each releasing the generous energies of the people and initiating an epoch of social concern and progressive change. There is a generational aspect to this. Each activist President was the child of an earlier age of action. F.D.R. and Truman were young men when T.R. and Wilson stirred the country, as Kennedy and Johnson were young men when F.D.R. was in the White House. Kennedy's own commitment to politics as the greatest and most honorable adventure similarly touched and formed a generation of young men and women in the 1960s. They were moved by his aspirations and shaped by his ideals. That generation's time is still to come.

If the thirty-year rhythm holds—1901, 1933, 1961—the next epoch of forward movement should begin about 1988 or 1992. When that time comes, and come it will, John Kennedy, seen from the crest of the next wave, will assume his true proportions as a humane and creative political leader.

Liberals and Deficits

MICHAEL KINSLEY

DECEMBER 31, 1983

One of the most dizzying things they try to make you believe in first-year economics is that the national debt is no cause for alarm because "we owe it to ourselves." As late as the 1976 edition of Paul Samuelson's famous textbook, talk about burdening future generations and analogies between the government's budget and a family's budget were dismissed as "the clichés of oldfangled shirt-sleeve economics," at home "in any club locker room or bar." The message was, leave that talk to the old fogies.

Who would have thought that this fogyish talk about the national debt would become the mainstay of Democratic political rhetoric? The temptation for Democrats to attack President Reagan's budget deficits is irresistible, of course, and mostly warranted. But for reasons both of honesty and of practical strategy, it's useful for Democrats to keep in mind exactly why Reagan's deficits are bad.

The basic Econ I point remains as true (albeit as hard to believe) as ever. A nation's debt to its own citizens is different from a family's debt to the bank. The debt itself doesn't make the nation as a whole any poorer, and deficit spending can even make the nation richer if used at the right time to stimulate a weak economy. Hysterical warnings about civic bankruptcy are just as silly now as they were when uttered by Republican fogies. But other things have changed since the glory days of Keynesianism.

One change is that we no longer just "owe it to ourselves." America will absorb about $30 billion of investment capital from abroad this year, and probably more than double that next year, a historic reversal from the days (two years ago) when America was a net capital exporter. All of this foreign capital doesn't go toward financing the national debt, but it replaces other money that does. This alleviates some of the problems that would otherwise be caused by huge deficits. But it means that this nation, just like a family, will have to pay off those loans with real resources some day.

There have been three other changes, two in the nature of the deficit and one in the nature of our thinking about it. First, the deficit has reached a size—$200 billion a year—that Samuelson never dreamed possible. Second, Keyne's idea was that deficits would give the economy a push in bad times; but this deficit will continue into good times. Right now, about half the deficit is caused by a still-weak economy, which reduces tax revenues and increases social welfare costs. This part is expected to shrink as the economy gets stronger over the next few years, but the other part—the "structural" deficit—is expected to get larger, so that the deficit will still be $200 billion in 1988, even if things are booming.

Third, Keynes was concerned with the "paradox of thrift," the danger that people would save too much money and the economy would be anemic. In America today, for a variety of reasons, our problem is the opposite. We need to discourage consumption and encourage savings so there will be more money to invest for the future.

It's clear to any sensible and honest person that these huge, undiminishing deficits will hurt our economy. What's not clear is exactly how. They could re-ignite inflation by overstimulating demand as the economy reaches full capacity. If the Federal Reserve Board moves to prevent this by squeezing the money supply, we'll tumble back into recession. And in any event, the deficit swallows up huge piles of capital that would otherwise go to private investment, thus reducing our future prosperity.

I would not hazard to guess whether Representative Jack Kemp was being stupid or dishonest when he wrote in the December 11 *New York Times* that "there is still no convincing evidence that deficits raise either inflation or interest rates." Treasury Secretary Donald Regan, a smart fellow, has been bluffing with similar pronouncements, accompanied by flurries of studies. Ordinarily these gentlemen are great evangelists of the free market, but on this matter they wish to repudiate the law of supply and demand. Interest rates are the price of money. When someone enters the market to buy up a large part of the available supply at any price—which is essentially what the government is doing in the market for capital—the price goes up.

So why have inflation and interest rates come down during the Reagan megadeficit years? Inflation came down because the Federal Reserve Board created a recession. Anyone can do that. As for interest rates, they have *not* come down. Real interest rates—the nominal rate minus the part that's just making up for erosion of the dollar—are higher than ever. Fifteen percent interest minus 12 percent inflation was a better deal than today's 9 percent minus 3 percent inflation. They would be even higher, except that the non-government demand for capital has been weak because of the recession. As private demand for capital increases, high interest rates will "crowd out" borrowers who (unlike the government) can't afford to pay any price or bear any burden for capital.

The biggest pile of government-issue malarkey on the subject of deficits has come from the President himself. On November 3, for example, Reagan told two lies he has repeated often: "We face those deficits because the Congress still spends too much." And, "I'm prepared to veto tax increases if they send them to my desk, no matter how they arrive."

Oh, really? And what if they arrive all gift-wrapped, with a little note that says, "Here, with love, is the tax increase you requested last year"? In the spring of 1983 the Reagan Administration proposed a "stand-by" tax increase for 1986, including a new energy tax and a 5 percent across-the-board income tax surcharge. "Stand-by" means that the tax will only be imposed if it proves to be necessary, based on statistical conditions only slightly more certain to occur than the sun rising tomorrow. All of the Administration's official predictions about future economic conditions *assume* this tax increase. Secretary Regan confirmed last week that a "contingent" tax increase will be proposed again this spring.

The transgression of Martin Feldstein, chairman of the President's Council of Economic Advisers, was not to propose a tax increase, but to point out that Reagan has already proposed one. That's why those who say Feldstein should resign if he disagrees with Administration policy miss the point. Feldstein agrees. It's Reagan who disagrees, or pretends to, in a brilliant feat of political legerdemain.

Reagan's second lie is that continuing huge deficits are the fault of a recalcitrant Congress, which refuses to cut spending. John Berry of *The Washington Post* reported last week that the budget Congress approved for fiscal 1984 is only $1.17 billion bigger than the one Reagan submitted. There was some very minor juggling of domestic and military spending, but the $200 billion deficit was just about exactly what Reagan requested.

More important, Reagan has never proposed enough spending cuts to balance the budget, even in the distant future. A chart prepared by Feldstein makes this clear. It predicts the general shape of the budget every year through 1988. Assuming a buoyant economy by that time, and current spending plans, Feldstein foresees a $210 billion deficit. Another column on the chart, labeled "Administration Policy," is the 1988 budget if the Reagan Administration gets every change it wants between now and then. This column shows a deficit of a mere $82.2 billion. About half the improvement, though—$61 billion—is that now-you-see-it, now-you-don't tax increase. Even if Congress goes along with every additional spending cut Reagan plans to request between now and 1988, and even if the economy is booming, without new taxes there will *still* be a deficit of almost $150 billion, according to the Administration's own figures.

Lately Feldstein has been trying to re-ingratiate himself with his employer by pointing out in speeches that "nearly two-thirds of the current structural deficit was inherited from the Carter Administration." What this means is that if it weren't for the recession we're still coming out of, Reagan's current deficit would only be half again larger than Carter's deficit in fiscal 1980. This is a devastatingly modest claim. By the same tortured calculation, Carter actually *reduced* the structural deficit by a quarter, from 2.7 percent of gross national product "inherited" from Gerald Ford in 1976 to 2.2 percent in 1980. Reagan has raised it to 3.4 percent.

What's worse, this comes despite Reagan's historic reversal of trends in spending for social welfare. Feldstein's second great offense against Reagan mythology has been to make clear that domestic spending is not to blame for the increasing chunk of the economy being swallowed by the federal deficit. Under changes in law *already enacted*, the share of G.N.P. taken by social programs other than Medicare and Social Security will have dropped from 9.3 percent in 1980 to 6.3 percent in 1988. This is about the level of the early 1960s. In other words, apart from Medicare, we're back to where we were before the Great Society. Even including Social Security and Medicare, domestic spending under current law will have dropped from 15 percent of G.N.P. in 1980 to 13 percent in 1988. Defense, by contrast, will have increased from 5.3 percent of G.N.P. to 7.7 percent, and revenues will have dropped from 20 percent to 19.5 percent. A bit of subtraction, and here we sit.

Feldstein's numbers constitute the temptation for the Democrats, and also the trap. Having beaten Reagan over the head with this chart, how do they propose to rewrite it? There are only two ways: cut spending or raise revenues.

The gap that needs to be closed is $210 billion in 1988, or 4.2 percent of G.N.P. Cut defense spending? Holding defense to its current share of G.N.P. (6.9 percent)—a proposal few leading Democrats would be dovish enough to support—gets you less than one-fifth of the way there. Even cutting defense back to its share in the bad old Carter days would close less than half the gap. There is no way to make a serious dent in the deficit by spending cuts without more deep chops in domestic programs. Medicare is the most logical target. Its share of G.N.P. is expected to rise from 1.2 percent in 1980 to 2 percent in 1988. But for a politician, the thought of publicly attacking Medicare takes most of the fun out of Reagan-bashing over the deficit.

The two leading Democratic Presidential candidates have already fallen into the biggest trap on the revenue side of the ledger. Both Walter Mondale and John Glenn have come out for delay or repeal of tax-bracket indexing, the only part of Reagan's tax cut that hasn't taken effect yet. It's due to start next year. Without indexing, inflation pushes people into higher tax brackets even if their real incomes don't increase. It's tempting, because the government gets extra revenues without an official tax increase. But repeal of indexing is a ludicrous stand for Democrats to take. Indexing is the tax break for *their* constituency.

Feldstein's figures show that despite Reagan's alleged tax cuts, the share of G.N.P. coming to the federal government in taxes has stayed at about 20 percent. That's because of "bracket creep" and because Reagan's cuts, which favored top brackets and income from capital, were offset by large increases in Social Security taxes, which fall only on wages up to middle-class levels. Most potential Democratic voters haven't gotten any tax cut. This powerful political message will be hard for Democrats to put across, though, if Republicans can accuse them of wanting to reinstitute bracket creep: a middle-class tax that barely affects the rich (because they are already in the top bracket), and doesn't affect corporations at all.

If political courage were in greater supply, there would be plenty of ways to help bring the budget into balance without being unfair, or risking our national security, or damaging the economy. (There were a few suggestions in the TRB column of October 10.) But all these ledger calculations reflect the same fallacy Samuelson attributes to the old fogies around the clubhouse—thinking of the government like a family in debt. If the real problem is finding more capital for productive investment, then the proper focus is on all government policies that affect the supply of and demand for capital. In this, the budget itself plays a surprisingly small role.

For example, the personal interest deduction will cost the government $36 billion in 1984. But by encouraging people to borrow money for consumption, it will drain far more than that from the capital markets. According to Lester Thurow in the December 22, 1983, *New York Review of Books*, private consumer borrowing eats up two-thirds of private savings in this country. Three steps forward, two steps back. Reducing or eliminating this subsidy could have a huge payoff.

By contrast, cutting Medicare by reforms such as raising the deductible may be largely self-defeating. This will reduce the federal deficit, but if people pay the difference out of their savings, the supply of capital will be reduced by an equal amount. (And if people *can't* pay the difference out of their savings, that's a good reason for pause.) Only by using its power as a large buyer and regulator to reduce health care costs can the government hope to direct significant sums away from this form of consumption and toward productive investment.

Then there is government spending that actually increases private consumption spending, such as the ludicrous farm price support system that costs us billions both as taxpayers and as consumers. Phasing it out would reduce government costs and leave also more money in family budgets, some of which would get saved.

At little or no apparent cost to itself, the federal government guarantees or actually provides loans to individuals and companies for various purposes such as new housing, encouraging exports, aiding small business, and coddling farmers even more. The Congressional Budget Office estimates that by 1988 such government-sponsored borrowing will be absorbing new capital at a rate of $134 billion a year. That's almost two-thirds of the expected budget deficit. These policies don't get nearly the scrutiny that direct federal spending gets, yet they are precisely the same drain on capital markets.

Finally, on a more positive note. Democrats shouldn't be afraid to note that a lot of government spending *is* productive investment. The proper analogy is not to a family but to a business. A business is not "living beyond its means" if it borrows money for investment that generates a higher return than the cost of credit. According to the General Accounting Office, almost a fifth of the 1982 federal budget—about $135 billion—was spent on capital investments, narrowly defined. This includes construction and repair of the nation's infrastructure, scientific research and development, and education and training. Our future prosperity depends on these investments just as much as on private outlays, and it is foolish to skimp on them just because they are paid for by the government.

Jerseygate

TRB FROM WASHINGTON

JUNE 18, 1984

We have reached a political nadir of some sort if the Democratic Party candidate for the leadership of the free world is chosen on the basis of a casual remark about New Jersey. Yet it seems possible history will record that Gary Hart lost his chance to be President when he stood with his wife, Lee, on a Los Angeles terrace and uttered these fateful words: "The deal is that we campaign separately; that's the bad news. The good news for her is she campaigns in California, and I campaign in New Jersey."

The TV networks played this incident very big, the analysts of the print media went to work on it, and it appears to have blossomed into a gaffe. This could cost Hart the New Jersey primary—and therefore, everyone agrees, any hope of the nomination.

The "gaffe" is now the principal dynamic mechanism of American politics, as interpreted by journalists. Each candidacy is born in a state of prelapsarian innocence, and the candidate then proceeds to commit gaffes. Journalists record each new gaffe, weigh it on their Gaffability Index ("major gaffe," "gaffe," "minor gaffe," "possible gaffe," all the way down to "ironically, could turn out to be a plus with certain interest groups"), and move the players forward or backward on the game board accordingly.

Hart's Jerseyblooper contained both of the key elements of the gaffe in its classically pure form. First, a "gaffe" occurs not when a politician lies, but when he tells the truth. The burden of Hart's remark was that, all else being equal, he'd rather spend a few springtime weeks in California than in New Jersey. Of course he would. So would I. So would Walter Mondale, no doubt, along with the vast majority of Americans, including, quite possibly, most residents of New Jersey. This doesn't mean that California is more important than New Jersey, or even a better place to live and raise a family. It certainly doesn't mean that people who live in California are superior to people who live in New Jersey. Quite the contrary. Just as youth is wasted on the young, California is wasted on

Californians. Hart's remark just means that California is more appealing than New Jersey as a place for someone from neither state to spend a few weeks.

The second element of the classic gaffe is that the subject matter should be trivial. Political journalism has evolved in somewhat the same direction as literary criticism, which is now dominated by people called deconstructionists. Deconstructionist criticism is indifferent to the literary value of the "text"—novel or poem or whatever—it is analyzing. The "text" is just grist for arcane and self-referential analysis. A work of no special merit is even preferable in a way, since it doesn't distract from the analysis, which is the real show.

Similarly, political journalism dwells in its own world of primaries and polls. If necessary, journalists can take a significant fact—such as Jesse Jackson's continuing embrace of the repellent Louis Farrakhan—drain it of all its moral implications, and turn it into a gaffe. But campaign mechanics make for preferable subject matter. And the ideal "text" for political journalism to chew on is an episode of no real meaning or importance—such as a small joke about New Jersey—which can then be analyzed without distraction exclusively in terms of its likely effect on the campaign. The analysis itself, of course, is what creates that effect: a triumph of criticism the deconstructionists can only envy.

Once the press certifies that a gaffe has been committed by any candidate, the rules call for a quick round of lying by all of them. Here too, Jerseygate followed the classic pattern. Walter Mondale, in his patented serial-monogamy style, proclaimed "I love New Jersey" and swore there's no place on earth he'd rather be. Hart asserted preposterously that all he'd really meant to complain of was having to fly across the country to meet his wife in California, rather than allowing her the pleasure of flying across the country to join him in New Jersey.

Journalists—stern enforcers of political etiquette—require politicians to tell these whoppers in order to put the campaign back on its proper course. Should a politician fail to lie at the first post-gaffe opportunity, the punishment would be headlines on the order of HART COMPOUNDS JERSEY GAFFE and MONDALE SPURNS JERSEY TOO.

So you can't blame Mondale for following the script. But you can blame him for a repeat performance the next day, when he began by saying he was "not going to press the point" regarding Hart's insufficient love of New Jersey, then repeated Hart's remark, repeated his own demand for an apology, and spent several minutes doing variations on the theme.

Mondale happened to be in New Jersey at the moment of Hart's gaffe. But Mondale is spending nearly twice as much time in California as in New Jersey in the period leading up to both state primaries. What a sacrifice!

And what should we make of what Mondale told a group in San Francisco in mid-May? "I saw this beautiful morning," he said, "and for one sane moment I thought I would withdraw from the race and spend the rest of my life right here." Right here? In California? Mondale seems to be saying that if he were sane, he would never step foot in his beloved New Jersey again. I think he should apologize. Sounds like a gaffe to me.

The Shlepic

ROBERT BRUSTEIN

MARCH 14, 1988

It could be argued that we no longer have theater on Broadway, we have only Events. And the blame for this rests squarely at the door of economics and the media. Recognizing that few people today are prepared to meet the soaring costs of theatergoing unless assured of a blockbuster, the press, television, and radio have been devoting more and more space to hyping special large-scale attractions. Anything that promises big sales through advance publicity receives massive pre-opening and post-opening coverage—features, double reviews, interviews, follow-ups, even audits of the income of its creators—until we are smothered under an avalanche of information we have no desire to know. This is a variant on the morphology of the hit, but it has grown to extravagant proportions. As Russell Baker noted in a recent column, people will buy tickets only to a show they can't get into. Success in the Broadway theater is based on a culture of scarcity.

By this measure, there would be a run even on Edsels were there a shortage of parts, and lots of theatrical Edsels have gone on the market lately masquerading as Rolls-Royces. Under such conditions, what can criticism do but fall into lockstep, praising what it has no power to alter? Even with bad reviews, the blockbuster continues to play to full houses and huge advance sales; even when heaped with scorn, the lachrymose engineer who manufactured the Event can row through his tears to the bank. By the end of the run, he probably owns the bank.

The critic-proof Event has resulted in a whole new theater genre which I call the "Shlepic." Often originating in England, and always costing millions, it takes New York by storm and runs for centuries to standing ovations. The earliest of these Shlepics was *Cats*, followed hard upon by *Les Misérables* and *Starlight Express*, with *Chess* and *Carrie* still to come. (Is it possible that *The Mahabharata* is an avant-garde version of the Shlepic?) The latest, and by far the most successful, in this series is *The Phantom of the Opera* by the only begetter of the genre, Andrew Lloyd

Webber. This musical generated $17 million in advance sales before it even opened, and now you can't buy a ticket until next Tish'a b'Av. Costing $8 million to produce, *The Phantom of the Opera* is not a musical play so much as the theatrical equivalent of a corporate merger. We follow the plot with less interest than its box-office reports; we can barely hear the music above the jingle of its cash register.

There are people moving around the stage of the Majestic, but the star of the show is obviously the chandelier. I've sometimes spoken of leaving a musical singing the set; this is the first time I've gone home singing the chandelier. What a piece of work! It may look like an ordinary object, sitting there lumpishly on the floor as you enter, but just when you're wondering why the set looks so drab, it rises laboriously from its moorings, like Old Deuteronomy's neon-flashing tire in *Cats*, and sails over your head to take its place amid transformed scenery, to the gasps of the audience. I'll say this for *The Phantom of the Opera*: You're never in doubt about where the production budget went. Most of it was lavished on this redoubtable piece of stage machinery, which makes another entrance at the end of the first act, gliding over our heads, executing a few barrel rolls and Immelmanns, then dropping gently if anticlimactically to the stage. I was disappointed when it failed to take a personal bow at the curtain call.

The Phantom of the Opera, as you doubtless know, is based on Gaston Leroux's 1911 variant on "Beauty and the Beast." As a literary work, it has as much value as the novels of Paul de Kock, but Leroux's feverish melodramatic plot was perfect material for silent films, where it gave Lon Chaney an opportunity to display one of his thousand faces. The hideousness of that disfigured face, as Chaney pumped and pounded away at his underground organ, is still the most memorable feature of the movie; and mimed silence is still the most appropriate medium for the plot. In the musical, the Phantom is allowed to express himself in song, through the overheated lyrics of Charles Hart and the supercharged music of Mr. Lloyd Webber, and although it is true that anything too silly to speak can be sung, I couldn't help longing for Mr. Chaney's golden silence. *The Phantom of the Opera* passes itself off as an opera about opera. It not only takes place in an opera house, it features nonstop singing and revolves around scenes from operatic works. But although this strategy gives the production designer (Maria Bjornson) ample opportunity to create some monumental sets and glittering costumes for simulations of works by Mozart, Verdi, Meyerbeer, and Massenet, Lloyd Webber's music, though also presumably based on operatic models, somehow always comes out sounding like a Puccini score clotted with damp Parmesan cheese. Here, the composer is still hung up between writing theatrical music and devising songs that might hit the charts. As usual, he delivers one such overplugged tune—in *Cats*, it was "Memory," in

The Phantom of the Opera, "The Music of the Night"—that lifts itself lyrically for a moment from the gluey mass of kitsch.

But *The Phantom of the Opera*, like other obnoxious offspring, is really meant to be seen, not heard. The story of a little girl from the *corps de ballet* who steps in and becomes a star when the diva resigns in a huff was more amusing in *42nd Street*. And the heroine's relationship with the Phantom—"a lonesome gargoyle who burns in hell"—is a weak variant on the story of Svengali and Trilby, with a sidelong glance at the Dracula myth. The plot also peeks at the myth of Pandora when, at the end of the first act, our overly curious heroine lifts the white plastic half-mask of the monster, who dragged her to his lair in the bowels of the opera house, to reveal his ghastly face. Maybe this is a latent reference to exposing the "ugly" hidden parts of the male anatomy; anyway, it had half the women in the audience swooning. The other half, I suspect, were fuming. The cheap perfume that permeates the evening comes from masochistic romantic novels, with their assumptions that women relish being ravished, dominated, and controlled.

Anyway, I think the heroine is meant to relish it, though in Sarah Brightman's impassive performance it is hard to know exactly what she is feeling. At the moment when the Phantom, placing a red noose around the neck of her bleached-blond boyfriend, is preparing to hoist him to the chandelier, Miss Brightman impulsively plants a wet kiss on the mug he calls ugly enough to "incur" even "a mother's fear and loathing." Dynamite! His vengeful heart melting, his hatred relenting, the Phantom frees the lover and sends the couple away, in a boat apparently borrowed from the prop shop of *Tales of Hoffmann*. Then, weeping copious tears over his gruesome topography, he sings "It's over now, the music of the night." Not quite over. Surrounded by pursuers, with all his exits blocked, the Phantom vanishes in a chair—leaving only his mask on the pillow and his character still available for the Shlepic sequel, *The Phantom Returns*.

Michael Crawford manages to play this operatic Elephant Man not only with a straight face, which is no small thing, but also with considerable passion, though I found his voice a little thin and reedy in the upper registers. The even more straight-faced Miss Brightman has a pleasant soprano, and the rest of the cast performs with that confident complacency that bespeaks certainty of extended employment. The contributions of the director, Harold Prince, and his lighting designer, Andrew Bridge, to this orgy of special effects have been properly celebrated. If you're a fan of laser-lighting shafts, flames shooting up from the floor, musty crypts, trick mirrors, stage elephants and bull-faced sphinxes, boat rides through a fog-shrouded lake festooned with glowing lights, and, above all, aeronautical chandeliers, it will be hard to find two more accomplished technical magicians in this hemisphere. But I remember a time, not long ago—in a Lloyd Webber musical called *Evita*, for one thing—when Prince owed more to the Berliner Ensemble than to Industrial Light and Magic, when he was able to astonish us with simple Brechtian elements rather than multimillion-dollar stage mechanisms. *The Phantom of the Opera* is a vulgar glitzorama, a parade of conspicuous consumption, a display of fake rococo for a transoceanic audience glutted with material goods. It suggests that something much more dangerous than a chandelier might be crashing onto the stage.

Washington Diarist: Merry FAXmas

HENRY FAIRLIE

JANUARY 2, 1989

If *TNR* were to choose a Man or Woman of the Year for its cover, my nomination for 1988 would be the five nuns of Discalced Carmelites of the Most Blessed Virgin Mary of Mount Carmel in Morris Township, New Jersey, who this fall barricaded themselves in their monastery in protest against the introduction of modern comforts to their cloistered life. The worldly distractions against which they revolted, all introduced by Mother Teresa Hewitt since she took over the monastery a year ago, include "television, newspapers, radio, snacks, and a high-tech lighting system in the chapel," according to the Catholic journal *Crisis*. These nuns are the sanest people of whom I have read all year, joyful models for us in this season of universal gorging and gouging. They are simply saying that they do not wish to clutter their lives. I never stroll through a shopping mall without observing that the display of goods includes almost none of the necessities of life. Shoes, we may think, are necessary; but then, of course, the *Discalced* Carmelites go unshod. The gross national product in America now feeds a gross national appetite for the conspicuous consumption of vanities. The "curse of plenty" against which Churchill warned is now a disease and daily distraction. The nuns are speaking to us. Perhaps it is the society as a whole that needs to take a vow of poverty.

In the last two decades one product that has come to be conspicuously and ravenously consumed is paper, and no city has a more voracious maw for it than Washington. *The Washington Post* the other day ran a story on "New Age Printing," the booming demand for "quick printing" and copying of many varieties. One local printer of 40 years' standing said: "Washington's appetite for paper is the hungriest I've seen." The electronic and other technological advances that were expected to create a paperless society have instead made it easier to commit words to print. This office is not alone in now having a nerve center that houses three gadgets: a copier; the printer for the word processors; and what is called a FAX, the silliest toy for adults yet invented. No nun would believe how much paper these machines spew forth in a day. It is no coincidence that the noise made by these machines is a chatter; the FAX even begins to chatter to itself in the middle of the night. On a much larger scale this is going on all over Washington. Why should the nuns not close their ears to the chatter that distracts us? As they might point out, things were said much more clearly when Moses had to carve the Ten Commandments on tablets of stone. In place of the printout machine and the FAX, in the new year, let us substitute slabs of granite and a chisel.

To supply our paper, forests must die. Yet in all the chatter around us we scarcely notice that Weyerhauser, the tree-slaughtering company, claims in its commercials to be "The Tree-Growing Company." In no Weyerhauser ad do you see a tree fall. Moreover, Weyerhauser appears also to be The Eagle Preservation Company and The Bambi Protection Company. We are surrounded by lies, and in the chatter do not notice them. GMAC calls itself "The Official Sponsor of the American Dream." Who appointed it the *official* sponsor? And how elevated is the Dream it finances? Without television, newspaper, and radio, the nuns will hear the tidings of comfort and joy this Christmas. We will be deafened to them by the hectoring disinformation of the ads of the merchandisers.

In a savage line in his poem "Bess," about an elderly woman who always helped her neighbors and is dying of cancer, William Stafford contrasts the significance of this local happening with "the grotesque fake importance of great national events" that usually seize the headlines. The words should be placed on the desks of every editor, anchorman, and columnist. It is no wonder that I noticed, when I traveled 13,000 miles by road around the country in 1984, that again and again ordinary Americans switched on the local news, then kept it on for the network news—with the sound turned off! Why should they, any more than the nuns, be subjected to the chatter? But the event that has seized the headlines this Christmas is not fake. The earthquake in Armenia makes national and ideological differences look trifling. It is also a reminder that, in however tragic a form, the Christ child was born to be the Prince of Peace. It is all the more sad, therefore, that not even for a few days could the Armenian protest leaders forgo the opportunity to press their political demands. The chatter of politics in the world today leads more and more to rage.

Since the problem has never occurred to me before, I have spent much of 1988 trying to discover why we say "Ooops!" when we almost bump into each other, or catch ourselves in some minor error. I calculate that I hear "Ooops!" 20 or 30 times a day, not least because the corridor in this office has a sharp L-turn, where I am constantly bumping into attractive young ladies. We each say "Ooops!" I have consulted every full dictionary. None helps. I have also called the press offices of various embassies, and found that in their countries people say something like "Ooops!" except for a rather snooty, firm French denial that they would never use the Franglais "Ooops!" I will personally award a bottle of vintage port of a fine year to any reader who can explain when "Ooops!" entered the language, and why we say "Ooops!" and not "Aaarps!" or "Uuups!"

The best news out of Washington in 1988 is that the Redskins are sunk. Nothing excites the Christmas spirit more than the sight of the proud and mighty being humbled. They join their humbled sporting cousins the Baltimore Orioles, the American League East cellar-dwellers just purchased for $70 million by a New York investor who has made his fortune by shifting around paper in lieu of money. Too bad the Orioles' new owner couldn't have spared some change for the New-York Historical Society. *The New York Times* recently carried yet another story about the Society's efforts to scrape together a few million to save it from insolvency, rescue some of its damaged archives and other treasures, and expand its role. When one estimates the numbers of enormously rich people and corporations who operate in New York, it is a shaming Christmas thought that they cannot adequately support the Historical Society of the most historical city in the United States, out of which they have gouged their millions. Baseball or history, FAX or facts? We know which our culture chooses. The five nuns chose better.

The Value of the Canon

IRVING HOWE

FEBRUARY 18, 1991

I.

Of all the disputes agitating the American campus, the one that seems to me especially significant is that over "the canon." What should be taught in the humanities and social sciences, especially in introductory courses? What is the place of the classics? How shall we respond to those professors who attack "Eurocentrism" and advocate "multiculturalism"? This is not the sort of tedious quarrel that now and then flutters through the academy; it involves matters of public urgency. I propose to see this dispute, at first, through a narrow, even sectarian lens, with the hope that you will come to accept my reasons for doing so.

Here, roughly, are the lines of division. On one side stand (too often, fall) the cultural "traditionalists," who may range politically across the entire spectrum. Opposing them is a heterogeneous grouping of mostly younger teachers, many of them veterans of the 1960s, which includes feminists, black activists, Marxists, deconstructionists, and various mixtures of these.

At some colleges and universities traditional survey courses of world and English literature, as also of social thought, have been scrapped or diluted. At others they are in peril. At still others they will be. What replaces them is sometimes a mere option of electives, sometimes "multicultural" courses introducing material from Third World cultures and thinning out an already thin sampling of Western writings, and sometimes courses geared especially to issues of class, race, and gender. Given the notorious lethargy of academic decision-making, there has probably been more clamor than change; but if there's enough clamor, there will be change.

University administrators, timorous by inclination, are seldom firm in behalf of principles regarding education. Subjected to enough pressure, many of them will buckle under. So will a good number of professors who vaguely subscribe to "the humanist tradition" but are not famously courageous in its defense. Academic liberalism has notable virtues, but combativeness is not often one of them. In the academy, whichever group goes on the offensive gains an advantage. Some of those who are now attacking "traditionalist" humanities and social science courses do so out of sincere persuasion; some, from a political agenda (what was at first solemnly and now is half-ironically called p.c.—politically correct); and some from an all-too-human readiness to follow the academic fashion that, for the moment, is "in."

Can we find a neutral term to designate the anti-traditionalists? I can't think of a satisfactory one, so I propose an unsatisfactory one: let's agree to call them the insurgents, though in fact they have won quite a few victories. In the academy these professors are often called "the left" or "the cultural left," and that is how many of them see themselves. But this is a comic misunderstanding, occasionally based on ignorance. In behalf of both their self-awareness and a decent clarity of debate, I want to show that in fact the socialist and Marxist traditions have been close to traditionalist views of culture. Not that the left hasn't had its share of ranters (I exclude Stalinists and hooligans) who, in the name of "the revolution," were intent upon jettisoning the culture of the past; but generally such types have been a mere marginal affliction treated with disdain.

Let me cite three major figures. Here is Georg Lukacs, the most influential Marxist critic of the twentieth century:

> Those who do not know Marxism may be surprised at the respect for *the classical heritage of mankind* which one finds in the really great representatives of that doctrine. (Emphasis added.)

Here is Leon Trotsky, arguing in 1924 against a group of Soviet writers who felt that as the builders of "a new society" they could dismiss the "reactionary culture" of the past:

> If I say that the importance of *The Divine Comedy* lies in the fact that it gives me an understanding of the state of mind of certain classes in a certain epoch, this means that I transform it into *a mere historical document*. . . . How is it thinkable that there should be not a historical but *a directly aesthetic relationship* between us and a medieval Italian book? This is explained by the fact that in class society, in spite of its changeability, there are certain common features. Works of art developed in a medieval Italian city can affect us too. What does this require?. . . That these feelings and moods shall have received such broad, intense, powerful expression as to have raised them above the limitations of the life of those days. (Emphasis added.)

Trotsky's remarks could serve as a reply to those American professors of literature who insist upon the omnipresence of ideology as it seeps into and perhaps saturates literary texts, and who scoff that only "formalists" believe that novels and poems have autonomous being and value. In arguing, as he did in his book *Literature and Revolution*, that art must be judged by "its own laws," Trotsky seems not at all p.c. Still less so is Antonio Gramsci, the Italian Marxist, whose austere opinions about education might make even our conservatives blanch:

> Latin and Greek were learnt through their grammar, mechanically, but the accusation of formalism and aridity is very unjust. . . . In education one is dealing with children in whom one has to inculcate certain habits of diligence, precision, poise (even physical poise), ability to concentrate on specific subjects, which cannot be acquired without the mechanical repetition of disciplined and methodical acts.

These are not the isolated ruminations of a few intellectuals; Lukacs, Trotsky, and Gramsci speak with authority for a view of culture prevalent in the various branches of the Marxist (and also, by the way, the non-Marxist) left. And that view informed many movements of the left. There were the Labor night schools in England bringing to industrial workers elements of the English cultural past; there was the once-famous Rand School of New York City; there were the reading circles that Jewish workers, in both Eastern Europe and American cities, formed to acquaint themselves with Tolstoy, Heine, and Zola. And in Ignazio Silone's novel *Bread and Wine* we have a poignant account of an underground cell in Rome during the Mussolini years that reads literary works as a way of holding itself together.

My interest here is not to vindicate socialism or Marxism—that is another matter. Nor is there anything sacrosanct about the opinions I have quoted or their authors. But it is surely worth establishing that the claims of many academic insurgents to be speaking from a left, let alone a Marxist, point of view are highly dubious. Very well, the more candid among them might reply, so we're not of the left, at least we're not of the "Eurocentric" left. To recognize that would at least help clear the atmosphere. More important, it might shrink the attractiveness of these people in what is perhaps the only area of American society where the label of "the left" retains some prestige.

What we are witnessing on the campus today is a strange mixture of American populist sentiment and French critical theorizing as they come together in behalf of "changing the subject." The populism provides an underlying structure of feeling, and the theorizing provides a dash of intellectual panache. The populism releases anti-elitist rhetoric, the theorizing releases highly elitist language.

American populism, with its deep suspicion of the making of distinctions of value, has found expression not only in native sages (Henry Ford:

"History is bunk") but also in the writings of a long line of intellectuals—indeed, it's only intellectuals who can give full expression to anti-intellectualism. Such sentiments have coursed through American literature, but only recently, since the counterculture of the 1960s, have they found a prominent place in the universities.

As for the French theorizing—metacritical, quasi-philosophical, and at times of a stupefying verbal opacity—it has provided a buttress for the academic insurgents. We are living at a time when all the once-regnant world systems that have sustained (also distorted) Western intellectual life, from theologies to ideologies, are taken to be in severe collapse. This leads to a mood of skepticism, an agnosticism of judgment, sometimes a world-weary nihilism in which even the most conventional minds begin to question both distinctions of value and the value of distinctions. If you can find projections of racial, class, and gender bias in both a Western by Louis L'Amour and a classical Greek play, and if you have decided to reject the "elitism" said to be at the core of literary distinctions, then you might as well teach the Western as the Greek play. You can make the same political points, and more easily, in "studying" the Western. And if you happen not to be well informed about Greek culture, it certainly makes things still easier.

I grew up with the conviction that what Georg Lukacs calls "the classical heritage of mankind" is a precious legacy. It came out of historical circumstances often appalling, filled with injustice and outrage. It was often, in consequence, alloyed with prejudice and flawed sympathies. Still, it was a heritage that had been salvaged from the nightmares, occasionally the glories, of history, and now we would make it "ours," we who came from poor and working-class families. This "heritage of mankind" (which also includes, of course, Romantic and modernist culture) had been denied to the masses of ordinary people, trained into the stupefaction of accepting, even celebrating, their cultural deprivations. One task of political consciousness was therefore to enable the masses to share in what had been salvaged from the past—the literature, art, music, thought—and thereby to reach an active relation with these. That is why many people, not just socialists but liberals, democrats, and those without political tags, kept struggling for universal education. It was not a given; it had to be won. Often, winning proved to be very hard.

Knowledge of the past, we felt, could humanize by promoting distance from ourselves and our narrow habits, and this could promote critical thought. Even partly to grasp a significant experience or literary work of the past would require historical imagination, a sense of other times, which entailed moral imagination, a sense of other ways. It would create a kinship with those who had come before us, hoping and suffering as we have, seeking through language, sound, and color to leave behind something of enduring value.

By now we can recognize that there was a certain naïveté in this outlook. The assumption of progress in education turned out to be as problematic as similar assumptions elsewhere in life. There was an underestimation of human recalcitrance and sloth. There was a failure to recognize what the twentieth century has taught us: that aesthetic sensibility by no means assures ethical value. There was little anticipation of the profitable industry of "mass culture," with its shallow kitsch and custom-made dreck. Nevertheless, insofar as we retain an attachment to the democratic idea, we must hold fast to an educational vision somewhat like the one I've sketched. Perhaps it is more an ideal to be approached than a goal to be achieved; no matter. I like the epigrammatic exaggeration, if it is an exaggeration, of John Dewey's remark that "the aim of education is to enable individuals to continue their education."

This vision of culture and education started, I suppose, at some point in the late eighteenth century or the early nineteenth century. It was part of a great sweep of human aspiration drawing upon Western traditions from the Renaissance to the Enlightenment. It spoke in behalf of such liberal values as the autonomy of the self, tolerance for a plurality of opinions, the rights of oppressed national and racial groups, and soon, the claims of the women's movements. To be sure, these values were frequently violated—that has been true for every society in every phase of world history. But the criticism of such violations largely invoked the declared values themselves, and this remains true for all our contemporary insurgencies. Some may sneer at "Western hegemony," but knowingly or not, they do so in the vocabulary of Western values.

By invoking the "classical heritage of mankind" I don't propose anything fixed and unalterable. Not at all. There are, say, seven or eight writers and a similar number of social thinkers who are of such preeminence that they must be placed at the very center of this heritage; but beyond that, plenty of room remains for disagreement. All traditions change, simply through survival. Some classics die. Who now reads Ariosto? A loss, but losses form part of tradition too. And new arrivals keep being added to the roster of classics—it is not handed down from Mt. Sinai or the University of Chicago. It is composed and fought over by cultivated men and women. In a course providing students a mere sample of literature, there should be included some black and women writers who, because of inherited bias, have been omitted in the past. Yet I think we must give a central position to what Professor John Searle in a recent *New York Review of Books* article specifies as "a certain Western intellectual tradition that goes from, say, Socrates to Wittgenstein in philosophy, and from Homer to James Joyce in literature. . . . It is essential to the liberal education of young men and women in the United States that they should receive some exposure to at least some of the great works of this intellectual tradition."

Nor is it true that most of the great works of the past are bleakly retrograde in outlook—to suppose that is a sign of cultural illiteracy. Bring together in a course on social thought selections from Plato and Aristotle, Machiavelli and Rousseau, Hobbes and Locke, Nietzsche and Freud, Marx and Mill, Jefferson and Dewey, and you have a wide variety of opinions, often clashing with one another, sometimes elusive and surprising, always richly complex. These are some of the thinkers with whom to begin, if only later to deviate from. At least as critical in outlook are many of the great poets and novelists. Is there a more penetrating historian of selfhood than Wordsworth? A more scathing critic of society than the late Dickens? A mind more devoted to ethical seriousness than George Eliot? A sharper critic of the corrupting effects of money than Balzac or Melville?

These writers don't necessarily endorse our current opinions and pieties—why should they? We read them for what Robert Frost calls "counterspeech," the power and brilliance of *other minds*, and if we can go "beyond" them, it is only because they are behind us.

What is being invoked here is not a stuffy obeisance before dead texts from a dead past, but rather a critical engagement with living texts from powerful minds still very much "active" in the present. And we should want our students to read Shakespeare and Tolstoy, Jane Austen and Kafka, Emily Dickinson and Leopold Senghor, not because they "support" one or another view of social revolution, feminism, and black self-esteem. They don't, in many instances; and we don't read them for the sake of enlisting them in a cause of our own. We should want students to read such writers so that they may learn to enjoy the activity of mind, the pleasure of forms, the beauty of language—in short, the arts in their own right.

By contrast, there is a recurrent clamor in the university for "relevance," a notion hard to resist (who wishes to be known as irrelevant?) but proceeding from an impoverished view of political life, and too often ephemeral in its excitements and transient in its impact. I recall seeing in the late 1960s large stacks of Eldridge Cleaver's *Soul on Ice* in the Stanford University bookstore. Hailed as supremely "relevant" and widely described as a work of genius, this book has fallen into disuse in a mere two decades. Cleaver himself drifted off into some sort of spiritualism, ceasing thereby to be "relevant." Where, then, is *Soul on Ice* today? What lasting value did it impart?

American culture is notorious for its indifference to the past. It suffers from the provincialism of the contemporary, veering wildly from fashion to fashion, each touted by the media and then quickly dismissed. But the past is the substance out of which the present has been formed, and to let it slip away from us is to acquiesce in the thinness that characterizes so much of our culture. Serious education must assume, in part, an adversarial stance toward the very society that sustains it—a democratic society makes the wager that it's worth supporting a culture of criticism. But if that criticism loses touch with the heritage of the past, it becomes weightless, a mere compendium of momentary complaints.

Several decades ago, when I began teaching, it could be assumed that entering freshmen had read in high school at least one play by Shakespeare and one novel by Dickens. That wasn't much, but it was something. These days, with the disintegration of the high schools, such an assumption can seldom be made. The really dedicated college teachers of literature feel that, given the bazaar of elective courses an entering student encounters and the propaganda in behalf of "relevance," there is likely to be only one opportunity to acquaint students with a smattering—indeed, the merest fragment—of the great works from the past. Such teachers take pleasure in watching the minds and sensibilities of young people opening up to a poem by Wordsworth, a story by Chekhov, a novel by Ellison. They feel they have planted a seed of responsiveness that, with time and luck, might continue to grow. And if this is said to be a missionary attitude, why should anyone quarrel with it?

II.

Let me now mention some of the objections one hears in academic circles to the views I have put down here, and then provide brief replies.

By requiring students to read what you call "classics" in introductory courses, you impose upon them a certain worldview—and that is an elitist act.

In some rudimentary but not very consequential sense, all education entails the "imposing" of values. There are people who say this is true even when children are taught to read and write, since it assumes that reading and writing are "good."

In its extreme version, this idea is not very interesting, since it is not clear how the human race could survive if there were not some "imposition" from one generation to the next. But in a more moderate version, it is an idea that touches upon genuine problems.

Much depends on the character of the individual teacher, the spirit in which he or she approaches a dialogue of Plato, an essay by Mill, a novel by D. H. Lawrence. These can be, and have been, used to pummel an ideological line into the heads of students (who often show a notable capacity for emptying them out again). Such pummeling is possible for all points of view but seems most likely in behalf of totalitarian politics and authoritarian theologies, which dispose their adherents to fanaticism. On the other hand, the texts I've mentioned, as well as many others, can be taught in a spirit of openness, so that students are trained to read carefully, think independently, and ask questions. Nor does this imply that the teacher hides his or her opinions. Being a teacher means having a certain authority, but the student should be able to confront that authority freely and critically. This is what we mean by liberal education—not that a teacher plumps for certain political programs, but that the teaching is done in a "liberal" (open, undogmatic) style.

I do not doubt that there are conservative and radical teachers who teach in this "liberal" spirit. When I was a student at City College in the late 1930s, I studied philosophy with a man who was either a member of the Communist Party or was "cheating it out of dues." Far from being the propagandist of the Party line, which Sidney Hook kept insisting was the necessary role of Communist teachers, this man was decent, humane, and tolerant. Freedom of thought prevailed in his classroom. He had, you might say, a "liberal" character, and perhaps his commitment to teaching as a vocation was stronger than his loyalty to the Party. Were such things not to happen now and then, universities would be intolerable.

If, then, a university proposes a few required courses so that ill-read students may at least glance at what they do not know, that isn't (necessarily) "elitist." Different teachers will approach the agreed-upon texts in different ways, and that is as it should be. If a leftist student gets "stuck" with a conservative teacher, or a conservative student with a leftist teacher, that's part of what education should be. The university is saying to its incoming students: "Here are some sources of wisdom and beauty that have survived the centuries. In time you may choose to abandon them, but first learn something about them."

Your list of classics includes only dead, white males, all tied in to notions and values of Western hegemony. Doesn't this narrow excessively the horizons of education?

All depends on how far forward you go to compose your list of classics. If you do not come closer to the present than the mid-eighteenth century, then of course there will not be many, or even any, women in your roster. If you go past the mid-eighteenth century to reach the present, it's not at all true that only "dead, white males" are to be included. For example—and this must hold for hundreds of other teachers also—I have taught and written about Jane Austen, Emily Brontë, Charlotte Brontë, Elizabeth Gaskell, George Eliot, Emily Dickinson, Edith Wharton, Katherine Anne Porter, Doris Lessing, and Flannery O'Connor. I could easily add a comparable list of black writers. Did this, in itself, make me a better teacher? I doubt it. Did it make me a better person? We still lack modes of evaluation subtle enough to say for sure.

The absence of women from the literature of earlier centuries is a result of historical inequities that have only partly been remedied in recent years. Virginia Woolf, in a brilliant passage in *A Room of One's Own*, approaches this problem by imagining Judith, Shakespeare's sister, perhaps equally gifted but prevented by the circumstances of her time from developing her gifts:

> Any woman born with a great gift in the sixteenth century would certainly have gone crazed, shot herself, or ended her days in some lonely cottage outside the village, half witch, half wizard, feared and mocked at. . . . A highly gifted girl who had tried to use her gift for poetry would have been so thwarted and hindered by other people, so tortured and pulled asunder by her own contrary instincts, that she must have lost her health and sanity . . .

The history that Virginia Woolf describes cannot be revoked. If we look at the great works of literature and thought through the centuries until about the mid-eighteenth century, we have to recognize that indeed they have been overwhelmingly the achievements of men. The circumstances in which these achievements occurred may be excoriated. The achievements remain precious.

To isolate a group of texts as the canon is to establish a hierarchy of bias, in behalf of which there can be no certainty of judgment.

There is mischief or confusion in the frequent use of the term "hierarchy" by the academic insurgents, a conflation of social and intellectual uses. A social hierarchy may entail a (mal)distribution of income and power, open to the usual criticisms; a literary "hierarchy" signifies a judgment, often based on historical experience, that some works are of supreme or abiding value, while others are of lesser value, and still others quite without value. To prefer Elizabeth Bishop to Judith Krantz is not of the same order as sanctioning the inequality of wealth in the United States. To prefer Shakespeare to Sidney Sheldon is not of the same order as approving the hierarchy of the nomenklatura in Communist dictatorships.

As for the claim that there is no certainty of judgment, all tastes being historically molded or individually subjective, I simply do not believe that the people who make it live by it. This is an "egalitarianism" of valuation that people of even moderate literacy know to be false and unworkable—the making of judgments, even if provisional and historically modulated, is inescapable in the life of culture. And if we cannot make judgments or demonstrate the grounds for our preferences, then we have no business teaching literature—we might just as well be teaching advertising—and there is no reason to have departments of literature.

The claim that there can be value-free teaching is a liberal deception or self-deception; so too the claim that there can be texts untouched by social and political bias. Politics or ideology is everywhere, and it's the better part of honesty to admit this.

If you look hard (or foolishly) enough, you can find political and social traces everywhere. But to see politics or ideology in all texts is to scrutinize the riches of literature through a single lens. If you choose, you can read all or almost all literary works through the single lens of religion. But what a sad impoverishment of the imagination, and what a violation of our sense of reality, this represents. Politics may be "in" everything, but not everything is politics. A good social critic will know which texts are inviting to a given approach and which it would be wise to leave to others.

To see politics everywhere is to diminish the weight of politics. A serious politics recognizes the limits of its reach; it deals with public affairs while leaving alone large spheres of existence; it seeks not to "totalize" its range of interest. Some serious thinkers believe that the ultimate aim of politics should be to render itself superfluous. That may seem an unrealizable goal; meanwhile, a good part of the struggle for freedom in recent decades has been to draw a line beyond which politics must not tread. The same holds, more or less, for literary study and the teaching of literature.

Wittingly or not, the traditional literary and intellectual canon was based on received elitist ideologies, the values of Western imperialism, racism, sexism, etc., and the teaching of the humanities was marked by corresponding biases. It is now necessary to enlarge the canon so that voices from Africa, Asia, and Latin America can be heard. This is especially important for minority students so that they may learn about their origins and thereby gain in self-esteem.

It is true that over the decades some university teaching has reflected inherited social biases—how, for better or worse, could it not? Most often this was due to the fact that many teachers shared the common beliefs of American society. But not all teachers! As long as those with critical views were allowed to speak freely, the situation, if not ideal, was one that people holding minority opinions and devoted to democratic norms had to accept.

Yet the picture drawn by some academic insurgents—that most teachers, until quite recently, were in the grip of the worst values of Western society—is overdrawn. I can testify that some of my school and college teachers a few decades ago, far from upholding Western imperialism or white supremacy, were sharply critical of American society, in some instances from a boldly reformist outlook. They taught us to care about literature both for its own sake and because, as they felt, it often helped confirm their worldviews. (And to love it even if it didn't confirm their worldviews.) One high school teacher introduced me to Hardy's *Jude the Obscure* as a novel showing how cruel society can be to rebels, and up to a point, she was right. At college, as a fervent anti-Stalinist Marxist, I wrote a thoughtless "class analysis" of Edmund Spenser's poetry for an English class, and the kindly instructor, whose politics were probably not very far from mine, suggested that there were more things in the world, especially as Spenser had seen it, than I could yet recognize. I mention these instances to suggest that there has always been a range of opinion among teachers, and if anything, the American academy has tilted more to the left than most other segments of our society. There were of course right-wing professors too; I remember an economics teacher we called "Steamboat" Fulton, the object of amiable ridicule among the students who nonetheless learned something from him.

Proposals to enlarge the curriculum to include non-Western writings—if made in good faith and not in behalf of an ideological campaign—are in principle to be respected. A course in ancient thought might well include a selection from Confucius; a course in the modern novel might well include a work by Tanizaki or García Márquez.

There are practical difficulties. Due to the erosion of requirements in many universities, those courses that survive are usually no more than a year or a semester in duration, so that there is danger of a diffusion to the point of incoherence. Such courses, if they are to have any value, must focus primarily on the intellectual and cultural traditions of Western society. That, like it or not, is where we come from and that is where we are. All of us who live in America are, to some extent, Western: it gets to us in our deepest and also our most trivial habits of thought and speech, in our sense of right and wrong, in our idealism and our cynicism.

As for the argument that minority students will gain in self-esteem through being exposed to writings by Africans and black Americans, it is hard to know. Might not entering minority students, some of them ill-prepared, gain a stronger sense of self-esteem by mastering the arts of writing and reading than by being told, as some are these days, that Plato and Aristotle plagiarized from an African source? Might not some black students feel as strong a sense of self-esteem by reading, say, Dostoyevsky and Malraux (which Ralph Ellison speaks of having done at a susceptible age) as by being confined to black writers? Is there not something grossly patronizing in the notion that while diverse literary studies are appropriate for middle-class white students, something else, racially determined, is required for the minorities? Richard Wright found sustenance in Dreiser, Ralph Ellison in Hemingway, Chinua Achebe in Eliot, Leopold Senghor in the whole of French poetry. Are there not unknown young Wrights and Ellisons, Achebes and Senghors in our universities who might also want to find their way to an individually achieved sense of culture?

In any case, is the main function of the humanities directly to inculcate self-esteem? Do we really know how this can be done? And if done by bounding the curriculum according to racial criteria, may that not perpetuate the very grounds for a lack of self-esteem? I do not know the answers to these questions, but do the advocates of multiculturalism?

One serious objection to "multicultural studies" remains: that it tends to segregate students into categories fixed by birth, upbringing, and obvious environment. Had my teachers tried to lead me toward certain writers because they were Jewish, I would have balked—I wanted to find my own way to Proust, Kafka, and Pirandello, writers who didn't need any racial credentials. Perhaps things are different with students today—we ought not to be dogmatic about these matters. But are there not shared norms of pride and independence among young people, whatever their race and color?

The jazz musician Wynton Marsalis testifies: "Everybody has two heritages, ethnic and human. The human aspects give art its real enduring power. . . . The racial aspect, that's a crutch so you don't have to go out into the world." David Bromwich raises an allied question: Should we wish "to legitimize the belief that the mind of a student deserves to survive in exactly the degree that it corresponds with one of the classes of socially constructed group minds? If I were a student today I would find this assumption frightening. It is, in truth, more than a license for conformity. It is a four-year sentence to conformity."

What you have been saying is pretty much the same as what conservatives say. Doesn't that make you feel uncomfortable?

No, it doesn't. There are conservatives—and conservatives. Some, like the editor of *The New Criterion*, are frantic ideologues with their own version of p.c., the classics as safeguard for the status quo. This is no more attractive than the current campus ideologizing. But there are also conservatives who make the necessary discriminations between using culture, as many have tried to use religion, as a kind of social therapy and seeing culture as a realm with its own values and rewards.

Similar differences hold with regard to the teaching of past thinkers. In a great figure like Edmund Burke you will find not only the persuasions of conservatism but also a critical spirit that does not readily lend itself to ideological coarseness. Even those of us who disagree with him fundamentally can learn from Burke the disciplines of argument and resources of language.

Let us suppose that in University X undergoing a curriculum debate there is rough agreement about which books to teach between professors of the democratic left and their conservative colleagues. Why should that trouble us—or them? We agree on a given matter, perhaps for different reasons. Or there may be a more or less shared belief in the idea of a liberal education. If there is, so much the better. If the agreement is momentary, the differences will emerge soon enough.

A Little Epilogue

A *New Republic* reader: "Good lord, you're becoming a virtuoso at pushing through open doors. All this carrying on just to convince us that students should read great books. It's so obvious. . . ."

I reply: "Dear reader, you couldn't be more right. But that is where we are."

The Child Monarch

HENDRIK HERTZBERG

SEPTEMBER 9, 1991

I.

Maybe the local time just seems slower because the current occupant of the White House is a hyperactive gland case. Anyhow, it's hard to believe that only a couple of years have passed since the Reagans went away. It was a touching moment, we now learn. "Look, honey," Ronnie whispered tenderly to Nancy as the helicopter banked back for one more sweep across the South Lawn, "there's our little shack." That's according to *An American Life*. According to *President Reagan: The Role of a Lifetime*, he whispered tenderly, "There's our little bungalow down there." Whatever.

It's taken a while for the full weirdness of the Reagan years to sink in. Not that the unnerving facts weren't available; but nobody—not even Reagan's political opponents—really wanted to face them. We've known for some time, for example, that Reagan's schedule was drawn up in consultation with an astrologer. Reagan's sacked chief of staff, Donald T. Regan, told us so in a book published a full eight months before the administration left office. Thanks to Nancy Reagan, Kitty Kelley, and now Lou Cannon, we've since learned about the weekly astrology classes Nancy took during the 1950s and '60s, the "zodiac parties" the Reagans attended in Hollywood, Nancy's annoyance when the White House astrologer insisted on being paid for her horoscopes, and the humiliation felt by aides such as James Baker, Richard Darman, and Michael Deaver at having to explain away absurd and arbitrary changes in the schedule that they knew were being made on the basis of supersecret astrological prognostications.

Cannon finds no evidence that astrology had any direct effects on substantive policy. But he finds plenty of evidence that this was a government of, by, and for the stars. And astrology, as it happens, is a pretty good metaphor for the peculiar qualities of that government and its peculiar central character.

Reagan, as portrayed in Cannon's book and in his own, is a childlike and sometimes childish man. His head is full of stories. He is unable to think analytically. He is ignorant. He has notions about the way things work, but he doesn't notice when these notions contradict each other. He has difficulty distinguishing between fantasy and reality. He believes fervently in happy endings. He is passive and fatalistic. He cannot admit error.

Within the White House, Reagan himself was consulted precisely as one consults a horoscope. To his frazzled assistants he had mystical power, but was not quite real. Like a soothsayer's chart, he required deciphering. "Reaganology," Cannon writes, "was largely based on whatever gleanings could be obtained from body language." The president's pronouncements in meetings, which usually took the form of anecdotes that might or might not be relevant to the matter at hand, were open to various interpretations. When the conversation ranged beyond the handful of *Animal Farm*-type certainties that made up what Cannon calls Reagan's "core beliefs" (taxes bad, defense good; government bad, markets good) Reagan was lost. Though the people who served with him respected him for his occult powers—his rapport with the television audience, his ability to read a text convincingly, the powerful simplicity of the core beliefs—they viewed his intellect with contempt. They thought he was a big baby, and they were right.

This is a point that Cannon makes over and over, in one way and another. His book is devastating and superb. He has covered Reagan for twenty-five years and is looked upon by Reagan's friends and enemies alike as a fair witness and an impartial judge. Having read not only Cannon's new blockbuster but also several thousand of his stories and columns in *The Washington Post*, I still have no idea if he is pro-Reagan or anti-Reagan. His only discernible ideological predisposition is that he has no ideological predisposition (though this ideologically predisposes him to underestimate ideology's importance, as well as to be more sympathetic to the administration's "pragmatists" than to its movement conservatives).

Cannon's book braids a biography of Reagan together with a detailed and lively account of Reagan's presidency. Much of it is necessarily about Reagan's advisers and Cabinet secretaries, for it was on them that the day-to-day burdens of the presidency actually fell. A good deal of what Cannon shows us about Reagan is seen through their eyes. It's quite a spectacle:

> The sad, shared secret of the Reagan White House was that no one in the presidential entourage had confidence in the judgment or capacities of the president.

> Pragmatists and conservatives alike treated Reagan as if he were a child monarch in need of constant protection.

> Reagan's reliance on metaphor and analogy for understanding made him vulnerable to arguments that were short on facts and long on theatrical gimmicks.
>
> He made sense of foreign policy through his long-developed habit of devising dramatic, all-purpose stories with moralistic messages, forceful plots, and well-developed heroes and villains.
>
> The more Reagan repeated a story, the more he believed it and the more he resisted information that undermined its premises.
>
> Ronald Reagan's subordinates often despaired of him because he seemed to inhabit a fantasy world where cinematic events competed for attention with reality.

And so on. Cannon stresses the movie angle as a way of understanding Reagan, which is interesting in light of how little public discussion of this angle there was during Reagan's twenty-five years as an active politician. Governor Pat Brown of California, whom Reagan unseated in his first bid for public office in 1966, humorously likened him to John Wilkes Booth. The joke backfired, but the "actor issue" was a perfectly legitimate one. If it is fair to examine how a candidate's background as a soldier or a corporate lawyer or a civil rights agitator might affect his habits of mind, then surely it was fair to ask if the mental habits instilled by spending most of one's time until the age of 53 dressing up in costumes and playing out elaborately mounted wish-fulfillment fantasies was good preparation for high office. But partly because it hadn't worked for Brown and partly because mentioning Reagan's profession somehow got classified as bigotry ("jobism," it might be called nowadays), the actor issue was never aired in any of Reagan's subsequent campaigns.

As president, Reagan spent a lot of time at the movies. According to Cannon, he saw some 350 feature films at Camp David alone. He also saw several more a month at the White House family theater, plus an unknown number in the private screening rooms of rich friends. And those were just the ones requiring the services of a projectionist. In addition, the Reagans watched TV every night they were free. Reagan loved war pictures. He had starred in several during World War II (*International Squadron, Rear Gunner*, and *For God and Country*, among others) and had absorbed hundreds more. Some of his best anecdotes—the B-17 pilot who cradles his wounded gunner's head in his arms as they ride their crippled plane down together; the black sailor who saves his white shipmates by grabbing a machine gun and swiveling to shoot a Japanese fighter out of the sky; the American Army officer (Reagan himself) who helps liberate the death camps—were twisted, hoked-up, or falsified versions of experiences that Reagan had encountered in movie theaters, not in real life.

We knew about Reagan and war movies. What Cannon adds is that Reagan loved peace movies, too. He couldn't stop talking about *War Games*, a Matthew Broderick vehicle about a teenage hacker who breaks into the NORAD computer and saves the world from being destroyed by trigger-happy Pentagon generals. He watched *The Day After*, the 1983 made-for-TV nuclear holocaust weepie that his own people spent weeks trying to discredit, and found it powerful and affecting. His strategic defense proposal was strikingly reminiscent of one of his own movies, *Murder in the Air* (1940), in which the future president, playing Secret Service agent Brass Bancroft, foils a foreign plot to steal the "Inertia Projector," an American ray gun that can shoot down distant enemy aircraft. And according to Colin Powell, Reagan's last national security adviser, Reagan's proposal to share strategic defense technology with the Soviets was inspired by *The Day the Earth Stood Still*, a gripping 1951 science fiction movie in which a flying saucer descends on Washington. The saucer disgorges Michael Rennie, the urbane representative of an advanced civilization, who warns earthlings to put aside their petty quarrels among themselves or face the consequences.

If the war-movie side of Reagan had been all there was to him, as many of us feared in the early 1980s, all of us might now be radioactive ash. But because he also had his peace-movie side, he turned out to be a somewhat less predictable and altogether less frightening character. He was, in fact, a precursor, a kind of spiritual grandfather, of what has become a standard Hollywood type: the autodidactic, self-righteous, "issue-oriented" star who is full of opinions about politics and who also dabbles in, and is fascinated by, "New Age" phenomena. These last, in Reagan's case, include (besides astrology) extrasensory perception, precognition, sci-fi, people from other planets, and prophecies about Armageddon. It was only natural for him to be interested in such things, given that the Reagans spent most of their lives (as Nancy puts it with screwball reasonableness in *My Turn*) "in the company of show-business people, where superstitions and other non-scientific beliefs are widespread and commonly accepted."

Reagan's staff kept most of the wigginess from spilling over into the public arena. "Here come the little green men again," Powell used to tell his staff whenever the subject arose of Reagan's preoccupation with how an alien invasion would unify the earth. Powell, Cannon writes dryly, "struggled diligently to keep interplanetary references out of Reagan's speeches." They couldn't be kept out of informal conversations, though—much to the bafflement of Mikhail Gorbachev, who, when Reagan started in about invasions from outer space at the 1985 summit in Geneva, politely changed the subject.

The wildest aspect of Reagan's premature New Agery was his obsession with the Battle of Armageddon. The closest anyone ever came to flushing out this particular bit of Reaganuttiness came during the second televised campaign debate in 1984, when Marvin Kalb asked Reagan if the matter of Armageddon had had any effect on American nuclear planning. Reagan just made it through his answer safely, saying that while he had engaged in "philosophical discussions" on the subject, "no one knows" whether "Armageddon is a thousand years away or the day after tomorrow," and therefore he had never "said we must plan according to Armageddon."

Had Walter Mondale picked up on this opening and used the rest of the debate, and maybe the rest of the campaign, to harass Reagan on what could have become the "Armageddon issue," the election might have been less one-sided. A little more drilling in Armageddon territory could have yielded a political gusher. Cannon has conducted his own archaeological dig into the matter and unearthed enough shards to warrant the conclusion that "Reagan is hooked on Armageddon." In 1968 Billy Graham visits Reagan and they talk about portents of the end of days. In 1970 Pat Boone brings a couple of radio evangelists to see Reagan in Sacramento, and one of them, seized by a supposed visitation of the Holy Spirit, prophesies rapturously that Reagan will be president and tells him about the approaching mother of all battles, and then listens as Reagan ticks off modern events, such as the founding of the State of Israel, that seem to fulfill the biblical preconditions for the big one. In 1971 Reagan tells his dinner partner, the president pro tem of the California Senate; that the end is nigh and that one of the portents is that Libya has gone Communist. In 1980 Reagan announces on Jim Bakker's TV show that "we may be the generation that sees Armageddon."

The obsession continues after Reagan is president. His national security aides grow used to hearing him talk about it. Robert McFarlane becomes convinced, in Cannon's words, "that Reagan's interest in anti-missile defense was the product of his interest in Armageddon." When Frank Carlucci tries to persuade Reagan that nuclear deterrence is a good thing, Reagan astonishes Carlucci by telling him about Armageddon. When Caspar Weinberger tries to make the same case, Reagan gives him the same Armageddon lecture. On March 28, 1987, at the Gridiron Club dinner, Reagan tells James McCartney of Knight-Ridder that because Chernobyl is the Ukrainian word for "wormwood" and Wormwood is the name of a flaming star in the Book of Revelation, the accident at the Soviet nuclear plant was a harbinger of Armageddon. (In a hilarious footnote, Cannon adds that Reagan, in telling the story to McCartney, misremembered the name of the star and called it

"Wedgewood." Shades of Nancy's china!) On May 5, 1989, Reagan tells Cannon that Israel's possession of the Temple Mount is a sign that Armageddon looms. There are other omens, too, he tells Cannon. What, for example? "Strange weather things."

II.

The book titled *An American Life* omits any mention of strange weather things. It is as much a star autobiography as a presidential memoir, but star autobiography of the pre-Geraldo type. There are no shocking confessions, no harrowing addictions, no twelve-step recoveries. This is *Photoplay* circa 1940, not *National Enquirer* circa 1990.

Has Reagan read this book? Besides the printed tome, there is also an audio version—two cassettes with a total running time of 180 minutes, on which Reagan, in his seductive announcer's voice, recites excerpts aloud. According to my calculation, the tapes represent about 32,000 of the roughly 260,000 words in the printed text. The evidence, then, is that Reagan has read at least 12 percent of his book. Trust, but verify.

The actual author of *An American Life*, as the opening acknowledgments more or less proclaim, is a "thoroughly professional team" of about two dozen people headed by Robert Lindsey, who has written several readable best-sellers. "Even though I am glad to have this book finished, I will miss my conversations with Bob," writes Reagan, or writes Bob, or writes somebody. There's no way, really, to be sure. Anyway, the conversations with Bob didn't yield much. Almost everything in the book could have been gleaned, perhaps was gleaned, from the public record—from newspapers, old speech and interview transcripts, other books, and White House news releases.

But if there are no revelations, there is a portrait—no, there are two portraits. On the surface is the golden personification of the American dream: the small-town lifeguard who saved seventy-seven people from drowning, the movie star who saved the girl and the day in many a B picture, the citizen-politician who saved the conservative movement from sullen irrelevance, the triumphal president who saved his country from drift and decline. Below the surface—but only a little below, since these depths are not very deep—is the child monarch, a person of stunning narcissism and unreflectiveness.

Reagan, as all the world knows, is a big-picture man. His famous "hands-off management style" seems to have evolved early and to have extended to the smallest details of his own life. His most politically potent qualities—the placidity of his temperament, the smooth-surfaced simplicity of his politics, the magical ease with which he waves away inconsistency and irresponsibility—are all related, first, to his ability to ignore contradictions (more precisely, his inability to notice them), and, second, to the effortlessness that has attended all his achievements.

"I was raised to believe that God has a plan for everyone and that seemingly random twists of fate are all a part of His plan," he writes. "My mother—a small woman with auburn hair and a sense of optimism that ran as deep as the cosmos—told me everything in life happened for a purpose. She said all things were part of God's Plan, even the most disheartening setbacks, and in the end, everything worked out for the best." But then, a few sentences later, he tells us what his father taught him: "that individuals determine their own destiny; that is, it's largely their own ambition and hard work that determine their fate in life."

Reagan is untroubled by the stark incompatibility of these two conceptions of will and destiny. He just forges blithely ahead, and before long it becomes clear which of the two views he finds more congenial:

> Then one of those series of small events began that make you wonder about God's Plan.

> Once again fate intervened—as if God was carrying out His plan with my name on it.

> Then one of those things happened that makes one wonder about God's having a plan for all of us.

> If ever God gave me evidence that He had a plan for me, it was the night He brought Nancy into my life.

And finally, as he and his wife emerge from the elevator on the second floor of the White House on the evening of the inaugural:

> I think it was only then, as Nancy and I walked hand in hand down the great Central Hall, that it hit home that I was president . . . it was only at this moment that I appreciated the enormity of what had happened to me.

Even the presidency was something that happened to Reagan. This is more than just the affectation of a becoming modesty. The political philosophy that Reagan adopted in his 40s may have stressed ambition and hard work, but Reagan himself has never had to do much more than go with the Plan. Even in his own telling, it is striking how easy he has had it (which makes his denunciations of "giveaway welfare programs" especially unattractive).

After graduating from Eureka College in 1932, he tells us, he was bitterly disappointed when someone else beat him out for a job running the sporting goods department at the local Montgomery Ward in Dixon, Illinois, for $12.50 a week. That's about it as far as reversals go. A few months later he was making $25 a week as a radio announcer, and then $75, and then, after a quick screen test taken during a trip to California to cover the Chicago Cubs in spring training for his radio station in 1937, $200 a week as a contract player at Warner's—the equivalent today, after taxes, of well over $100,000 a year.

Reagan was 26 when he arrived in Hollywood in the depths of the Depression, and after that it was just a matter of adding zeroes to his income. Even World War II was easy for him. Lieutenant Reagan spent it narrating training films for the Army Air Force at a movie studio in Culver City. His first picture after his discharge involved riding horses, which made it, he writes, "like a welcome-home gift." Of course, he was already home. He had been home all along—though he genuinely believed, at the time and after, that he had been to war.

In 1954, after Reagan's movie career had begun to falter, the Plan intervened in the form of an offer to serve as the host of a television series, "General Electric Theater," and to give speeches at GE plants as a company spokesman. Taking this job, perhaps more than any other decision Reagan ever made, was what made him president. Reagan had turned down other TV offers because, as he notes shrewdly in *An American Life*, "most television series expired after two or three years, and from then on, audiences—and producers—tended to think of you only as the character you'd played in the TV series." Being the host, however, was different. It put him before the public every week for eight years (plus another two years as the host of *Death Valley Days*), not as a cowpoke or a private eye or a bumbling husband, but as a congenial, dignified man in a business suit, a man called Ronald Reagan.

Cannon's book stresses Reagan's pride in his acting and his movie career, but Reagan's book confirms Christopher Matthews's insight that Reagan's real calling in life was not as an actor but as an announcer—and, by extension, as a giver of speeches. Reagan offers no reflections on the craft of acting, but plenty on the craft of announcing and speechmaking. (Can you picture the young Reagan waiting on tables for a chance to play Hamlet? Neither can I.) The speeches for GE became The Speech, a compendium of free enterprise bromides and fabulous anecdotes about government waste that he polished to a high gloss in hundreds of repetitions, and which, when he delivered it on national television in 1964 on behalf of Barry Goldwater, led to the governorship of California and eventually the presidency of the United States.

III.

Characteristically, Reagan sees no contradiction between the cozy cartel system of the Hollywood studios in which he prospered and the cutthroat laissez-faire doctrine he would later espouse. On the contrary, he deplores the antitrust suit that forced producers "to make movies purely on the speculation theaters would want to show them." This kind of ideological incoherence contributes to Reagan's opacity about just when and how he became a conservative. His wife is more straightforward on this point. Referring to Reagan's years shilling for GE in the middle and late 1950s, she wrote in *My Turn*: "It was during this period that Ronnie gradually changed his political views."

From Nancy's account, and from Cannon's, it seems clear that during his GE spokesman days Reagan became persuaded by the sound of his own voice, which was also his master's. More flatteringly to himself, Reagan depicts the change as starting much earlier. He pretends to recall, anachronistically, that as a small-town boy he learned "to know people as individuals, not as blocs or members of special interest groups." He claims, improbably, that his support for Franklin D. Roosevelt was a function of FDR's call in 1932 for a cut in federal spending. While making a picture in England in 1949 he observes, omnisciently, "how the welfare state sapped incentive to work from many people in a wonderful and dynamic country." He makes much of having called on the Democrats to nominate Dwight D. Eisenhower for president, but this was a popular position within Americans for Democratic Action, the leading liberal pressure group of the day. (The ADA ticket was Ike and William O. Douglas.)

Reagan also portrays his battles with Hollywood Communists in the Screen Actors Guild, the United World Federalists, the American Veterans Committee, and other organizations as a factor in his conversion to conservative Republicanism. This makes a nice, heroic-sounding story, but it's demonstrably untrue. He writes that "after the war, I'd shared the orthodox liberal view that Communists—if there really *were* any—were liberals who were temporarily off track, and whatever they were, they didn't pose much of a threat to me or anyone." But this was *not* the "orthodox," i.e., mainstream, liberal view. By 1946, and unmistakably by 1950, the great majority of American liberals, leftists, and Democrats were firmly anti-Communist. This was the case even in Hollywood, where a fair amount of poolside Stalinism (like today's hot-tub Sandinismo) persisted right through the mid-1950s.

Reagan after the war was a dupe, an enthusiastic joiner of Communist front groups. He expresses no remorse about this. On the contrary, in his memoir you can almost hear the fond, indulgent chuckle in his voice as he describes himself during this period. He "was speaking out against the rise of neofascism in America." He "joined just about any organization I could find that guaranteed to save the world." But heck, he just "hadn't given much thought to the threat of communism." Darn that headstrong, idealistic Reagan kid anyway—somebody forgot to tell him about the Moscow trials. In any case, he doesn't mention such things in explaining his awakening to the problem of communism. Instead he recounts a visit from a couple of FBI agents and his agreement to become an informer for them. ("They asked if they could meet with me periodically to discuss some of the things that were going on in Hollywood. I said of course they could.")

Whatever his reasons for turning against communism, he remained left of center long after he did so. As late as 1952, by which date he had been publicly denouncing Communists for six years, the Los Angeles County Democratic Central Committee declined to endorse him for an open House seat because they thought he was *too* liberal. It's tantalizing to speculate on what might have been had the Democrats of Los Angeles not made this bonehead decision. Would Representative Reagan have become Senator Reagan? Might he have ended up as JFK's running mate? Would he have drifted to the right and become a marginal crank like Sam Yorty? Or would he have stayed left and won the White House four or eight years earlier than he did? And—most delicious thought of all—would the ultimate sneer-word of today's conservatives be not McGovernism or Carterism, but Reaganism?

The fact that Reagan converted to anti-communism long before he converted to conservatism may have had an important consequence. Evil though he thought the empire was, his conservatism did not depend on an emotional attachment to a permanent, Manichaean East-West struggle. This may be one reason why he was so much readier than were the ideologues among his aides when Gorbachev came along and announced that the struggle was over.

Reagan is not, nor has he ever been, ideologically sophisticated. He was a sentimental liberal who became a sentimental conservative. His liberalism was a product of inertia combined with a vague sympathy for the little guy; his conservatism was a product of convenience combined with sympathy for guys who weren't so little—the GE managers and executives who had his ear for eight years. ("By 1960, I realized the real enemy wasn't big business, it was big government.") This lack of intellectual sophistication—an inability to think, really—is one of the themes of Cannon's book that manifests itself over and over again in Reagan's book. For example, when he becomes governor of California, two years after the Watts riots, Reagan decides to "find out what was going on" by paying secret visits to black families around the state:

> One of the first things I heard was a complaint that blacks weren't being given a fair shot at jobs in state government. I looked into it and confirmed that virtually the only blacks employed by the state were janitors or those working in other menial positions, largely because state civil service tests were slanted against them.

His response was to change "the testing and job evaluation procedures" to make up for the fact that "blacks just hadn't had the opportunity to get the same kind of schooling as other Californians"—in other words, to rewrite the tests and the qualifications so as to guarantee equality of outcome. A good-hearted act, no doubt about it; but Reagan shows absolutely no awareness that this aggressive instance of affirmative action is precisely the sort of thing that his Justice Department would soon enough denounce as an affront to American values.

Another example. A lodestar of the Reagan administration's foreign policy was the distinction between authoritarian regimes, which are by nature reformable because they permit competing centers of social power to exist, and totalitarian regimes, which are by nature unreformable because all power has been seized, or is in the process of being seized, by a party-state professing a messianic ideology that claims a total monopoly on truth. This analysis was the heart of a famous article by Jeane Kirkpatrick in *Commentary* in 1980. Reagan was so impressed by this piece that he made Kirkpatrick his ambassador to the United Nations.

The doctrine of the immutability of totalitarian regimes has turned out to have no predictive power, and it was therefore a poor basis for long-term policy; but the analytic distinction between the two types of dictatorship was sound enough. The idea that there's a difference between plain old undemocratic governments, however brutal, and those with totalitarian pretensions is not hard to grasp. Furthermore, this idea underlay some of the Reagan administration's most important foreign policy innovations. Even so, it comes as no real surprise that the authoritarian-totalitarian distinction was utterly lost on Reagan. Discussing policy options for the hemisphere in *An American Life*, he writes:

> Sure, we could send in the troops, but the threat of communism wouldn't diminish until the people's standard of living was improved and the totalitarian countries of Latin America gave them more freedom.

Discussing the Falklands War, he writes:

> Margaret Thatcher, I think, had no choice but to stand up to the generals who cynically squandered the lives of young Argentineans solely to prolong the life of a corrupt and iron-fisted totalitarian government.

The Argentine military junta, remember, was Kirkpatrick's beau ideal of authoritarian government. And the totalitarian prototype in the Kirkpatrick scheme was pre-Gorbachevian Soviet communism, which Reagan describes as a system of—what else?—"authoritarian rule."

Or perhaps it isn't Reagan but his "thoroughly professional team" that is confused. I must acknowledge that the sentences quoted above are not recited on the cassettes, so there is no hard proof that Reagan was ever familiar with them. But *An American Life* does have passages that Reagan can be credited not only with having read, but with having written. These are excerpts from a diary that he seems to have kept as president, of which a total of about forty pages are scattered through the ghosted text.

To appreciate fully the flavor of these diary entries, one needs to sample more than one or two. The three entries below are given in their entirety. They are typical. I categorically deny that I am being unfair:

> *Feb. 22*
>
> Lunch on issues. I'm convinced of the need to address the people on our budget and the economy. The press has done a job on us and the polls show its effect. The people are confused about economic program. They've been told it has failed and it has just started.
>
> *June 30*
>
> Word came that the hostages were going to leave in a Red Cross motorcade for Damascus. It was a long ride. We then were told that celebrations in small villages along their route were delaying them. About a quarter to three our time, they arrived at the Sheraton hotel in Damascus.
>
> Out to George Shultz's home for dinner with George and O'Bie. A very nice and finally relaxed dinner. Before that, however, I spoke to the nation on TV from the Oval Office, then George took questions in the press room. When I spoke our people were just leaving Syrian air space in a military aircraft.
>
> *Sept. 26*
>
> High spot was swearing in of Chief Justice Rehnquist and Justice Scalia in the East Room. After lunch meeting with George S., Cap. W., and Bill Casey plus our White House people, Don R., John P., etc. It was a sum up of where we stand in the negotiations between George and Shevardnadze. The difference between us is their desire to make it look like a trade for Daniloff and their spy Zakharov. We'll trade Zakharov but for Soviet dissidents. We settled on our bottom line points beyond which we won't budge. Then we picked up Nancy and helicoptered to Ft. Meade for the opening of the new National Security Agency complex. I spoke to the NSA employees. Then we helicoptered to Camp David and topped the day with a swim.

The entries from the diary that were chosen for publication in *An American Life* are presumably the best of the lot, and this is as good as they get. One can imagine the sick disappointment of Lindsey and the rest of the team when they got their first look at them. There are no portraits of friends and enemies, no thumbnail sketches, no gossip, no peeves, no wisecracks, no outbursts of principle, no anecdotes—no nothing, really, except simple-minded digests of news bulletins and appointment logs. For authenticity's sake, the team has left in a few grammatical howlers and preserved a Reagan habit, which some will find endearing, of taking the hyphens out of compound phrases like "tight rope," "plane side," and "heart breaking" and saving them up for use in low-octane swear words, such as "h--l" and "d--m" (hang on, shouldn't that be "d-m-"?).

Many entries combine childish diction with childish thinking, as in this reflection on the flap over the visit to the Waffen SS cemetery at Bitburg, Germany:

> I still think we were right. Yes. The German soldiers were the enemy and part of the whole Nazi hate era. But we won and we killed those soldiers. What is wrong with saying, "Let's never be enemies again"? Would Helmut be wrong if he visited Arlington Cemetery on one of his U.S. visits?

And then this follow-up, after Kohl suggested that they balance the Bitburg ceremony with a tour of Dachau:

> Helmut may very well have solved our problem re the Holocaust.

And then there is this innocuous reference to a negotiation on the budget:

> The big thing today was a meeting with Tip, Howard Bohling, Jim Wright, Jim Baker, Ed Meese, Don Regan, and Dave Stockman.

The problem is that Howard Bohling wasn't at the meeting, or on the planet. Our diarist is conflating two of the actual attendees, Howard Baker and Richard Bolling. Are the identities of these men a mere detail? You could say that about Bolling, a mere representative (though a prominent one) and a Democrat to boot. But Senator (and Majority Leader) Baker was the second-most-powerful figure in the Republican Party. He would later become Reagan's chief of staff. It is deeply weird that the president was so vague about who he was.

The emptiness of Reagan's diary is one of many indications that the president's narcissism was of the babyish, not the Byronic, variety. And a happy baby he was. His perfect obliviousness to the feelings and the thoughts of others protected him from emotional turmoil. And his emotional tranquillity in turn helped to cushion him from what otherwise might have been the political impact of the contrast between his beliefs and his life. He listed "family" first among his public values, yet his emotional remoteness so wounded his own children that during the White House years three of them published books attacking him. And he treated his closest aides, Cannon tells us, "as indifferently as he did his children." Once they left his employ, they would never hear from him again.

There were times when Reagan's lack of self-awareness was merely goofy. At other times, however, his inability to see himself clearly takes on a somewhat more unpleasant edge. Consider this anecdote:

> I've never liked hunting, simply killing an animal for the pleasure of it, but I have always enjoyed and collected unusual guns; I love target shooting, and have always kept a gun for protection at home. As I had done when I was governor, I sometimes did some target shooting with the Secret Service agents who accompanied us to the ranch, and occasionally managed to amaze them with my marksmanship. We have a small pond on the ranch that sometimes attracts small black snakes, and every now and then, one would stick its head up out of the water for a second or two. After I'd see one, I'd go into the house and come back with a .38 revolver, go into a little crouch, and wait for the next snake to rise up. Then I'd shoot.
>
> Well, since I was thirty feet or more from the lake, the Secret Service agents were shocked that I was able to hit the snake every time. They'd shake their heads and say to each other, "How the hell does he do it?"
>
> What they didn't know was that my pistol was loaded with shells containing bird shot—like a shotgun—instead of a conventional slug. I kept my secret for a while, but finally decided to fess up and tell them about the bird shot.

This little story has a chilling, brightly lit creepiness, like something out of David Lynch. Its trajectory, from Reagan's pious and no doubt sincere disavowal of killing animals for pleasure to his almost sensuous description of the fun of blowing the heads off inoffending water snakes (and doing it in an unsporting manner, too), suggests an obliviousness that is potentially sinister. One begins to suspect that, for all his generic charm, Reagan may not be such a nice guy after all. We are dealing here with the same insensibility that enables Reagan to believe that he never traded arms for hostages, that the deficit was all the Democrats' fault, that his economic policies helped the poor at the expense of the rich.

IV.

But wait. If he was dumb, superstitious, childish, inattentive, passive, narcissistic, and oblivious, how come he won the cold war?

Good question. The answer, in two words, is Mikhail Gorbachev. Reagan, always lucky, was never luckier than to find himself president of the United States at just the moment when a Soviet leader decided to lift the pall of fear and lies from his empire, thus permitting the system's accumulated absurdities and contradictions to come into plain view and to shake it to pieces.

Everyone agrees that the West, led by the United States, deserves credit for creating the conditions under which this could happen. But in order to assign to Ronald Reagan the lion's share—that is, to assign to this particular president more than the equal slice of credit that is due each of the eight postwar presidents who carried out the Western policies of containment, nuclear deterrence, conventional military readiness, support for NATO, support for non-Communist economic development, and political and diplomatic opposition to Soviet expansionism—you have to believe that the *marginal* differences between Reagan's policies and his predecessors' were the ones that brought about the Gorbachev breakthrough.

These marginal differences included bigger increases in military spending; intransigence in, if not outright hostility to, arms control negotiations; an emphasis on ideological attacks on Leninism in American public diplomacy; suspension of the anti-Soviet grain embargo; assistance to the guerrillas fighting the Soviet-supported Sandinista regime in Nicaragua; a somewhat more aggressive program of military aid to the Afghani *mujaheddin* than might otherwise have been pursued (though this program was begun under the Democrats and was popular with both parties); the anti-missile defense proposal; and the military interventions in Lebanon and Grenada. The effect, such as it was, of these policies on changes within the Soviet Union was probably mixed.

Reagan's admirers argue that the American military buildup encouraged Soviet reform by persuading Gorbachev that the arms race was a pointless rathole. Still, it could also be argued that the buildup retarded reform by strengthening the worst-case paranoids within the Soviet military. More plausible than either argument is the view that Gorbachev's determination to disengage from the cold war was the product of forces far deeper and stronger than whether American military spending increased a lot or a little during the early 1980s, that the forces that made and unmade Gorbachev were indigenous, historical, Russian.

Nor were the other Reagan policy innovations—whether "hawkish" like the contra obsession or "dovish" like the grain-embargo cancellation, whether wise like the president's vigorous rhetorical opposition to Leninist ideology or foolish like the Lebanon fiasco—truly central to the epochal decisions being made in the Kremlin. And the argument that these innovations were decisive requires us to believe that without them Gorbachev would not have come to power; or that he would have come to power, but would not have embarked on the path of glasnost and perestroika; or that he would have embarked on this path, but would have been deflected or replaced long before he could follow it as far as he did. None of these propositions seems plausible to me.

The issue of nuclear weapons increasingly occupied Reagan's attention, and it presents a special case. How much he knew about the topic was the subject of much speculation while he was in office. Cannon shows that Reagan's ignorance was actually more comprehensive than many of us suspected. The president did not know that submarines carried nuclear missiles, or that bombers carried them. He did not know that land-based ballistic missiles made up a much larger proportion of the Soviet nuclear force than the American one, and therefore he did not realize that his proposal for halving the numbers of such missiles on both sides was far from being the even-handed basis for serious negotiation he believed it to be. Though he had campaigned against the "window of vulnerability"—the alleged ease with which a Soviet first strike could destroy America's land-based missiles—he did not know that his own plan to put such missiles in stationary silos would open the "window" wider.

Throughout Reagan's first term his strings were being pulled by officials who privately opposed the whole idea of arms control agreements with the Soviet Union because they thought such agreements weakened the West's will to resist. These officials concocted bargaining positions that the Soviets could be relied upon to reject, which is exactly what the Soviets did under Brezhnev, Andropov, and Chernenko. Then along came Gorbachev. He wanted a deal so badly that he systematically probed until he found a question Washington was unable not to take yes for an answer to. And so the "zero option" for European-based intermediate-range missiles—a proposal that the Defense Department had crafted to be unacceptable—became, presto chango, the great and crowning achievement of Ronald Reagan's foreign policy.

Whatever happens in the aftermath of the coup in Moscow, the central achievements of the Gorbachev years—the dissolution of the Soviet Union's Eastern European empire, the demolition of Leninist ideology, and the defusing of East-West confrontation—will almost certainly remain. Could Gorbachev have done all this without Reagan? Probably, yes—but he probably couldn't have done it without accepting Reagan's (that is, the West's) view of the cold war. Gorbachev recognized that the cause of the cold war was not superpower tensions or capitalist encirclement or the arms race, let alone the international class struggle. The cause of the cold war was simply the Soviet Union's refusal to become a "normal" country. As a corollary, Gorbachev recognized that the Soviet Union faced no military threat from the West, however bulging Western arsenals might be. So he knew he could accept what his predecessors would have seen as preposterously disadvantageous arms control deals without putting his country's physical security at risk.

There was another point of agreement between Gorbachev and Reagan. They both thought Gorbachev's country was redeemable. Reagan had a recurring daydream that someday he would take a Soviet leader up in his helicopter and together they would fly low over an American suburb. The Soviet leader would see the tidy little houses of American workers, with their plastic pools out back and a car or two out front, and he would decide that maybe it was time to scrap communism and try a little democracy and free enterprise instead. Is this sentimental fantasy really so different from what actually happened?

When Reagan called the Soviet Union an "evil empire" and "the focus of evil in the modern world," conservative op-ed writers expressed their satisfaction that at last we had a president who had a moral vocabulary and a tragic sense of history, a president who recognized that some political systems are irredeemably tyrannical and aggressive, a president who rejected the contemptible claptrap that attributes every international conflict to "lack of understanding." These commentators, and many of their friends inside the Reagan administration, saw Gorbachev as simply cleverer than his predecessors, and therefore more dangerous. Reagan did not agree. When he said "evil," he just meant bad. He didn't really believe in immutable malevolence. The villains of Reagan's world were like the ones in Frank Capra's movies: capable of change once they saw the light. Reagan thought that Gorbachev was a pretty good guy.

As president, of course, Reagan was the ex officio high priest of the nuclear cult. He was followed everywhere he went by a military aide handcuffed to the "football," the sacred object containing the codes that would enable him to launch the final conflagration. And the propinquity of the thermonuclear Excalibur gave him, in this one area of policy, a consciousness of personal power unparalleled in history and shared only with his Soviet counterpart. By the same token, the rituals of nuclear summitry required his personal participation, and he found the drama irresistible.

Resplendent in the vestments of the nuclear episcopate, Reagan announced his astonishing heresies. In 1983, just when the whole of the conservative foreign policy establishment, and many centrist and liberal nuclear worthies besides, had geared up to defend the morality of nuclear deterrence against freezeniks, Catholic moralists, Euro-accommodationists, and other unsound elements, the president proclaimed that nuclear deterrence was . . . immoral. To replace it, he proposed an exotic space shield that would protect America (and why not Russia, too?) against nuclear attack.

Whatever progress is ultimately made in anti-missile defense technology, the idea of an impenetrable space shield was then, and remains today, a lunatic notion. The notion's provenance was lunatic, too. "The dream," writes Cannon, "was the product of Reagan's imagination, perhaps of Brass Bancroft and the Inertia Projector and *The Day the Earth Stood Still*, and certainly of the vivid prophecy of Armageddon that Reagan accepted as a valid forecast of the nuclear age." SDI was pure Reagan.

Useless as SDI would be as a shield against a determined missile attack, it would not be at all useless as a supplement to a first strike launched by the side that possessed it. This—plus a superstitious awe of American technology—was why SDI alarmed the Russians. Reagan did not understand this. He thought they were lying when they said they were worried about Americans attacking them with nuclear weapons, because they had to know Americans would never do such a thing. McFarlane, who didn't think they were lying, saw how the dross of Reagan's "dream" could be turned into gold. In a negotiating ploy so one-sided that he privately called it "The Sting," the United States would abandon SDI—a research program of dubious practicability—in exchange for the destruction of thousands of actually existing Soviet nuclear weapons. McFarlane didn't mind that Reagan kept saying SDI was not a bargaining chip, because every such avowal drove up its value as a bargaining chip.

McFarlane didn't realize that the old boy meant what he said. And Reagan had another dream, which prompted him to utter another heresy, the most dangerous one that the priesthood could imagine. He said he wanted to rid the world of nuclear weapons altogether. Total nuclear disarmament was a silly old chestnut of cold war propaganda, especially Soviet propaganda. But Reagan believed in it. He had said so in a number of speeches before he became president, but no one paid any attention because everyone assumed that it was just drivel that he'd thrown in to soften his right-wing image. As president, Reagan continued to believe in the desirability of complete nuclear disarmament, even after it was explained to him that nuclear weapons were good because they had kept the peace for forty years. His advisers, he writes in *An American Life*, included "people at the Pentagon who claimed a nuclear war was 'winnable.' I thought they were crazy."

Reagan knew that his own secretary of defense, for example, was "strongly against" nuclear disarmament. Still, he told Gorbachev that he wanted exactly that. In October 1986, at the Reykjavik summit, the principals agreed on principles: the Soviet Union and the United States would scrap all their ballistic missiles within five years and all the rest of their nukes within ten. The only thing that stood in the way of the deal was SDI. Gorbachev wanted it confined to the laboratory, and he simply refused to take seriously Reagan's offer to share it. Reagan, all accounts agree, became angry—so angry he stalked out of the room while Gorbachev was still talking to him. The session, and the summit, ended. Reagan's "dreams" had fratricided, like incoming missiles bunched too closely together. He and Gorbachev had to settle for the Euromissile treaty, which would be signed a year later.

Cannon blames Reagan for the failure at Reykjavik. "Reagan," Cannon writes, "clung to his competing dreams of a world without nuclear weapons and a world in which people would be protected from nuclear war by an anti-missile defense." But were these "dreams" really so inherently contradictory? If both sides still had nuclear arsenals, then SDI would indeed be "destabilizing," because it would create an obvious, if conjectural, temptation to strike first: smash the other side's forces, and even a leaky defense might be enough to repel what was left. But if "a world without nuclear weapons" were actually to be achieved, then might not shared anti-missile defenses (of a suitably modest kind) be just what Reagan was saying they'd be—insurance against cheaters or crazies?

In retrospect, it's clear (at least to me) that both Reagan and Gorbachev blundered at Reykjavik. If one of them had given in, both superpowers might be dismantling the last of their ballistic missiles right now. But Gorbachev's stubbornness was less excusable than Reagan's. Gorbachev should have realized that it didn't much matter what he conceded about SDI: once nuclear disarmament was a reality, there would be little political support in the United States for spending hundreds of billions of dollars on exotic space lasers designed to shoot down weapons that were being eliminated anyhow. Gorbachev should have tried to understand why Reagan was so angry: SDI was Reagan's baby, Reagan's pride was at stake, and therefore Reagan was the one who was overvaluing it. Gorbachev should also have realized that Reagan meant what he said about sharing the technology, that on this point, as on the space shield itself, Reagan was willing to brave ridicule and the weight of expert opinion.

All this is, admittedly, a little moot. Once Gorbachev decided to forgo rule by terror, the arms race was going to melt away no matter what anyone else did. The peace that reigns between the United States and the Soviet Union is obviously more of Gorbachev's making than of Reagan's, whereas Reagan alone is responsible for a domestic legacy that includes, besides a wonderful revival of the American Spirit, a soul-crushing national debt, an ignoble Supreme Court, stark economic stratification, mounting racial fear, the impoverishment of public institutions, and a make-my-day brand of social discourse that revels in ugly contempt for losers. Yet none of that (except the debt) is a surprise. We—those of us who voted against him—knew he was going to be that way from the start.

Reagan was the plaything of whichever of his aides most deftly pushed his hot buttons, but on the nuclear question he lurched into leadership—and that *was* a surprise. The same ignorance that made him a pawn in the struggles among his advisers also made him a savant—an idiot savant, to be sure—in the surreal universe of nuclear strategy. He may not have known which end of the missile has the warhead on it, but he was an expert on the end of the world.

It was Reagan's genius to paste a smiley-face on Armageddon's grinning skull. It turned out he didn't view the biblical account of Armageddon as a prophecy of something inevitable, let alone desirable. He viewed it as a sci-fi story, a cautionary tale about a big awful disaster that could and should be prevented. This is a misreading of the text of the Book of Revelation, but Hollywood always rewrites the classics. Too many downbeat endings.

And how was Armageddon to be prevented—or, rather, who was to prevent it? Something McFarlane observed about Reagan is instructive on this point. "He sees himself as a romantic, heroic figure who believes in the power of a hero to overcome even Armageddon," McFarlane told Cannon. "I think it may come from Hollywood. Wherever it came from, he believes that the power of a person and an idea could change the outcome of something even as terrible as Armageddon. . . . He didn't see himself as God, but he saw himself as a heroic figure on earth." Not as God, but maybe as God's sidekick.

Perhaps, in true Hollywood style, there will be a sequel. The happy ending was not the only unusual feature of our hero's interpretation of the tale of Armageddon. "As Reagan understood the story," Cannon notes, deadpan, "Russia would be defeated by an acclaimed leader of the West who would be revealed as the Antichrist." Residents of Pacific Palisades, beware of strange weather things. What rough and chuckling beast, its hour come round at last, slouches toward Beverly Hills to be born?

Clinton for President

EDITORIAL

NOVEMBER 9, 1992

For the better part of two decades, it has been difficult to view the election of a Democrat to the White House as anything but a mixed blessing. For the last four elections, the editors of this magazine have supported a series of Democratic candidates (with the exception of John Anderson in 1980), more out of loyalty than enthusiasm. Looking back, our endorsements progressively honed the art of faint praise, and were written for the most part in a tone of caution and even, in some cases, scarcely concealed dread. The candidates were in every case the lesser of two evils, people for whom the reconstruction of liberalism and the restoration of effective government were decent enough ideas, but ones which always took second billing to the exigencies of Democratic Party politics. We hope—and increasingly believe—that those days of equivocation can now come to an end. In endorsing Bill Clinton and Al Gore, we are not simply voting our hopes over our fears. Least of all are we affirming some party loyalty. We are expressing our belief that they offer the best chance in a generation to bring reform and renewal to a country that desperately needs both.

That opportunity is one that should appeal to principled liberals and conservatives alike. At this ideologically diverse magazine, it has prompted an unnerving and unusual consensus in favor of a political change. Even conservatives must now acknowledge that the Bush administration has proved to be a humiliating end to a curiously inglorious era. In retrospect, conservative government failed even on its own terms. Where social problems came from government, Republicans had neither the courage to abolish nor the interest to reform it. The welfare system, which had come under searching and legitimate scrutiny from conservatives, was left virtually intact. Middle-class entitlements are untouched. Domestic discretionary spending ballooned, and the proportion of government money that is consumed by transfer payments has grown at the expense of the money geared toward infrastructure and investment.

To be sure, much of the current discontent with Bush's economic record is overblown. Bush has suffered with the business cycle; manufacturing is not in the crisis both Ross Perot and Bill Clinton claim; productivity has increased; inflation and interest rates have both been brought down. Moreover, Bush wisely avoided any panic measures to stimulate an economy slowly recovering from its accumulation of private debt. But the president was unable to explain this to the country or to justify his economic prudence, because it would have amounted to a disowning of Ronald Reagan's recklessness and therefore alienated a large section of his base. And this failure to be candid points to a deeper failing. The president has failed to address—let alone tackle—the longer-term causes for American economic sluggishness: the deficit and the need to retrain American workers in the face of a fast-changing globalized economy. If in many areas Bush's restraint was economically prudent, in others it has jeopardized our economic future.

Moreover, when Bush seeks to revive himself, as he did in his State of the Union address last January, this economic dishonesty is compounded by the holograms of ideology: capital gains tax cuts, enterprise zones, a line-item veto, "family values," or some pathetic nonsense about a deficit reduction check-off on tax returns. These slogans are by now an excuse for gross policy lapses, not a means to put them right; after twelve years they reflect less the reality of the American economy than an empty ritual of inaction.

It took the president three years to provide a health care package. Even now, he has done little to promote educational reform or welfare overhaul. With the former, the president has lazily intoned the mantra "choice" while giving only token support to his innovative education secretary. With the latter, he has basically let underfunded local initiatives go on autopilot, showing interest only when the subject provoked a healthy response from focus groups as the campaign loomed. His domestic policy centers on a capital gains tax cut and the panacea of enterprise zones: the first an impediment to a free market and the second a way of postponing effective intervention in the inner city. Meanwhile, the real problems mount.

Frankly, we can see no consistency or meaning in George Bush's domestic record, except a fitful effort to appease public opinion and to win re-election. If he returns to the White House, even this excuse for action will disappear. He represents at this point an almost uniquely ill-suited option for the country. He does not have the credibility to start over; nor does he have a mandate, even from conservatives, to carry on. He has delivered neither fiscal restraint nor effective government. His economic plan for the future—cobbled together by James Baker's aides in the days after the convention—carries no weight, since it comes from a president who has long seen economics as a mere adjunct to his short-term political needs.

In foreign affairs, the record is scarcely better. The pristine anti-communism of the early 1980s, which this magazine supported, has since buckled under the weight of its own success. By 1986 Reagan was beginning to embrace the post-cold war world with a fervor that would soon remove a central prop from Republican ascendancy. Bush inherited this precarious political legacy and bungled it. Instead of embracing the democratic revolutions of the late 1980s and using them to formulate a clearly pro-democratic foreign policy, Bush lapsed into an incoherent diplomatic realism. For two years he expended his full energies on sustaining the corpse of the Soviet Union past its natural life and backed the genocidal regime of Saddam Hussein over the democratic government of Israel. His instincts in foreign policy were geared toward the extension of the status quo, whether in Beijing or Belgrade, even in the face of momentous historical shifts. Bush misjudged Eastern Europe; he misread Russia; he built up Saddam, only to engage in a massive effort to halt him; his early support of Maastricht now seems foolhardy, and his appeasement of Beijing morally indefensible. To be sure, no disasters—except the invasion of Kuwait—occurred on his watch. But there was no positive movement in the evolution of American foreign policy either; and no persuasive account of America's post-cold war role in the decades ahead. In its absence, the country runs the risk of a slide into cynicism and fitfulness in its dealings abroad, a trend that Bush deplores but has done his own peculiar best to accelerate.

Bush has done to conservatism what no liberal opponent could have done: he has destroyed it from within. By infusing it with layer upon layer of intellectual dishonesty, he has reduced it to an expedient for the extension of his own power, its positive arguments distilled into the empty code words of Houston, its intellectual legacy reduced to a shrill husk of exclusion. His administration is, in short, degenerate. No wonder in the last few weeks it has not so much faltered as collapsed.

This time, mercifully, there is an alternative. It is not a rival ideology but a practical engagement with the legacy of the last twelve years, an engagement that could and should appeal across traditional ideological lines. Its guiding principle is an attempt to apply the old liberal principles of effective government and civic equality in a world where both seem to be in terminal decline. For the past two decades this magazine, among others, has been engaged in an attempt to give this principle intellectual heft and political realism. We make no apologies for this effort, however Sisyphean the task has sometimes seemed. We refuse to believe that government has no role to play in rescuing our cities from collapse, in turning our welfare system from one of dependency to one of responsibility, in retraining workers who are left behind by the global economy. We continue to uphold the idea that Americans are open to duty and service to their fellow citizens, and that our government and our president are central to that civic enterprise. And we think that in Bill Clinton and Al Gore, we may finally have found the men who have the intellectual edge and moral intuition to put these old and new ideas into practice.

Their philosophy is not, as any reader of these pages will surely know, a reprise of entitlement liberalism. Clinton's economic program is remarkable for its eschewal of the easy palliatives of redistribution. He proposes to raise taxes only on those earning more than $200,000. As rich-soaking goes, this is a mild step (compare it with the Labour Party's doomed tax plans in Britain earlier this year). It's a non-destructive and partial reversal of the regressive tax changes that began in the late Carter years with the capital gains cut and the increase in the payroll tax and continued with the Reagan cuts of 1981. We also like the fact that his plan contains little redistributionist rhetoric, preferring instead to talk about public investment; and that he intends to make it impossible for welfare to be "a way of life" by limiting cash assistance to two years, after which recipients would be required to work. His campaign platform and his Arkansas record suggest that he knows he must tackle the entrenched interests in education and health care if he is to achieve higher levels of excellence and greater access in both. In all these areas, Clinton understands from experience that liberalism will only succeed if it recognizes the follies of its past; if it sees government as something to be reinvented rather than promoted; if it recognizes that citizenship is as much a matter of responsibilities as it is of rights.

On the deficit, we worry that Clinton is too blithe about its fast-growing threat to our economic health. But we are confident that in office he will be forced to make the hard choices on entitlements, because a Democratic Congress and a Democratic president will be unable to avoid accountability any longer. We see no essential conflict between this and a strategy of government investment; indeed, the two are complementary. Clinton should forgo a desperate dash for growth in his first year in order to lay the deficit-cutting groundwork for more sustainable growth in his fourth. The emphasis he has rightly put on education, training, and investment has always been a long-term strategy. He should keep his eyes on the prize and not imperil it with short-term reflation. And besides, Clinton must surely recognize that it will not help him at all to have two years of growth at the beginning of his first term and an economic collapse at the end.

On social policy, the same virtuous dynamic may also kick in. Clinton will be accountable for effective health care reform in a way no Republican president could be. His grasp of policy detail and his public commitment to control health care costs are the best insurance we have that a transition to universal health insurance will not fall prey to the special interests of the health care lobby. Not only will he lose the excuse of gridlock, he will also have the Nixon-goes-to-China card of a Democrat having to prove his lean government credentials. The same political dynamic that allowed him to confront the National Education Association in Arkansas will operate in Washington to an even greater degree.

Clinton is also more in touch with the cultural reality of today's America than is his opponent. In our view, this matters. It matters that he recognizes women as active and equal participants in the workplace and politics. It matters that his marriage is a partnership, like most Americans'. It matters that he has had daily, working experience with people of a different race; that his relationship with gay Americans is one of familiarity and respect. If the traumatic issues of race, gender, and sexuality are to be addressed with any honesty in our politics and culture, they must be addressed by people who have nothing to prove but their engagement with the issues. Clinton is one of the few men in our public life whose integrity on these matters is unquestionable. That is why he could take on Sister Souljah's hatred without impugning his commitment to racial equality; and why he has been able to insist on equal rights for homosexuals without losing the respect of Reagan Democrats. This kind of integrity is an asset in any human being. In a president, it represents a rare opportunity to find a realistic truce in our cultural and racial wars.

Abroad, we find Clinton's internationalism a refreshing change from the narrow confines of Scowcroftism. To be sure, on military matters he does not have the experience of Sam Nunn or the wonkery of Gary Hart. But he comes from a wing of the party that has resisted the liberal impulse to treat the Defense Department as a way to fund other social programs and to see foreign relations as an area where the recourse to military intervention is regarded as taboo. He also has a vice president with considerable foreign policy credentials. On Bosnia and the Middle East, Clinton's instincts have so far been sound. His foreign policy addresses at the beginning of this campaign reflected a deep understanding of this country's need to remain engaged in Europe and Asia, to refocus our defenses rather than run them down.

Much has been said in this campaign about the question of character. We believe it tells in Clinton's favor. He has shown the character to emerge from a difficult childhood to take advantage of some of the best education the world has to offer; he has shown the ability not merely to package his politics, but to think through the intricacies of policy that support it; in the primaries, he showed dignity and perseverance in the midst of an unconscionable invasion of his privacy; in his public career he has weathered five terms of elective office with a creditable and dogged record of public service. On the most important matter of judgment so far, he picked Al Gore to be his running mate. It was a choice that showed Clinton's ability not only to act freely of the interest group politics of the Democratic Party, but to recognize a man with complementary expertise and intuition, whose mastery of policy detail (especially in the areas of defense and technology) is also married with a steadiness of touch. If Clinton runs his administration as well as he has run this campaign, then we have little to fear about his temperamental ability to bear the burdens of high office.

Of all the sicknesses affecting our politics, the most profound is our inability to be honest. On the deficit, the underclass, race, we have long been engaged in an elaborate ritual of denial. This ritual, intensified by the distraction of the last four years, should stop now. We sense in the public engagement of the last few months that Americans are ready to elect an administration that is finally accountable, that will no longer have the excuse of an opposing Congress to avoid action, that will engage the complicated, practical problems of our country, that will be directly answerable for its failures. Clinton, heaven knows, is not perfect. He has a tendency, as we have noted before, to avoid hard truths. But the choice now is between watching an exhausted president perpetuate four more years of cynicism and keeping an intelligent, committed politician honest. We choose the latter.

PART III

Race:
"The Crisis of Caste"

The Freight-Car Case

EDMUND WILSON

AUGUST 26, 1931

Not since the Sacco-Vanzetti case has any question concerning justice in the American courts received so much attention both in the United States and abroad, as the "Scottsboro case" involving eight young Negroes sentenced to death for alleged assaults upon two young white women. In the following article Edmund Wilson describes the circumstances of the alleged crime and of the subsequent trial. —THE EDITORS

Chattanooga, Tennessee

Old low sordid Southern brick buildings, among which a few hotels, insurance companies and banks have expanded into big modern bulks as if with sporadic effort; business streets that suddenly lapse into nigger cabins; a surrounding wilderness of mills that manufacture fifteen-hundred different articles, from locomotives to coffins and snuff; and a vast smudge of nigger dwellings—six Negroes to one white in Chattanooga. "Hell's Half-Acre" in the mill district is a place people don't dare go at night; it is calculated that among the niggers there is an average of a murder a day. In Chattanooga, the manufacturers, enslaving the Negro almost as completely as the planters did before the Civil War, have kept him in his African squalor and produced a super-squalor of Southern slackness mixed with factory grime.

The night of March 24, two white girls from Huntsville, Alabama, came into Chattanooga on a box-car. According to the testimony of one of them at the trial in which they afterwards figured, they had some boys along; and according to the general report they were well known to be prostitutes. It is alleged that they had been in the habit of living in the Negro quarters and that one of them had not long before been arrested for "hugging" a Negro on the street. Victoria Price represented herself as having been married twice; Ruby Bates said she had never been married. They both dipped snuff.

The girls said that they had spent that night at the house of a woman they knew in Chattanooga. They left about 10:45 the next morning on a freight-train bound for Memphis, traveling in a low roofless car known as a "gondola": the gondola was about two-thirds full of gravel. The girls had bobbed hair and wore overalls. In the same car were about half a dozen white boys.

At Stevenson, Alabama, just across the state line, about twenty colored boys got in and scattered through the train. They were a miscellaneous lot of hoboes—like the white boys and the girls, from the bottom layer of that far-southern society. Only one of the nine afterwards arrested was able even to write his name. Some of them said they were on their way to Memphis to look for jobs on the river boats. In some cases, they were friends traveling together; in others, they did not know each other.

What happened on the train is uncertain. Apparently one of the white boys, walking along the top of a box-car, stumbled over one of the Negroes and threatened to throw him off the train. At any rate, ill feeling was created and presently the colored boys came trooping down into the gondola. One of them had a gun and another a knife, and the white boys were outnumbered. Some kind of fight evidently took place and the white boys either jumped off or were put off the train—all except one who slipped down between the cars, was rescued by one of the Negroes and stayed on.

The group who had been put off were furious and one of them had a cut head. This boy went to the nearest railroad station and told the telegrapher that the niggers had tried to murder them; and the telegrapher, very indignant, telephoned ahead to have the niggers taken off the train.

So that when the train arrived at Paint Rock, the sheriff and a band of deputies boarded the train and arrested nine of the boys. The others had disappeared. The Negroes supposed at first that they were being arrested for bumming a ride. One boy was found in an empty car, where he said he had been riding by himself ever since the train left Chattanooga. Four others had been traveling on an oil car and said that, though there had been some sort of disturbance along the train, they hadn't known what it was about. It seems reasonable to suppose that, if any violence had occurred, the boys responsible had escaped from the train. The one with the pistol was never found. And the authorities could find no evidence of foul play beyond the cut head of the boy who had complained.

But there were the two white girls alone on the train with a gang of niggers. The authorities demanded of the girls whether the niggers hadn't attacked them and the girls at first denied it. But under pressure of repeated questioning and prompting, they confessed that they had been raped. The doctor who examined the girls found proof that they had been having sexual intercourse, but no reason to conclude that they had been roughly handled except one small bruise on one of them which might equally well have been caused by traveling on gravel.

The boys were put in jail at Paint Rock, but when a mob gathered and threatened to lynch them, they were removed to the town of Gadsden. In their cells, they went mad with fury—yelled wildly and beat on the doors and tore up their beds and bedding. They told their lawyers that they had been led from their cells at Gadsden by a lieutenant of the National Guard, then handcuffed in pairs and clubbed by people brought in from the streets. On April 6 they were put on trial at Scottsboro, Alabama, the county seat of Jackson County.

A few days before the trial, *The Chattanooga News* had expressed itself as follows:

> How much farther apart than night and day are the nine men who perpetrated those frightful deeds and a normal, kind-hearted man who guards his little family and toils through the day, going home to loved ones at night with a song in his heart. How is it possible that in the vesture of man can exist souls like those nine, while others in the vesture of man can dream such beauty as Keats dreamed, or can paint as did Raphael?

And *The Scottsboro Progressive Age* congratulated "the people of Jackson County upon their conduct during the past few days when their patience and chivalry were severely taxed. If ever there was an excuse for taking the law into their own hands, surely this was one."

At any rate, the fifteen thousand or so inhabitants of Scottsboro and the hillbillies of the surrounding countryside have ordinarily very little excitement and it was a long time since anything had come their way like nine niggers accused of rape. The day of the trial was celebrated like a festival; it was also fair day and horse-trading day. There were about ten thousand people in Scottsboro. The poor whites had come in with their guns prepared to slaughter the boys then and there and were only prevented by the state militia, who guarded the courthouse with drawn bayonets, tear-gas bombs and machine-guns. What with the bugle-music of changing guard, the brass band from the local hosiery mill playing "The Star-Spangled Banner" and "Dixie" and a parade of twenty-eight Ford trucks with a phonograph and amplifier at the head, organized by an enterprising agent who had seized the occasion to stimulate slow sales, the town was in a delirium of gaiety.

In the meantime, inside the courthouse, Ruby Bates and Virginia Price were testifying that the colored boys had held them down in the gondola and raped them: each had been raped by exactly six. The white boy who had remained in the car corroborated their testimony to the extent of asserting that he had seen the Negroes have intercourse with the girls, and three of the Negroes testified that they had seen other Negroes attack the girls—though they afterwards told the lawyers that they had been induced to do this by the court officials who had promised to have them let off if they did.

The other white boys had either fled or been told to disappear, as they were never produced.

Eight of the boys were immediately found guilty and sentenced to death in the electric chair. At the announcement of the first two verdicts, the brass band struck up outside and the crowd enthusiastically applauded. Only the youngest boy—fourteen (the oldest was only twenty)—got off with a mistrial. On account of his youth, the prosecutor had asked in his case for life imprisonment. Yet, notwithstanding this clemency of the state, eight of the jury demanded electrocution. One of the other boys had also said originally that he was fourteen, but apparently as a result of threats or violence, later asserted that he was nineteen. It had been feared that he would get off with the penitentiary.

It had been an excessively difficult matter to get anyone to defend the boys. Each of the seven lawyers who composed the Scottsboro bar had been assigned in turn to the defendants and all except one had gotten out of it. A Mr. Wimbley, an attorney for the Alabama Power Company, is said to have remarked that the Power Company had enough juice to burn all nine of the defendants. The only person who was willing to take their case even to preserve the formal decency of the law was Mr. Milo C. Moody. Mr. Moody is, from all reports, by way of being the town heretic. He has never hesitated to take up unpopular positions, but he is old now and in competition with the brass band and the Ford agent's amplifier, was not able to do much for his clients.

In the meantime, however, the Scottsboro case had attracted the attention of an intelligent Negro doctor in Chattanooga, Dr. P. A. Stephens. Dr. Stephens brought it to the attention of the Interdenominational Alliance of Colored Ministers and they raised the inadequate sum of $50.08 and appealed to Mr. Stephen R. Roddy, a Chattanooga attorney, to defend the nine boys. Mr. Roddy is young and conventional—yet not so conventional that he wasn't willing, on the offer of very modest remuneration, to go down to Scottsboro to see whether anything could be done. When he appeared in the courtroom, Judge Hawkins hastened to announce that if Mr. Roddy would conduct the defense, the Scottsboro bar would be released. Mr. Roddy replied, however, that he had been merely sent by the colored ministers to observe. Fresh from getting through the crowd and the guard and with the music of the brass band in his ears, he decided that there was no hope for a postponement and, a member of the Tennessee bar, he was unfamiliar with Alabama procedure. He asked to be associated with Mr. Moody in the defense. At the end of the trials, he put on the stand the commander of the National Guard and one of the court officials and had them testify that the ovation which followed the announcement of the first two verdicts was so loud that the other jurors couldn't have failed to overhear it.

But Dr. Stephens and the colored ministers were not the only people interested in the Scottsboro case. The Communists had recently been active in Chattanooga and on February 10 three of them had been arrested for attempting to hold a street demonstration. They were tried during the last week of March and all found guilty of violating the Sedition Statute, a law which, dating originally from 1796, had never before been applied, construed or noticed during the whole hundred and thirty-five years of Tennessee's history. A motion for a new trial, however, was made, and on April 18 Judge Lusk of the criminal court, in an opinion which, handed down in the state which had declared the illegality of the teaching of evolution in the schools, might serve as a model to the courts of New York, set aside the verdict of the jury and granted the defendants a new trial. He pointed out that the defendants had been arrested before they had had a chance to make any subversive speeches and that in any case "membership in the Communist party and adherence to its principles" had been "recognized as lawful" by the inclusion of its candidates in the Tennessee ballots. "This case," Judge Lusk concluded, "has given the Court much concern. As a lover of the institutions of this state and nation, I look with deep concern upon the activities of subversive agitators of every sort. But, in meeting these movements, we must demonstrate our superiority to them by keeping, ourselves, within the law. The best way, in my judgment, to combat Communism, or any other movement inimical to our institutions, is to show, if we can, that the injustices which they charge against us are, in fact, nonexistent."

In the meantime the Communists in Chattanooga had heard about the arrest of the nine Negroes and had gone down to Scottsboro the day of the trial. One of the principal aims of the American Communists at the present time is to enlist the support of the Southern Negroes. In the "Thesis and Resolutions for the Seventh National Convention of the Communist Party of the United States," held in March–April 1930, the following policy is emphatically laid down:

> The building and the work of the party cannot be effective without a serious change in its attitude and practices in regard to the work among the Negro masses and the transformation of passivity and underestimation into active defense and leadership of the struggles of the Negro masses. The party must be made to express in energetic action its consciousness that a revolutionary struggle of the American workers for power is impossible without revolutionary unity of the Negro and white proletariat. To achieve this unity and to win for Communist leadership also the masses of Negro workers, the party must root out all traces of a formal approach to

> Negro work. . . . The influence of white chauvinism is still felt in the party and has recently manifested itself in St. Louis (opposition in the fraction to a correct Bolshevik line on Negro work). . . . Also wrong, however, is the tendency, displayed by some Negro comrades (which they have since corrected more or less completely) to surrender to the propaganda of the Negro bourgeoisie and petty-bourgeois intellectuals of race-hatred directed against all whites without distinction of class.
>
> Protest against the special oppression to which Negroes are subjected must take the form of intensive political campaigns and mass organization to fight against lynching. Negro workers and farmers persecuted on the basis of race discrimination must be accepted and treated as class-struggle victims. . . .
>
> The party must openly and unreservedly fight for the right of Negroes for self-determination in the South, where Negroes comprise a majority of the population. . . . As the Negro liberation movement develops, it will, in the territories and states with a majority of Negro population, take more and more the form of a struggle against the rule of the white bourgeoisie, for self-determination. . . .
>
> Unless our Negro program is concretized and energetically pushed, the work of our party in winning the majority of the working class will be fruitless in the North as well as in the South.

The Communists assigned to Chattanooga, therefore, seized upon the Scottsboro case as an ideal instrument for realizing this program. The first thing that they did was to get their defense organization, the International Labor Defense, to send Judge Hawkins a telegram which irritated and amazed him, in which they described the cases against the Negroes as a "frame-up" and a "legal lynching" and told the Judge they would "hold him responsible." Then, after the trial, the I.L.D. went to Mr. Roddy and asked him to undertake an energetic and spectacular defense. According to Mr. Roddy, they went through all the gestures of taking him up into a high place and showing him the kingdoms of the earth. They told him he had the opportunity of becoming a national figure, a second Clarence Darrow—a dream, one gathers, entirely alien to Mr. Roddy's ambitions. He asked how they proposed to pay him. They explained that they would raise the money by holding meetings among the Negroes and getting them to contribute to a defense fund. This idea seemed distasteful to Mr. Roddy—and the I.L.D. representatives had begun to arouse his suspicions: one of them, who had said he was a lawyer, had in the course of a discussion of the trials, inquired whether the defendants had been "arraigned" yet. Mr. Roddy refused to have anything to do with the International Labor Defense.

The I.L.D. next went to the attorney who had so efficiently defended the arrested Communists. Mr. George W. Chamlee is quite a different type from Mr. Roddy. A shrewd lawyer and a clever man, humorous, worldly-wise, deep in the politics of the state and able to see every side of every question, he is by way of being a local character: he works by himself, forms his own opinions and pursues his own ends, and is not infrequently found in opposition to the conventional elements of the community. Some years ago, he made himself conspicuous by defending street-car strikers; and he has represented both radicals and Negroes when it would have been difficult to get another Chattanooga lawyer to take their cases. At the same time, as a candidate for office, he has undoubtedly derived political support both from the Negroes and from organized labor. And on the other hand, he once scored an equal triumph by getting off a group of Tennesseans convicted of a lynching whose cases had been appealed to the supreme court. At the recent trial of the Communist agitators, when the prosecutor attempted to make much of the fact that the defendants were avowedly in favor of the overthrow of the government and had forsworn loyalty to the American flag, Mr. Chamlee reminded him that both their grandfathers, having fought in the Civil War, had repudiated the federal government and professed allegiance to the flag of the Confederacy.

Following the local custom, the Communist papers give Mr. Chamlee the title of "General"; but he has never been a general in the military sense: he was attorney general of Tennessee for eight years. In the last Democratic primaries he ran for renomination against Mr. Roddy, the Democratic county chairman. Both were defeated by a third candidate, but Mr. Roddy got more votes than Mr. Chamlee—and it may be that political rivalries have contributed to the antagonisms which have developed in the course of the Scottsboro case.

At any rate, the situation has been complicated by another element. Dr. Stephens had been approached by the International Labor Defense and he had at first cooperated with them. But their obvious tone of propaganda had, he says, aroused his suspicions and he and the colored ministers had finally broken off relations with them. Dr. Stephens had written for advice and information to the headquarters in New York of the National Association for the Advancement of Colored People, and the result was that two entirely separate and mutually hostile defense campaigns got under way.

Precisely what is the history of the split between the N.A.A.C.P. and the I.L.D. it is difficult to find out. But its underlying causes are sufficiently plain. The National Association for the Advancement of Colored People is a nonpolitical organization, which, under the leadership of Mr. Walter White, has in many cases been admirably successful in protecting the legal rights of Negroes. In the Arkansas riot cases of 1925, where seventy-nine Negro share-croppers and tenant farmers, who had attempted to sue their landlords for money due them, had been charged with insurrection and condemned either to long prison terms or to death, the N.A.A.C.P. fought the verdicts and caused the Supreme Court to reverse its decision (made in the Leo Frank case) and to hold that if it could be shown that a trial had been dominated by the fear of a mob, the conviction could be overruled. The N.A.A.C.P. works quietly and by conventional methods. Its general tendency is to encourage the Negroes to approximate to white respectability, so that they may compete in the same fields and claim the same rights. The aims of the Communists have been indicated. The rupture between the two organizations was inevitable—as it seems to have been inevitable between the International Labor Defense and the American Civil Liberties Union after Gastonia—as it seems to be inevitable at the present stage wherever Communists and bourgeois liberals attempt to work together. Whatever the immediate occasion of the break, the result invariably seems to be that the liberals end by accusing the Communists of disingenuous or jesuitical tactics, of diverting money raised for special defense funds to Communist propaganda, of prejudicing their particular causes by waving the red flag too openly and of being willing and even eager to make martyrs to provide atrocities for *The Daily Worker* and *The Labor Defender* and so inflame the class-consciousness of their public; while the Communists, on their side, accuse the liberals of insincerity or timidity, of sacrificing their causes by sticking too closely to the conventional machinery and trusting to the fair play of capitalist courts, of being unwilling to deal with fundamentals for fear of antagonizing the rich persons or foundations who subsidize them and of attempting to mislead the proletariat as to the latter's interests in order to safeguard their own bourgeois positions.

William Pickens, the colored secretary of the N.A.A.C.P., began by endorsing the efforts of the I.L.D. He wrote a letter to *The Daily Worker* in which he asserted that "the only ultimate salvation for black and white workers" was "in their united defense, one of the other." It was not long, however, before he had taken the position—in conformity with the official policy of the N.A.A.C.P.—that the Communists were ruining the boys' chances by adding anti-Red prejudice to race prejudice; while the Communists were denouncing Mr. Roddy as a member of the Ku Klux Klan who had done his best to help "the Southern boss lynchers railroad the boys to the electric chair" and Mr. White as a betrayer of the Negro, who would never have come into the case at all if the rank and file of his organization had not insisted on it and who was now in it not to save the victims but merely to connive with the authorities by getting their sentence commuted to life imprisonment.

Mr. Pickens and Mr. White went to Scottsboro and Chattanooga on their own account and took steps to engage new counsel. A ludicrous and pathetic contest began between the Communists and the N.A.A.C.P. to get the parents of the sentenced boys to endorse their respective organizations and to authorize their respective lawyers to defend them. The N.A.A.C.P. accused the Communists of having carried off certain members of the families of the defendants and of keeping them in hiding so that nobody else could get at them; and the Communists charged the N.A.A.C.P. with having induced the Negroes to sign statements which they couldn't read and which had never been read to them. Before the motion for a new trial had been made, the bewildered prisoners and their relations had been persuaded to sign and repudiate a variety of documents. The Communists, who were counting on the case as a crucial stroke in their campaign to win the Negroes, labored particularly hard over the families of the boys. They brought two of the mothers to New York and had them speak at the meetings which they were now holding there and elsewhere, South, North, East and West, in their effort to raise funds and recruit Communists. One of them, returning to Chattanooga, wrote to her late entertainers as follows:

> Well I sure miss you all but I was just homesick. I'm sorry I was that way, but after all I love the Reds. I can't be treated any better than the Reds has treated me. And I am a Red too. I tell the white and I tell the black I am not getting back of nothing else. I mean to be with you all as long as I live. . . . Well, I am looking for you to come to see me like you said. You can't realize how highly I appreciate the kindness you all did for me. . . . I hope next time I be to see you all I will be less worried. I never stayed away from my family that long for I think my children don't get along without me. . . . Give all the Reds my love for I love them all.
>
> My daughter Sybil says she thanks you all for the kindness you did for me and she works only two days a week and anything she can do on her spare days she will be glad to do so. Will close now.
>
> From one of the Reds, Janie Patterson.

Another of the mothers wrote as follows:

> My dear friend, organ of the League of Struggle for Negro Rights. This is Azie Powell's mother. I was away from home at the time those men was out to see me. I was out trying to collect some money what a man owes me to defend for my boy. . . .
>
> From birth I has work hard plowing, farming by myself for a living for my children. Have had no help supporting them. So sorry, deeply sorry to my heart that my boy was framed up in this. I am almost crazy, can't eat, can't sleep, just want to work all the time, so weak I don't see how I can stand much longer. Living on the will of the Lord. . . .
>
> Azie was raised on a farm, he was born on a farm, got one little girl seven years of age already has heart trouble. Have two boys, two girls in all with no father assisting. Poor me, poor me, so burdened down with trouble, if I could only see my baby Azie once more. Lord have mercy on my poor boy in Birmingham. My boy is only fourteen, will be fifteen

November 10.

Poor me, worked hard every day of my life, can't make a living hardly to save my life. . . .

From Josephine Powell, Atlanta, Ga.

P.S.—Not knowing what to say or what to do for the best.

The Communists held mass meetings and parades, had a demonstration in Harlem broken up by the police, protested to the President, sent ninety-some telegrams to the Governor and organized an "All-Southern Conference" at Chattanooga, at which the Communist leaders were arrested.

Two parties appeared among the Negroes: those who were persuaded by the arguments of the Communists or were excited by communism as a new form of revivalism (the meetings were often held in churches) and those who, from conservatism, willingness to mind their place or prudence about keeping on the safe side of the whites, were opposed to the Communist agitation. In one case, a married woman named Bessie Ball, who had attended a Communist meeting with the man who lived next door and had been elected a delegate to the All-Southern Conference, was beaten up when she got home by her husband, who had heeded the counsels of the respectable Negro preachers. When his daughter had him arrested the next day, the judge congratulated him on his conduct and advised him to use a shotgun on the Reds and call the police if they gave him any trouble. The wife was fined $10 and the house of the man next door was raided and he and his mother arrested, but afterwards released. When the latter couple got back home, they were visited by their neighbor, Mr. Ball, who had just been given *carte blanche* by the court: Mr. Ball, finding a copy of *The Liberator,* the Negro Communist paper, proceeded to tear it up. When the Communist mother protested, he hit her over the head with a wooden block. Later, he shot at the son with the shotgun prescribed by the judge. Both were arrested again on charges of felonious assault with intent to kill. Mr. Ball was soon released, but the Communist kept in jail.

On May 14, Robert Minor complained in *The Daily Worker* that "one of the most serious mass campaigns that the party has ever undertaken" had, in spite of success at agitation, not succeeded in organizing "a united front from the bottom—a united front of the rank and file masses of Negro people and black and white workers." He outlined a more energetic program and ended by calling upon "every District and every Section and Unit to throw itself with full strength and devotion into this campaign, which can very well prove to be an epoch-making one in the struggle of the Negro masses and the working class."

The more docile Negroes were scared: Negroes were practically never to be found on freight-trains any more and white people in Scottsboro said they almost had to shake hands with their servants every morning in order to persuade them that they meant them no harm. The white Southerners, of course, resented both the Communists and the N.A.A.C.P. as interference in their affairs from the North. On one occasion, *The Jackson County Sentinel* announced that they would "have no editorial this week on the 'Negro Trial' matter. We just couldn't do one without getting mad as hell." "The International Labor Defense of New Yawk and Rusha" had told them that they "must have Negro jurors on any jury trying the blacks if they are to get 'their rights.' A Negro juror in Jackson County would be a curiosity—and some curiosities are embalmed, you know."

A change of venue to another county was first promised by the Court, then denied. A hearing on motions for new trials was set for June 5. Mr. Roddy, Mr. Chamlee and Mr. Joseph Brodsky, an I.L.D. attorney, all appeared in court. Some of the jurors were cross-examined with a view to making them admit that they had been aware of the brass band and the demonstration outside during the trials and Mr. Chamlee filed a motion for new trials, asserting that the indictments were vague and mentioned no exact facts or dates; that bias had been present in the case; that the defendants had had no chance to employ counsel; that the jury had been prejudiced and had included no Negroes; that the defense were in possession of newly discovered evidence; that it had been impossible at the trials to question Virginia Price as to whether or not she practised prostitution; that the Negroes at the time they were arrested had displayed no consciousness of guilt; that the state had failed to produce the white boys; that there must originally have been on the train from fifteen to eighteen colored boys and that if any crime had been committed, there was no certainty it had not been committed by the boys who had gotten away; that the ride from Stevenson to Paint Rock could only have taken forty or fifty minutes and that it would have been impossible for a fight and twelve rapes to take place in so short a time.

The hearing was the occasion in Scottsboro for another popular demonstration. Mr. Chamlee brought a bodyguard along and Mr. Brodsky was kept in the building for two or three hours after the hearing was over until the crowd outside had dispersed. Judge Hawkins, who has to depend for his reelection on the voters of Jackson County, denied the motions for new trials.

The defense will appeal the case to the supreme court of Alabama and, if they are unsuccessful, will appeal it to the Supreme Court of the United States.

In the meantime, the Communists in Alabama had continued to work at their program. The Negro share-croppers were miserably paid and the

Communists stimulated them to organize. On July 16, the Share-Croppers' Union held a meeting in a church at Camp Hill of which one of the objects was to protest over the Scottsboro case. A white posse came to break it up and as a result the sheriff was shot, a Negro picket was shot and killed, four Negroes disappeared and thirty-four were arrested on charges which range from carrying concealed weapons to conspiring to commit a felony.

Theodore Dreiser has lent his name to a committee to raise funds for the I.L.D. in connection with the Scottsboro case and a German committee has recently been organized with the names of Einstein, Thomas Mann and Lion Feuchtwanger.

Whatever happened in that open freight-car in broad daylight on a heap of gravel, Ruby Bates and Virginia Price would never have made any trouble about it. The complaint of one white boy has sent it across the world. And for Einstein, Dreiser and Mann in their studies, the kind of differences which exist between one race of people and another seem as negligible as they do to the most ignorant, the least fastidious types of our civilization who have no social position, even the meanest, to keep up. Between them lie all those planes of humanity where the antagonism between hoboes in a freight-car bursts empires and lays commonwealths waste.

The Riot in Harlem

HAMILTON BASSO

APRIL 3, 1935

Lino Rivera is a Puerto Rican Negro who is sixteen years old. He lives in Harlem and has no job. He sometimes runs errands for a Harlem theater and has done other odd jobs. On the afternoon of March 19, after attending a motion-picture show, he went into a Kress store on West One Hundred and Twenty-fifth Street, one of Harlem's principal thoroughfares. He passed a counter displaying hardware and saw a knife he liked. The knife cost ten cents. Rivera decided to lift it and slipped it in his pocket. A clerk saw him and took the knife away. He held the boy by the arm and began to push him out of the store. The boy said:

"I can walk. You don't have to push me."

"Don't talk back," the clerk answered. "You ought to be glad I'm not going to have you arrested."

The clerk continued to push the boy and Rivera protested again. A small crowd gathered around them.

"I told you not to push me," the boy said.

"Don't get fresh," the clerk said. "If you do, I'll call a cop."

"What's he done?" asked a woman in the crowd.

"I ain't done nothing," the boy said.

"The hell you haven't," said the clerk.

A second clerk came up and now the two of them began to struggle with the boy. He clung to a post and began to kick at the two men who tried to pull him away. The crowd became larger. Voices rose in protest.

"What they fighting with that boy for?"

"What you done, boy?"

"I ain't done nothing," the boy shouted.

"They ain't got no right to treat that boy that way."

The two men pulled the boy from the post and began to drag him away. The boy fought and kicked and bit. He bit one of the men on the thumb and the other on the wrist. The man who was bitten on the thumb began to bleed. He shouted: "I'm going to take you down to the basement and beat hell out of you."

The boy was taken to the basement, still fighting with his captors, but less violently now, and a conference was held with a few policemen who had appeared. It was decided, finally, to let the boy go free. He was taken to the back door and turned loose. He ran straight home.

Meanwhile, in the store, the anger and resentment of the crowd had mounted. A woman screamed that they were beating the boy to death and that rumor, spreading, reached a second crowd that had gathered before the store. Threats of violence began to be heard. A speaker started to address the crowd. Policemen reached the scene and tried to break up the gathering. The people refused to move. The speaker continued his harangue. He urged the people to hold their ground.

In the store, now a scene of considerable confusion, the crowd waited for the boy to reappear. He did not and the notion that he was being beaten in the basement seemed to be confirmed. Men in the crowd suggested that they go and free the boy. Women became hysterical. In the excitement a counter was turned over. Some of the employees, becoming frightened at the temper of the crowd, began to leave.

Then, its siren shrieking through the streets, an ambulance stopped before the store. It had been called for the man whose finger had been bitten, but the crowd, its anger growing every minute, thought that it had come to take the boy to the hospital. It began to surge into the store. Three other speakers had joined the first orator and one of them had mounted a ladder. A policeman started toward the man on the ladder and the first fighting began.

With the appearance of the ambulance, the crowd was convinced that the boy had been brutally beaten. It was now well out of hand and the policemen on duty sent in a call for reinforcements. A brick crashed through a window. The spread of splintering glass was lost in the roar of the crowd. And then, further to substantiate the idea that the boy had been beaten, a hearse appeared. Now it was believed that the boy had been killed. The crowd, yelling with rage, poured into the store.

It was about this time, perhaps an hour and a half after the boy was first caught, that leaflets were circulated through the crowd. These leaflets, mimeographed, were worded as follows:

CHILD BRUTALLY BEATEN
WOMAN ATTACKED BY BOSS AND COPS
CHILD NEAR DEATH

One hour ago a twelve-year-old Negro boy was brutally beaten by the management of Kress's Five and Ten Cent Store.

> Boy is near death. He was mercilessly beaten because they thought he had "stolen" a five-cent knife.
>
> A Negro woman who sprang to the defense of the boy had her arms broken by these thugs and was then arrested.
>
> Workers! Negro and White!
>
> Protest against this lynch attack on innocent Negro People!
>
> Demand the release of the boy and the woman!
>
> Demand the immediate arrest of the manager responsible for this lynch attack!
>
> Don't buy at Kress's!
>
> Stop police brutality in Harlem!
>
> ISSUED BY YOUNG LIBERATORS.

How much these leaflets contributed to the trouble cannot be determined. The opinion in Harlem, after the riot, was that they contributed a great deal. Their appearance, regardless of who was responsible for them, was certainly thoughtless and ill advised. With the crowd already in a sullen mood, with the air full of threats and wild rumors, the positive statement that the boy had been brutally beaten, along with a woman who tried to help him, was not likely to restore any calm or reason. It may be said that the flare-up in Harlem would have occurred whether they were distributed or not. It is equally true, however, that the trouble reached the proportions of a riot, and a race riot, only after they were placed in the hands of the crowd.

To believe, however, that the purpose of these leaflets was deliberately to provoke a race riot, that it was carefully calculated and planned by the Communists, is to believe in the stupid Red scare of the Hearst press. That they helped to rouse the crowds to violence is true. That the violence might have been less if they had not appeared is also true. But not they, or any other leaflet, would have precipitated such trouble if Harlem had not already been smoldering with anger and resentment.

To begin with, Harlem is from 55 to 60 percent unemployed. Many of its inhabitants, before the Depression, were employed as house servants or as attendants in hotels. Others worked in the building trades, as elevator men, as waiters and dishwashers in restaurants. Not all Harlem Negroes, contrary to the impression to be gained from a number of novels, are orchestra leaders and nightclub entertainers. They have been hit perhaps harder than any other group in New York. Many of them have not had work in four years.

Relief has been inadequate. Charges have been made that it is one-third lower in Harlem than elsewhere. Some unemployed Negroes say they have to wait days, and some say weeks, before getting assistance. Relief administration has been entirely in the hands white persons whose knowledge and understanding of the Negro is limited. White investigators have caused much antagonism and bad feeling. There have been quarrels and recriminations and, in some instances, fist-fights and brawls.

As a result of the Depression, Negro families have been forced to combine their resources and live together. Congestion and miserable living conditions have resulted. While there is no legal restriction of Negroes to any one district in New York City they are forced to live in Harlem because landlords in other parts of the city refuse to rent to them. Harlem landlords have taken advantage of this situation to raise rents to exorbitant heights. It is common knowledge that an apartment worth $25 rents for $40 or even $50 in Harlem. Some of these apartments have not been renovated or improved in years. Many of them even lack toilet conveniences.

A certain portion of the Harlem population, during the boom, was relatively prosperous. During 1919 and 1920, Negroes living in Harlem took title to over five million dollars' worth of real estate. Most of this investment has been lost. One Negro leader in Harlem states that there is hardly a bank in New York that will renew mortgages on property owned or occupied by Negroes; and, if they are renewed, the rate of interest charged is higher than that charged to whites.

The greatest cause of resentment is the discrimination shown in the matter of employment. Many stores in Harlem will not employ Negro help, chief among these being the three large five-and-ten-cent stores on One Hundred and Twenty-fifth Street. As a protest against this, boycotting organizations have been formed, among them the Negro Industrial and Clerical Alliance and the Citizens' Committee for Fair Play. These organizations, by use of the boycott, seek to get jobs for the members of their organizations in those stores discriminating against the Negro.

It was these things that formed the background of the Harlem riot. One Negro, in discussing the affair, said he was surprised that trouble had not broken out before this. It has been brewing for a long time. The chance apprehension of a boy, the spread of a rumor that seemed to have a basis in fact, was only the accident that set off the anger of a section of society that has suffered through five years of depression. If the New York City government wishes to prevent a recurrence of the Harlem riot, it had best go to the root of the trouble and not attempt to place the onus of a tragic incident upon any one radical group.

Who Is Qualified?

STOKELY CARMICHAEL

JANUARY 8, 1966

[Poverty] is no longer associated with immigrant groups with high aspirations; it is identified with those whose social existence makes it more and more difficult to break out into the larger society. At the same time, the educational requirements of the economy are increasing.

—MICHAEL HARRINGTON, ***The Other America***

Lowndes County, Alabama

I wouldn't be the first to point out the American capacity for self-delusion. One of the main reasons for the criticism of American society by the Students for a Democratic Society, the Student Nonviolent Coordinating Committee and other groups is that our society is exclusive while maintaining that it is inclusive. Although automation has prompted some rethinking about the Alger myth and upward mobility, few people are realistic about the ways in which one legally can "make it" here—or who can make it.

The real ways are three: by having money, by knowing the right people, and by education. The first two methods cannot be acknowledged by most of our citizens or our government because they are not available to everyone and we want to think that everyone has equal opportunity in the United States. Therefore, Americans compensate themselves by saying that at least there is education, and that is available to anyone who cares enough.

The panacea for lack of opportunity is education, as is the panacea for prejudice. But just how available is it? If every 16-year-old in the nation was motivated to attend high school, he could not: there are not enough schools, not enough physical space. As for college, less than one-quarter of the population ever gets there. The financial barrier is too high; even the cheapest state college charges fees which are impossible for the poor. Scholarships serve only the gifted. To make matters worse, many universities and colleges are already fighting off the mob by making entry more difficult: City College in New York, for example, has raised the academic average required for acceptance by several points. It is getting harder, not easier, for the poor to be included here. For the Negro, there is an additional problem. He is not psychologically attuned to think of college as a goal. Society has taught him to set short sights for himself, and so he does.

Hard work was once considered a fourth way to climb the ladder, and some Americans still see it as a possibility. Automation should have buried that once and for all: you can't start as an elevator operator and move up to be the president of the company, because there are—or soon will be—buttons instead of operators. Actually, the hard work method was finished off before automation—but until today only a handful of social critics had the nerve to say that ours was a nation of classes. You have to start ahead of the pack to make that climb.

Think now of the Southern Negro, driven off the land in increasing numbers today, coming to the Northern city. He can hardly be compared to previous immigrants, most of whom brought skills with them. Others took menial work until they could save up and open "a little shop." The Southern Negro arrives; is he to pick cotton in Manhattan? He finds the menial work automated and the "little shop" gobbled up by supermarkets. He is, in fact, unemployable—from the Mississippi Delta to Watts. As for finding work in the new factories of the "changing South," he can forget it; if anything, those factories will be more automated than others. As for education, he probably cannot even read or write because Southern Negro elementary schools are that bad. You have to pass tests to get into college; he doesn't even have the education to get an education. Civil rights protest has not materially benefited the masses of Negroes; it has helped those who were already just a little ahead. The main result of that protest has been an opening up of the society to Negroes who had one of the criteria for upward mobility. Jobs have opened up, but they are mainly the jobs on Madison Avenue or Wall Street—which require education. Housing has opened up, but mainly in the "better neighborhoods." In a sense, the Negroes helped by protest have been those who never wanted to be Negroes. Americans who would point to the occasional Negro in his $30,000 suburban home or his sports car and say, "He made it," should have met the Mississippi lady of color who said to me in 1962: "The food that Ralph Bunche eats doesn't fill my stomach."

The South is not some odd, unique corner of this nation; it is super-America. The Negro is not some "minority group," but a microcosm of the excluded. A white boy may sit with me watching the President on television, and think: "I could be President." No such thought would have occurred to this black boy or any other. In fact the white boy is wrong: he doesn't have much chance either of becoming President. Unless he has money, the right contacts or education, he too will be excluded. Racism is real enough in the

United States, but exclusion is not based on race. There may be proportionately fewer Negroes than whites among the included; and Negroes are, of course, "last to be hired, first to be fired." But the number of excluded whites is vast. The three criteria for upward mobility apply brutally to black and white everywhere.

Let me make one thing clear: I am not saying that the goal is for Negroes and other excluded persons to be allowed to join the middle-class mainstream of American society as we see it today. Aside from the fact that at least some Negroes don't want that, such inclusion is impossible under present circumstances. For a real end to exclusion in American society, that society would have to be so radically changed that the goal cannot really be defined as inclusion. "They talk about participating in the mainstream," said a Brooklyn College faculty member recently at a teach-in on the antipoverty program, "when they don't realize that the mainstream is the very cause of their troubles."

Education is one major form (and means) of exclusion; politics is another. Who plays politics in this country? People who have one of the three qualifications for inclusion. They tell us: "Register to vote and take over the political machines." But this is farcical; the only people who take over the machines are other political mechanics.

If there is doubt about the existence of exclusion from politics, the passage of the 1965 Voting Act should have established it. That legislation passed only because most Americans had finally recognized that such exclusion did exist. Readers familiar with the congressional challenge of the Mississippi Freedom Democratic Party will remember the exclusion—political and even physical—experienced by that group of Southern Negroes. But most Americans do not see that the Voting Act hasn't solved the problem. Recent reports of the Civil Rights Commission and other groups point up the need to send more federal examiners and to inform Negroes of their rights if the Act is to be meaningful. Yet the attitude of the Justice Department suggests that the government is not yet willing to take the initiative necessary for registering Negroes who are not already free from fear and aware of their rights.

The three criteria mentioned here—money, who you know, and especially education—are what people mean when they use the word *qualified.* After the Watts uprising, committees were assigned to study the causes and make recommendations. These were composed of the "experts on Negroes," the "qualified." I am not opposed to the presence on such committees of intellectuals and professionals, or merely making a parallel objection to poverty boards which don't include the poor. My objection is to the basic approach, which excludes the unqualified.

Again, the Southern Negro is not unique but a microcosm. He has been shamed into distrusting his own capacity to grow and lead and articulate. He has been shamed from birth by his skin, his poverty, his ignorance and even his speech. Whom does he see on television? Who gets projected in politics? The Lindsays and the Rockefellers and even the Martin Luther Kings—but not the Fannie Lou Hamers. That is why it was so important to project her during the MFDP challenge. Sharecroppers can identify with her. She opens up the hope that they too can be projected, because she says all the things that they have been saying to themselves—but she is heard. Mrs. Hamer's significance is very different from Dr. King's. One hears white people say of Dr. King: "He is so intelligent, so articulate." Of Mrs. Hamer they say: "What a beautiful soul"—implying, that she lacks analytical intelligence. To some extent, and sadly, Mrs. Hamer has come to accept this vision of herself. Those who know her and others like her, feel that her intelligence is just as great and her analysis as sharp. But Dr. King has one of the three qualifications—education. This is no criticism of the man, but of the society.

When SNCC first went to work in Lowndes County, Alabama, which is 80 percent Negro by census figures, I—a "qualified" person by virtue of my college education—used to say to the black people there that they should register to vote and then make their voices heard. They could assert their rights, take over the power structure. This was the prescription of the qualified. But these people said they didn't want to do that; they did not think they could; they did not even want to enter a machine headed by George Wallace. To them politics meant Wallace, Sheriff Jim Clark and Tom Coleman, who had been accused of the murder of Jonathan Daniels. To them the Democratic Party didn't mean LBJ, but a crew of racist bullies and killers. Entering politics meant, until last summer, confronting the tools of Wallace: the county registrars who had flunked Negroes consistently for years.

They asked if something different could not be created. They wanted to redefine politics, make up new rules, and play the game with some personal integrity. Out of a negative force, fear, grew the positive drive to think new.

SNCC's research department provided the tool: the possibility, under an unusual Alabama law, of a group of citizens in any county becoming a political party in that county by running candidates for county offices and getting 20 percent of the vote. Having done that, the county party can go on to become a state party by running candidates for state office and polling 20 percent of that vote. Thus, educated people (SNCC research) suggested an answer by providing the *information*. But the Alabamans had known what kind of way they wanted to take. They needed to be given confidence and to be told how to do it.

Local "freedom parties" are now being organized in 10 counties stretching across Alabama's Black Belt, with plans to do this in 12 more counties. Together, they contain 40 percent of the potential state vote. Given the Flowers-Wallace contest, which must come, the balance of power could lie with those counties. But the true excitement of this development lies in what it means for the people themselves.

The meetings of the executive committees of these county parties are open. The parties will hold county conventions and draw up platforms in April of 1966. Later, candidates will be nominated who must support those platforms. In conventional politics it is the candidates who spell out the platform (*i.e.*, make promises); in Alabama candidates won't have to outpromise each other, but simply represent.

Right now, workshops are being held to prepare for the future: 150 black Alabamans have already learned about the duties of a county sheriff and a tax assessor, with more to come. Very few citizens anywhere in this country know what such duties are.

Some say it is romantic to place faith in "the masses" as a force for radical change. But the people who say this are the "qualified." Alabama Negroes are beginning to believe they don't need to be qualified to get involved in politics. People long accustomed to self-contempt are beginning to believe in their own voice.

Others might say we are leading the black people of Alabama down the road to frustration. Perhaps power politics will eventually overwhelm the freedom parties and the would-be Negro sheriffs. But there are reasons why this might not happen in Alabama. In counties with Negro majorities, there could be a black sheriff elected next year. Even a Governor Wallace will have to deal with him. SNCC learned from the Mississippi Freedom Democratic Party experience that the Southern Negro doesn't have to cast his lot with the national Democratic Party in order to be recognized as a force which must be dealt with. The Johnson Administration pushed through the Voting Act on the assumption that Negroes would automatically line up with its party. But their allegiance is not quite guaranteed. In New York they cast crucial votes for Lindsay, and in the South both Democrats and Republicans are now vying for the Negro vote.

I have hope for this nation. But it is not based on the idea of an American consensus favorable to progress; James Baldwin's idea of the Negro as the conscience of the country is closer to the truth. The majority view is a lie, based on a premise of upward mobility which doesn't exist for most Americans. They may think the government is at least dealing with basic problems (racial injustice, poverty), but it cannot solve them when it starts from the wrong premise.

The status quo persists because there are no ways up from the bottom. When improvements within the system have been made, they resulted from pressure—pressure from below. Nothing has been given away; governments don't hand out justice because it's a nice thing to do. People must struggle and die first: Goodman, Schwerner and Chaney, and, in the county where I am working, Mrs. Viola Liuzzo and Jonathan Daniels.

President Johnson's concept of the Great Society is preposterous. The definition comes from him, as does the means of entering that society. Excluded people must acquire the opportunity to redefine what the Great Society is, and then it may have meaning. I place my own hope for the United States in the growth of belief among the unqualified that they are in fact qualified: they can articulate and be responsible and hold power.

Watts—Waiting for D-Day

ANDREW KOPKIND

JUNE 11, 1966

Los Angeles

Toward the end of these warm, dusty spring afternoons, small knots of men begin to form at street corners, in front of liquor stores and pool halls, and on the stoops of shabby houses all over south central Los Angeles—a vast undefined area which is "Watts" to everyone who doesn't live there. School is out; jobs are over. It has been another day of frustration and failure and, overall, boredom. Students and the marginally employed mix with the dropouts, the permanently idle and the hustlers. The whites—merchants and social workers, mostly—scurry home to the western and northern suburbs. What is left is the police and "us."

Ten months after the riots or the revolt (depending on where or who you are), Watts is still in a state of siege. The police keep order by their numbers, the extent of their weaponry, and the sophistication of their tactics. They cruise the avenues all night long, breaking up gatherings, arresting as many as possible, searching everyone who looks suspicious. And almost everyone looks suspicious. Few men in Watts do not know how to spread-eagle against a wall or a police car; they have learned from experience.

From time to time the siege is broken. In March, two people were killed in an extended battle that some people call "Watts II." Now, the incidents hardly rate front-page treatment. Deep in the *Los Angeles Times* are stories such as the one last week that began: "Angry crowds hurled rocks and bottles at police in two Negro areas of the city early Saturday. . . ." The tension is below the surface, but there is an almost universal belief another "explosion" is inevitable.

It is that belief, as much as anything, that could produce "Watts III." Both sides are girding for war. The police have developed new anti-riot tactics: at the call of "Code 77" (the Watts precinct number) they move out in troop carriers bristling with shotguns. The young Negroes of the ghetto have their battle plans, too: gangs are organized to converge on one preselected target, then scatter in souped-up cars and regroup at the next unannounced site for another attack. Naturally, neither side wants to be the first to charge. But in the context of a mounting arms race (there are rumors that Molotov cocktails are being prepared and cached, and most Negro men have guns) an "accident" could trigger a fresh revolt.

It almost happened last month. On May 7, police officer Jerold M. Bova shot and killed a Watts Negro, Leonard Deadwyler, after a 40-block auto chase up Avalon Boulevard. Deadwyler's pregnant wife claimed she was having labor pains and her husband was speeding her to the hospital (the car had a white handkerchief, as a signal of distress, tied to the radio antenna). Bova said he was justified in stopping the car (his cruiser forced it to a halt) and approaching the passengers with a loaded .38 revolver. Bova reached in through the window of the passenger's side, across Mrs. Deadwyler, and stuck the gun in the Negro's side. The next instant Deadwyler was shot. Bova claimed the car "lurched" and the gun discharged accidentally. Mrs. Deadwyler said Bova was negligent. The Negroes of Watts called it murder.

There were rallies and rioting after the killing, and an ad hoc "Committee to End Legalized Murder by the Cops" was set up. Two *Newsweek* reporters covering a riot at a liquor store were beaten. Then the police moved in and "busted" four young Negroes who seemed to be among the ringleaders. One of them, Tommy Jacquette, was picked up for "suspicion of robbery," but by the time the police were through, that charge was dropped and he was booked for "inciting to riot," and three other attendant charges. The arrests did not do much to reduce tensions; predictably, they had the opposite effect. White social workers and sympathetic white journalists were warned by their Negro friends to keep clear of Watts.

The coroner's inquest into the Deadwyler case lasted eight days. Last week the nine-man jury (in good Hollywood style it included one Negro, one Oriental, one woman) found the homicide "accidental," and the district attorney dropped the case. But the Negroes in Watts were not in a charitable mood. Tuesday night, they went on a window-smashing rampage.

A lot of chickens (in a phrase much appreciated in Watts) are coming home to roost. No matter how such incidents may be explained in white society, every time a white man kills a Negro (or is even mildly disrespectful, for that matter) the difficulty of building an integrated community becomes that much closer to impossibility. As it is, black alienation from white Los Angeles is almost total.

What is "happening in Watts"—the question everyone here asks—is a strong surge of the black nationalist tide. It is a logical response to the conditions of the ghetto: the powerlessness of the Negro, and the unwillingness of the whites to move toward "integration" on anything more than a token basis. The McCone Commission Report—issued last December to explain the nature of the August revolt and suggest some kinds of solutions—was discouragingly inadequate on both counts. It placed much of the responsibility on the Negro, who couldn't cope with "the conditions of city life" (Bayard Rustin pointed out that the city couldn't cope with the conditions of Negro life). There were some things that the city could do to help out: build a hospital, run a bus line through Watts to employment centers, put cafeterias and libraries in the all-Negro schools. But at bottom, the Report seemed to say, the conflict was some sort of communications breakdown; nothing wrong that a human relations commission and some bricks and mortar couldn't cure.

The McCone solutions have not yet been implemented, although there are bond issues on the ballot this month for school improvements and a new hospital. One new bus line has received federal funds, and there are some human relations committees floating around. But it would be hard to find a Negro in Los Angeles who has the slightest faith that the Report's recommendations, even if they were all effected, could make a significant difference in ghetto life. "There's been a complete failure of white leadership," a white businessman active in civic affairs told me. "No one understands that the Negroes just can't stand being second-class citizens anymore. Patching up living conditions or finding a few people jobs won't help."

The nationalist "reaction" focuses on that state of second-classness. There had been a base of nationalist feeling before that: the Muslims had a large and militant membership, and they had had violent battles with the police. But the August revolts charged the entire Negro population with that sense of "black power" that combines dignity, pride, hatred of whites and Negro brotherhood.

In Watts, there is no single form for its expression. There are organizations like SLANT (Self-Leadership for All Nationalities Today), Us (a somewhat cultish but powerful following of Malcolm X), the Black Muslims, the Afro-American Citizens' Council, the Self Determination Committee, the Afro-American Culture Association and more. It is hard to estimate their numbers (SLANT, which is Tommy Jacquette's group, has about 500 young members), but the important point is not members but sentiment. They catch the deepest aspirations in the ghetto, and they can command the "troops" when the crisis comes.

Nationalist feeling goes beyond these particular clubs. It permeates even the "moderate" institutions, the self-help organizations, the community development agencies, the Teen Posts. Many of them are moving to all-black staffs; whites are relegated to minor posts, as helpers or "resource people."

"What's happening in Watts is what's happening in the rest of America," a nationalist leader told me. "The ghetto is no promised land. There are no jobs to be integrated into. There's no way to move to the so-called integrated areas. The accepted liberal means don't work. The white power structure has no intention of giving up anything without demands, and power yields only to power. I want to see black people organized for power—now. There are enough black people in Los Angeles right now to have a great amount of power *as blacks*. Every other ethnic group in America did it—the Jews, the Italians, the Irish, all of them. The black people have to do it even more, because they were slaves and they started with absolutely no power at all. The feeling is there, though the organizational unity isn't there yet. But the only healthy sign is the feeling of black unity, the feeling that people will have to look to themselves for the solution to their problems."

There is no single ideological line for "black nationalism." SLANT's Tommy Jacquette, for instance, calls himself "more liberal" than others because he sees nationalism as a more or less temporary stage: black men (they all disdain the "slave" word "Negro") have to build up their own community before integration is anything more than continued subservience. Jacquette does not isolate himself from whites; but if they want to help, he recommends that they work in their own worlds, trying to force changes within white society that could allow Negroes acceptance as equals.

But the line moves quickly to extreme positions. As it does, behavior as well as philosophy becomes more removed from white standards. Leaders of Us wear green felt "bubas" (a sort of poncho, of no particular national origin) to set themselves apart (their followers sometimes wear Malcolm X sweatshirts). "Black" is the common referent for all that is good or true. There are black holidays (Malcolm's Birthday, the Sacrifice of Malcolm, Uhuru Day), black language (Swahili), black schools (teaching "soul," nationalist doctrine), black history and, in a sense, black logic.

"You can't mix with the power structure that you're going to deal with," Us's chief, Ron Karenga, explains. Karenga, a 24-year-old graduate student (African linguistics) at UCLA, speaks with a biting, slyly contemptuous air of an old mandarin. "We can't share power that we don't have. We could some day share city or state power, but not community power." At a youth rally after the Deadwyler killing, Karenga said, "We are free men. We have our own language. We are making our own customs and we name ourselves. Only slaves and dogs are named by their masters" (Karenga's name used to be Everett).

The Deadwyler case, Karenga thinks, "could be the catalyst that sets off a community-wide revolt."

White Los Angeles is convinced that the Negroes want another violent revolt, and black Watts is sure the whites will provoke it. Observers who have wandered around the 77th Precinct say the mood of the police swings from deep hatred to deep fear of the Negroes. The Negroes feel much the same way, in reverse.

On both sides there are increasing pressures to keep the lid on. For the whites, another blowup could upset an already delicate political situation—there are state, congressional and county elections this year, and Watts is a major issue in all of them. Governor Brown, for one, has an overriding interest in at least the semblance of tranquillity in Watts. He has suffered criticism on the subject from all sides; the whites think he was too weak with the Negroes, and the Negroes think that in deference to white prejudice and frugality he has failed to seek bold reforms. He is sensitive to the charge that his office did not quickly call up the National Guard last August (Brown was initially out of the country, and much of the blame rests with Lt. Gov. Glenn Anderson). He is said to be a little quicker on the trigger these days. In the wake of the Deadwyler killing, National Guardsmen were alerted and advance men were moved into the area in the middle of the night. Brown sends aides into Watts to "talk things over" with Negro militants, and while nothing tangible comes of the conversations, the Negroes are pulled into a talking situation.

On the ghetto Negroes' side, there are new organizational pressures for "cooling it" that did not exist before last August. Watts was the paradigm non-community. It had a wide variety of leaders and practically no followers. In the past year, the traditional leadership has been discarded—first went the clergymen, then the politicians, and the older civil rights chiefs who used to talk mainly to the whites. There are rudiments of new kinds of organization, but it is barely visible (especially to the white eye). "Before August there were gangs," Tommy Jacquette explained; "now they're organizations." There are also the new self-help agencies, like Operation Bootstrap ("Learn Baby, Learn") which does job training, literacy, and personal behavior education in a strongly nationalist atmosphere. The local poverty program has funded the Westminster Neighborhood Association and the Neighborhood Adult Participation Project which sponsors training and education projects, block and tenant organizations and various social services. Local residents are hired (including some of the most active young militants) and they quickly develop an interest in community stability. The activist groups perhaps would not mind a good fight—if they could lead it. But none of them feels that they are yet in a secure leadership position. For the time being, they all would rather keep things just below boiling-point.

There is nothing very important being done to change people's lives in Watts, and until there is, outbursts of fresh violence should be expected. The official war on poverty has some $33 million to spend (after long delays in funding because of Mayor Samuel Yorty's political shenanigans with the board of directors), but few Watts Negroes can see where it all goes. Actually, two-thirds of it shores up the public schools, a program which is, in the phrase of a poverty program official in Washington, "like flushing it down the drain." The Teen Posts, Westminster and NAPP have some potentially helpful programs, but they are so far mired in the general administrative mess and rendered practically useless by the inadequacy of funds. Sargent Shriver has been shopping for a new L.A. poverty czar, but at least two of those asked have said privately that Shriver would not assure them of his political support for whatever "controversial" activities they might try.

Times are bad in the power broker business; many of the middlemen seem to be losing their accounts. In Watts, the whites—and even the middle-class Negroes—cannot do much to win the confidence of the ghetto. There is suspicion all around. One Watts nationalist leader told me, when I called for an interview, "I don't think you'd give us a fair shake because like most liberals you're probably a Jew and very sensitive to anti-Semitism, and you just don't want to understand black nationalism." The impression is strong that, in every way, it is already too late in Watts.

Although whites will be increasingly irrelevant in the ghetto, it does not mean the death of "leadership." Ignored for years, natural leaders are now quickly rising to the top. On the first day of the Deadwyler inquest hundreds of furious Watts residents jammed into the courtroom and threatened, if only by their presence, to break up the proceedings. Appeals from stern and respectable whites failed. Finally, a black man in a Malcolm X shirt climbed into the judge's chair and directed the scores of Negro clergymen to get out. They did. Then, he said, the rest of the black folk (without special business in the court) could go, too. The people filed peacefully into the corridor, and the man in the Malcolm X shirt climbed down.

Death of a Dropout

JANET SIDEMAN

JUNE 3, 1967

In early May, newspapers reported that Clarence Brooker, age 19, Negro, was accidentally killed by a policeman in the Northeast section of Washington, D.C. A policeman was patrolling his regular beat, when he saw a group of boys milling about the street. Complaints from shopkeepers had already been received about them. The policeman stopped in front of the group and one of the boys, Clarence Brooker, dropped a bag of cookies onto the sidewalk. The bag broke, the crushed cookies were strewn over the street, the policeman attempted to arrest Brooker for disorderly conduct. There was a struggle and a chase, two shots were fired, and the boy was finally apprehended. It is unclear where he died, but the policeman was surprised that Clarence Brooker was dead at all. No one had realized that he had a bullet in his back, since there was no external bleeding. An investigation was demanded and the case is now before a grand jury. Among other items of interest mentioned in the reporting was that Clarence Brooker, besides having a police record, was also a high school dropout—one of many. (The dropout rate in the District's senior high schools last year was 12.3 percent.)

About two years ago I taught eleventh grade English in a Northeast Washington high school that had a special program for dropouts. Clarence Brooker was one of my students. The program had an all Negro enrollment. Most of the students lived in the Northeast ghetto section.

On the opening day of school I was informed that, although books had been ordered, they had not yet arrived, and I should not count on them arriving at all. When I met the class, I asked them to write about something they enjoyed doing or that interested them. I mentioned that we would have no books for a while, but if I knew what they liked, I could base class work on this. They kept asking when the books would come. I said I didn't know, but you didn't have to carry a book to school in order to learn.

The students began writing, and after about 15 minutes, some began handing their papers in. The girls returned to their desks and sat, staring into space. The boys were more restless, and some got up and left the room. Browsing through the papers, I remarked that no one had crossed anything out or erased. You expect changes in written work. All the compositions were about half a page and in beautiful "penmanship." The letters were even, perfectly formed and slanted from left to right. The right-hand margins were as straight as a ruler. The compositions could be "classified" (using the professional jargon) as those that "demonstrated skills had not been learned" and those that were "literate." Here is an example of the former:

"Well I like everyone in the class. I have no pick. I am new here but that don't mean that I take of myself. The reason I here is because I drop out of school but I well like it here. The thing that interest me most is getting of school and having my diploma so I can say that I lest finish school without having to shy."

The other group wrote pieces something thing like this:

"My name is - - - - -. My address is - - - - -. I like school a little. My favorite subjects are English and Math. My favorite sports are softball and football. I would like to finish school and become a clerk-typist. I came here because I know how hard it is to get a good job without a high school diploma. And I wouldn't want to be referred to as a drop-out. I don't think it's going to be hard to finish school because I'm beginning to like going here."

Clarence Brooker was one of the first to finish, and after he brought the paper to my desk, he wandered from the room, returned, and roamed up and down the aisles, looking to see what the others were writing.

He had wide shoulders and was very muscular, which made him seem taller than he was. The photo of him in the newspapers gave the impression that he looked dull and impassive, but he had a very expressive face. His handwriting was clear, almost feminine because he paid such attention to details. The Os and As were perfect circles, the loops of the Ys and Gs were of equal length. His name was written in the upper right-hand corner, the date beneath it of equal length. "English XI" was in the left-hand corner, "Composition" in the middle.

"My interest is girls, booze and money, but the reason I came back is because I want my diploma. My diploma will help me very much in the future.

"My plan in the near future is to join the Air Force, and in order to join, I have to have my diploma.

"After I finish my service career, my other three interests will go into effect."

So from the English teacher's viewpoint Clarence was way ahead of the game—he was literate. That is, he conjugated verbs properly, he knew when to begin a new paragraph, he even had a good "clincher sentence," and the textbook tells us this is one of the most difficult problems in writing a composition. He had followed the assignment, he told me what interested him. He even had a bit of originality left in him. One of the better students in the class. So why had he dropped out? Because school had no relation to his life.

Dropouts are like nonchurchgoers; both might feel guilty or worried, but they soon discover their everyday lives are not altered by nonattendance. They can sleep late. There are no immediate consequences, and the future? Well, that is a long way off. Who knows if it was the air force that brought Clarence Brooker back? Anyway he carried an additional burden. He had more energy than was good for him and he didn't know what to do with it. That's the last thing you want from the congregation. They're only required to know when to rise, when to kneel, and to wait patiently while the organist finds the right page.

A few days later I requested another piece of writing. I began the sermon by asking the class to try to put their feelings into words. If they were interested in something, they should try to examine why. My words were stilted, but 30 wary faces do not make you very relaxed. "You have a language as a means of guiding and controlling your lives, so you can express ideas and understand situations. Do you think you would be able to have thoughts without a language?" I concluded. The girls dutifully began writing their names and the date at the top of the blue-lined paper. Clarence Brooker and some boys around him started laughing and yawning. What was the trouble? Clarence answered for them. They were bored. They knew what interested them, but I would never let them write about it. Yes I would, what was it?

"Sex," Clarence answered.

"You can write about it, but since I want you to put feelings into words, you might think I was trying to pry into your private lives, and that is not what I intended. Maybe you would feel freer with something less personal." He insisted that was what they really wanted to write about, and I agreed. Could they use a dictionary? Of course, that's what it was there for. Clarence had a perpetual grin on his face and after some writing would mutter something to those around him. The dictionary was passed from desk to desk. Snickers went around the room, pounding on desks, glances to see who would begin first.

"The point of this is to use words, not noise."

I was uneasy, maybe I had overstimulated them. Teachers are always warned about this. The boys had been discipline problems before, the girls were pregnant or already mothers. It is important that limitations be set. Clarence was one of the first to finish, and waved his paper in the air as he brought it up. The bell rang while he was grabbing a pen away from one of the boys who had not yet finished. But nothing was produced that was stimulating, let alone overstimulating. The majority of the papers were definitions from the dictionary, with some moralizing attached.

"Sex is a division into male and female, relating to reproductive organs. Sex should mainly be active among adults who are married, but it doesn't always happen that way."

Here is the one Clarence Brooker wrote:

"Sex is, or shall I say, can be a form of both pleasure and relaxation. To me, sex is a *need* that has to be fulfilled by a member of the opposite sex. Some people use sex as a plaything, but sex should be regarded as being essential to life.

"Birth control pills should be abolished and so should abortions. Women getting rid of children should be sentenced to jail because it's a form of murder."

Grammatically correct, and the most original within the framework of the class, but not radically different. One newspaper article reported that Clarence committed rape and other sexual offenses, but his composition gives no hint of that. It is quite respectable today to consider sex a *need*, and many people agree with Clarence's view of birth control.

The next day the students wanted to hear the compositions and I read a few. They were very disappointed. I asked them if they could explain why, since they obviously had strong feelings about things, they could not express them in writing. The listlessness had begun, the wandering in and out, the slamming of the door, tapping feet. Their explanation was that they shouldn't be doing any writing or discussing at all.

"We want to get down to work." What was the definition of work in 11th-grade English? Spelling, grammar, nouns, tests. And when are we going to get books?

I went to the central English department to see if I could get a book used by other D.C. schools. There happened to be one lying around, with Eleventh Grade English on it in capital letters.

"With this type of student, your classwork must have intensive structure," I was told. "Since it is lacking in the homes, the schools must provide it."

A lesson from the book was mimeographed. The sheets were passed out, heads were bent, *Adverbs* written in the center of the lined paper, numbers one to 20 to the right of the red vertical margin line. Correct the following sentences. (1) The parts of this camp stove fit together very simple. . . .

It was very peaceful. All the pens were moving in unison, a studious classroom scene. Then Clarence Brooker was finished. If we had had books, I could have told him to begin the next lesson. He left the room, returned, wandered about. I told him I would correct his paper with him. Wasn't I going to grade it? I wrote an A in red ink. Wasn't I going to enter it in the record book? It was entered. Most of the students had done well. What was interesting was that students who could barely construct a sentence in a composition were able to recognize the incorrect use of an adverb in an isolated sentence. A student told me he was unable to pass the written part of the Civil Service Exam, would I give him additional work in grammar? I showed him one of his tests, where he was able to "correct the following verb forms," and substitute "I am" for "I is." Yet he always said "I is" and always wrote it in compositions. I never was able to convince him that the solution was not in additional exercises.

If the students could have defined what education meant to them, they would not have used words like understanding, ideas, or thought, for only words that could be attached to "things" had any meaning to them. They must have work. Work comes from a book and can be numbered and titled. A grade can be set down on paper and you can amass a collection of these papers to prove that you have been to school.

But what do you do with someone like Clarence Brooker, who is smart, who has this energy? He wanted work, but he wouldn't wait patiently when he finished, and he refused any other alternative. The class had been in session two weeks, and I decided to keep on mimeographing lessons for a while. I wasn't getting to know the class too well because Clarence was occupying most of my time. The wandering had developed into explosive noises. He wrote on other students' papers, he mimicked them. I spoke to him many times. Yes, he really wanted his diploma, he really did want to join the air force. He was very nice, his eyes responded to what I was saying. From a distance you would have thought we were having a conversation. You do very well in your work, maybe it's time for you to begin something new. Yes ma'am. Bring a book, any book, to class. Yes ma'am. He never did. Bring a book from the school library. Yes ma'am. He never went, he just wandered around the halls.

I asked another teacher if he had any "behavior problems."

"I never let them start," he answered. "From the first day, if there's any trouble, out they go. That's the only way to treat these kids. If you don't show them who's boss, they'll walk right over you. Besides, it's not fair to the rest of the class."

The school social worker said, "These children need authority because they don't get it on the outside. If the teacher doesn't show he is in control, it becomes very frightening for them."

I asked the principal if Clarence could be transferred to another class with a male teacher.

"We can't do it. He has to have eleventh-grade English to graduate. Just drop him if he disrupts the class."

His classmates didn't have much sympathy with Clarence either. A girl spoke to me about him after class. "I know I shouldn't tell you how to run things, but you shouldn't let that boy in the class. We can't get any work done."

"But don't you think it's important that we try and see if we can't work something out with students like that?"

"I don't know about that. All I know is he's keeping me from learning."

So I hadn't followed the rules. I hadn't asserted my authority as teacher. If I could not make Clarence sit still, he had to be dropped. I had done neither, therefore he was walking all over me, which was to be expected.

"You really want to join the air force?"

"Yes."

"And you need a high school diploma to do that?"

"Yes."

"Then as a favor to me, I want you to think about something. Will you explain to yourself how you can want something badly, and yet, at the same time, do something that you know will give you the very opposite of what you want?"

"I'll try to stick it out," he answered. I had not got through at all. He didn't appear for the next few days, then came in late, left, then banged on the door glass until I started to go toward him. It dragged on for a few more days, then he was dropped. The policeman stationed in the building was instructed not to let him enter. I looked up his record to see what his other classes were and discovered that his other teachers had dropped him weeks before.

When I discussed this with other teachers and friends, I was advised not to take it personally. I didn't, and that's what made it so disquieting. I would have felt better if Clarence had been personally hostile, for that would have meant he had formed some opinion, passed some judgment.

Perhaps it is useless to investigate who was to blame for putting Clarence Brooker and hundreds of other dropouts on the street. The Negro child's education must be structured, it must be consistent. So he is taught to identify abstractions with visual things on the assumption that abstractions are too much for him to handle. He then becomes dependent on material symbols and equipment, and then in the cruelest inconsistency of all, is provided with schools that have substandard equipment, and little or no material to satisfy this dependency. His private life is full of tension and conflict, so he is given work where tension and conflict are eliminated and he never learns to cope with them.

He faces inequality, therefore he is taught conformity, which is mistaken for equality. He never conceives of a class as a miniature community, where people of different character and ability have to live together. And he never experiences equality, since he must have authority, which by its very definition means that someone is above him.

Well, one May evening Clarence Brooker, who was too smart for his own good and couldn't stick it out, dropped a bag of cookies in front of a policeman and was shot. Did he know why he dropped it? The policeman symbolized authority? But this authority wasn't going to be walked over, he carried a gun to prove it. If he were not a dropout, would Clarence be alive today? Who can say? He got an A on his adverbs. He knew that the parts of this camp stove fit together very simply.

Busing: What's to Be Done?

ALEXANDER M. BICKEL

SEPTEMBER 30, 1972

President Nixon and the Republican platform are inflating busing as a political issue, and Senator McGovern and the Democratic platform seek to deflate it. The deflationary effort is not only less likely to succeed, it is also the less responsible form of political behavior. For if busing as such is a false issue, it has come to symbolize a real one: namely, what is the proper objective of federal policy toward racial concentration—or separation, or isolation—in the public schools, and beyond that, what are the proper priorities of federal policy in primary and secondary education?

The federal courts are well along toward a transition from enforcing what could still properly be called segregation to undertaking, in the South and in many places elsewhere, the integration of schools, so that they will be racially balanced. This is a policy that requires busing, and it is this policy that Mr. Nixon and the Republican platform oppose when they oppose busing. It is the issue raised by this policy that Senator McGovern and the Democratic platform evade when they seek to deflate the busing controversy by their characterization of busing as an acceptable method of desegregation. Of course it is, but we are past desegregating the schools in most places in the South and elsewhere. Should federal policy now be to integrate them?

An affirmative answer to this question necessarily means we have set priorities. Integrating the schools—which the federal government will have to do nationally or not at all—is likely, once it is undertaken, to be all we will be doing in primary and secondary education for the next decade or more. It is an absorbing task. If it is equally a moral imperative to abolish racial concentration in schools resulting from housing patterns, from demographic changes and other factors as it is to disestablish legally enforced segregation, then perhaps the question whether to proceed with racial dispersal answers itself. So it may also if integration is a necessary, or necessarily the best, means of improving the education of lower-class black children.

But there is a moral difference between what housing patterns do to schools, even where those patterns were encouraged by past government policies, and what a legally enforced system of rigid segregation does to schools. There is a moral difference at least sufficient to render relevant a further inquiry into the costs that a policy of integration must incur, into its prospects of success, and into its value as a means of improving the education of black children.

Not the most sanguine reading of the available data can lead to the conclusion that the attainment of racial balance in the schools is the only or always necessarily the most effective way to improve the education of black children. On the other hand, the demography of many areas is such that the rather delicate conditions of balance in which alone educational improvement can even be hoped for are unattainable. Nearly half the black population in the country is concentrated in 50 cities, and a third of the total in 15. This is not a Northern pattern. It is nationwide. The 50 cities include such places of great black concentration as Baltimore, Houston, New Orleans, Atlanta, St. Louis, Memphis, Dallas, Birmingham, Jacksonville, Kansas City and Richmond. And of course Washington, D.C. In these places and places like them, only extensive busing across district lines can have any impact at all, and its costs are high. It entails not only the expenditure of funds, which are in short supply and could be put to other uses, but of political, moral and administrative resources, which are also not in unlimited supply, and for which other fruitful employment could also be found. And since we are not prepared to pay the additional costs of closing private schools or incorporating them into the public system, or of restricting the freedom of residential choice which the middle class enjoys, busing not infrequently fails to achieve its end, even after all its other costs have been borne.

What, then, is to be done? Congress passed a rider to the Higher Education Bill last summer ordering that lower-court decrees be stayed pending appeal, rather than being implemented immediately as has been the practice in cases where busing is used for the purpose of achieving racial balance. But this is a stopgap, and not very effective as such either, because busing decrees do not generally avow a purpose to achieve racial balance; they still speak the language of desegregation, even though they have often actually made the transition to integration. Other anti-busing measures—the President's, or the harsher one passed in the House, which is now up for consideration in the Senate—are also stopgaps, though in another sense. They are stopgaps because they are negative. They are not a school policy; they seek to ensure the absence of a school policy. Moreover, they encounter constitutional difficulties. In many applications, they are in conflict with decisions of the Supreme Court—the *Swann* case and companion cases of 1971, and the *Emporia* and *Scotland Neck* decisions of last June.

Now in one sense, that does not mean that the House bill is unconstitutional, or that the President acted unlawfully in proposing his bill. In the last analysis, nothing is unconstitutional until there is a judicial decree saying so on particular facts. Such a decree must be obeyed. Until then there are predictions and opinions, and Congress and the President are not only entitled to their own predictions and opinions, they are entitled to hold opinions contrary to those expressed by the Supreme Court, and to give statutory form to their own opinions in the hope that the Supreme Court will be persuaded to see the error of its ways and will reverse itself.

But if our system of government is to work well and retain the confidence of our people, and if the institutions of our government are not to destroy each other in chaotic conflict, Congress and the President ought to provoke a direct clash with the Supreme Court only as a very last, almost despairing resort. For only two outcomes of such a clash are possible. Either the Supreme Court digs in its heels and dashes popular expectations that Congress and the President have raised, thus discrediting Congress and the President, or itself, or more likely both. Or the Court surrenders, reverses itself, and leaves the indelible impression, at least for a generation, that it is not independent, that it does not follow the law and its own precedents, but rather the election returns. Neither result is beneficial.

The constitutional difficulty, moreover, is even greater. The President's bill and the House bill are supported as exercises of a power of Congress to control the Supreme Court by prescribing the remedies that the Court may administer. In other words, the argument is that without reversing itself, the Supreme Court could hold that Congress has the necessary power to lay down the law that the Court is bound to apply.

On analysis, I think this argument questions *Marbury* v. *Madison* itself, the very foundation of the power of judicial review. No one can guarantee that a majority of the Court would reject this claim to supreme legislative power. The Court has seldom been presented with this sort of challenge, in my judgment never with quite the challenge embodied in the House bill, and except as one reasons one's way to the proper conclusion from *Marbury* v. *Madison* itself, this has happily been a grey area of constitutional law. The question is not whether the congressional assertion of power to prescribe remedies would be held unconstitutional, but whether it should be, and what kind of pervasive change in the basic structure of our federal institutions, going well beyond the busing problem and affecting myriad other matters, we will have worked if the assertion of congressional power is accepted.

The President—so one had judged, for example, from his position on the 18-year-old vote issue, when he opposed trying to deal with it legislatively—is an institutional and constitutional conservative. So are many congressmen who voted for the House bill. But that bill, as well as the

President's proposal, are recklessly radical in undertaking to alter the balance of power between the judiciary and the political institutions of the federal government.

Congress, it is said, though it cannot overrule the judicial definition of the substance of constitutional rights, has power to prescribe appropriate remedies for effectuating them, and to forbid the courts to employ other remedies. But in one of the companion cases to the *Swann* case of 1971, the Supreme Court had before it a North Carolina statute that provided as follows:

> No student shall be assigned or compelled to attend any school on account of race, creed, color or national origin, or for the purpose of creating a balance or ratio of race, religion, or national origins. Involuntary busing of students in contravention of this article is prohibited, and public funds shall not be used for any such busing.

The Court declared the statute unconstitutional because it operated "to hinder vindication of federal Constitutional guarantees."

Not only the prohibition of assignments of students on account of race, but even the prohibition against assignments for the purpose of creating racial balance, said the Court, "must inevitably conflict with the duty of school authorities to disestablish dual school systems." For even though racial balance was not mandated by the Constitution, some ratios were likely in many cases to be useful starting points in the shaping of a remedy. An absolute prohibition of ratios, even as a starting point, interfered unconstitutionally with the shaping of appropriate remedies. An absolute prohibition of busing of students assigned on the basis of race "will similarly hamper" the fashioning of effective remedies for constitutional violations. Bus transportation; said the Court, as it had noted in its main opinion in the *Swann* case, "has long been an integral part of all public educational systems, and it is unlikely that a truly effective remedy could be devised without continued reliance upon it."

Can Congress do what North Carolina could not? Section five of the 14th Amendment gives Congress enforcement power. But there is clear historical evidence that section five was not meant to change the relationship between Congress and the judiciary. It merely confirmed, as do other amendments, general legislative power that Congress possesses anyway. That power enables Congress to dictate to the courts a choice among remedies, or to create new ones and substitute them for remedies the courts have been administering. But Congress ought not be held to have power to take away a remedy for a constitutional violation in circumstances in which the courts have decided that it is the only and the essential remedy, for which nothing can be substituted—and for which, for that matter, Congress provides no substitute. If Congress has this power, it has in fact, if not in form, the power to alter the substance of most constitutional rights, not merely the right to go to one or another school. If such a power is upheld, the school bus will have traveled to a far destination.

What Congress and the President can do, the only thing they can do without inviting a constitutional crisis, and what they must do is to try to change the reality on which the courts have been acting, rather than trying to alter the decisions the courts have been making. Congress and the President should address themselves not to the courts, but to the problems of primary and secondary education. These problems—affecting many private as well as public schools—include poor educational results as well as racial isolation. Busing and racial balance won't solve them in most places. And there is no panacea that will solve them everywhere. Hence no categorical national policy is possible. What is possible is federal help for coherent, well-planned local efforts to improve primary and secondary education.

Few such efforts are now being made, and federal programs are not designed to induce them. Federal programs are themselves incoherent, as they have to be, since no one is in possession of a panacea to be administered nationally. But they are at the same time over-administered from Washington—just enough to transmit their own incoherence from the national level, where it is inevitable, to the local level where it is disastrous and avoidable. A thousand flowers—to borrow a saying—should bloom, but they should not bloom at random and untended in every school district. Conditions vary, but one condition is universal, and it is that if a school district uses a pot of federal money to buy three TV sets, two speech specialists and four other assorted devices one year, a little more or a little less of a different assortment the next year, and so forth, nothing at all will happen that makes a substantial difference.

Something might happen if the school district were required to look at itself in organized fashion, and consult its customers in committees that are sure to include representatives of all of them; and if it were then required to present a 10-year plan for self-improvement, taking into view the community's entire primary and secondary educational process, drawing on private as well as public resources, and seeking to enhance the process in both private and public schools. Such a plan would include measures to alleviate racial inbalance, it might include interracial educational projects involving children from private and public schools who are otherwise left in place, it might include school decentralization, it might include voucher projects opening a choice among schools that only the well-to-do enjoy now, and it would presumably include many things no one has yet tried. It would in any event embody a common local judgment—not a judge's and not a federal administrator's—of the direction of school policy over a foreseeable period of time.

Federal money would then be concentrated as a bloc grant and committed to the plan. A measure of supervisory federal controls would remain necessary, and the plan itself would need HEW approval before funds would flow into it. But the degree of federal control and administration would be greatly reduced from the present level.

There is a bill—HR 13552, introduced by Representatives Preyer (D, N.C.) and Udall (D, Ariz.)—that carries out the suggestion discussed above. Suppose it were enacted, would it have any chance of diverting the inexorable movement of the judicial bus? Well, the Supreme Court can see what others perceive. There is no reason to believe that a majority of the justices have a doctrinaire attachment to maximum integration. That is not why they order it. They order it for different reasons.

District judges before whom school suits are brought are made to confront what is usually a wasteland: a school district deteriorating in every way, sinking deeper and deeper into racial isolation, and doing nothing about it. So the judge orders integration and busing. That is all he can do, short of throwing up his hands, which after 18 years in the school business he no longer thinks he may do. The record of the wasteland and of the judge's response to it then moves up to the Supreme Court. There the doctrinal pull of *Brown* v. *Board of Education* again exerts its force, a principled line between any case and the one immediately preceding it is hard to find—if we said desegregation, why not more desegregation?—and what happens is what we have seen happen. But if Congress and the President, instead of fighting the courts, try to get school districts to fight the reality to which the courts have been reacting, and manage to present courts in the future with school districts embarked on concentrated long-range reforms, then, without needing to renege on prior decisions and without accepting any impairment of the general function of judicial review, courts will be able to say that they are now faced with new facts, with a new reality, which no longer calls for the old remedies. And the Supreme Court will agree. Or so—candor compels one to add—so one would expect.

The Court's Affirmative Action

EDITORIAL

JULY 8 & 15, 1978

When Allan Bakke applied to the UC/Davis medical school for the second time (according to Mr. Justice Powell's opinion issued last week), he had the misfortune to be interviewed by the man he'd sent a letter to complaining about discriminatory treatment the first time around. This man, a Dr. Lowrey, wrote that he found Bakke "rather limited in his approach" and that he was disturbed by Bakke's "very definite opinions which were based more on his personal viewpoints than upon a study of the total problem." As a consequence of his disapproval of Bakke's opinions, Dr. Lowrey gave Bakke a lower rating than the five others who reviewed his application, and probably as a consequence of that one low rating under Davis's elaborate quasi-numerical admissions system, Bakke was not admitted.

Having probably been denied admission to medical school because of his strongly held opinions, Allan Bakke will now be admitted for the same reason. The United States Supreme Court, after invalidating Davis's minority admissions program, held that since Davis can't prove it wasn't this program that kept Allan Bakke out, they must let him in. But the courts aren't about to apply that standard retroactively to everyone who was ever denied admission to an institution with a now-disqualified affirmative action program. Essentially, Bakke is getting favored treatment for bringing what the Court regards as a socially useful piece of litigation.

All of which says two things about the social system that produced last week's landmark case of *University of California Regents* v. *Bakke*. One is that life will always be unfair and capricious in ways even the Supreme Court is not equipped to deal with. The second is that it's a remarkable arrangement—as any foreigner will tell you in amazement—to leave this kind of social decision up to the courts.

On this occasion the Supreme Court seemed as uncomfortable with the arrangement as anybody. And it is not clear exactly what the court decided; there was no majority for any one view. Still, by our reading, if each of the nine justices really means what he said it will be the very rare affirmative action program that is disqualified under the *Bakke* standards. Government institutions and institutions receiving federal aid will be able to continue almost all their current efforts to help minorities, especially if they're willing to engage in a bit of dissembling to satisfy Justice Powell, the swing vote.

The court broke down this way. Four justices—Brennan, White, Marshall and Blackmun—believe that "reverse discrimination" programs of almost any sort do not violate either the Constitution or the 1964 Civil Rights Act. Another four—Stevens, Burger, Stewart and Rehnquist—believe that any discrimination on the basis of race, however benign, by an institution receiving federal aid violates the Civil Rights Act; therefore these four said it was unnecessary to discuss the constitutional question. The ninth justice—Powell—believes that it is permissible for institutions to take race into account as a "factor" in their admissions decisions, but that Davis's system of reserving 16 places for minorities goes too far in institutionalizing explicit racial discrimination. He particularly admires the subtle way they do it at Harvard.

The result, after some simple addition, is that five justices believe the Constitution permits almost all current forms of "affirmative action," and four have expressed no opinion on the subject (limiting their discussion to explicit quotas under the Civil Rights Act). This hardly reflects what the Reverend Jesse Jackson was quick to identify the day of the decision as "a shift in mood from redemption to punishment."

The majority justices struggle mightily to fit the very modern problem of discrimination in *favor* of formerly disadvantaged minorities into their traditional analysis of the 14th Amendment's "equal protection" clause. The clause itself simply forbids a state to "deny to any person within its jurisdiction the equal protection of the laws." The Supreme Court has developed what constitutional scholars call a "two-tiered analysis" to flesh out the Constitution's slender admonition. Since every state action benefits some people more than others, the vast majority of such actions are entitled to only "ordinary scrutiny." But those that affect "fundamental rights" or benefit people on the basis of a "suspect classification" get "strict scrutiny." There's been a lot of legal erudition spent on what's the difference between these two types of "scrutiny," but the practical effect has been that state actions discriminating in unsuspicious ways (between criminals and noncriminals, for example) are upheld while suspicious forms of discrimination are knocked down. Discrimination on the basis of race has always been the clearest "suspect classification."

Justice Powell and the other four justices who discuss the constitutional question have two very different explanations of why state actions making distinctions on the basis of race are not automatically invalid in the case of "reverse" or "benign" discrimination. The theory of Brennan, White,

Marshall and Blackmun is that a racial discrimination that operates to the disadvantage of whites is not as suspect as one that operates against blacks or other minorities. The purpose of the equal protection clause, by this line of thinking, is to protect the "discrete and insular minority" (to quote from a 1938 Supreme Court footnote that is the most famous footnote in American jurisprudence); it is intended to help the kind of group that is least able to protect its own interests through the political process, and so must be protected from the tyranny of the majority. Whites simply do not qualify for this special constitutional protection. Therefore the justices propose that "racial classifications established for ostensibly benign purposes" be subject only to a sort of middle level of scrutiny, which they describe as "strict and searching" but not necessarily "fatal." Under this standard any affirmative action or reverse discrimination program could survive as long as it did not stigmatize or burden any group "least well represented in the political process." That is to say, you could not reserve places for Chicanos by denying them explicitly to blacks.

Justice Powell's theory is that racial distinctions are equally suspect no matter whose ox is gored, but in the case of most affirmative action programs the suspect classification endures "strict scrutiny" and survives it. (The last time an explicit racial classification survived allegedly "strict scrutiny" was in the Supreme Court case upholding the internment of Japanese-Americans during World War II.) Powell believes that a university's need to maintain a diverse student body is a "substantial" enough goal to justify even a suspect racial classification, but the particular method the institution chooses must be "necessary" to the achievement of that goal. Powell doesn't consider rigid quotas "necessary," when other affirmative action methods are available. This is why he voted to invalidate the Davis scheme, while upholding the general right of institutions to use race as a "factor" in their admission decisions.

Since Powell is the determining vote on today's court, it is important to try to understand how far he is willing to go in approving affirmative action programs. His objection seems to be not to quotas alone, but to a system that doesn't treat "each applicant as an individual in the admissions process." What he likes is "an admissions program . . . flexible enough to consider all pertinent elements of diversity in light of the particular qualifications of each applicant, and to place them on the same footing for consideration, although not necessarily according them the same weight." What he doesn't like is: "a classification that imposes disadvantages upon persons like [Allan Bakke], who bear no responsibility for whatever harm the beneficiaries of the special admissions program are thought to have suffered." The coming legal battle over specific affirmative action programs will be fought over these phrases. What about a system that uses a rigid formula of some sort for admissions, and automatically adds 10 percent to the minority score but has no set number of minority students in mind? Is this really constitutionally different from a system (like Harvard's) that weighs race along with other factors but doesn't use a mechanical formula for any of them?

One oddity of Justice Powell's opinion is his suggestion that *any* form of reverse discrimination—even quotas—is lawful if it has been ordered as a remedy following a judicial, legislative or administrative finding of past racial discrimination. This is a loophole big enough to drive a bus through—and indeed its purpose is to preserve earlier court decisions upholding busing and other explicitly racial remedies for civil rights violations. But it creates the anomalous possibility that UC/Davis could reinstitute its minority quota program if, say, the University of California Board of Regents were to issue an official finding that the university had in the past discriminated against minorities in medical school admissions. Surely, there are few institutions that could not substantiate such a self-incrimination if they wished to impose a rigid reverse discrimination system on themselves as a "remedy."

We share Justice Powell's belief that the crucial moral issue in the debate over affirmative action is protection of the individual. (See "Disadvantaged Groups, Individual Rights," *TNR*, October 15.) The trouble with many affirmative action programs—certainly the trouble with quota systems such as the one at Davis—is that they substitute simplistic group identifications for evaluations of individual worth. There are two problems with such programs. One is that they demean and insult both those who are admitted and those who are excluded as a result. The other is that they encourage group hostility and suspicion in society at large.

Justice Powell wrote last week that the United States has become a nation of minorities. "Each had to struggle—and to some extent struggles still—to overcome the prejudices not of a monolithic majority, but a 'majority' composed of various minority groups of whom it was said—perhaps unfairly in many cases—that a shared characteristic was a willingness to disadvantage other groups." This is the underside of the ethnic diversity that is one of our nation's greatest strengths. A crude emphasis on group characteristics rather than individual strengths by institutions dispensing society's favors encourages this unsavory, competitive aspect of groupthink. In the long run it undermines the generous desire to help disadvantaged *individuals* for which Americans of all groups are justly renowned.

March to Nowhere

EDITORIAL

SEPTEMBER 19 & 26, 1983

To most Americans over forty—perhaps even over thirty-five—the 1963 March on Washington is an incandescent memory. It was one of those events one tells one's children about. It was also a turning point in the history of the United States, after which the country's civil institutions would, on the issue of race, finally and however painfully be brought into line with its civil religion: individuals were not to be excluded from the political life of the republic, not to be barred from the doors of economic opportunity and social advancement, not to have their claims weigh less on the scales of justice simply on account of color.

What made that outpouring of humanity in the summer sun twenty years ago an event in the long annals of race relations in America as significant as the Emancipation Proclamation? At least three factors are to be noted. The first was the moral authority of the aggrieved and of their grievance: mass suffering so pointless, disenfranchisement so arbitrary, hopes so elemental. The second was the urgency of their cause: despite a liberal Administration that would have preferred to equivocate on race as previous liberal Administrations had, the country could no longer ignore those turned away by law and custom from what both Constitution and ideology pledged would be open to all. The gravity of their militancy, the solemnity of their endurance, constituted in the end a great illumination. The third was a man who was—and in our era there has been only one American who authentically merited the appellation—a charismatic personality.

Of course, the movement was much more than one man. But in the mind and soul of Martin Luther King Jr., and in his voice—that voice which may have pierced heaven as certainly as it pierced the walls of callousness on earth, came together the experiences of workers and dreamers so inspired and so often disdained that one does not exaggerate in thinking of them as a species of saints. Dr. King was the first black man in our history—let there be many such!—who had in his legions more whites than blacks. This mass movement of whites as well as of blacks is his distinctive achievement, not because it is better to lead whites than it is to lead blacks, but because without whites stirred to join with blacks in redressing the wrongs done them, those wrongs could never be redressed.

In the fifteen years since the assassination of Dr. King, other black leaders have tried, so to speak, to raise his spirit from the dead, evoke his eloquence, muster his sway. Some of these efforts have been poignant, others silly, still others cynical. The flame cannot be kept alive by self-serving words, and certainly not by actions out of character with the love for America that shines through Dr. King's 1963 speech. Since his death the civil rights leadership has been without a leader. Not that there haven't been pretenders, some of whom had derided him while he lived and for precisely those of his qualities—the courage of the nonviolent preeminent among them—which had won him and them the victories upon which other victories were to be built.

It is instructive and also saddening to recapitulate some of this desultory history. The Student Nonviolent Coordinating Committee dissolved in its rancor toward whites; some of its most prominent leaders scattered—to Africa, to just this side of the asylum, to a political atrophy so total it could be the consequence only of the kind of Jacobin ambition that preceded it. And after years of litigation and unseemly squabbles with its associated Legal Defense Fund, the N.A.A.C.P. does not even know who actually has responsibility for its own operations; some of the community's most respected luminaries have taken to the general press to counsel institutional suicide, desperate but telling advice. Another organization with an identity crisis is the Congress of Racial Equality, the very existence of which is a matter of dispute; suffice it to say that the visionary figure of its early years, James Farmer, was long since gone when the successor leadership found itself in trouble with the New York authorities for cheating on its contributors and its purposes. Mr. Farmer now devotes himself to what has proven the hardest and probably the most necessary public cause, that of integrated housing—a cause which does not interest many in the black leadership (sadly, it does not interest others either) because integrated neighborhoods would threaten the safe seats of the ensconced black politicians. CORE's Floyd McKissick, it will be remembered, tumbled to Richard Nixon for empty promises, as the Southern Christian Leadership Conference's Ralph Abernathy tumbled to Ronald Reagan for even emptier ones.

Because S.C.L.C. was Dr. King's organization, its disintegration is the most poignant. Jesse Jackson struck out on his own out of Chicago; he had a scheme rather than a dream. The scheme seems to work, but to what purpose? In Atlanta, S.C.L.C. has flailed around for more than a decade in search of an issue and a constituency, its activities often an embarrassment even to its well-wishers. Its one asset, the memory of Martin Luther King, having been pressed into promiscuous service, was not appreciating. Coretta King, the faithful widow, sensed the opportunity offered by the twentieth anniversary of Dr. King's great movement—the movement's great moment—and called for a commemoration. Neither in the black leadership nor at the grass roots was there much enthusiasm for a march. But once the idea was announced and the date set, there was no way to resist it; only the Urban League, steadier in its work than the others, declined to participate. In the end, many of those who went to this year's march did so not only to honor the memory of 1963, and not only to support "Jobs, Peace, Freedom" (who could be against them in the abstract?), but also to keep an expression of black protest from falling on its face. Even so, the crowd was smaller than the number that turned out either for labor's 1981 Solidarity Day march in Washington or for the nuclear freeze demonstration in New York last year.

What this malaise in the black leadership reflects is the absence of a vivid moral vision. The absence of that vision is in turn expressed in whatever the leadership undertakes. But there are always individuals and groups at the edges of our political life ready to compensate for the absence of moral clarity with their own sectarian causes. So this march may just be another enterprise, vaguely well intentioned, that became a holding company of ideological sectarianisms. Surely it is another case of manipulation and exploitation of blacks with their organizational needs by whites with their organizational agendas. What, after all, has a speech given in behalf of the Democratic Revolutionary Front of El Salvador got to do with Dr. King's message of nonviolence? What sort of "freedom" is meant when among the speakers and among the conveners and planners are long-time apologists for some of the bloodiest tyrannies of the age? With what ethical credentials does James Abourezk, one-time vicar of the Ayatollah Khomeini in the United States, speak for justice? Why was a representative of the pseudo-pacifist Greenham Common Women's Peace Encampment, which routinely speaks of the American "occupation" of Britain, given a platform to speak in the shadow of Abraham Lincoln, who waged war for a free Union? What is the ideology of the Native American who spoke up for the persecuted Indians of Guatemala but failed to notice the persecuted Indians of Nicaragua? Why did no one mention the Poles?

At least one thing can be said for this motley collection of issues, causes, and allies. This year's march does show that "black nationalism" or separatism is for all intents and purposes dead. In 1963 there was tension between "moderates" like Dr. King and "militants" like John Lewis (a genuinely wise man, now a city councilman in Atlanta). In the following decade, black nationalism flowered (perhaps more strongly in the media than in the community). At SNCC, Mr. Lewis was forced out as insufficiently militant by Stokely Carmichael, who gave way to H. Rap Brown, who was displaced by the Black Panthers, and so on down a diminishing line that has now petered out in the courtroom where a defendant in the Nanuet murder-robbery case is demanding to be tried as a prisoner of war. The phenomena of mau-mauing, of guilt-tripping white liberals, of separatist fantasies, of dashiki-clad jive—these have pretty much run their course. The dream of integration may have lost much of its luster, but the dream of separation has lost even more. The "salt and pepper" constituency that so moved Josephine Baker at the 1963 march, and for whose future she shrewdly feared, has now in some measure been restored. There was no visible racial tension at the march, and that is certainly a good thing. May it also be an auguring.

A symmetrical paradox underlies the assessments by right and left as to whether (and how much) progress against the confines of discrimination has actually been made by black people during the last twenty years. Conservatives say that so much progress has been made that there is virtually nothing left to protest; at the same time they question wholesale the effectiveness of the programs under which much of the progress was actually achieved. Radicals, and some liberals, too, maintain that ours is a relentlessly racist society, questioning whether much progress has been made at all—and suggesting, falsely, that the civil rights movement has been a failure.

Let us review (and revel in) some of the progress that *has* been made. The legal edifice of segregation no longer exists. Twenty years ago blacks could be, and were, legally denied the right to be served in a public restaurant, to stay in a public hotel, to use a public restroom, to sit in a seat of their choice on a public bus. Blacks were quasi-legally denied the right to vote throughout most of the South. All that has utterly changed. Even in Mississippi, the two contenders in the Democratic runoff for governor courted black voters, wanted them to register and to vote; and if, here and there, one still finds reason to send in federal officials to guarantee access to the polls, it is, and everyone knows it, less an omen of the future than a remnant of the past. In thousands of communities across the country, black and white children attend integrated schools—some of them through successful and, in many places, quite uncontroversial, busing programs.

The massive achievements are not simply in the legal sphere. In elite universities and law firms, the barriers to black advancement have crumbled. In various professions newly recruited blacks now command higher salaries than whites, according to the fine old market theory of supply and demand. In these areas, the one impediment to greater black progress is still—and how could it have been otherwise so soon after the political triumph of civil rights?—a shortage of adequately trained individuals. Already troubled black colleges, for example, have suffered from competitive raiding of their faculties by more prestigious institutions. Sometimes, it should be admitted, unqualified blacks advance; that's another sign of parity with whites whose individual progress is, of course, also not always according to the strictest meritocratic standards. New laws and new customs have anointed a class of arbitrarily selected black businessmen to profit from public and private contracts, sometimes not competitively and not always in seemly fashion. An enormous black middle class has emerged which may amount to the most startling and startlingly fast demographic revolution in American history. None of this can truthfully be denied. (The organizers of this march know this, yet their call asserts, preposterously, that there is a "rising tide of extremism" and a serious revival of the Ku Klux Klan. The white sheet hysteria is a contrivance of people who want to be heard and funded but really have nothing to say.)

A particularly striking achievement of these last years is the emergence of elected black politicians whose margins of victory—sometimes whose fundamental bases of support—come from whites. These politicians, especially the big-city mayors, are today perhaps the most important black leaders in the country. Few of them were prominent in the march. Their concerns are those of practical justice; and, alas, even black mayors of big cities must sometimes cut budgets. The intoxicating fantasies of the march about cutting the defense budget by 25 percent will not pay the salaries of any laid-off school teacher or firefighter. The elected black leadership, particularly in the cities, must engage in a brand of coalition-building rather different from the facile ideologized coalitions that appeared on the Mall. One reason that the most pragmatic, which is to say the most practical and programmatic, of these politicians are discomfited by Jesse Jackson's possible candidacy for the Presidency is that they see it (his personal hustling aside) as intruding the heady and illusionary slogans of the frustrated black streets onto the relatively more concrete politics of realistic coalitions and compromise.

Nonetheless, the frustrated black streets and the need for coalitions with liberal whites are the immediate polar constraints within which these politicians work. For all the advances made by blacks into the middle and upper middle classes, the realities at the bottom of the black social ladder may never have been grimmer. The fact that there are black millionaires does nothing to elevate the life of the black poor. No group's rich really elevate its poor unless and until its communal institutions establish bonds of loyalty that move downward in the hierarchy as well as upward; this has not yet happened in black America. Even the importance of the achieving black role model seems to have been overestimated as an instrument for mobilizing the dormant ambitions of the black poor. The black professional class, the black professoriat, the black entrepreneurial vanguard have simply not taken responsibility for their own. There is not at this crucial stage in the development of the black community even a single thoughtful and deeply honest publication among black intellectuals—there is hardly a forum of any sort in this vein—willing to engage in those necessary acts of painful self-criticism without which neither intellectual clarity about the black social condition nor concrete understanding of how to alter it will be attained.

The statistical indices of black (and non-black) poverty are rising; and if there were some psychological index of black poverty the reality it would illumine would be terribly dispiriting. Barely half of black men over sixteen are employed. Some of this unemployment is a direct function of government policy and temporary or permanent economic trends. But many of these are unemployed because they are unemployable—not because they are indolent but because they are, perhaps even in some clinical sense, depressed. That's what cumulative poverty does. It breeds generation upon generation of excluded, hopeless, chronically dependent people. The policies that derive from the Reaganite doctrine of the stone heart exacerbate and intensify this often inarticulated suffering. But they are not its fundamental causes.

Reagan as political target is a convenient and useful improvisation. His draconian cuts in expenditures for special education, for example, have already impeded the practical adventure of learning for precisely those youngsters who require additional help and inspiration. It is, after all, a truism that not everyone comes to the doors of opportunity without need of further assistance. Of course, this one instance of social parsimony does not exhaust the ways in which the present Administration has turned its back on the poor in order to pave the way for the greater prosperity of the speculating castes. Never in our history has more of the sparse supply of investment capital been funneled to nonproductive, unnecessary, and socially disfiguring tax shelter ventures. So Reagan as political target is also a status quite deserved, though it is for us still a little much to hear him routinely depicted as the warmongering focus of absolute evil by folk who have embraced, let us say, Yasir Arafat as a man of peace, or who trip grudgingly over their words in naming men like Yuri Andropov and Fidel Castro for what they are.

One of the unexamined assumptions of the march is support for affirmative action in employment and schooling—an unexceptionable notion when it means vigorously recruiting qualified black applicants, a controversial (and, to us, unacceptable) one when it means, as it often does, quotas. It is revealing to recall what quotas meant in the past: an arbitrary exclusion of Jews or Orientals from jobs and schools where their ability to perform was never doubted. Quotas now mean an arbitrary inclusion of minority individuals in positions where the ability to perform is precisely at issue. An inevitable corollary is the exclusion of others whose performance is not in question. Which brings us to the problem of coalition-building. How are stable and deeply rooted liberal alliances with trade unions—rather than perfunctory and symbolic appearances by trade union leaders—to be secured when quotas undermine the hard-won and justified principle of seniority in the workplace? The vesting of blacks and other minorities with corporate rights to a precise share of the goods of society is a significant departure from our constitutional and philosophical tradition, which recognizes no legal entitlements or rights to groups but only to individuals. This departure has already motivated other racial and ethnic groups to make unprecedented corporate claims on the public weal. It is a sure formula for inflaming and perpetrating intergroup hatred. And it won't work for the black poor. Their children are done no service by having teachers whose appointment has been secured through less exacting requirements. And what does anyone think is the consequence of the application of racial quotas in public housing projects—those grim urban fortresses of despair—whereby blacks are plucked from the end of a long chronological waiting list to make sure that there are 20 percent of them and 10 percent Hispanics in the least dreary of the dreary apartments? How explain that to depressed whites? And how justify it? Maybe the overachieving Jewish lad whose "rightful" place at the Harvard Law School will be taken by a somewhat less overachieving black lad (and, in any case, not usually from disadvantaged background) will end up at the University of Chicago; it may not be fair—and the question of fairness is an important question!—but it's probably no great tragedy. And it won't end up in violence on the streets either. Not so other applications of quotas, which are the more invidious because they extract society's concessions to black people as compensation for past wrongs from other people—not inordinately privileged people, by the way, and wholly innocent of enforcing or profiting from the black condition. And what kind of a patchwork country would we be, how open would the doors of opportunity be, if each group—black, Jewish, Italian, Irish, Chinese, Chicano, etc.—had its mandated portion of Columbia Medical School graduates, federal judges, magazine editors, airline pilots?

Let us anticipate that "Reaganism is obliterated from the face of this earth," as one speaker at the march characterized its goal. Let us contemplate that Fritz Mondale is elected President with a good liberal Congress, with many more blacks in it than in the current one. Let us even imagine for the moment that the next President is not Mr. Mondale, or even Alan Cranston, but Jesse Jackson—and that he turns out to surprise everyone with the soundness of his political imagination. Let us assume, then, that there won't be an MX, but a nuclear freeze instead. What, five or ten years hence, will be the situation of the black poor? There is a specter at once haunting and inhibiting the economic and social progress of black Americans. It is almost impossible to allude to it without being accused of racism. But it is a tragic truth on which the indices of black poverty, statistical and psychological, are based. There is an epidemic—the metaphor of pathology is not inappropriate, for what is involved is the health of the black community—of single-parent families, unmarried mothers, deserting fathers. Recent figures from the Bureau of the Census show the extent of the epidemic. Forty-one percent of black families are headed by women without husbands present, up almost a third in the last decade. The divorce rate among blacks has more than doubled in a decade, and is now double that of whites. The percentage of black children living in one-parent homes rose from 32 percent to 49 percent in the same period; these children's homes may account for close to 80 percent of the black poor. It's obvious why these families are poorer: none of them has income from two wage earners, few from even one. Most are supported by the welfare system. Even more to the point is the social contagion of teenage pregnancies, which would only be exacerbated were the Administration's war on the abortion option to succeed. But even with widely available birth control information and publicly funded abortions (not exactly an ideal expenditure of social capital), the demographics tell a terrible story, presage a worse one: young women, girls really, still children themselves having children, passing on depression and helplessness from generation to generation. According to a study in the May/June issue of *Family Planning Perspectives*, a publication of the Guttmacher Institute, the fertility rate of black teenagers in the United States is by far the highest in the developed world. For every thousand black females under nineteen, most of them unmarried, there are 515 children born into all kinds of disadvantages of life: inadequate mothering or worse, the absence of a father, the chintzy and humiliating public dole as the most common source of income, the trap of dependence. Among teenagers between fourteen and seventeen in the West, black fertility exceeds the next highest rate by a factor of 2.5 to 1. For unmarried mothers of all ages the ratio of black to white is almost 5 to 1; for ages fifteen to nineteen, the ratio is almost 6 to 1. This is a demographic disaster—nothing less.

A convener of the Washington march and the Delegate to Congress from the District of Columbia, Walter Fauntroy, dismisses the connection between black poverty and black family structure. Some hard-hearted on the right say it is the whole story. It is, alas, much of the story, that part of it not easily affected by even the most farsighted and generous public expenditures and public attitudes. But it should not embarrass black people or the black leadership. The disintegration of the black family, once so stable, is another of the consequences of our indifferent—no, cruel—past. But this is 1983, not the years of slavery, or of the post-Reconstruction racist consolidation, or of the disruptive migrations northward. Though it won't be easy, someone must begin to address the problem now, and it probably should be blacks first. And a march of all the causes on the left does little more than divert attention from what makes miserable the most miserable of our black brothers and sisters.

Uneasy Holiday

TAYLOR BRANCH

FEBRUARY 3, 1986

There was always a special patriotism to the speeches of Martin Luther King. No other American orator could bring audiences to their feet by reciting three full stanzas of "My Country, 'Tis of Thee." From there he often soared across the American landscape in perorations calling on freedom to ring "from the granite peaks of New Hampshire . . . from the mighty Alleghenies of Pennsylvania . . . from the snowcapped Rockies of Colorado . . . from Lookout Mountain in Tennessee! Let it ring . . . from Stone Mountain in Georgia!" On through Southern states in whose capitol buildings black people dared not seek a drink of water, King rang freedom bells, touching his audiences with ecstatic boldness. "And when that happens," he said finally, "all of God's children—black men and white men, Jews and Gentiles, Catholics and Protestants—will be able to go ahead and sing with new meaning, 'Free at last! Free at last! Thank God Almighty I'm free at last!'"

On January 20 King's own name will be tolled from those hilltops. Children will let fly balloons in Maryland and Arizona. World leaders will pay their respects at his tomb in Atlanta, and pilgrims will retrace the steps of his marches. By act of Congress, duly signed by the president, his birthday will be celebrated as our tenth federal holiday on the third Monday of this and every succeeding January. Officially, King's Birthday joins New Year's Day, Christmas, Labor Day, Independence Day, and the other five working days on which the government closes its doors.

The enshrinement is a remarkable phenomenon. It is accomplished less than 18 years after King's murder, in the month when he would have turned but 57 years of age. By contrast, George Washington's birthday was not made a federal holiday until 1879, 80 years after his death. The gestation period for Columbus Day was 176 years, from its origins in 1792 as a private festivity at Tammany Hall to its official adoption by Congress in 1968. Lincoln, whose birthday is celebrated in 32 states, came closest to federal recognition in 1920, but Southerners killed the House bill in the Senate.

Ironically, the creation of the holiday owes something to a negative trend in contemporary race relations. In 1983 the Reagan administration was proposing tax exemptions for segregated schools, delaying an extension of the Voting Rights Act, and mounting an attack on all affirmative action programs as "quotas," which exacerbated antagonisms between blacks and Jews. Some Republican leaders, fearing that their entire party was headed toward extinction among black voters, resolved to make amends for these injuries with a holiday. The leaders of the King Holiday Commission are aware of such limitations to their support. They know they are not riding an unmixed tide of national sentiment, and that some of King's admirers and detractors alike regard his new day as a political gesture, a throwaway holiday for blacks. In death as in life, King's followers struggle for recognition while King himself reaches for something deeper and almost unfathomable. All this makes for an uneasy new holiday, mysterious in origin and meaning.

Even in the context of previous holiday politics, the enactment of the King holiday legislation in 1983 stands out as a paradox. It was both routine and explosively controversial. With scarcely a flicker of outside notice, the bill reached the House floor under a suspension of the rules and passed 338 to 90. Howard Baker, then the Senate's Republican leader, decided to bypass the Senate committee process and place the House bill directly on the voting calendar, in a procedure normally reserved for minor business. The bill passed 78 to 22. Every Southern Democrat except John Stennis of Mississippi voted for it. So did Strom Thurmond, Jeremiah Denton, and Paul Laxalt—three of the four conservative Republicans who had issued a report opposing the holiday as premature and too costly. The minority opposition was concentrated in the arid Western states, where black voters are rare. President Reagan signed the measure less than three months after it came to the House.

Whisked into law, the King holiday matter receded. Neither President Reagan nor the news media did much to herald the approach of the holiday. Congress stalled for nearly a year before creating a commission to plan the first celebration, and then provided no money, staff, or office space. Coretta Scott King, Senator Robert Dole, Senator Edward Kennedy, and the other commissioners were obliged to go begging for a Washington headquarters, until HUD Secretary Samuel R. Pierce donated spare rooms in the HUD building. Pierce's generosity provided another of many ironies buried in the holiday politics. More than 20 years ago, when top FBI officials launched a covert campaign to brand King a "fraud, demagogue and moral scoundrel," they sought to replace him as a national leader of American black people with Samuel R. Pierce, who was then a Republican lawyer in New York.

Contempt for King still exists. It flashed during the Senate's consideration of the holiday legislation in 1983, giving evidence that the quiet dispatch of that business was anything but routine. Senator Jesse Helms of North Carolina attacked King as a communist sympathizer or worse, and in seeking to open sealed FBI files on King he relished the point that it was a liberal attorney general, Robert Kennedy, who had authorized the original wiretaps. This provoked an emotional response from Senator Edward Kennedy. "If Robert Kennedy were alive today, he would be the first person to say that it was wrong ever to wiretap Martin Luther King," he declared. When Helms doggedly challenged the Senate to debate the secret history of those wiretaps, Senator Daniel Patrick Moynihan flung Helms's packet of FBI material to the Senate floor with an angry shout that it was "filth." There were gasps from the gallery when Senator Bill Bradley said that it was impossible for him to give Helms "the due respect of a colleague." Speakers on both sides acknowledged an "atmosphere of tension" on the Senate floor. It was due, one Senator said edgily, to "a number of circumstances that we are all aware of." Race, scandal, war, communism, money, religion—all the most volatile subjects of political discourse converged to shake the Senate briefly from its famous languid decorum.

President Reagan performed no better at his press conference that same day. When a reporter asked whether he thought King had been a communist sympathizer, the president replied, "Well, we'll know in about 35 years, won't we?" He meant that the answer had to await the court-ordered date for the unsealing of the FBI bugging material. This fatuous remark so stunned the assembled reporters that there followed only one feeble question about "where the logic is here." President Reagan, while announcing that he would sign legislation honoring King above nearly all the Founding Fathers, reserved judgment about King's basic loyalty to the country.

The press conference backed swiftly away from a moment that was not only searingly awkward but fundamentally misinformed. The sealed records from King's FBI file do not address the question of King's political allegiance. Those records, by the tens of thousands of pages, are available for public inspection in the FBI Reading Room. The sealed ones are about King's personal life, especially his extramarital sex life, as intercepted by FBI bugs and wiretaps. Out of ignorance, or perhaps extreme reluctance to touch the delicate issue of the sex lives of political leaders, none of the major news media mentioned this glaring discrepancy between the public description of the records and their actual content. By passing along this error, which was common to President Reagan's remark and to Senator Helms's campaign to unseal the records, those who framed the public debate over the King holiday fostered the slanderous misimpression that King's entire public career might have been a spy's ruse.

It is also possible that the politicians were speaking more manipulatively in code, knowing that to harp on secrets buried in FBI files might quicken by suggestion the vague but widespread rumors about King's private life. Even Senator Helms did not dare to address this subject directly, however, and this was perhaps his only area of agreement with King's most ardent supporters. Skittishness about speaking personally of King is almost universal. His enemies seem to fear that to do so would backfire, or expose their utter lack of knowledge about him as a human being, while his admirers seem to fear that anything less than perfect will slide or be twisted into degradation.

Questions of identity dissolve in the insecurities of race. It is well to remember that King lived nearly his entire life calling himself a Negro instead of a black man. The very name of his race was in flux, and for most of his years the personal attributes of Negroes were virtually invisible within the white culture. He forced himself upon the world as a political issue. During his lifetime there was little appetite or conditioning to absorb more about him.

Relatively few blacks and practically no whites ever knew, for instance, that King was anything but a champion among his fellow black Baptist preachers in the huge, six million-member National Baptist Convention. This was the center of King's church heritage, where both his father and grandfather had achieved national reputations. The convention's annual meetings were advertised as the largest gatherings of black people under one roof anywhere in the world—up to 20,000 preachers, deacons, choristers, and laymen from the richest and most powerful institution of the black culture, meeting in an atmosphere crossed between that of a giant synod and a national political convention.

When King and his civil rights forces moved to take over the convention at Kansas City in 1961, they were repulsed in an ugly riot during which one preacher was killed. The victorious conservative president blamed King publicly for the riot, threw the power of the organized church against most of King's civil rights initiatives, and remained in power another 20 years, long enough to support Ronald Reagan for president. King, effectively accused of murder and excommunicated from his own national church, withdrew from the convention for the remainder of his life. This bitter experience blocked his career ambitions as a churchman and drove him toward the unpleasant conclusion that a majority of his peers never would embrace his nonviolent resistance. Within a few months he went to Albany, Georgia—alone, without the legions of Convention Baptists he had hoped to marshal—and was swept up in his first sustained campaign of civil disobedience to the segregation laws.

None of this registered in public. One might have expected the segregationist press to trumpet the news that King was implicated in the violent and shameful debacle, and that his fellow black preachers rejected his plans for integration. The chasm between the races was so wide, however, that the shattering conflict at Kansas City was a silent event to the white world, which made a habit of noticing King only when he could not be avoided. Unfamiliarity and discomfort blotted out the texture of King's life amid black preachers, among many other central aspects of his personality.

Yet when a Justice Department official simply offered him an automobile ride in the autumn of 1963, a front-page scandal erupted over charges of government favoritism for black leaders. The sensitivities of race exposed King to bizarre disparities of perception. His political genius lay in his strength to maintain balanced judgment under constant bombardment from a wide range of forces—J. Edgar Hoover, the conservative Baptist incumbent, King's contentious aides, his conscience, his bitter rivals within the civil rights movement, Southern governors, condemned prisoners appealing for his help—always knowing that his every deed and statement might be magnified or reduced a thousand times by the trick mirrors of race. Similarly, his gift as an orator lay in his ability to deliver the same speech in a way that would move both urban sophisticates who wanted to hear about Camus and unlettered church folk who wanted to hear about the furniture in heaven.

Now we are beginning to fashion a holiday mythology based on images that covered the cocoon of King's life. Almost inevitably, he is being celebrated for his achievements as they registered in the majority culture—for his great marches and civil rights laws, and for the Nobel Peace Prize. He is seen as the epitome of black success, rising from utter obscurity to the heights of international acclaim: just as Lincoln overcame his log cabin origins, so King conquered the limitations of racism. Like all myths, these contain truth, but in King's case they threaten to distort the inner progression of his life and to rob the new holiday of its true meaning. To celebrate King as the paramount black political symbol makes him a brittle icon—a counterpart to Britain's Prince Charles. From the core of King's religious belief to the edge of his political triumphs, his life was about status and human pride, but by his own lights the story ran counter to most of the King mythology.

The young King is generally portrayed as a well-educated but conventional Southern Baptist minister, whose transformation into a man of stature began suddenly when the Montgomery bus boycott made him a celebrity in national race politics. In fact, by inheritance and oratorical gifts, King was a prince within his national church long before the 1955 boycott. While still a student, he established a reputation that brought him invitations to preach in the largest black churches—New York congregations claiming up to 10,000 members. When he left college to attend a Pennsylvania seminary in 1948, he was the only member of his integrated class wealthy enough to support himself without at least part-time work.

Until midway through his career, King remained something of a dandy.

He wore expensive clothes, savored the opera, and dabbled at golf. He never gave up dramatic late entrances and other showmanship techniques of a master preacher, and he was accomplished in the formal etiquette—reminiscent of Renaissance court diplomacy—by which his preacher's fraternity managed and divided clerical prerogatives. Congregations ceremoniously presented him and his colleagues with wooden gift boxes stuffed with cash; special tributes to the ministers lasted hours. The preacher was a monarch, cut to the figure of Moses.

King embodied this role at the same time he rebelled against it. From the beginning he warned against the special temptations of success among a status-hungry people, denouncing the predilection of his fellow preachers for long Cadillacs. As glory fountained up beneath him, these harsh warnings from his own personal theology loomed ever larger in his life. He preached that privileged people require special discipline to be at peace with justice. His wife recalled that "his conscience fairly devoured him."

By family training he was extremely sensitive to shadings of his public image, which he labored adeptly to manage. In the 1950s he maneuvered to become the first black civil rights leader to meet with Eisenhower, and his 1964 trip to visit the pope was at least partly a promotional tour, conceived in awareness that the Norwegian Parliament was considering him for the Nobel Prize. He had given up his fanciest clothes, however, and nearly all his money. He never bought a Cadillac. Within minutes of hearing he would receive the prize, he announced that he would give the $250,000 purse to the movement. By then jealousy was poisoning some of his dearest friendships, and he knew that FBI officials were working diligently to blackmail or disgrace him with intercepted evidence of his extramarital affairs. King pledged to give them up—but failed. These personal ordeals, though central to the furnace of his character, did not change the direction of his public record. He returned from Oslo almost directly to the jails of Selma, Alabama, to begin the campaign for the Voting Rights Act, which transformed American politics by enfranchising black citizens in the rural South.

There followed the three years that foreshadowed the surly mood of American politics after his death. The most influential civil rights leaders repudiated his protest against the war in Vietnam. The editors of *Life* called his first major Vietnam speech "a demagogic slander that sounded like a script for Radio Hanoi." Meanwhile, the spirit of his movement disintegrated amid riots, repression, and the surge of black pride. Black opinion leaders began to speak of nonviolence, and of King, with condescension. White intellectuals ignored him as a tediously religious Uncle Tom. His literary agent sent word that New York publishers expressed no interest in a new book by King on any subject. King kept moving away from the "mountain-top" of Oslo. While other aspiring leaders of both races kept clamoring for their moments in the White House, King stopped going at all. "He's canceled two engagements with me, and I don't understand it," President Johnson complained in a private memo. At the end, King was not in the company of white presidents or black elites, but marching with the garbagemen of Memphis.

He had the driven energy to help lift a people to a new identity and position of respect, and in the process he acquired what is commonly regarded as the highest honor in the Western world. This is the storybook side of King, which has its place. But the more revealing side lies in his determination to reclaim the common level of humanity. He resisted not just the expectation but the insistent demands of his peers that he allow himself to be feted and toasted as a symbol of hard-earned prestige. Instead, he pushed his way back down to jail, to new battles that left him nearly a pariah, and finally to the garbage strike in Memphis. The proud young doctor forged a prophet's humility out of his determination to leave behind what he called "a committed life." This downward thrust makes him a transcendent figure rather than merely a romantic one. In this respect, it is a disquieting sign that the official literature for the new King holiday seldom mentions the crucible years after he won the Nobel Prize.

Inescapably, the meaning of King's life springs from religion as much as politics. Born into a culture in which the pulpit was the key to riches as well as salvation, he struggled with religion as preachers' kids often do, having grown up privy to both the trade secrets of the business and its claim to ultimate reality. His religious beliefs never were orthodox. He studied at a seminary teeming with freethinking professors who doubted, for instance, the existence of the historical Moses—on the ground that no Moses character had been located in Egyptian or Persian texts covering that era. King adapted to such skepticism more readily than most of his classmates, because he was searching for an honest way to recover from a prolonged spell of blanket disbelief. In particular, he was troubled by liberal theology's answer to the age-old problem of reconciling the idea of God with the presence of evil in the world. He rejected the progressive notion that intellectual and scientific progress could steadily reduce evil, and thereby the need to explain it. Although such an outlook was ascribed almost automatically to King and Social Gospel crusaders, he stubbornly refused to believe that education or comfort made people less sinful. On the contrary, he thought these attainments fed the central moral sin of pride.

Not until late in his studies did King find a way to join his yearning for justice in the world to an idea of God in the universe. He fixed upon the theory that from human self-centeredness comes an ingrained capacity for "enemy thinking," or self-justifying moral codes. These accommodate the removal or blotting out of people, as in racial segregation. In extreme form they can invert morality altogether, as when the most heinous sins of ordinary life become the sacred duty of soldiers, Klansmen, or terrorists. King merely resolved that it was possible, by supreme acts of faith and human will, to combat enemy thinking without falling prey to it, to affirm that "the arm of the moral universe is long, but it bends toward justice." By such efforts, he sought to uphold the existence of God. Far from being a comfortable or conventional theology, this was nearly a desperate one, linking King's personal religious doubts not only to the plight of his race but also to the fate of the bomb-threatened globe.

For years before and after his famous "I Have a Dream" speech of 1963, King identified the American dream with Jefferson's familiar credo from the Declaration of Independence: "All men are created equal . . . endowed by their creator with certain inalienable rights." He praised the passage for its universalism, and then he praised it also for "something else" at its center—"something ultimately distinguishes democracy from systems of government which make the state an end within itself." The dream, he said, "affirms that there are certain basic rights that are neither conferred by nor derived from the state." This idea was dear to him. He interpreted it to mean that religion and democratic politics are united in their purest essences and yearnings, beneath all the imperfections of doctrine. The politician should acknowledge a mission derived from the spirit, not from worldliness. The preacher should be out in the world defending the endowments of the creator. And the individualism inherent in the rights—"life, liberty, and the pursuit of happiness"—embraced both the personalism of King's own religious belief and the freedom-dream of his politics.

King's version of the dream had nothing to do with the tinsel of prestige or windfall riches. Indeed, he sought to reclaim the sacredness of free human character in a country he saw as glutted with wealth and power. His deity was a personal God whose benevolence could be believed, communicated—even demonstrated—as when his crowds responded to the cry of his favorite prophet, Amos, to "let judgment run down as waters, and righteousness as a mighty stream!" This was the spirit of the civil rights movement, which lived in the bottomless passion of his speeches.

Time can narcotize even national holidays, turning cherished historical moments into sale-a-thons, binges, highway casualty statistics. Still, holidays are among a nation's fundamental traditions. Like hidden blood vessels, they carry life sources so vital to a culture that we can be oblivious to their meaning until crisis or inspiration flushes it scarlet to the surface. Arbitrarily, to mark and measure the passage of time, we have fixed the new year upon a certain day in early winter, in a celebration dating from Roman sacrifices to the two-faced God, Janus. Almost as arbitrarily, a church council in what we call the fourth century selected December 25 as the birth date for Jesus of Nazareth, and for 16 centuries since then the Christmas birthday celebration has stood handsomely among the winter festivals of the world's major religions.

King's holiday is yet a blink against these swaths of time, but already it stands out among the nation's permanent landmarks. With the holiday calendar and the monument grounds of the capital city filling toward capacity, it appears that during its formative two centuries the government of the United States constructed three major political monuments—to Washington, to Jefferson, and to Lincoln. Most of Washington's parks and traffic circles are named for military leaders of the Civil War era. The six House and Senate office buildings are named for 20th-century legislators of modest historical resonance—Cannon, Longworth, Rayburn, Russell, Dirksen, and Hart. And among the eight purely American holidays, beyond the two imported from the ancient Mediterranean, King's Birthday alone stands in honor of a preacher, a Ph.D., a black man, and a martyr who was wiretapped and reviled by officials of the same government that elevated him. King never held or sought public office, but he shaped more sweeping political change than any politician or private citizen of his era. He did not live out the American dream, as is obvious from his short, tormented biography. But for his age he did reinterpret the nation's precious freedoms along the edge between religion and politics, where the country was founded. For this he earned his holiday.

A glance around the country—from the liberated, resurgent South to the faces in mayors' seats, office buildings, television shows, and even college sports arenas—confirms the magnitude of the transformation wrought by King and his movement. We are that much further from South Africa. A glance there, or to the Middle East, or to eruptions of race hatred in Philadelphia and other cities, confirms that a renewal of that spirit could not be wasted. This is what the holiday is for. King was a black leader but never a parochial one. The boundless vision of his message touched people far beyond his camp and sowed changes more profound than political accommodation.

Ed Bethune, a little-known, last-term congressman, brought a small sign of it to the floor of the House of Representatives. "Mr. Speaker, as a Republican and a former FBI agent, I rise in strong support of the Martin Luther King holiday bill," he said. After describing the travail of the civil rights movement in his home state of Arkansas, he continued: "And do you know what we learned out of all that? The great changes are not made here in the legislative chambers or in the judicial halls. The great changes in this world are made in the hearts and minds of men and women. Attitudes are so important. I think that this holiday for Martin Luther King will give us an annual opportunity to recommit ourselves to the proposition that all men are created equal. It will nourish the spirit of reconciliation that we need so desperately in this country right now."

The Crisis of Caste

C. VANN WOODWARD

NOVEMBER 6, 1989

Outbursts of racial tension or violence in America usually coincide with disparagement of past efforts to improve relations and predictions of worse things to come. It might help to place recent outbursts in perspective by recalling some past experiences. On August 11, 1965, just five days after the civil rights movement had reached its peak with the signing of the Voting Rights Act, a riot broke out in the Watts section of Los Angeles. It raged for a week, left 34 dead (all but three of them blacks), injured more than a thousand, and required military occupation of 46 square miles to halt the violence. Watts was followed by 150 major riots and hundreds of minor ones that summer and the next three summers. Cities were aflame all over the country. The worst of the riots and the bloodiest of the century occurred in Detroit in July 1967. Forty-three were killed, 14 square miles of the city were gutted by fire, and 15,000 troops were brought in to bring the riot to a halt.

Historical analogies can be as misleading as helpful, but some are unavoidable. Comparisons between the 1860s and the 1960s in the history of American race relations have proved all but irresistible when the civil rights movement comes under discussion. The two peaks of progress that face each other across the century challenge comparison, as do the shadows that they cast before them. By calling the civil rights movement "The Second Reconstruction," in an article for *Harper's* in April 1965, I should say that I intended the comparison as a warning rather than a prediction. It was to suggest that if the soaring promises and expectations of 1965 were followed by the complacency, neglect, and betrayal that prevailed after the promises of 1865, we might face once more the failure and reaction that disgraced the First Reconstruction. Although it is impossible to believe that the analogy will hold up to the extent of predicting for the 1990s the horrors of the 1890s that wiped out the gains of the First Reconstruction, it must be admitted that there are some signs pointing that way.

Before turning to them, however, it is important to give full acknowledgment to such progress as has been made. One way of summing that up is by quoting Chief Justice Earl Warren's description of the situation of black people in the South and in some measure in other parts of the country during the early 1950s:

> They could not live where they desired, they could not work where white people worked, except in menial positions. . . . They could not use the same rest rooms, drinking fountains, or telephone booths. They could not eat in the same restaurants, sleep in the same hotels, be treated in the same hospitals. . . . They could not attend the same public schools. . . . They were denied admission to any university attended by whites, whether public or private.
>
> They were denied the right to sit on juries even when their own lives, freedom, or property were involved. . . .
>
> They were segregated on buses, street cars, trains, ships, and airplanes and terminals of all kinds. They were not allowed to vote.

Granted that the wrongs are slow to be redressed and the rights have yet to be fully restored, the mere enumeration of wrongs to be righted should curb hasty dismissal of past achievements in the struggle against the Jim Crow system. Granted too that the gains black people have made during the last 30 or 40 years in schooling, in earnings, in the military services, in the occupations and the professions, in elective and appointive offices and in politics generally, have been limited and remain far lower than the levels whites have long enjoyed, they are nevertheless of undeniable importance. The same is true, both as to the progress and its limits, of advances in the harmony of relations between races at some levels. No amount of cynicism should be permitted to dismiss these gains. Having registered and underscored those concessions, we are on firmer ground in assessing recent evidence of a contrary sort, evidence of stagnation and retrogression in many areas, some of which had earlier seen years of gratifying progress.

If Gunnar Myrdal's *American Dilemma* (1944) and the Kerner Report (1968) were landmarks in the history of the Second Reconstruction, a new book titled *A Common Destiny: Blacks in American Society* (1989) may earn comparable status in time. The work of a committee of social scientists, it lacks the readability of its predecessors and will not likely have the public attention they received, but its findings are not to be overlooked. Throughout its pages, reluctantly recorded, run negative and pessimistic themes. Several of these are caught in the following passage:

> Since the mid-1970s, many signs of stagnation or even retrogression have appeared in some important measures of income, health, education, and conditions of black community and family life: increased poverty, a decrease in college enrollment of blacks, an increased proportion of

households headed by poor single women, and continuing high unemployment of both men and women. After a decade and a half of devoting great attention but little pragmatic action to these conditions, they have reached a critical stage.

The decline of recent years in many of the areas mentioned here—health, income, schooling—has often been preceded by a period of striking improvement that has been suddenly halted or reversed. And improvement at the upper end of the economic scale has been accompanied by decline at the lower end, where the great majority of the black population is located. This polarizing tendency is illustrated by changes in family income. While black families with incomes over $50,000 grew from 4.7 percent in 1970 to 8.8 percent in 1986 (when 22 percent of white families were in that category), black families with incomes of less than $10,000 grew from 26.8 to 30.2 percent. And while annual earnings of black male college graduates rose 6 percent, blacks with high school degrees fell 5 percent further behind.

In education black students made substantial progress in several ways up to the early or mid-1970s, but since then they have stalled or declined. In higher education the percentage of undergraduate, graduate, and faculty blacks has declined generally. The rate of black high school graduates attending college rose rapidly to 48 percent in 1977, only to fall to 36.5 percent in 1986. Slippage and declines in status and rating in economic, health, and other categories in addition to education follow upon years of remarkable advance.

There appears to be no plausible reason to doubt a considerable increase among whites in acceptance of the right of blacks to equal opportunity, but endorsement of principle is often accompanied by rejection of measures designed to achieve the principle. Large-scale desegregation of schools occurred in the South in the 1960s and 1970s, but the pace has slowed, and the amount of racial separation remains high outside the South. Even within desegregated schools means are often found to keep black and white students separated. Access to housing has increased for blacks in some parts of the country, but residential segregation in metropolitan areas remains about as high as it was in the 1960s. Black participation has appreciably increased in sports, entertainment, arts, and public schools, but apart from the Army, this has not meant true integration or the elimination of racial separation in American life. The prospects for achieving those goals appear remote, and there seems to be no reasonable hope in the foreseeable future for colorblind assimilation.

To speak of racial averages among blacks in the last decade or more is to speak in terms of slippage, stagnation, or retrogression. That is discouraging enough, but those terms prove wholly inadequate when we turn to what is happening in the urban ghetto and the inner-city population. On that subject a vocabulary of crisis is required. Demographers have coined the term "hypersegregation" to describe the phenomenon. This is race relations without any relations between races—almost total segregation. It was rapid urbanization of blacks in smaller numbers that brought on the Jim Crow system in the South in the first place. More extensive in the North than in the South at first, Jim Crow began to be enforced and rigidly regimented by law in the South in the 1880s. These laws continued to be elaborated in the decades following. But that was a century or more ago, and laws to enforce the system have long since been declared unconstitutional. Now we are told in a disturbing recent study that "racial segregation in this country is deeper and more profound than previous attempts to study it had indicated."

This study represents an exhaustive investigation of 22,000 neighborhoods, in 60 cities, including ten large Northern metropolitan areas that contain 29 percent of the urban black population of the country. The work was directed by Douglas S. Massey and Nancy A. Denton of the University of Chicago and published in the August 1989 issue of *Demography*. Hypersegregation not only greatly accentuates the level of segregation for blacks in any dimension but markedly increases the number of ways and areas to which segregation extends. Black patterns of fertility, marriage, and family have diverged more sharply from the mainstream in the last decade, while poverty and unemployment are increasingly concentrated in the black inner city. Even "black ghetto speech has grown progressively more distinct from the standard English" of whites. The result is a vicious circle in which the longer blacks are made victims of the white stereotypes that foster hypersegregation, the more they appear to conform to the stereotypes that were used to justify segregation in the first place, and the deeper victims sink in isolation.

The plight of the hypersegregated cannot be understood, of course, without taking into account the environment in which they are trapped. That includes the disintegrating families and the multiplication of female-headed households, fatherless children, child mothers, and homeless people. They live in streets brutalized by crime amid people crazed by drugs. They live in communities deserted by the strong, the able, and the resourceful members who were liberated by the success of the civil rights movement they once led, and promptly got out. Among these were some individuals with political talents who have become mayors of increasing numbers of our largest cities. This is not to blame them for what happened in the inner cities, but the coincidence of their rise and the increase of hypersegregation does illustrate the paradox of the civil rights movement. The unliberated at the same time find less and less concern for their plight in the higher courts, in the federal administration, and in a country where racial segregation is regaining wide acceptance and resistance to it increasingly seems not worth the trouble, even among its victims.

The terms "class" and "underclass" are constantly used in reference to blacks in the more hopeless ranks. Yet the condition of these people is not adequately defined by the socioeconomic determinants of class, such as unemployment and poverty. Hispanic Americans are often lumped with Afro-Americans, and among the lower ranks they do have many class characteristics in common with blacks. But the study of hypersegregation made extensive comparisons of blacks and Hispanics and found marked differences in the degree and the multiplicity of ways in which blacks were penalized and excluded. "Blacks are thus unique in experiencing multidimensional hypersegregation," Massey and Denton point out. Slow and reluctant to admit the existence of class distinctions in their democracy, Americans are now faced with entrenched realities of caste distinctions.

The analogy between the outcome of the first Reconstruction and the second, between what followed in the 1890s and may follow in the 1990s, remains what it was when it was first made in April 1965, a warning rather than a prediction. But in the intervening quarter century, the warning signals have kept multiplying.

PART IV

Fights: "What Do the Liberals Hope For?"

Liberalism vs. War

HERBERT CROLY

DECEMBER 8, 1920

The editor of The New Republic *is profoundly distressed to discover that liberalism has undergone an eclipse since 1912 when the bulk of the Progressives turned to Wilson as their Moses. Mr. Croly attributes this eclipse chiefly "to the unreality which liberals have allowed to pervade liberalism." Close at hand is a much clearer and better reason. The temporary knell of American liberalism was sounded the minute its false leader put it into the war. This fact naturally does not appeal to* The New Republic, *because its editors have boasted that they helped to put the country into the struggle . . .*

—*THE NATION* OF NOVEMBER 3RD, 1920

In the foregoing passage *The Nation* puts a drastic interpretation upon the relation between liberalism and war. The two are absolutely incompatible. Liberalism necessarily languishes in so far as it approves of war and necessarily thrives in so far as it opposes war. The rule applies to all liberalism and to all war, and it provides, consequently, a standard with which to measure the behavior of liberals during the late war. The existing eclipse of liberalism is due, not to the war itself or to any essential defect of liberal doctrine and practice as clues to human liberation, but to the unnecessary endorsement of the war by liberals. If they had chosen to oppose the war, liberalism instead of suffering from an eclipse, would now shine like a star in the Heavens for the guidance of those who are seeking salvation.

This interpretation of the relation between liberalism and war seems to be finding favor with an increasing number of people and under the circumstances its popularity is not unnatural. Considering the nature of the Treaty of Versailles, the grave probability of future wars and the irremediable calamities which are in consequence overtaking the lives of so many innocent and helpless human beings, pro-war liberals have much to explain. They usually explain it by dwelling on the greater calamities which would have resulted from the refusal to fight, and the retort has manifest force. But it is not sufficient. Pro-war liberals were not satisfied with the defeat of German militarism. They insisted on military victory as the necessary agency of certain positive political purposes: and up to date they have not succeeded in accomplishing as the result of victory any of these positive political benefits. Moreover they are for the most part blind or indifferent to the damage which their failure has done to the credit of traditional liberalism. In view of this apparent ignorance of their own failure by so many pro-war liberals, it is no wonder that the dogma of the absolute incompatibility between liberalism and war is coming to the surface. If they wish to restore their credit, they will have to pay more attention to the discrepancies in their record. They will have to either shift liberalism to new and stronger ground or repair the manifest breaches in their defenses.

Liberals deserve the eclipse from which liberalism is suffering. But they do not deserve it merely because they did not oppose the war. When the war came, they were in no position effectively and creditably to oppose it. Liberalism had not lived up to the opportunities and the necessities of its own ideal. By neglecting to contrive a positive moral and political substitute for war, it had condemned itself in the event of a general war to a Hobson's choice. The choice did not consist, as *The Nation* implies, between a clear good and an unmitigated evil but between two evils, of which the greater was not necessarily the will to fight on the side of the western Powers.

It is the business of liberals to use science for the purpose of humanizing man in society. In so far as the promoters of such an ideal find a sufficient excuse for endorsing war, the compulsion constitutes a grave impeachment of liberalism. Yet the endorsement of any war does not sound the "knell" of any and all liberalism. The sense in which war sounds the "knell" of liberalism depends upon the specific meanings which we attach to the words "war" and "liberalism." When war and the preparation for war become equivalent to systematic and authoritative militarism, war does sound not merely the temporary but the permanent "knell" of anything like liberalism. But wars sometimes occur without creating or implying militarism or at least without implying the kind and amount of militarism which is dangerous to our traditional anaemic liberalism. Wars have even occurred whose purposes and effects are inimical to militarism and helpful in the long run to what is known as liberalism. In this class I should place the war which Great Britain carried on against Napoleonic imperialism, the war which Napoleon III waged against Austria-Hungary on behalf of north Italian independence and the war which Lincoln insisted on fighting in order to prevent the South from perpetuating the institution of slavery on American soil.

If war may sometimes constitute from the point of view of existing liberalism the less of two evils, it cannot be as fatal for liberals to approve of a war and as profitable for them to oppose a war as the Nation alleges. It depends on the war. In the instances of the Crimean and the Boer Wars, groups of British liberals increased their own credit and did a little something to vindicate liberalism by opposing unjustifiable appeals to arms. But the two instances do not establish the rule. Although I admire Charles James Fox for his sympathy with the French Revolution and the precocious gallantry of his devotion to liberal ideals, his opposition to the dogged British determination to fight Napoleon I was, I think, an example of poor judgment. Take another case. Admitting that the American government could and should have avoided the Spanish-American War, its support by liberals did not sound the "knell" of contemporary American liberalism. On the contrary the very man who most enthusiastically approved the morality of forcing war on Spain in order to liberate Cuba was the man who during the following fourteen years contributed more than any other political leader to the immediate vitality of American liberalism.

Coming down to our own day the "knell" which has sounded for progressivism in this country is no doubt associated with American participation in the Great War. Yet, so far as I can see, the approval or the disapproval by progressives of American belligerency has little or nothing to do with this particular doom. In America and Great Britain the majority of liberals approved the war and a minority opposed it. But the dissenting minority are just as deservedly and completely suffering from an eclipse as are the orthodox majority. In the case of the socialists in America the majority opposed the war and a minority approved it. But the dissenting majority are suffering from the same kind of political impotence as are the complacent majority. The pacifist socialists are as much divided among themselves and are as incapable of digging out of their minds a positive moral compensation for war as are the pro-war liberals. After a careful survey of the position of liberalism in all countries where a liberal party existed at the outbreak of the war, I am unable to trace any superiority in enlightenment, prestige, serviceability or authority to anti-war as compared to pro-war liberals. The plain fact is that the Great War caught liberalism unprepared just as it caught socialism, capitalism, democracy and the Christian Church unprepared. In the midst of the general ruin the less credit any group of liberals takes for holding to one particular line of action, the more likely they are to understand why liberalism has failed to reap the fruits of victory, why it is now impotent and how it can in the future do more to redeem the promise which it has held out to the peoples of the enhancement of human life in this world.

The Great War was not an episode in the history of mankind for which a nation or an individual could escape responsibility by being too good to fight. It originated in a fundamental delinquency of Christian civilization, the moral penalty of which both liberals and conservatives, bourgeois and socialists must necessarily share. The civilized peoples of the West had allowed the appropriation of their noblest modern achievement, which is the increase of knowledge and the improvement of technology, by irresponsible centers of class and national power. They had permitted, that is, an increasing divorce between science and religion at the very moment when science was better qualified than ever before either to liberate or to oppress mankind. The consequences of this divorce were particularly tragic in the case of liberals and Christians. For liberalism is an attempt to use knowledge in the interest of human fulfillment, and without the ultimate integrity and the complete conviction which only the service of religious truth could bring, liberalism was bound to flinch from dealing with the deeper emergencies of civilization. As for Christians, in so far as Christianity concerned itself with human fulfillment in this world, the dedication of science to the satisfaction of distracting secular interests condemned the Christian Church to impotence.

When the Great War came it revealed with awful emphasis and finality the lack of integrity in the authoritative moral standards of modern civilization. It imposed a distressing choice both on Christians and liberals, but it certainly did not impose on them the moral necessity of non-participation. For a nation or an individual to refuse to play a positive part in the unfulfilled moral conflict of their civilization because of a conscientious objection to war in general was not unlike a refusal to participate in a worldly life because of a conscientious objection to the Fall of Man. I do not mean by the analogy that a small people like the Dutch or the Swiss who were privileged to stay out were under any obligation to go in. Neither am I claiming that the conscientious objector should not have followed the dictates of his conscience. But the peoples which stayed out escaped the common liability only because they happened to be insignificant centers of organized political and industrial power; and the conscientious objector was a sufficiently close analogue of the virgin who could not preserve her purity without committing suicide. The nation or the individual which escaped was lucky, but under the circumstances the price of its good fortune was impotence. Although the sufferings of the conscientious objector were honorable to the sufferers, their tears will not water the soil of a new and more humane civilization.

If there is any truth in this, it applies particularly to the case of America and of individual Americans. There was nothing in our history which prepared us or forced us to participate in the war. On the contrary, the ancestors of millions of Americans crossed the Atlantic partly to escape this kind of liability. We went in apparently more as a matter of deliberate choice than did any other people. Yet the decision was not as much a matter of choice as it seemed. Although the American people had displayed a more active interest in avoiding war than had the European peoples, they had never travelled far in providing a positive substitute for it. They had never qualified themselves by superior moral energy and enlightened humanity to escape from the fatal liability to accept war at times as the less of two evils and an effective agency for the accomplishment of their national purposes. Their comparatively pacific point of view was born of a happy accident of geographical position, and when the Great War came, this accident waxed insignificant compared with the equally cherished accident of their huge size. The American nation happened to be a center of political industrial and military power of unique importance. Its interference in the war on one or the other side was certain to be decisive. Its refusal to interfere in the war was certain to be no less decisive. In a real sense it could not stay out. If the American government had refused to fight after one belligerent had threatened the maritime routes upon the inviolability of which American security rested, Americans would have had to shoulder a plain responsibility for the victory of militarism. The refusal would not have made for pacification either in this country or in Europe. On the contrary, the morally aggressive fraction of the American people would have been so chagrined by the frustration of its pugnacity that they could and would have used the victory of militarism in Europe in order to cultivate militarism in America.

A growing apprehension of the decisive effect of American economic power upon the issue of the war, no matter whether the nation went in or stayed out, persuaded the editors of *The New Republic* as early as the spring of 1916 to urge American intervention, but intervention conditioned on the acceptance by the Allies of a program of international conciliation. A year later the intervention actually took place. The President preceded it with a declared program which looked in the direction of ultimate conciliation. France, Great Britain and Italy never accepted this program and the American government never pressed them to accept it. This radical diversity of aims persisted until the end of the fighting. When the victory came the divergent political purposes prevented the embodiment of a program of pacification in the Treaty of Peace in spite of the clear and specific obligation to do so under the terms of the armistice. The plan of the pro-war American liberals failed in its immediate object; and those who had contended for intervention in the expectation that American influence would make for permanent pacification must admit to a serious miscalculation. They had urged their countrymen to abandon a cherished national tradition and pay a terrific price for the purpose of promoting world peace, and after the price was paid they were unable to obtain the delivery of the promised goods.

The miscalculation in my own case consisted chiefly in false anticipation of what the psychology of the American people would be under the strain of fighting in a world war. Realizing their comparatively pacific attitude, their indisposition to intervene in a European quarrel and their freedom from many of the interests, the traditions and the institutions which characterized the European power states, I assumed that they would preserve even during so terrible a war a somewhat disinterested American point of view. I assumed that the American people would take as much interest in the declared political objects of the war as they would in their exertions on behalf of military victory. These suppositions proved to be wrong. Although the President continued to wave his program of pacification as a justification for paying the utmost price for military victory, the American nation as a whole thought only of victory and little of its supposed political objects; and as long as the fighting lasted both the government and public opinion were intoxicated with propaganda and discouraged any attempt to clarify and to popularize the politics of the war by honest discussion. When victory came the American people were both divided and unenlightened as to the best method of turning it to account. President Wilson sailed for France severely handicapped by the opposition and misunderstanding of his fellow-countrymen. The insecurity of his position betrayed him into the fatal error of consenting to a vindictive Treaty which rendered future inter-class and international wars inevitable in payment for the acceptance by Europe of a League to guarantee nominal peace. But by this time he had entirely lost touch with his fellow-countrymen. They had quickly reacted from their artificially hot fit of pro-European belligerency and had replaced it with a cold suspicion of European entanglements. They interpreted the League, not as a League of Peace, but as an effort to impose on America a permanent obligation to send American soldiers to fight in European quarrels. As soon as they got a chance they repudiated the League without paying any attention to the solemn warning of President Wilson that they thereby rendered unfruitful the American treasure and blood which they had spent so lavishly in France.

Are we justified in concluding as a result of the election that the effort to move towards the goal of permanent pacification by the route of American intervention has proved to be an utter failure? I do not believe we are. The issue remains open. The pro-war liberals anticipated that by going into war explicitly on behalf of a pacific purpose, the American people would pledge themselves to support a positive substitute for war as a solvent of international quarrels and an agency of international action. That idea is far from dead. It has more vitality than it had previous to American intervention. The American people are recovering from their war neurosis. As the memory of it fades away they are regaining some of their visions. They are waking up to the consequences and the responsibilities of their part in the victory. They have rejected the specific plan whereby President Wilson proposed to redeem the responsibility, but while rejecting the plan they are moving plainly in the direction of recognizing the obligation. For they rejected the League in part at least because, as they were told, it did not redeem the obligation, and during the course of the election discussion the opponents of the League, except a few utter irreconcilables, came more and more explicitly to acknowledge the need of the cooperation by Americans with European nations in providing an effective substitute for war. If the Harding administration fails to move in the direction of permanent pacification, it will frustrate a wish of the American people which will hereafter become increasingly articulate and aggressive.

The positive and the permanent justification of American intervention from the liberal point of view consists in the extent to which it committed America to initiating and participating in the coming experiments in pacific international organization. Non-intervention would have confirmed an unreal isolation, the excuse for which could only consist in an equally unreal and offensive claim to American moral superiority. Intervention was an irrevocable acknowledgment by America of the existence of a joint destiny for America and Europe and a joint responsibility for the delinquencies of civilization and for the welfare of the peoples. It gave reality to ties, debts and common memories which will prevent the American people from resuming the irresponsibility of their former attitude. It associates one of the most strenuous flights of the American national consciousness with an effort, made in alliance with a part of Europe, to keep the peace among nations. The association may fade away, but it will not fade away as long as the American people continue to cherish liberal and humane ideals as an essential part of their national democratic tradition.

In this sense pro-war liberalism has a case, but it is a precarious case of which its advocates have no reason to feel certain or proud. For that reason they are, in so far as they realize the vulnerability of their own position, bound in honor to do what they can to prepare in other ways against a repetition of the disaster of a general war and of a Hobson's choice between two evils. There are other ways in which they can prepare. An international association for the preservation of peace is not the only or even the most promising means of doing away with war as a plausible agency for the accomplishment of purposes in themselves desirable. It is still more important, as our experience in the late war so clearly proved, to build up within nations centers of moral self-possession which may help to make them too good to fight in the one realistic meaning of that phrase. A nation which is too good to fight must be able and willing to accomplish by other and more humane instruments the desirable objects which the world has hitherto accomplished by war. The vitality of any international association for the prevention of war will depend upon the extent to which human people can build up an enduring foundation for peace in the moral and social psychology of the participating nations.

The article on "The Eclipse of Progressivism," which *The Nation* dismissed with a sneer, was an unpretentious attempt to indicate the route whereby the American national consciousness could attain a valid moral and psychological substitute for war and a foundation of peace. It dealt, indeed, with war between classes rather than war between nations, but it clearly aimed at the conclusion that a nation which can overcome war between classes will have attained a degree of moral self-possession which will enable it to invalidate the moral and political pretexts for wars between nations. The authorization by conscious collective consent of semi-independent but cooperating classes within a nation erects the surest safeguard against the kind of headstrong mob rule in which war so often originates and whose flare-up in this country during the recent war was so largely responsible for the disappointing end of its crusade in Europe. The class whose increasing recognition as an estate in the American Republic will help most effectively to create a better moral and social balance in American national life is that of the salaried and wage-earning workers. It was British labor, allied in part with British liberalism and organized both for political and economic action, which recently forbade the British government either to continue or to resume hostilities against Russia. With this object lesson particularly in mind my purpose was to arouse American liberals to the need of purging our own liberalism of its existing association with a dominant class whose psychology is determined by the practice of acquisition and exclusive possession and whose interests are opposed to the fulfillment of a humane liberal ideal. In attributing the present eclipse of progressivism to the "unreality which liberals have fastened on liberalism," I was referring explicitly to their inability to transcend class shibboleths and their consequent bondage in the end to a psychology of disassociation and a law of irreconcilable conflict.

Assuming that the editor of *The Nation* calls himself a liberal, he has challenged this explanation of the eclipse of American liberalism only to confirm it. His dissent is a perfect product of the unreal attitude towards fundamental issues which so frequently condemns liberalism not only to impotence but to peevish and irrelevant fault-finding. He did not stop to consider the reasons I had urged in favor of the proposed explanation and the relation of those reasons to the future prevention of war, but jumped immediately to a "clearer and better" reason. This clearer and better reason proved to be a dogma about the antagonism between all liberalism and all war which erroneously assumed that both liberalism and war were fixed quantities and which by failing to discriminate between adequate and inadequate liberalism prevented the word from standing in this connection for significant reality. Liberalism must obtain reality from the ability of liberals to place knowledge at the service of human liberation. But liberals who propose to get rid of war by conscious dissent while at the same time ignoring its roots in moral and social psychology are seeking human liberation by cultivating obscurantism rather than enlightenment. They must in the end either compromise with war or impotently protest against it. They do not bring to the task of human amelioration in this world the knowledge of human nature and the ability to control its individual and social behavior which enables them to put up a successful contest against the object of their own detestation.

What Do the Liberals Hope For?

EDMUND WILSON vs. STUART CHASE

FEBRUARY 10, 1932

I.

It is curious to read today the writings of the American liberals in the days just before the depression. No matter how realistic they seemed to be, they all had a way of ending in bursts of language that left you blank.

Consider, for example, the conclusion of Stuart Chase's pamphlet on *Waste and the Machine Age.* Stuart Chase is perhaps the vividest writer of the liberal camp; he has an unusual knack of making statistics take shape as things and people. And in *The Tragedy of Waste* and his other books he worked stubbornly to disillusion us with the blessings of the American "prosperity" era. But here is his final message:

> I see before us three alternatives. We can drift with the tide as at present. We can adopt some simple formula like "government by business" or "state socialism" and thus attempt to run a dreadnaught with a donkey engine. Or we can face the full implications of the machine, relying on no formulas, with nothing to guide us but our naked intelligence and a will to conquer.
>
> The stars, alas, predict the first; Russia proved the futility of the second when the Marxian formula gave way to the New Economic Policy; the last is the great adventure—the boldest, most exhilarating, most dangerous adventure that ever challenged the intelligence and spirit of mankind. From our brains have sprung a billion horses, now running wild and almost certain sooner or later to run amuck. Where are the rulers with their whirling ropes; where the light-hearted youths to mount, be thrown and rise to mount again?

But what did all this mean? Evidently, what was lacking was not light-hearted youths—the colleges and schools were full of them—but any explicit directions to them on the part of Stuart Chase.

And here is the conclusion of Walter Lippmann's chapter on "The Business of the Great Society" in *A Preface to Morals*—a book which gives an excellent account of the situation of the intelligent modern man who finds that all the moral motives have evaporated:

> The more perfectly we understand the implications of the machine technology upon which our civilization is based, the easier it will be for us to live with it. We shall discern the ideals of our industry in the necessities of industry itself. They are the direction in which it must evolve if it is to fulfill itself. That is what ideals are. They are not hallucinations. They are not a collection of pretty and casual preferences. Ideals are an imaginative understanding of that which is desirable in that which is possible. As we discern the ideals of the machine technology we can consciously pursue them, knowing that we are not vainly trying to impose our casual prejudices, but that we are in harmony with the age we live in.

But what did this really mean? What is this Machine Technology which is apotheosized as a transcendent being with ideals to which it is necessary for human beings to adapt themselves? One had supposed that man, the tool-making animal, had himself created technique and that it existed only in so far as he practised it. "In harmony with the age we live in"—but are not we—the Lippmanns and the people who read him—the age we live in as much as anybody? Mr. Lippmann, having shown out the old-time God, ushers in a new and much less plausible one called "Machine Technology" in whose awful sight even he, the professional political philosopher, cannot presume to play an authoritative part in the age in which he lives!

Finally, here is the conclusion of the Beards' *Rise of American Civilization.* Mr. Charles A. Beard is one of the best American writers of his generation and *The Rise of American Civilization* is a masterpiece of economy and organization. Never perhaps has an immense historical subject been more beautifully and completely articulated in so small a compass. And never have the proportions of popular legend been altered with a bolder and firmer hand. With the Beards, every sentence, every clause, carries its cool facts as the sentences in other books carry nouns and verbs—and the fighting of the Civil War shrinks to three pages while the origins of the forces that produced it take up a couple of hundred. When the Beards got to the end of their story, however, they could only write a brilliant essay on the present—no doubt the best of all the essays because it was the work of wider-ranging as well as more concrete minds than the woolly generalizations that used to come out in the magazines in such quantities; but—what was disappointing—they could only end this essay as follows:

> If the generality of opinion, as distinguished from that of poignant specialists, was taken into account, there was no doubt about the nature of the future in America. [They still talk like historians writing about the past, but evidently they are giving their own opinion about the present.] The most common note of assurance was belief in unlimited progress—the continuous fulfilment of the historic idea which had slowly risen through the eighteenth and nineteenth centuries to a position of commanding authority. Concretely it meant an invulnerable faith in democracy, in the ability of the undistinguished masses, as contrasted with heroes and classes, to meet by reasonably competent methods the issues raised in the flow of time—a faith in the efficacy of that new and mysterious instrument of the modern mind, "the invention of invention," moving from one technological triumph to another, overcoming the exhaustion of crude natural resources and energies, effecting an ever wider distribution of the blessings of civilization—health, security, material goods, knowledge, leisure and esthetic appreciation, and through the cumulative forces of intellectual and artistic reactions, conjuring from the vasty deeps of the nameless and unknown creative imagination of the noblest order, subduing physical things to the empire of the spirit—doubting not the capacity of the Power that had summoned into being all patterns of the past and present, living and dead, to fulfill its endless destiny.
>
> If so, it is the dawn, not the dusk, of the gods.

Again, what did this mean? Mr. Beard may not have wanted to run the danger of being mistaken for a "poignant specialist," but one had expected something more definite from him than this. The "invulnerable faith in democracy" of his peroration seems a little out of place at the end of a history which has been so largely preoccupied with extremely undemocratic situations of group-conflict and group-exploitation; and the "faith in the efficacy of that new and mysterious instrument of the human mind, 'the invention of invention,' moving from one technological triumph to another," etc., seems more incongruous still. "That new and mysterious instrument"—"the more perfectly we understand the implications of the machine technology." Mr. Beard, who has just been pointing out to us with such acumen how every political movement, every artistic tendency, every migration, every war, has depended on somebody's interest, finally makes everybody's interest depend on an apotheosized abstraction—that "new and mysterious instrument" that moves "from one technological triumph to another" and conjures "from the vasty deeps of the nameless and unknown creative imagination of the noblest order."

"If so"—but if what?—"it is the dawn, not the dusk, of the gods." What gods? And why this talk of dusk?

II.

One accepted this sort of thing before the depression even though one could never see quite what it meant nor how it followed from what went before. And one has no right to complain about it now: it is too easy to be wise after the event.

But it is rather disquieting today to find Mr. Lippmann, Mr. Beard and Mr. Chase still continuing in the same vein. Mr. Chase's "Declaration of Independence" in *Harper's* is a meditation which, though full of all kinds of admirable sentiments expressed with considerable eloquence, seems to take place a long way off from the scene of action: "America is too fine a land to be longer drugged by the infantile slogans and dazzled by the glittering gadgets of shoddy speculators. It deserves a civilization as great as its majestic distances, its rolling prairies, its mighty rivers and massed sierras," etc. He appeals to the "intelligent minority" to act their age and escape from the standards of golf-playing country-club-joining suburban society. But what to do? In the name of what?

Mr. Beard in an article in the same number of *Harper's* in which he recommends as "much planning" as "is necessary," winds up with a vision of the future even giddier than that at the end of his history: "And, to paraphrase Milton, methinks puissant America, mewing her mighty youth, will yet kindle her undazzled eyes at the full midday beam, purge and unscale her long abused sight, while timorous and flocking birds, with those that love the twilight, flutter about amazed at what she means, and in their envious gabble would prognosticate a year of sects and schisms." But what does Mr. Beard think she means? Unless she receives a sudden revelation, I don't see how she is to avoid a year or many years as the battleground of sects and schisms who want her to mean different things. And in two articles in *Scribner's,* "Rushlights in Our Darkness" and "A Search for a Center," he does little to supply this revelation. He tells us that about all we can do is fall back on a "philosophy of ethical reconciliation"—which the old master of social actualities then proceeds to adumbrate in a void from which the social actualities of the present have been completely swept away.

And Mr. Lippmann, trusting nowadays in the bankers and attempting tactfully to slip a few liberal notions into the minds of *Herald Tribune* readers, is coming to chill us more and more with the suspicion that all his beautiful diplomacy has ended in his coming back from the ride with the liberal inside and the smile on the face of the banker.

One of the most striking things about all these writers is their avoidance of the subject of socialism and communism, or their misrepresentation, when they do touch on it, of what is going on in Russia. According to Chase in the passage quoted above, the Russians "proved the futility" of socialism "when the Marxian formula gave way to the New Economic Policy." But the

N.E.P. period has passed and the Five Year Plan is in its fourth year. Mr. Chase changes the subject to Mexico and seems to imply that we should all be much better off if we were able to live as if modern industry didn't exist. More recently, however, he has gone so far as to contrast the balance-sheet of the Soviets with that of the United States.

Mr. Beard, whose American history up to the very last pages might almost be an elaboration of certain passages on capitalist expansion in *Das Kapital,* is evidently so anxious to fight shy of communism that in his article reviewing proposed policies of social salvation he barely mentions the philosophy of the Soviets, though he discusses Mussolini at length.

In an earlier article in *The Forum*—"A 'Five Year Plan' for America"—he makes the following points against Russian communism: that its policy of planning was "an afterthought and never would have been even partially realized had it not been for the technological assistance of Western capitalism"; that "the Russian plan" is not a real plan anyway, because "for more than ten years the Russian government has pursued a zigzag course, trying one expedient after another"; and that "it rules by tyranny and terror, with secret police, espionage and arbitrary executions." Well, why on earth should the first two of these facts be put forward, as Beard does specifically put them forward, as objections to "a dictatorship in the name of the proletariat"? As a matter of fact, Marx had said that communism would have to make use of the technological developments of capitalism. That, in fact, is one of his principal points; so that there is little sense in Beard's statement that the Bolsheviks "laid aside Marx" and "took up Frederick Winslow Taylor": industrial efficiency as it existed before Taylor appeared to give his name to it is what *Das Kapital* is mostly about. In any case, what difference does it make whether the Bolsheviks' idea of planning was an afterthought or not?—and what is there damaging about their having been obliged to follow a zigzag course? Why should it be a matter for surprise or reproach that they could not establish communism overnight? And as for the third item of his indictment, what on earth makes Mr. Beard talk as if the capitalist government of the United States did not rule "by tyranny and terror, with secret police, espionage and arbitrary executions"? Mr. Beard must know that the "personal liberty" which he asserts that the American tradition safeguards but thinks that the Soviets suppress, is not today worth a cent as soon as you step out of your owning-class orbit, and that you are lucky if you do not land in jail or get run out of town or shot, like the reporters, Brookwood organizers and American Civil Liberties representatives who tried to lend a hand at Harlan or Lawrence. In his later article, he gets around communism by treating it as if it were merely a form like another of the belief in pure economics: "Economics in Russia," he says, "did not automatically supply the great illumination." But it is not economics as a pure science which is the issue: it is economics in the sense of the difference in standards of living between an exploiting and an exploited class; it is economics in the sense of the attempt to abolish such social classes. It seems absurd to say it of a man of Mr. Beard's record and attainments, but it looks as if Marx and Lenin were playing the part of bogies upon which all these writers were having a hard time to shut their doors. In a recent article in *The New Republic* on the promotion of the German navy under the Empire, Mr. Beard made a point at the beginning of reassuring his readers that the facts he was about to reveal would not give any comfort to the Marxists, and then went on to describe a case of the exploitation of patriotism by capital which illustrated Marx's theory superbly.

And Mr. Lippmann has shown himself the master of them all by exalting himself to a plane where he is able to tell the readers of *The Herald Tribune* that Russian society is the same thing as American, but only as yet in a lower stage of development.

III.

Not that these writers do not, so far as one can tell, contemplate that American society shall ultimately adopt some form of socialism. Mr. Lippmann, in "A Preface to Morals," expressed the belief that American business was on its way to socializing itself. And there was a common assumption among liberals before the slump that America was working toward the same goal as Russia by an inverse capitalistic process. That was, in fact, the liberal's only excuse for being.

The attitude is very clearly seen in *The Autobiography of Lincoln Steffens,* published only last year. In this extraordinarily interesting book, we have the story of an American born in the sixties who acutely studies at first hand and in all its ramifications the corruption of the American social structure, who watches the political reform movements from the inside and who finally comes to the conclusion, as the result of contact with Socialists and Single-Taxers, that it is the economic system and not merely the crimes of bad men in office which is responsible for the social diseases of the time; who consorts with the American radicals of the early years of the century; beholds the Mexican revolution, for lack of fundamental socialist principles, lapse back into the hands of the privileged classes; sees the Kerensky revolution in Russia superseded by the Bolsheviks, who base their policy upon Marxist principles—greatly to the dismay of many American socialists, who are horrified by the actual spectacle of the realization of their aims; but finally returns to the United States to find his boyhood home in California inhabited by a liberal Governor who refuses to pardon Mooney and Billings, only to base his hopes of American salvation on Henry Ford's high wages and the calling by Hoover after the first stock-market crash of a conference of leading business men, and even to look comfortably forward to a time when the bootleggers shall have grown out of their "criminal stage" and "having bought their way all through politics to a place beside the power trust and the railroads," established themselves as a respectable trust. He even reaches a point of enthusiasm where he is able to say of the autobiographical baloney ghost-written by Samuel Crowther for Ford that "it might well be the Bible, as Ford is the prophet, of business."

I do not know whether Mr. Steffens still so confidently swears by this Bible. I have heard intimations that he does not. But these opinions, even after the depression had commenced, on the part of a man of Mr. Steffens' unusual intelligence and remarkably wide social and political experience, are significant of the effects of American "prosperity" psychology on the minds of our political critics.

Ford the prophet had become our favorite myth—conjured up by the acuteness of our need to get some kind of democratic hero out of our advanced and inflated stage of capitalism. George Soule, in an article in *The Virginia Quarterly,* has shown how, though the Ford of legend never really existed, it was found necessary to invent him. It had been the custom of capitalism in the past to save money in manufacturing as far as the unions would let it by paying labor as little as possible: it did not have the imagination to foresee that, with so many people thus impoverished, few would be able to buy its products. Ford, for reasons which from the best accounts were by no means primarily dictated by overflowing benevolence toward labor (the opportunity for big publicity and for holding out a bait to strong and rapid workers), undertook without union pressure (he had forbidden organization in his factories) to raise the workers' pay. He also undertook to bring a luxury within the reach of the masses. At the time of the voyage of the Peace Ship, moreover, he had lent himself in what seems to have been a real burst of magnanimity to the projects of certain internationalists. But how could we have hoped that Ford's few eccentric gleams of idealism and democratic feeling would transform or meant the beginning of a transformation of the vast greedy system which he understood so little? Under pressure from his business back home, he got cold feet on the Peace Ship before it landed; and since then the system has been steadily transforming him into its own harsh and narrow likeness. Today he is as badly off as anyone, and his workers have had to pay for his losses like the workers in any other plant.

Who today in any camp on the left can have the optimism to believe that capitalism is capable of reforming itself? And who today can look forward with confidence to any outcome from the present chaos short of the establishment of a socialistic society—not like the Russian: how could it be? America is not Russia—but with this in common with Russia: that it shall aim to abolish social classes and private enterprise for private profit?

IV.

Yet these liberals, who presumably aim at socialism, still apparently pin great hopes on the capitalists.

They draw up schemes for "planned economies" which are designed to preserve the capitalist system while eliminating some of its worst features—though so far as one can tell from what they write, they haven't the ghost of an idea of an agency to put even these into effect. The liberals of today are not a part of a progressive movement like the liberals of the Wilson-Roosevelt era. One can only suppose that they are hoping for some such movement, though it is not clear where it is coming from, nor why, after Roosevelt and Wilson, they should expect it to accomplish what they want. Assume even that Franklin Roosevelt is made President at the next election—assume even that he is induced to pay attention to the proposals of one of the liberal "plans." Isn't it evident that these proposals would ultimately be reduced to the same status as Herbert Croly's *Promise of American Life* by the time it had been brayed in the mortar of Roosevelt's campaign speeches or as George Record's socialism by the time it had been filtered through Wilson? Since there is no Wilson or T. R. in sight, would they even fare so well? It would be the capitalists, not the liberals, who would do the planning; and they would plan to save their own skins at the expense of whoever had to bleed.

Roosevelt and Wilson were both owning-class men who, though their imaginations went somewhat beyond their class, never did anything seriously to injure its interests. They tried to save the system they were on top of by a few reforms and a great deal of sheer hot air. Now what one wants to ask the liberals of today is how they can hope to get a new creative statesmanship out of the psychology of that owning-class. One wonders to how great an extent they may have come to share that psychology themselves.

For one feels, as one reads them today, that, in spite of their expressions of moral and esthetic dissatisfaction, they are still sold like other middle-class Americans on the values of the middle-class world which they criticize. You will look in vain in any of their recent utterances for any really damaging attack on these values. Stuart Chase has come out strongly in favor of the Americans' playing less golf; but he manages to sound as smug as if he were playing golf every day. Desperate capitalists who, finding their system breaking up in their hands and searching their hearts as to how they ought to act, should they consult Mr. Chase in *Harper's,* would be likely to conclude that American life was sounder and more placid than they had supposed. And when Walter Lippmann tells people over the radio that "we must face some more reduction in the costs of retail goods, of rents and of labor," there is no question whom he means by "we." Mr. Lippmann's "we" are not the workers who have to face having their wages reduced, but the employers who have to face reducing them. And Mr. Lippmann is ready to do anything in his power to help them muster the morale to face it.

Without, no doubt, being conscious of it, these writers seem unwilling to face the implications of the middle-class acceptance of the status quo—which involves at the present time the forcing-down of the working class below the bare subsistence level in order that the owning-class may not be obliged to sacrifice comforts and luxuries—a state of things always easy to ignore for the reason noted by Henry George after the depression of the seventies: that to force people down below a certain level is to force them out of existence altogether. In any case, you hear very little about it in what these students of society have been writing.

In fact, though they are better informed and more enlightened than the average American business man, their imagination does not extend much further nor their logic cut much deeper. Their political thinking is mediocre because their solidarity is middle-class. And this is a disappointment to one who has read them in the past with profit. Writers of their intellectual eminence have no business to succumb to the influence of standards of living. What is at the bottom of the capitalist crisis is class differences in standards of living with the special habits and ideas they involve and of which it is as hard for the ordinary person to divest himself as for the leopard to change his spots. It is hard for anybody; but if our professional illuminati can't break through them to some larger grasp of the world which is cracking up around us, we deserve all to be cooked together.

—EDMUND WILSON

Mr. Chase Replies

This is a free country—more or less—and Mr. Wilson has as good a right to attack me for my economic views as a Presbyterian has to attack an agnostic. He has recently been converted to one of the forms of communism, and safe in the arms of Marx can take pot shots at those outside the compound. I do not feel, however, that his shots are very well aimed. Overcome with zeal, he has fired his clods too fast.

He implies that I am, first, a hopeless, middle-class liberal, second, a defamer of Soviet Russia; he implies, third, that I have nothing to offer in the current depression. He cites one essay from *Harper's Magazine,* and part of a sentence from a pamphlet, as the twin pillars upon which his indictment rests. The essay was a highly personal reaction to a number of American living conditions which I do not happen to like. It was sincere but hardly profound. To take it as an expression of a final economic philosophy is grossly unfair. In reading the sentence which had to do with Russia, Mr. Wilson completely misinterpreted my meaning, though I do not think he intended it deliberately. I cited Russia as an example of the futility of slogans. In 1921 Lenin found that pure socialism would not work, and introduced an area of private trading, much of which remains. Whether it will work ultimately remains to be seen. One would not be surprised if it did. My point was to show that dogma seldom survives the pragmatic test at any given testing period.

If Mr. Wilson had taken time to read carefully only a small part of what I have written in the last few years, his indictment would perforce be cast in other and more intellectually competent terms. I do not care to waste anybody's time arguing about a private declaration of independence or half a sentence. But to a true bill I will argue indefinitely. I propose to recast the indictment, with or without Mr. Wilson's permission:

> Chase is a man difficult to place. He is obviously not an orthodox liberal, for he supports the Russian dictatorship, and repeatedly hints at the benefits of an economic dictatorship in this country. The hints include a recent article in *The Nation* entitled "If I Were Dictator." He seldom mentions free speech, free press or political reform, while the majesties of political democracy and the ballot leave him cold. His criticism of the going economic system has been unremitting and severe. He has catalogued its appalling wastes with considerable industry; he has done his best to undermine the theory and the practice of commercial salesmanship; he has presented item by item the mismanagement of machine technology in the modern world; he has analyzed Coolidge prosperity quantitatively and found it largely myth; he has documented unemployment, overproduction, the lack of integrity in a pecuniary civilization; he has flashed a sidelight from the handicraft economy of Mexico as a count in the bill of technological abuses—while recognizing the offsetting evils of a handicraft regime, and the utter impossibility of retreat to that regime. He has visited Russia, and returned enormously excited by the Gosplan, and not at all perturbed, like his friend Roger Baldwin, by the G.P.U. He has defended the Russian economic experiment consistently and on occasion belligerently.
>
> Since the market crash of 1929, he has made a number of reasonably drastic proposals for revamping the industrial structure, including mandatory national and regional planning, the social control of new investment, the breaking up of large incomes and large inheritances, regulation and profit limitation of all corporations affected with a public interest, compulsory unemployment insurance, a complete shift in the division of the national income to the end that workers receive far more, absentee owners far less. He obviously has no faith whatever in the profit motive as an automatic guide to economic well being.
>
> Such, briefly, is Chase's official record. He has been attacking the whole American economic structure, until many are sick and tired of listening to him. Now, why in the name of all the gods does he not announce himself, call that structure capitalism, identify his remedies as

> planks in the platform of socialism? Or better, why, in view of his analysis, does he not refuse to waste his time with palliatives and planks, but come out for communism and a clean sweep? Why all the hedging and crawling; the refusal to call a spade a spade?

Well, I'll tell you, Mr. Edmund Wilson. While you were dissecting Proust and other literary gentlemen—and a very pretty job you did—I was dissecting the industrial structure. For almost twenty years I've been at that job. I have been off and on a devout single-taxer, a member of the pre-war Socialist Party, a devotee of Consumers' Co-operation, a convert to Guild Socialism, a near Communist. I found good in all these theories, but none could I accept as an act of faith, or as a sovereign remedy. Their tidy syllogisms, framed so long ago, were forever being punctured before my eyes by a new invention, a new financial move, a new industrial method, new findings by the anthropologists and the psychologists, a new hundred million horse power. I tried hard to make the facts fit the syllogisms and they would not fit. Ah, what I should have been saved in peace of mind if they only had.

They would not fit, Mr. Edmund Wilson—neither the standard definitions of capitalism, socialism, communism, nor the standard analyses, nor the classical remedies. It is probable at the present time, for instance, that more than half the economic activity of this country is in the zone of collectivism, broadly interpreted, rather than in the zone of free competition and traditional capitalism. I do not use these words, because I do not know what they mean, save in the muzziest way. If I appeal now to the middle class, particularly the technician, it is because a decade of working with the labor movement has taught me that for the moment most of American labor is spiritually bankrupt. If I often disregard the severe canons of the Marxian class struggle, it is because those lines, to date, are blurred and unrecognizable over great portions of the American industrial front, sharp as they may be in Europe, and because a more dynamic conception is mandatory here.

Some years ago I came to the conclusion that we were not going to resolve the problems of poverty, waste and human degradation in America by employing these standard dogmas. Somebody had to find out what was really going on, not what Karl Marx, seventy years ago, said might go on. He was a good guesser, but seventy years is a long time. Somebody had to find a new analysis to fit the American scene, the American temperament, molded by the frontier and a world of a billion horse power. I am looking for a synthesis a good way ahead of your orthodox communism, Mr. Wilson, and yet one which can begin to work. Now; here. I may not find it, but I shall keep on looking until I die. It does not matter. Others are looking too. Some day it will be found.

—STUART CHASE

Brumaire: The Soviet Union as a Fascist State

VINCENT SHEEAN

NOVEMBER 8, 1939

The political evolution of the Soviet Union for the past twenty years has been observed with anxious attention in all countries where freedom of information, thought and expression is still permitted to exist. There has grown up a bias in favor of the Soviet Union, based upon the magnitude of the historic effort made there, which in many cases overrides serious disagreement with the basic theories of that effort. It has seemed to innumerable liberals and radicals that a special patience and understanding should be accorded that struggle to construct a socialist or socializing political economy in a country so huge, barbarous and ill suited to the experiment.

In the despair of the European masses, who have seen capitalism, democracy, Christianity and Marxian socialism alike ruinously incapable of solving the contradictions of their society and providing an equal and just freedom for the inhabitants of the earth, the solutions adopted by the Russian Revolution and its post-revolutionary regime have successively and often illogically represented the only hope discernible. I say successively and often illogically because in fact the Russian solutions have in the course of these twenty years also contradicted each other and objectively failed without shaking the faith of great numbers of people, workers and intellectuals, in the vitality and ultimately correct direction of the Russian effort. The faith to which I refer has been strong enough to withstand contemplation of the most horrifying and bloodthirsty terrorism of modern times because, and simply because, the end has seemed good.

The moral authority of international communism among workers and intellectuals of the Left—among non-communists—has been based upon this obstinate faith, and not upon the practical achievement or intellectual superiority of the Communists. In fact, it is very easy to prove that a much greater economic development has been attained in America by quite different means; the fact is obvious. It is also easy to dispose of present-day communist pretensions to intellectual authority, since communist thought and expression are enslaved to tactical command and in no case present a free analysis. The moral authority of the international communist movement among radicals and liberals who did not belong to it has been, I believe, based upon a consideration of ends, and therefore existed—where it did exist—by virtue of a vote of confidence, an act of faith.

Of faith in what? In the ends? But ends are nothing susceptible of present proof. In what, then, except the men who pursue those ends—and in their steadfastness, their just appreciation of historic force, their ability and their honesty? In that, and in the philosophic system they profess to serve, although, as I have said before, many who have honored the Soviet Union and hoped in it do not accept all of its basic theories. The Soviet effort, its ends and the men who pursue them, have all benefited by a purely emotional attraction in all parts of the world, and most of all by the aching void in the heart and soul of other systems. Throughout these twenty years the Soviet Union, by posing as "the socialist fatherland," has commanded a certain special loyalty among all those innumerable varieties of liberal and radical who were not Communists but expected a good result from the Soviet effort internally and externally. To some degree radicals, whether workers or intellectuals, had two countries, their own and the Soviet Union; and the fact that most of them knew nothing whatever about the Soviet Union did not materially weaken their attachment to it in idea.

Meanwhile the Soviet Union itself has been steadily evolving in a sense which becomes evident only upon a retrospective view. Starting with equalitarian Jacobinism as its emotional power, Marxian socialism as its official philosophy and a handful of inexperienced intellectuals as the executants of the experiment, it traversed the period called "war communism" (the effort to "win socialism by assault") under Lenin and Trotsky and then subsided into the New Economic Policy, a modified form of private capitalism under state control, aiming at state capitalism rather than outright socialism. The debates upon whether the aim was "state capitalism" or "state socialism" showed, at this period, the beginnings of a Bolshevik scholasticism which was afterwards to reach fantastic development.

After the downfall of Trotsky in 1927, his program of industrialization was taken over by the victors and promulgated in the first Five Year Plan (1928–33), which was pushed through to a qualified success by means of the most tyrannical control of every worker in Russia. The second Five Year Plan carried the process further, and passed from heavy industry to consumers' goods, for which an immense population—impoverished by years of war and revolution—had to be reeducated in the name of "culture" before they knew that they even wanted consumers' goods. A program of collectivization in agriculture was enforced from 1931 onwards by means of the most ghastly sacrifices, in which six or seven million peasants are believed to have died of starvation in the Ukraine alone. This industrialization and this collectivization are, in actual fact, the achievements of the Soviet regime, and upon their solidity and permanence must be based any claim which the regime may have to historic consideration as a socialist advance. When all the smoke has blown away—say in twenty or thirty or forty years—this may indeed prove to be a solid achievement.

But the course of the political evolution has in fact been the central phenomenon. No reflective person outside the Soviet Union assumes that it is necessary to murder millions of people to produce an industrialization program. It would not have been necessary in the Soviet Union under a different political development. Nor is it necessary to enforce agrarian collectivization in a way which brings about the death of six million people from starvation. These monstrous sacrifices have been entailed by the haste, waste and inefficiency of a terrorized bureaucracy operating under naked political control—that is, under the orders of power unrestrained and irresponsible, concentrated more and more into the hands of a single man. In the political field the development of the tyranny of that one man, by successive phases from 1927 to 1939, has abolished every vestige of Soviet democracy and even of democracy inside the Russian Communist Party, has solidified the new social classes and expropriated the workers—immensely increased in number by industrialization—for the benefit of the state, bureaucracy and army, the precise organisms which it was the aim of the Russian Revolution to suppress. Every vital principle of socialism from Marx to Lenin has been, it seems to me, vitiated, perverted or ignored. To this process from 1927 to 1939, as it is seen in retrospect, I apply the description intended in revolutionary literature by the word Thermidor. Stalin's Thermidor—drawn out over twelve years—is now at last completed, and this month, October, 1939, is his Brumaire.

All socialist thought since Marx has been haunted by the dread of Thermidor and Brumaire. The ninth Thermidor, Year II, in the French Revolutionary calendar, was the date (July 27, 1794) when the terror was halted and with it the Revolution, giving way to a progressively moderating development under new masters. The eighteenth Brumaire, five years later (November 9, 1799), was the *coup d'état* of Napoleon Bonaparte which ended the French Republic and established the successful general as First Consul.

Such developments have been considered dangerously probable by all socialist theoreticians including Marx, Engels, Lenin, Rosa Luxemburg, Trotsky and Stalin himself. What has confused observers of the Stalinist Thermidor through its long, cautious evolution is, in part, the terror, which increased instead of decreasing after 1927, and in fact reached its peak of wholesale carnage only last year; and in part also the fact that Stalin's political course—by zigzags to the Left and zigzags to the Right—is concealed under expert mystifications which make its significance apparent only after its results are irremediable.

Historic analogies, so dear to the Bolshevik theorists, are not actually of much use except in simplification for the cultural illiterates who accept communist tutelage. Obviously there is no resemblance of nature between the tyrant Stalin and the tyrant Bonaparte, and there is little resemblance of historic circumstance between October, 1939, and the eighteenth Brumaire. What is a constant factor, and can be used, is the significance of these words, Thermidor and Brumaire, in revolutionary ideology. Taking Thermidor to be the process of arrest-and-reverse of the revolutionary machine—and ignoring its effect on the terror, which is a circumstance incident to revolutions and not inherent at a particular stage—and Brumaire to be its consummation in a personal tyranny, I believe it is now clear that the first process has been completed and the second begun. Ignoring every precept of revolutionary thought from Robespierre through Marx, Engels, Lenin, Trotsky and even his earlier self, Stalin has, as a personal dictator of an enslaved and terrorized state, embarked upon a militarist expansion the end of which cannot be seen by any person now living. This is therefore a fantastic dialectical abuse, and is the exact kind of policy reprobated by Lenin under the name of adventurism. The end, which was to have justified the means, has in fact exposed the hideousness of the means, and at this tremendous corner in human history we must all look back—since we cannot see around the corner—and evaluate. Readers of Dante must be reminded at this stage of the poet's halt in a high place, when Virgil says to him:

Volgi gli occhi in giue:
buon ti sarà, per tranquilar la via,
veder lo letto delle piante tue.

What are the results of the twelve years' Thermidor inside the Soviet Union? A measure of industrialization and of agrarian collectivization has been achieved at the cost of millions of lives; the workers have lost every liberty hitherto known to man, and can choose neither their place, times nor kinds of work; they cannot organize, strike or protest in any way; the prison and the knout are installed in factory and collective farm. Their compensations (such as they are) are of a purely fascist nature, consisting in the psychological and social delusions of the mass meeting, chauvinism, competitive sacrifice and self-congratulation. In the socialist realm, in economy, what is the objective result of such a cruelly intensified development? Quite plainly this: that surplus value, which is the very center and meaning of the Marxian socialist system, has been brutally augmented by all the capitalist devices hitherto discovered, applied with ruthless force to a helpless proletariat, and expropriated to the uses of a bureaucratic state and army which thus constitute a new class of expropriators. The human and economic waste has been colossal, more, probably, than any nation has ever known in twenty years of its history; and the enslavement of the proletariat and peasantry, which no longer have even the right of movement from one part of the same district to another, is without parallel in the records of mankind. It would be difficult to imagine how the Marxian effort at socialist reconstruction could have gone further astray.

This economic enslavement has been promoted by a prolonged terroristic repression which, attacking first the *ancien régime*, then non-communist forces of the Left, then obstructionists in industry and agriculture, and later all the Bolsheviks, whatever their rank in the party hierarchy, who dared to protest, has now generalized itself into a machine for striking down anybody who in any way displeases the master of all power or those whom he temporarily trusts to do his bidding. This process, like the counter-revolutionary economic and social program, has been gradual—so gradual that for a long time it could be minimized as historically necessary or incidental. Its essential character has, when we examine it over the twelve years of Stalin's Thermidor, been that of the struggle of one man to achieve and retain absolute power.

At first he struggled by means of party organization and intrigue—striving, by appointments, dismissals, organizational manipulations, to discredit his opponents and strip them of influence. Later, when the machinery of terror had passed completely under his control, he extended the death penalty to an indefinite multitude of offenses and applied it *from the age of twelve.* Thus he was able, in the last phase—that which began in 1936 and is just now ended—to exterminate the vestiges of independence inside the Russian Communist Party by shooting all elements that showed any sign of thought, and to replace them by political and cultural illiterates who would accept without question any dictum, however absurd, of the mightiest of all tsars. The directors of Cheka and Ogpu, succeeding each other by murdering their predecessors, created a system of espionage and lightning punishment which deprived all correspondence, conversation and discussion of their privacy, obliterated the last traces of critical vitality and sent millions of Russians by one route or another to oblivion. The *oubliette* is the most exact figure, indeed, for the last phase of the terror, since the Munich agreement in September, 1938; for during the past year the victims of the terror have not even received trials, however farcical. They have simply vanished off the face of the earth, and none dares question why or how. Among them were many of the most unscrupulous servants Stalin ever possessed; and among them, also, were some of the sincerest and most devoted revolutionaries who ever lived.

In the intellectual sphere, Stalin's Thermidor has deadened activity but claimed as its own any incidental achievement that might have been attained by individual talent and work. Thus the whole of history has been falsified, the earlier socialist and communist works outlawed, a new version of "Leninism" prepared and forced upon the semi-literate mass; philosophical teaching and in the end even scientific teaching have been put under tactical orders; and yet any noteworthy "stunts," like Pavlov's experiments or the Polar flights of the aviators, have been claimed, by a fantasy of self-congratulation, as Soviet achievements. It is well known that Professor Pavlov was a bitter anti-Bolshevik and never ceased throughout his life to complain of the regime in Russia, and it is high time that somebody said so in print. He and other "heroes" of the regime have been, as often as not, prisoners of it, and speculation can only boggle at the thought of what they have suffered in attempting to work under such conditions.

The gradual but progressive solidification of Stalinism and its succinct eventual characterization as a counter-revolutionary and anti-socialist regime akin to fascism, have been accompanied by the inevitable deification of the dictator. This began on a large scale in 1929. Since then millions of statues, portraits and effigies of the dictator have been installed throughout the Soviet Union, his name has been given to many towns and villages, factories and farms, his personal existence (birthdays, etc.) hieratically impressed upon the people in tsarist or fascist style, and his august person surrounded by such sickening adulation as only a Roman emperor could have accepted. This was a logical (and perhaps, in origin, tactical) development of the mummification of Lenin. Lenin himself was violently opposed to any such nonsense about individual leaders, particularly of a materialist revolution. Krupskaya, his widow, once remarked in 1927 that if Lenin were alive now he would be in prison. Alive or dead, he is in fact in prison—in the prison of Stalinist fascism, the negation of everything he meant in life.

EDITOR'S NOTE: This was the first of two articles by Vincent Sheean. The second appeared in the November 15, 1939, issue.

Common Sense about Russia

EDITORIAL

NOVEMBER 15, 1939

There are few writers on international affairs whose views will command more respect among those of progressive leanings than Vincent Sheean. Readers of his books and articles know that he knows his Europe and—before 1927—knew his Russia at first hand. They also have learned to rely on his warm feeling for the plain people of the world, and especially for those engaged in building better things for the future, or in resisting oppression. He has never been above the battle. In Spain, for instance, he was not just a reporter. He also worked hard and long, as did so many other Americans of good will, to arouse the public to the meaning of the Loyalist cause, to expose the lies which sought to blacken it, to succor the victims of the defeat.

When Mr. Sheean decides to testify against the Soviet Union, as he has in the two articles written for *The New Republic*, his testimony therefore cannot be discounted as was that of some of the others who have done so in the past. He does not harbor a congenital hostility to the Russian experiment, concealed beneath a veneer which is rubbed off by the first experience of discomfort. He cannot be accused of personal grudges. He is not a captious critic, or an unreliable factionalist always shifting loyalties. He can see beneath surfaces and is not put off by superficial disappointments. He would never have become disillusioned because the Bolsheviks did not create Utopia overnight or were slow and clumsy in solving their enormous difficulties.

Nevertheless we sense what seems to us a certain lack of realism in his point of view, which is shared by many. His articles make it clear that his adverse judgment was precipitated by the action of the Soviet government in the war crisis. This action was so contrary to previous communist professions, and was so shocking to those who had been girding themselves for the fight against Hitlerism as the most hateful phenomenon in the modern world, that it created a revolution in emotional attitudes. In none does this revolution strike deeper than in those who have made their own the international aims to which they thought the Soviet Union was pledged. The firmer their devotion to these aims, the more profound is their revulsion at what they feel is a betrayal. And, since the Soviet government could act in this way abroad, every doubt about its internal policy is resolved against it. At last the hypocrite is disclosed for what he is. The alternative to this revulsion is a sort of blind religious faith, trusting in a divine wisdom that it cannot understand.

There has long been a tendency among intellectuals to be either "for" or "against" the Soviet Union; to demand that it be regarded either as all white or all black. Any attempt at a really critical view was branded as lack of clarity or "liberal confusion." Those who, like *The New Republic,* saw some good things and some bad were condemned as Stalinists whenever they expressed a favorable judgment, and as Trotskyists or bourgeois reactionaries whenever they expressed an unfavorable one. This tendency is now intensified. Things are seen, in this excitement of war, more than ever disguised under labels and categories, and the chief preoccupation of many is now to pass a final moral judgment upon Soviet communism. This is only natural, since communism offered itself as the one true way of social salvation, permitting no deviation or dissent. And, as Mr. Sheean points out, it was the last resort of those who had been balked and disillusioned by other systems.

To us, however, it seems that partisanship of this kind makes it impossible to understand what has happened. One is not so bitterly disillusioned about Soviet foreign policy, for instance, if one never accepted the drive for "collective security" as an article of faith, but rather saw in it a device of Moscow's foreign policy. *The New Republic* is in this position, because it opposed collective security as a policy for this country and was always extremely dubious about its success in Europe.

When Litvinov's line was adopted by the Soviet Foreign Office, it was as sharp a break with the past and as much a contradiction of former Bolshevik theory as the later shift from collective security to the friendship with Hitler. Leading Communists had never trusted capitalist nations to keep their promises and had always expected another imperialist war. They thought the League of Nations was a joke. Their main concern was to preserve the Soviet Union against attack, and, doubtless, to profit from the quarrels of others. These opinions were not changed when the USSR joined the League and Litvinov began his skillful campaign for resistance to aggressors. When at the same time the Comintern took its new line of coöperating with democratic forces in other countries to oppose fascist aggression, it acted mainly as an adjunct to the diplomatic maneuver.

The secret of the whole business was that the Soviet Union feared an attack by Hitler, probably with the aid of Italy and Japan, possibly also with the backing of Britain and France. If it could convince the Western powers that Hitler was the chief enemy it could split its opponents and deflect the aggression. Collective security through the League was the obvious weapon for the purpose. If it could be put across, Hitler's attack might be prevented entirely, but if Hitler did attack, the Soviet Union would have allies. It was a good, hard-headed piece of *Realpolitik*, comparable with the strategy of any other European foreign office. The ideological mumbo-jumbo in which it was clothed was an instance of the thoroughness with which the Soviet forces follow through any line adopted. The propaganda carried masses of people along with it, including many devout Communists, but it was sunk without a trace when Stalin decided that collective security would not work.

And he had good reasons for deciding this, as everyone will now admit. The marvel is that he flogged the dead horse for so long. There was never any chance that the United States would join the parade. Collective security suffered an uninterrupted series of defeats—in Ethiopia, in Austria, in Spain. Munich gave it the final blow. After that, what reason had the Kremlin to believe that the policy was serviceable any more? Britain and France seemed to have no will to resist; they had furthermore deprived themselves of enormous strategical advantages. It was plain enough that the leading powers in both Western democracies were more afraid of Stalin than of Hitler. Even after their change of front, their attempt to win Moscow into an alliance was a half-hearted one. The blunders of Baldwin, Chamberlain and Daladier virtually forced Stalin into isolation.

And there he was, back where he started. The time-honored tactic of any politician is, if he cannot make a good deal with one side, to make it with the other. No dependable allies would safeguard the Soviet Union against attack, and so, he thought, it must fortify itself. In a series of brilliant strokes, Stalin utilized Hitler's plight to entrench himself in Poland, in the Baltic, in the Balkans. Military motives ruled, regardless of concern for other peoples. The defense of Leningrad and of the Ukraine was immensely strengthened. The Comintern has done its part, by retreating from the popular front and dropping anti-fascism, to return to the old anti-imperialist-war revolutionary position.

It is only when one looks at these moves through an ideological fog that they are hard to understand. The Soviet Foreign Office is no more altruistic than those in London, Paris, Berlin and Rome. But also it is no more villainous. We do not believe that Stalin has started out on a Napoleonic career of conquest. The dangers of war are too great on the home front, as he must well know. It is, of course, conceivable that he would make this mistake; anything is conceivable in this crazy world. But the Soviet economy does not require additional territory except for defense of weak boundaries, and the time for military assistance to world revolution has not arrived. What is going on now is pressure discreetly applied where it can produce immediate results, and diplomatic intrigue of the old familiar kind.

At home, the Stalin dictatorship has mowed down a succession of enemies and potential enemies, together with many innocent persons, by the old conspiratorial technique of espionage and terrorism. It had been the hope of those who saw some good in the Russian Revolution that this ugly repression would gradually die out, and be replaced by a political system more in consonance with socialist ideals. There were times when this seemed to be occurring. At any rate, the terror affected for a long time mainly those prominent in politics, leaving the great body of the people untouched except by the general censorship of ideas and the tutelage of the monolithic political system.

Old Bolsheviks might be liquidated, but industries were growing, labor had shorter hours and higher wages, the standard of living was slowly rising, social services spread, popular education was established. The many volumes recording careful observation of revolutionary improvements in Russia cannot be thrown away on account of the recent events. The last purges, however, beginning after the assassination of Kirov, seem to have reached so far down as to have pretty thoroughly disorganized the management of Soviet economy. So good a correspondent as G. E. R. Gedye of *The New York Times* describes a difficulty in obtaining ordinary articles of clothing in Moscow which indicates a great deterioration since 1935 and 1936. Apparently the effort of Stalin to keep himself in power by terroristic methods, killing off or removing or frightening whole ranks of people who had developed ability to do things, has seriously inhibited the advance of Soviet society. Nevertheless it seems extreme to say, as Mr. Sheean does, that "the workers have lost every liberty hitherto known to man," or that "the prison and the knout are installed in factory and collective farm," or that surplus value "has been brutally augmented by all the capitalist devices hitherto discovered, applied with ruthless force to a helpless proletariat, and expropriated" for the use of a new class of expropriators. If anything like this is true, then the Soviet state must be so weak internally as not to inspire fear in anyone. It certainly could not endure a war.

There are doubtless Red devils and Red angels, but on the average Communists are simply human beings who should be judged and dealt with as such. We must look beyond their words to their intentions, just as we do with other politicians. Wide-eyed simple faith will not do. We must recognize, too, that Communists in this country dance to the tune Moscow plays, no matter how honest they may be as individuals. That does not mean they ought to be outlawed or persecuted; political terror is just what we dislike most in Russia. But Moscow is not playing our tune; it is playing its own, as any but a fanatic would expect it to do. It does not and has not for a long time sincerely represented any genuine international movement, and it is not a secure repository of the trust of workers or intellectuals in other nations, any more than is London or Paris or Berlin. Yet there are institutions and ideas everywhere in the world that are worthy of respect; there are persons in more than one country who can cooperate as free and independent human beings. The tract for the times is merely that the ambitious attempt of the Comintern to create a monopoly of these precious values has gone bankrupt.

The Corruption of Liberalism

LEWIS MUMFORD

APRIL 29, 1940

As an economic creed, liberalism was undermined by imperialism and monopoly before the nineteenth century closed. But as a personal and social philosophy, liberalism has been dissolving before our eyes only during the past decade. The liberal lacks confidence in himself and in his vision of life. He has shown in every country where the attacks on liberalism have been forceful that he either does not possess stable convictions, or that he lacks the insight and the courage that would enable him to defend them. Continually hoping for the best, the liberal remains unprepared to face the worst; and on the brink of what may turn out another Dark Ages, he continues to scan the horizon for signs of dawn.

The record of liberalism during the last decade has been one of shameful evasion and inept retreat.

Liberalism has compromised with despotism because despotism promised economic benefits to the masses—an old device of despotism. In the case of Soviet Russia liberals continued to preserve an embarrassed silence about the notorious plight of freedom and justice in that country because they had esthetic scruples about appearing to align themselves with those forces in America that opposed Russia for purely reactionary reasons. So they preferred to be tacitly on the side of the greater despots, like Stalin and Hitler, in order to be free of any taint of association with the minor despots of American capitalism. In international affairs liberalism has likewise graciously lent support to the forces of barbarism, in an effort to give the devil his due. And on the theory that war is the worst of evils, the liberals have tearfully acquiesced in the rule of those who, as Blake said, would "forever depress mental and prolong corporeal war."

Liberalism has been on the side of passivism, in the face of danger; it has been on the side of appeasement, when confronted with aggressive acts of injustice; and finally, in America today, as in England yesterday, liberalism has been on the side of "isolation," when confronted with the imminent threat of a worldwide upsurgence of barbarism. Today liberals, by their unwillingness to admit the consequences of a victory by Hitler and Stalin, are emotionally on the side of "peace"—when peace, so-called, at this moment means capitulation to the forces that will not merely wipe out liberalism, but will overthrow certain precious principles with which one element of liberalism has been indelibly associated: freedom of thought, belief in an objective reason, belief in human dignity.

The weakness and confusion and self-betrayal of liberalism during the crisis that has now come to a head, provide one of the most pitiable spectacles that these pitiful times have shown.

Unable to take the measure of our present catastrophe and unable, because of their inner doubts and contradictions and subtleties to make effective decisions, liberals have lost most of their essential convictions, for ideals remain real only when one continues to realize them. Liberals no longer act as if justice mattered, as if truth mattered, as if right mattered, as if humanity as a whole were any concern of theirs: the truth is they no longer dare to act. During the period of the United Front, liberals accepted the leadership of a small communist minority, fanatical, unscrupulous, deeply contemptuous of essential human values, incredibly stupid in tactics and incredibly arrogant in matters of intellectual belief; they accepted this leadership simply because the Communists, alone among the political groups, had firm convictions and the courage to act on them.

Now that the moral treachery of the Communists has placed them alongside their natural tactical allies, the Fascists, many of these liberals have, on practical points at issue, even drifted into a covert defense of Hitlerism. They show far more distrust of the English and French and Finnish peoples, who are resisting the barbarians, than they do of the German and Russian masses who follow, blindly, stupidly, irrationally, without access to any sources of objective fact, the leadership of Hitler and Stalin. These liberals were against Chamberlain when he sought to appease the fascist powers; and they are still against Chamberlain, now that he has reversed his old position. To comfort themselves and keep to their illusions, they concoct imaginary situations in which Stalin suddenly reverses his obvious plans and undermines Hitler—as if anything would be gained for humanity by substituting one impudent dictator for two. . . . In their imaginary world, these liberals are always right; in the real world, they have been consistently wrong. So victimized are some of these liberals by their protective illusions and self-deceptions that it is easy to predict that they will presently swallow without a grimace Hitler's hoax that Nazi Germany is defending the masses against the "capitalist plutocracies."

The Romans used to say that the worst results come about through the corruption of what is good; and one may say this about the present state of liberalism. But the defects of liberalism are not due to isolated mistakes of judgment that individual liberals have made; they are due to fatal deficiencies that go to the very roots of liberal philosophy. Unfortunately, liberalism's weaknesses are so debilitating that they not merely undermine its own will-to-survive, but they may also give up elements in a longer human tradition, on whose maintenance our very civilization depends.

Liberalism is a very mixed body of doctrine. So it is important that, in discussing its errors, we should detach its essential and enduring values from those which have characterized a particular age, class or group.

Like democracy, with which it has close historic affiliation, liberalism during the last generation has been subject to a violent assault. This came originally from the Marxian revolutionaries of the Left; but the blows were doubled through the triumphant action of the fascist revolutionaries of the Right. By now these extremes have met in their attack on liberalism.

According to the Marxian critics, liberalism arose at the same time as capitalism; and therefore, liberalism is doomed to disappear when capitalism is overthrown. From the Marxian point of view, ideas are but the shadows of existing economic institutions: human liberty depends upon freedom of investment, freedom of trade. One might think, to hear a Marxian critic, that the concept of freedom had never been framed before the Manchester school came into existence.

So the anti-liberals, pretending mainly to attack capitalism, have also attacked the belief in the worth and dignity of the individual personality: they have undermined the notion of *Humanity*, extending beyond race, creed, class or other boundaries. So, too, they have sought to wipe out the concept of an impersonal law, built up by slow accretions that reach back into an ancient past, forming a coherent pattern tending toward justice. The anti-liberals have upheld, rather, the one-sided personal rule of a party or a man. In Germany and Spain the basic concept of law has been so completely overthrown that a man may be tried and convicted for a crime that did not exist in law at the time he committed it.

Now the universal elements in liberalism, the moralizing elements, are the real objects of the fascist attacks. These universal elements arose long before modern capitalism; they were part of the larger human tradition, embodied in the folkways of the Jews, in the experimental philosophy of the Greeks, in the secular practices of the Roman Empire, in the sacred doctrines of the Christian Church, in the philosophies of the great post-medieval humanists. The Marxian notion that ideas are always the shadows of the existing economic institutions runs bluntly against facts precisely at this point. For although a culture forms a related organic whole, a residue is left in each period and place which tends to become part of the general heritage of mankind. This residue is relatively small in amount but infinitely precious; and no single class or people can create it or be its sole keeper.

The effort to equate Manchester liberalism with the humanist traditions of personal responsibility, personal freedom and personal expression is sometimes shared by the defenders of capitalistic privilege; that is the gross fallacy of those who try to tie together private capitalism and "the American way." But these notions are false, whether held by the absolutists of private property or by the absolutists who would challenge the regime of private property. The most important principles in liberalism do not cling exclusively to liberalism: what gives them their strength is their universality and their historic continuity. Confucius, Socrates, Plato, Aristotle, testify to them no less than Jefferson and Mill. Liberalism took over this humanist tradition, revamped it, and finally united it to a new body of hopes and beliefs that grew up in the eighteenth century.

This second element in liberalism, which seems to many people as important as the first, rests upon a quite different set of premises. Liberalism in this sense was symbolically a child of Voltaire and Rousseau: the Voltaire who thought that the craft of priests was responsible for the misery of the world, and the Rousseau who thought that man was born naturally good and had been corrupted only by evil institutions. It was likewise a by-product of the inventors and industrialists of the period, who, concentrating upon the improvement of the means of life, thought sincerely that the ends of living would more or less take care of themselves.

This pragmatic liberalism, which I shall here distinguish from the ideal liberalism, was vastly preoccupied with the machinery of life. It was characteristic of this creed to overemphasize the part played by political and mechanical invention, by abstract thought and practical contrivance. And accordingly it minimized the role of instinct, tradition, history; it was unaware of the dark forces of the unconscious; it was suspicious of either the capricious or the incalculable, for the only universe it could rule was a measured one, and the only type of human character it could understand was the utilitarian one. That there are modes of insight into man and into the cosmos which science does not possess, the liberal did not suspect; he took for granted that the emotional and spiritual life of man needs no other foundation than the rational, utilitarian activities associated with the getting of a living. Hence, finally, liberalism's progressive neglect of the fields of esthetics, ethics and religion: these matters were left to traditional thinkers, with the confident belief that they would eventually drop out of existence, mere vestiges of the race's childhood. On the whole most liberals today have produced no effective thought in any of these fields; and they live, as it were, on the debris of past dogmas and buried formulations. Unconscious, for example, of the sources of their ethical ideas, they pick up more or less what happens to be lying around them, without any effort at consistency or clarity, still less at creativeness: here a scrap left over from childhood, there a fragment of Kant or Bentham, or again a dash of Machiavelli, pacifist Quakers one moment and quaking Nietzscheans the next.

In short, it is not unfair to say that the pragmatic liberal has taken the world of personality, the world of values, feelings, emotions, wishes, purposes, for granted. He assumed either that this world did not exist, or that it was relatively unimportant; at all events, if it did exist, it could be safely left to itself, without cultivation. For him men were essentially good, and only faulty economic and political institutions—defects purely in the mechanism of society—kept them from becoming better. That there might be internal obstacles to external improvement seemed to him absurd. That there was as large a field for imaginative design and rational discipline in the building of a personality as in the building of a skyscraper did not occur to him. Unfortunately, immature personalities, irrational personalities, demoralized personalities are as inevitable as weeds in an uncultivated garden when no deliberate attempt is made to provide a constructive basis for personal development.

Behind this failure to establish, on a fresh basis, a normative discipline for the personality was a singular optimism—the belief that it was not needed. Did not liberalism imply an emancipation from the empty institutional religion, from the saws, precepts, moralizings of the past? Did this not mean that "science," which confessedly despised norms, would eventually supply all the guidance necessary for human conduct? Such was the innocence of the liberal that those who were indifferent to ethical values thought of themselves as realists. They could hardly understand William James when he called emotionality the *sine qua non* of moral perception. But the fact was that the most old-fashioned theologian, with a sense of human guilt and human error, was by far the better realist. Though the theologian's view of the external world might be scientifically weak, his view of the internal world, the world of value and personality, included an understanding of constant human phenomena—sin, corruption, evil—on which the liberal closed his eyes.

Pragmatic liberalism did not believe in a world where the questions of good and evil were not incidental but of radical importance. Its adherents thought that they would presently abolish the evils inherent in life by popularizing anesthetics and by extending the blessings of the machine. They did not believe in the personal life. That was outmoded. Esthetic interests, moral discipline, the habits of contemplation and evaluation, all this seemed mere spiritual gymnastics: they preferred more physical exercises. By activity (busy work) pragmatic liberals kept their eyes manfully on the mere surface of living. They did not believe that any sensible man would, except when he made his will, face the more ultimate facts of existence. For them, the appraisal of death was a neurotic symptom; happily, science's steady advances in hygiene and medicine might postpone further and further that unpleasant occasion itself.

This failure to deal with first and last things, to confront, except in a hurried, shamefaced way, the essential facts of life and death, has been responsible for some of the slippery thinking on the subject of war that has characterized liberals recently. One of them, in private conversation, told me that he could not face a political decision which might lead to war and thereby bring about the death of other human beings. When I objected that the failure to make such a decision in the present international crisis would possibly lead to the less fruitful death of the same human beings six months or six years hence, he confessed that any extra time spared for the private enjoyment of life today seemed that much gained. I do not doubt the honesty of this liberal; but it is obvious that he has ceased to live in a meaningful world. For a meaningful world is one that holds a future that extends beyond the incomplete personal life of the individual; so that a life sacrificed at the right moment is a life well spent, while a life too carefully hoarded, too ignominiously preserved, may be a life utterly wasted.

Is it any wonder, then, that pragmatic liberalism has been incapable of making firm ethical judgments or of implementing them with action? Its color-blindness to moral values is its most serious weakness today; hence it cannot distinguish between barbarism and civilization. Indeed, it is even inclined to pass a more favorable verdict on barbarism when it shows superiority in material organization. Refusing to recognize the crucial problem of evil, those who follow this creed are incapable of coping with the intentions of evil men: they look in vain for merely intellectual mistakes to account for the conduct of those who have chosen to flout man's long efforts to become civilized. Evil for the pragmatic liberal has no positive dimensions: he conceives it as a mere lack of something whose presence would be good. Poverty is an evil, because it indicates the lack of a good, namely riches. For this kind of liberal, the most heinous fact about a war is not the evil intentions and purposes that one or both sides may disclose: it is mainly the needless waste of material, the unbearable amount of human suffering, the premature deaths.

Lacking any true insight into these stubborn facts of human experience—corruption, evil, irrational desire—liberals also fail to understand that evil often lies beyond purely rational treatment, that a mere inquiry into causes, mere reasonableness and sweetness in one's attitude, may not only fail to cure an evil disposition but may aggravate it. Now, unfortunately, there are times when an attitude of intellectual humility and sympathy is entirely inappropriate to the press of a particular situation. There are times when active resistance or coercion is the only safeguard against the conduct of men who mean ill against human society. The alternative to coercion is what the religious call conversion, salvation, grace, on the part of the offender. That, too, is essentially a pre-rational process, not hostile to reason, but proceeding by a short cut into an area that reason cannot directly touch. Liberals tend to minimize the effectiveness of both coercion and conversion, both force and grace; but it is hard to point to any large and significant social change in which both elements did not play a part.

Coercion is, of course, no substitute for intelligent inquiry and no cure in itself for anti-social conduct. But just as there are maladies in the human body which call for surgery rather than diet—though diet, if applied at an early stage, might have been sufficient—so there are moments of crisis in society when anti-social groups or nations that resist the ordinary methods of persuasion and compromise must be dealt with by coercion. In such moments, to hesitate, to temporize, only gives the disease a deeper hold on the organism; and to center one's efforts upon changing the mind of one's opponent, by opposing reason to his irrationality, and to overlook the elementary precaution of depriving him of his weapons for attacking one, is to commit a fatal offense against the very method one seeks to uphold.

The liberal's notion that reasoning in the spirit of affable compromise is the only truly human way of meeting one's opponent overlooks the important part played by force and grace. And his unctuous notion that evil must not seriously be combated because the person who attempts to oppose it may ultimately have to use physical force, and will become soiled by the act of fighting, is a gospel of despair. This belief is the core of his defeatist response to Nazism; it means a practice turning the world over to the rule of the violent, the brutal and the inhuman, who have no such fine scruples, because the humane are too dainty in their virtue to submit to any possible assault on it. Now the dangers are real: force *does* brutalize the users of it; when blood is spilt, anger rises and reason temporarily disappears. Hence force is not to be used daily in the body politic, like food or exercise; it is only to be used in an emergency, like medicine or the surgeon's knife. Fascism is barbarous, not because it uses force, but because it *prefers* force to rational accommodation: it deliberately turns mental and physical coercion into human nature's daily food.

But to surrender in advance, to take no step because one may make a false step, is to pursue an illusory perfection and to achieve an actual paralysis. Force cannot be left behind, no matter how humane and rational our standards of conduct. He who under no circumstances and for no human purpose will resort to force, abandons the possibility of justice and freedom. The German socialists took their legalistic pacifism seriously; they got their reward in the concentration camp. The English Laborites, following the nerveless Tory leadership, took the same position in international affairs; and that led not alone to the betrayal of Czecho-Slovakia but to the present endangerment of Western civilization itself.

Despite these sinister examples, the same guileless reasoning has been driving our American liberals into a position of queasy non-resistance, on the ground that the only motive that could sanction our immediate opposition to Hitlerism would be our belief that those opposing him now were angels. People who think in these terms are secretly complimenting themselves upon virtues and purities that neither they nor their countrymen possess; they are guilty of that most typical liberal sin, the sin of Pharisaism. It is because we, too, are not without guilt that we may, in the interest of preserving humanity from more abject humiliations, oppose Hitler and Stalin with a clean heart. To be too virtuous to live is one of the characteristic moral perversions of liberalism in our generation.

The essential moral weakness of liberalism, which I have only glanced at here, is coupled with a larger weakness in the liberal philosophy. Along with liberalism's admirable respect for rational science and experimental practice, goes an overvaluation of intellectual activities as such, and an undervaluation of the emotional and affective sides of life. In the liberal theology, emotions and feelings have taken the place of a personal devil. Now as every good psychologist knows, and as Count Korzybski has ably demonstrated, emotions and feelings, associated with the most devious and remote body processes, are involved in all thought. Reason and emotion are inseparable: their detachment is a practical device of limited use. Thought that is empty of emotion and feeling, that bears no organic relation to life, is just as foreign to effective reason as emotion that is disproportionate to the stimulus or is without intellectual foundations and references. The body, the unconscious, the pre-rational are all important to sound thought. But because the liberal has sought no positive discipline for emotion and feeling, there is an open breach between his affective life and his intellectual interests. His first impulse in any situation is to get rid of emotion because it may cause him to go wrong. Unfortunately for his effort to achieve poise, a purely intellectual judgment, eviscerated of emotional reference, often causes wry miscalculations. The calmness and sang-froid of Benes was perhaps his most serious weakness during the long period before the Munich crisis; ominously, it repeated the self-defeating mood of Bruening, in the days preceding his removal. Instead of priding himself on not being "carried away by his emotions," the liberal should rather be a little alarmed because he often has no emotions that could, under any conceivable circumstances, carry him away.

This is not a new criticism. Graham Wallas lectured on the subject twenty years ago. He showed that in all valid thinking that referred to human situations it was important to be able to use the emotions, not to put them into cold storage. Liberalism, by and large, has prided itself upon its colorlessness and its emotional neutrality; and this liberal suspicion of passion is partly responsible for the liberal's ineptitude for action. In a friendly world, pragmatic liberalism leads to nothing worse than a tepid and boring life; but in a hostile world, it may easily lead to death. If one meets a poisonous snake in one's path it is important, for a *rational* reaction, to have a prompt emotion of fear; for fear releases the flow of adrenaline into the bloodstream, and that will not merely put the organism on the alert but will give it the extra strength either to run away or to attack. Merely to look at the snake abstractedly, without sensing danger and experiencing fear, may lead to the highly irrational step of permitting the snake to draw near without being on guard against the reptile's bite. The liberal's lack of a sense of danger when confronted by the avowed programs and the devastating achievements of the totalitarian regimes is one cause of society's rapid disintegration.

Liberalism under its assumption that men ideally should think without emotion or feeling deprives itself of the capacity to be human. This is one of the gravest features of the present crisis; the cold withdrawal of human feeling by the liberals today is almost as terrible a crime against civilization as the active inhumanity of the fascists. And that withdrawal is responsible for liberalism's deep-seated impotence.

Closely allied with the liberal's emotional anesthesia is his incurable optimism—a wrinkled smile left over from the eighteenth century, when, in the first flush of confidence, the possibilities of human advance seemed boundless. This optimism belonged to a constructive and expanding age: in its inception, it was a healthy reaction against the moldering institutions and precedents of the past. But it has become an unfortunate handicap in a period when destructive forces are gaining the upper hand, and when, in the approaching stabilization of population and industry, the malevolence of the human will, on the part of the propertied classes, may at critical moments—as already in Germany and Italy—give unlimited power to those who represent barbarism. Destruction, malice, violence, hold no temptation for the liberal; and in the kindness of his heart, he cannot bring himself to believe that they may viciously influence the conduct of any large part of mankind. The liberals could not understand that the gift of Czecho-Slovakia to Nazi Germany could not appease Hitler: that one might as well offer the carcass of a dead deer in a butcher store to a hunter who seeks the animal as prey—the meat being valued chiefly as a symbol of his prowess. And that is why the talk of mere economic adjustments that would enable the fascist states to live at peace with the rest of the world is muddled nonsense; it assumes, contrary to fact, that fascism springs out of rational motives and pursues concrete utilitarian ends. The bad arrangements of the peace of Versailles did not by themselves create fascism, nor will the best results of a magnanimous peace conference be able at once to wipe out its destructive impulses and undermine its irrational philosophy. Unfortunately it is not in Ricardo or Marx or Lenin, but in Dante and Shakespeare and Dostoevsky, that an understanding of the true sources of fascism are to be found. Economic explanations reflected a reality in the nineteenth century; they disguise a reality—the claim to barbaric conquest—today.

During the last ten years, the optimism of the liberals has remained unshaken. The incurable tendency of the liberal is to believe the best about everybody: to hope when there is no reason to hope, and to exhibit the nicest moral qualms, the most delicate intellectual scruples, in situations that demand that he wade in and coarsely exert his utmost effort. We now face a world that is on the brink, perhaps of another Dark Age; and because a Dark Age is not included in the liberal chronology, liberalism glibly refuses to accept the evidence of its senses. Like the sun-dial, it cannot tell time on a stormy day. So, habitually, the pragmatic liberals brand those whose eyes are open to the human devastation around them as "hysterical," "mystical," "having concealed fascist tendencies," or—taking a leaf from the Hitlerites—as "warmongers."

Now one must remember that liberalism has two sides. There is an ideal liberalism, deeply rooted in the example and experience of humanity: a doctrine that commands the allegiance of all well disposed men. And there is a transient doctrine of liberalism, the pragmatic side, which grew up in the eighteenth century out of a rather adolescent pride in the scientific conquest of nature and the invention of power machinery: this is the side that emphasizes the utilitarian aspects of life that concentrates on purely intellectual issues, and that, in its exclusive concern for tolerance and "open-mindedness" is ready to extend its benevolent protection to those who openly oppose the very purposes of civilization. What is important in ideal liberalism are elements like the great Roman notion of *Humanity*, united in the pursuit of freedom and justice, embracing all races and conditions. This ideal is radically opposed at every point to the autarchy advocated by the Fascists; and it is no less opposed to the isolationism, moral and physical and political, advocated by most American liberals—a passive milk-and-water version of the Fascist's contemptuous attitude toward the rest of the human race.

Plainly the liberal who proposes to do nothing on behalf of humanity until the lives of individual Americans are actually threatened by a fascist military invasion will have very little left to save. For life is not worth fighting for: bare life is worthless. Justice is worth fighting for, order is worth fighting for, culture—the cooperation and the communion of the peoples of the world—is worth fighting for: these universal principles and values give purpose and direction to human life. At present, the liberals are so completely deflated and debunked, they have unconsciously swallowed so many of the systematic lies and beliefs of barbarism, that they lack the will to struggle for the essential principles of ideal liberalism: justice, freedom, truth. By clinging to the myth of isolationism, they are helping to create that insane national pride and that moral callousness out of which fascism so easily flowers.

What is the result? Pragmatic liberalism has flatly betrayed ideal liberalism. The values that belong to the latter have been compromised away, vitiated, ruthlessly cast overboard. The permanent heritage of liberalism has been bartered for the essentially ignoble notion of national security, in itself a gross illusion. These liberals are loath to conceive of the present war as one waged by barbarism against civilization. Though many of them were moved by the plight of the Spanish Republicans, they have managed to insulate themselves from any human feeling over the fate of the humiliated and bullied Czechs, the tortured Jews, the murdered Poles, the basely threatened Finns—or the French and English who may next face extermination—just as many of them have managed to keep supremely cool about the horrors that have befallen the Chinese. They have eyes and they see not; they have ears and they hear not; and in their deliberate withholding of themselves from the plight of humanity they have even betrayed their own narrow values, for they are witnessing the dissolution of those worldwide cooperations upon which the growth of science, technics and industrial wealth depends. This corruption has bitten deep into pragmatic liberalism. The isolationism of a Charles Beard or a Stuart Chase or a Quincy Howe is indeed almost as much a sign of barbarism as the doctrines of a Rosenberg or a Gottfried Feder. No doubt the American liberals mean well; their good intentions are traditional. But they cling to the monstrous illusion that they can save themselves and their country by cutting themselves off—to use Hawthorne's words in *Ethan Brand*—from the magnetic chain of humanity. Their success would spell the end of every human hope they still share.

In a disintegrating world, pragmatic liberalism has lost its integrity but retained its limitations. The moral ardor of the eighteenth-century liberals, who faced difficult odds, strove mightily, risked much, has gone. The isolationism that is preached by our liberals today means fascism tomorrow. Their passivism today means militarism tomorrow. Their emphasis upon mere security today—and this applies especially to the current American youth movement—means the acceptance of despotism tomorrow. While their complacency, their emotional tepidity, their virtuous circumspectness, *their unwillingness to defend civilization with all its faults and all its capacity for rectifying those faults*, means barbarism tomorrow. Meanwhile, the ideal values of liberalism lack support and the human horizon contracts before our eyes. While the barbarians brazenly attack our civilization, those who should now be exerting every fiber to defend it are covertly attacking it, too. On the latter falls the heavier guilt.

What are the prospects, then, for the Western World's surviving the present crisis, with even a handful of the scientific discoveries, the inventions, the literary and esthetic and scholarly achievements, the humanizing patterns of life, that the last three centuries so magnificently created or expanded? On any candid view, the prospects are poor. Barbarism has seized the initiative and is on the march. But as the crisis sharpens, as the evils that threaten us become more formidable, one possibility remains, born of the crisis itself: the psychological possibility of a large-scale conversion. Are the pragmatic liberals shattered enough yet to be ready for a reintegration? Are they capable of rededicating themselves to the tasks of ideal liberalism? If so, there is at least a ray of hope: the optimism of pathology, a commonplace of both religion and psychoanalysis.

To achieve a new basis for personal development and communal action, the liberal need not abandon his earlier concern for science, mechanism, the rational organization of society. But he can no longer regard the world that is embraced by these things as complete or all-sufficient. The world of political action must transcend that of the Economic Man: it must be as large as the fully developed human personality itself. No mere revision of Marxism, no mere ingenious political program with a few socialistic planks added or taken away, no attempt to make five disparate economic systems produce profit in a community where new social motives must take the place of dwindling or absent profits—none of these shallow dodges will suffice. What is demanded is a recrystallization of the positive values of life, and an understanding of the basic issues of good and evil, of power and form, of force and grace, in the actual world. In short: the crisis presses toward a social conversion, deep-seated, organic, religious in its essence, so that no part of personal or political existence will be untouched by it: a conversion that will transcend the arid pragmatism that has served as a substitute religion. For only the living—those for whom the world has meaning—can continue to live, and willingly make the fierce sacrifices and heroic efforts the present moment demands.

To the disoriented liberals of today one must repeat the advice that Krishna offered Arjuna on the eve of battle, as reported in the *Bhagavad-Gita.* Like the liberals, Arjuna hesitated, debated, had specious moral scruples, remembered his relatives and friends on the other side, clung to the hope of safety in a situation that did not permit him to enjoy it. Victory, Krishna pointed out, is never guaranteed beforehand; and what is more, it is irrelevant to the issue one must face. What is important is that one should attend to the overwhelming duty of the moment, in a spirit of clear-sighted understanding. "Counting gain or loss as one, prepare for battle!" In that spirit—*only* in that spirit—can civilization still be saved.

Mr. Mumford and the Liberals

EDITORIAL

APRIL 29, 1940

That ill-defined personage, the liberal, has been the target for many heavy projectiles in recent years. He had long been inured to opposition from the believers in tradition and orthodoxy. Even hotter fire has recently flamed from radical innovators on Right and Left—Fascists, Nazis and Communists. But the liberal, partial to reasonableness and understanding though he is, thrives on battle. He should not be disconcerted even when one of his own kind swings into action with a volley squarely at his front. For after all it was self-searching, as opposed to acceptance of a hand-me-down uniform, that made him a liberal in the first place. Nevertheless he may be deeply disturbed by the implication in Lewis Mumford's eloquent philippic on "The Corruption of Liberalism," in this issue of *The New Republic,* that like Tennyson's noble but slightly ridiculous Six Hundred he not only sees cannon to right of him, cannon to left of him, cannon in front of him, but is riding into the valley of death without good reason why.

Many a reader of the article who has classified himself as liberal will be puzzled by an apparent lack of direction in Mr. Mumford's fire. Surely it is not the modern liberal who in childish optimism has been believing in an automatic millennium, but the sentimental Victorian and his descendant, the complacent apologist for "the American system." The doleful prophecies of the liberals have for years made them shunned as spoilsports or even traitors. It is not the liberal who has failed hotly to feel the menace of Mussolini and Hitler, but the opponents of change and action, the beneficiaries of settled institutions. One would think, to read Mr. Mumford, that Baldwin, Chamberlain, Henderson, Daladier and Bonnet were leading liberals, or that the editors of *The New Statesman* in England, *L'Oeuvre* in France and *The New Republic* and *The Nation* in the United States were responsible for the surrender of Austria, Czecho-Slovakia, Spain, Poland and Finland.

It would be beneath the dignity of the subject, however, to ride scatheless out of the battle merely because of Mr. Mumford's faulty aim. He raises issues that need to be confronted, not dodged. One of these is the relationship of emotion and reason, and another, growing out of that, is the question whether the solid values of liberalism—concerning which Mr. Mumford and some of his readers are undoubtedly in agreement—are being betrayed by liberals because of a lack of depth, courage, vision, or whatever it is that is required to defend them.

On the issue of sterile intellectualism there is much danger of becoming trapped into superficial conclusions. There is, as Mr. Mumford points out, a shallow way of thinking and living in which strong emotions are repressed rather than acknowledged and used. Such a habit tends to futility in action, not to speak of pathology in the individual. But this type of character is not a special mark of those who hold liberal opinions. It can be found in every group in society. One must not, moreover, confuse this personality trait, as Mr. Mumford seems to do, with the error in thought which held that man is by nature good and needs only the guidance of reason in order to choose the better way. Though the error lay at the root of mistakes in liberal and other nineteenth-century philosophies, it was held by many with strong emotional capacities and balanced personalities. The theologians and others who denied it not only suffered often from twisted emotional lives, but were guilty of as great a fallacy—that man was a victim of original sin, and that punishment and the exploitation of a sense of guilt were necessary for his redemption.

Modern psychology, and especially Freud, have indeed revealed emotional depths in the personality which most people do not like to recognize, and these buried emotions include some that, if unadjusted and undisciplined, may seem like the incarnation of evil—such as murderous aggression. But the appeal to Freud will not bear out the conclusion that the proper remedy is a reversion to moral condemnation of the mentally immature. It is, of course, elementary that sane persons need to defend themselves against dangerous psychotics, and that there are crises when force is the only possible defense. Yet no doctor would maintain that straitjackets and iron shackles have any therapeutic value; as a matter of fact such instruments of restraint are little used nowadays in mental hospitals. The only possible means of salvation for the emotionally sick is one that the liberals and scientific humanists would thoroughly approve—an objective and sympathetic understanding. We have every reason to suppose that something like this is true concerning the evils manifest in modern society.

The recognition of the large part played by emotions in human life does not lead soundly to the conclusion that uninhibited or disoriented emotional reaction is the route to health and safety. The Nazis themselves are guilty of setting primitive emotional impulses against reason, and glorifying the former by contrast. This gives rise to an obscurantist and destructive mysticism. Critics like Mr. Mumford are in danger of making the same mistake. He has, in his understanding of the subject, taken only the first step—that emotions, however disagreeable or discreditable, should be recognized rather than repressed. But he seems to have stopped there, rather than going on to understand that a main purpose of recognizing them is to coordinate them, by use of the reasoning faculties, and so to be capable of dealing effectively with reality. Mr. Mumford's own example of the fear of snakes can be turned against him. Mere common observation would show him that capacity to escape or cure snakebite is not proportional to the amount of unreasoning terror inspired in the individual by the sight of a snake.

All this may seem remote from the subject which apparently is closest to Mr. Mumford's heart—hatred of isolation. But since he chose not to discuss directly the wisdom of entering the war, but rather on broader grounds to impugn the characters of those who are against participation, this discussion has been the relevant one.

There are, of course, isolationists who lightly decline to recognize unpleasant facts or to feel anything about what is going on in the world outside their own political boundaries. But Mr. Mumford should be the last to deny that it is possible to feel deeply, and intelligently as well, about the waste and horror of war—not just the killing of the best of a whole generation but the traumata to which millions of personalities and the most precious institutions are subjected by it. He should take more pains to remember the deep shock to the sense of human dignity which was suffered by the incurring of such losses twenty-five years ago for causes which turned out to be deception and illusion. And he ought to admit that it may be as false to principle to blind oneself to the crimes and deficiencies of those who today rule Britain and France because of belief in the cause one hopes they are fighting for, as it was five years ago to ignore the crimes and deficiencies of the rulers of Russia because of emotional dedication to the declared aims of the Russian Revolution.

It is a tragic and momentous decision before which the leaders of America stand in the present months. The deepest and best in them, and in the liberal tradition, lend at least as much force to the impulse to fulfill the potentialities of human life in their own country as they do to fighting evil in Europe, at the risk of great loss. Nothing will be gained in the task of choosing the right course by refusing to admit the validity of emotions on both sides. One does not win integration or dignity by denying the existence of inner emotional conflict, and making up for the repression of one side by overcompensation on the other. What is required is a course of thought and action that will give outlet not merely to hatred and fear but to the creative drives as well. It is not out of the question to harmonize them all in an effective program which will have the desired influence in the objective world. It is not a mark of barren isolationism to believe with all one's heart and soul that the best contribution Americans can make to the future of humanity is to fulfill democracy in the United States.

Limits of the New Left

CHRISTOPHER JENCKS

OCTOBER 21, 1967

Week before last, I reported on a meeting in Czechoslovakia between 40 Americans and two delegations of Vietnamese revolutionaries. That report concentrated on the Vietnamese side of the dialogue; now I want to say something about the Americans there. The majority were young and came from what is now irrevocably christened the "New Left." Some were active in the antiwar movement, organizing teach-ins, writing, helping set up protest groups and fomenting draft resistance. Others were working with poor whites and blacks on grievances only obliquely related to the war; they knew relatively little about Vietnam when they arrived in Bratislava. But they all saw the war as an inevitable by-product of some ill-defined sickness in the American system, which could only be cured by radical political remedies. They were contemptuous of liberals who regard the war as a colossal blunder and who think that when the war is over America will get on with rehabilitating a flawed but redeemable society. For this reason almost all the young radicals at Bratislava were slightly scornful of the traditional "peace movement," which they regard as ideologically naïve and politically ineffective. They had little in common with the clergymen and pacifists from the pre-Vietnam peace movement who were also in Bratislava, except distaste for the war.

To me, the most stricking fact about the young radicals was the extent to which they identified with the Viet Cong. This identification was almost entirely confined to people born after the outbreak of World War II. I myself am only a few years older, have been bitterly critical of the war and support the National Liberation Front in the limited sense that I would rather let it take power than continue either the war or the present Thieu-Ky regime. Yet I do not feel instinctively allied to the NLF, and I know hardly anyone else my age who does. Indeed, I would say that inability to identify with the Viet Cong is one of the obvious differences between the generation which came to political consciousness under Eisenhower, as I did, and the generation which worked out its political position under John Kennedy and Lyndon Johnson, as the young radicals at Bratislava had.

This New Left sympathy for the NLF is not based on any similarity of style or of temperament. The Vietnamese revolutionaries we met were not the joyless Communist apparatchiks whom the Soviet Union would send to such a meeting, but they were dignified, restrained, disciplined and apparently selfless—about as unlike the loose-tongued, anarchistic, spontaneous Americans as any group could conceivably be. It was easy to respect their courage and patience under incredibly difficult conditions, and to find them personally charming, but it would not be very easy for a young American to establish an intimate personal friendship with or psychological understanding of such strangers. Nor do I think most of the Americans at Bratislava would find life in post-revolutionary Vietnam congenial; on the contrary, I suspect most would find themselves in opposition fairly soon. The common bond between the New Left and the NLF is not, then, a common dream or a common experience, but a common enemy: the U.S. government, the system, the Establishment. The young radicals' admiration for the NLF stems from the feeling that the NLF is resisting The Enemy successfully, whereas they are not.

Speaking for the older generation at Bratislava, David Dellinger said to the Vietnamese at one point, "You are Vietnamese and you love Vietnam. You must remember that we are Americans and we love America too, even though we oppose our government's policies with all our strength." The young man next to me groaned at this expression of patriotic sentiment, and as I looked around the room at the other American faces I got the impression that he was not alone in his feeling that almost anything non-American was likely to be better than almost anything American.

The historical failures of American radicalism are, I think, linked in important ways to this distaste for American culture and American institutions. One reason why the radical revival of the early 1960's captured the American imagination and achieved modest success was that it seemed so completely native, so true to the professed high purposes of the Republic. It appealed to the Constitution, to schoolbook stories of what America should be, to injustices which troubled millions of decent citizens.

But the New Left has never numbered patience among its virtues; it soured on America once it became clear that radical change, rather amorphously defined, would be neither quick nor easy. If America could not undo the evil consequences of racism in a few years, then America was hopeless. If America could not restrain its military, if it could not support revolutions in the underdeveloped countries, then America was a positive menace and the primary task of our time was to contain American power. Having begun a few years earlier with great residual faith in the American people, and a conviction that "the people" had strengths from which a new better society might be built, many of the young radicals moved to the conclusion that Americans as a whole were hopelessly complacent, corrupt and self-centered. This view is not yet universal in the New Left, but it seems to be gaining ground. The result was a dramatic contrast at Bratislava between optimistic, confident Vietnamese and pessimistic, self-deprecating Americans. They sang "We Shall Overcome," but it was a nostalgic tribute to an earlier era, not an expression of confidence in the future.

The central weakness of the New Left, it seems to me, is its attitude toward authority. This came out clearly two years ago when this journal asked a number of young radicals to describe what they thought was wrong with America and what should be done about it. The essays were almost monotonous in their insistence that the people have no voice in decisions which affect their lives; that they are powerless.

That is true, but it is by no means a universal complaint. The toiling masses of Marxist memory still toil, but they do not seem to feel oppressed by the institutions within which they live. On the contrary, most defend these institutions staunchly. If, for example, you ask poor people what is wrong with America, they will usually complain about the *results* of decisions which affect their lives, not the *process* by which the decisions are made. They want good schools or good housing; relatively few of them want a voice in the operation of these facilities if the results are satisfactory. The New Left, however, cares more about how a decision gets made than about what the decision is. The Free Speech Movement at Berkeley exemplified this outlook. Very few Berkeley students had any real interest in whether the university allowed political advocacy on its property. But many came to resent the university's making such decisions arbitrarily without consulting anyone, and thousands enjoyed participating in the struggle to alter the rules.

An allergy to paternalism is not unique to the New Left, but young radicals of the kind who went to Bratislava have taken it more seriously than most anyone in my generation and more seriously than most of their peers. It is this which has driven many into total opposition to the American way of life, which, they say, is largely shaped by big organizations and involves passive dependence on enormous numbers of remote experts, bureaucracies and commercial enterprises. Their opposition has led a growing minority to talk about the need for a revolution in America—though no one has any clear idea who would organize such a revolution, or whom it would bring to power, or how post-revolutionary America would be organized. It is this opposition, too, which has made the young radicals cynical about the anti-communism of their elders, forgetting that many liberal anti-Communists were also anti-authoritarian. They are ready to support any sort of attack on the American establishment, even if it is launched by Vietnamese guerrillas with whom the New Left has only the most remote ideological or cultural kinship.

How widespread is this readiness to identify with "the enemy?" The militant, embittered sentiments described above are probably confined to one or two percent of the younger generation. But I think the basic attitudes which lead the activists to sympathy for the Viet Cong are quite general among the young, and that their impact is only beginning to be felt.

These are children of the 1940s, raised in relatively permissive middle-class homes where authority was supposed to be rational rather than arbitrary. Unlike earlier generations of Americans, their parents were reluctant to take advantage of their monopoly on physical, economic and legal power. Their youngsters were free to challenge the legitimacy of parental authority from an early age, by arguing that their parents were not using their power reasonably or wisely. Not only that, but such challenges often succeeded. Even when they failed, the children often curbed their parents' power indirectly by refusing to join in a consensus which defined certain rules as sensible and just. Without such a consensus many parents felt reluctant to impose their will, and in many cases found it impossible even when they tried.

The emphasis on consensus and rationality in these young people's upbringing was accompanied by reliance on new forms of discipline. The distinctive feature of a "permissive" home is not that "anything goes." It is that the limits are supposed to be set by the child's internalized sense of what is reasonable and unreasonable. In order to keep up this pretense, overt sanctions and punishments are frowned on. Instead, if the child behaves in what the parents regard as an unreasonable fashion, they retaliate by making the child feel he has hurt them, has let them down. Such a threat was doubtless terrifying to the very young. As they grew older, however, children discovered that they too could use such weapons. Children fear rejection, but so do parents, at least in modern America. A child who acted as if he hated his mother could frequently reduce her to tears. This leads to a system of mutual deterrence, which makes parents hesitate to use their ultimate power and produces an unprecedented equality in relations between the generations.

Such children emerged into the larger society with relatively little experience of authority structures based solely on superior force. Yet this is almost always the ultimate source of authority in large groups and organizations. Confronted with such authority these young people's first reaction was to resort to the tricks they had learned at home. First they tried reason. Racism, they argued, was a violation of the Constitution; the Saigon government was founded on a violation of the Geneva Agreements; and so forth. Such arguments had some success on the racial front, but virtually none on foreign policy. When this tactic failed the young radicals tried withholding love and approval from their elders. This was both the origin and the effect of the protest marches and of civil disobedience—a technique known to all children in all times. Like reason and legalism, emotional confrontations proved moderately effective as weapons against racism. The liberal leaders of the national establishment wanted the young to love and admire them. They did not want to play the tyrannical father and enforce order with a paddle. (Small-town Southern elites came from an older tradition, and felt no more embarrassed by using force against protesters than they did about spanking their children.) Civil disobedience has not yet been tried on a large scale to curb the Vietnam war, but the small efforts to date have not had much effect.

The failure of the techniques learned in permissive, middle-class homes has brought a crisis in America's radical movement. Ghetto Negroes have turned naturally to violence, for they have mostly been raised on it. Young middle-class whites, on the other hand, find violence almost impossible. The radicals must, therefore, either abandon the struggle and retreat into cynicism and privatism or else compete with other adults for control over the apparatus of the state—which means, ultimately, control over the apparatus of violence and coercion. One way to do this might theoretically be violent revolution, but as a practical matter this seems infeasible, undesirable, and an escape from reality. America is not Vietnam. The only real alternative seems to be creating political organizations capable of taking power, first locally and eventually nationally.

Yet it is precisely here that the young radicals' distrust of all authority becomes an apparently insuperable problem. They are allergic to leadership, hierarchy and discipline. They want a movement of small insurgent "cells," organized around mutual trust, equality and respect for every man's individuality. These are appealing values. They are, indeed, my own. But I doubt that they can lead to the creation of political organizations capable of winning and wielding power.

If the children of permissive, middle-class parents are unwilling or unable to participate in established political institutions, or if their distaste and alienation from the whole pattern of American life makes it difficult for them to communicate with a relatively complacent and chauvanistic majority, who *will* exercise power in America? The most likely answer is that power will go by default to conservatives and reactionaries from more traditional backgrounds, who are less allergic to leadership, more willing to submit to the discipline of political organization, readier to make the compromises inherent in the assumption and exercise of power. This seems especially likely if the U.S. fails to suppress the South Vietnamese revolution and withdraws. Any such about-face in Vietnam could produce a right-wing reaction even stronger than the one produced by the collapse of nationalist

China and the stalemate in Korea. The older generation of liberals and radicals showed no great capacity for withstanding such onslaughts in the late 1940s and early 1950s. If the younger generation is also temperamentally incapable of organizing itself so as to withstand a right-wing revival, America may be headed for an era of repression which will make McCarthyism seem relatively innocuous.

Matthew Arnold and the Cold War

LEON WIESELTIER

DECEMBER 27, 1982

In a century of artistic and critical heterodoxy, there has been a striking orthodoxy, which is the faith in modernism. It is almost always deemed to have embodied the century's most essential energies, to have constituted its contribution to the unfolding of the human spirit in art. The full force of the modernist faith, however, is most dramatically apparent in the dizzying history of its intellectual and political alliances. Modernism has attended the most diverse visions of society. Mystics, revolutionaries, royalists, Marxists, liberals, conservatives—all, at one time or another, have instantiated the modernist creed, and looked to it as the natural complement in culture of their creed in politics. To this list there must now be added a new intellectual species—actually a subspecies—the neoconservatives. At a time when the political fortunes of neoconservatism, and of the social and economic forces in American society that it has supported, may be mercifully on the wane, there has recently appeared *The New Criterion*, edited by Hilton Kramer, the first neoconservative journal of culture.

Nowhere in *The New Criterion* is there any mention of the old *Criterion*, which was also called *The New Criterion*, the review edited by T. S. Eliot from 1921 to 1939. This may seem a little odd, because the new shares more than its title with the old; it shares also its general thesis, which is the affinity of high art for conservative politics. Perhaps the editors of the new review were reluctant to invoke its predecessor because they know how brutally this thesis was refuted by events after 1939, when high art saved nobody from low deeds. In fact some of the philosophical and aesthetic grounds for these low deeds were prepared by *The Criterion*'s contributors. There is not much political glory, then, to be borrowed from it. But there is another reason for *The New Criterion*'s reticence about its namesake, which is that it does not exactly reproduce its position. *The Criterion* married modernism to monarchism. *The New Criterion* marries modernism to capitalism, and to the middle class.

The marriage of modernism to capitalism is a retort to the marriage of modernism to Marxism. *The New Criterion*'s quarrel is not with *The Criterion* of the 1930s, but with *Partisan Review* of the 1940s—with the generation of intellectuals that preceded Kramer's, that believed simultaneously in socialism and the highest soundings of sensibility. The socialism was hardly revolutionary; it was analytic, a criticism of the capitalist constructions of social and cultural life, and it was utterly unillusioned about what the criticism of capitalism had brought about when it was realized in Russia. The socialism was in many ways indistinguishable from liberalism. The more it tended toward liberalism, the more it tended toward the middle class, and the more it tended toward the middle class, the more it tended toward what Lionel Trilling called "variousness, possibility, complexity, and difficulty." Now comes *The New Criterion*, with a new twist. It proposes to defend capitalism from the point of view of art, and modernism from the point of view of politics.

The New Criterion's first point about contemporary culture is that it has been politicized. "We are still living in the aftermath of the insidious assault on mind that was one of the most repulsive features of the radical movement of the Sixties." Thus the editors, in the introduction to their journal. The assault on mind, they argue, takes place in the name of "ideology or publicity, or some pernicious combination of the two." The ideology is Marxism and, more generally, anti-Americanism. It is responsible, in the first place, for the degradation of art criticism into "propaganda." And as the criticism of art goes, so goes the criticism of literature. "Political purposes are increasingly infiltrating literature," writes Joseph Epstein.

> So thoroughly politicized has contemporary literary life become that most people assume it is the literary man's duty to be on the side of revolution, to find the United States racist and the members of the middle class either desperate dogs or insensate swine.

Or, as the editors write, "what it seems to come down to is a fervent wish on the part of many writers to dissociate themselves from the capitalist society in which we live," when in fact

> capitalism, for all its many flaws, has proved to be the greatest safeguard of democratic institutions and the best guarantee of intellectual and artistic freedom . . . that the modern world has given us.

The editors conclude their statement of purpose with the demand that "the first condition of any serious criticism of the arts in the contemporary world" must be "that it is now only in a democratic society like ours that the values of high art can be expected to survive and prosper."

Capitalism certainly has the best record on democracy. The rest is false.

American writing, for example, has hardly declared war on the middle class. The spiritual condition of that class is the subject of Saul Bellow and John Cheever, who have surely contributed more to the national literature than E. L. Doctorow and Robert Coover have taken away; and there is no more persuasive proof of the reputation of the middle class than the reputation of John Updike, the poet of its smugness, whose work does more than anything produced by the "political" writers to give the adversary attitude a good name. And since when is the adversary attitude toward the middle class a betrayal of the literary vocation? It is, quite the contrary, the novel's mother's milk. For two centuries novelists have been composing the annals of bourgeois airlessness, and not the maker of Emma Bovary, nor the maker of Effi Briest, nor the maker of Anna Karenina, ever called for the class to be destroyed. The neoconservative charge against contemporary literature is a commonplace about modern literature, except in the use to which it is put. This use is the political delegitimation of doubt. It is not treason to your class, however, to tell the full truth about it, especially if you continue within it. ("One should live like a bourgeois and think like a demi-god" was how Flaubert put it.) The worst you can be accused of is bad faith, but bad faith may be all there is for those who love truth and hate revolution. In this sense it is especially outrageous when the neoconservatives bash Roland Barthes, that really indispensable writer. It was Barthes who taught his time that the bourgeoisie's facts of nature are really facts of culture; but it was he who lingered, more than anyone since Proust, over the possibilities of happiness contained in those facts.

It is not the case that literary criticism has surrendered to politics, either. American criticism does not suffer from too excessive an engagement with the world outside the word; it is, if anything, trapped in textuality. But then the neoconservatives think so, too. They have it both ways. They like to trash structuralists and deconstructionists for "proving that reality doesn't exist," as Epstein writes; and then they trash them for acting like literature doesn't exist, for making it stoop before politics. Damned at the superstructure and damned at the base. The truth is that not all formalism is sterile and not all Marxism is insurrectionary, that aestheticism has no necessary relation to anti-Americanism, that there are good critical reasons for staying at the surface and good critical reasons for going below.

What's more, there is a difference between the criticism of the political and ideological position of a writer, which belongs to the war of ideas, and the inquiry into the political and ideological function of literature, which belongs to the theory of culture. The latter is not a politicization of criticism. It is compatible, quite the contrary, with the most contradictory politics and ideologies. And it is a field into which American criticism has only recently entered. American criticism has finally transcended the dreary debate between "form" and "content" and gone on to really interesting questions about the intersection of the two. Some of the critics of American criticism, however, have not; and some of them think that an idea is refuted when it is called "fashionable" or "exotic," and that any idea that was introduced into American criticism in translation, and between the Port Huron statement and the 1980 election, is already wrong.

But something more fundamental is false—*The New Criterion*'s premise that "it is only in a democratic society like ours that the values of high art can be expected to survive and prosper." The history of the relationship between democracy and culture is considerably more complicated. The values of high art have survived in this political system, but they have not always prospered. A democracy usually puts downward pressures upon culture. This is inevitable wherever arithmetic is a measure of authority. The spirit of creation is not the spirit of consensus; or, as Seferis gently put it, "art is for all men, never for the masses." For this reason, popular culture is a constant threat to high culture, a threat about which *The New Criterion* is terribly worried.

It is not for the sake of art, however, that political systems are designed. Democracy and art is a subject that must be handled carefully. The view that there is an essential connection between political legitimacy and the products of the imagination has been a motive for all sorts of wickedness. Art is a form of election, an uncommonly strenuous effort of the spirit. It was the revolutionary achievement of liberalism in the seventeenth century, however, to do away with election as the basis of enfranchisement in society. This was part of its more general expulsion of the soul from politics. There are conservatives who want this liberalism repealed, who desire that the soul be returned to politics, who believe that it is still a requirement of political systems that they satisfy spiritual needs. The neoconservatives are not yet among them. But they appear not to appreciate that a demotion of culture followed from the secularity of democracy, that the fortunes of art are uncertain in a society that is philosophically opposed to public rewards for spiritual privilege. Democracy must be defended, but on other grounds.

"What text, what painting, what symphony, would shake the edifice of American politics?" George Steiner recently asked. It is an unfair question, because art should not be asked to. Art is not impossible in a democracy; it is only impeded. But there is a historical truth behind Steiner's question, which is that the fortunes of art have been furthered also in undemocratic societies. Communism has been a condition of the work of Milosz, Kundera, Brodsky, Konrad, to name only the living, and fascism a condition of the work of Borges, García Márquez, Vargas Llosa. These are (in *The New*

Criterion's favorite phrase) "serious" writers all. The history of the relationship between tyranny and culture, then, is also complicated. But this must be properly understood. The inspiration that dictators visit upon writers sweetens nothing, obviously. It is not even an irony. It is a crime—not least a crime upon the writer. "Polish books have only one subject," Milosz wrote gravely in a poem to Lech Walesa. It is precisely in undemocratic societies that art is politicized, not by the artist but by the society. The artist starts as a slave to public subjects, and the dissident artist, too. The real triumph over tyranny, therefore, is not a poem about freedom, but a poem about love—a poem that neither submits nor resists, because it takes freedom for granted. Not the right politics, but no politics. The greatness of the United States in the matter of culture may be described this way—it is a place for no politics, a place for private subjects. When liberalism separated the soul from society, it made the fate of the soul into a private subject; and when it made the fate of the soul into a private subject, it prepared for the writers of our time an argument against the totalitarian nature of our time's tyranny. The indifference of American society to art irritates some Americans, but it is for this indifference that some of the Russians are here. They dreamed of a place where politicians don't read poetry.

Democracy's purpose with respect to "high art," then, is not to need it. That is the good news, and the bad. Politics is not expected; and just as the artists and the writers must not rely upon the powers, the powers must not rely upon the artists and the writers. In the 1960s the attempt was made to enroll culture in the service of anti-Americanism. Now the attempt is made to enroll culture in the service of pro-Americanism. Why is the love of capitalism any less damaging to art than the hatred of capitalism? Or the service of one ideology better for criticism than the service of another? It is the service itself that is the problem. Politicization is politicization. As citizens of this country, its writers and artists have all the duties of citizenship, but the duties of citizenship do not include their work. That is theirs. When freedom is real, it is forgotten. For this reason democracy is always in danger, because it is not always busy with its own defense. But part of what it defends is the freedom to forget about freedom. This is the basis in the real world for the neoconservatives' fear, but there is not much, at least in the realm of culture, that they may do about it.

"It is time to apply a new criterion to the discussion of our cultural life—a criterion of truth." So say the editors. Naturally nobody is against "truth," but there is more that must be said. It was said by Andrei Sinyavsky, in his brilliant essay "The Literary Process in Russia," which appeared in 1976 in the first English collection from *Kontinent*.

> It is at this point that literature must be on its guard and not give way to the seductive spell of speaking the truth and nothing but the truth. . . .

This attitude is one of the chronic failings of the nineteenth century, which we have inherited from two books with interrogative titles: *Who Is to Blame?* and *What Is to Be Done?* We are again faced by the eternal Russian dilemma: Where is your allegiance, you professional purveyors of culture? Whose side are you on? Are you for the truth, or the official lie? When the question is put like that, the writer has no choice but to answer proudly: for truth! And that is the only fitting reply in such a situation. But in proclaiming oneself to be on the side of truth, it is worthwhile remembering what Stalin said when some brave members of the Union of Writers asked him to explain once and for all what socialist realism was, and how, in practical terms, to attain those glittering heights. Without taking a moment's thought or batting an eyelid, the leader replied: "Write the truth—and that will be socialist realism!"

The point has been reached when we should fear the truth, lest it hang round our necks again like an albatross. Let the writer refuse to tell lies, but let him create fiction—and in disregard of any kind of "realism." Otherwise all this promising, liberated literature will again be reduced to a recital of the torments we suffer and the remedies we offer in their place. It will revert to those questions: "What is to be done?" and "Who is to blame?" And everything will again fall to pieces and it will begin all over again: "liberation movement," "naturalist school," "realist school," and as the natural culmination we will end up again with "Party literature," with writers, in Lenin's words, acting as "screws and cogwheels" in the "common proletarian cause." It would be a good thing to avoid all that; to refrain from offering ready-made recipes. Having exorcised ourselves from the lie, we have no right to succumb to the temptation of the truth. . . . We must put a stop to our cringing and currying favor with that hectoring taskmaster—reality! After all, we *are* writers, artists in words.

Not lies, but fiction. It is a kind of Hippocratic oath for writers. I have cited it at such length because of the moral achievement it represents—this was written by a Russian writer. If the distinction can be made over there, it can be made over here. If in the Soviet Union, where lies are necessary to live, where they keep you in your job and out of jail, a writer has a right to something other than "truth," then a writer has a right to it in the United States, too. We have truth, so let us have fiction. But "a criterion of truth" is not a criterion of fiction. It is really a criterion of utility, of political and ideological utility.

The neoconservatives are in a pretty tight spot. They must find a way to mobilize the moral resources of this country without mocking them. They are correct to claim that democracy has difficulty in recognizing its enemies, that it puts itself at a psychological disadvantage. And the cure that they propose, this "new criterion," is not quite worse than the disease, as their critics claim; they are not McCarthy. Still, the strain they propose for the imagination is not just. If the writer in the Soviet Union cannot write as he pleases because the Soviet Union is totalitarian, and the writer in the United States cannot write as he pleases because the Soviet Union is totalitarian, where on earth can he write as he pleases?

There was much literary glory in the old *Criterion*. In its first issue there appeared *The Wasteland*, which for a literary magazine is a good start. Later issues introduced to English readers the work of Proust. Yeats, Lawrence, Joyce, Lewis, and Pound were published in its pages. In this respect, too, the *Criteria* will forever differ. Not merely because the age is poorer—for that the neoconservatives cannot take the rap. What distinguishes *The New Criterion* from its predecessor, already in its first issue, is its philistine air. (The excerpt from Elias Canetti's memoirs included in the issue is like china in a bull shop.) Consider Joseph Epstein's essay on "The Literary Life Today," a long rant in which it is established that there is nothing. "Contemporary literature has not been able to produce a towering literary figure"; "so few American masterpieces have been produced in the last quarter-century"; "one is hard pressed to think of an important literary critic"; "ours has been an age without great literary magazines"; "the literary intellectual is disappearing"; "there no longer seems much reason to look to Europe for any sort of cultural guidance or literary example"; and so on. This is not criticism; it is accounting. And consider Epstein's argument against certain schools of literary theory: "It is all very ingenious, this work of structuralists, semiologists, Foucaultists; it is also all very boring." With this the man thinks something mental has been accomplished.

We may conclude from this manner of discussing literature not merely that the nattering nabobs of negativism are no longer on the left. We may conclude also that at the heart of the neoconservative concern for tradition there is a deep longing for an official culture. What else does this mourning for masterpieces and towering figures mean? Epstein needs a canon, because without a canon he has no bearings. He cannot abide the inconclusive condition of culture in the present, which is always the condition of culture in the present—it leaves him too exposed to art's elements, too unprotected by opinion, too much at the mercy of his eye and his mind. Instead, he wants the reading of masterpieces by towering figures—a certified experience of art.

But this is philistinism with a twist—philistinism in the defense of modernism. The defense of modernism is a major objective of the neoconservative campaign in culture, and it is the subject of the most intellectually impressive article in *The New Criterion*'s first issue, Hilton Kramer's "Postmodern: art and culture in the 1980s." Kramer traces with great lucidity the birth of modernism in the revolt against bourgeois philistinism, and proceeds to protect it against postmodernism, the recent revivals of bourgeois modes of art and design, which he interprets as the summation in a single style of the attack on "the concept of seriousness" in the 1960s. But if the spirit of modernism was assaulted from the left then, it is assaulted from the right now—and in the pages of Kramer's journal. For Epstein's fear of the new, his contempt for those who are trying to do without formulas, or without *his* formulas, amounts to a yearning for an Academy. It is status raised to an aesthetic value, and meanness of spirit raised to a principle of culture. The friend of masterpieces is not quite the friend of art.

It is in Kramer's contributions that the main themes of this analysis of culture are best developed. He writes to praise "seriousness" and to bury the 1960s. He claims that the cultural agenda of those years was to "sever the link between high culture and high seriousness" by proposing an essentially facetious aesthetic, known as "Camp"; and his discussion of the consequences of "Camp" in the decade that followed is illuminating. But Kramer, too, goes too far. Not everything postmodern is political, and not everything postmodern is a joke. Kramer may not like the buildings of Michael Graves or the poems of John Ashbery, but there is certainly "seriousness" within them, and a disciplined evaluation of the past.

The most unsatisfactory aspect of Kramer's analysis is his failure to face up to the contradiction between the marriage of modernism and capitalism, on the one hand, and the history of their relations, on the other. These relations have not been harmonious. The adversary attitude to which Kramer is politically opposed had a basis in reality. Modernism *was* a cultural insurrection, and sometimes also a social insurrection, and sometimes even a political insurrection. Indeed, Kramer has written many times in sympathy with the modernist defiance of the commercial class; and he has written many times in sorrow about the domestication of that defiance. Postmodernism, in his view, is a "yearning" for the bourgeois satisfactions that have been destroyed. But then it is the accommodations of postmodernism that must be resisted, not the anger of modernism. The truth is that capitalism has not sustained modernism, but swallowed it. The natural ally of capitalism is precisely postmodernism. Modernism lives with capitalism in an inauthentic state, but postmodernism lives with it authentically. The careers of Philip Johnson and Andy Warhol make this plain. Theirs is the art that is most hospitable to the profits point of view, that has replaced "seriousness" with social expression, and artistic profundity with an eye for the main chance. They are the artists who have precisely the attitude of acceptance that Kramer seems to feel is appropriate. The debate about the styles must be joined on aesthetic grounds, then, not on the grounds of economic or social theory. Modernism cannot be helped by capitalism, because capitalism helps something else. And capitalism cannot be justified by modernism, because modernism is not in the business of making such justifications. It is an art of opposition.

It should be apparent that the controlling critical notion of the neoconservatives, the talismanic term that will drive whole decades away, is "seriousness"; and, like "truth," nobody is against "seriousness." But the source of neoconservative "seriousness" is rather interesting. It is Matthew Arnold. Arnold is everywhere. Last spring Joseph Epstein published an earlier version of his *New Criterion* essay in *Commentary* in which he set forth the premises of his kind of *pompier* criticism. The essay was called "Matthew Arnold and The Resistance"; "Matthew Arnold has become perhaps more important than ever before," he announced. That is because "standards, for him, were essential," whereas "standards in literary matters have been shaky for a long while now." Epstein cited Arnold's "The Literary Influence of Academies" approvingly, for its regret that there existed in England "no body of opinion . . . strong enough to set up a standard." Then there appeared in the September issue of *The Atlantic* Hilton Kramer's attack on Susan Sontag's attack on "the Matthew Arnold idea of culture"; Kramer went on to defend "the Matthew Arnold idea of culture" against what he called "the Oscar Wilde idea of culture" (as if the author of *intentions* was just another flimsy aesthete). And now in *The New Criterion*, in a revaluation of F. R. Leavis, Norman Podhoretz adduces Arnold as the final authority on "the exercise of discrimination."

Leavis, not Trilling. There's the rub. The return of Matthew Arnold is not the return of Lionel Trilling, even if it was Trilling who taught Arnold to this generation. These are all Trilling's wayward sons. (The neoconservatives' Trilling problem is too large to go into here. Suffice it to say that it is rather classically Freudian: the father was slain in Norman Podhoretz's *Breaking Ranks* and deified in William Barrett's *The Truants*.) They are his wayward sons not least because they did not learn their lessons well. In their hands Arnold is diminished. He is emphatically not the man who lamented that

> our organs of criticism are organs of men and parties having practical ends to serve, and with them these practical ends are the first thing and the play of mind the second; so much play of mind as is compatible with the prosecution of these practical ends is all that is wanted.

The ideal of seriousness is not Arnold's only ideal. It comports in his criticism with the ideal of disinterestedness, which he defined as "a free play of the mind on all subjects which it touches." This is not the spirit of *The New Criterion*. It has practical ends to serve. It will not be accused of "variousness, possibility, complexity, and difficulty." The substance of art is not opinion, and the pleasure art provides is not the pleasure of being right.

The Case for the Contras

EDITORIAL

MARCH 24, 1986

The upcoming vote in Congress on military aid to the Nicaraguan *contras* is one of the most important foreign policy votes of the decade. The future of Central America hinges on its outcome.

The position of the *contras* is precarious. They certainly have people: anywhere from 14,000 to 20,000, depending on whom you believe. That represents about twice the number of guerrillas in El Salvador, a country with about twice the population of Nicaragua. And about three times the number of Sandinista troops at the time of the overthrow of Somoza.

They also have people on the home front. Not even the most anti-*contra*-aid congressman denies that the Sandinistas have become extremely unpopular. Among those strongly opposed to Sandinista rule is the Church, the most popular institution in Nicaraguan society. The pope's divisions are not the only disaffected. These now include ordinary people deprived of the necessities of life in a wrecked economy; the business and middle classes, which have been denied the promises of freedom; and many intellectuals, some in exile, who don't relish life as functionaries of that state. The *contras,* a peasant army, themselves represent the deep resentment in the countryside at Sandinista offenses to tradition and religion. Add to that the general uprising of the Mitkitos against Sandinista colonialism, and you have a vast popular opposition. These are the people whose hopes would be betrayed by the liquidation of the armed resistance and the consolidation of Sandinista rule, which will be the inevitable result of an American denial of military aid to the *contras.*

But if they are so many, why haven't they already won? For the same reason Solidarity, ten million strong, lost in Poland. Under Leninist regimes, Philippine-style "people power" does not do terribly well. Nor do vastly outgunned, out-trained guerrilla armies do well against Cuban-Soviet-style military machines.

The Soviets have poured something on the order of $500 million in arms into Nicaragua in the last five years. Since 1984 the U.S. has been prevented from sending the *contras* a penny's worth of arms. The recent delivery of helicopter gunships to the Sandinistas, reportedly piloted in combat by Cubans, has been decisive. It has made it extremely difficult for the *contras* to move and to resupply. In the absence of antiaircraft weaponry, they are quite defenseless.

As a result, *contra* advances and successes in the past several years are being reversed. In the last six months, particularly since the introduction of the MI-24 gunships, all but between 3,000 and 6,000 *contras* have been driven from Nicaragua. The rest are in Honduran camps waiting for arms. In civil wars numbers alone can't determine the outcome, particularly if one's side is barely armed.

And also barely trained. Again out of congressional scrupulousness, the U.S. military has been prohibited from training and professionalizing the *contra* forces, as it has done in El Salvador with a resulting marked improvement in the country's human rights record. It is somewhat paradoxical to argue that we shouldn't be training the *contras* because they are so undisciplined when one of the major reasons this peasant army remains undisciplined is that the U.S. military is prohibited from training it.

Thus the upcoming vote will be critical. Without military aide, the *contras* will fight and bleed perhaps for some time longer, but without hope. First to wither will be the armed resistance, overcome by vastly superior Soviet-supplied firepower. Then, just as certainly, the unarmed resistance, demoralized and abandoned, will follow, leaving the Sandinistas in total, permanent control of Nicaragua.

What's so bad about that? What, after all, does the resistance hope to achieve? Sandinista defense minister Humberto Ortega explained it well when, in 1981, he denounced former Sandinista junta member Alfonso Robelo as an enemy of the revolution. "The democracy that Robelo asks," charged Ortega, "is . . . that they [the bourgeoisie, presumably] have the army, the power, and that we Sandinistas be what the left is in Costa Rica, a sector, an organization that is free to move about, that publishes its newspaper." In other words, Robelo wants, for Nicaragua, Costa Rican–style democracy, where all the political tendencies, including the left, are free to compete for (rotating) power. For Humberto Ortega, such a program amounts to political criminality. It is what made the Sandinistas push Robelo out of the junta, crush his party, and drive him to exile and resistance. Robelo is now one of the three leaders of the *contra* political leadership, the United Nicaraguan Opposition, known as UNO.

What is at stake in this civil war is any hope for a democratic Nicaragua. The end of the *contras* means the end of that hope. And a ban on military aid will likely mean, sooner or later, the end of the *contras*.

One would think that House Democrats, who for years have been urging, pushing, encouraging, threatening, and finally celebrating the return of democracy in the Philippines, would be equally eager to see democracy returned to Nicaragua. But they are not. Why? They put up a case that we find, for an issue of this gravity, stunningly weak.

By what right does the U.S. try to bring democracy to a place where it enforced dictatorship for so long? This is the "because of our tainted history we have no moral standing" argument. It is mystifying. The United States stood by the dictatorship in Haiti for at least three decades. Does this mean that we should therefore have ruled ourselves morally ineligible to assist in the transition to democracy? The United States ruled the Philippines as a colony for nearly five decades, then stood by a dictator for the last two. Does that mean that the United States should have disqualified itself from aiding the restoration of democracy?

Certainly the U.S. has a very blemished history in Nicaragua. It is equally certain that our aims now are different than they were 60, even 20, years ago. As in Guatemala and El Salvador, as in the Philippines and Haiti and other places where our history is stained, in Nicaragua the relevant question is American intentions today, not Teddy Roosevelt's at the time of the building of the Panama Canal.

We have no right to try to impose democracy on another country. After the Philippines and Haiti, and the general self-congratulatory jubilation of liberals and conservatives alike over two triumphs of American diplomacy, this argument stands exposed as camouflage. Those who advocate dramatic American intervention in pro-American dictatorships should not be suddenly stricken with scrupulousness about the sanctity of sovereignty when intervention is proposed in states ruled by pro-Soviet Leninists.

But one situation involves peaceful change; the other war. If in Nicaragua transition to democracy were possible without war, we too would oppose any fighting. But that option does not exist. Does anyone believe that the Sandinistas will ever peacefully transfer power or permit a free allocation of power by election?

The contras can't win. This argument is invariably heard from those who vote again and again to cut off aid to the *contras.* Yes, unarmed they can't win. Maybe House Democrats expect Nicaraguan democrats to win by lying down in front of Sandinista tanks, Philippines style.

Can the *contras* win the way the North Vietnamese won in South Vietnam? No, but they can win in the way the Sandinistas won in Managua. They could win not by rolling over the Sandinista army, but by controlling the countryside, which would in turn help undermine what little urban support the Sandinistas have. A Leninist regime with a conscript army on the defensive, losing the countryside and undermined in the city, would ultimately find its situation untenable.

The contras are not democrats but Somacistas. It is true that some top commanders are ex-Guardia. But even the most conservative (and powerful) of the three political leaders, Adolfo Calero, was a longtime opponent of Somoza and jailed for his efforts. The other UNO leader, Arturo Cruz, an impeccable democrat, says the *contras* represent "the revolt of Nicaraguans against oppression by other Nicaraguans." One doesn't raise an army of 15,000 peasants with promises of restoring a universally despised dictatorship.

We should try diplomacy, not force. The United States should be working out with the Sandinistas some kind of diplomatic arrangement under the umbrella of Contadora. This imagined solution to Sandinista regional power and ambitions is a parchment barrier: the Sandinistas are given free rein within their borders, and in return, they promise not to trespass on anyone else's. Certainly we can expect Sandinistas to adhere initially to such a nonaggression or revolution-with-frontiers agreement. Time enough for the *contras* to wither away and be repatriated in Miami. At which point the Sandinistas will be secure in the knowledge that no future opponents are ever going to risk their lives in a second insurgency, having seen the first one out. With a free hand, does anyone imagine that they will adhere to their agreements any more than, say, the Vietnamese adhered to theirs? We have experience with Sandinista parchment. In 1979 they pledged to the Organization of American States to establish an open, democratic, and pluralistic society.

It takes willful blindness to imagine that some kind of paper agreement with the Sandinistas that allows them to consolidate their power will ensure stability in Central America. In fact, the opposite is almost certainly the case. A highly militarized, highly disciplined country with by far the largest army in Central America, with ideological ambitions stretching far beyond its borders, and supported by Cuba and the Soviet Union, is bound to be a source of constant instability in a region of weak and fledgling democracies.

The neighboring countries seem to want a Contadora solution. What does one expect from, say, Costa Rica, a country with no army facing a 50,000-man military across its border? It sees a starved insurgency, an isolationist U.S. Congress, and a rising military power in Managua. Does one expect Costa Rica publicly to come out in support of overthrowing its neighbor, given the odds now that its neighbor will be in power permanently? Of course such countries will make muted public statements. But as many of the leaders of these weak democracies told the Kissinger Commission and others since, they are desperate to see the United States get rid of the Sandinistas for them.

What is the government of Colombia, one of the original Contadora countries, to say? It publicly denies but privately knows that an assault on its Palace of Justice and the massacre of its Supreme Court was carried out by M-19 guerrillas with weapons of Nicaraguan origin. It knows that Sandinista *comandante* Tomas Borges attended a mass, complete with an M-19 flag draped over the alter, for the guerrillas killer in that raid. The reach of the Sandinistas is impressive. Latin American governments, many of which face left-wing insurgencies, are hardly likely to make themselves more of a target by public calls for the Yankees to save them from communists.

The contra policy is driving the Sandinistas into the hands of the Soviets. It is hard for Americans to believe that some people act out of ideological conviction. Look, therefore, at what the Sandinistas did long before there was a Reagan, long before there were *contras.* In one year the Carter administration gave them aid the equivalent of half of what Somoza received in 16 years, and during that time they systematically eliminated their democratic allies and aligned themselves with the Soviets.

On June 23, 1981, Humberto Ortega said to Sandinista army and militia officers: "We are saying that Marxism-Leninism is the scientific doctrine that guides our revolution, the instrument of analysis of our Vanguard for understanding [the revolution's] historic process and for carrying out the revolution. . . ." He then asserted that the FSLN had made the pact with the moderate opposition only for the purposes of getting rid of Somoza, holding off U.S. intervention, and keeping the economy in place.

It is remarkable that for House Democrats Sandinista ideological commitment requires constant theatrical demonstration. It took Daniel Ortega's flight to Moscow a few days after a *contra* vote last year to dramatize Managua's connection with Moscow. You can be sure that this time Ortega's handlers will take away his American Express card until after the vote. Don't expect to see him visiting New York for eyewear or Moscow for hardware until the coast is clear.

The Cubans and Soviets will match our escalation. This is the counsel of pure defeatism. It cedes to the Soviets the power to set the level of violence and superpower commitment on the North American continent. It is, in effect, to say that the Soviet will annex Nicaragua exceeds that of the United States to prevent it from happening. The prophecy is, of course, self-fulfilling.

The contras will draw the United States into the war. Probably the root argument, certainly the one on which Tip O'Neill hangs his hat. Its origin is the fear of another Vietnam and the isolationist hope that if we only will stay out of this fight no harm will come to us.

But nothing is more likely to force American military intervention than the consolidation of an aggressive, highly militarized, pro-Soviet regime in the area. The *contras* want to do their own fighting. Cut them off, and the only body in the hemisphere able to restrain the Sandinistas will be in the U.S. Army. Of course, American military involvement can never be ruled out. But destroying the only indigenous armed opposition to the Nicaraguans hardly seems the way to prevent it.

And what will be more likely to bring about American military involvement? Even Democrats argue that the United States has a vital interest in preventing the establishment of a Soviet base in Nicaragua. Even Democrats would call for American military action in that situation. Walter Mondale, for example, suggested a quarantine. When tried in October 1962, that idea brought us closer to World War III than any other moment in postwar history. A democratic Nicaragua is the only guarantee that the threat will not materialize.

The consolidation of the Sandinistas will lead to a second Cuba on the mainland, or more precisely, to an enlarged first Cuba. As Robelo recalls, during his days in the ruling junta no important decision was ever made without the assent of the Cuban invariably present at the meeting. Even those who think it sentimental for the United States to concern itself with the state of pluralism and democracy in other countries must recognize what a strategic defeat the establishment of a Soviet satellite in Central America would constitute for the United States.

We do not have any illusions about the tragedy that is civil war and the suffering it causes. Guerrilla war is of necessity nasty, brutish, and long. And this peasant army, ill-trained and ill-equipped, is hardly a perfect model for insurgency. But our choice is this model—which could be vastly improved in combat effectiveness and discipline if given sufficient American aid and training—or none.

We believe that preventing the establishment of a Leninist dictatorship in Nicaragua is a goal worthy of American support, and those willing to fight for this cause are deserving of American assistance. A decision to support one side in a civil war is not one to be taken lightly. We come to it in the full realization that, whatever tragedy it brings, the liquidation of the democratic side of Nicaraguan civil war will bring infinitely more tragedy to Nicaragua, to Central America, and ultimately to the rest of the hemisphere.

Correspondence: *The* Contra-*versy*

CONTRIBUTING EDITORS

APRIL 14, 1986

To the editors:

We disagree with *The New Republic's* editorial unconditionally endorsing President Reagan's policy of military aid to the Nicaraguan *contras.*

This disagreement is not rooted in isolationism, defeatism, willful blindness, or a double standard of "scrupulousness" about the sovereignty of "states rules by pro-Soviet Leninists"—the only motives the editorial permits to opponents of *contra* aid. Nor is our view rooted in any illusions that left-wing dictatorships are somehow morally superior to right-wing ones. Rather, it stems from a judgment that the means the administration proposes—themselves morally dubious—cannot accomplish the ends it envisions.

TNR brushes aside the large body of evidence, from both official and unofficial sources, that even with massive American aid the *contra* army will be militarily and politically unable to achieve the goal of overthrowing the Sandinista regime and replacing it with a liberal democratic government on the Costa Rican model.

For all practical purposes, the leadership of the *contras* continues to be dominated by antidemocratic supporters of the former Somoza regime. The great majority of their military commanders are former National Guardsmen. Their record of human rights violations has been amply documented by such independent investigators as Amnesty International and Americas Watch.

We do not question the democratic credentials of Arturo Cruz—or, for that matter, of Rubén Zamora, who occupies a position in the political arm of the Salvadoran guerrilla movement analogous to that of Cruz in the Nicaraguan one. But as *The New Republic* has repeatedly pointed out with reference to El Salvador, at the moment of guerrilla triumph the democrats who adorn the letterheads will be pushed out by the thugs who control the guns.

It may be that none of the imaginable American policies toward Nicaragua could succeed in imposing a pluralist democratic system upon that country—including the policy we favor, which would combine political and economic pressure, negotiations, and aid and encouragement to democracies in the region. We do think, however, that our policy would stand a far better chance than the one recommended by Reagan and TNR of achieving the second U.S. goal: preventing Nicaragua from becoming a heavily armed, aggressive Soviet military surrogate on the American continent.

Managua long ago agreed to the outlines of a settlement that would, among other things, prohibit foreign military bases and advisers, institute negotiations aimed at reducing regional armaments levels, and create joint mechanisms to prevent and resolve border disputes. Such a deal can almost certainly still be struck. It would forestall the strategic disaster TNR fears. And because its terms would be easily verifiable, it would not have to rely on trust.

Some time ago, in a lead editorial ("Sticks and Sticking Points," August 15 & 22, 1983), *The New Republic* endorsed the relatively mild step of symbolic American naval maneuvers in Central American waters. The magazine then added in conclusion:

"If, however, the Administration has really no intention of negotiating with Nicaragua, but is preparing for a general Central American war, which will inevitably involve American boys, then we have a right to know now. In that case we would be forced to join the opposition to the Administration, and oppose all U.S. military activities in the area, as the lesser of two evils.

"When a government takes steps as decisive and potentially dangerous as those taken by President Reagan, the country deserves to be informed of the ultimate direction of that policy. If for negotiations, genuine and sincere, the Administration will gain support from much of the democratic center. If for military victory, then we join with others in saying no."

Two-and-a-half years later, negotiations have yet to be seriously tried, military victory has become the express goal of administration policy, and *The New Republic* is saying yes. Despite the dissents of TRB and Jefferson Morley, the magazine recommends fomenting a proxy war it admits would be "of necessity nasty, brutish and long." And if the proxies cannot win? *TNR*'s answer is that "American military involvement can never be ruled out." Such "involvement" would be catastrophic for many reasons, but there is no sign the American people would support it. The most likely outcome of the administration's policy, then, is military retreat and strategic failure—failure that the administration is already preemptively blaming upon those who have been warning it all along against the consequences of its folly. As contributing editors of *The New Republic,* we remain committed to continuing discussion of this issue in its pages. But as for the bankrupt policy the magazine editorially endorses, "we join with the others in saying no."

ABRAHAM BRUMBERG, ROBERT COLES, HENRY FAIRLIE, HENDRIK HERTZBERG, VINT LAWRENCE, R. W. B. LEWIS, MARK CRISPIN MILLER, ROBERT B. REICH, RONALD STEEL, RICHARD L. STROUT, ANNE TYLER, MICHAEL WALZER, C. VANN WOODWARD

Index